LEADERSHIP ON THE FEDERAL BENCH

Leadership on the Federal Bench

THE CRAFT AND ACTIVISM OF JACK WEINSTEIN

By Jeffrey B. Morris

Oxford University Press, Inc., publishes works that further Oxford University's objective of excellence
in research, scholarship, and education.

Oxford   New York
Auckland   Cape Town   Dar es Salaam   Hong Kong   Karachi   Kuala Lumpur   Madrid   Melbourne
Mexico City   Nairobi   New Delhi   Shanghai   Taipei   Toronto

With offi ces in
Argentina   Austria   Brazil   Chile   Czech Republic   France   Greece   Guatemala   Hungary   Italy
Japan   Poland   Portugal   Singapore   South Korea   Switzerland   Thailand   Turkey   Ukraine
Vietnam

Published by Oxford University Press, Inc.
198 Madison Avenue, New York, New York 10016

Oxford is a registered trademark of Oxford University Press
Oxford University Press is a registered trademark of Oxford University Press, Inc.

Library of Congress Cataloging-in-Publication Data

Morris, Jeffrey Brandon, 1941-
  Leadership on the federal bench : the craft and activism of Jack Weinstein / Jeffrey B. Morris.
    p. cm.
  Includes bibliographical references and index.
  ISBN 978-0-19-977241-4 (hardback : alk. paper)
  1. Weinstein, Jack B. 2. United States. District Court (New York : Eastern District)–Biography.
  3. Judges–New York (State)–Biography. I. Title.
  KF373.W3485M67 2011
  347.73'14092--dc22
  [B]
                                                                        2011005306

Note to Readers
This is publication is designed to provide accurate and authoritative information in regard to the subject
matter covered. It is based upon sources believed to be accurate and reliable and is intended to be current
as of the time it was written. It is sold with the understanding that the publisher is not engaged in rendering
legal, accounting, or other professional services. If legal advice or other expert assistance is required, the
services of a competent professional person should be sought. Also, to confirm that the information has
not been affected or changed by recent developments, traditional legal research techniques should be used,
including checking primary sources where appropriate.

*(Based on the Declaration of Principles jointly adopted by a Committee of the
American Bar Association and a Committee of Publishers and Associations.)*

You may order this or any other Oxford University Press publication by
visiting the Oxford University Press website at www.oup.com

IN LOVING MEMORY OF SARA E. ROBINSON,

MATILDA MORRIS AND SOPHIE RODMON

Contents

Preface

⌇ ───

THE CHAIN OF events that led to this book began in the summer of 1993 in Judge Jack Weinstein's study. A few days earlier, I had responded to a telephone call from Judge Weinstein, who appeared to be seeking advice about putting his papers in order for his "retirement." When we spoke, it seemed to me that what he might be seeking was a vehicle for putting his career in perspective, so I suggested we undertake an oral history together. What I may have had in mind was the then current "model" of oral histories of judges: two to four sessions focusing primarily on events prior to appointment to the bench with comparatively little discussion of cases.

Judge Weinstein and I agreed to undertake an oral history without discussing the number of sessions, but we also agreed that we would deal with cases he had decided. We each prepared for our first session by reading all of his published opinions from his first year on the bench. We both enjoyed that first session so much that we agreed to go through his entire judicial career (then some twenty-five years) discussing all published opinions and those unpublished opinions that he considered of interest. In the first go-round (1993–1994), we had twenty-three sessions ranging from two to three hours in length. Judge Weinstein would provide me with one or two years' worth of opinions, which I would read during the week or two between sessions. While I struggled to complete my "assignments," Judge Weinstein, being Jack Weinstein, would arise at 5:30 in the morning, and after spending an hour rowing in Long Island Sound, *would* review all of the opinions before we met at nine or nine-thirty.

When we did meet, each of us sat with large notebooks in his study overlooking Long Island Sound and conversed. There was no question he refused to answer. Everything was on the record. We each taped the sessions; always hoping that at least one machine was working. (In all of our sessions, we probably lost a total of forty-five minutes to an hour, but the technology always made us feel insecure.) We generally worked uninterrupted except for a brief phone call or two or the occasional arrival of a faxed draft opinion. During the week following each session, Judge Weinstein's secretary typed up the transcript and mailed it to me. Judge Weinstein looked over the transcripts, but the only corrections he made were for spelling and grammar. Very early in the sessions, we agreed that we would jointly own the oral history, which we were assuming would be the only product of our sessions, but we also agreed that at least one copy of the oral history would be available where it could be seen and used by anyone without limitations.

In the decade following the early sessions, we met several times to update the oral history. The only significant change that occurred in the form of the sessions occurred relatively soon after we began, when Judge Weinstein would begin a taping by discussing with me interesting developments in his work since the previous session. During the most recent tapings (as of the summer of 2010), we covered all cases decided to that date. I also used the occasions to raise questions that had arisen during the final revision of this book.

The Weinstein oral history reflects systematic attention to each case upon which he had written, as well as some where the decision was oral, but a transcript was available. Cases of transient consequence were usually discussed only briefly. With the biggest cases—generally the class actions, where there were dozens of opinions or more—we tended to discuss the litigation as a whole, only focusing upon particularly significant opinions. Throughout the tapings, the judge would discuss what he remembered of the parties and lawyers, how the case played out, and its significance. His memory was and is extraordinary. The reader should be aware that at the time this book was copyedited Judge Weinstein was still sitting on the bench and carrying a full load in his ninetieth year.

Not only opinions were read. Sometimes Judge Weinstein included in his opinion notebooks, excerpts from the trial or sentencing transcripts or the Court of Appeals opinion (and Supreme Court opinion) reviewing the case. In any event, I read published Court of Appeals opinions from all Weinstein cases as well as those cases which led to a decision on the merits by the Supreme Court. Many unpublished opinions on LEXIS and WESTLAW were also read and discussed. I also read a high percentage of Judge Weinstein's books, law review articles, and speeches.

It is fair to say that neither of us ever lost enthusiasm for this undertaking. During the first series of interviews—twenty-three in all—there was no suggestion that a book would come out of it, just the understanding that the oral history would, when completed, be available to all interested parties. Later, my involvement with several book projects, including histories of the U. S. Courts of Appeal for the District of Columbia and Eighth Circuits, made such thoughts of a book on Judge Weinstein unrealistic. However, by the time I had completed my book on the Eighth Circuit, I had decided that a book should be written, because as a lawyer/political scientist and legal historian, I could see that the richness of material in the Weinstein Oral History could be employed to look not just at Weinstein's career but also at the opportunities federal district judges have to influence public policy, and how these can be realized by an unusually talented jurist.

The reader may well desire a straight answer to whether this book is in some way an "authorized" biography. That is a difficult question to answer. Judge Weinstein made available any material I requested at all times. Furthermore, a large part of this book could not have been written without the oral history. Apart from any anticipated substantive value of a book, without the oral history and its resonances, the joy of this endeavor could not have been realized, and I would not have entertained such a large undertaking.

On the other hand, with one brief response to be described momentarily, Jack Weinstein never gave (and was never asked to give) any suggestions about the contents of this book. Jack Weinstein is as independent as anyone I have ever met. He also respects the independence and professionalism of others. There was, however, one stray moment, though, when I asked Judge Weinstein whether he had any thoughts about the shape of the book. He replied, "Make it as critical as possible."

The Weinstein Oral History and the judge's other writings were but one of the sources to which I looked in writing this book. In the first place, I came to this book having already written a considerable amount about the lower federal courts. The extent of my readings of the histories of federal district courts and biographies of district judges are indicated in the footnotes to my introductions. For this book, I also read widely on sentencing, the history of the New York City schools, the battle over the Shoreham Nuclear Reactor, and class actions. I employed newspaper files, law review articles, and interviews.

It should be noted that writing a book on Jack Weinstein has special difficulties. His rate of production continues to be such that, reminiscent of the Red Queen in *Alice in Wonderland*, one must read as fast as one can to stay in the same place. To give but one example, over a Fourth of July weekend, I completed writing a small section of a chapter that had taken weeks to research. Finishing it with a sigh of relief and just for fun, I searched on the Internet for "Judge Weinstein." That search immediately turned up the unwelcome information that just two days before he had handed down a two-hundred-fifty-page opinion in that litigation.

As many have found out, working with Jack Weinstein has enormous rewards. He is so thorough that one can assume that he has thought through every aspect of every question before he writes or speaks. He does not dissimulate. I also have often thought how nice it would be to be treated with as much respect by my students as I have been by Judge Weinstein. Finally, he is a most engaging personality whose enormous charm makes being in his presence unusually pleasurable.

The contents of the Weinstein Oral History allow for considerable thought about the role of the federal district courts, the possibilities that attach to judging at the trial level, and the particular contributions of one remarkable judge. It is true that seeing the potential for creativity in the work of a district judge through the career of Jack Weinstein is something like what it must have been to look at the possibilities for choreography in a piece of music through the eyes of George Balanchine. They both used the same vocabulary and building blocks as everyone else in their professions. They were exposed to the same stimulus from the music (or briefs) that their colleagues have been. Their tasks were essentially the same as their fellow choreographers or judges. Yet, each could create a product the quality of which was far above others in the same profession or at least could produce such a product far more often than anyone else in the same profession. Weinstein is so productive, so prolific, so thorough, and so compassionate that he is virtually *sui generis* even though he faces the same challenges that other judges confront.

Nevertheless, this book permits the reader to come closer to observing different facets of federal district judging than any other book. This book attempts to suggest the points of opportunity where a district judge can influence the outcome of cases. It permits insight into the factors—personal and situational—that influence the judging of cases and permits the reader to observe a judge discussing the effect of *his* background on his decision-making rather than having to depend entirely upon statistical analysis of the proclivities of large numbers of judges. The reader can see the personal factors that influence a judge in handling cases without giving short shrift to the legal factors.

The introductory chapter of this book attempts to explain why it was written at all. It responds to the questions of why a study of the work of district judges focuses on Judge Weinstein and why federal district courts deserve serious consideration in a book. The next chapter, the first full chapter of the book, deals essentially with what the job of a district judge entails. That is followed by a chapter devoted to Weinstein's life before he became a judge and the qualifications he had for the bench. The third chapter looks at some of the external factors that may have conditioned Weinstein's work as a judge—national political developments, changes in judicial administration, and the possible impact of the district where Weinstein judges, the Eastern District of New York. The fourth chapter focuses upon the characteristics of Weinstein's judging and considers the generally accepted view that he is a judicial activist.

Chapters 5 through 7 and Chapter 9 discuss the more important decisions for each of the four decades Weinstein has been on the bench. (Chapter 9 actually covers the period 1997 to date.) Chapters 8, 10, and 11 deal with some of Weinstein's most important and interesting work—Chapter 8 with his battle over the Federal Sentencing Guidelines and chapters 10 and 11 on class actions and mass torts. The final chapter offers some concluding thoughts on Weinstein's career.

In a book that took as much time and effort as this one, an author runs up many debts that deserve acknowledgment. The first is, of course, to Judge Jack Weinstein himself, his law clerks and his ever helpful secretaries, Evelyn Hoffman and Jean Capobianco. Second, to my wife, Dona B. Morris, a political scientist and attorney, who read the manuscript with very great care and a shrewd eye, and whose numerous suggestions greatly improved the manuscript. I am also deeply indebted to Dean Larry Raful of Touro Law Center and Gary Shaw, vice dean during most of the time this book was being written, for their ability to find a second sabbatical leave for me as well as for their genuine interest in this book. As usual, I am also very much in debt to the able staff of the Touro Law Library for their assistance, especially to the associate director, Beth Mobley, and to April Schwartz, the law librarian. I must also express indebtedness of Roger Newman, a distinguished scholar and editor, who has been spotting amazingly valuable information from the legal literature for me for some four decades. In this project, he also made some very valuable suggestions. My colleague Patricia Rooney graciously joined me in the ungrateful task of reading the page proof.

I am also indebted to a number of colleagues who commented thoughtfully on the original draft conclusions of the book: Hal Abramson, Fabio Arcila, Marianne Artusio, Rodger Citron, Howard Glickstein, Alan Hornstein, Eileen Kaufman, Lynn Kramer, Deborah Post, Doug Scherer, Martin Schwartz, Tom Schweitzer, and Rena Seplowitz. Their suggestions were helpful to me not only for the revision of that chapter, but in the revising of the book. My colleagues Citron and Peter Davis made useful suggestions for Chapter 1. I must also acknowledge my colleague Richard Klein not only for his enthusiastic interest in the book, but for his marked ability in finding mentions of Judge Weinstein's work in the most unusual places.

Due to the long gestation period of this book, I received some research assistance from a great number of students. The work of three was of particular value: Stacy Walpin, a graduate of George Washington University Law School, Peter La Piana and Shari Newman. A fourth, Barbara Burke, had a unique understanding of what I was trying to do in this book and made some vital suggestions in the later stages of the writing. In addition, Elizabeth Athenas and Craig Szustkiewicz assisted with the proofreading of the book.

Finally, I must also again express deep appreciation to my wife, Dona, but this time along with my son, David, and my daughter, Deborah, for bearing with me during the years of absorption in this book.

Note: The Weinstein Oral History and Other Sources

1. There are presently two copies of Weinstein Oral History: one possessed by Judge Jack Weinstein and one by me. It is my expectation that when this book is published, copies of the entire oral history will be given to the Columbia University libraries and to the law library of Touro Law School.
2. The Weinstein Oral History is paginated 1-1415, the next 76 pages are 1415-1 to 1415-28; Then 1415a to 1415-2; Then 1415-AA to 1415-VV. At that point, page numbers resume at 1416.
3. Those items which are indicated in footnotes as being in possession of the author are still in my possession. At a later time, I will deposit them in one of the law libraries that have the oral history.

Note on Footnotes

I have departed from normal legal footnoting in several respects:

1. In citing to Weinstein cases as district judge, I have not indicated which district court. With the rarest of exceptions, all citations to his district court decisions are from the Eastern District of New York. I have replaced "E.D.N.Y." with the date the opinion was issued.
2. Some unpublished opinions, transcripts of court sessions, and the like come from large loose-leaf notebooks that are in Judge Weinstein's chambers. Several examples demonstrate how they are cited:

   1990 Op. NB Op. 4—Fourth opinion in Weinstein's 1990 note book holding decisions
   1990 Sp. NB Sp 7—1990 Speech Notebook, speech Number 7

3. Almost all of the appeals court decisions referred to are those of the U.S. Court of Appeals for the Second Circuit. In place of noting the court in the footnote citations, I have indicated by abbreviations the judges who sat on the panel. I have indicated the last names of district or visiting judges who are part of a Court of Appeals panel, but I have not identified them further. If any other Court of Appeals is involved, I have indicated the circuit.

Abbreviations

Alti—Francis X. Altimari
Cab—Jose A. Cabranes
Calab—Guido Calabresi
Card—Richard J. Cardamone
WJF—Wilfred Feinberg
Gur—Murray Gurfein
HJF—Henry Friendly
IRK—Irving R. Kaufman
JLO—James L. Oakes
Katz—Robert Katzmann
Living—Deborah Ann Livingston
Lumb—J. Edward Lumbard
Mans—Walter Mansfield
McL—Joseph M. McLaughlin
Mesk—Thomas J. Meskill
Mull—William Hughes Mulligan
New—Jon O. Newman
Pool—Rosemary S. Pooler
Soto—Sonia Sotomayor
Timb—William H. Timbers
VanG—Ellsworth A. Van Graafeiland
Walk—John Walker, Jr.
Win—Ralph K. Winter, Jr.

The full last name of these Court of Appeals judges is given:

Murray I. Gurfein
Peter W. Hall
Paul Hays
Dennis G. Jacobs
Amalya L. Kearse
Pierre N. Leval
Gerard E. Lynch
Roger Jeffrey Miner
Leonard P. Moore
Lawrence W. Pierce
George C. Pratt
Reene Raggi
Robert A. Sack
Chester J. Straub

Introduction

Jack B. Weinstein and the Work of the Federal District Courts

WHY WRITE A book about the judging of Jack B. Weinstein?[1] In his fifth decade as a federal judge at the age of eighty-nine, Weinstein was still working prodigiously. Weinstein's reputation among knowledgeable legal observers is both formidable and controversial. His reputation is based not only upon his work as a judge but also upon scholarship that has encompassed both the theoretical and the practical. For almost a half-century, he has been a central figure in the law of evidence, federal civil procedure, and New York State civil practice. Weinstein has produced a practice code, major treatises, and casebooks. He has written hundreds of articles not only in the areas already mentioned, but dealing with mass tort law, legal ethics, institutional litigation, sentencing, and public education. He has served on dozens of committees and boards including the Presidential Commission on Catastrophic Nuclear Accidents, the Carnegie Commission on Science, Technology, and Government, and the Task Force on Science and Technology in Judicial and Regulatory Decision-Making.[2]

As a district judge, Weinstein has made important contributions in a multitude of fields from evidence to civil rights to criminal sentencing, but perhaps has had the greatest impact in the field of class actions.

---

[1] See, e.g., Richard A. Posner, *Judicial Biography*, 70 N.Y.U. L. REV. 502, 512 (1995); Richard A. Posner, *The Learned Hand Biography and the Question of Judicial Greatness*, 104 YALE L.J. 511 (1994).

[2] "In Recognition of the Honorable Jack B. Weinstein," Edward J. Devitt Distinguished Service to Justice Award, June 17, 1994 [hereinafter, Devitt Award]. *See also* Judicial Conference, Second Judicial Circuit of the United States, 160 F.R.D. 287 (June 17, 1994) (available on Westlaw).

Kenneth Feinberg, special master of the September 11th Victim Compensation Fund (and named by President Barack Obama as an independent administrator of the $20 billion fund set up by BP to compensate victims of the oil spill in the Gulf of Mexico) says, "I think Judge Weinstein has made more of an impact on American law than any judge alive." Professor Alan Dershowitz has called him "[t]he most important Federal Judge in the last quarter century."[3] Secretary of State Hillary Rodham Clinton said, "Judge Weinstein has literally made the law, and has done so with great distinction for many years."[4] Thurgood Marshall, in no way known for flowery tributes, wrote to Weinstein, "You have, more than anyone I know of, contributed your share to the work of the federal judiciary."[5]

On the other hand, there are distinguished appellate judges, as well as accomplished lawyers, who have been and are quite critical of Weinstein's judicial work. He is charged with departing from the independence and detachment required of a judge, making too much law, and being too innovative. Weinstein has been called a "'philosopher king'" who fashioned 'something out of nothing.'"[6] His former colleague and now member of the Court of Appeals, Joseph M. McLaughlin, jested, but with some truth, that Weinstein was a man who "never saw an innovation he didn't like."[7] Activist, innovator, and lawmaker, Weinstein has never hidden his liberalism. J. Edgar Hoover, after reading a memorandum about Weinstein's acquittal of an alleged bank robber because the government could not prove that he had caused fear or intimidation, a requirement of the statute, scribbled, "This Weinstein is certainly a disgrace."[8] Even admirers have written of his work in mass torts as "a combination of prestidigitation and rank insubordination."[9] He has been reversed by the Court of Appeals for the Second Circuit in a number of major cases.

[3] William Glaberson, *A Judge Shows Who's the Boss*, N.Y. TIMES, July 20, 1997, at 21, 24.

[4] Hillary Rodham Clinton, *Tribute to Charles Black*, 111 YALE L.J. 1911 (2002). Weinstein received a 9.2 rating (out of 10), close to the top nationally, in *The Robing Room*, a new website for lawyers to rate judges based on sixteen references, *available at* http://www.therobingroom.com. One criminal defense lawyer commented: "Wonderful human being. Defendants respect him and the way he carries his duties. He treats everyone with respect and is knowledgeable in all aspects of the law." Another wrote, "Simply the best. Loves lawyers. Great demeanor. Knows who he is and has no ego issue, as long as you know he is too. Did I mention brilliant?" A third commented, "The Gold Standard." However, another stated, "if he is 'result-oriented,' isn't that next to lawlessness?" (Comments 4292, 3992, 1179, 1722 in *id.*).

[5] Joseph Goldstein, *New View of Brown v. Board Unlikely to Sway One Judge*, NEW YORK SUN, July 9, 2007, at 4.

[6] Comment of Aaron Twerski, *The House that Jack Built*, BROOKLYN LAW NOTES 6–7 (Spring 2002); *See* discussion of critics *in* Martha Minow, *Judge for the Situation: Judge Jack Weinstein, Creator of Temporary Administrative Agencies*, 97 COLUM. L. REV. 2010, 1010–2011.

[7] James L. Oakes, *Jack Weinstein and His Love-Hate Relationship with the Court of Appeals*, 97 COLUM. L. REV. 1951 (1997).

[8] Jack B. Weinstein FBI file, Dec. 16, 1970 (in possession of the author).

[9] Peter Schuck's assessment summed up in Burt Neuborne, *Innovation in the Interstices of the Final Judgment Rule: A Demurrer to Professor Burbank*, 97 COLUM. L. REV. 2091, 2095 n.20 (1997).

Yet, virtually everybody agrees that Weinstein is a brilliant and creative jurist, energetic and compassionate, scholarly and pragmatic, highly organized and extremely efficient. Weinstein has seven honorary degrees and has received a bevy of awards given by bar associations. The *National Law Journal* named him "Lawyer of the Year" in 1993.[10] The issue of the *Columbia Law Review* dedicated to him to commemorate his thirtieth anniversary on the bench contained tributes to him from Justice Stephen Breyer, Second Circuit Court of Appeals Judge James L. Oakes, and two law school deans, among others.[11] There were also seven substantive articles related to his work.

When he received the Edward J. Devitt Award in 1993, the highest accolade that federal judges give to one of their number, Weinstein was honored for outstanding contributions to justice as a developer of the law, a teacher of the law, a writer, and a judge.[12] The citation continued:

> Like all great judges he knows that he is dealing with real people and real problems. His law-making and law-giving are not simply an intellectual exercise; they are and have been a splendidly crafted use of his legal talents to solve existing problems and to make the solution of future problems easier to ascertain and easier to apply.[13]

If Weinstein has been a "quintessential activist judge," at least he has been a most thoughtful activist, grappling in opinions, speeches, and articles with many of the most difficult problems gripping the legal system.[14] There is no question that, in addition to his scholarship in civil procedure, he has, as judge and scholar, greatly influenced developments in many other fields of law. His management of the most complex cases, particularly mass tort cases, has been extraordinarily influential. Overall, he has been one of the nation's most innovative judges of the past fifty years introducing "countless improvements into New York State and federal law."[15] He is known for "controlling

---

[10] *Lawyer of the Year, Jack Weinstein: A Jurist Who Is Willing to Lead*, 16 NAT'L L.J. No. 17–18 (Dec. 27, 1993–Jan. 3, 1994), at 53.

[11] A Special Issue Dedicated to Judge Jack B. Weinstein, 97 COLUM L. REV. 1946–2209 (November 1997).

[12] Devitt Award, *supra* note 2, at 2. The recipients for the award are selected "whose decisions are characterized by wisdom, humanity and commitment to the rule of law; whose writings demonstrate scholarship and dedication to the judicial process; and whose activities have helped to improve the administration of justice, to advance the rule of law, to reinforce collegial ties within the judicial branch, or to strengthen civic ties within local, national, and international communities." According to the award criteria, bench, bar and community alike would willingly entrust that judge with the most complex cases of the most far-reaching import. 35 *Third Branch* (March 2003).

[13] Edward J. Devitt Distinguished Service to Justice Award, 12th Annual, In Recognition of the Honorable Jack B. Weinstein, June 17, 1994 (Bolton Landing, New York).

[14] Arnold H. Lubasch, *Jack Weinstein: Creative U.S. Judge Who Disdains Robe and High Bench*, N.Y. TIMES, May 28, 1991, at B5.

[15] John C. Goldberg, *Misconduct, Misfortune, and Just Compensation: Weinstein on Courts*, 97 COLUM. L. REV. 2034, 2035 (1997).

every molecule in his courtroom" and for efficiency in managing his docket.[16] It is this combination of craft, activism and courage—a willingness to stick his neck out over and over—that makes Weinstein such an interesting vehicle for studying the work of federal district courts and its impact.

This book, then, will be a study of Jack Weinstein as a district judge; of a man and his life in the law. Though it will not omit discussion of his life prior to reaching the bench or of his off-the-bench life while he has been a judge (especially where his life experiences have affected his decision-making), we will look at his decisions and other writings, to his conception of the judicial function, his beliefs and values, his competence, the artistry which has marked his work and his impact as judge on law and politics.[17]

At the same time, though, this book will try to fulfill a second broad goal—to illuminate the work of federal district judges more generally. If Weinstein is in many ways unique as a judge, he nevertheless shares important aspects of his role with every other district judge: dealing with routine cases which reinforce appreciation for process; owning a frontline view of the social, economic, and political problems which lead to lawsuits and trustee for the reputation and integrity of the federal courts.[18]

THE WORK OF FEDERAL DISTRICT JUDGES

The work of the federal district courts has not been the subject of much study. Those who have written about courts and judges—especially nonlawyers—have generally directed their attention to the work of the Supreme Court of the United States, although that has changed somewhat in the past two generations.

Yet, federal district courts are important legal *and* political institutions. For about a half-century federal district judges have contributed mightily to the protection of constitutional rights and to ensuring that governmental institutions—state and local as well as federal—act under the rule of law. An obvious example is Frank M. Johnson, judge of the Middle District of Alabama for over two decades (the one district judge who has received considerable study), who became legendary not only for steadfastly enforcing school desegregation and voting rights, but also for assuming control of Alabama's prisons, mental hospitals, and state police to rectify violations of rights protected by the U.S. Constitution.

Judge Johnson is not alone in American legal chronicles. Other courageous district judges who come immediately to mind are Judge John M. Woolsey of the Southern

---

[16] Glaberson, *supra* note 3, at 21.
[17] Charles Fairman, *Introduction, Symposium on the Writing of Judicial Biography*, 24 IND. L.J. 363, 364 (1949).
[18] Fritz, CHRISTIAN G. FRITZ, FEDERAL JUSTICE IN CALIFORNIA: THE COURT OF OGDEN HOFFMAN 1851–1891 (1991), xff.

District of New York who prevented the U.S. Customs Service from embargoing the importation of James Joyce's *Ulysses*; Ronald Davies, judge of the District of North Dakota, sitting by designation in Little Rock, who upheld the desegregation of Central High School when Governor Orval Faubus was attempting to close the school; Murray Gurfein and Gerhard Gesell who rebuffed attempts to prevent publication of the *Pentagon Papers*; and, perhaps most notably, Judge John J. Sirica, who faced down the President of the United States over the Watergate tapes.

In the forty years Jack B. Weinstein has been on the bench, federal district judges in the District of Columbia have presided over "state trials" involving Watergate, the Iran-Contra affair, and "Libbygate." Other district judges aroused controversy throughout the land by strict construction of the National Environmental Protection Act and the Endangered Species Act. In addition to Frank Johnson, a number of judges supervised the running of prisons, mental hospitals, and other governmental institutions. If the period immediately after 9/11 was not notably marked by judicial courage, a few district judges—Shira Scheindlin of the Southern District of New York and Gladys Kessler of the District of Columbia among them—refused to defer to the Bush administration's assertions of emergency power.

Most of the attention district courts receive from the general public falls into a few (usually) dramatic categories—political trials during which defendants and their attorneys often seek to use the trial as a sounding board or perhaps to bait the judge to bring about a mistrial or reversal; trials of public officials for corruption and of leaders of organized crime; last-minute requests for restraining orders to stay or prevent executions, projects arguably harming the environment, desegregation of schools or labor walkouts; remedial orders to end constitutional violations in prisons and other public institutions. The district judge's moments in the sun are few in number, even in lengthy careers.

Yet, as the primary intake point for the federal court system, district courts are the principal "gatekeepers" for the federal courts. Generally, it is the district courts which finally determine whether there is federal jurisdiction; whether the party bringing the case has standing; whether the defendants are entitled to immunity from suit; whether the Eleventh Amendment or rules of comity are properly invoked to bar a suit against a state or whether an action has been brought before the statute of limitations ran out. By managing cases on his/her docket, a federal judge may narrow or widen the scope of issues to be decided at trial. When ruling on motions and encouraging settlement, the district judge often exerts a major influence on whether a litigant will continue to seek a decision in court.[19]

---

[19] On gate-keeping, *see* C. K. Rowland & Bridget Jeffery Todd, *Where You Stand Depends on Who Sits: Platform Promises and Judicial Gatekeeping in the Federal Judicial Courts*, 53 J. POL. 175,177 (1991). Lawrence Baum, *The Judicial Gatekeeping Function*, in COURTS, LAW, AND THE JUDICIAL PROCESS 128ff (S. Sidney Ulmer ed., 1981); Lawrence Baum, *The Judicial Gatekeeping Function*, in AMERICAN COURT SYSTEMS 125, 126 (Sheldon Goldman & Austin Sarat, 1970).

There are, to be sure, particular problems in studying the work of the federal district courts—beginning with the number of judges (over 900)[20] who handle over 230,000 cases annually and the number of cases (averaging well over 300 cases per authorized judgeship a year). In addition, the published opinions of a district judge may deal only with a single issue and that issue may not represent in any way the difficulty or importance of the case. Uncaptured by opinions, buried in lengthy records, or lost to history may be such important aspects of the work of district judges as the influence of the judge on the lawyering of the case; his role in settlement; his dignity and fairness in the courtroom; the alacrity with which he handles objections to the admission of evidence.

The literature about district courts and district judges is very small compared with the importance of those courts. The judges themselves have not created a revealing literature. Law professors have focused upon jurisdictional issues, matters of judicial administration, and case studies concerning the efficacy of major structural litigation, producing several full-length case studies and anthologies of shorter case studies.[21] When law professors who have been former law clerks write of the judges they've worked for, the tone is almost always laudatory. Political scientists have concentrated heavily on the appointment process,[22] quantitative analysis of the relationship between background variables and decisions, role perception, and the implementation of decisions.[23]

Yet, there are about a dozen judicial biographies[24] and approximately the same number of histories of district courts which have appeared in the

---

[20] As of December 2008, there were 678 authorized district court judgeships and several hundred senior judges. Some of the authorized judgeships were vacant, pending appointment and confirmation of new appointees.

[21] Donald L. Howowitz, The Courts and Social Policy (1977); Phillip J. Cooper, Hard Judicial Choices: Federal District Court Judges and State and Local Officials (1988); Gerald N. Rosenberg, The Hollow Hope: Can Courts Bring about Social Change? (1991), R. Shep Melnick, Regulation and the Courts: The Case of the Clean Air Act (1983); Limits of Justice: The Courts' Role in School Desegregation (Howard I. Kalodner & James J. Fishman eds.) (1978); Justice and School Systems: The Role of the Courts in Education Litigation (Barbara Flicker ed.) (1990).

[22] See particularly Sheldon Goldman: Picking Federal Judges: Lower Court Selection from Roosevelt through Reagan (1999).

[23] See Austin Sarat, Judging in Trial Courts: An Exploratory Study, 39 J. Pol. 368ff; 388ff (1977).

[24] Frank R. Kammerer, Justice: A Judicial Biography (1991); Ronald J. Bacigal, May It Please the Court: A Biography of Robert T. Merhige, Jr. (1992); Louise Ann Fisch, Reynoldo G. Garza, The First Mexican-American Federal Judge (1996); Barbara Ann Atwood, A Courtroom of Her Own: The Life and Work of Judge Mary Anne Richey (1998); Jace Weaver, Then to the Rock Let Me Fly: Judge Luther Bohanon and Judicial Activism (1993); Harry J. Stein, Gus J. Solomon (2006); William Nelson, In Pursuit of Right and Justice: Edward Weinfeld as Lawyer and Judge (2004); Jack Bass, Taming the Storm: The Life and Times of Judge Frank. M. Johnson, Jr. and the South's Fight over Civil Rights (1993); Robert Francis Kennedy, Jr., Judge Frank M. Johnson, Jr., A Biography (1978); Frank Sikora, The Judge: The Life and Opinions of Alabama's Frank M. Johnson, Jr. (1992); Tinsley E. Yarbrough, Judge Frank Johnson and Human Rights in Alabama (1987); Arthur Selwyn Miller, A "Capacity for Outrage": The Judicial Odyssey of J. Skelly Wright (1984); Tinsely Yarborough, A Passion

past generation.[25] Generally, the biographies tend to focus on a limited number of cases. The histories understandably give relatively little attention to the contemporary work of the district court. A rounded contemporary picture of district judging rarely has appeared.

It should be noted, however, that in the past generation, much has happened to make the study of district judges somewhat easier. Computerized legal databases facilitate almost instant compilation of a given judge's complete list of opinions. The computer has made it unnecessary to go through every page of every volume of *Federal Supplement* and *Federal Rules Decisions* during the working life of a judge to compile a complete list of opinions. Now it can be done in seconds. Many unpublished opinions are now available through LEXIS or reproduced by specialized services. Google is, of course, invaluable. In addition, hundreds of oral histories of district judges have been produced and available. There is a published guide to these oral histories as well as an anthology based on them, which sheds light on prejudicial careers, the factors leading to their appointment, the transition to the bench, the

FOR JUSTICE: J. WATIES WARING AND CIVIL RIGHTS (1987); FEDERAL BAR FOUNDATION, EDWARD WEINFELD: A JUDICIOUS LIFE (1998); FEDERAL BAR FOUNDATION, GLIMPSES OF WALTER MANSFIELD (1995). *See also* SHELDON ENGELMAYER & ROBERT WAGMAN, LORD'S JUSTICE (1985); VERNA C. CORGAN, THE RHETORIC OF JUDGE MILES WELTON LORD (1995); FRITZ, *supra* note 18; WILLIAM DWYER, *IPSE DIXIT*: HOW THE WORLD LOOKS TO A FEDERAL JUDGE (2007); CHARLES M. HAAR, MASTERING BOSTON HARBOR: COURTS, DOLPHINS AND IMPERILED WATERS (2005). There are also books with brief biographies of judges who sat in a particular district. *See, e.g.*, PEGGY J. TESLOW, HISTORY OF THE UNITED STATES DISTRICT COURT FOR THE DISTRICT OF SOUTH DAKOTA (1991); ARDELL THARALDSON, PATRONAGE: HISTORIES AND BIOGRAPHIES OF NORTH DAKOTA'S FEDERAL JUDGES (2002). *See also* THE FEDERAL COURTS OF THE TENTH CIRCUIT: A HISTORY (James K. Logan ed.) (1992).

[25] *See* RICHARD CAHAN, A COURT THAT SHAPED AMERICA: CHICAGO'S FEDERAL DISTRICT COURT FROM ABE LINCOLN TO ABBIE HOFFMAN (2002); LAWRENCE H. LARSEN, FEDERAL JUDGES IN WESTERN MISSOURI (1994); KERMIT L. HALL & ERIC W. RISE, FROM LOCAL COURTS TO NATIONAL TRIBUNALS; THE FEDERAL DISTRICT COURTS OF FLORIDA, 1821–1990 (1991); TONY FREYER & TIMOTHY DIXON, DEMOCRACY AND JUDICIAL INDEPENDENCE: A HISTORY OF THE FEDERAL COURTS OF ALABAMA, 1820–1994 (1995); CHARLES L. ZELDEN, JUSTICE LIES IN THE DISTRICT: THE U.S. DISTRICT COURT, SOUTHERN DISTRICT OF TEXAS, 1902–1960 (1993); STEVEN HARMON WILSON, THE RISE OF JUDICIAL MANAGEMENT IN THE U.S. DISTRICT COURT, SOUTHERN DISTRICT OF TEXAS, 1955–2000 (2002); GEORGE W. GELB & DONALD B. KITE SR., FEDERAL JUSTICE IN INDIANA: THE HISTORY OF THE UNITED STATES DISTRICT COURT FOR THE SOUTHERN DISTRICT OF INDIANA (2007); ROBERTA SUE ALEXANDER, A PLACE OF RECOURSE: A HISTORY OF THE U.S. DISTRICT COURT FOR THE SOUTHERN DISTRICT OF OHIO, 1803–2003 (2005); THE FIRST DUTY: A HISTORY OF THE U.S. DISTRICT COURT FOR OREGON (Carolyn Buan ed. 1993); PATRICIA E. BRAKE, JUSTICE IN THE VALLEY: A BICENTENNIAL PERSPECTIVE OF THE UNITED STATES DISTRICT COURT FOR THE EASTERN DISTRICT OF TENNESSEE (1998); PETER GRAHAM FISH, FEDERAL JUSTICE IN THE MID-ATLANTIC SOUTH: UNITED STATES COURTS FROM MARYLAND TO THE CAROLINAS, 1789–1835 (N.D.); MARY K. TACHAU, FEDERAL COURTS IN THE EARLY REPUBLIC: KENTUCKY 1789–1816 (1978); MARK EDWARD LENDER, "THIS HONORABLE COURT": THE UNITED STATES DISTRICT COURT FOR THE DISTRICT OF NEW JERSEY, 1789–2000 (2006); MATTHEW F. MCGUIRE, AN ANECDOTAL HISTORY OF THE UNITED STATES DISTRICT COURT FOR THE DISTRICT OF COLUMBIA (N.D.); JEFFREY BRANDON MORRIS, CALMLY TO POISE THE SCALES OF JUSTICE: A HISTORY OF THE COURTS OF THE DISTRICT OF COLUMBIA CIRCUIT (1991); FEDERAL BAR COUNCIL FOUNDATION, UNITED STATES COURTS IN THE SECOND CIRCUIT (1992); CHRISTIAN G. FRITZ, M. GRIFFITH, & J. M. HUNTER, A JUDICIAL ODYSSEY: FEDERAL COURT IN SANTA CLARA, SAN BENITO, SANTA CRUZ, AND MONTEREY COUNTIES (1985).

nature of the job, and the opinion-writing process.[26] There is also a guide to collections of the papers of federal judges.[27] In addition, many judges are open to interviews and generous with their time.

WHY STUDY THE WORK OF DISTRICT COURTS BY CONCENTRATING ON THE CAREER OF A SINGLE JUDGE?

While some judges and scholars have criticized the focus on a single judge via biography as an uneconomical and unscientific way to study the judicial process,[28] biography has been used to describe the role of courts in the political system, place judges and courts in the context of their time, and describe and explain the linkage between person, process, and policy. Such a study can reconstruct the values that have influenced judicial decision-making and provide useful data for a wide range of scholars.[29]

This book is not intended as a full-scale biography. Rather its focus upon a single judge offers the opportunity to describe what trial judges do and the political implications of their work. Focusing on a single person permits us to offer a portrait of his/her private character, legal productivity, and ethical standards, hopefully producing a portrait of a human being rather than an artificial and sterile model.

While presenting a portrait of a most unusual trial judge, this book will attempt to test observations and generalizations made by other scholars about courts and attempt to answer (or provide data for others to answer) questions about the work of federal trial judges. Looking at a single judge permits an in-depth study of which characteristics are valuable for a judicial career. We will also consider the strategies and tools available to achieve policy goals and what judicial activism means at the trial level. By focusing upon a unique trial judge, we can consider the potential which a single district judge can have for influence outside his or her district. This also permits an inquiry as to whether extrajudicial activities of a district judge may distract from judicial work or add to its quality. It is this author's hope that from this book, the reader will not only learn something about Jack Weinstein, but more generally about the federal district courts.

---

[26] WILLIAM DOMNARSKI, FEDERAL JUDGES REVEALED (2009).

[27] Directory of Manuscript Collections Related to Federal Judges, 1789–1997 (Federal Judicial Center 1998).

[28] See the discussion in J. Woodford Howard, Judicial Biography and the Behavioral Persuasion, paper delivered at 1969 Meeting of the American Political Science Association, at 10 [hereinafter Howard, Judicial Biography].

[29] J. Woodford Howard, Jr., Commentary, 70 N.Y.U. L. REV. 533, 536–37 (1995). J. Woodford Howard, Jr., Alpheus T. Mason and the Art of Judicial Biography, 8 CONST. COMMENT. 41, 45 (1991). J. Woodford Howard, Jr., Judicial Biography, supra note 28, at 7.

While working on this book, the author has interviewed a number of persons who have played important roles in Jack Weinstein's career, and read the well over one thousand Weinstein opinions, as well as his books, articles, and speeches. I have also made heavy use of the transcripts of discussions I had with Judge Weinstein beginning in 1993. The Weinstein oral history is one of the most extensive oral histories made of a federal judge, certainly the most extensive by a federal district judge. In it, Weinstein attempts to do what few judges have done—to publicly reflect on what he has done and why he acted as he did.[30] While the applicable law and facts, of course, affect judicial decision-making, so do aspects of the judge's values and previous experience. The Weinstein oral history allows a virtually unparalleled opportunity to look at both the legal factors and the personal factors that affected the decisions of a distinguished judge throughout a career spanning more than four decades.[31]

---

[30] "Comprehensive and sustained commentary on the judging process does not flow easily from the judicial pen." FRANK M. COFFIN, THE WAYS OF A JUDGE 12 (1980). As Felix Frankfurter put it, the "power of searching analysis of what it is they are doing rarely seems to be possessed by judges." OF LAW AND MEN 32 (1956).

[31] It is intended that the transcripts of the more than 1750-page oral history will be open to any interested person in the Oral History Office at Columbia University and the law library of Touro College Jacob D. Fuchsberg Law Center. No strings are attached by either Judge Weinstein or me to the use of this material by others.

1

"All The Facts of Real Life Revealed in Our Work":

The "Job" of a Federal District Judge[1]

IT IS NOT unusual for a Court of Appeals judge to state that the work of a trial judge offers "a much richer experience" than serving on an appellate court. One such judge was a Devitt Award recipient, Edward Tamm, who served on both the U.S. District Court for the District of Columbia and the U.S. Court of Appeals for the District of Columbia Circuit, and who spoke fondly of the district judge's daily contact with lawyers, witnesses, and juries and of dealing basically with the "people's problems."[2] After all, the federal district courts are the "workhorses of the federal judiciary," where "litigants meet in open combat," witnesses are heard, jurors used, and "facts are determined."[3]

Published opinions reveal but a small part of the federal trial judge's work.[4] Indeed, for many trial judges, opinions are of secondary importance. Trial judges write relatively few published opinions. Even presiding over trials is a comparatively small part of their work. District judges not only adjudicate disputes over facts and law and act as umpires during trials, but negotiate, administer, and sometimes perform a significant

---

[1] Jack B. Weinstein Oral History, at 279.

[2] 1 Oral History of Judge Edward Tamm 12 (Nov. 12, 1983); 2 Oral History of Edward Tamm 3 (Dec. 29, 1983); Gerhard Gesell, *Perspectives on the Judiciary*, 39 AM.U. L. REV. 490 (1990); 1 Tamm Oral History 12–13; 2 Tamm Oral History 3.

[3] KEVIN L. LYLES, THE GATEKEEPERS: FEDERAL DISTRICT COURTS IN THE POLITICAL PROCESS 3 (1997).

[4] *See* C. K. ROWLAND & ROBERT A. CARP, POLITICS AND JUDGMENT IN FEDERAL DISTRICT COURTS 16 (1996).

political role.[5] J. Woodford Howard, biographer of District, Court of Appeals, and Supreme court judges, tells us that justice in a case requires "an active manager with broad discretion and powers to keep various actors ... litigants, lawyers, witnesses, jurors" within their proper role.[6]

Because of the absence of available descriptions of the work of federal district judges,[7] it seems appropriate to provide such a description before delving into Jack B. Weinstein's career.

First, it should be noted the life of a district judge is hurried and the flow of cases unending. Day in and day out, the district judge has hundreds of cases on his docket. Some of those cases disappear from the docket without meaningful judicial work as parties fail to pursue them or they settle without judicial intervention. Weekly, perhaps even daily, the judge and his staff (two or three law clerks, a judicial assistant, and courtroom deputy (an employee of the clerk of court's office) will be processing a number of cases—monitoring them, responding to pretrial and posttrial motions, holding pretrial conferences to schedule or possibly settle cases, presiding over trials (although that has become relatively rare), sentencing criminal defendants, and writing opinions or findings of fact.

The federal district courts use an individual calendar whereby, ordinarily, cases are randomly assigned to individual judges, who are responsible for them from the time of assignment (close to the time of filing of the complaint) until final judgment. A civil case begins with a complaint filed in the office of the clerk of the district court by the plaintiff. Jurisdiction is obtained over the defendant by the service of process. The defendant has twenty days to file an "answer" to the complaint (the United States government has sixty days). The answer sets up the defendant's response to each allegation in the complaint and may offer affirmative defenses. At the time, the defendant may also assert a counter-claim against the plaintiff or a cross-claim against a third party.[8] At the pleading stage, the defendant may move to dismiss the complaint; for example, on the ground that the court has no jurisdiction over the case. After the pleading stage,

[5] LAWRENCE BAUM, AMERICAN COURTS: PROCESS AND POLICY 133–37; JOHN PAUL RYAN ET AL., AMERICAN TRIAL JUDGES 3ff (1980); DAVID W. NEUBAUER, JUDICIAL PROCESS: LAW COURTS AND POLITICS IN THE UNITED STATES 153ff (1991).

[6] J. Woodford Howard, *Judge Harold R. Medina: The "Freshman," Years*, 69 JUDICATURE 127, 133 (October–November 1985) [hereinafter, Howard, *Freshman*].

[7] *But see* José A. Cabranes, Judging: Some Reflections on the Work of the Federal Courts, Remarks at Touro College, Jacob B. Fuchsberg Law Center, Huntington, N.Y. (Mar. 1, 1993).

[8] *See* FEDERAL JUDICIAL CENTER, BENCHBOOK FOR U.S. DISTRICT COURT JUDGES (1996; 4th ed. with March 2000 revisions) [hereinafter, BENCHBOOK FOR DISTRICT JUDGES]; CALVERT G. CHIPCHASE, FEDERAL DISTRICT COURT LAW CLERK HANDBOOK (2007); FEDERAL JUDICIAL CENTER, LAW CLERK HANDBOOK (Sylvan A. Sobel, Jr., 2d ed. 2007), THE ELEMENTS OF CASE MANAGEMENT: A POCKET GUIDE FOR JUDGES (William W. Schwarzer & Alan Hirsch eds., 2006); Administrative Office of the United States Courts, *A Journalist's Guide to the Federal Courts* (N.D.), *available at* http://www.uscourts.gov [hereinafter, *Journalist's Guide*]; JENNIFER EVANS MARSH, THE USE OF VISITING JUDGES IN THE FEDERAL DISTRICT COURTS: A GUIDE FOR JUDGES AND COURT PERSONNEL (2001, updated 2003); FEDERAL JUDICIAL CENTER, DESKBOOK FOR CHIEF JUDGES OF U.S. DISTRICT COURTS (3d ed. 2003).

either party may move for a judgment on the pleadings. If the motion to dismiss and/or the motion for judgment on the pleadings are not granted, the case will proceed.

The district judge has the obligation to "manage" the cases before him for several reasons: to achieve more timely justice by keeping his docket moving, to curtail discovery abuse, and to facilitate settlement. Early in the process, attorneys for the parties to the case may engage in motion practice. For example, the parties may make motions to dismiss based upon failure to state a claim, lack of jurisdiction, improper venue or failure to join a party, contending that the court lacks jurisdiction over the case or that there is no legal basis for relief, to transfer the case because it has been brought in the wrong venue, to join other parties in the lawsuit.

If the case survives these early motions, other motions may follow for discovery of information possessed by the other side through depositions, written interrogatories, or the production of documents. The opposing side may oppose such motions for discovery or move to obtain a protective order. Possibly as early as just after the answer is filed or after discovery is complete, a Rule 56 motion for summary judgment may be filed—that, as a matter of law, the plaintiff's case is insufficient to go to trial—often containing voluminous amounts of documentary, affidavit, and deposition evidence. The motion for summary judgment is often the most decisive motion in a civil case for claims will be dismissed, if there is no genuine issue as to any material fact and the movant is entitled to judgment as a matter of law. The judge may grant that motion in whole or in part or deny it entirely.[9] Much of the pre-trial process culminates in motions for summary judgment. The trial's court's decision, even where the court denies the motion, is critical to resolving the dispute. Even when the motion is denied, the parties are now aware that they face the expensive process of going to trial, which may encourage settlement.

If the case is going to trial, before the trial there will be motions dealing with the admissibility of evidence at trial, such as hearsay testimony, the scope of expert opinion, or assertions of privilege (such as attorney-client privilege), some of which may require expedited treatment.[10] While considerably less than 5 percent of all civil actions reach trial,[11] the judge may have to decide motions in most civil cases.

Thus, unless the district judge has exercised his option to refer aspects of the pre-trial to a magistrate judge before trial or settlement, he will have dealt with a variety of motions—some complex, many not. Each, except those decided from the bench, will require an order disposing of the motion.[12] Some motions may require evidentiary hearings; some may not. Some are handled simply by a judge scribbling nothing more

---

[9] Kenneth C. Broodoo & Douglas H. Haldfitis, *Practice in the Federal District Courts from the Law Clerk's Perspective: The Rules Behind the Rules*, 43 BAYLOR L. REV. 333, 354 (1991) [hereinafter, Broodoo].

[10] Ralph Johnson, *Focus on Judge Mark R. Kravitz*, 11 FED. BAR COUNC. NEWS No. 3, at 3, 7–10 (June 2004).

[11] Less than 1.8 percent in 2003. *See* STEPHEN SUBRIN & MARGARET Y. K. WOO, LITIGATING IN AMERICA: CIVIL PRACTICE IN CONTEXT 240 (2006).

[12] ALVIN B. RUBIN & LAURA B. B. BARTELL, LAW CLERK HANDBOOK 29, 145 (rev. ed.1989).

than "granted" or "denied" on the papers or by a quick ruling from the bench; others may require a detailed written opinion. Some rulings may be of little significance even to the parties, while others may greatly affect how speedily the case reaches disposition by adding or decreasing the incentives to settle, the direction and substance of settlement, or the outcome of the trial. But, even decisions as simple as whether to give one side more time may, when decided, permit a party to harass or exhaust his opponent, while a motion to extend discovery may make it possible for a plaintiff to "find" a theory for his lawsuit. Rulings on such motions are generally immune from appellate reversal and opinions on them rarely are published.[13]

Much of the work of district judges takes place in their chambers rather than in their courtroom. In chambers they read motions, discuss issues with law clerks, and draft and re-draft orders, judgments, and opinions. It is there that they hold informal status conferences with the attorneys in each case and the final pretrial conference.

The final pretrial conference is mandated by Rule 16 of the Federal Rules of Civil Procedure. It is typically held after discovery is complete or nearly complete, to lay bare the heart of the dispute and to narrow the issues as much as possible. At the final pretrial conference, the court is alerted to the status of any settlement negotiations and may at the meeting strongly encourage resolution of the dispute before trial.[14]

The purpose of the conference is to simplify the issues to be determined at trial, to avoid the production of unnecessary evidence, to limit the number of expert witnesses, and to discuss settlement. The joint pretrial order is the final and determinative integration of the parties' pleadings.

Settlements greatly affect the district court's ability to manage its workload. Judges vary in attitudes toward their participation in settlement negotiations. A judge can encourage settlements during the pretrial period by setting a trial date early in the process, having parties as well as attorneys present during pretrial discussions, initiating settlement discussions, suggesting a settlement figure, meeting separately with different sides, and refusing to grant postponements once the trial date is reached.[15] Notable examples of Judge Jack Weinstein's involvement in settlement negotiations occurred in the cases involving the Shoreham Nuclear Reactor (*see* Chapter 7) and Agent Orange (*see* Chapter 10).

Thus, during the pretrial process, the judge will have had the opportunity to assist the attorneys in framing the issues and enabling the development of the facts; to simplify and expedite the proceedings by limiting the number of potential witnesses and the issues needing proof; and to make sure that a meaningful and complete record will

---

[13] ROWLAND & CARP, *supra* note 4, at 122.

[14] RUBIN & BARTELL, *supra* note 12, at 37–39; Broodoo, *supra* note 9, at 382.

[15] Joel B. Grossman et al., *Dimensions of Institutional Participation: Who Uses the Courts, and How?*, 44 J. POL. 107 n.39 (February 1982).

be developed if an appeal is anticipated.[16] The district judge might also recommend the use of other methods of dispute resolution—nonbinding mediation, nonbinding arbitration, a facilitator, or a summary jury trial (an abbreviated trial presented to an advisory jury which renders a nonbinding verdict).[17]

Managing is, thus, an important part of the job of a district judge, a task which, as the distinguished district judge of the District Court for the District of Columbia District, Judge Gerhard Gesell, pithily pointed out, "has nothing to do with pure rules of law, but . . . a lot to do with knowing how trial courts work."[18]

The function of a district judge that is most visible to the general public is presiding over trials. Some judges are happiest in the courtroom. Judge Harold Medina's biographer tells us that Medina "loved being King of the Courtroom"; "the routines and rituals of trials—hearing testimony, watching witnesses and litigants, hassling with counsel—were human dramas to him."[19] But not all able district judges are as enamored with trials or at least with the way trials are conducted. Judge Marvin Frankel of the Southern District of New York, a law school classmate of Weinstein's and a distinguished judge in his own right, could be quite critical, stating that, "the trial judge spends a good deal of his time solemnly watching clear, deliberate, entirely proper efforts by skilled professionals to block the attainment of [truth] . . ."[20]

In a jury trial, one major function of the district judge is to preside over the selection of the jury. Jury selection may be conducted by the judge or left in the hands of the attorney; however, the judge retains the final authority to decide which questions can be asked of potential jurors. Once the trial begins, the district judge also rules on the admissibility of evidence and the acceptability of questions lawyers ask of witnesses. The final judgment rule guarantees that appeals during trials are rare, essentially limited to interlocutory orders, orders denying intervention, and collateral orders. The trial judge also decides motions for judgment as a matter of law, which may be made when a party has been fully heard on an issue during a jury trial. Such motions can be renewed after the jury verdict.

In a jury trial, the trial judge should deliver a clear, comprehensive, fair, and useful charge to the jury, summarizing the case, pinpointing the chief issues, and instructing the jury on the applicable law. The jury charge is crucial. Parties file proposed joint jury instructions which they have agreed to and supplementary instructions on points upon which they have not agreed. Each counsel must be given the opportunity out of

---

[16] Charles E. Wyzanski, Jr., The Importance of the Trial Judge [Letter from Wyzanski to Senator Leverett Saltonstall, Jan. 12, 1959], *in* COURTS, JUDGES, AND POLITICS 355 (Walter F. Murphy & C. Herman Pritchett eds., 2d ed. 1974).

[17] ROBERTA SUE ALEXANDER, A PLACE OF RECOURSE: A HISTORY OF THE U.S. DISTRICT COURT FOR THE SOUTHERN DISTRICT OF OHIO, 1803–2003, at 147–51 (2005).

[18] Gesell, *supra* note 2, at 490.

[19] Howard, *Freshman, supra* note, 6 at 133.

[20] Marvin E. Frankel, *The Adversary Judge, in* JUDGES ON JUDGING 63 at 67 (David M. O'Brien, ed., 1997).

the presence of the jury to make objections to the proposed charge and will object again after the charge is given to preserve the issue for appeal.

During a bench trial (a trial without a jury), the trial judge as the finder of fact must determine the credibility of witnesses. At the end of the trial, he issues his findings of fact and conclusions of law (written or oral). The distinguished legal historian, J. Willard Hurst, wrote that "craftsmanship holds itself nowhere more surely than in the handling of facts. In the hands of a first-rate judge the statement of the facts of a case seems almost itself to declare the proper result."[21] This will be seen as one of Weinstein's greatest strengths. Such fact-finding is essentially immune from appellate scrutiny.

At the trial of both civil and criminal cases, the judge performs another important role. He is the guardian of the appearance of fairness and the maintenance of authority. Judge Charles Wyzanski of the District of Massachusetts wrote that the judge must conduct a trial in such a way "that the jurors, the witnesses, the counsel and the spectators not only follow the red threads of fact and law, but leave the courtroom persuaded of the fairness of the procedure and the high responsibility of courts and judges in advancing the values we cherish most deeply."[22] Wyzanski saw the trial judge as "a teacher of parties, witnesses . . . and even casual visitors to his court. His conduct of the trial may fashion and sustain the moral principles of the community . . . his character and personal distinction, open to daily inspection in his courtroom, constitute the guarantees of due process."[23]

After trial, either party may file posttrial motions. These motions may include one for relief from the judgment, such as a motion for judgment not withstanding the verdict, motions for a new trial, and motions for attorneys' fees and costs. The judgment may require the judge to stay its execution by setting a *supersedeas* bond or a bond for costs.[24]

The criminal process proceeds much more swiftly, in part because of deadlines set by the Speedy Trial Act.[25] A criminal case can begin several ways, including an arrest with or without a warrant followed by filing of a complaint ("information") sworn to by the U.S. Attorney or federal law enforcement officer or by an arrest on a warrant issued upon indictment. After the defendant's arrest, he will make an initial appearance in court where he will be informed of the charges he faces as well as his rights. Counsel will be appointed if the defendant is too poor to afford one, and bail may be set. There will then be a preliminary examination at which the government will present its

---

[21] J. Willard Hurst, *Who Is the "Great" Appellate Judge?*, 24 IND. L.J. 399 (1949).

[22] Charles E. Wyzanski, Jr., *A Trial Judge, in* WHEREAS—A JUDGE'S PREMISES 3 at 4 [hereinafter, Wyzanski, WHEREAS].

[23] Wyzanski, *The Importance of the Trial Judge, supra* note 16, at 355.

[24] [Federal Judicial Center], HANDBOOK FOR FEDERAL JUDGES' SECRETARIES 123 (rev. September 1985) [hereinafter, SECRETARIES HANDBOOK].

[25] Speedy Trial Act of 1974, P.L. 93–619, 88 Stat. 2076, 18 U.S.C. 3161–74. The law has been amended a number of times.

evidence to a magistrate judge or a district judge, who will determine if there is probable cause that the defendant committed a crime. If probable cause is found, there will be a detention hearing to determine whether the defendant may be released on his own recognizance or on an unsecured personal bond. Finally, the district judge or magistrate judge will handle the arraignment at which the defendant's plea is taken and at which he may request a jury trial. If the defendant waives trial by jury, the judge must determine that the accused understands the implications of the waiver and is mentally competent to do so.[26] If the defendant knowingly and voluntarily pleads guilty or *nolo contendere*, the matter proceeds to sentencing. At the arraignment, some judges also schedule dates for hearings on motions and the date for the trial. If there is more than one defendant and several wish to use the same attorney, the judge must inquire into potential conflicts of interest.[27] These four hearings—the initial appearance, the preliminary hearing, the detention hearing, and the arraignment—may be held by magistrate judges or district court judges or a combination of the two. Throughout the process, the judge must continue to monitor the defendant's competence to stand trial, to be sentenced, and, if acquitted by a plea of insanity, to decide whether he should be institutionalized.[28]

Unless the defendant(s) has pleaded guilty, prior to the criminal trial there may be a considerable number of motions, generally on paper. They may include motions to challenge the sufficiency of the indictment by way of a motion to dismiss; to challenge jurisdiction or venue; to discover evidence; and, perhaps most importantly, to suppress evidence because of violations of the Fourth, Fifth, or Sixth Amendments of the U.S. Constitution. In a criminal case, there may be an early omnibus hearing to determine which motions will be filed, to simplify the issues to be tried, and to expedite full disclosure of evidence. Thus, in criminal cases, the decisive events often occur before trial—the appointment of counsel, setting of bail, and motions to suppress evidence.

Throughout the pretrial and the trial as well, the judge must be careful not to permit prejudicial publicity.[29] He or she must oversee the impaneling of the jury and make whatever special arrangements are necessary for the jury and the press. At the trial, after the prosecution has presented evidence, the defense will make a Rule 29 motion, asking the judge to acquit the defendant because the prosecution's evidence is insufficient to sustain a conviction. Such a motion may also be made after the conclusion of the testimony of defense witnesses.

Assuming these motions have not been granted, the judge, after the closing arguments, must charge the jury. While the jury is deliberating, if it has questions about

---

[26] BENCHBOOK FOR DISTRICT JUDGES, *supra* note 8, at 31.

[27] *Id.* at 25.

[28] *Id.* at 53ff.

[29] Charles E. Wyzanski, Jr., *A Trial Judge's Freedom & Responsibility, in* Wyzanski, WHEREAS, 9 at 16 (1965).

the evidence or the judge's instructions, it may communicate them to the judge by note. The judge then will discuss with the attorneys what the answer to the note should be, calls the jury back into the courtroom and, respond to its queries. If the jury says it is hopelessly deadlocked, the judge will typically give the jury an Allen charge, urging jurors to reconsider and try again to reach a verdict.[30]

After the jury renders a verdict, there will be posttrial motions for a new trial and for arrest of judgment. Sentencing will be preceded by a pre-sentence investigation report by a court probation officer. Sentencing practices during Jack Weinstein's tenure are the subject of Chapter 8 of this book.

As with civil cases, very few criminal cases go to trial. The number of criminal trials has dropped startlingly. In 1962, there were 5,097 criminal trials in the federal courts. By 2002, there were only 3,574, despite a doubling of criminal filings.[31]

"Big cases" pose great challenges for the district judge. Many of the most difficult occur in class actions and other aggregative litigation such as mass tort cases; institutional litigation involving the operation of schools, prisons, and mental hospitals; multidefendant criminal cases and high-profile litigation such as trials for political corruption; and "political trials" with unruly defendants and attorneys. When there are consent decrees entered in cases involving public institutions, judges may have to administer them for years. This may also occur in class actions where hundreds of millions of dollars may be distributed.

District judges also are called upon to deal with emergency petitions for temporary restraining orders; extensive litigation involving state and federal prisoners (most of it *pro se*); pleas for reduction of sentences; and civil rights complaints.[32] District judges also perform what arguably are "appellate functions"—reviewing decisions, references, or recommendations of other officials and institutions: magistrate judges, bankruptcy courts, as well as some administrative agencies; Social Security disability matters.[33]

District judges sit with other district judges very rarely—in those instances where a three-judge district court is necessary (this happened more often early in Weinstein's tenure)[34] and, even more rarely, *en banc*. Most district judges sit more often with the Court of Appeals.

Among other tasks district judges perform is committee work for the district court itself, for the Circuit Judicial Council, and for the Judicial Conference of the

---

[30] *Journalist's Guide, supra* note 8, at 22.

[31] Patricia Lee Refo, *Opening Statement: The Vanishing Trial*, 30 LITIG. 2 (Winter 2004).

[32] SECRETARIES HANDBOOK, *supra* note 24, at 45–47.

[33] RICHARD A. POSNER, THE FEDERAL COURTS: CRISIS AND REFORM 26 (1985).

[34] At the time Weinstein was appointed to the bench, three-judge district courts were required when the constitutionality of acts of Congress and of the states was questioned. Appeals from three-judge district courts went directly to the U.S. Supreme Court. At present, such district courts are required only where the reapportionments of congressional and state legislative districts are at issue and in certain cases under the Voting Rights Act.

United States. They also deal with matters connected with grand juries, wiretaps, naturalization, and extradition.[35] District judges traditionally engage in such activities as speaking before or at least attending meetings of bar associations, presiding over law school moot court competitions, and speaking to civic groups.

SOME REFLECTIONS ON THE JOB OF FEDERAL DISTRICT JUDGE

Trial judging differs considerably from appellate judging.[36] In spite of presiding over a courtroom with lawyers, litigants, jurors, reporters, and court-watchers, as Edward Weinfeld of the Southern District of New York, one of the finest trial judges of the twentieth century put it, the trial judge "treads a lonely path. Often times it is a soul-searching vigil."[37] As Weinfeld's colleague for a brief time (before elevation to the Court of Appeals), Harold Medina, said, the trial judge is "a soloist," who almost always acts alone.[38]

The trial judge may well be alone when he receives an application for a temporary restraining order in a highly charged case involving a strike in a vital economic sector or a desegregation order on the eve of the opening of school. That was where Judge Walter Bastian was when he received at home a motion to temporarily restrain President Harry Truman's seizure of the nation's steel mills.[39] Murray Gurfein had been on the bench less than a week when he was asked to prevent publication of the Pentagon Papers.[40] Sometimes there are enormous pressures to bear alone. Just recall John J. Sirica during the Watergate trials. On the other hand, district judges may well have greater public visibility than the generally anonymous judges of the Court of Appeals, but with that visibility may come more than a dollop of obloquy as Judge W. Arthur Garrity, Jr. experienced during the controversy over desegregation of the Boston school system.[41]

---

[35] STEVEN FLANDERS, THE 1979 FEDERAL DISTRICT COURT TIME STUDY 89–90 (October 1980).

[36] Weinstein has singled out three major differences: (1) the district court is far more people-connected than appellate courts; (2) district judges have much greater control of the pace of their work; (3) their life is independent and solitary. Weinstein Oral History, *supra* note 1, at 1480.

Judge Jose Cabranes, a district judge for the District of Connecticut before elevation to the Court of Appeals for the Second Circuit, has pointed to certain critical facts affecting the decision-making process of trial judges: time, or lack of it; the instinctive impulse to build an appeal-proof record; the occasional necessity of making a quick decision even if possibly wrong; and the occasional willingness to apply to a particular issue whatever principles of law the parties agree on. Cabranes, *supra* note 7, at 11–12.

District judges must file quarterly reports of matters taken "under advisement" for some time. WILLIAM I. KITCHIN, FEDERAL DISTRICT JUDGES: ANALYSIS OF JUDICIAL PERCEPTIONS 68 (1978).

[37] FEDERAL BAR FOUNDATION, EDWARD WEINFELD: A JUDICIOUS LIFE 63 (1998).

[38] Howard, *Freshman, supra* note 6, at 151.

[39] MAEVA MARCUS, TRUMAN AND THE STEEL SEIZURE 102 (1977).

[40] *See United States v. New York Times Co.*, 328 F. Supp. 324 (1971).

[41] Carey Goldberg, *Judge W. Arthur Garrity, Jr. Is Dead at 79*, N.Y. TIMES, Sept. 18, 1999.

The pace of a district judge is always hurried. There is little time to philosophize. Motions proliferate. Cases press hard. A trial requires rapid decision-making amidst constant tension between being timely and being well enough informed.[42] Even if the rule is unclear, the decision must be made. The trial must continue. On appeal, the troublesome issues may stand out, at trial they come up quickly and have not been sifted from the trivial.[43]

Judge George T. McDermott, who served as a district judge of the District of Kansas and, later, as a member of the U.S. Court of Appeals for the Tenth Circuit, thought that:

> [T]he District bench is the most difficult and most trying position of them all. A district judge must make his mistakes quick. He cannot take several weeks time out, in the midst of a trial, to figure a way to go wrong, a prerogative of all Courts of Appeals.[44]

Of course, for every case with political or legal drama, there may be hundreds of cases that are more routine. Yet, federal judges must be generalists, going from case to case in highly disparate fields.[45] Richard Posner has written, judges "know very little about most of the disputes that come before them; and to know that you don't know is a sign of intelligence, not necessarily one of timidity."[46] Jack Weinstein found that overcoming that ignorance was one of the most pleasurable parts of being a district judge.

The judge is the manager of a small group located in chambers. That group, his staff, ordinarily includes two law clerks, a secretary, a courtroom deputy, and a court reporter. The judge is responsible for matters connected with his "space"—his chambers and his courtroom. It is there that the judge oversees the flow of paper. The rise of case management and the development of support staffs have led to criticism of "bureaucratization." In recent years, formal adversarial procedures have come to be downplayed in the federal courts in the interest of increasing case dispositions. Judicial procedures are now geared more toward flexibility and informality—negotiation and bargaining, settlements, as well as alternative mechanisms of dispute resolution such as arbitration and mediation.[47] Concurrently, a considerable number of supporting

---

[42] Cabranes, *supra* note 7, at 11–12.

[43] Wyzanski, *A Trial Judge's Freedom and Responsibility*, *supra* note 29, at 21.

[44] Harry F. Tepker, *The Judges of the Court of Appeals*, *in* THE FEDERAL COURTS OF THE TENTH CIRCUIT: A HISTORY 318, 343 (James K. Logan ed., 1992).

[45] GERALD N. ROSENBERG, THE HOLLOW HOPE: CAN COURTS BRING ABOUT SOCIAL CHANGE 16 (1991).

[46] Richard A. Poser, *The Learned Hand Biography and the Question of Judicial* Greatness, 104 YALE L. J. 511, 530 (1994).

[47] WOLF HEYDEBRAND & CARROLL SERON, RATIONING JUSTICE: THE POLITICAL ECONOMY OF THE FEDERAL DISTRICT COURTS 188 (1990).

personnel have been added—magistrate judges, bankruptcy judges, and more law clerks.

The subject of district judges as lawmakers is discussed in Chapter 4. For now, we can say that the average district judge "makes" relatively little law that is applicable to those other than the parties before him. Trial court opinions have limited precedential effect even in the district of its author. Generally, trial judges follow or adapt substantive law made by higher courts. Most of their published opinions involve gatekeeping matters, motions for summary judgment, and institutional litigation. Most trial judges do not leave a jurisprudential mark.

It should be noted when we turn to Jack Weinstein's judicial record that even in those areas where district judges exercise a wide range of discretionary authority immune from appeal, their reach is limited by the quality of the evidence, the arguments of the lawyers, the relevance and clarity of appellate precedent, and, occasionally, by decisions in related cases by their colleagues from their district.

THE POINTS OF OPPORTUNITY

When can a particular district judge make a difference? What are the "points of opportunity," when, as the result of ability and style, a trial judge can make an important difference—either to the parties before him, to the profile of the litigation, and, sometimes, to the development of public policy?

The pretrial period offers the judge the opportunity to shape the case. The breadth or narrowness with which he or she approaches gate-keeping matters—jurisdiction, ripeness, mootness, political question, immunity, abstention—may prove crucial. A judge's decision to certify a class raises the profile of the litigation and may well benefit plaintiffs.[48] Allowing parties to intervene, keeping parties in the case, and inviting friend of the court (*amicus curiae*) briefs can focus attention on the case and achieve greater flexibility with remedies.

Through control of discovery, a judge can shape the case by narrowing or widening the scope of the issues to be decided at trial. The trial judge may ask for briefs on particular issues which he deems important that may yield a decision on an issue little considered by the parties in originally preparing for trial. By permitting or encouraging the attorneys to develop the facts so as to make a meaningful and complete record, a trial judge can make it possible for an important issue to be addressed fully on appeal. Pretrial rulings can dramatically change the balance of probable trial outcomes as well as affect the incentives each side has to settle the case.[49] Clearly, a district judge's

---

[48] *See* Jack B. Weinstein, *Some Reflections on the "Abusiveness" of Class Actions, Excerpts from a Symposium before the Judicial Conference of the Fifth Judicial Circuit*, 58 F.R.D. 299, 300. (Available on Westlaw)

[49] ROWLAND & CARP, *supra* note 4, at 122; Lawrence Baum, *The Judicial Gatekeeping Function, in* COURTS, LAW, AND JUDICIAL PROCESSES 128ff (S. Sidney Ulmer ed., 1981).

decision on a motion for summary judgment will determine the result of the case, unless there is an appeal.

At trial, the judge may intervene to protect a party who is poorly represented. The ultimate result of a case may be affected by the trial judge's willingness to risk, or his strategic sense of how to avoid, reversal through tailoring findings of fact, issuing limited rulings of law, or employing alternate bases for decisions. Sometimes a decision on the admission of evidence may prove decisive. Reversals may be minimized by the doctrine of "harmless error." In practice, excepting major motions such as summary judgment, reversals ordinarily occur when important evidence has been excluded, when the charge is erroneous as to substantive law, and where there has been patent unfairness or deprivation of a constitutional right.[50]

Other characteristics of a judge's work may greatly affect the quality of the trial, though not necessarily the results: his control of the courtroom, how he "handles" lawyers and jurors, his command of the law of evidence and federal procedure and his agility with them. In the "big case" with high-profile defendants, political trials, and the like, the handling of the media may prove crucial.[51]

With litigation involving public institutions, the judge may make a major difference in his choice of remedy and the manner in which he oversees it. In civil rights cases, a judge's handling of attorneys' fees may encourage or discourage more litigation.[52]

In criminal cases, the major points of opportunity for a district judge lie with appointment of trial counsel; fixing bail which may affect a defendant's desire to plead; making sure a plea is voluntary; determining the defendant's competence to stand trial; ruling on suppression motions; presiding over a fair trial; and, even during the Sentencing Guidelines era, sentencing.

Part of the difficulty of assessing the work of a district court is that much of what trial judges do that is significant—controlling the case; attempting to produce settlement; presiding over jury and bench trials with dignity and fairness; dealing with motions effectively; producing convincing findings of fact—are extremely difficult to assess unless the pretrial and trial are personally observed throughout many cases by an astute observer with a legal education. Few have that time.

THE TOOLS OF A DISTRICT JUDGE

The powers of a district judge to enforce his rulings are varied. They include dismissal, summary judgment, or judgment not withstanding the verdict. In appropriate cases, a district judge may issue temporary restraining orders, preliminary and permanent injunctions, declaratory judgments, the writs of *habeas corpus* and mandamus.

---

[50] *United States v. Antonelli Fireworks Co.*, 155 F.2d 631, 642, 644, 665–66.

[51] *See* discussion of *Hart v. Community Bd.*, 383 F. Supp. 699 (Jan. 28, 1974) in Chapter 5.

[52] *See Zimmermann v. Schweiker*, 575 F. Supp. 1436, 1440 (Dec. 5, 1983), discussed in Chapter 6.

Furthermore, a district court judge may even have the power to stay his own decisions and assess attorneys' fees.

Where criminal cases are concerned, the judge's weapons include dismissal, sentencing, and ordering restitution. To deal with difficult attorneys, the district judge has the power under the Federal Rules of Civil Procedure to grant sanctions and the power of contempt, which can also be used to deal with difficult witnesses and parties. To deal with a recalcitrant witness, a judge also has the capacity to grant immunity.[53]

FEDERAL DISTRICT JUDGES AND THE POLITICAL PROCESS

Courts perform functions central to the modern state: regime legitimation, policy-making, social control.[54] In the United States, the federal courts are instruments of national power.[55] No party appears before a federal judge more than the government of the United States. District courts enforce the policies of the federal government and confer legitimacy on its activities. Ordinarily, they are a centralizing agent enforcing the supremacy and uniformity of federal law and federal rights and are used to secure compliance with policies created in other sectors of the political system. The district judge implements statutes (legislative policies) and appellate court decisions and enforces other norms. As the major intake point for cases in the federal judiciary, the federal district courts are very much a part of the American political process.

But the federal courts have come to do more than this. If not before, certainly by the 1960s, the federal courts had become a symbol of and a weapon used by the government to protect the rights of the individual. The federal courts monitor institutions of government and attempt to assure equal treatment and governmental "fair play," keeping agencies within their constitutional and statutory limits.

The federal courts also provide a forum in which people may seek to advance their goals of directing governmental actions and allocating societal resources.[56] Through equitable remedies, judges can impose policy judgments on administrators and elected officials. Judicial decisions determine who gets what, when, and how.[57] Their decisions resolve disputes, enforce norms, and allocate social values. The federal courts may not be able to *command* social change, but they are able to speed it up or slow it down. They have also become a safety valve, providing a forum for outraged individuals or groups

---

[53] F.R.C.P. 37, 70; 18 U.S.C. 6002, 6003.

[54] Herbert Jacob, Introduction *in* COURTS, LAW, AND POLITICS IN COMPARATIVE PERSPECTIVE 1, 3 (Herbert Jacob, Erhard Blankenburg, et al. eds., 1996).

[55] Edward A. Purcell, Jr., *Reconsidering the Frankfurtian Paradigm: Reflections on Histories of Lower Federal Courts*, 24 L & SOC.INQ. 679, 687 (1999).

[56] HERBERT JACOB, DEBTORS IN COURT 16 (1969); LAWRENCE BAUM, THE PUZZLE OF JUDICIAL BEHAVIOR 66 (2000).

[57] *See* ALEC STONE, THE BIRTH OF JUDICIAL POLITICS IN FRANCE 7, 10–15 (1992).

to vent their disapproval of the actions of government (federal, state, or local), their employers, and others.[58]

In the course of their work—by enforcing norms, adjudicating conflicts, and mediating between the government and citizens[59]—district judges inevitably make policy affecting not only the litigants before them but also others, sometimes *many* others.

It was around the time Jack Weinstein was appointed as a judge that Americans were coming more and more to expect that in litigation brought both by public interest groups and individuals, and, sometimes, by the government, that the federal courts would perform as ombudsmen for minorities and the poor, and began to turn to them often to correct malfunctions of the political system, which other parts of the federal and state governments seemed unable or unwilling to correct.[60] While not every federal judge views his or her role as actively resolving problems kept in abeyance by state governments, Congress, and the federal government, a large number do. A colleague of Jack Weinstein on the Eastern District bench, Judge I. Leo Glasser, who is considerably more risk averse than Jack Weinstein, spoke eloquently about this role of the federal courts when he discussed *pro se* litigation some years ago:

> People just walk in and start lawsuits. I think its great . . . even if it is a pain in the neck. It's just wonderful—they can go in and say, "I want my rights vindicated." It is a tribute to the system.[61]

This was a role for the federal courts Jack Weinstein had little trouble embracing.

---

[58] Purcell, *supra* note 58, at 687; Harry P. Stumpf, American Judicial Politics 54, 454ff (1988); Samuel Krislov, The Supreme Court in The Political Process 34 (1965); David S. Clark, *Adjudication to Administration: A Statistical Analysis of Federal District Courts in the Twentieth* Century, 55 S. Cal. L. Rev. 65 (1981); Kenneth M. Dolbeare, Trial Courts in Urban Politics 113ff (1967).

[59] Christopher E. Smith, Politics and the Judicial Process 7ff (2d ed. 1997).

[60] Henry J. Friendly, Federal Jurisdiction: A General View 71 (1973).

[61] JBM Interview with Judge I. Leo Glasser, May 17, 1990. Of course, much litigation brought by *pro se* litigants is intended to remedy their own grievances.

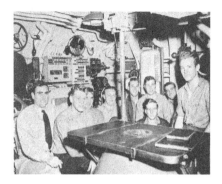

2

The Years Before Appointment to the Bench, 1921–1967

THE FEDERAL DISTRICT COURTS leave unusually wide room for a judge's individual qual-ities to be reflected in their work.[1] Part of the purpose of this book is to demonstrate how Jack B. Weinstein's abilities, characteristics, and life experience have affected his judging both in general and in particular and produced a judicial product that is widely believed to be remarkable.

Jack Weinstein's family history is similar to that of tens of thousands of descendants of Eastern European Jews, whose forbearers emigrated to the United States around the turn of the twentieth century and whose offspring, two generations down the line, would assimilate almost completely, attain professional distinction, believe strongly in tolerance and social reform, and dedicate their lives in large part to that goal.

On his father's side, Jack Weinstein's grandfather, Michael Weinstein, was a tailor in Beregszasz, a small, mainly Jewish town, located before the First World War in Hungary, but now known as Beregovo in the Ukraine. Michael Weinstein, one of eight children, married Miriam Gruenstein (Jack B. Weinstein's paternal grandmother). One of those children, H. Louis Weinstein, would be Jack Weinstein's father. Weinstein's paternal grandfather and grandmother, her sister, much of her sister's family, and some of his grandfather's ultimately came to the United States (some of them illegally) early in the twentieth century.[2]

---

[1] Lawrence Baum, American Courts 149 (1986).

[2] Weinstein Oral History, at 1795–96. Some of Weinstein's family settled in Israel, including Israel Yarkoni, now in his late eighties, who left Europe after Munich. Yarkoni fought in Greece with the British Army,

Weinstein's paternal grandparents lived in a squalid tenement on the Lower East Side of New York. Michael Weinstein got a job tailoring in a sweatshop, while Weinstein's grandmother, Miriam, stayed home and took care of the children, who went to work as soon as they could.[3] Years later that family grew somewhat more affluent and moved to East Harlem, which had a large Jewish community. Judge Weinstein's first memory is of visiting his grandparents' walk-up apartment, a railroad flat.[4] Later, they moved to Bensonhurst in Brooklyn. Weinstein's grandfather may have had a small pension from his union, but he was largely supported by his family and by going to the cemetery to pray for people for which he received alms. Weinstein's grandmother died in the late 1930s of diabetes. Weinstein remembers her as "a beautiful, petite lady," who lived into her nineties.[5]

Jack Weinstein's mother's family came from the city of Bialystock in the Russian Pale. Jack Weinstein's maternal grandfather's father was a blacksmith, who is said to have dropped dead working at his forge at age 101.[6] According to family legend, Jack Weinstein's grandfather, Gershon (George) Brodach, warned by a friendly policeman that he was going to be arrested the next day for injudicious comments about the tsar on a street corner, fled Russia in a horse-drawn wagon, but not before the sixteen-year-old boy was married to Channah (Hannah) Figarsky, who was a year younger.[7] It is said that Gershon and Channah were carried out of Russia in potato sacks.[8]

Gershon and Channah made their way to Brooklyn, where they joined those members of the Figarsky family who already had emigrated. Gershon and Channah donned packs and sold tobacco, gloves, and other necessaries to sailors in Brooklyn's great port. Gershon came to earn a modest living as a ship chandler.[9] Eventually, the couple came to live in a simple three-story brick house on Rodney Street in the Williamsburg section of Brooklyn (and later in Bensonhurst), raising seven children. Both Gershon and Channah spoke Yiddish and Hebrew as well as Russian. Gershon was literate in English.[10] Jack Weinstein remembers his grandmother, who lived into her late eighties, "as a sweet person with a perpetual smile and the invariable message,

---

in the Stern Gang, and in Israel's war for independence. Yarkoni rose to the rank of colonel and ultimately became an aide to the president of Israel. *See* Weinstein Interview of November 11, 2005. *See* also Weinstein Oral History, at 1524–39.

[3] Weinstein Oral History, at 1796.

[4] *Id.* at 1796.

[5] *Id.* at 1796–97.

[6] Much of this is based upon Jack B. Weinstein, First Rough Notes for Sketch of Memoir 3 (Apr. 20, 2006) (unpublished manuscript in possession of author) [hereinafter, Weinstein, First Rough Notes].

[7] Jack B. Weinstein, Untitled Eulogy to his Mother, at 1 (Nov. 2, 1984) [hereinafter referred to as Weinstein, Eulogy].

[8] *Id.* at 1; Jack B. Weinstein, Remarks at Ellis Island Naturalization Ceremony, Brooklyn, N.Y., July 3, 1986, at 1.

[9] Weinstein Oral History, at 669.

[10] Interview of Jack B. Weinstein by author, July 9, 2010.

'Griese everybody'" ["Give everyone my regards."] when they left her home with the fruit and cake she forced on them.

Betsy Brodach, the daughter of Gershon and Channah Brodach, was born in Brooklyn, but her earliest memories were of a farmhouse "with the apple blossoms outside her windows and chickens in her yard."[11] After a brief stay on a farm in Rhode Island, the family returned to the Williamsburg section of Brooklyn, where Gershon Brodach took up shoe-repairing. Jack Weinstein remembers hearing the "whining twirly machines" and watching his grandfather cut the leather on his apron with a sharp knife, nail the soles to the leather, and grind them, all while holding extra nails in his mouth.[12]

During Prohibition, Gershon Brodach ran a wine-making establishment and also made a few barrels of whiskey annually. Jack Weinstein enjoyed his "grandpa's taking" him by trolley to the Wallabout Market where vendors could gather next to the Brooklyn Navy Yard to sell their wares. He eagerly awaited their jaunts over the Williamsburg Bridge to visit the run-down tenements, narrow streets, and throngs of merchants on the Lower East Side, to purchase food and clothes for the family.[13]

Jack Weinstein remembers his father, H. Louis Weinstein (1898–1950), as bright and athletic. Weinstein describes him as slender and "fairly tall" (five feet, ten inches), a "distinguished looking man with a 'red mustache . . . and a smiling, pleasant face.'"[14] H. Louis probably finished grade school, but at the age of twelve he was carrying vests from factory to factory on Manhattan's East Side, leaving his back somewhat "humped over."[15] At about age eighteen, he got a job at the main branch of the U.S. Post Office in Manhattan.

Jack Weinstein has identified his father as his most important mentor—"a man who worked extremely hard to provide a stable home for his family while maintaining an impish, prankster's sense of humor."[16] Louis Weinstein would go work for the National Cash Register Company. He became its top salesman on Long Island and, ultimately, sales manager for all of Long Island; supervising between one hundred and one hundred fifty salesmen before his premature death.

Jack Weinstein has said that he had turned down an appointment to the U.S. District Court for the Southern District of New York because at the time he didn't want to be a federal judge, but, when offered the Eastern District of New York—essentially his father's old sales territory—he accepted.[17] When he lectured at the University of

---

[11] Weinstein, First Rough Notes, *supra* note 6, at 3.

[12] *Id.* at 8.

[13] George Broadach would die of a fall from his roof during the Second World War. It was not clear whether it was an accident or suicide. Weinstein, First Rough Notes, *supra* note 6, at 4.

[14] *Id.* at 1.

[15] Weinstein Oral History, at 1415C.

[16] Steven M. Gold & Peter G. Eikenberry, *Focus on: Judge Weinstein*, 8 FED. B. COUNCIL NEWS 1, 3 (December 2001).

[17] Weinstein Oral History, at 1189.

Dayton Law School in 1994, Weinstein visited the site of the factory of the National Cash Register Company and that of the Sugar Camp where H. Lou was trained some seventy years before.[18] The Dayton visit, he said, probably resulted in "my coming to terms with my longstanding mourning for my father," who had died of a heart attack and stroke in 1950.[19]

Weinstein's father was more even-tempered and social than his mother. Louis Weinstein enjoyed the fruits of America and the modern industrial economy, but Weinstein believes that his mother felt she was cheated out of an education.[20] Bessie Brodach (1901–1984), had five sisters and two brothers. Living in a brownstone in Williamsburg, Bessie grew up among sailors and farmers, peddlers and policemen, saloon keepers and rabbis.[21] The valedictorian of her sixth grade class, Bessie was extremely bright. Her teacher begged Bessie's parents to let her go on to high school, but she was not permitted to continue for fear that she would be overeducated for her prescribed status in life.[22] Instead, she was put to work stripping feathers for women's hats, using the false papers of her older sister to get the job.[23]

Bessie Brodach was a woman of many talents. Her oldest son believes that "[S]he would have been an equivalent to a judge or doctor today."[24] Unfortunately, those paths were not open to her, and she would feel dissatisfied with her life.[25] Weinstein believes that he was affected by the fact that neither of his parents received the opportunities they might have had under other circumstances.[26]

Although, as Jack Weinstein relates it, it was considered shameful for the women of that time and class to have to work and a reflection "on her man." Bessie, without drawing attention, modeled. She had bit parts in some Broadway plays with her sons. She brought home heavy briefcases of letters to the lovelorn, which she answered and she matched singles who wrote in; she advised young men on how to improve their bodies when they paid for courses on muscle building for weaklings. She developed recipes for a sugar company and cooked lunches for the executives.[27]

She also wheeled Weinstein's sister, Naomi, in a baby carriage three-quarters of a mile twice a day so that she could give her father-in-law insulin shots.[28]

---

[18] *Id.* at 1189.

[19] *Id.* at 1188.

[20] Weinstein, First Rough Notes, *supra* note 6, at 13.

[21] Weinstein, Eulogy, *supra* note 7, at 1.

[22] *Id.*

[23] Weinstein Oral History, at 991.

[24] Interview of Jack B. Weinstein by William Glaberson, July 7, 1997, at 48 [hereinafter Glaberson Interview].

[25] *Id.* at 47.

[26] *Id.* at 46–47.

[27] Weinstein, Eulogy, *supra* note 7, at 3.

[28] Weinstein, First Rough Notes, *supra* note 6, at 14.

After her husband's death, Bessie took her high school equivalency exams and then attended nursing school. For many years, she was a floor nurse in hospitals and old age homes. Working into her seventies, she also took courses in creative writing and Indian anthropology and gave lessons in spoken and written English. In her eighties, Bessie was reading voraciously, lecturing on nutrition, baby sitting, and beginning to work on her memoirs and on a book about bringing up children.[29] A great reader, her personal library would form the core of the Bessie Brodach Weinstein Jury Library (books made available for jurors) at the Eastern District courthouse.[30]

And, according to her son, Bessie remained a beauty. Jack Weinstein said this in his eulogy: "Men pursued her, first by trolley and auto and later in wheelchairs."[31] Indeed, one of them was her uncle, a successful businessman. She did marry twice more, but unsuccessfully. Weinstein moved her in her last years to an apartment on the sixteenth floor of Brooklyn's St. George Hotel, close to the federal courthouse. When his mother visited the court, Jack Weinstein arranged to be telephoned from the lobby so he would have time to slip on robes, which he knew she enjoyed seeing him in. One day, when Weinstein went to look in on his mother, he discovered her on the floor having suffered a stroke. She died at age eighty-six on October 30, 1984.

H. Lou met Bessie at Coney Island during the period he was working for the post office. They married when he was twenty and she almost eighteen. Shortly after their marriage, H. Lou and Bessie moved to Wichita to care for Louis's newly widowed sister and her two children.

Wichita in 1921 was little more than a village, which had a substantial Indian reservation nearby. Soon after the couple arrived there, Bessie became pregnant. She gave birth to Jack Weinstein in a Catholic hospital on August 10, 1921. His father brought in a rabbi from St. Louis to do the circumcision.[32]

Lou learned to hunt and fish in Wichita. He retained his love of fishing throughout his life; often angling in Sheepshead Bay and Sandy Hook with Jack. Bessie, who already was able to cook Russian and Hungarian–style, became highly skilled in American cooking. "Kosher" was not her watchword. She cooked with pork fat and other foods forbidden to those Jews who keep kosher. She even served pork, telling her husband that it was "light beef."[33] In his eulogy, Jack Weinstein, with pardonable pride spoke of his mother making "the fastest and best apple and lemon meringue pies in the West."[34]

Befriended by their Christian neighbors, by nuns in the hospital where Weinstein was born, and by some Native Americans, the Weinstein's became assimilated

---

[29] *Id.* at 5.

[30] Weinstein, First Rough Notes, *supra* note 6, at 4; Weinstein Eulogy, *supra* note 7, at 5.

[31] Weinstein, Eulogy, *supra* note 7, at 5.

[32] *Id.* at 5.

[33] *Id.* at 6.

[34] Weinstein, Eulogy, *supra* note 7, at 2.

Americans in the West. Their Wichita stay gave the family a stamp of Mid-America which would contrast with the more narrowly circumscribed Jewish immigrants and first-generation working husbands and housewives Jack knew as an older child.[35]

Nevertheless, after more than five years in Wichita, Jack's parents were homesick and lonely for their warm, extended families and friends and returned permanently to New York, when Jack was four and one-half. By this time, Jack had two siblings—his brother, William, and his sister, Naomi (later Naomi Weinstein Duckler).[36]

Shortly after returning to New York, H. Lou Weinstein left for Dayton where he attended the National Cash Register training school. Jack and his mother lived briefly with Lou's parents in a railroad flat in East Harlem and Bessie's parents at Rodney Avenue and Wyeth Street in Williamsburg. Later, Lou and Bessie had a small apartment on St. John's Place in Brooklyn. Around 1926 Jack's parents purchased a semi-attached brick house among the vegetable farms of Bensonhurst on Eighth Street between Bay Parkway and Avenue "O." The house had a large coal-burning stove in the basement and a twenty-by-twenty bin where coal was delivered down a chute. It was Jack Weinstein's job to shovel the coal in the morning and evening, remove the ashes, and take the ash barrel up to the front of the house, where the garbage men collected it. With her Kansas experience fresh in mind, his mother started a small garden with vegetables, a few fruit trees, and a walnut tree.

WEINSTEIN'S EARLY YEARS

Childhood

Three things stand out from Weinstein's reflections on his childhood: how happy it seems to have been, his troubles at school, and his love affair with Brooklyn.

Weinstein attributes his own self-assurance and positive nature to growing up in a warm atmosphere in which he was doted upon by his parents, three young, unmarried aunts, his two uncles, grandparents, and other landsmen. Both of his parents had been "the favorites" of their warm families and Jack, less than five years old when his parents moved back to Brooklyn, was not only his parents' first child, but the family's first grandchild and its darling. As a child, he says, he could do no wrong amidst the Weinstein clan.[37]

---

[35] Weinstein Oral History, at 1794.

[36] *Id.* at 1415Q, 1415S.

[37] Glaberson Interview, *supra* note 24, at 44; Weinstein Oral History, at 670; Weinstein, First Rough Notes, *supra* note 6, at 9. One uncle drove a Yellow Cab; the other was a peddler.
  It is interesting to see the similarity between Weinstein and the first Chief Justice of Israel, Simon Agranat: Agranat, "the first child and first grandchild in his extended family was much loved and cherished during his childhood and he reciprocated this affection . . . . He grew up in an atmosphere of optimism." *See* PRIMA LAHAV, JUDGMENT IN JERUSALEM: CHIEF JUSTICE SIMON AGRANAT AND THE ZIONIST CENTURY 7, 9 (1997).

This is not to suggest that young Weinstein was a saint. He could be a manipulator. On his way to have his appendix out, he threatened "to kick and scream and not go into the operating room" unless he was given a sailboat to use in Prospect Park. His Aunt Flo got it for him. Many years later, at the ceremony in which he swore in Elizabeth Holtzman as District Attorney of Kings County, he confessed, "I have never been able to believe that the statute of limitations has run on my filching potatoes to roast as mickeys in the lots of Bensonhurst."[38]

Jack Weinstein was raised in a loving and supportive American Jewish household that was neither really poor, nor middle class either.[39] His family was socio-economically part of an Italo-American working-class community, which included ironmongers, painters, peddlers, and taxi-drivers.[40] Although Weinstein had worked from the time he was eight,[41] until the Great Depression life was relatively easy for his family. His father prospered at work and so did their life in Bensonhurst. There were outings to Coney Island with frankfurters at Nathan's and free tickets to Luna Park. His mother took Jack to the Brooklyn Children's Museum, the Metropolitan Museum of Art, the Museum of Natural History, and concerts. The nuclear family made trips to Asbury Park and Atlantic City. His parents were an "extremely loving couple" and the many cousins, aunts, and uncles dined together at least once or twice a week.[42]

However, the Great Depression wiped out the family's savings and, in the early 1930s, Lou lost his job. He struggled with a second-hand cash register and supply business in a small store on Jamaica Avenue, and the rest of the family also worked. Bessie worked at odd jobs without letting the neighbors know that she had a husband who could not support his family. Among those jobs was as a cook for a large sugar company. She made lunch for the executives and brought the leftovers home. Jack Weinstein delivered groceries, worked as a stock boy, sold the *Saturday Evening Post*, and awakened at 4:30 in the morning to help deliver milk, a job for which he received a dollar a day plus a quart of milk. He had an entrepreneurial streak—while following the milk wagon, he collected droppings to be sold as fertilizer. He also earned money going door to door selling clothes pins that he found on the ground and arranged

[38] Jack B. Weinstein, Remarks at Induction Ceremony, Elizabeth Holtzman as District Attorney, Kings County 1 (Dec. 30, 1981) (copy in possession of the author).

[39] Manuscript draft of Interview of Jack Weinstein by James Vescovi for Columbia Law School Report Alumni Magazine enclosed with Memorandum to Weinstein from Vescovi, Aug. 14, 1997, at 3 (copy in possession of author) [hereinafter Vescovi Interview].

[40] Weinstein Oral History, at 674.

[41] *Benchmark*, NEW YORKER, May 3, 1993, at 34–36.

[42] Weinstein, First Rough Notes, *supra* note 6, at 20–21.

into packs.[43] "It was," Jack Weinstein says, "always the practice in his family to work at as many jobs at the same time as possible."[44]

Some of Jack's work also had intangible compensation. He and his mother acted on Broadway in such shows as *Subway Express* and *I Love an Actress*.[45] He also tried out for many other shows including *Peter Pan* with Eva La Gallienne.[46] Weinstein relates that "for years I used to smell the Max Factor cold cream and grease paint" and he always has had "a sense of excitement and expectation when the curtain rises."[47] Years later, while investigating Weinstein's background prior to his appointment to the bench, the FBI's New York bureau admitted to its failure: "Applicant's employment as an actor in the Broadway theaters was not verified since he performed when he was seven to nine years of age."[48] Weinstein also made an unsuccessful screen test for an appearance in the *Our Gang* comedies, but did appear on the stage of the Metropolitan Opera as a supernumerary[49] and was able to see many plays and films free of charge.

By the age of nine, Weinstein was acting on Broadway and commuting by himself, returning to Bensonhurst at eleven at night. Between matinees and evening performances, Weinstein shot marbles with his cousins (also involved in various ways with the theater) at the curb at 42nd Street near Broadway.

Jack Weinstein's experience at school was a different story. Bessie Weinstein convinced the teachers at the public school that she had attended to admit Jack to first grade when he was four years old. Unready, he dropped out. The following year, he went to P.S. 205 in Bensonhurst, three blocks from his home. His schooling was marked by academic and disciplinary problems. Weinstein has said that he "was not very good at the alphabet or writing or reading."[50] He still was not ready for school and could not catch on. Indeed, his father asked him, "Are you the dumbest in the class, Jackie?" Jack replied quite seriously, "No, Dad, I think I am the second dumbest."[51] He was left back in fourth grade, having to attend summer school. He was also a wise-acre, talking out of turn and making jokes.[52] His parents often came to school to plead for him, and he was even threatened with being placed in the "ungraded class"—the class for the mentally impaired.

---

[43] Eugene H. Nickerson, *Jack B. Weinstein: The Early Years*, 97 COLUM. L. REV. 1958 (1997).

[44] Weinstein Oral History, at 1415V; Glaberson Interview, *supra* note 24, at 44; Robert Kolker, *High Caliber Justice*, N.Y. MAGAZINE, Apr. 5, 1999, at 33, 35.

[45] Nickerson, *Supra* note 43, at 1928, 1960.

[46] Weinstein, First Rough Draft, *supra* note 6, at 21.

[47] Jack B. Weinstein, Memoir—First Supplemental Memorandum, Excerpt 2, at 7.

[48] U.S. Department of Justice, Federal Bureau of Investigation, Files HQ-89-7007, HQ72-2745, 77 HQ470, at 24–25 (Oct. 3, 1966). Jack B. Weinstein FBI file, Sept. 30, 1966 (in possession of the author) [hereinafter Weinstein FBI file].

[49] Speech on Retirement of Brother Bill, May 30, 1995, at 4 (in possession of the author).

[50] Weinstein Oral History, *supra* note 44, at 18.

[51] *Id.* at 18–19.

[52] *Id.* at 491–92.

Although Weinstein had a fifth grade teacher he "truly loved" and did well in that class,[53] it was not until junior high school that he finally "caught on." There, he scored extremely high on an intelligence test and was skipped a grade. Such childhood experiences were much with him a half-century later when a series of major cases involving the New York City public schools came to him. Litigation raised issues of: treatment of the emotionally handicapped, faculty segregation, bilingual education, and the use of federal funds in the New York City public schools.[54] He commented:

> . . . I did have something in my own background which gave me some sensitivity to what could happen to a kid who got yanked out and sent to a school far from his neighborhood where there were loads of kids who didn't want to learn.[55]

When Weinstein graduated from Lincoln High School, Weinstein's Aunt Lillian, who was working for Byrne Express and Trucking Company, convinced Al Byrne to give Weinstein, who was fifteen, a job. The small company picked up freight in Williamsburg, at Manhattan's piers, and in the train yards close to Bush Terminal and delivered it to various small factories that were in and around what is now a park next to the U.S. Courthouse on Cadman Plaza in Brooklyn. Assisted by his uncle, an Irish political leader, Byrne's business was expanding.[56]

Weinstein was paid $14 for a sixty-hour week—answering the telephone and typing letters and bills in the company's office located under the Brooklyn Bridge. Later, he helped with the loading and unloading of freight. Still later, when Byrne became an executive in the trucking association, Weinstein helped write his speeches. Early in his judicial career, Weinstein handled *Byrnes Express and Trucking Co. v. Drivers & Chauffeurs Local Union 816*.[57] In that case, he denied Byrnes's petition for an injunction, although Weinstein delayed his order several days. The decision ended their warm relations. Weinstein now thinks that as a matter of ethics he should have disqualified himself from the case.[58]

The influence on Weinstein of his work for the trucking company should not be underestimated. He had grown up in the kind of community where people worked with their hands and that experience was reinforced. He worked closely with the truckers, fished with them, drank beer with them, wrote letters for them, and enjoyed their company. When he was a judge, he still remembered how such things had worked as the payoffs in the trucking industry and the matriarchal relationships in Italian-American families. He drew upon that background in a case involving income tax

---

[53] Weinstein, First Rough Notes, *supra* note 6, at 18.

[54] *See especially* Chapter 6, but also chapters 4 and 9.

[55] Weinstein Oral History, at 492–93.

[56] Weinstein Oral History, at 9.

[57] *Byrnes Express and Trucking Co. v. Drivers & Chauffeurs & Chauffeurs Local 816*, 1987 U.S. Dist. LEXIS 8958 (Nov. 27, 1967).

[58] Weinstein Oral History, at 588ff.

evasion in a matriarchal Italian family. The defendant was a naïve young trucker. Weinstein granted a rare directed verdict of acquittal because "it was clear to me that the mother was running the show."[59]

In another case, a large paint company had taken the right to sell its paint from a small paint store. The old man who owned the store and his son, a painter, were seeking an injunction. A decision for the plaintiff would not have been unreasonable, but it did not happen in Weinstein's court. The hearing on the injunction was conducted around a table. The president of the corporation was there in a very fine suit and tie. Weinstein asked the two painters to let him see their hands—both of them had "very heavily calloused hands with paint stains embedded," workmen "just a half a run up from poor workers." They reminded him of the many workers on the trucks who had the same kind of heavy calloused hands and large forearms from lifting the heavy bales and crates. Weinstein said he believed their hands rather than the mouths of those connected with the paint company and granted the injunction on the theory that under equity, rights were not to be terminated improvidently. The Court of Appeals (a fine panel: James L. Oakes, George Pratt, and Pierre Leval) vacated Weinstein's injunction.[60] However, Weinstein still cannot "get this picture out of mind" of the "high priced counsel taking away" the livelihood of that old man coming in with heavy, heavy hands with the paint and the acids.[61]

Weinstein attended Brooklyn College at night while working for Byrne during the day. He did his homework on the Williamsburg Bridge, "while the tugboats below spewed up their smoke and coal cinders"; "little particles of unburnt coal would get blown up on the bridge and got into my eyes and I would have to brush it off my papers."[62] Byrne and his men wanted Weinstein to succeed in college. Byrne gave him time off to study for examinations. The men "were excited about knowing somebody who was actually going to college,"[63] Weinstein recalls. "And all of the men, none of them had more than an elementary education, they all supported me."[64] The men took pride in his school work and, later, in his naval decoration.[65]

Of Brooklyn College, Weinstein recalls: "It was wonderful: a philosophy course on existentialism and metaphysics and Aristotle and mathematics and history and physics and all these intellectual things coming for a couple of hours each night was just so exciting."[66] When classes ended, he would walk the couple of miles to get home and would then get up at 5:30 a.m. to work. One would think that working fulltime, attending classes, studying, and commuting would leave little time for college life. Even so,

---

[59] See United States v. Melillo, 275 F. Supp. 314 (1967); Weinstein Oral History, at 28–31.

[60] See Alan Skop, Inc. v. Benjamin Moore, Inc., 909 F. 2d 59 (1990: PC: Oakes-Pratt-Leval).

[61] Weinstein Oral History, at 191–94. See also id., at 1018.

[62] Weinstein, First Rough Notes, supra note 6, at 24; Weinstein Oral History, at 1800.

[63] Weinstein Oral History, at 58–59.

[64] Elizabeth Stull, Judge Weinstein's 40th Anniversary on the Bench, BROOKLYN EAGLE, Apr. 26, 2007.

[65] Weinstein, First Rough Notes, supra note 6, at 22–23.

[66] Weinstein Oral History, at 1798.

he reminisced: "Those were wonderful years at the college . . . This was the place where my wife and I met, where we laughed and agonized with friends . . . over the world's problems together, and where we acquired habits of learning and study . . . that have carried many of us to positions we never dreamed we would achieve."[67]

But it was with the Byrnes Company at the docks that Weinstein "learned the meaning of strikes, payoffs and what it meant for company and men alike to be right on the margin of economic viability." When, as a judge, he handled public housing cases, he recalled the effect upon a trucker making $34 a week of a labor agreement under which a small increase raised his salary too much to be able to stay in public housing.[68]

He saw things, too, that he did not forget. He had observed "a good deal of minor crime."[69] Once he lectured a law clerk who had chided him for wasting time corresponding with prisoners: "I guess, you know, they haven't had your opportunities or advantages . . . You could be in their position . . . I could have slipped into that position, although I had a very strong family."[70] And: "They helped me. They remind me that, except for the grace of God, there go I. I came up from a rough neighborhood. I was brought up in Bensonhurst where the Mafia was regnant when I was a child."[71] This makes Weinstein more understanding of those who had slipped and then found themselves before him for sentencing, just as his experiences with members of his family who entered the country illegally to escape persecution make him more understanding of the plight of immigrants.[72]

Weinstein has never lost his emotional connection to the working class community within which he grew up and those with whom he worked in his high school and college years. He remembers that these were people that really needed an advocate.[73]

It is conventional wisdom of political science that judges bring with them to the bench certain local values that subsequently affect their policy-making patterns.[74] Certainly, the sights and sounds of the Brooklyn of his youth remain palpable when talking with Weinstein today, and they clearly have been with him throughout his career. He speaks vividly of the vegetable gardens of Bensonhurst, of the trolley ride to the Wallabout Market (where the Brooklyn Navy Yard, the site of many of the asbestos

---

[67] Jack B. Weinstein, Speech before Brooklyn College Alumni Association, "Alumnus of the Year Award," New York, Oct. 26, 1968, at 2.

  Weinstein says that his politics were to the left in this period; that he paraded on behalf of Spain's leftist government; that he attended a few communist meetings in the neighborhood, but found them too "foreign oriented" and "dogmatic." Weinstein Oral History, at 1799.

[68] Transcript of Videotaped Interview of Jack B. Weinstein by Gordon Mehler, Oct. 10, 2006 (on file with author) [hereinafter Mehler Videotaped Interview].

[69] Weinstein Oral History, at 49, 720.

[70] Weinstein Oral History, at 33.

[71] Mehler Videotaped Interview, *supra* note 68, at 10.

[72] Weinstein Oral History, at 1425, 1472.

[73] Vescovi Interview, *supra* note 39, at 6.

[74] In this context, that means regional and state values. *See* ROBERT A. KARP & RONALD STRIDHAM, THE FEDERAL COURTS 130 (3rd ed. 1998).

cases he would preside over, would be built).[75] He recalls his outings to Coney Island with its brick houses and wooden bungalows and Feldman's, the German beer garden restaurant, where his father would take him at the end of the day.[76] One lens through which he perceives New York is as a collection of villages, with ethnicity a very important part of those villages.[77]

The Brooklyn of Weinstein's youth was still a major manufacturing center with thousands of small companies—pump manufacturers, metal stamping shops, print shops—as well as a few large companies, and it possessed vital transportation links with the rest of the nation—the trains and train yards and the ships and tugs.[78] Those memories of the Brooklyn of his youth impacted upon his judicial work not only by engaging his interest and framing the way he looks at facts, but also by deepening the perspective with which he views the extraordinary diversity of cases that come before him. A case involving the Wassau Sick Society brought back his walk home from Brooklyn College passing by the Washington Cemetery.[79] His perspective on a diversity case involving the possible negligence of New York City for not putting up signs in Spanish on a beach beyond Sheepshead Bay differed from that of the Court of Appeals, because he remembered the beaches.[80] Coney Island would be the site of the major school desegregation case Weinstein handled. His affection for those who worked in the Brooklyn Navy Yard conditioned his handling of the asbestos cases.[81] Needless to say, values are embedded in these experiences.

Wartime

When America became involved in the Second World War, Weinstein immediately attempted to enlist in the Naval Air Force. However, he was turned down because of hay fever. Volunteering for the regular navy, he was told that, if he could graduate from college by fall, he could go to naval cadet school and become an officer. Quitting his job, Weinstein took some forty credits in the spring and summer sessions at Brooklyn College—he says that "It was like being on vacation after all the work he had done"[82]— and graduated *magna cum laude* after a total of seven years of study. It should be no surprise that this man, who has received seven honorary degrees, including ones from

---

[75] When he received the Devitt Award, Weinstein gave the money to the children's playroom at Long Island Hospital in Brooklyn, mentioning at the ceremony the connection of his parents and grandparents to the community. Presentation of Devitt Award, 160 F.R.D. 287, 355, 356 (1994) (available on Westlaw).

[76] Weinstein Oral History, at 278, 280, 1035.

[77] *Id.* at 948.

[78] *Id.* at 49, 674.

[79] *Id.* at 874, 1035.

[80] *Id.* at 861.

[81] *Id.* at 668, 673, 674.

[82] *Id.* at 1799.

Columbia and Yale, believes "absolutely in free education as the ladder to rise above poverty and ignorance."[83]

Weinstein had ninety days of training at Columbia University in the autumn of 1943. Receiving high grades, he was assigned to study electronics and radar at Harvard and M.I.T. for seven months. He performed his electronics experiments in Harvard Law School's Austin Hall.

Having done well once again in "school," Weinstein then had a choice of assignments. He volunteered to enter the submarine corps, the branch of the navy that required the greatest technological skill, because of its high pay and because he believed that, if he came home alive, that it would be less likely that he would come home maimed.[84]

After attending submarine school in New London, Connecticut, he flew to San Francisco, Hawaii, and then Midway, where he awaited assignment to a sub by doing some radar repair work, fishing, and watching the "gooney birds."[85] After a short stint on a submarine tender, he was assigned to the USS *Jallao* (SS 368), a new submarine. Weinstein met it in September 1944 in Pearl Harbor.

There is an "official" history of the USS *Jallao*,[86] and Weinstein has written of his experiences in a twenty-six-page letter,[87] but we dare not tarry too long on board this vessel. In less than a year, the sub participated in the Battle of Leyte Gulf and traveled in the North Pacific, the heavily mined Korea Strait, the Yellow Sea, Manchurian Coast, Saipan, the Marshall Islands, and the Sea of Japan. There were long patrols with occasional misses and failed torpedoes.[88] Among Weinstein's memories are those of a terrible typhoon with waves "at least as high as a five story building," of "deep purple fog," of a huge whale one hundred feet off the port bow, and of round mines seen through sonar.[89]

The *Jallao* sank two Japanese cruisers, one for which Lt. (jg) J. B. Weinstein received a letter of commendation and the other on August 11, 1945. The first "kill" occurred during the ship's first patrol during the battle of Leyte Gulf as part of a spread of submarines designed to catch retreating Japanese forces. The radar was reading so well that it picked up a cruiser at the phenomenal distance of approximately 35,000 yards. For that, the radar officer, Weinstein, received a letter of commendation.[90] The sub

---

[83] Transcript of NPR News Interview of Jack B. Weinstein by Juan Williams, 50th Anniversary, *Brown v. Board of Ed.* [sic] 8 (Nov. 30, 2003) [hereinafter NPR Interview].

[84] Weinstein, First Rough Notes, *supra* note 6, at 28.

[85] *Id.* at 30.

[86] "U.S.S. JALLAO—Ship's History: Pre-Commissioning and Commissioning" [In the possession of the author, this document appears to be a government document that was once classified].

[87] Letter from Jack B. Weinstein to William Stegman, Nov. 13, 1997 (in possession of the author) [hereinafter Weinstein to Stegman letter].

[88] U.S.S. JALLAO—Ship's History, *supra* note 86; Anthony M. Destefano, *Salvaging a Legend of World War II*, NEWSDAY, Aug. 22, 2006, at A15; Weinstein, First Rough Notes, *supra* note 6, at 33.

[89] Weinstein to Stegman letter, *supra* note 87, at 4, 6, 7, 9.

[90] Weinstein, First Rough Notes, *supra* note 6, at 31.

participated in other torpedo attacks, was injured by the screw of one of the ships it was escorting, and rescued five airmen floating in a raft after they had been shot down by the Japanese. Weinstein himself saved the life of a sailor who was going overboard.

After the dropping of the second atomic bomb, radar on the *Jallao* picked up a vessel traveling from mainland China toward Japan. It might have been a passenger vessel or possibly a freighter. Weinstein remembers approaching the captain of the ship and saying, to him, "'Captain, the war is almost over. The ship is probably carrying refugees from Manchuria back to Japan including women and children—do we really have to sink it?'" Weinstein records that the captain replied, rather sadly, "'I'm sorry, Jack, but those are my orders. I have no alternative.'" Action ceased four days later. The USS *Jallao* arrived in San Francisco on September 2.[91]

Weinstein had been in the navy almost four years. Besides the Letter of Commendation, he left having been awarded the Submarine Qualification Pin, the Submarine Combat Pin with two Gold Stars, the American Area Service Medal, the Asiatic-Pacific Areas Service Medal with one star, a Commendation Ribbon, and the World War II Victory Medal.[92]

In the navy, Weinstein demonstrated his ability to work with rough characters and to deal with intermittent anti-Semitism. As officer of the deck, his natural self-confidence matured into a habit of command. Weinstein's wartime experiences shaped his attitude toward the draft, influenced his approach to cases involving mail censorship, contributed to his understanding of litigation involving bomb sights and electronics, and added to his enjoyment of maritime cases.[93] He also remembers the Second World War as "a segregated war . . . when the only black on board my boat was a steward, snickered at by some of the men and officers because he was trying to study algebra and asked elementary questions."[94]

Like many of his generation, Weinstein viewed his service in the military as "not only an obligation but a high opportunity to serve the country."[95] Perhaps paradoxically, Weinstein's service in the Second World War left him unsympathetic to the problems of the Selective Service during the war in Vietnam. "My own feeling," he said, "was if somebody didn't want to be a member of the armed forces he probably wasn't going to be a good soldier. Certainly, if I was in my submarine and I was standing next

[91] Weinstein, First Rough Notes, *supra* note 6, at 13–14.

    Weinstein was in the ward room on the submarine tender *Proteus* at Midway when Franklin D. Roosevelt's death was announced. He began to cry, but was "amazed and much chagrined to hear a substantial number of officers clap and shout to applaud his death." Jack B. Weinstein, First Supplemental Memorandum, Excerpt 1, at 1–2 (in possession of author).

[92] Weinstein FBI file, *supra* note 48, at 6.

[93] *See, e.g.,* Weinstein Oral History, at 443; *Wilson v. United States*, 1978 U.S. Dist. LEXIS 19505 (Feb. 17, 1978) at *17.

[94] *See* Jack N. Weinstein, "Law Day Speech," Nassau County Bar Association, rev. draft, Feb. 26, 2003 [for speech given May 1, 2003!] [in possession of author].

[95] Weinstein Oral History, at 64.

to somebody who was in there reluctantly and wanted to get out, I wouldn't want him around me."[96]

Undoubtedly, the war contributed to Weinstein's deep patriotism—for over forty years he has annually attended the Memorial Day parade in his hometown of Great Neck[97]—but it is always leavened by the skepticism most Jews have of government. In one of his cases, Weinstein held that anti-abortion protestors had a right to participate in the Town of Hempstead's Memorial Day Parade.[98] Although generally believing that courts should not interfere with internal military discipline, he held in 1991 that the transfer of a soldier because of his opposition to the war violated his First Amendment rights.[99] In 1978, remembering the mail censorship he had to perform on the submarine, Weinstein held that censorship of the mail of leftists was unconstitutional.[100] When, more than four decades later, mass tort claims came before him involving the effects of asbestos on those who worked in the Brooklyn Naval Yard, Weinstein "felt a sense of affection for those [who] had built our great navy in World War 2."[101]

It should be noted that Weinstein's brother, Bill, was a master sergeant during the Battle of the Bulge. Neither Jack nor Bill nor anyone else in Weinstein's extended family in the United States died or was wounded in the war, but those who had remained in Hungary, Russia, and Poland were decimated.[102]

YEARS OF PROFESSIONAL GROWTH

Law School

While he was in the navy, although he had never met a lawyer or seen a law, Weinstein decided to go to law school. There was a wide choice of fields in which he could have undertaken graduate study. His college degree had been in economics, but Weinstein also had abilities in advanced physics and mathematics and an interest in medicine.[103] To pass the time on the submarine, Weinstein had asked his mother to send him books, specifying that he wanted some on law. One she sent was the classic, *The Common Law* of Oliver Wendell Holmes, which the young sailor read while the sub was in the Japanese Sea. He did not, apparently, understand much of it, but he was fascinated by it. On board the USS *Jallao*, there was an officer who had attended the University of

---

[96] *Id.*

[97] *Id.* at 498.

[98] *North Shore Right to Life Committee v. Manhasset Post No. 304*, 452 F. Supp. 834 (June 9, 1984).

[99] *Cortright v. Resor*, 325 F. Supp. 797 (Mar. 23, 1971).

[100] *Wilson v. United States*, 1978 U.S. Dist. LEXIS 19505 (Feb. 17, 1978).

[101] Weinstein Oral History, at 1348.

[102] Addendum to Weinstein, First Rough Notes (June 9, 2006), at 2; Interview of Israel Yarkoni by Jack B. Weinstein, at 3 (Oct. 26, 2005); Weinstein Oral History, at 1475.

[103] Weinstein Oral History, at 971–72.

Pennsylvania School of Law, who encouraged Weinstein to study law. Weinstein finally decided that law seemed the best way to use all the background that he had, or as he put it, "The advantage of being a lawyer is that you can use everything."[104]

Weinstein had six months free after he was released from duty and before law school was to begin. He used it to act as a contract terminator settling the claims of those who had contracted to deliver huge amounts of munitions and equipment for the navy, but whose materials were no longer needed. Foreshadowing his later work in class actions, he cut fees and costs of lawyers and accountants. Working in uniform in Philadelphia and New York, he received what we might term some paralegal training.[105]

On October 10, 1946, even before he left the navy, Weinstein married Evelyn Horowitz (b. 1922), a year younger than he. Weinstein had been admitted to the Harvard Law School, but Evelyn was pregnant and the couple wanted to stay in New York near their families.[106] Beginning in the fall of 1946, Weinstein attended Columbia Law School; graduating in 1948. Weinstein's close association with Columbia Law School has lasted throughout his career. He said, "Columbia has done so much for me . . . and had provided the opportunity for such a full and satisfying life of the mind, body and spirit."[107] Even today, Weinstein feels deep appreciation for "all those wonderful teachers and scholars who tried to imbue us with a sense of the majesty of the law through their example"[108] and credits many of his insights on the bench to particular professors and courses.[109] Generally, Weinstein has great praise for the men who taught him at Columbia. For example, he said of Jerome Michael and Dean Young B. Smith:

> Jerry on equity who I relied on in writing my recent gun opinion and in the Manville Asbestos case; Young B. Smith who spent a term on ancient *Rylands v. Fletcher* and *Buick v. McPherson*, the cases that underlie all my mass tort work . . . [110]

While Weinstein has warm memories of student life at Columbia, he admits that the law school had some drawbacks. Some classes in the postwar accelerated two-year program were as large as three hundred. Half the curriculum was fixed. The faculty was very demanding, so demanding in fact that a number of students complained about abuses in the use of the Socratic Method.[111] Responding, the law school set up

---

[104] Weinstein Oral History, at 979; Mehler Videotaped Interview, *supra* note 68, at 3; Vescovi Interview, *supra* note 73, at 4; Weinstein, First Rough Notes, *supra* note 6, at 30.

[105] Weinstein Oral History, at 699.

[106] Weinstein Oral History, at 1809.

[107] Weinstein, First Rough Notes, *supra* note 6, at 26.

[108] Jack B. Weinstein, A Few Memories, Speech at 55th Reunion, Columbia Law School Class '48 (Oct. 23, 2003), at 1.

[109] Interestingly, Weinstein did not take courses in Constitutional Law, Federal Jurisdiction, and Administrative Law. Interview of Jack B. Weinstein by author, July 9, 2010.

[110] *Id.* at 1–2. *See also* Jack B. Weinstein, *Jerome M. Michael, in* THE YALE BIOGRAPHICAL DICTIONARY OF AMERICAN LAW 380–81 (Roger K. Newman ed., 2009).

[111] Weinstein was not among them.

an associates program in which young graduates acted as teaching assistants. The year following his graduation, Weinstein was one of the first seven associates in the program.[112]

As an associate, Weinstein worked closely with Julius Goebel, who taught a required course, Development of Legal Institutions (DLI). Goebel was a difficult man, a curmudgeon, nasty to women and minorities, but Weinstein felt he had a real interest in students and he liked him.[113] Goebel probably had the greatest impact on Weinstein's judging of all his professors, offering an expansive view of equity and the powers of the chancellor, which Weinstein would come to find quite congenial:

> Ultimately, in my work on the court, I found that the material on the development of legal institutions and the development of equity in that course and a separate law school course on equity were among the most valuable that I had had. They taught me how flexible legal institutions could be in a time of change and stress. They encouraged me to undertake a revision of the practice and evidence and to develop new procedural devices and to ignore some of the old ones . . . [114]

Clerkship with Stanley Fuld

It is not quite correct to say that Stanley Fuld was Jack Weinstein's "mentor"— Weinstein's talents are great and throughout his entire career he has marched to his own drummer. However, it is fair to say that Fuld probably had the greatest influence on Weinstein's professional career.

At the recommendation of Dean Young B. Smith of Columbia Law School, Stanley Fuld hired Weinstein to serve as his law clerk for the school year 1949–50, succeeding Weinstein's future long-time Columbia colleague, Maurice Rosenberg.

Fuld then was in the early stages of a career on the New York Court of Appeals, which lasted from 1946 to the end of 1973 (Chief Judge, 1967–1973). Fuld and Roger Traynor, Chief Justice of the California Supreme Court, were the preeminent state jurists of the middle third of the twentieth century.[115] Regarded as one of Benjamin Cardozo's heirs,[116] Fuld wrote major opinions in criminal law and procedure[117] conflict

---

[112] Weinstein Oral History, at 9.

[113] Weinstein, First Rough Notes, *supra* note 6, at 35. The negative judgments are as much the author's as Weinstein's.

[114] Weinstein Oral History, at 1354, 1335A, 1384, 875. On Weinstein's use of equity, see particularly the discussion of the asbestos litigation, Chapter 11.

[115] *See* Jeffrey B. Morris, *The American Jewish Judge: An Appraisal on the Occasion of the Bicentennial*, 38 Jew. Soc. Stud. 195, 214 (1976).

[116] Bernard S. Meyer Et Al., The History of the New York Court of Appeals 16 (2006).

[117] *People v. Donovan*, 13 N.Y. 2d 148 (1963).

of laws,[118] contracts, torts, and desegregation and on the First Amendment.[119] He also contributed significantly to broadening the protection of rights in the New York State Constitution. Although during the Nixon administration, Fuld was mentioned in the press as under consideration for U.S. Supreme Court vacancies, it is not likely that Fuld, a moderate and civil-liberties-conscious Republican, was seriously considered.

Weinstein considered his clerkship "like being dropped onto Mount Olympus by parachute."[120] Fifty years after the clerkship, Weinstein wrote of Fuld's judging:

> No passive reverence for the law guided Fuld's chambers. Rather, robust research of *every* jurisdiction's law on *every* relevant point and the interminable writing and rewriting required by the master left little time for sleep. De rigueur were innumerable typewritten drafts and repeated galley and page proof revision until, finally, the opinion was torn from the judge's hands and locked between hard covers and glued back, safe from his tinkerings . . . [121]

Nevertheless, it must not have been very much fun. Fuld, a perfectionist, could put his opinions through thirty drafts and was abusive to his clerks. He took personal offense at any error a law clerk made and Weinstein, like other Fuld clerks was, from time to time, fired in a fit of pique and then rehired.[122]

In his eulogy to Fuld, Weinstein tried to explain Fuld's difficult and demanding behavior toward his clerks:

> It was that he was protecting this Goddess, the common law from a succession of bumpkins who were soiling her pristine garment with their inadequate research and lack of understanding of the law.[123]

Yet, the six–foot, two-inch war veteran wept in chambers from Fuld's abuse and refused to spend a second year with him. Weinstein explained: "I did not want to stay for more than a year. I had taken more abuse than I wanted. I had a child. I was almost thirty and I wanted to get out and practice."[124]

Nevertheless, Weinstein did spend a second year with Fuld. When Weinstein's successor as clerk broke under the strain, at Fuld's pleading Weinstein came back informally

---

[118] *See, e.g., Babcock v. Jackson*, 12 N.Y. 2d 473 (1963). *See also* Willis M. Reese, *Chief Judge Fuld and Choice of Law*, 71 COLUM. L. REV. 548 (1971).

[119] *Oliver v. Postel*, 30 N.Y. 2d 171 (1972).

[120] Jack B. Weinstein, Honorable Stanley Fuld, Sept. 22, 2003, at 1.

[121] Jack B. Weinstein, *The New York Court of Appeals in the Eyes of a Neophyte*, 48 SYRACUSE. L. REV. 1469 at 1469 (1998).

[122] Weinstein Oral History, at 216–17, 348.

[123] Weinstein, Honorable Stanley Fuld, *supra* note 120, at 3; Weinstein, *The Honorable Stanley H. Fuld*, 1 HIST. SOC'Y CTS. ST. N.Y. 1, 10 (Spring/Summer 2004).

[124] Weinstein Oral History, at 1581; *see also id.*, at 1415V.

and without salary. That year exemplifies the extraordinary energy that has marked Weinstein's career. Weinstein worked on Fuld's cases from six to nine-thirty or ten in the morning; spent the rest of the day at his law practice and worked on legislative matters in the evening for State Senator Seymour Halpern. Some of those evenings were spent in Albany, but much correspondence and drafting was done in New York City.[125]

In the end, Weinstein emerged lifelong friends with Fuld. Weinstein would often pay tribute to Fuld, who died in 2004 at the age of ninety-nine. From Fuld Weinstein learned that "you had to take a fresh look at the law as well as the facts in each case and you had to adjust the law to new realities."[126] From Fuld's treatment of New York's second and third offender laws, Weinstein learned how to mitigate some of the harshness of criminal laws through analysis of the law and the facts, methods upon which he drew with extraordinary creativity in his battle against the Federal Sentencing Guidelines. From Fuld's exhumation of the writ of *Coram Nobis*,[127] Weinstein saw the possibilities for the use of the writ of *habeas corpus* in federal court.[128] Perhaps most important, though, Fuld, who had been renowned when he handled appeals for the District Attorney's Office of New York County under Thomas Dewey, impressed upon Weinstein the high standards which should be demanded of the government before anyone could be sent to prison.

Weinstein acknowledges the influence of this "consummate craftsman" on his own opinion writing: emphasizing the facts, slanting them without misleading; using simple and clear prose ("sparer and leaner than Cardozo") largely free of textual footnoting; never oversimplifying the law and polishing opinions endlessly right into the page proofs (when there still were page proofs!).[129] Fuld wrote to convince the bar, the public, and particularly scholars, but also for "the person who reads and runs." Of the effect on Weinstein:

When I became a judge I tried unsuccessfully, to measure up to Fuld's standards. As I finish each opinion I have a mental image of Fuld taking out his pen to improve it. I couldn't help thinking, "I know it should be better, Stanley. I did the best I could."[130]

Still another indication of Fuld's impact on Weinstein, accentuated by his work on the reform of state procedure and his experience as an advisor in the state legislature

---

[125] Weinstein Oral History, at 1415Y, 1809; Weinstein, First Rough Notes, *supra* note 6, at 39ff.

[126] Weinstein Oral History, at 227.

[127] A writ calling the attention of the trial court to facts which do not appear on the record despite the exercise of reasonable diligence by the defendant and which, if known and established at the crime a judgment was rendered, would have resulted in a different judgment.

[128] Weinstein Oral History, at 325, 748, 979. *See* Fuld's opinion in *People v. Olah*, 200 N.Y. 96 (1949).

[129] Weinstein Oral History, at 59, 69–70, 78, 171, 213, 214, 224, 431.

[130] Jack B. Weinstein, Memorial Address 8 (Sept. 22, 2003) [copy in possession of author]. *See also* Jack B. Weinstein, *In Memoriam—Stanley H. Fuld*, 104 COLUM. L. REV. 253, 255 (2004); Jack B. Weinstein, *The Honorable Stanley H. Fuld*, 1 HIST. SOC'Y CTS. N.Y. 1, 11 (Spring–Summer 2004).

and at the New York State constitutional convention, is the great respect Weinstein has for New York State laws and courts.[131]

In two areas, however, Fuld would *not* be Weinstein's model. The first was in the treatment of law clerks. Second, was Fuld's lack of interest in court administration while Chief Judge. As will be seen in Chapter 5, when Weinstein chose to run for Chief Judge of the New York Court of Appeals in 1973 to succeed Fuld, among his reasons was his awareness of the need for a Chief Judge who would be a strong administrative leader of the state court system, something that Fuld had not been.[132]

Experience in Practice

In addition to his clerkship with Stanley Fuld and his career at Columbia as an associate (1948–1949) and a professor (beginning in 1952), Weinstein had a rich variety of experiences between his graduation from law school and the beginning of his career on the bench on May 1, 1967. Among other things, Weinstein was engaged in the private practice of law; involved in the drafting of the briefs for *Brown v. Board of Education I and;* instead of, drafted both the revised New York State Motor Vehicle and Traffic Law and the New York's Civil Practice Law and Rules; wrote or edited five books, including a multivolume treatise on New York State practice; served as County Attorney for Nassau County and was heavily involved in attempts to rewrite the state constitution.

Weinstein's experience in the private practice of law was relatively brief. In the summer before he clerked with Judge Fuld, he worked for the small firm of Demov, Callaghan & Morris, which was beginning to specialize in commercial real estate. The young Roy Cohn, then an Assistant U.S. Attorney, directed much business to the firm.[133] After the end of his clerkship with Fuld, Weinstein had some trouble finding a job. Anti-Semitism narrowed his opportunities. He was offered a position as a tax lawyer at Cravath Swain & Moore, but had no interest in that field.[134] Instead, Weinstein began an association with William Rosenfeld, a single practitioner, which would become a partnership. Almost immediately, Weinstein received referrals from his former professors, Herbert Wechsler and Walter Gellhorn, as well as from one brother-in-law. The family connection to the firm became even closer when his brother, Bill, married Rosenfeld's secretary. During the time he worked with Rosenfeld (1950–1952), Weinstein handled derivative actions, a capital case with Whitman Knapp by appointment of the Court of Appeals,[135] and other matters.

---

[131] *See* Weinstein Oral History, at 221, 602.

[132] *Id.* at 602, 1271, 1283.

[133] Weinstein Oral History, at 1415V.

[134] Weinstein, First Rough Notes, *supra* note 6, at 36–37.

[135] *People v. Kelly*, 302 N.Y.512 (1951); 304 N.Y. 662 (1952). Knapp and Weinstein won a reversal, but their probably insane client was found guilty in the second trial and was executed. The defendant wanted to be executed so he could go see his paramour in heaven and continue the discussion he had started with

Weinstein's private practice "quickly moved into a public practice."[136] Though already a member of a Democratic Club in Manhattan, Weinstein was hired by State Senator Seymour Halpern, a Republican. For Halpern, he handled Republican election matters, drafted legislation, and served as Special Counsel to the New York Joint Committee on Motor Vehicle Problems. In that position, Weinstein would redraft the motor vehicle law, as well as many other bills.[137] Weinstein's experience with the legislature explains why he never used the term "legislative intent" for "[m]ost legislators had no idea at all what was going on in Albany."[138]

Columbia Professor

Weinstein must have built up a good deal of respect and good will among his professors, for he became the first person appointed to the faculty as part of the postwar expansion. Weinstein accepted the offer immediately:

The opportunity to be with brilliant minds and learn more about the law was something I just couldn't forego. For a young kid brought up in relative poverty, it was like dropping into heaven.[139]

In 1952, Columbia was probably the third most prestigious law school in the United States, but it was facing significant problems. "Columbia lacked the money, the space, the faculty and the new curriculum required to cope."[140] The demands the law school placed on its students were too great.[141] However, in a short time, a new dean, William Warren, raised money for a new building and for a major expansion of the faculty. The curriculum grew from a few subjects "to scores of seminars as diverse as the burgeoning law."[142]

Yet, "it was a tight band of only a dozen or so dedicated professors,"[143] who lunched together around a round table every day.[144] They were a brilliant group of achievers and achievers-to-be. Noel Dowling's casebook on constitutional law was "'the Bible.'"

---

her that had led him to kill her. *See* Weinstein, First Rough Notes, *supra* note 6, at 42; Weinstein Oral History, at 1415AA.

[136] Mehler Videotaped Interview, *supra* note 68, at 4.

[137] Weinstein, First Rough Notes, *supra* note 6, at 41.

[138] *Id.* at 42.

[139] Arnold H. Lubash, *Jack Weinstein: Creative U.S. Judge Who Disdains Robe and High Bench*, N.Y. TIMES, May 28, 1991, at B5.

[140] Jack B. Weinstein, *In Memoriam: William C. Warren*, 101 COLUM. L. REV. 456 (2001).

[141] Jack B. Weinstein, Five Minutes on the Way the Law School Was in 1952 When I Arrived as a Faculty Appointee, remarks at The Way We Were Luncheon, Nov. 30, 2004, at 4–5. [hereinafter Weinstein, Five Minutes].

[142] Jack B. Weinstein, William C. Warren, *supra* note 140.

[143] *Id.* at 2. *See also* Jack B. Weinstein, A Few Memories on Student Days, remarks at Columbia Law School 2–4 (Oct. 23, 2003).

[144] Weinstein Oral History, at 14.

Karl Llewellyn was finishing his great work on sales. Young B. Smith was head of the New York Law Revision Commission. Herbert Wechsler was about to become responsible for the writing of the Model Penal Code. Milton Handler was on his way to dominating the field of antitrust. The specialist in international law, Phillip Jessup, would ultimately sit on the International Court of Justice.[145]

Weinstein was brought to the law school to teach corporate law (with the influential New Dealer, A. A. Berle), criminal law, and accounting. When Jerome Michael died in 1954, Weinstein was asked to take over Michael's courses in evidence and procedure and Michael's seminar on trial practice. Weinstein did not have much knowledge in any of these areas.[146] Shortly thereafter, he would take over Walter Gellhorn's clinical seminar and, later, state constitutional law.

Weinstein would continue to teach two courses a semester at Columbia Law School for three decades after he became a judge. He was not just a part-time adjunct.[147] He would teach either evidence or civil procedure every semester as well as a seminar. He found that the teaching was useful for judging because, as he put it, "teaching gives you a broad view of fields that is sometimes lacking if you depend only upon briefs or particular litigation."[148] Believing that the way to learn is to put together materials for courses one teaches,[149] Weinstein, with Maurice Rosenberg, edited a casebook in civil procedure which was published in 1962.[150] Having the opportunity to think about whole subjects provided consistency for Weinstein, while other judges might have to pick at the subject piecemeal, case by case.[151]

Weinstein's Columbia colleagues would be a part of Weinstein's life *as a judge*. He appointed his colleague, Louis Lusky, to represent defendants in cases involving fugitives from the draft.[152] He used Curtis Berger as special master in the Coney Island school segregation case.[153] He sent opinions regularly to Willis Reese, Herbert Wechsler, and Louis Henkin[154] and officiated at the remarriage of the dying Allan Farnsworth.[155] He would make use of many former students in his judicial work. For example, he appointed two of them, who had distinguished careers, to the board of directors of the Johns Manville Trust.[156] Among his students at Columbia was Ruth Bader Ginsburg, who studied evidence with him.

---

[145] *See* Weinstein, Five Minutes, *supra* note 141, at 2–4.

[146] Weinstein, First Rough Notes 6, *supra* note 6, at 44; Weinstein Oral History, at 1415Z, 51.

[147] Through the 1998–99 academic year. That year he prepared a brand new set of materials for teaching Civil Procedure. Interview of Jack B. Weinstein by author, July 9, 2010.

[148] Mehler Videotaped Interview, *supra* note 68, at 7. *See also* Weinstein Oral History, at 140ff.

[149] Weinstein Oral History, at 792.

[150] MAURICE ROSENBERG & JACK B. WEINSTEIN, ELEMENTS OF CIVIL PROCEDURE (1962).

[151] Weinstein Oral History, at 157.

[152] *United States v. Lockwood*, 382 F. Supp. 1111 (Sept. 30, 1974).

[153] *Hart v. Community School Bd.*, 383 F. Supp. 699 (Jan. 28, 1974). *See also* Weinstein Oral History, at 278.

[154] *Id.* at 199, 967, 1113.

[155] *Id.* at 1705.

[156] *Id.* at 135.

Brown v. Board of Education

Jack Weinstein's early teaching career led to his involvement in what probably was the most important litigation of the twentieth century, *Brown v. Board of Education*. He was one of the attorneys who worked and was listed "of counsel" on the National Association for the Advancement of Colored People's (NAACP) brief in the main case.[157] Weinstein was brought into the legal effort after *Brown* was set down for reargument in 1953. Weinstein's involvement in *Brown* began just as he was about to take over his colleague Walter Gellhorn's clinical seminar, Problems in Current Civil Rights Litigation, a seminar in which students received one-half point credit for legal work for such civil rights organizations as the American Civil Liberties Union, the American Jewish Congress, and the NAACP. Gellhorn took Weinstein to a meeting that Thurgood Marshall asked him to chair. Impressing Marshall by dictating the consensus once it had been reached, Weinstein was welcomed and became part of a team which included such notables as Marshall, Robert Carter, Constance Baker Motley, Jack Greenberg, James Nabrit, William T. Coleman, and Charles Black.

Weinstein recalls Marshall drawing lawyers, historians, social scientists, social psychologists, and financiers into the fray. Marshall "cajoled, he threatened, he joked."[158] It was, Weinstein said, "our privilege to work for him during the years when he burned with a bright incandescence . . . "[159] Weinstein worked days when he could and nights at the library of the City Bar and at the nearby Algonquin Hotel, where he often stayed over. Weinstein minimizes his role, stating that he was always used "in a very low level capacity, almost like a young associate in a law firm" or, as he expressed it at a different time: "I was just a general purpose associate floor sweeper."[160] Weinstein has admitted his error in strongly opposing the inclusion of Kenneth Clark's research in the brief; research that provided a basis for the High Court's holding.[161]

For Weinstein, the experience of working on *Brown* was personally transformative. He had met few, if any African-Americans in his public school, in Brooklyn College's night classes, or on his segregated submarine. Thurgood Marshall "was really the first African American I had any close association with."[162] Certainly, the experience with *Brown* influenced his dealing with New York City school cases, especially the Coney Island school case discussed in Chapter 4.

---

[157] Four cases were decided in *Brown v. Board of Education*, 347 U.S. 483 (1954); 349 U.S. 294 (1955).

[158] Jack B. Weinstein, Reflections on *Brown v. Board of Education*, Remarks at Court of Appeals for the Second Circuit, New York City (Feb. 9, 2004) 7–8 (copy is possession of author).

[159] *Id.*

[160] Interview of Jack B. Weinstein by Juan Williams in *Thurgood Marshall; 50th Anniversary Brown v. Board of Education*, NPR NEWS Interview transcript, Nov. 20, 2003, at 2, 5, 18 [hereinafter NPR Interview]. *See also* Weinstein, Reflections on *Brown v. Board of Education*, supra note 158, at 8.

[161] *See Brown v. Board of Ed.*, 347 U.S. 483, 495 n.11 (1954).

[162] NPR Interview, *supra* note 160, at 9–10. President Jimmy Carter invited Weinstein to the White House reception observing the twenty-fifth anniversary of *Brown v. Board of Education*.

Government Service, Scholarship, and Politics

By 1954, Weinstein was consultant to and reporter for the New York Temporary Commission on Courts, popularly known as the Tweed Commission after Harrison Tweed, a leading figure in the New York Bar. The Tweed Commission was the driving force behind what still remains the last significant revision of the Judiciary Article of the New York State Constitution. The Commission's recommendations for structural and procedural reform of the judicial system were approved by the electorate in 1961.[163] The new Judiciary Article for the state constitution created what was called a "Unified Court System," establishing various trial courts and the Administrative Board of the Judicial Conference. It conferred various administrative powers on the four Appellate Divisions.[164]

The Tweed Commission was supposed to look at the administration of justice in the state and to make recommendations in four areas: congestion and delay, cost of litigation, organization, and administration of the court system and practice and procedure. The Commission also spun off an Advisory Committee on Practice and Procedure formed to overhaul the Civil Practice Act and Rules.[165] As part of the process, a series of "persuasive and definitive studies" were undertaken by Weinstein, Harold Korn (director of research), and Donald Distler (associate reporter) over a five-year period. Distler was later succeeded by Arthur Miller.[166] The Advisory Committee completely revised New York State Practice. Weinstein was the primary draftsman of the revised New York Civil Practice Law and Rules (CPLR); a task, Professor Geoffrey Hazard wrote, that Weinstein performed superbly.[167]

The aim of the framers of the CPLR was simplification and liberalization. The old New York Civil Practice Act and Rules of Civil Practice were carefully rearranged. Drastic changes were made in the area of personal jurisdiction, extending the reach of New York courts.[168] However, an effort to transfer the principal authority for procedural rule-making to the courts failed, as did a number of other proposed major reforms.[169]

While working on the CPLR, Weinstein gathered materials for what became an eight-volume treatise on New York civil procedure, which he edited with Korn

---

[163] New York State Unified Court System, Press Release, July 17, 2007, *available at* http://www.courts.state. ny.us/press/pr2006_16.shtml.

[164] New York's intermediate appellate court.

[165] Geoffrey Hazard, Book Review, 78 HARV. L. REV. 1305, 1306 (1965) (reviewing JACK B. WEINSTEIN, HAROLD KORN & ARTHUR MILLER, NEW YORK CIVIL PRACTICE (1963)). On the work, *see* Weinstein Oral History, at 1803.

[166] Hazard, Book Review, *supra* note 165, at 1306.

[167] Geoffrey C. Hazard, Jr., *Reflections on Judge Weinstein's Ethical Dilemmas in Mass Tort Litigation*, 8 NW. U. L. REV. 569, (1994). On the treatise, *see* Weinstein Oral History, at 1803.

[168] Hazard, Book Review, *supra* note 165, at 1306.

[169] Hazard, Book Review, *supra* note 165, at 1308.

and Miller. Weinstein also published a manual on New York civil procedure.[170] His decision to write a treatise and manual was "based on the need to make sure that it [the CPLR] was properly construed." As one reviewer wrote, "The authors . . . hold their protective hands over it [CPLR] in an attempt to save it from destruction, misconstruction, and misapplication . . . ."[171] Weinstein believes that the treatise, which is still in use as a basic resource, had a major impact on getting the CPLR started right.[172]

The treatise was intended to aid New York judges and attorneys in solving day-to-day problems arising under the CPLR. It was praised by Charles Breitel, who later became Chief Judge of the New York Court of Appeals, as vastly superior to previous treatises on the defunct Civil Practice Act.[173] Others lauded it for its thoroughness and practicality,[174] calling it "carefully considered, well-organized, and well written."[175] Professor Adolf Homburger said that, "In scope of coverage, originality of approach and depth of analysis, it measures up to the highest standards" and will "take its well-earned place among the important treatises of legal science."[176]

Weinstein took an active role in the creation of the Federal Rules of Evidence. Having revised a leading evidence casebook,[177] Weinstein was appointed to the Advisory Committee to the Judicial Conference Committee on Evidence by Earl Warren in 1966.[178] After the Rules were promulgated, Weinstein repeated what he had done with the CPLR sharing authorship of a treatise and a manual on evidence with Margaret Berger, a former law clerk and professor at Brooklyn Law School.[179] Weinstein, thus, was able to influence to some degree the interpretation by judges of the evidence rules in their formative years, while providing an important work for practitioners.

---

[170] JACK B. WEINSTEIN, HAROLD L. KORN, & ARTHUR R. MILLER, NEW YORK CIVIL PRACTICE (1963); JACK B. WEINSTEIN, HAROLD L. KORN, & ARTHUR R. MILLER, MANUAL OF NEW YORK CIVIL PROCEDURE (1967).

[171] Adolf Homburger, Book Review, 112 U. PA. L. REV. 1222, 1235 (1964) (reviewing JACK WEINSTEIN, HAROLD KORN, & ARTHUR MILLER, NEW YORK CIVIL PRACTICE (1963)).

[172] Weinstein Oral History, at 1804.

[173] Charles Breitel, Book Review, 64 COLUM. L. REV. 974, 976 (1964) (reviewing JACK B. WEINSTEIN ET AL., NEW YORK CIVIL PRACTICE (1963–64)).

[174] Arthur Lenhoff, *A New Procedural Code in New York*, 13 BUFF. L. REV. 119, 132 (1963–64) (reviewing JACK B. WEINSTEIN ET AL., NEW YORK CIVIL PRACTICE (1963)).

[175] Jack H. Friedenthal, Book Review of NEW YORK CIVIL PRACTICE (1963), 49 MINN. L. REV. 220 (1964).

[176] Homburger, *supra* note 171, at 1238.

[177] EDMUND M. MORGAN, JOHN M. MAGUIRE, & JACK B. WEINSTEIN, CASES AND MATERIALS ON EVIDENCE (5th ed. 1957); revised with other collaborators in 1964 and 1970; also various annual supplements containing statutory and rules changes. James Bradley Thayer had edited the first edition in 1892. Weinstein pruned and reanalyzed the fourth edition. *See* Weinstein Oral History, at 1415EE–FF. *See also* MORGAN, MAGUIRE, & WEINSTEIN, BASIC PROBLEMS OF STATE AND FEDERAL EVIDENCE (5th ed. Weinstein rev. 1976).

[178] NEW YORK TIMES, Mar. 8, 1966.

[179] *See* Weinstein Oral History, at 1804–05. *And see* JACK B. WEINSTEIN & MARGARET BERGER, WEINSTEIN'S EVIDENCE [7 vol.] (1975, 1979) with annual supplements. *See also* JACK B. WEINSTEIN & MARGARET BERGER, WEINSTEIN'S EVIDENCE MANUAL [2 vol.] (1987); JACK B. WEINSTEIN & MARGARET BERGER, WEINSTEIN'S EVIDENCE MANUAL (student ed. 1987).

During the fifteen years before he was appointed to the bench, besides his works on evidence and New York practice, Weinstein had also written or edited two books on the New York State Constitution[180] and written over three dozen articles on such subjects as traffic safety, conflict of laws, drugs, hearsay, search and seizure, and legal assistance for the indigent.

County Attorney (1963–1965)

Weinstein's activist tendencies were demonstrated during the two years he served as County Attorney for Nassau County. In that position, he actively sought to use his office as an instrument to assist the modernization of the county and to see that the populace would be treated fairly and respectfully.[181]

Eugene Nickerson, the first Democrat elected Nassau County Executive in a half-century, was a liberal activist, a decent blue-blooded social reformer. Nickerson's first County Attorney was Bert Hartnett, whom Weinstein had known from Brooklyn College, Columbia Law School (where he was his classmate and fellow associate) and as a neighbor. Leaving the job to go into practice, Hartnett suggested Weinstein as his replacement.[182]

With a population of 1.4 million, Nassau County was then the fastest growing county in the United States. A maze of local governments existed within the county: three towns, two cities, and numerous villages as well as numerous water, garbage, and fire districts.[183] Nickerson brought clean government and attempted with considerable success to have built the infrastructure the county needed—new and wider roads, parks, hospitals, beaches, and the Nassau Coliseum. He also sought to provide new housing opportunities for the poor and minorities, a reformed welfare system, and other public services.[184]

Weinstein found being County Attorney "a fascinating job."[185] He saw his role as facilitating Nickerson's activist governing, defending the county, and assisting Nickerson's political career.[186] Of course, much of the work was handling legal matters. He directed a staff of thirty attorneys, which represented every county department—police,

---

[180] JACK B. WEINSTEIN, ESSAYS ON THE NEW YORK CONSTITUTION (1966); JACK B. WEINSTEIN, A NEW CONSTITUTION MEETING TODAY'S NEEDS AND TOMORROW'S CHALLENGES (March 1967).

[181] Eugene H. Nickerson *Jack B. Weinstein: The Early Years*, 97 COLUM. L. REV. 1958, 1959 (1997) [hereinafter Nickerson, *Weinstein Early Years*]. *See also* William S. Siegel, *Tax Certiorari and Condemnation: Jack B. Weinstein's Legacy as Nassau County Attorney*, N.Y.L.J. (Apr. 3, 2007).

[182] Weinstein, First Rough Notes, *supra* note 6, at 49; Jack B. Weinstein, *In Memoriam—Eugene H. Nickerson*, 102 COLUM L. REV. 1193 (2002) [hereinafter Weinstein, *In Memoriam—Eugene Nickerson*].

[183] Nickerson, *Weinstein Early Years*, *supra* note 181, at 1959.

[184] Weinstein, *In Memoriam—Eugene Nickerson*, *supra* note 182, at 1194–97; William D. Siegel, *Tax Certiorari and Condemnation: Jack B. Weinstein's Legacy as Nassau County Attorney*, 237 N.Y.L.J. 20 (Apr. 13, 2007).

[185] Weinstein, First Rough Notes, *supra* note 6, at 50.

[186] Weinstein has related how he warded off a blandishment from Roy Cohn, stating, "I'm protecting somebody who could be a gubernatorial candidate, and I'm not going to let anything happen while I'm here

engineering, condemnation, social welfare, etc.[187] From his position, Weinstein launched social action projects including expansion of legal services to the poor, constitutional reform, and apportionment.[188]

During the years Nickerson was County Executive, the Nassau County Democratic Party consciously made use of the courts as a part of a comprehensive program to appeal for popular support. The Democrats did this by using the courts to maintain procedural fairness and openness in town government and to ensure accountability in order to gain strength and compete evenly with the dominant Republicans.[189]

Nickerson and Weinstein met with strong opposition from Republican partisans as well as police unions, the sheriff, and the doctors and administrators of the county hospital.[190] One of their staunchest opponents, a major thorn in their side, was Nassau County District Attorney William Cahn. Weinstein, in one of the rare sharply critical assessments of individuals in his oral history, stated that Cahn was "a terrible character: harsh and abusive when he had power and arrogant."[191] Weinstein constantly fought with Cahn, who tried unsuccessfully to get Nickerson removed from office for allegedly interfering with Cahn's investigation of the county jail.[192]

The most notorious episode involving Cahn occurred when he seized the entire press run (10,000 copies) of the *Evergreen Review* because, he claimed, it was pornographic. A civil suit against the county was brought in the U.S. District Court for the Eastern District. Weinstein was forced to defend Cahn because of the county's potential liability. A three-judge district court which included Weinstein's Columbia Law School colleague, Paul Hays, and two future colleagues on the Eastern District bench, John R. Bartels and George Rosling, enjoined the seizure.[193] Ultimately, Cahn released all but three copies.[194]

Cahn was later convicted in the Eastern District for fraud connected with his travel expenditures and disbarred. Weinstein says that he came to feel sorry for him and told Cahn to use his name on his application for readmission to the bar. The Appellate Division turned down the application.[195]

---

on my watch that will, at all, create a problem for him. That's one of the main things I'm here for." Weinstein Oral History, at 882.

[187] Weinstein, First Rough Notes, *supra* note 6, at 50–51.

[188] Meyer *et al.*, *supra* note 116, at 26–27.

[189] KENNETH M. DOLBEARE, TRIAL COURTS IN URBAN POLITICS 50–51 (1967).

[190] Weinstein, *In Memoriam–Eugene Nickerson*, *supra* note 182, at 1196–97.

[191] Weinstein Oral History, at 628ff.

[192] *Id.* at 30, 682ff; Jack B. Weinstein, Memoir—First Supplemental Memorandum 5–6 (in possession of author) (hereinafter Weinstein, Memoir).

[193] *Evergreen Review, Inc. v. Cahn*, 230 F. Supp. 498 (June 11, 1964).

[194] Jack B. Weinstein, First Supplemental Memorandum, Excerpt 2 in Weinstein, Memoir, at 1–5 (in possession of author); Weinstein, *In Memoriam–Eugene Nickerson*, *supra* note 182, at 1959.

[195] Jack B. Weinstein, Memoir, First Supplemental Memorandum, in Weinstein, Memoir, *supra* note 194, at 10.

One quintessential Weinstein accomplishment as County Attorney was his reform of the manner in which the county handled condemnations of private property for public purposes. After he saw that an elderly couple was going to receive what Weinstein believed was too little money for their property from the county, he phoned them and suggested a much fairer settlement. Nickerson suggested, however, that he ought to "keep it under wraps" for, if the Republicans every found about it, "'we were both goners.'"[196]

However, Weinstein went further, taking whatever actions he could to change the tactics and procedures of his office in condemnation proceedings to ensure fair treatment of property owners. He revealed the appraisals the government had made of properties. He contracted with his Columbia Law School colleague, Curtis Berger, and St. Johns University Law School professor, Patrick Rohan, to study the county's land acquisition procedures. This study led to a user-friendly system, which included advance payments to property owners.

The endeavor as County Attorney that probably had the greatest impact on Weinstein's later career was the brief he wrote for the suburbs in the leading "one-man, one-vote" case in New York State, *WMCA v. Lomenzo*.[197] As a result of his work in the *WMCA* case, Weinstein came to represent the Democratic Party in reapportionment matters throughout the state.[198]

The most important achievement of Weinstein's tenure as County Attorney was his leadership of a group of government officials and community leaders who created Nassau County Legal Services, one of the first community legal services "storefronts" in the nation.[199] Reading in the newspapers that there was money in Washington for legal services, Weinstein "high-tailed" it down to Washington to secure funding from the Kennedy administration. His philosophy was simple: "It's a Hobbesian World out there. The rich have little trouble moving through society. It's the poor who need help."[200]

Under state law the State's Appellate Division, Second Department had to approve the new "law firm." Opposition surfaced from conservative members of the bar and some African-American attorneys. Meetings turned nasty. Proponents of legal services were accused of "bringing socialism to the county, of subverting the client-attorney

---

[196] *Id.* at 10.

[197] *WMCA v. Lomenzo*, 377 U.S. 633 (1964). *See also* CALVIN B. T. LEE, ONE MAN, ONE VOTE: WMCA AND THE STRUGGLE FOR EQUAL REPRESENTATION 123, 146 (1967).

[198] A number of persons were involved in the litigation that would factor importantly in Weinstein's career, including Trivia, Stanley Fuld, Orrin Judd, and Leonard Sands.
    Among other major endeavors of the County Attorney's Office while Weinstein held the office were brokering a deal to mitigate the degree of housing discrimination on Long Island and Weinstein's recommendation to raise assessments on vacant land, which raised much money without adding to the burdens of home owners.

[199] Francis J. Flaherty, *The Living Legend of New York's Eastern District: A "Classic Liberal" on the Bench*, NAT'L L.J. 2 (Nov. 22, 1982).

[200] Vescovi Interview, *supra* note 73 at 5 (fax pagination).

relationship . . . and of taking bread out of the mouths of attorneys."[201] The opposition sought to disbar Weinstein.[202] The Presiding Justice of the Second Department passionately opposed the plan. Weinstein served him with a petition for mandamus, which he threw back at Weinstein. The conflict almost became physical.[203] Weinstein remembers that after he phoned Stanley Fuld and possibly State Attorney General Louis Lefkowitz, opposition disintegrated. Weinstein was the first chairman of the board.[204]

During the ceremony in which he received an award from the American Jewish Committee in 1967, Weinstein stated:

> I merely did the minimum that was required in my position as County Attorney. Had we done less I and others would have justly been subjected to the most severe criticism.[205]

In 1992, Weinstein spoke at the twenty-fifth anniversary dinner of the Nassau-Suffolk Law Services Committee. Two hundred fifty people attended.[206]

What was the impact of Weinstein's experience as County Attorney on his professional future and, ultimately, on his judging? For his immediate future, Weinstein had made valuable contacts in the New York Democratic Party. In the longer run, the county job gave Weinstein familiarity with a number of areas of law that he would later deal with on the bench, including government contracts and municipal insurance.[207] He also got a realistic view of how party politics works[208] and came to believe that ordinary plaintiffs "very often" "could not get a square deal" in zoning cases in the state courts because Republican lawyers, who controlled judgeships, were in touch with real estate interests.[209] He also received an on-the-ground familiarity with Nassau County and a greater appreciation of the need to give practical help to the poor, which later would lead him to personally fund a number of services within the Eastern

---

[201] NASSAU LAWYER, February 1992, at 6.

[202] *Message from Jeffrey Seigel*, in Nassau/Suffolk Law Services Committee, LAW SERVICES NEWS (March/April 2004), at 1; Weinstein, First Rough Notes, *supra* note 6, at 51; Glaberson Interview, *supra* note 24, at 13; Jack B. Weinstein, *The Poor's Right to Equal Access to the Courts*, 13 CONN. L. REV. 651, 658 (1981).

[203] Some say it did. Interview with Tom Maligno, Fall 2008.

[204] Weinstein Oral History, at 1781–83; NASSAU LAWYER, February 1992, at 6. *See* Jack B. Weinstein, All People Are Entitled to the Assistance of Lawyers in Civil as Well as Criminal Matters, Speech to Association of the Bar of New York City 16 (Mar. 30, 1976). *See also* Jack B. Weinstein, *Delivery of Legal Services Reviewed*, N.Y.L.J. (May 2–3, 1974).

[205] Jack B. Weinstein, Speech Accepting Award of American Jewish Committee, Garden City, May 11, 1967 (delivery copy with emendations), at 1.

[206] NASSAU LAWYER, February 1992, at 6.

[207] Weinstein Oral History, at 57. *See also Royal Ins. v. Ru-Wal*, 918 F. Supp. 647 (Mar. 12, 1966).

[208] Weinstein Oral History, at 89. *See Anderson v. Meisser*, 285 F. Supp. 974 (June 15, 1968).

[209] *See Lerner v. Town of Islip*, 272 F. Supp. 664 (Aug. 19, 1967).

District court.[210] In addition, he came to understand that the school system in the suburbs was "the center for the whole community."[211] He also established personal relationships that would be helpful to him in complex cases such as that involving the Shoreham Nuclear reactor,[212] and he developed a lasting friendship with Nickerson, who would join him on the bench of the Eastern District.[213]

After his service as Nassau County Attorney, Weinstein became advisor to the New York State Commission on Reform and Simplification of the [State] Constitution (for which he prepared a draft constitution) and then to the Constitutional Convention itself. Although he ran unsuccessfully to be a convention delegate from Nassau County, at the convention, Weinstein would work closely with the Speaker of the State Assembly and President of the Convention, Anthony Travia. Travia, too, would become a colleague of Weinstein's on the bench of the Eastern District.

Personality

Jack and Evelyn Horowitz Weinstein have been married since 1946. A graduate of Brooklyn College and the Columbia University School of Social Work, "Evie" Weinstein is a psychiatric social worker. She has worked with Jewish asthmatic children, the Red Cross and, after the Second World War, established a clinic for former members of the armed forces suffering from what we would call post-traumatic stress syndrome. She was a social worker at Long Island Jewish Hospital and head of the social service department of North Shore Hospital she organized the state-funded ombuds service in Nassau County and trained many who worked in the program.

Evelyn Weinstein also cofounded Community Advocates (which is concerned with issues related to the welfare and mental health system in Nassau County), and the Nassau Action Coalition, which helps the aged, the disabled, the blind, and welfare recipients. The recipient of a truckload of awards and citations, she remains active in social work and political advocacy, and she has received the Social Worker of the Year award in Nassau County. Active in advocacy for the poor at the town, county, state and national level, Evelyn Weinstein was a delegate to the White House Conference on Education and the Second International Conference on Aging.[214] Mrs. Weinstein is a passionate liberal, who formed a woman's organization to protest the Vietnam War.

---

[210] Glaberson Interview, *supra* note 24, at 14.

[211] *See Kramer v. Union Free Sch. Dist. No. 15*, 282 F. Supp. 70, 75, 76–77 (Jan. 30, 1968), *rev'd*, 395 U.S. 621 (1969); Weinstein Oral History, at 76ff.

[212] Weinstein Oral History, at 934. *See* Chapter 7.

[213] Weinstein Oral History, at 142, 764. Nickerson and Weinstein had neighboring offices in the courthouse, and the two men would constantly visit each other and talk. After Nickerson's death, Weinstein, in his oral history repeated several times how much he missed him. *See, e.g., id.* at 1608–09.

[214] [Program for] Co-Pay, Inc. 30th Annual Dinner Dance; Karen Weisberg, *The Grand Dames of Great Neck*, GREAT NECK REC., c. 1981 (copy in possession of the author).

Jack and Evelyn Weinstein have three children: Seth George (born October 3, 1946) when Weinstein was a law student, Michael David (born August 1, 1951), and Howard Lewis (born July 7, 1954). Seth has had a varied and interesting career, which has included teaching in Harlem, working in television, selling Christmas trees, sailing across the Atlantic Ocean, and starting a rare gem import business. Presently building and rehabilitating commercial and residential structures, he is married to an international dress designer. Michael, who lives in Eugene, Oregon, is a physician who does trauma work and has set up clinics to serve indigent people. He is married to Donna Kay Spurlock, also a physician, and they have two children, Kelsey and Luke. Howard is a successful importer of goods from China, who lives in Connecticut, and is married to Deborah Davies.[215] Jack Weinstein's brother Bill has three children and six grandchildren. His sister Naomi has four children and three grandchildren.

At six feet two inches and built like a linebacker, Weinstein still has the ability to "command awe and respect without distance."[216] Looking at him, one remarks on his big, fuzzy eyebrows and the twinkle in his eyes. Always active physically—he has sailed, jogged, cross-country skied, and played tennis in his eighties—he still goes to the gym every day and continues to row in the Long Island Sound inlet that adjoins his home. In the sixteen years the author has had lengthy conversations with him, not once has he heard a complaint of a physical ailment nor has he ever seen him discouraged.

A poor sleeper, he gets up in the middle of the night to make changes in drafts of speeches or opinions.[217] Even when he does sleep well, he has, throughout most of his career, arisen before 5 or 5:30 a.m. to tinker with a speech, row, or be in his office by 6:30.

Weinstein's energy is legendary. When he was writing his treatises, he worked seven days a week from five-thirty in the morning to eleven p.m. or midnight.[218] That energy has marked his entire career. Dean Joan Wexler of Brooklyn Law School has said that "[H]is stream of letters, speeches, articles, sermons, reports, bar activities, law reform efforts, and commentary is endless."[219] "I've always done," Weinstein says, "more than one thing at a time."[220] As we have seen, after he became a judge, he continued teaching at Columbia Law School essentially full-time.[221] If he can no longer work twenty hours a day, day after day, week after week,[222] still, well past his eightieth birthday, he volunteered to take the entire backlog (ultimately, he took five hundred) of prisoner *habeas corpus* petitions in the Eastern District and, with the help of a special master, resolved

---

[215] Weinstein, First Rough Notes, *supra* note 6, at 55–56.

[216] David W. Leebron, *To Jack, Son of Colombia*, 97 COLUM.L.REV.1965 (1992).

[217] Weinstein Oral History, at 900, 1615.

[218] *Id.* at 812.

[219] Joan G. Wexler, *In Praise of Jack B. Weinstein*, 97 COLUM. L. REV. 1968, 1970 (1997).

[220] *Benchmark*, NEW YORKER, May 3, 1993, at 34, 35.

[221] Weinstein, First Rough Notes, *supra* note 6, at 53.

[222] Weinstein Oral History, at 812.

them in a matter of months. He had "caught up for everybody."[223] Even when dealing with the massive *Agent Orange* litigation, "his [case] terminations continued at the same rate. Almost always he has conducted the most civil trials in the district and in some years, his total hours on trial were the greatest in the country."[224] Asked about this, he simply said, "I dispose of my cases. I take my share out of the wheel, but I get rid of them faster than most."[225] Weinstein believes that his district does not need more judges. Part of that is based on his view that magistrate judges should be entrusted with more responsibilities. But he believes that "[t]e basic problem is that we don't have enough work."[226] Weinstein may well forget that not every colleague is a Weinstein.

Among the other traits that come rapidly to mind after spending time with Jack Weinstein are his enjoyment of his work, enthusiasm, self-confidence modified by genuine modesty, courage, a positive view of people, compassion, dislike of authority, and fierce independence. Jimmy Breslin writes that "he brings so much nobility and warmth and common sense into the law that people who drop in his courtroom wish not to leave."[227] He can, however, get angry. Professor Linda Mullenix of the University of Texas Law School, a sharp academic critic of Weinstein's work, was the object of such wrath and reports: "If he gets mad at you and yells at you, it's kind of like God booming." But she adds, "I have to tell you . . . he's the only man who's ever yelled at me and then apologized in a handwritten note."[228]

Richard Posner, judge of the U.S. Court of Appeals for the Seventh Circuit and, arguably, the only federal judge more productive than Weinstein, has said that "the capacity to find your docket interesting is not the least important attribute of an outstanding judge."[229] In his seventy-seventh year, speaking at Columbia Law School, Weinstein said:

> After a third of a century and tens of thousands of cases, I continue to look forward to each day's courthouse surprises. I can hardly wait to get in each morning and peer in the kaleidoscope of life, constantly changing in color and form.[230]

He has told his clerks, tongue in cheek: "these are not real people, remember, who are testifying. There is somebody up there from central casting who is sending them

---

[223] Weinstein Oral History, at 1725.

[224] *Id.* at 753.

[225] *Id.* at 1701.

[226] *Id.* at 1725.

[227] JIMMY BRESLIN, THE GOOD RAT 30 (2008).

[228] Kolker, *supra* note 44, at 37.

[229] Richard A. Posner, *The Learned Hand Biography and the Question of Judicial Greatness*, 104 YALE L.J. 523 (1994).

[230] Jack B. Weinstein, Family: Lawyer; Genus: Judge; Species: Trial Judge, Symposium on Judges, Columbia Law School Spring Reunion Panel, May 1, 1999, at 5.

down here for our amusement and education."[231] He has also said, "Every morning I get in and I say, 'I am going to make another mistake today because there is something new we haven't heard of.'"[232]

At eighty-nine, his intellectual curiosity is enormous. He reads half a dozen magazines and dozens of professional periodicals and borrows large numbers of books from the Great Neck Public library.[233] About that curiosity, Joan Wexler, a former Weinstein clerk, told of her interview for a clerkship with Weinstein:

> He was interested in my graduate studies. He was interested in my teaching career before law school . . . He was interested in my law review note. I finally caught on. He was interested in everything . . . new cases, evidence, theories, children—they all excite him."[234]

When Weinstein was involved in the asbestos cases—he was about seventy years old at the time—he found himself "continuing to consider new practices and new substantive law . . . . To try to understand why our American judges could use their powers so flexibly. I began to consider powers of equity judges, the chancellors of Medieval England and how their techniques were carried over to modern times."[235]

Some observers have reported that:

> Federal district judges appear to be rather lonely figures feeling distant from their immediate associates—that those federal judges often experienced sensations of great personal inadequacy in meeting the high standards of their judicial colleagues.[236]

Not so with Weinstein! After his experience with Stanley Fuld, Weinstein "had no desire to work under stress" with "someone demanding and intellectually superior." He said, "I would not have been able to work under somebody. I just had to be my own person." He "wanted to work where he was wholly in charge."[237] It is not clear whom Weinstein might have worked for who could have been his intellectual superior.[238] But there is no question of his comfort in running his own show.

---

[231] Mehler Videotaped Interview, *supra* note 68, at 12.

[232] Glaberson Interview, *supra* note 24, at 7.

[233] Weinstein Oral History, at 1520, 1722.

[234] Wexler, *supra* note 219, at 1968.

[235] JACK B. WEINSTEIN, INDIVIDUAL JUSTICE IN MASS TORT LITIGATION xii (1995).

[236] Robert A. Carp, *The Scope and Function of Intra-Circuit Judicial Communication: A Case Study of the Eighth Circuit*, 6 L. & SOC'Y 405, 420–21 (1972). *See also* Paul D. Carrington, *U.S. Courts of Appeals and U.S. District Courts: Relationships in the Future, in* THE FEDERAL APPELLATE JUDICIARY IN THE TWENTY-FIRST CENTURY 69 (Cynthia Harrison & Russell R. Wheeler eds., 1989).

[237] Weinstein Oral History, at 791; Weinstein, First Rough Notes, *supra* note 6, at 48.

[238] He did name Professor Herbert Wechsler of Columbia Law School as one.

Warren Burger used to explain that at least part of John Marshall's achievements was the result of a man whose energy was not wasted in deep inner conflicts.[239] While Jack Weinstein appears to be a much more psychologically complex figure than Marshall, nevertheless, his positive approach to life seems to have made an inexhaustible flow of his energy possible. His insecurities are few—one being some discomfort in social situations, such as making small talk and remembering names.[240] Weinstein does agonize over some of his cases—especially sentencing—but not to the point of being dilatory. And in the courtroom, he is decisive.

Weinstein's extraordinary self-confidence can be confused with vanity or arrogance. Of the public law litigation he handled involving an institution for the developmentally disabled, he reflected, "I knew exactly what I want[ed] to do right from the outset, I mean, right or wrong, I have a strong sense that this is the way it should be handled. And if I foul up, the Court of Appeals will correct me."[241]

This is a man with "chutzpah." Weinstein had no compunctions about writing to the U.S. Attorney four times in two and one-half weeks seeking to advise her, among other matters, to post warnings in various languages in airports about currency reporting requirements and expressing his view that the government should take responsibility for notifying an arrested foreign national of his consular notification rights at indictment or when he first pleads.[242] He wrote FBI Director, William H. Webster, to indicate his disappointment at FBI witnesses and the weaknesses of their scientific proof exhibited at trial.[243]

Weinstein's unusual (for a judge) willingness to fearlessly go out on a limb has led to an oft-told courthouse joke: "God has been seeing a psychiatrist lately because He thinks he is Jack Weinstein."[244] Weinstein himself enjoys such stories and tells them on himself, but it should be pointed out that while he has a great deal of self-confidence, he does not belittle others. When asked by the *New York Times* for his opinion of two potential Supreme Court appointees, he told the newspaper that both were worthy candidates, noting, "I'd be proud to be reversed by either one of them."[245]

Some of that self-confidence is the result of his enormous range of experience and knowledge. One day, John C. Goldberg, then a Weinstein clerk, was taking a walk with Weinstein, when a car made a turn that Goldberg said was illegal. Weinstein replied, "'When I and my colleagues drafted the New York Motor Vehicle Law, we intended that

---

[239] This occurred several times in the presence of the author when he was working for the Chief Justice.

[240] *See* Weinstein Oral History, at 705–06.

[241] Weinstein Oral History, at 707.

[242] Letters from Jack W. Weinstein to Roslynn R. Mauskopf, Feb. 19, 2003 (twice), Feb. 20, 2003, and March 7, 2003 (copies in possession of this author). *See also* Sentencing Hearing, *United States v. Hoyos*, CR-83-0014 discussed in N.Y. DAILY NEWS, Mar. 10, 1983.

[243] Letter from Jack B. Weinstein to William H. Webster, Feb. 27, 1979. *See also* Webster to Weinstein, June 6, 1979. Both letters can be found in Weinstein's FBI file (copy in possession of author).

[244] Glaberson Interview, *supra* note 24, at 21.

[245] NEW YORK TIMES, May 30, 1993, at 24.

to be permissible.'"[246] Other times, it is just the result of irrepressible wit. In the late 1970s, after Weinstein sentenced the head of the United Paper Workers Union to three years in prison for embezzlement, the defendant's lawyer argued, "'The President of the United States got an absolute pardon. To put this man in jail makes a mockery of justice.'" Replied Weinstein (undoubtedly deadpan), "But Mr. Nixon was not before me."[247] At another time, Weinstein related how he achieves settlements: "Whenever I have a case that is difficult, I say to the lawyers, 'Have you considered the choice of law problems in this case? Go out into the hallway and discuss them.'"[248]

Most federal judges "labor in obscurity,"[249] but not Weinstein. He does not isolate himself from the press and, indeed, often makes good copy. His desire to speak out derives in some measure from strong self-identification as an educator and a member of the academy. He has taught throughout his career. In some of his courses in mass torts, he has accepted students from several area law schools.[250] When he held his seminars at the court, he used the cases "much as you would in grand rounds if you were a medical person to illustrate the problem."[251] He also is attentive to the scholarship of law professors. Further, he has strongly supported the use of law students as part-time law clerks and urged stipends for summer interns. He saw the part-time clerkship program as providing "useful research assistance," but its "main purpose would be to permit judges to provide law students with an understanding of courts and the way litigation is conducted."[252] The desire to teach extends to children. Weinstein has visited P.S. 8 in Brooklyn to teach. During the sentencing of Colombo capo Pasquale (Patsy) Amato, a kindergarten class sat in the jury box in Weinstein's classroom.[253]

Some of Weinstein's desire to speak out comes from the obligation he feels to share with public officials or the general public what he has learned from his unique vantage point. That desire to educate is deep. Regarding accepting an award at a Second Circuit Conference, he said, "I never try to miss an opportunity to say something substantive."[254] Speaking of an aspect of the asbestos litigation, he told me, "The matter . . . is of continuing importance to me and I want the public to understand the problem as I see it."[255] The bench, after all, can be a bully pulpit.[256] Asked about Justice

---

[246] Glaberson Interview, *supra* note 24, at 21, 24.

[247] NEW YORK TIMES, Nov. 21, 1978, at B2.

[248] PETER SCHUCK, AGENT ORANGE ON TRIAL 55 (1987).

[249] LAWRENCE BAUM, JUDGES AND THEIR AUDIENCES 169 (2006).

[250] N.Y.L.J., Oct. 8, 1992; Weinstein Oral History, at 1677.

[251] Weinstein Oral History, at 468.

[252] Jack B. Weinstein & William B. Bonvillian, *Law Students as Part-time Law Clerks*, 15 JUDGES J. 58, 59–60. *See also* Jack B. Weinstein & William M. Bonvillian, *Part-time Clerkship Program in Federal Courts for Law Students*, 68 F.R.D. 265 (1976) (available of Westlaw). *See also* Weinstein Oral History, at 1726–27.

[253] NEW YORK DAILY NEWS, Jan. 26, 1993; Weinstein Oral History, at 1702.

[254] Weinstein Oral History, at 1256.

[255] *Id.* at 518.

[256] Max Widener review of LOUISE ANN FISCH, ALL RISE: REYNALDO G. GARZA, THE FIRST MEXICAN AMERICAN FEDERAL JUDGE (1996) *in* H-LAW, http://www.h-net.org/~law/reviews/fischla.htm.

Ruth Bader Ginsburg's statement that effective judges will speak in a moderate and restrained voice, Weinstein responded, "It's one thing, however, to speak when you're on an appellate court and another when you see people day after day in your courtroom who are being destroyed because they haven't had proper guidance . . . If I cannot say what I see happening, who in the world is going to say it?"[257]

There is no doubt that Weinstein is "less risk-adverse than many judges."[258] He believes that judges are there to take risks. Weinstein says that he "really doesn't care very much what people think or certainly what my superiors think."[259] As we shall see, he has been reversed relatively often in some of his important cases.[260]

There can be little doubt of the former submariner's physical courage. After a threat was made to him in court, "cool and unruffled, the judge slowly repeated the words to the court stenographer for the record."[261]

On the other hand, it takes some time to realize that when Weinstein is lionized for his achievements, as his wife, Evelyn, said, "I always think he doesn't think he's done enough."[262] Weinstein says: "I never thought a poor boy who had to go to night school and work on the docks to obtain enough money for his shoes would ever be in this great position."[263] He says that he still feels that, "I wish I were smarter and had more energy. I'd be in a position to really take advantage of my position and really do something decent for a change. Yes, I still have that feeling."[264] He has a deep sense of obligation toward the community.[265]

Weinstein is also quite self-critical. He said to me one time: "I don't have very much doubt that I'm as susceptible as anybody else and maybe more so to publicity and to the enjoyment of having a lot of money I'm giving away [as he did in the *Agent Orange* case]."[266] Of his performance today, he says, "I'm not as good a judge as I was in the first few years . . . I see a deterioration in what I consider the standard of demeanor and judicial competence."[267] He realizes that once he had "worked" and "saw workers and what was going on. I saw people in the gutter." But, "[n]ow I'm out of touch. I'm rich

[257] NEW YORK NEWSDAY Interview with Jack B. Weinstein: *Communities Control Better than Courts*, NEWSDAY, July 6, 1933, at 61.

[258] Peter Bowles, *Tough Talk from the Bench*, N.Y. NEWSDAY, NY-Q, Nov. 14, 1993, at 1, 5, 6; Weinstein Oral History, at 1408.

[259] Mehler Videotaped Interview, *supra* note 68, at 13.

[260] Charles T. Kimmett, *Rethinking Mass Tort Law*, 105 YALE L. J. 1713 (1996) (reviewing JACK B. WEINSTEIN, INDIVIDUAL JUSTICE AND MASS TORT LITIGATION (1995)).

[261] PETER SCHUCK, AGENT ORANGE ON TRIAL 215 (1987). Yet, one fear that Weinstein has admitted to was avoiding traveling to the USSR because he feared he would fall into the clutches of the KGB and not have available to him a document in English stating his alleged crime. NEW YORK TIMES, Mar. 8, 1993.

[262] Glaberson Interview, *supra* note 24, at 24.

[263] Kenneth P. Nolan, *Weinstein on the Courts*, 3 LITIGATION 24, 26 (Feb. 1992).

[264] Weinstein Oral History, at 1415NN.

[265] Weinstein Oral History, at 389.

[266] Weinstein Oral History, at 578. *See also id.* at 519–20.

[267] *Id.* at 811.

now. I have rich friends, a job, full insurance and a life as free of stress as possible. That's not the kind of person that you would want to make important decisions affecting everyone."[268]

Before we suggested that "putting people down" is not a Weinstein trait. Weinstein's view of people is generous. After brilliance and self-confidence, the most characteristic Weinstein traits are compassion and empathy. While many judges and attorneys gripe about incivility and lack of preparation of members of the bar, Weinstein says that in his courtroom, the lawyers are "just wonderful" and "the very models of practicing attorneys." For him, "lawyers ask their questions crisply and do not ask the same questions over and over again." When asked to what he attributed such stellar behavior, apparently not as common in other courtrooms, Weinstein replies (presumably deadpan) with a variation of the Jewish prayer, "I cause my countenance to shine upon them."[269]

He has an eye that constantly discerns good traits in groups not normally thought of for good traits or for organizations not normally praised by liberals—the bureaucracy of the New York City Board of Education,[270] the general level of competence of those handling supplemental security income (SSI) claims,[271] Selective Service boards, even Mafia leaders who have close family ties. His view of Congress is positive—praising it for doing "an excellent job" with well thought-out and well-drafted statutes in many areas.[272]

He supposes that people would think "[it] incomprehensible that a judge should like, on a personal basis, some of the people before him."[273] Of one defendant he said, "I rather liked this guy though he was a crook and drug dealer. He was other wise a charming fellow."[274] Of the Dominican women convicted in a major welfare fraud scandal, he said, " . . . you don't want to destroy these mothers because you destroy the family. In many cases, they're very good mothers. These mothers were stealing, except with [sic] possibly one, not for themselves but to give their children something better."[275]

Of course, Weinstein's affection for people is reflected in his judging. Of one perennial *pro se* litigant he relates:

Normally, most judges would have thrown him out of court but I kind of like the old guy—so I would always let him come in and start his case and not require him

[268] *Id.* at 1723.

[269] Interview of Jack B. Weinstein with Jeffrey B. Morris, April 20, 2010. Rather than criticizing lawyers, Weinstein praises them for their good work, refers to them as "distinguished members of the bar" and he says, they then play the role expected of them. *Id.*

[270] Weinstein Oral History, at 117.

[271] *Id.* at 766.

[272] *Id.* at 1487.

[273] *Id.* at 362.

[274] Weinstein Oral History, at 1606.

[275] *Id.* at 1150. There are some limits to Weinstein's empathy. Of a terrorist who set off car bombs he said, "I really have no compassion for a guy that would have killed hundreds, really hundreds of people with [his] bombs. *Id.* at 1362–63. Of one dangerous drug dealer who came before him, he said, "Some of these people are dreadful people." *Id.* at 1333.

to pay fees. Then I would listen to him a little while and tell him he was improving in his capacity as a *pro se* litigant and then I would dismiss it. He was generally quite pleased with me. An interview with him appeared in the *New York Times* at one point and he said that the judge indicated that he was improving all the time.[276]

There was a rabbi from Poland who kept walking into his chambers deeply concerned about his naturalization certificate because it was dated "A.D." [Year of the Lord—measured from Jesus Christ's birth]. Weinstein described him as "a very nice man with a big beard [who] wasn't going to cause any trouble, but he felt very strongly about it." Weinstein tried unsuccessfully to talk him out of it, but he said it was a matter of religion and he was constitutionally protected. He kept walking in and talking to the judge's secretary. Weinstein tells the rest: "So I came up with this idea that I would draw up a certificate, which would say he was admitted as a citizen on August 25th, 'the 250th year of the United States of America's independence.' I would keep the certificate in a vault and give him a copy if he needed it." Weinstein then wrote an unpublished opinion and gave him a copy. "And he walked out happy and that was the end of it." Weinstein reflected with a big smile, "My view is that . . . these are all customers and [we] try to keep the customers happy."[277]

Perhaps the most salient characteristic of Weinstein-the-Judge is his stress on the "human face of the law." He has said: "You have humanity coming into court. You have people in trouble. The judge acts in a compassionate human way to show that the law isn't all that rigid and cruel."[278] He has a deep concern for others and the ability to put himself in their shoes. To sentence a Mafia defendant with cancer, Weinstein went to the hospital so that the defendant could continue treatment. After the sentencing, he put his arm around the grief-stricken family.[279] Two weeks after 9/11, Weinstein wrote then Chief Judge Edward Korman about plans for improved security in the courthouse:

> We should, I believe, to the extent possible, avoid the air of the court house as fortress . . . . Many people coming to our building are tense, concerned and confused. They need our reassurance and help.[280]

His compassion is seen most in mass tort, Social Security disability cases, and sentencings, but it shows up in many other places. At the closing of the *Suffolk County*

---

[276] *Id.* at 1328.

[277] *Id.* at 640–43, esp. 643.

[278] Weinstein Oral History, at 1367–68.

[279] *Id.* at 1208.

[280] Letter from Jack B.Weinstein to Chief Judge Edward Korman, Sept. 26, 2001 (in possession of author).

Developmentally Disabled case,[281] he recalled the "horrors that I first observed and then came home and wept."[282] He has often referred to the daughters of DES mothers, "who are now unable to have children of their own," to the Vietnam veterans frightened by the effects of herbicides on their progeny, and to the former Brooklyn Navy Yard workers ravaged with asbestos-related diseases.[283]

Weinstein believes deeply that *everyone* is entitled to "a little expression of esteem" and speaks movingly about his visits to prisons, when the inmates "had their arms through bars when they found out that I was a federal judge, begging me to do something about their case . . .."[284] "I was a human being they could reach out to."[285] A judge acts, he has said, in a "compassionate way to show that the law isn't all that rigid and cruel."[286] Of cases brought by prisoners, he says, "We ought to in some way touch them and say, 'Look, we know you're a human being. We know you're there, we feel we would like to help you. [But], there's nothing we can do, but O.K. keep trying and we respect you as a person.'"[287] Just listening to people and demonstrating sympathy and empathy, he says, is important. When he settled the DES cases, he called in the plaintiffs and talked to them, as he had done with the relatives of the children in the *Suffolk County Developmentally Disabled* case and he would do in other cases.[288]

Sentencings, especially of those who were convicted of low-level drug charges under the Sentencing Guidelines were particularly difficult for him. "It's just too overwhelming . . . This sense of the cruelty that I was involved in."[289] About to sentence a defendant to a substantial term and worried about it, Weinstein awakened in the middle of the night and said, "'God, I can't let this happen.'"[290] When for a time he refused to take drug cases, he called himself in a speech at Cardozo Law School, "a tired old judge who had temporarily filled his quota of remorselessness."[291] Weinstein gives cookies to a defendant's child after sentencing "primarily to assuage my own sense of the cruelty I had been party to."[292]

Undoubtedly, this compassion has led him to sentencings that could not be squared with case authority. One defendant he sent to the Metropolitan Correction Center "so he'll be able to see his kids."[293] He has had children come up to the table where he is

---

[281] *See, e.g., Society for Goodwill to Retarded Children v. Cuomo* 652 F. Supp. 515 (Jan. 27, 1987).

[282] Weinstein Oral History, at 1026–27. *See also* NEWSDAY, June 11, 1993, at 24.

[283] *See* Weinstein Oral History, at 755.

[284] *Id.* at 11–12.

[285] *Id.* at 331.

[286] *Id.* at 1367–68.

[287] *Id.* at 33.

[288] *Id.* at 675.

[289] *Id.* at 325.

[290] *Id.* at 1157.

[291] *Id.*

[292] *Id.* at 316–17.

[293] *Id.* at 593.

sentencing and explained that he hoped that: "Even if the AUSA [Assistant U.S. Attorney] was inclined to appeal when he came into court, the thought that the Court of Appeals will see this tape, would dissuade him."[294]

His empathy is not limited to criminal defendants. For one man who was in court to try to avoid eviction, there was nothing he could do because the eviction was legally proper. Weinstein says, "I clearly couldn't do anything for him—so I gave him twenty bucks."[295] Much of his judicial activism is, perhaps, less a reflection of any specific agenda, than the product of a deeply held conviction that judges must apply the law with compassion and respect for individuals involved in the cases before them.

Weinstein has a long history of philanthropy. In the Eastern District he created a foundation to provide medical services or examinations necessary for an attorney to properly represent a *pro se* prisoner or for those involved in Social Security disability cases. He also set up a contingency fund for anyone who needs help when they come into court (or into probation) for food, coffee, or a place to sleep that night.[296] He sends books, Supreme Court reports, and advance sheets regularly to the Suffolk County jail.[297] It comes, in part, he says from "just sitting across the table in sentencing. You just get a sense sometimes for the desperation of these people. They are real people."[298]

Weinstein writes about a thousand or more notes a year to acquaintances and to those who send him their scholarship. He sends those he cares about letters, speeches, articles, sermons, and reports, among other items.[299] His graciousness can be seen over and over in his letters. For example, he sent a letter to the *Harvard Law Review* praising the publication of a note by a student, which, Weinstein said, would have been enjoyed by the great figures on the law of evidence who had been on the Harvard Law faculty, whom he went on to name.[300] His evaluations of candidates for tenure are generous.[301] He tells his clerks, "if we ever can cite an article by a friend, we should. So, if my clerks have written anything, I'd put them in an opinion at one point or another . . . . It's a sign of affection."[302] Still, his intellect is so alive and his desire to educate so great that he can even find time to write a professor from the Puget Sound

---

[294] *Id.* at 1157.

[295] *Id.* at 896–97.

[296] Stephen Breyer, *Tribute to the Honorable Jack Weinstein*, 97 COLUM. L. REV. 1947, 1948 (1997); Weinstein Oral History, at 304. *See also* Weinstein Oral History, at 303ff.

[297] Weinstein Oral History, at 303, 1329.

[298] *Id.* at 307. On the use of the Devitt Award money, *see* Presentation of Devitt Award, Judicial Confence, Second Judicial Circuit of United States, 160 F.R.D. 287, 355–56 (available on Westlaw).

[299] Dean Joan Wexler's Remarks, Judge Weinstein's 40th Anniversary 6 (Apr. 6, 2007). The author can certainly personally attest to this!

[300] Jack B. Weinstein letter to Singer, via HARVANO LAW REVIEW at 4 (copy in possession of author).

[301] Jack B. Weinstein letter to Dean Jesse Choper, Feb. 23, 1986 (copy in possession of author).

[302] Weinstein Oral History, at 255, 1677.

Law School whom he did not know, but who made a sweeping statement about hearsay with which he disagreed.[303]

There are many tales of his thoughtfulness. During a cold, gale-driven storm that occurred while he was Chief Judge, Weinstein invited demonstrators protesting President Ronald Reagan's economic policies to spend the night in the lobby of the U.S. Courthouse, so long as they wouldn't demonstrate in the courthouse. He was quoted in the *New York Times* saying, "'I don't know who they are or what they stand for. I would have done it for anyone.'"[304]

In his now classic book, *Presidential Character*,[305] James David Barber compared four types of Presidents. The passive-positive President (such as Warren G. Harding) who searches for affection, seeks to be loved, and is easily manipulated. The passive-negative President (such as Dwight D. Eisenhower) who responds rather than initiates. The active-negative President (such as Woodrow Wilson or Richard Nixon) who seeks power as a means to self-realization, expending great energy on tasks but deriving little joy from them. The active-positive President (such as Franklin D. Roosevelt or John F. Kennedy) who is an optimist with high self-esteem, energy, and self-confidence. Actively shaping his environment rather than being passively molded by it, the active-positive President enjoys the vigorous exercise of presidential power. He seeks out, even creates, opportunities for action rather than waiting for the action to come to him. He is willing to risk defeats and is able to learn from them, but does not engage in all-or-nothing crusades. Full of vigor and with a real sense of humor, the active-positive President enjoys the exercise of power, dealing well with anxiety, frustration, and guilt. He likes to be the center of attention and cares about results.[306] Whether or not Barber's methodology can properly be adapted to judges, his description of the active-positive President appears to fit Jack B. Weinstein "to a T."

Weinstein's "Jewishness"

One further aspect of Weinstein's background is that he is Jewish. His paternal grandfather was strictly orthodox. His maternal grandfather was a skeptic. The judge's Americanized father did not think too much of organized religion nor did his mother. His family did not keep kosher.[307] Young Jack went to school on religious holidays and, as a child he had little Jewish training. Weinstein is not a "religious" Jew. He does not believe in God or the afterlife. His nod to kosher is not to eat pork.[308] Yet, his children

---

[303] Weinstein Oral History, at 467.

[304] NEW YORK TIMES, Oct. 26, 1982.

[305] JAMES DAVID BARBER, THE PRESIDENTIAL CHARACTER *in passim* (4th ed. 1992).

[306] BARBER, *supra* note 305, *in passim*, esp. at 267.

[307] Weinstein Oral History, at 1415L.

[308] *Id.* at 342. Weinstein relates that when he was practicing law and saying Kaddish for his father at a little schul on 42nd Street in Manhattan, that "[i]t was my duty fairly regularly to go out on the street and dragoon people who looked Jewish into participating with us as part of the minyan." Jack B. Weinstein,

were bar mitzvahed, and he celebrates Jewish holidays, donates to the synagogue, and identifies himself as a "member of the tribe." He relates that his father encountered a good deal of anti-Semitism. The judge himself encountered some at the Byrne Company, in the navy, and when looking for his first legal job. What Weinstein feels is an historical connection to the Jewish people, a sense of historical continuity going back almost to the beginning of civilization.[309]

This, however, is only the beginning of a description of Weinstein's ethnic identity which, like so many things with Weinstein, has been characterized by enormous involvements. Like many Jews, Weinstein has been heavily engaged in philanthropic activities. His contributions to non-Jewish charities are described in different places in this book. As for Jewish charities, besides monetary contributions, during his career Weinstein chaired the Federation of Jewish Philanthropies' Committee for Soviet Jewry,[310] served as a trustee of the board of the Federation of Jewish Philanthropies, and chaired their subcommittee on services to new Jewish-Americans, for whom he also gave talks and moderated programs. He has often given sermons at Temple Emanuel Great Neck, and has spoken at other synagogues on Long Island. Between 1978 and 1985, for example, he spoke at synagogues at least nine times.[311]

The important question, though, is the conscious and unconscious impact of Weinstein's Jewish identity and background on his judging. There is, of course, a great Jewish tradition of studying the law, viewing it as dynamic, made for man, and as a vehicle for the improvement of mankind on earth. In an article published more than thirty years ago, I suggested that the most prominent American Jewish judges had shared three things: a refusal to sanctify formulae and a distrust of shibboleth, a consensus on the principle that the law must meet the needs of contemporary society, and a belief that social justice can be promoted through the interpretation of the law. It appeared that on average Jewish judges seemed to have engaged in far more than the normal amount of extrajudicial activities. Among such activities were writings opening the judicial process for examination by the public; a sort of bearing witness from the inside. Many American Jewish judges have made important contributions to civil liberties and some of those judges were arguably in the prophetic tradition, fighting for justice and righteousness regardless of the risks of unpopularity.

I contended that elements of being Jewish had blended with a special brand of Americanism, one that might be anticipated from traditional outsiders who very much desired to belong, yielding an Americanism rooted in Thomas Jefferson, Thomas Paine, Henry David Thoreau, and Abraham Lincoln; one characterized by tolerance and egalitarianism. This led to the shaping of a jurisprudence based upon the compatibility of

---

Sixty Minutes in Great Neck, Adult Education Program of Great Neck 3 (Mar. 5, 1980) [hereinafter Weinstein, Great Neck]. *See also* Interview of Jack B. Weinstein by Jeffrey B. Morris, May 30, 1990.

[309] Interview of Jack B. Weinstein by Jeffrey B. Morris, November 19, 2010.

[310] Weinstein Oral History, at 1682–83.

[311] This is based on speeches in Weinstein's notebooks for those years. *See, e.g.,* Remarks at Installation of William D. Siegel, Temple Or-Elohim, Jericho, N.Y., June 17, 1983, Speech 18.

Old Testament beliefs and the philosophies of the Founding Fathers, yielding a jurisprudence which gave them and their brethren greater security, while expanding the parameters of freedom for all their fellow-citizens.[312]

In the three decades since I made the foregoing observations, many American Jews, like many members of other ethnic groups, have given somewhat less attention to assimilation and somewhat more to ethnic identity; significant growth has taken place in Conservative and Orthodox Judaism, and American Jews as a group have become proportionately less liberal than in the past. As a result, I have come to doubt the applicability of those generalizations made in 1976. *Nevertheless*, the characteristics of the American Jewish judge as described in that article seem to fit Weinstein snugly.

Going back to Weinstein's work on the New York Civil Practice Law and Rules, we see a conscious belief that law is dynamic and must be made to fit the needs of the present. Weinstein's refusal to sanctify formulae can be seen throughout his career both before he was on the bench and during his time on the bench most obviously in his attempts to work around many of the decisions of the Court of Appeals.

Weinstein, who attributes to his Jewish background his dislike of authority, made the connection between his Jewishness and his judging in a sermon:

> Jews, who have known oppression from the days of the Pharaohs to those of the commissars, above all others, should bear in mind that the poor, the oppressed, the widowed, the orphaned, those unable to fend for themselves, look to us for protection.[313]

Weinstein, as Jew and judge, has sought to help the oppressed achieve social justice through interpretation of the law.

Further, Weinstein, like Cardozo, Brandeis, Jerome Frank, David L. Bazelon, and others, has engaged in extensive extrajudicial activities, especially speeches and writings, using them to promote the different goals of his activities. Like the judges mentioned in this paragraph (save Brandeis), Weinstein has opened up the judicial process for examination by the public, based upon, quite possibly, the objectivity gained from feeling to at least some degree standing outside society.[314]

---

[312] *See* Morris, *The American Jewish Judge, supra* note 115.

[313] Letter from Jack B. Weinstein to Jeffrey B. Morris, Nov. 23, 2010, confirming the substance of his remarks at Temple Emanuel, Great Neck, Mar. 30, 1979 entitled Some Aspects of American Law and Jewish Life. *See also* Jack B. Weinstein, Remarks at the Dedication of the New Building of Temple Emanuel, Great Neck, N.Y. Sept. 27, 1967, p. 1 (copies in possession of author).

[314] "We stand outside of non-Jewish society in the light of all this [long Jewish] history and we can, therefore, look with a clearer and a more objective eye at the institutions around us." Weinstein, Great Neck, *supra* note 308, at 7. On Weinstein's Jewishness, *see also* Weinstein Oral History, 342, 377; Interview of Jack B. Weinstein by Jeffrey B. Morris, May 30, 1990; Glaberson Interview, *supra* note 24, at 47, 49.

Appointment to the Bench

Weinstein does not seem to have waged the lengthy campaign for the bench that the literature suggests is the norm.[315] His involvement in the attempt to revise the New York State Constitution brought him to the attention of Robert Kennedy, who had been acquainted with him since 1961 or 1962 through the State Democratic Committee. Weinstein was involved in Democratic Party politics at the state level through Jack English, the chairman of the Nassau County Democratic Party, especially in matters of voting and reapportionment. Later, he wrote a one-page legal memorandum for English stating that Robert Kennedy could run for the Senate in New York.[316]

When Kennedy was in the Senate, Weinstein began to draft legislation for him, even using his Washington office at night. At one point, Kennedy wanted Weinstein to be the Democratic candidate for State Attorney General, but that ran afoul of the need for ethnic and geographic ticket-balancing. The columnist, Jimmy Breslin, has written that Kennedy took this as a personal defeat.[317] Kennedy offered to nominate him as a district judge for the Southern District of New York,[318] but Weinstein was so heavily involved with the revision of the state constitution,[319] his writing, teaching, and revision of the Federal Rules of Evidence, that he turned him down and recommended his Columbia classmate, Marvin Frankel, who was appointed. Weinstein says that, at the time, municipal and state governments were much more important to him than the federal government because of their greater impact on the people.[320]

However, when some months later Kennedy offered to recommend his appointment to the bench of the Eastern District to the vacancy left by the retirement of Leo F. Rayfiel, Weinstein was of a different mind. Although he had asked Kennedy to hold off until the Constitutional Convention ended, he "quickly became fed up" with the convention (particularly because the delegates didn't want to do anything about the state justice system) and indicated he wanted the appointment to go ahead.[321] He was also moved by the idea of sitting in what was his father's old territory and aware that it was unlikely that he would get a third chance for the bench.[322] Accompanied to his confirmation hearing by Senators Kennedy and Javits,[323] Weinstein only had to answer a single question: "Did you have a pleasant trip to Washington?"[324]

---

[315] *See, e.g.,* WILLIAM DOMNARSKI, FEDERAL JUDGES REVEALED 83ff (2009).

[316] Jimmy Breslin, *A Kennedy Hand Needed in City,* NEWSDAY, July 19, 1999, at A6.

[317] *Id.* at A6.

[318] Weinstein was not acquainted with New York's other senator, Jacob K. Javits.

[319] Weinstein prepared all the working paper for Anthony Travia, who presided over the convention. Weinstein Oral History, at 1787.

[320] *Id.* at 10. *See also* COLUMBIA LAW SCHOOL NEWS, Oct. 4, 1966, at 1. *See also* Weinstein Oral History, 1784ff.

[321] *Id.* at 1788.

[322] Weinstein, First Rough Notes, *supra* note 6, at 52–53; Vescovi Interview, *supra* note 39, at 27.

[323] When Weinstein took senior status on the bench in 1993, he paid courtesy calls on New York's then senators, Daniel Patrick Moynihan and Alphonse D'Amato, as well as on Senator Edward Kennedy. Weinstein Oral History, 1791.

[324] Weinstein Oral History, at 1788.

WEINSTEIN'S QUALIFICATIONS FOR THE BENCH

Weinstein has said, "Everything in your background prepares you to be a judge."[325] Weinstein was particularly well qualified for the federal bench. In an interview during the FBI investigation preceding Weinstein's appointment, Louis H. Henkin[326] advised "that the applicant possesses all the attributes necessary for the duties of a federal judge."[327] All his colleagues essentially agreed, and there was strong support from Jack Greenberg and Marvin Frankel. The Chief Judge of the Eastern District, Joseph C. Zavatt, stated that "[T]here is no other person in the Eastern District of New York that he would rather see as a member of the Federal bench."[328] The most distinguished judge on the Eastern District at the time, John F. Dooling, spoke of Weinstein as "a top flight lawyer of excellent reputation and . . . his ability is well known."[329] In the end, the FBI reported that "Federal and local judges, bar association officials, fellow professors, civil rights and religious leaders, highly recommend applicant. They describe him as a prodigious worker with a judicial temperament, stable and well-adjusted. His character, reputation and loyalty were not questioned."[330]

Speaking at Weinstein's investiture, Stanley Fuld stated:

He has excelled as a practicing lawyer, a law school teacher, a public official, a draftsman par excellence of statute and constitution, a writer of innumerable articles as practical as they are scholarly and the author of the authoritative text on practice and procedure in our state.[331]

Almost everybody who serves as a federal district judge has political experience and, as we have seen, so did Weinstein—working for both parties in the legislature, as County Attorney, and as advisor to the Constitutional Convention. He also had considerable knowledge of New York State politics and politicians. He not only was admired by the senator from New York who was responsible for making the recommendation to the President for the judgeship but also was well acquainted with state party officials and well known to state bar groups. As a judge, he would be able to work well on

---

[325] Mahler Videotaped Interview, *supra* note 68 at 3. *Compare with* Harold Medina's statement: "The work of a federal judge is just what my whole career has fitted me to do." J. WOODFORD HOWARD, COURTS OF APPEALS IN THE FEDERAL JUDICIAL SYSTEM 96 (1981).

[326] Professor Louis Henkin of Columbia Law School.

[327] U.S. Department of Justice, Federal Bureau of Investigation, File 89-HO-7007, NY 77-12248, FOIPA No. 997432, at 42.

[328] *Id.* (citing interview of Joseph C. Zavatt, Sept. 28, 1966, at 42–43).

[329] *Id.* at 44f.

[330] *Id.* (citing Mr. Gates to W. V. Cleveland, Memorandum of Oct. 12, 1966 and Jack Bertrand Weinstein Department applicant U.S. District Judge Eastern District of New York).

[331] Transcript of Ceremonies Attending the Induction of Honorable Jack B. Weinstein as District Judge for the Eastern District of New York, May 5, 1967, 16 at 17.

matters of judicial administration with such dissimilar politicians as Mario Cuomo and Alphonse D'Amato.

Most of those political activities, though, required first-rate skills as an attorney. At the age of 45, Weinstein was unusually well qualified as a lawyer. Though he did not have extensive experience in private practice, over nearly two decades he had made his mark as a government lawyer and through doing *pro bono* work.

As a full professor at one of the nation's leading law schools, he had mastered a number of fields of law and thought deeply about them.[332] He would draw upon his Columbia connection often for law clerks, special masters, and trustees. He had become an important legal scholar, but a very practical one—especially in two fields essential to judging: evidence and civil procedure. Ironically, while he probably knew more about New York procedure than any attorney in the state, it would be the federal bench on which he would sit. Nevertheless, he knew federal practice well from his teaching.[333] He also had written on conflicts of law, pretrial discovery, searches and seizures, and reapportionment.

His experience as County Attorney had exposed him to a wide variety of law, and he had considerable experience drafting other laws including the motor vehicle laws, the State Credit Crime Act of 1966, and the Interstate and International Practice Act (which he co-edited).[334] As Nassau County Attorney, Weinstein had demonstrated administrative talent which, though not thought much about at the time, would prove invaluable when he handled the *Agent Orange* fund. In addition to all this, he had apprenticed under one of American's great creative judges, a perfectionist who also wrote well.

The two things that were primarily missing from Weinstein's background at the time of his appointment were: extensive litigation experience[335] and strong grounding in the traditional specialties of the federal courts: admiralty, copyright, patent, labor, and administrative law. The absence of litigation experience was mitigated by his knowledge of evidence and civil procedure. His knowledge of New York State law would turn out to be valuable in diversity and *habeas corpus* cases.[336] By the time he was appointed to the bench, he was playing an important role in drafting the new Federal Rules of Evidence. As for the traditional federal specialties, they were, at the time, giving way on the docket to much greater involvement with constitutional law and statutory interpretation. Further, Weinstein had enormous intellectual curiosity and the ability to learn very rapidly.[337] His rapid-fire mind augured well for his

---

[332] Weinstein Oral History, at 157.

[333] Weinstein Oral History, at 18.

[334] In Recognition of the Honorable Jack B. Weinstein, 12th Annual Edward J. Devitt Distinguished Service to Justice Award 2 (June 17, 1994).

[335] Weinstein did not argue in what were probably his two most important cases, *People v. Kelly*, 502 N.Y. 512 (1951) and *WMCA v. Lomenzo*, 377 U.S. 633 (1964). On the latter case, *see* LEE, *supra* note 197, at 60, 131.

[336] Weinstein Oral History, at 10.

[337] *Id.* at 18.

courtroom work, and he had the habit of command. He also had the habit of writing. This would be one judge without pen paralysis. It might be added that he knew much of his geographic jurisdiction well.

Timing is terribly important in judicial appointments. In Weinstein's case, he was the right age when the Democrats controlled the White House, and New York State had a powerful senator who respected him and must have seen him as a brilliant, hard-nosed liberal. Weinstein's scholarly achievements would also have appealed to Robert F. Kennedy. This was an era where there was, on the whole, no great pressure to appoint minorities and women on the bench and long before the era where ideological battles would make activist liberals or activist conservatives difficult to confirm. Further, Weinstein's connections to Seymour Halpern, the state senator for whom Weinstein had worked who was in Congress at the time, may well have impressed New York's Republican senator, Jacob Javits, who himself was a liberal.

The only items in the FBI investigation that might have given some senators pause were Weinstein's representation in 1959 of a graduate student who took the Fifth Amendment before the House Committee on Un-American Activities;[338] being included as one of two hundred fifty professors (including such eminent scholars as Harold Urey, C. Van Woodward, Foster Rhea Dulles, and Walter Gellhorn) urging abolition of that committee;[339] and acting as *amicus curiae* for the New York Civil Liberties Union when it opposed the City Board of Education's attempt to get the state supreme court to overrule an anti-informer decision.[340] However, his FBI report indicated that "during September 1966, several confidential informants who are familiar with certain phases of Communist Party activities in the New York City area advised that they had no knowledge of the applicant or his relatives."[341]

What Kind of Judge Would Weinstein Have Been Expected to Make?

Those who knew Weinstein in 1967 saw a strong personality who was likely to dominate his courtroom and pull few punches. Virtually everyone who has observed Weinstein throughout his career has referred to his confidence, decisiveness, independence, and courage. Weinstein could absorb tremendous amounts of material and retain it for extremely long periods of time. He had close to a photographic memory.[342] He had achieved renown as a scholar, but his energy allowed him involvements in practical professional work and public affairs. He was and is a man who derives great pleasure from what he does and could have been expected to enjoy his work. One would

---

[338] Weinstein Oral History, at 131.

[339] N.Y. TIMES, Mar. 20, 1961.

[340] *See* FBI Director to SACS, NY, Albany, Washington Field, Oct. 3, 1966, in Weinstein FBI file, *supra* note 48.

[341] Weinstein FBI file, *supra* note 48 at 68. *See also id.* at 65, 70A, 70B, 71.

[342] Interview of Morris Schneider, Deputy County Attorney under Weinstein and later, County Attorney, in Weinstein FBI file, Jack Bertrand Weinstein, File 77-47024, 9/30/66. Filed Office File 77-12248.

also have anticipated enormous intellectual curiosity. By 1967 he already had a fairly lengthy record of professional concern for the less fortunate including his work on *Brown v. Board of Education*, his efforts as a volunteer for Legal Aid and the New York Civil Liberties Union, his and activities as Nassau County Attorney.

In retrospect, it is clear that Weinstein came to the bench with some traits that anyone would look for in a fine judge: an outstanding legal mind, intellectual curiosity, energy, decisiveness, thoroughness, independence, and felicity of literary style. Beyond this, though, there were other traits which contributed to a most unusual career. Among them were innovativeness, both in doctrinal and procedural matters; a profound belief that the law must show its human face; extraordinary fecundity and variety in off-the-bench speeches and writings as well as the use he might make of those speeches and writings to "sell" his jurisprudential ideas; ability to be "good copy" for the press; executive energy.

Perhaps at the time no one would have predicted the "Weinstein opinions"—long, scholarly, utterly thorough—or his predeliction for creating legal theories for the use of attorneys appearing before him. Nor is it likely that they would have foreseen his unique style, the product of paradoxical traits: profound dignity coupled with puckish wit; unshaken self-confidence joined to considerable modesty, self-criticism, and praise for others; professions that he does not care who wins a case coupled with profound personal agony when unable to do something for a needy litigant; bristling independence and dislike of authority while holding a position on a lower ring of the judicial ladder; unusual care for craftsmanship coupled with a willingness (at times a pride in) to be reversed. Such traits have produced a judicial career that is *sui generis*.

As for Weinstein himself, his memory is that: "I was fully comfortable the minute I got on the bench."[343]

---

[343] Weinstein Oral History, at 18.

3

The Political and Legal Environment within which Jack Weinstein

Judged: Nation and District, 1967 to Date

NO JUDGE IS an island. A judge performs in a world marked by laws and limited by previous decisions. He reads and hears arguments of counsel. Lawyers, government officials, and the general public have expectations of him. The district within which he sits provides the mix of cases he has to decide as well as the environment within which his decisions will be received. Nor can a judge be unaware of the times in which he lives—the national political and socio-economic climate.

A judge's performance is the result of the interaction between his abilities, values, and personality with the tasks presented to him by the "outside" environment. That environment affects the mix of cases a district judge confronts, but also, to some degree, the substance of the decisions he makes. The principal national factors of that environment are (1) the substantive laws passed by Congress; (2) law enforcement policies of the Department of Justice and the local U.S. Attorney; (3) decisions of the Supreme Court and Circuit Court of Appeals; (4) the rules and procedures made by the Congress and the U.S. Judicial Conference; (5) the national political environment; and (6) the social and economic environment. But the work of the judge is also affected by the particular local district culture—the politics and socio-economic conditions that produce cases and influence outcomes.

In this chapter, we will look first at the major national developments which affected the courts during the period 1967 to date. We, then, will explore district political culture and how being in the Eastern District of New York may have impacted Jack Weinstein's judging.

THE ERA

When Jack B. Weinstein, a political liberal, became a judge, moderate liberalism was becoming the prevailing philosophy on the federal bench in most parts of the United States.[1] By the late 1960s, the federal courts had become a forum where groups came seeking to accelerate social or political change or to redress a variety of claimed wrongs. The Supreme Court under Earl Warren had made path-breaking decisions in the areas of racial civil rights and legislative apportionment and had applied the Bill of Rights to state action. The Warren Court had made it much easier to get into the federal courts by revamping doctrines impeding access and had revitalized the 1871 Civil Rights Act[2] so that it became a prime vehicle to test state actions affecting rights. The Supreme Court had also sanctioned the use of the writ of *habeas corpus* to review state criminal proceedings for constitutional violations. In addition, the Federal Rules of Civil Procedure were amended in 1966 to facilitate the bringing of class actions.

This momentum was generally sustained during much of the 1970s in the lower federal courts, even though the election of Richard Nixon began a rightward trend that has lasted over forty years. Yet, during the early years of the Nixon administration with Kennedy-Johnson appointees on the bench and the growth of a liberal public interest bar, there were liberal results in many important cases.[3] In addition, in the early years of the Burger Court, Supreme Court decisions derived from cases the Court had decided in the 1960s or by expansion of them by the lower federal courts, opened up new areas of civil rights litigation and extended the Equal Protection Clause to encompass gender, alienage, and illegitimacy. Lower federal court judges began to abandon the "hands-off doctrine," under which judges deferred to the "expertise" of the custodians of prisons, jails, and mental hospitals and, because of the failures of state governments to improve those institutions, began to take a more active role in their management.[4]

Thus, during Weinstein's first decade on the bench (1967–1976), he was judging in a jurisprudential environment which generally embraced greater access to the federal courts, receptivity to modification of traditional principles of federalism, generous readings of the Equal Protection Clause, and expansion of procedural due process. Many federal judges demonstrated a willingness to employ the equitable powers of the district court to oversee public institutions and government services and employment

---

[1] ROBERT & CARP A. C. K. ROWLAND, POLICYMAKING AND POLITICS IN THE FEDERAL COURTS 45 (1983).

[2] 42 U.S.C. §1983.

[3] There were important laws dealing with occupational safety and consumer protection. Among the rights creating statutes were the National Environmental Protection Act and the Education for All Handicapped Children Act. Access to the courts was facilitated by the Civil Rights Attorneys Fee Award Act of 1976. P.L.94-599, 90 Stat. 2641, 42 U.S.C. §1988 (1976).

[4] MARK EDWARD LENDER, "THIS HONORABLE COURT": THE UNITED STATES DISTRICT COURT FOR THE DISTRICT OF NEW JERSEY, 1789–2000, at 225 (2006).

practices.[5] In addition, class actions began to be used by the federal courts in mass tort cases.[6]

During Weinstein's second decade on the bench, the nation and its federal court system became more conservative in the 1980s, more often supporting both state and federal governments in criminal and First Amendment cases, limiting expansion of the Equal Protection Clause and the breadth of the right to privacy, and often siding with the states in clashes with the federal government. The power of the lower courts was reined in in a number of respects, most notably in desegregation cases.

This growing conservatism led to a judicial environment less friendly to Weinstein's judicial philosophy, especially in the criminal law, which was marked by passage of harsh federal criminal statutes. The Comprehensive Crime Control Act of 1984 overhauled the federal sentencing system and revised bail and forfeiture practices, addressing as well controlled substances, terrorism, and certain economic offenses.[7] In its wake came the Comprehensive Forfeiture Act of 1984[8] and the establishment of a new national sentencing commission. Judges of virtually every persuasion were strongly critical of the role the federal courts had to play in drug cases, arguing that such cases trivialized and distorted federal justice and, once the Federal Sentencing Guidelines were adopted, that the courts had been made parties to cruel injustice. The dominance of the Sentencing Guidelines lasted until they were made entirely discretionary in 2007.[9]

As national politics became increasingly bitter, tensions between the federal courts and Congress grew. During Weinstein's first decade on the bench, there had been tensions over low judicial salaries, over statutes increasing the workload of the federal courts without providing the manpower to deal with it, and over "interference" with the way the courts conducted their business.[10] Tensions between the courts and Congress were further exacerbated during Weinstein's third decade on the bench (1987–1997) by growing national polarization. Members of Congress made vitriolic attacks on federal judges. Congressional hearings were held to educate the citizenry about "judicial abuses." Legislation was introduced aimed at limiting the powers of the

---

[5] *See* Laurie Bennett Mapes, *A Period of Complexity 1950–1991, in* THE FIRST DUTY: A HISTORY OF THE U.S. DISTRICT COURT FOR OREGON 223, 225 (Carolyn M. Buan ed., 1993).

[6] ROBERTA SUE ALEXANDER, A PLACE OF RECOURSE: A HISTORY OF THE U.S. DISTRICT COURT FOR THE SOUTHERN DISTRICT OF OHIO, 1803–2003, at 189ff.

[7] P.L. 98–473.

[8] 98 Stat. 1837.

[9] *See Apprendi v. New Jersey*, 530 U.S. 466 (2000); *Blakely v. New Jersey*, 542 U.S. 296 (2004); *United States v. Booker* and *United States v. Fanfan*, 543 U.S. 220 (2005). In *Booker* and *Fanfan*, the Court held that the sentencing guidelines could not be mandatory. On December 10, 2007, the Supreme Court restored the broad sentencing discretion district judges once had. *See Gall v. United States*, 552 U.S. 38 (2007) and *Kimbrough v. United States*, 552 U.S. 85 (2007).

[10] STEVEN HARMON WILSON, THE RISE OF JUDICIAL MANAGEMENT IN THE U.S. DISTRICT COURT, SOUTHERN DISTRICT OF TEXAS, 1955–2000, at 233ff (2002).

courts and at undermining their independence. Proposals were made to strip them of jurisdiction. Wars were waged over the confirmation of lower court nominees.

Even more harsh legislation was passed in the 1990s dealing with crime and immigration. Several of these statutes, which would impact significantly on Weinstein's judging, need brief discussion here. The Anti-Terrorism and Effective Death Penalty Act of 1996 (AEDPA)[11] streamlined *habeas corpus* procedures, making it much more difficult for federal prisoners to overturn state convictions on federal constitutional grounds. A one-year deadline was set for the filing of *habeas* petitions, the number of successive petitions was limited, and the review of state prisoner petitions was prohibited if claims had been adjudicated on the merits in state courts.[12]

The Illegal Immigration Reform and Immigrant Responsibility Act of 1996 took a tough stance toward aliens. Class actions to challenge practices of the Immigration and Naturalization Service were prohibited as was judicial review of some of the discretionary decisions of the Attorney General. The definition of an aggravated felony for which an alien could be deported became much harsher.[13]

The Prison Litigation Reform Act of 1996[14] greatly changed almost every aspect of federal court procedures then being used in litigation over prison conditions, making it more difficult to file *in forma pauperis* petitions and to obtain payments for special masters.[15]

By the end of Weinstein's third decade on the bench (1997), a yawning gulf caused by profound differences over social issues divided the two major political parties. The federal courts had become an important political battleground (especially the process of appointing judges) for these differences, and a punching bag for politicians.

The trend continued through the administration of George W. Bush. One example was the 2003 PROTECT Act.[16] Intended to protect children from (particularly computer-generated) pornography, the law was enacted in thirty days without consideration of the views of the judiciary. In the statute, Congress indicated in no uncertain terms that the federal courts had been making too many downward departures in sentencing. Seeking to threaten individual judges, the Justice Department was authorized to monitor the rates at which individual judges imposed sentences falling below the guideline range. Requesting information on downward departures on a judge-by-judge basis was a veiled threat that federal judges whose record was out of the mainstream might face impeachment.[17]

---

[11] P.L. 104–132.

[12] 26 *Third Branch* No. 11 (November 1996).

[13] *Id.*

[14] *Id.*; P.L. 104-134.

[15] 29 *Third Branch* No. 69 June 1996); 29 *Third Branch* No. 11 (November 1996).

[16] Prosecutorial Remedies and Other Tools to End the Exploitation of Children Today Act of April 30, 2003, 108 P.L. 21, 117 Stat. 650. The Act provided protection for children by expanding to national coverage a rapid response system to find kidnapped children.

[17] William H. State of the Judiciary, 36 *Third Branch* No. 1 (January 2004); Adam M. Liptak, *New Bill on Abduction Alerts Would Curb Judges' Powers*, N.Y. TIMES, Apr. 18, 2003.

Yet, even during the period after 1990, Congress continued to pass laws which could be enforced in federal courts and created new statutory rights, although this happened far less frequently than before.[18]

THE WORK OF THE FEDERAL COURTS, 1967–2007

Between 1967 and 2007, the workload of the federal courts increased enormously. While Congress did attempt to assist the federal courts, it was usually after long delays and by increasing the number of judges, law clerks and staff. From August 1968 to August 2007, the number of federal judges doubled as new judgeships were created in 1968, 1970, 1978, 1984, and 1990. Congress also upgraded U.S. Commissioners to U.S. Magistrates and enlarged their responsibilities. Later, they were given the more digni- fied title of "magistrate judges" and their responsibilities increased.[19]

Although the path was circuitous, involving legislation passed in 1978 and 1984 and a major Supreme Court decision, the status of bankruptcy referees was elevated. Their title was changed to bankruptcy judges and their responsibilities increased. Bankruptcy judges remained adjuncts to the district courts with only somewhat greater powers than before. The power to appoint bankruptcy judges was moved from the district courts to the Court of Appeals.[20]

Congress also increased the number of support personnel in the courts, including law clerks, district executives, and central legal staff. In 1986, the minimum dollar amount necessary for the federal courts to hear a diversity action was raised from $10,000 to $50,000 (and in 1996 raised again to $75,000). During this period, Congress continued to chip away at the power of the judicial branch to run its own affairs with statutes such as the Judicial Conduct and Disability Act of 1980 and the Federal Civil Justice Reform Act of 1990, which encouraged methods for cutting costs and delays.

During this forty-year period, the mission of the federal courts began to be trans- formed from adjudication to negotiation. Case management and managerial judging laid greater stress on informal procedures and the use of bureaucratic support than

---

[18] Among the laws creating rights were the Americans with Disabilities Act of 1990, the Civil Rights Act of 1991, and the Family and Medical Leave Act of 1993. *See* 33 *The Third Branch* (December 2001). Ironically, although members of Congress had been quite critical of the way class actions were being handled in the federal courts, the Class Action Fairness Act of 2005 (CAFA) was adopted providing class action litigants (including defendants) broad access to federal courts, which were perceived as fairer than state courts. The law also attempted to protect the interest of individual class members and tried to curb the enor- mous legal fees often received by plaintiffs' attorneys. GT ALERT: New Federal Legislation: The Class Action Fairness Act of Feb. 18, 2005 (March 2005), http://www.gtlaw.com/pub/alerts/2005/0302.asp.

[19] Magistrate Act of 1969, 82 Stat. 1107, 28 U.S.C. 631–39 (1982), 28 U.S.C. §604, 18 U.S.C. §3060, 3401–02; Federal Magistrate Act of 1976, 90 Stat. 1729; Federal Magistrate Act of 1979, 93 Stat. 643; Judicial Improvements Act of Dec. 1, 1990, P.L. 101–650, 104 Stat. 5089. *See* WILSON, *supra* note 10, at 356.

[20] Bankruptcy Reform Act of 1978, 92 Stat. 2549; *Northern Pipeline Constr. Co. v. Marathon Pipe Line Co.*, 458 U.S. 50 (1982). Bankruptcy Amendments and Federal Judgeship Act of 1984, 98 Stat. 333.

preparing for a formal trial.[21] Speed and efficiency, informality, and routinization began to prevail over traditional adjudication.[22] That trend was fostered by a change in the Federal Rules of Civil Procedure in 1983 including settlement as one of the topics for discussion at the omnibus pretrial hearing.

Among the most profound changes affecting federal judges during the period between 1967 and 2007 was the result of technological developments. The federal court system was automated in the mid-1990s.[23] Judges, lawyers, and jurors trying cases can now have a transcript in front of them in mini-seconds as a result of Real Time court reporting and transcription.[24] Courtrooms now have an integrated CD-ROM, video, and audio capability, which allows lawyers to present their cases on videotape, audiotape, or through CD-ROM players attached to their personal computers. Judges no longer have to wade through ceiling-high documentary exhibits and lug them home in the evening.[25]

DISTRICT CULTURE

The caseload a district judge manages is in some measure a product of local factors. Although the caseloads of all district courts are affected by the Constitution, Supreme Court decisions, laws passed by Congress, and the limits on federal jurisdiction, the mix of cases in any one district is also influenced by the characteristics of that particular district. These characteristics include geography, demographics, socio-economic conditions, and the amount of governmental activity.[26] A district's mix of cases may be affected by local factors and these factors may have some effect on how decision-making takes place. In addition, local factors may have some impact of the outcomes of litigation as well as on the way decisions are received.[27]

The environmental characteristics of a jurisdiction affect the application of federal law and what type of cases end up in federal court.[28] The extensive coastline of Florida and its proximity to the Caribbean and the Gulf of Mexico, for example, has led to many cases involving smuggling and immigrants throughout the history of its three

---

[21] Mayer N. Zald, Foreword, WOLF HEYDEBRAND & CARROLL SERON, RATIONING JUSTICE at vii. *See also id.* at 136.

[22] WOLF HEYDEBRAND & CARRLL SERON, RATIONALIZING JUSTICE 3 (1990).

[23] 38 *Third Branch* No. 4 (April 2006).

[24] 37 *Third Branch* No. 12 (December 2005).

[25] 35 *Third Branch* No. 11 (November 2000). *See also* 34 *Third Branch* No. 8 (August 1999) and http://www. pacer.psc.uscourts.gov.

[26] In one study of five federal courts, tort cases ranged from 18 percent of the docket to 77 percent, business regulation cases from 10 percent to 39.5 percent of the docket, and public law cases from 15 percent to 52 percent. Joel B. Grossman, Herbert M. Kritzer et al., *Dimensions of Institutional Participation: Who Uses the Courts, and How?*, 44 J. POL. 86, 1010 (February 1982). *See also* CHARLES H. SHELDON, THE AMERICAN JUDICIAL PROCESS: MODELS AND APPROACHES at 18ff (1974).

[27] *See* SHELDON GOLDMAN & THOMAS P. JAHNIGE, THE FEDERAL COURTS AS A POLITICAL SYSTEM 1–7 (1971); HEYDEBRAND & SERON, *supra* note 22, at 10.

[28] HEYDEBRAND & SERON, *supra* note 22, at 32.

district courts.[29] In the Border Division of the Southern District of Texas, the typical caseload has been immigration violations, customs, and narcotics smuggling.[30] Because of its location in Washington, D.C., the U.S. District Court for the District of Columbia traditionally has been the major forum for politically salient lawsuits against the heads of federal executive departments.[31]

Demographic characteristics also matter. One study concluded with the finding that 60 percent of the variance in personal injury cases from district to district was explainable by demographic factors and industrialization.[32] The racial and ethnic makeup of a district, itself affected by the amount of immigration legal and illegal, can be another significant factor that impacts the court's docket.[33] To choose a simple example, the District of South Dakota hears relatively few cases, but among them are a much higher percentage of cases involving Native Americans than most other American jurisdictions and a far greater number than all four of New York's districts taken together.

Socio-economic factors affect the mix. Complex civil cases may result from the presence of large corporations.[34] The presence or absence of certain industries affects, for example, the number and type of patent, copyright, trademark, and securities cases.

The amount of government activity in a district affects the number and type of regulatory cases and white-collar prosecutions. Complex civil filings in the district court are often the result of corporate mergers or the interaction of corporations and government agencies.[35] The number of complex civil and criminal cases will probably vary with the size of the government presence.[36]

The mix of cases may also be affected by the degree of urbanization; the lawlessness or lawfulness of the inhabitants and the susceptibility of their local public officials to corruption; the density of the lawyer population, the demand for attorneys, and their caliber; the number and type of organizations in the district who can afford to litigate; and the reputation of the state court system.[37] In addition to the effects of geography, demographic factors, commerce and communications, and the size and activity of its governmental presence, the Eastern District of New York is greatly affected by the temptations to crime in the district and the vitality of its bar.

---

[29] Kermit Hall & Eric W. Rise, From Local Courts to National Tribunals: The Federal District Courts of Florida, 1821–1990, at 2; Edward A. Purcell, Jr., *Reconsidering the Frankfurtian Paradigm: Reflections on Histories of Lower Federal Courts*, 24 Law & Soc. Inquiry 679 (1999).

[30] Charles L. Zelden, Justice Lies in the District: The U.S. District Court, Southern District of Texas, at 1 (1993); Wilson, *supra* note 10, at 93ff.

[31] *See* Jeffrey Brandon Morris, Calmly to Poise the Scales of Justice: A History of the Courts of the District of Columbia Circuit, *in passim* (2001).

[32] Hydebrand & Seron, *supra* note 22, at 79.

[33] Barbara B. Yarnold, Politics and the Courts: Toward a General Theory of Public Law 1–20 (1982).

[34] Heydebrand & Seron, *supra* note 22, at 318, 69.

[35] *Id.* at 318, 69.

[36] *Id.* at 64, 66.

[37] *Id.* at 79.

Geography—The Eastern District of New York, surrounded by water, is made up of two islands. One island, Staten Island, a borough of New York City, contributes relatively little to the case mix of the Eastern District because of its small population and relative lack of commerce. However, Long Island, the largest island in the continental United States, some 118 miles long, stretches from "the great blue fish grounds of Fisher's Island and Montauk Point" to the Bay of New York.[38] While parts of Staten Island might be described as suburban, the two boroughs of New York City that are on Long Island, Queens, and Brooklyn, are densely populated. Directly east of Queens is Nassau County, a quintessential suburb. The easternmost part of the district, Suffolk County, is part suburban, part rural, and part luxurious vacation center. In the past forty years, both Nassau and Suffolk Counties have sustained vigorous growth.

The Eastern District embraces Coney Island, Fire Island, and Montauk Point. Much of the district is blessed with natural beauty: sparkling waters and glorious beaches, salt marshes and sand dunes, and the verdant tree-shaded hills of the North Shore of Long Island.[39] Once upon a time, the 350 miles of the Eastern District's coastline, the Long Island Sound, the bays, the East River, and the Atlantic Ocean yielded important admiralty and maritime litigation. While that is no longer true, these days the District's waters and coastline are the subject of environmental litigation. The number of cases and the significance of those cases are accentuated by the high quality of life enjoyed by residents of Nassau and Suffolk Counties. The sheer physical beauty and recreational attractiveness of the area has drawn many middle-class residents and owners of second homes many of whom have taken an active role in protecting the environment from potential threats. The proximity of Long Island's suburbs to important public interest law firms and lawyers, as well as to Wall Street law firms ready to undertake *pro bono* work, undoubtedly contributes to the frequency of environmental litigation in the District.

Demographics—New York City is a city of contrasts and complexity. There may be no more complex and rich a concentration of racial and ethnic diversity than is found in the Eastern District, especially in Queens and Brooklyn. This reflects, in part, the significance of New York as a port of entry for immigrants. The U.S. District Court for the Eastern District naturalizes more Americans than any other court. By 1990, over a million aliens had individually petitioned for and been admitted to U.S. citizenship by the Eastern District.[40] Judge Eugene Nickerson thought that:

> Perhaps because so many of our residents come to us from other lands, yearning to be free, the Eastern District is more often the forum where the

---

[38] Jack B. Weinstein, Opening Address before the United States Parole Commission Tri-District Seminar for Probation Officers, Brooklyn, N.Y. 1 (Jan. 26, 1983).

[39] BERNIE BOOKBINDER, LONG ISLAND PEOPLE AND PLACES PAST AND PRESENT 244 (1983); DIANE KETCHAM, LONG ISLAND SHORES OF PLENTY: AN ECONOMIC CELEBRATION 22 (1988).

[40] By 1990, over a million aliens had individually petitioned for and had been admitted to U.S. citizenship by the Eastern District court. Special Session Commemorating the 125th Anniversary of the United States District Court for the Eastern District of New York (Mar. 22, 1990).

individual, poor or immigrant though he may be, seeks to realize America's promise of liberty.[41]

Socio-Economic Factors—If the Eastern District were just a collection of attractive geographical and recreational features with a large immigrant population, it might have little more to interest us than the district courts for the Districts of Wyoming or Maine. It is primarily Brooklyn and Queens, two boroughs with more than half the population and area of New York City, the most dynamic city in the world, that have provided the Eastern District (and, therefore, Weinstein) with most of his significant cases. Brooklyn and Queens are part of a city that is the commercial and communications capital of the United States. The vitality of commerce in Nassau County, an important center of business with large office complexes, industrial parks, and medical offices, has also yielded significant litigation, as have the agricultural, fishing, and recreation industries (and fragile environment) of Suffolk County.

The Eastern District presents a great many temptations to engage in illegal activity. The District's two large airports have succeeded the port of New York as the nation's greatest port of entry for both persons and goods. Attempts to smuggle large quantities of drugs into the United States are very much a part of life here and are reflected on the docket of the federal court.[42] A *New Yorker* article termed the Eastern District a "cynosure for avant-garde American criminals."[43] The New York waterfront, the extraordinary amount of construction, the sanitation industry, the automobile body shops, the amount of goods delivered by truck, have made Brooklyn and Queens in particular important places of business for major organized crime families, whose leaders live in all five counties that constitute the District. As Eastern District Judge Raymond J. Dearie pointed out: "They live here; eat here; sleep here; die here."[44] More recently, New York's potent symbolic targets have made it a magnet for Islamic terrorists.

Governmental Activity—The Eastern District of New York is home to a large number of federal, state, and local government offices. Because no city in the United States undertakes to provide more services than New York City—police and fire protection, public school and higher education, transportation, and recreational activities, New York City has been the object of frequent and important litigation in the Eastern District. While the state court system has been greatly improved since Weinstein ran

---

[41] Eugene H. Nickerson, *United States District Court for the Eastern District of New York: Footnotes to Its History, in* UNITED STATES COURTS IN THE SECOND CIRCUIT 24 at 36 (Federal Bar Council 1992).

[42] Weinstein has written in an opinion: "The judges of the district—which once contained a great port and now contains a great international airport—have had wide experience with the importation of drugs in all its variations." *United States v. Shonubi*, 895 F. Supp. 460, 511 (Aug. 4, 1995), *vacated by*, 103 F.3d 1085 (2d Cir. 1997).

[43] NEW YORKER, Aug. 4, 1997, at 37, 38.

[44] Interview of Raymond J. Dearie by the author, June 1990.

for Chief Judge of the state in 1973[45] and pointed to such weaknesses of the state court system as delays of more than one year in trying accused criminals and a housing court where people were not adequately informed of their rights, much of what the New York State courts do is affected by a lack of resources. Actions brought by prisoners in New York constituted much of the docket of the Eastern District during Weinstein's tenure.

Quality of the Bar—Still another important factor impacting on the work of the Eastern District is the density of the lawyer population and caliber of the bar. The quality of the U.S. Attorney's Office is particularly significant. Since early in Weinstein's tenure, able U.S. Attorneys (many now judges of the Eastern District) transformed the caliber of their office with the appointment of excellent lawyers. In addition, since the 1970s the presence of a superior organized Crime Task Force ensured frequent, important criminal cases.[46] As the City of New York is the defendant in many civil cases, it is no small matter that the City has traditionally been defended by a strong, large, and professional law office. In addition, the density and homogeneity of the population have led to a plethora of organizations in the New York area that litigate, while the already large number of able lawyers from the five counties of the District are replenished by many Manhattan attorneys who cross the East River to handle litigation.[47]

In sum, Jack Weinstein was appointed to judge in a district that was densely populated and heterogeneous, bumptious and adversarial, extraordinarily dynamic, and accustomed to being at the forefront of intellectual, cultural, economic, and social change. This was and is the place where Jack Weinstein lived and worked, where he was rooted, and which he loved.

Impact of the District Legal Culture on Decision-Making

As each federal district is a separate, largely self-contained unit with relatively little administrative connection to other districts and relatively little direction and coordination from above, this lack of centralization and coordination helps maintain some of the individuality.[48] It is hard, though, to assess whether the "legal culture" of the Eastern District of New York has an impact on the court's decision-making. Does it affect how the court handles its work?[49] How might the "district culture" affect the way a judge makes decisions or affect the outcomes of those decisions?

---

[45] Weinstein now thinks more highly of the handling of criminal cases in the state courts than in the federal courts. *See* Weinstein Oral History, at 1643; In re: Habeas Corpus Cases, 03-Misc.-0066 (Dec. 11, 2003), at 5 (copy in possession of author).

[46] Letter from James H. Lehmann to Dear Fellow Yale Student, at 3 (1982) (in possession of author).

[47] In addition, in New York, as in many states, there is a tendency for attorneys when, they can, to file in federal rather than state court because of shorter delays, better resources, and the belief that the average judge is more able.

[48] RICHARD J. RICHARDSON & KENNETH N. VINES, THE POLITICS OF FEDERAL COURTS 93 (1970).

[49] HENRY R. GLICK, COURTS, POLITICS, AND JUSTICE 67 (1983).

We know too little about district culture and its effects. We do know that it is reinforced and perpetuated because experienced trial judges from the district are the primary socializing agents for new judges. We may assume that judges also learn local methods of operation from experienced members of the court staff. Local attitudes may also be conveyed by contact with state judges, local civic officials, and attorneys and through the local press.[50]

It seems likely that the impact of local ways of operating have a greater impact in isolated districts where a small number of judges are housed in the same courthouse. When asked a generation ago what distinguished the Eastern District from other district courts, the judges largely tended to contrast it with the U.S. District Court for the Southern District of New York. Judge Arthur D. Spatt stated, for example, that it was a little more of a "hometown court."[51] We do know that as late as the middle 1970s, there appears to have been a good deal of interaction among the judges of the Eastern District. At that time, a committee of the Association of the Bar of the City of New York commented on the "esprit de corps" of the judges.[52] Almost all the judges met each morning over coffee before commencing the day's business and discussed the day's business. This was one place where new judges were "socialized."[53] When Weinstein first came on the bench, before sentencing, a panel of three judges would discuss each sentence. In complex situations, all the judges participated. Weinstein mourns the loss of these sessions in the Eastern District, which came to an end due to the growth in the size of the court and as the result of the Federal Sentencing Guidelines.[54]

The Eastern District of New York today is one of the largest district courts in the nation with twenty-six regular and senior judges. Its judges have chambers in three locations. The author, after talking with about a dozen Eastern District judges in 1990 was unable to find any particularly unique decision-making practices, style, or folkways except in comparison with the much larger Southern District of New York.

Yet, it is important to remember that, while national factors—Supreme Court decisions, federal statutes, administrative regulations, and the nature of federal jurisdiction, along with the homogenizing effects of transportation and communications—press hard for uniformity of decisions by district judges, decisions are still affected by

---

[50] CARP & ROWLAND, *supra* note 1, at 88–89. STEPHEN J. EARLY, CONSTITUTIONAL COURTS OF THE U.S. 98 (1977). Even during their first generation, Kentucky's federal courts developed an identifiable style that was manifest in its proceedings and disposition of the caseload. *See* MARY K. BONSTEEL TACHAU, FEDERAL COURTS IN THE EARLY REPUBLIC: KENTUCKY 1789–1816 (1978).

[51] Interview by the author, May 1990. During a round of interviews with the judges of the Eastern District in 1990, the author was unable to find any particularly unique decision-making practices, style, or folkways except the contrast with the larger Southern District of New York.

[52] Committee on the Federal Courts, Civil Caseload Management in the U.S. District Court for the Eastern District of New York, 31 REC. ASS'N B. CITY N.Y. 663, 669 (1976).

[53] *Id.* at 669.

[54] Jack B. Weinstein, Judge Jacob Mishler: Coffee, Cake and Sympathy, Memorial [Ceremony] 2 (May 21, 2004) [hereinafter Weinstein, Mishler]. Since the Sentencing Guidelines have become advisory, Eastern District judges do consult with other judges on some sentences.

local factors—by local needs, local politics, the attitudes of local officials, and sometimes by the assumptions, attitudes, and practices which characterize a district's elite
bench and bar.[55] After all, federal court organization is based on state and regional
boundaries.[56] The system of appointment of district judges usually (dominated by sen-
atorial influence) emphasizes local experience and background. Inevitably, district
judges bring to the bench certain local values and orientations. Many studies have
documented the assertion that in close cases, a "judge's personal values, the tradition
and practice of their own district or circuit, or the values and attitudes of their particular region do enter into judicial decision-making practices"[57] and that federal district
judges can be influenced to a significant extent by the social and economic conditions,
values and structures of political power within their local district.[58]

The classic studies of the impact of localism on decisions involved the reactions of
Southern District judges to the civil rights decisions of the U.S. Supreme Court in the
1950s and 1960s and demonstrated that almost all of the federal district judges could
not divorce themselves from their Southern milieu.[59]

While it is better not to rely heavily on generalizations based on race cases in the
South of the 1950s and 1960s,[60] yet, more recently two political scientists who have

---

[55] Purcell, *supra* note 29, at 716–17. After reading the histories of district courts, most written in the last
two decades, Edward A. Purcell saw the "theme of localism," of judges and lawyers shaped by local and
regional values.

[56] RICHARDSON & VINES, *supra* note 48, at 61, 71; ROBERT A. CARP & RONALD STRIDHAM, THE FEDERAL
COURTS 231 (2nd ed. 1991).

[57] ROBERT A. CARP & C.K. ROWLAND, POLICYMAKING AND POLITICS IN THE FEDERAL DISTRICT COURTS vii
(1983).

[58] *See generally* ROBERT A. CARP & C.K. ROWLAND, POLITICS AND JUDGMENT IN FEDERAL DISTRICT
COURTS vii (1996). *See also* CARP & STRIDHAM, *supra* note 57; J. EISENSTEIN, POLITICS AND THE LEGAL
PROCESS 149–59 (1973). *See also* studies of petit juries in Kentucky in the decades after the framing
of the Constitution and of the way judges of the Southern District of Texas fostered the economic
growth of the Southeast Texas. MARY K. BONSTEEL TACHAU, FEDERAL COURTS IN THE EARLY REPUBLIC
1788–1816, at 148 (1978). Mary K. Bonsteel Tachau, 2290 Cases: The Kentucky Federal Courts 1789–1816,
paper delivered before Organization of American Historians, at 6 (1976); ZELDEN, *supra* note 30, at 53,
134. *See also* Beverly Blair Cook, *Sentencing the Unpatriotic: Federal Trial Judges in Wisconsin during Four
Wars, in* THE QUEST FOR SOCIAL JUSTICE: THE MORRIS FROMKIN MEMORIAL LECTURES 1970–1980 at 73,
122 (Ralph M. Aderman ed.) and Herbert M Kritzer, *Political Correlates of the Behavior of Federal District
Judges*, 40 J. POL. 25, 48 (1978).

[59] JACK W. PELTASON, FIFTY-EIGHT LONELY MEN (1961). Kenneth Vines, too, stressed that judicial policies
are formulated by judges with strong local connections, administered by a locally appointed court staff,
and service a clientele usually drawn from the district. RICHARDSON & VINES, *supra* note 48, at 46, 73, 98;
Kenneth N. Vines, *Federal District Judges and Race Relations in the South, in* AMERICAN COURT SYSTEMS
376, 381–82 (Sheldon Goldman & Austin Sarat eds., 1978). *See also* MITCHELL S. G. KLEIN, LAW, COURTS
AND POLICY 128 (1984).

[60] Writing about Southern judges in 1970, Michael W. Giles and Thomas G. Walker found no substantial
relationship either from a judge's social background characteristics, environmental factors, or community and school district. Giles & Walker, *Judicial Policy-Making and Southern School Segregation, in*
COURTS, LAW, AND JUDICIAL PROCESSES 469, 477ff (S. Sidney Ulmer ed., 1981).

made a number of studies of district courts and judges, continue to assert that district judges are "highly representative of their respective regional and local cultures."[61]

Thus, we can only say this much with confidence: When federal judges in a local setting are required to resolve controversial disputes between local majoritarian values and national constitutional values,[62] the judges, products in some measure of local influence, ties, outlook, and local political organizations, may be influenced to some extent by the social and economic conditions, values, and structures of political power within their districts.[63]

State political culture, too, must have some influence, not only because districts are contained within states—in half of the states the district and state boundaries are identical—but because federal judges are called upon to apply state law in diversity and Section 1983 cases and mix socially with state judges at bar meetings. Thus, there are pressures to synchronize judicial behavior so that it is uniform throughout the state.[64] In these ways, national values, filtered through local courts, may become modified or partially ignored.[65]

The largest numbers of decisions in the Eastern District of New York come from a densely packed urban area. Political scientists have demonstrated that urban districts are likely to produce more liberal judicial opinions because urban centers tend to be more liberal and that is where the judges are likely to have grown up and worked. In addition, the most prestigious bar association in the area of the Eastern District (the Association of the Bar of the City of New York[66]), once stuffy and conservative, was transformed during the period of Weinstein's judgeship to one that was liberal and inclusive.[67] If anything, most of the other bar associations are more liberal. Political officials in the area tend to be more liberal than such officials nationally. The regional Court of Appeals, the U.S. Court of Appeals for the Second Circuit,[68] has traditionally been one of the most liberal circuits. The large number of state and federal judges in New York, plus the high visibility of other political actors, guarantees judges in the area relative anonymity so that any single judge will be under less political pressure when rendering an unpopular decision.[69] That probably has had no influence on the staunchly independent Jack Weinstein.

[61] CARP & ROWLAND *supra* note 1, at 84ff; YARNOLD, *supra* note 33, at 17. In 1982 Wenner found that geographic location influenced both Congressmen and federal court judges in their consideration of environmental issues. *Id. But see* ROWLAND & CARP, *supra* note 1, at 9 and *see* Purcell, *supra* note 29, at 716.

[62] C. K. ROWLAND & ROBERT A. CARP, POLITICS AND JUDGMENT IN FEDERAL DISTRICT COURTS 58 (1996).

[63] SHELDON, *supra* note 26, at 180; EISENSTEIN, *supra* note 58, at 149; EARLY, *supra* note 53, at 89.

[64] CARP & ROWLAND, POLICYMAKING AND POLITICS IN THE FEDERAL DISTRICT COURTS 92–93 (1983).

[65] RICHARDSON & VINES, *supra* note 48, at 175. *See also id.* at 38–39.

[66] Recently renamed the "New York City Bar."

[67] Jeffrey B. Morris, *"Making Sure We Are True To Our Founders": The Association of the Bar of the City of New York, in passim* (1997).

[68] In this book, the U.S. Court of Appeals for the Second Circuit may, from time to time, be referred to as the "Second Circuit."

[69] CARP & ROWLAND, *supra* note 1, at 130, 127; ROWLAND & CARP, *supra* note 62, at 85.

With all this in their background, we can say that the judges of the Eastern District of New York have generally been more protective of civil rights and liberties than the judges in most American jurisdictions and more tolerant of dissent.

ADMINISTRATIVE DEVELOPMENTS IN THE EASTERN DISTRICT, 1967–2007

During Jack Weinstein's tenure, the Eastern District of New York has become much busier and much bigger. The jump in caseload can be dated from 1968. By 1975, filings had increased by two-thirds over 1968. By 1980, filings had climbed an additional 40 percent. Civil cases had tripled, many of them *pro se*. As elsewhere, the increase in caseload in the Eastern District was dealt with by creating Article III judgeships, magistrate judges, and more law clerks and other judicial personnel. When Weinstein arrived there were eight judgeships. All of the judges sat in Brooklyn. By 2007, there were twenty-four judges sitting in two widely separated courthouses. Along with more Article III judges, there were more magistrate judges, more bankruptcy judges, more law clerks, and more staff.[70] As in other districts, there was a move from traditional adjudication through adversarial proceedings to more informal administrative processing.

The first important change in the way of doing judicial business in the Eastern District after Weinstein arrived was the adoption in 1969 of the individual calendar system for assigning civil and criminal cases in place of the master calendar.[71] The individual calendar system approach increased judicial efficiency by fostering the judges' familiarity with assigned cases.[72] Weinstein found this very helpful for his judging.[73]

Criminal cases pressed hard in the 1970s. Weighted criminal filings went up threefold from 1966 to 1975. By 1975 the Eastern District was giving more time to criminal cases than any other district in the nation.[74] A series of "Speedy Trial" rules, affected the criminal docket: the first imposed by the Circuit Judicial Council (1971); the second by the District itself (Plan for Achieving Prompt Disposition of Criminal Cases) (1973); and the third by Congress, the Speedy Trial Act of 1974.[75] Around the same time, the U.S. Attorney's Office, no longer a home for patronage appointments, began to go after political corruption and white-collar and organized crime.

---

[70] Weinstein, Judge Jacob Mishler, *supra* note 54, at 1.

[71] Under the individual calendar system, all aspects of a case are assigned to a particular judge promptly after the case is filed.

[72] The individual calendar system went into effect on October 1, 1969. *See* Committee on the Federal Courts, *supra* note 52, at 663–64. *See United States v. Lockwood*, 382 F. Supp. 1111 (Sept. 30, 1974).

[73] *See* Chapter 5.

[74] Annual Report United States Courts for the Second Circuit Fiscal Year 1975, at 44 (December 1975); United States Courts Second Circuit Report 1977 at 4, 36–37 (1977).

[75] Committee on the Federal Courts, *supra* note 52, at 666.

During the years Weinstein was Chief Judge (1980–1988), the court issued local rules and standing orders emphasizing practicality and civility during pretrial proceedings. Some of those rules and standing orders eventually became part of the Federal Rules of Civil Procedure.[76] During Weinstein's tenure as Chief Judge, the court also instituted a program of using magistrates to oversee all discovery in civil cases.[77] In 1981 Weinstein announced an Eastern District program for legal assistance to the poor in civil cases, probably the first in the federal courts. A special panel of lawyers was set up to provide free legal counseling to all poor people filing civil suits.[78]

That year, with two vacancies in the Eastern District and Judge Jacob Mishler temporarily limited, Weinstein declared a "speedy trial emergency" during which civil cases could have been suspended to allow the court to comply with the Speedy Trial Act.[79]

For much of the period, lack of courthouse space has been another problem. The Eastern District was caught up in the controversy involving the judiciary and Congress over the costs of a mammoth $5 billion national courthouse construction program to house the judges and staff that had been added to the judiciary to keep up with the case flow. There were space emergencies declared in 1989, 1992, and 2001. As the former circuit executive for the Second Circuit, Steven Flanders, wrote in 1998:

> Judges and their courtroom deputy clerks . . . are regularly on the hunt for a courtroom for the next trial, the next long-scheduled sentencing, the next pretrial conference, the next hearing.[80]

A federal courthouse opened in Central Islip in the year 2000, but the new facilities in the greatly enlarged main courthouse of the district in Brooklyn was not ready for several more years.

CONCLUSIONS[81]

While it does not seem that Weinstein's judging was greatly affected by the growing national conservatism until the late 1980s, after that there can be no doubt that he was agonizing over by one of its manifestations, guideline sentencing. The agony would stimulate his creativity as he tried to create reversal-proof downward departures from

---

[76] Steven M. Gold & Peter G. Eikenberry, *Focus on Judge Weinstein*, FED. B. COUNCIL NEWS, December 2001, at 1, 3.

[77] JACK B. WEINSTEIN, INDIVIDUAL JUSTICE IN MASS TORT LITIGATION 130 (1995).

[78] NEW YORK DAILY NEWS, July 9, 1981; *NEWSDAY*, July 8, 1981.

[79] N.Y.L.J., Aug. 1, 1982, at 1.

[80] Steven Flanders, *Eastern District at a Crisis Point*, 5 FED. B. COUNCIL NEWS, December 1998, at 4.

[81] I acknowledge my indebtedness in writing this section to John Phillip Reid's brilliant book on a judge remarkably different from Weinstein: *An American Judge: Marmaduke Dent of West Virginia* (1968).

the Guidelines, a story recounted in Chapter 8. In Chapter 9, we will observe how Weinstein attempted to tame the effects of two more harsh statutes, the Anti-Terrorism and Effective Death Penalty Act of 1996 and the Illegal Immigration Reform and Immigrant Responsibility Act of the same year.

It cannot be said that the enormous increase in the caseload of the district court fazed him in any way, nor did Supreme Court decisions limiting access to the federal courts. He continued to welcome and take seriously prisoner petitions, Section 1983 lawsuits, Social Security disability, and other cases brought *pro se*. Although other federal judges complained about the number of mundane cases they had to decide, Weinstein did not join their number. Rather, he derived great stimulation from seeing and hearing the parties before him and from educating himself in the diverse problems they brought to the court. Even frivolous lawsuits and eccentric plaintiffs provided him with another learning experience or, at least, an amusing story. Every day Weinstein comes to his office, he seems to find another exciting challenge.

If the national political climate was more conservative than Weinstein would have preferred, other aspects of the environment in which he did his judging were favorable. He arrived on the federal bench when the era of important state lawmaking had passed and the "great" questions of public law were coming to the federal courts. He did his judging in a dynamic jurisdiction offering challenging and important cases involving the environment, immigration, the mob, and New York City government among others. Weinstein was fortunate to work in a large, sophisticated district with a distinguished bar; in a milieu where vigorous, powerful personalities armed with chutzpah fared well. In spite of reversals and criticism, Weinstein produced work that was, on the whole, not unwelcome to bench, bar, and legal academics, and he came to be widely admired.

4

Characteristics of Jack Weinstein's Judging

THIS OBSERVER FINDS ten major characteristics of the judging of Jack Weinstein. None of the ten is unique to judges. However, when taken together and executed with panache, they have made Weinstein's judging *sui generis*.

As seen here, the major characteristics of Weinstein's judicial career are: (1) an ability to sustain extraordinarily high productivity; (2) a reliance upon a rich smorgasbord of sources when deciding cases; (3) a mastery of the craft of opinion writing which reflects an insistence on thoroughness and an elegant and catchy style; (4) a view of his role as a lawmaker, who makes decisions on the basis of a wide variety of factors; (5) a deep concern for and awareness of the humanity of the parties who come before him; (6) a capacity to shape and sometimes to transform cases by putting ingenious procedural strategies into the minds of attorneys appearing before him; (7) a fierce judicial independence; (8) a vigorous participation in a striking range of extrajudicial activities; (9) an unusual innovativeness encompassing not only the use of new technology in the courtroom but also striking creativity in employing procedural rules and making substantive law; (10) a capacity to gain attention for his ideas, decisions, and activities. In the first part of this chapter, we will consider each of these characteristics, while in the second part, we will consider the appropriateness of the label "judicial activist," which has often been applied to Weinstein.

Weinstein's *productivity* as a judge is the result of a quick and absorptive mind, an ability to sustain extraordinarily hard work and the fact that Weinstein requires less sleep than most human beings. During his early years on the bench, he continued teaching two courses a semester at Columbia, completed his evidence treatise, revised and updated his casebooks and wrote twenty-eight law review articles. He also took an active role on the Advisory Committee of the Judicial Conference, which was creating the Federal Rules of Evidence, and gave numerous speeches. Yet, even as an inexperienced judge, he led all federal district judges in the number of cases terminated and in the number of trial days and hours.

After more than forty years on the bench and reaching eighty-nine years of age, Weinstein has barely slowed down. Attorneys find that he still works very hard, that he is demanding, and that they need to be very well prepared when before him.[1] Undoubtedly his productivity has been facilitated by the great enjoyment he has always taken from his job, which permits him to study a variety of problems and see the many kinds of people before him.[2] It also reflects a very happy life at home. Such productivity is also the result of rarely putting off decisions. While he admits to insecurity about some things and agonizing over sentences, Weinstein says, "When it comes to making a decision in court or in an opinion, I do it."[3]

Along with his deep knowledge of substantive law, procedure, and evidence, in many cases Weinstein digs into a *rich variety of other sources*. "The judge," he has said, "has to be sensitive to the world at large."[4] Weinstein came to the bench with a strong background in history, philosophy, science, and mathematics, which he supplements to understand particular cases.[5] Gifted with extraordinary intellectual curiosity, Weinstein is an omnivorous reader and quick study, who often has been able to overcome the difficulty federal trial judges' face in dealing with the wide range of problems that come before them.[6] In his most celebrated case, *Agent Orange*, for example, he displayed a remarkable grasp of the technical literature on chemical toxicity.[7]

Weinstein brings to his cases more than book knowledge. More than most judges, he relies on site visits. He says that he can "feel the situation better if he actually sees it, smells it and feels it," that he finds it "easier to understand what is at stake when I can see and hear the real people concerned in their own setting."[8] It has been argued that there may be large, indirect benefits from on-the-spot visits [to prisons] by judges, so that they may talk with staff and others and take the time to observe, in order to

---

[1] Jack B. Weinstein, 1 ALMANAC FED. JUDICIARY 101 at 104 (1997).

[2] "It's as if, I often tell my law clerks, the people before us are sent by central casting in the sky for our edification about the human spirit." Judson Hand, *Black Robes Are a Skimpy Buffer against the Outside World*, SUNDAY STAR-LEDGER OF NEWARK, May 9, 1999.

[3] *See also* Weinstein Oral History, at 230.

[4] Discussion on Class and Multiple-Party Actions, Atsuo Nugano & Jack B. Weinstein, New York, Feb. 25, 2010 [original version] (copy in possession of the author) [hereinafter Nugano-Weinstein Discussion].

[5] He has claimed in recent years that, while he had no difficult handling patent cases when he first came to the bench, science had gotten so complicated that he could no longer understand what was in *Scientific American*. Weinstein Oral History, at 1588.

[6] See the concern that has been expressed about the limits of judicial knowledge in structural-institutional litigation. *Compare* DONALD L. HOROWITZ, THE COURTS AND SOCIAL POLICY 30ff (1977) and GERALD N. ROSENBERG, THE HOLLOW HOPE: CAN COURTS BRING ABOUT SOCIAL CHANGE 20 (1991) *with* Weinstein, Oral History, at 345.

[7] *See* PETER SCHUCK, AGENT ORANGE ON TRIAL 117 (1987).

[8] WEINSTEIN, INDIVIDUAL JUSTICE IN MASS TORT LITIGATION 99 (1995).

better understand and to harness the organizational culture of the institutions they are trying to change.[9] Former law clerk Joan Wexler, speaking of the Coney Island school case, remembers, "He wanted to go see, so we went to Coney Island." We "took the subway. It was typical of the way he did things. We went and talked to people."[10] With law clerks and lawyers in tow, he crawled into all of the boilers at the Shoreham Nuclear Reactor.[11] While handling the case involving the treatment of the emotionally disabled in the New York City schools, Weinstein visited schools in every borough.[12] Weinstein visited the Suffolk County Developmentally Disabled Center, which he was overseeing, several times and spoke at its closing ceremony.[13] He has returned to the sites of some cases long after the cases were over.[14] Weinstein has also held hearings in jails, mental hospitals, and state courtrooms.

A third characteristic of Weinstein's judging is his mastery of the *craft of opinion writing*. The "Weinstein opinion" emerged during his early years on the bench. It is formidable—long (sometimes very long), utterly thorough, and graced with scintillating prose. It does not have footnotes; citations are placed in the text.[15] More than occasionally, the opinion is long enough to be preceded by a table of contents and sometimes it includes appendices, photographs, a glossary, or a chart.

While district judges are often too pressed to write many opinions, that is not true of Weinstein who uses the time others don't have to pursue his own judicial interests and make his views available to others.[16]

Weinstein learned how to carefully shape the facts in his opinions from Stanley Fuld:

I learned early, under Fuld [Weinstein also credits Whitman Knapp], how to write a statement of the facts and I work on it. I work at the statement of facts more than I work at the statement of law . . . Fuld's view . . . is that when you state the facts, which have to be absolutely accurate, it depends on how you put them, you

---

[9] John J. DiIulio, Jr., *Conclusion: What Judges Can Do to Improve Prisons and Jails, in* Courts, Corrections and The Constitution 287, 313 (John J. DiIulio ed., 1990).

[10] Joseph Goldstein, *New View of Brown v. Board Unlikely to Sway the Judge*, N.Y. Sun, July 9, 2007, at 4.

[11] Weinstein Oral History, at 932.

[12] *Id.* at 486ff.

[13] *Id.* at 513, 1028.

[14] *Id.* at 636ff. Weinstein has also tried cases and held hearings all over the Eastern District, including jails and even a state courtroom. *Id.* at 760, 933, 1283–84.

[15] Weinstein Oral History, at 12, 13, 68–70, 214. Weinstein's academic scholarship is heavily footnoted. Weinstein often uses a technique of issuing a preliminary memorandum quickly, so the case is decided and the appeal process can get started. Then, he polishes it up and issues a final opinion weeks later. This must be differentiated from his use of "tentative opinions" to keep the parties aware of his thinking, which is subject to refinement and change, but which also may keep his views immunized from review.

[16] Transcript of videotaped interview of Jack B. Weinstein by Gordon Mehler, Oct. 10, 2006 at 4 (on file with author) [hereinafter Mehler Videotaped Interview].

should be able to understand what the ruling is going to be without hearing what the law is. This is all accurate.[17]

During his first decade on the bench, Weinstein used opinions to figure things out, to master areas of law, to discuss a problem, help others learn. Sometimes he tried to lay down guidelines for himself and other judges.[18] For example, in *United States v. ex rel. Thurmond v. Mancusi*,[19] a *habeas* case, Weinstein was "trying to figure out what habeas was all about and I put it all in an opinion as a kind of a learning process . . .. While I was learning, as a teacher I was [writing] it down trying to help others."[20]

Characteristic of both Weinstein's opinions and his other writings, in fact, in all his work, is his thoroughness. To offer an example: an article co-authored with a law clerk on the use of interns in the federal courts ("parttime student clerkships") included a discussion of the legislative history of a federal statute which, in turn, encompassed treatment of an opinion of the Attorney General and case law; discussion of the Canons of Judicial Ethics; a proposed district rule; and forms for appointment and for designating clearance.[21] A recent posting on a blog indicates how well known Weinstein's thoroughness is: "A briefing order that reads like a law review article can only emanate from the chambers of EDNY Judge Jack B. Weinstein."[22]

During his first decade on the bench, the thoroughness of his work was particularly evident in the field of evidence, an area where he had a full understanding of the philosophy underlying the field and where he drew quite openly from his experiences with the Advisory Committee on the Rules of Evidence.

In *United States v. Smith*, for example, Weinstein refused to raise the physician-patient privilege to the level of a constitutional right. With the privilege "in a state of development," he thought it unwise to "freeze it into a constitutional form not amendable by rule, statute, or further case law development." Rather, "[c]ourts and legislatures must be given reasonable freedom to develop new approaches to questions of

---

[17] Weinstein Oral History, at 1176. *But see id.* at 171: "Fuld was a master of stating the facts in the findings . . . so that you were led to the proper result." However, *see id.* at 751 for Weinstein's admission of twisting facts to keep a boy out of prison. *See also id.* at 191 and 102.

[18] Sometimes he even wrote opinions for discussion in his evidence class. *See* Weinstein Oral History, at 87, discussing *United States v. Barbati*, 284 F. Supp. 489 (Apr. 26, 1968). Weinstein Oral History, at 311. *See In re Grand Jury Subpoena of Alfonso Persico*, 522 F.2d 41 (June 19, 1975: *JBW-Smith-Timbers*); Weinstein Oral History, at 311.

[19] 275 F. Supp. 508 (Sept. 14, 1967).

[20] Weinstein Oral History, at 7. *See also id.* at 68, 92, 1234.

[21] Jack B. Weinstein & Wm. B. Bonvillian, *A Part-time Clerkship Program in Federal Courts for Law Students*, 68 F.R.D. 265 (available at Westlaw). *See also* Jack B. Weinstein, *Proper and Improper Interactions Between Bench and Law School: Law Student Practice, Law Student Clerkships and Rules for Admission to the Federal Bar*, 50 ST. JOHNS L. REV. 441 (1976) [hereinafter, Weinstein, Proper and Improper Interactions].

[22] Http://www.nyfederalcriminalpractice.com/2008/02/edny-judge-sets-stage-for-nota.html (Feb. 8, 2008). The case involved the interaction between restitution orders, forfeiture orders, and payments victims receive from other sources.

testimonial privilege."[23] Procedural opinions were another area in which Weinstein's thoroughness and command was particularly evident.[24]

Weinstein's opinions are marked by both elegant and catchy *prose*. Writing, for example, in a prosecution for tax evasion case involving possibly tainted evidence, he said: "In the case before us a more appropriate simile than the 'fruit of the poisonous tree' . . . is, perhaps, that of a tree nourished by both pure and polluted waters."[25] Another example comes from an area some might consider to be the law's driest, jurisdiction:

> A corporation such as plaintiff which does business in more than one state may be compared to a man with his trunk and head in one state and his limbs and fingers spread over many others. If one finger is bruised, the whole body— including each of the fingers—is weakened. Most would agree, however, that injury is localized in one finger. Similarly, a corporation, when beset by unfair competition in one or more states, is weakened wherever it does business, but businessmen would generally agree that their injury was the "loss of business where the customers" are located.[26]

Over the years, Weinstein has published opinions he believed were useful precedents, those involving new issues, those he spent a lot of time on and those helpful for teaching. Some opinions were written because they presented the perfect case to address the problem.[27] Some were written "only because I was amused by it."[28] But, some have been attempts to create at the district court level what were essentially appellate dissents aimed at the future.[29]

Professor J. Woodford Howard of Johns Hopkins University aptly stated that judging is "perhaps the most role-conscious of professions."[30] *Judicial role* has captured the attention of political scientists.

A *role orientation* is a judge's beliefs about the proper kind of behavior a judge should exhibit. Those beliefs are in some measure influenced by the set of normative

---

[23] 425 F. Supp. 1038, 1054–55 (Nov. 24, 1976). *See also United States v. Mackey*, 405 F. Supp. 854 (Nov. 14, 1975). *See also United States v. Barbati*, 284 F. Supp. 409, 412 (Apr. 26, 1968) and *United States v. Iconetti*, 406 F. Supp. 554, 559 (Jan. 8, 1976).

[24] *See, e.g., Stromillo v. Merrill Lynch, Pierce, Fenner & Smyth*, 54 F.R.D. 396 (Dec. 29, 1971). *See also, e.g., Lemberger v. Westinghouse Elec. Corp.*, 1976 U.S. Dist. LEXIS 12506 (November 1976 [sic]).

[25] *United States v. Schipiani*, 289 F. Supp. 43 (July 26, 1968).

[26] *Spectacular Promotions, Inc. v. Radio Station WING*, 272 F. Supp. 734, 737 (Sept. 1, 1967).

[27] Weinstein Oral History, at 1241.

[28] Weinstein Oral History, at 152; *United States v. Brown*, 70-CR-445, 1970 NB 346 (Dec. 1, 1970).

[29] Mehler Videotaped Interview, *supra* note 17, at 14. In addition to publication in West's published reports, Weinstein puts some opinions on LEXIS or Westlaw, but much of his work never sees the light of day. An enormous number of decisions are made orally and are available only online or through the hearing transcript, although some written opinions are converted from oral statements at hearings. Weinstein Oral History, at 1582–83.

[30] J. Woodford Howard, Jr., *Commentary*, 70 N.Y.U. LAW REV. 533, 545 (1995).

expectations others have regarding the proper behavior of those who sit on the bench. The most obvious example is the expectation that when one leaves legal practice and becomes a judge, the judge is expected to abandon being an advocate and instead be a neutral arbiter. The judge's role orientation specifies the criteria upon which his or her decisions are made, the variables that can legitimately be allowed to influence decision-making and the priorities among them.[31]

Role must be distinguished from function. As part of their job, all federal district judges perform functions such as deciding cases, managing caseloads, and writing opinions.[32] Parts of their functions are the application and interpretation of laws, the enforcement of norms, the resolution of disputes and the legitimation of governmental acts.[33]

Judges are expected to be independent, resolve conflicts neutrally, and act objectively and ethically as well as to decide cases swiftly and efficiently, control their courtroom, and act in a dignified manner both within and outside of court.[34]

The characteristics of a trial court affect a federal district judge's view of his role. Generally, trial judges are more concerned than their appellate brethren with fact-finding, following precedent, clearing the docket, ascertaining truth, and seeking justice in *immediate* cases. They anticipate that changes in case law will [largely] come from above.[35]

However, judges and most observers differ on the purposes of the courts and the manner in which the decision-making function is carried out. Scholars have found that most federal judges are "law interpreters," who believe in a modest role for the courts, accepting the norms of judicial restraint and emphasizing respect for precedent. They do not believe that judges should substitute their wisdom for the actions of the elected branches and that they should eschew making innovative decisions.[36]

Far fewer district judges view their role as "law makers."[37] Such judges contend that they can and must make law some of the time because appellate court precedents are often ambiguous or do not cover all situations. When they interpret statutes, judges

[31] James L. Gibson, *Judges' Role Orientations, Attitudes and Decisions, in* COURTS, LAW AND JUDICIAL PROCESSES 150, 152 (S. Sidney Ulmer ed. 1981). *See also* G. ALAN TARR, JUDICIAL PROCESS AND JUDICIAL POLICYMAKING 265–67 (4th ed. 2006). *See also* CHRISTOPHER E. SMITH, COURTS, POLITICS AND THE JUDICIAL PROCESS 202 (1997); LAWRENCE BAUM, THE PUZZLE OF JUDICIAL BEHAVIOR 845 (1997).

[32] LAWRENCE BAUM, AMERICAN COURTS, PROCESS AND POLICY (1986); FRANK M. COFFIN, THE WAYS OF A JUDGE 198 (1980).

[33] WOLF HYDEBRAND & CARROLL SERON, RATIONALIZING JUSTICE: THE POLITICAL ECONOMY OF FEDERAL DISTRICT COURTS 20 (1990). *See also* WILLIAM I. KITCHIN, FEDERAL DISTRICT JUDGES: AN ANALYSIS OF ROLE PERCEPTIONS 46 (1978); J. WOODFORD HOWARD, COURTS OF APPEALS IN THE FEDERAL JUDICIAL SYSTEM 13 (1981); BAUM, AMERICAN COURTS, *supra* note 32, at 134–37.

[34] TARR, *supra* note 31, at 265–67. *See also* GLICK, SUPREME COURTS IN STATE POLITICS 55–68 (1971).

[35] CHRISTIAN G. FRITZ, FEDERAL JUSTICE IN CALIFORNIA: THE COURT OF OGDEN HOFFMAN 1851–1891, at xii (1981); CHARLES H. SHELDON, THE AMERICAN JUDICIAL PROCESS: MODELS AND APPROACHES 85–86 (1974).

[36] ROBERT A. CARP & RONALD STRIDHAM, THE FEDERAL COURTS 164 (2d ed. 1991). *See also* DAVID W. NEUBAUER, JUDICIAL PROCESS: LAW, COURTS AND POLITICS IN THE UNITED STATES 360 (1991).

[37] SHELDON, *supra* note 35, at 89; GLICK, *supra* note 34, at 50.

find that the language of the statutes is often ambiguous and that legislative intent is frequently impossible to discern.[38]

District judges also disagree as to how they should go about their decision-making. There are the "mechanists" who view decision-making as merely the process of applying correct, readily apparent answers to legal questions; "formalists," who believe that judges ought to arrive at their decisions through well-established procedures; and "realists," who admit to making decisions on the basis of a wide variety of factors beyond the limits of legal training and procedures.[39]

Jack Weinstein has given serious consideration to his role as a federal district judge. His views differ from the norm and are far more complex than those discussed above; the result, perhaps of reliance by scholars on short interviews or questionnaires and because Weinstein has written much from which his views can be gleaned.

Although taken out of context, a few quotations may suggest his candor and how different his views are from the views of most other judges:

> My problem may well be that I still haven't decided whether I'm a professor a judge . . . [40]
>
> [To a litigant] "I can't do anything more for you. I'm gonna act as a judge from now on.[41]
>
> If the vacuum is there, it seems to me there ought to be a role for the judge.[42]

There is no question that Weinstein sees case-processing as an important part of his role. He takes it seriously and has always been remarkably productive. But, beyond this, Weinstein is an unabashed[43] lawmaker. For example, he has said recently:

> The concept that "judges don't make law" is a myth. It is equivalent to the concept of the emperor who walks the streets naked, but is told by his subjects that

---

[38] Marc Galanter et al., *The Crusading Judge: Judicial Activism in Trial Courts*, 52 S. CAL. L. REV. 699, 711ff (1978–1979); Glick, *supra* note 34, at 50. Some scholars have found that there are some judges who simply see themselves as "case processors" whose goal is efficient management of their dockets. Their major concern is task performance. This observer does not view this as a separate role since there are many law interpreters and lawmakers who consider this an important role applying to them. *See* Kitchen, *supra* note 33, at 39ff, 98–99; SHELDON, *supra* note 35, at 90; Glick, *supra* note 34, at 31; Carp & Stridham, *supra* note 36, at 164. Other purposive roles have been posited. We mention here only one other—that of "conflict resolver" whose major goal is to resolve conflicts fairly (or dispense justice).

[39] These decisional roles came out of studies of state courts at various levels. SHELDON, *supra* note 35, at 91–92; GLICK, *supra* note 34, at 72.

[40] Jack B. Weinstein Oral History, at 519.

[41] *Id.* at 605, quoting Peter Schuck.

[42] *Id.* at 394.

[43] Weinstein Oral History, at 312. *See* Weinstein's unsuccessful effort to dismiss a case on *Brady* grounds because the police had not told the prosecutor about an important piece of information. He was reversed. Weinstein Oral History, at 458. *See also* Weinstein Oral History, at 52ff. *See also id.* at 101ff, 207. Whatever ground he has broken is limited by a lack of authority over any other judge or court. *See* Conclusions, *infra.*

he is adorned with wonderful clothing . . . law is made and remade in our courts—good, bad, and neutral—necessarily.[44]

Weinstein has always been interested in "moving the law" and has often broken new ground in substantive law. Weinstein "finds many more gaps in the law—precedents not on all fours and ambiguous statutes—than other judges. He also believes that there constantly are new issues that have not yet been decided."[45] There can be little doubt that Weinstein's "law making" while professor—the Civil Practice Law and Rules (CPLR) and treatises in particular—as well as his experience with the creation of the Federal Rules of Evidence has made him more sensitive to the gaps in the law judges must fill.

Weinstein has far less compunction about departing from precedent than almost any other respected federal district judge. One such example from early in his career is *Matter of Holliday's Tax Services*. There, Weinstein held that the one shareholder of a small closely-held corporation could appear without an attorney in a bankruptcy proceeding. Faced with a virtually unbroken line of state and federal cases employing the rule that a corporation can only appear by an attorney, Weinstein modified the absolute rule in bankruptcy cases based upon "the inherent power of a Court to supervise the proper administration of justice." "A person's day in court is," Weinstein said, "more important than the convenience of the judges."[46]

Furthermore, where decision-making is concerned, Weinstein is an open "realist," who admits to making decisions on the basis of a wide variety of factors. Weinstein believes that judges should "draw upon their life experience, trust their judgment about right and wrong and strive to reach just results, even if the results do not readily flow from the most obvious and literal reading of applicable case law."[47]

What hangs over Weinstein's view of his role as a judge is his close identification with what he calls the "postwar role of the federal courts . . . to protect the injured who come before them against those who have caused or are causing unjustifiable harm." This is what he believes the United States as a nation will be remembered for. It is "my view," he has said "that it is the United States system of justice, equality and due process that will be remembered as the country's greatest contribution to the improvement of humanity."[48] He has said that "to aid the weak and suffering delineates the

---

[44] Jack B. Weinstein, Making Law in Mass Torts and Other Things, Speech to Law Clerks and Student Interns, Eastern District of New York, July 16, 2009, at 2–3.

[45] Transcript of Interview of Jack B. Weinstein by William Glaberson 4 (July 7, 1997) [hereinafter Glaberson Interview].

[46] *In the Matter of Holliday's Tax Serv. Inc.* 417 F. Supp. 182, 183, 184 (June 24, 1976). *See also* N.Y.L.J., June 28, 1976.

[47] Steven M. Gold & Peter G. Eikenberry, *Focus on Judge Weinstein*, FED. B. COUNCIL NEWS, December 2001, at 1, 3–4.

[48] *See* Jack B. Weinstein, *Proselytizers for our Rule of Law*, 28 BROOK. J. INT'L.L. 675, 677 (2003), Memorandum based upon speech at New York City Bar, Meeting of Association for Study of the United States System and the Global Legal Order (SUNSGLO), Nov. 14, 2002). Another time, he remarked, "Like the Greeks

primary duty of American law."[49] For Weinstein, the law must be protective of those who otherwise would be without power to protect themselves. He has also said, "Wherever I see a chance to improve the administration of justice or to correct an injustice I will utilize whatever powers I have."[50] He has admitted: "That's in my background. I can't escape it. What it leads to always in every one of these cases is the question: what can I do for the individual—the person who is suffering, or may not be suffering, but thinks she is suffering."[51]

Courts, he says, exist to help people. People should have access to them. Judges have responsibility for people and the law should be protective of those who otherwise would be without the power to protect themselves. Certainly, there are other federal judges who believe this. But, it has rarely been laid out more eloquently, maintained so consistently, and perhaps none have translated it into decisions with such craft.

In addition to his concern that courts should be protective of those who are without the power to protect themselves, there is a corollary, which might be labeled an unusually *deep sense of humanity*, pervading Weinstein's judging. It has shown up repeatedly, especially in sentencing, Social Security disability and immigration cases. Warning that "the psychological and emotional distance between the judge and those who are in court must not be allowed too become too great,"[52] Weinstein insists that the law must have a human face. One of his complaints about the Court of Appeals is that they miss the humanity that comes with trial judging. Weinstein sees the courtroom as a place where the individual participates in government and the administration of justice on an intimate level. He not only asks how courts can help people, but also how can *he* dignify the individual litigant. He has stressed that the defendant about to be

---

with philosophy and sculpture, the Romans with governmental organization and engineering, and the Hebrews with monotheism, we can with effort and foresight, make equal justice for all one of our lasting contributions to civilization." Jack B. Weinstein "Adverse Effect on Budget Cuts on Justice in the Federal Courts." American Bar Association, Panel on Gramm-Rudman-Hollings: The Impact of Federal Budget Cutting on the Practice of Law and the Justice System, New York City, Aug. 10, 1986, p.2 (in possession of author); *see also* Jack B. Weinstein, Speech before Alumni Association of St. John's University School of Law, April 27, 1984, at 9 (in possession of author).

[49] James Vescovi, Distinguished Columbian: Jack Weinstein '48 (copy of draft to appear in *Columbia Law School Report Alumni Magazine* Aug. 14, 1997) [copy in possession of author].

[50] Question and Answer Session, Practicing Law Institute, Prisoners' Rights Seminar, Barbizon Hotel, New York City, Oct. 16, 1972. (copy in possession of author)

[51] *Judge Jack B. Weinstein, Tort Litigation and the Public Good: A Roundtable Discussion to Honor One of America's Great Trial Judges on the Occasion of his 80th Birthday*, 12 J.L. & POL'Y 149, 172 (2003) [hereinafter *80th Birthday Roundtable*].

[52] *See* Symposium, Judge Jack B. Weinstein, *The Role of Judges in a Government Of, By and For the People: Notes for the Fifty-Eighth Cardozo Lecture*, 30 CARDOZO L. REV. 1, 226 (2008).

sentenced is a *human being*. The disabled in SSDI cases are entitled to clear explanations if they are turned down by the agency. In mass tort actions, he asks:

> What can the court system do to avoid the rigidity of matrixes that treat people, not as if they were individual human beings, but as if they were just marked as numbers (as were so many holocaust victims?) That's the problem for me.[53]
>
> How should we address a mass societal problem . . . and give each individual who is hurt a sense that, yes, somebody has heard *me*, somebody has listened to *me*, somebody has tried to compensate me, somebody cares about me.[54]

Often what people most need, he has said, "is a hearing, a forum, a sense that we understand their fears, heeds and aspirations." Even after Weinstein closed all the DES cases, he held a hearing for the DES daughters—to listen and to explain the role the legal system performed in those cases.[55]

The impact of judges on the development of the litigation strategy of attorneys during pretrial proceedings has generally not been discussed in the literature. One of the most remarkable characteristics of Weinstein's judging is his ability to *shape, develop, and sometimes transform cases* before him. Weinstein is a master at doing this not only through invitations in his opinions, but also through hints made to lawyers or, sometimes, even by helping lawyers make their case. He plants ingenious procedural strategies or complex legal theories into the minds of attorneys appearing before him, who, when smart enough to follow, are able to allow Weinstein to move the case his way. A plaintiff's lawyer commented in the gun class action.[56] "I have to say, I'd never seen Judge Weinstein so happy and beatific as the day he got the market share evidence. 'Not happy for the plaintiff—just happy that he was watching the case unfold, maybe in the way he envisioned it years before.'"[57] That this trait was evident very early in Weinstein's tenure can be seen in Chapter 5, in the discussion of the *Kahane* and the *Salzmann* cases.[58] Lawyers in Weinstein's court have come to anticipate that he will take the initiative in shaping the suit because he will have considered matters two steps in front of everybody else. Further, he may appreciate the interrelationship of apparently disparate matters that others have missed, and he is likely to explore innovative substantive norms or will mold things to turn out his way.[59]

---

[53] *80th Birthday Roundtable*, *supra* note 51, at 172.

[54] WEINSTEIN, INDIVIDUAL JUSTICE IN MASS TORT LITIGATION, *supra* note 8, at 167.

[55] *See In re: DES Litigation*, Hearing, July 14, 2009 (transcript in possession of author).

[56] *See* Chapter 11.

[57] Robert Kolker, *High Caliber Justice*, NEW YORK, Apr. 5, 1999, at 33, 36–37.

[58] *See, e.g., United States v. Lockwood*, 382 F. Supp. 1111 (Sept. 30, 1974), 336 F. Supp. 734 (1974); *Kahane v. United States*, 75-C-624, JBW Op. NB 798-827 (Aug. 14, 1975). *See also*, Weinstein Oral History, at 49.

[59] Martha Minow, *Judge for the Situation: Judge Jack Weinstein: Creator of Temporary Administrative Agencies*, 97 COLUM. L. REV. 2010, 2018 (1997).

It has not been uncommon for Weinstein, for example, to suggest a motion to an attorney, who would never have thought of it and then, should the motion be made, Weinstein, of course, grants it. As his colleague, Edward Korman, has said of Weinstein's work:

> Well, you come up with these crazy ideas that you dreamed up yourself. Then . . . you would suggest to the attorney that he make a motion when they didn't even want to make a motion and then you would do these things.[60]

Sometimes, however, getting through to the attorneys is not easy. In the complex litigation involving the liability of manufacturers of light cigarettes, Weinstein says plaintiffs' counsel were:

> . . . taking the position that every single smoker was defrauded. Well, it's absurd . . . I'm telling them they are not going to a jury unless they come forward with substantial evidence and a theory. So, I've continually expanded and extended discovery in order to give them a chance.[61]

Perhaps Weinstein's most unique trait as a judge is his ability to take a very ordinary case and make it very important. Weinstein has the analytical vision to recast mundane issues brought to him by lawyers into important issues that somehow they did not see. As an appellate judge, Benjamin Cardozo had that "gift vouchsafed to few judges"—to "make silk purses out of sow's ears."[62] So, too, Weinstein also has enlarged the importance of cases before him by certifying classes, asking for briefs on particular questions and by inviting *amici* into the case.[63] In *David v. Heckler*,[64] discussed in Chapter 6, Weinstein, with the aid of able attorneys, transformed a case brought in Queens Small Claims Court involving a Medicare reimbursement claim into a national class action. In *Nicholson v. Williams*,[65] discussed in Chapter 9, Weinstein took a lawsuit involving New York City's policy of removing children from mothers after they were

---

[60] Quoted by Weinstein in Weinstein Oral History, at 643. Korman was referring in particular to the political corruption case of Representative Frederick Richmond, Chapter 5. Even when Weinstein doesn't greatly alter the shape of case, lawyers are aware of the awesome tools he brings to it. The *Yellow Pages* case, *supra*, was an unfair competition case involving the yellow pages telephone directories, Weinstein's settlement efforts included negotiations, the employment of special masters, and an opinion written only to achieve settlement. *See Verizon Directories Corp. v. Yellow Book U.S.A.*, 338 F. Supp. 2d 422 (Oct. 7, 2004).

[61] Weinstein Oral History at 1532.

[62] RICHARD A. POSNER, CARDOZO: A STUDY IN REPUTATION 47 (1995). "The little case, the ordinary case is a constant occasion and vehicle for creative activity, for the shaping and on-going reshaping of our case law." KARL LLEWELLYN, THE COMMON LAW TRADITION 99 (1960).

[63] *City of New York v. Heckler*, 589 F. Supp. 1494 (June 22, 1984); *Nicholson v. Williams*, 203 F. Supp. 153, 165 (Mar. 18, 2002); *United States v. Mosquera*, 816 F. Supp. 168, 171 (Mar. 16, 1993).

[64] 591 F. Supp. 1033 (July 11, 1984). *See* Weinstein Oral History, at 762ff.

[65] 203 F. Supp. 2d 153 (Mar. 18, 2002).

battered by their husbands or boyfriends and transformed it into a case that was closely watched by child welfare organizations all over the county. He did so in part by certifying the case as a class action[66] and inviting *amicus curiae* from all over the country to illuminate the issue of the constitutionality of the City's policy for him. Indeed, as described in Chapter 10 and 11, Weinstein has repeatedly used the class action structure to attempt to achieve practical remedies in mass tort actions.

In the course of transforming cases, Weinstein has been willing to depart from the traditional adversary system and to assume a heavy burden of the workload to get the attorneys before him to change their approach.[67] He also has been criticized by distinguished observers, such as Dean Martha Minow of the Harvard Law School, who faulted Weinstein for trying "to respond as a problem-solver, to the entire situation before him." He has, she said, repeatedly crafted a role as "judge for the situation" with a "penchant for engineering big solutions to big problems."[68]

Weinstein also shapes cases in his courtroom in smaller ways. In some areas, such as evidence, attorneys come to him, saying, "Well, it just seems wrong judge. I'm not sure why, but you're the expert, so you figure out a way to do the right thing." As Weinstein tells it, sometimes he helps them and sometimes he doesn't.[69]

Weinstein is known to advise attorneys during the jury selection process—presumably in order to achieve a fair jury—by saying to them, "So and so looks like trouble" or "don't we think we need a few men or women or blacks etc.?" and then arrange to strike the jurors himself.[70] When a welfare mother came to a hearing in a multidefendant welfare fraud case wearing diamond rings and a fur coat, Weinstein whispered to an attorney, "The next time she comes in, tell her to wear a cloth coat." He was afraid that the press would play her display of wealth up to the detriment of the other mothers.[71]

A seventh characteristic of Weinstein's judicial career is his *fierce independence*. While independence should be an important role attribute for all federal judges, Weinstein's is particularly fierce and includes within it considerable independence from high courts or regional and national institutions of judicial administration.

He recalls that:

> . . . I always felt from the day I got in that I was the Article III judge of the same Constitutional stature as the whole legislature and the President in my sphere . . . [72]

---

[66] N.Y.L.J., Mar. 22, 2001, at 1, 2.

[67] *See* J. Woodford Howard, Jr., *Adjudication Considered as a Process of Conflict Resolution: A Variation on Separation of Powers*, 18 J. Pub. L. 339, 370 (1969).

[68] Minow, *supra* note 59, at 2011.

[69] Weinstein Oral History, at 561.

[70] Jack B. Weinstein letter to Robert B. Propst, Oct. 3, 1986 (copy in possession of author).

[71] Weinstein Oral History, at 1151.

[72] *Id.* at 612–13.

I was the Article III judge. An independent branch of government . . . . I didn't care what anybody else was doing, what the Court of Appeals was doing. I'd listen to them, but I had an enormous sense of independence. I think that's so important.[73]

For Weinstein, this has included a certain independence from the Court of Appeals for the Second Circuit in substantive matters.

As we have already seen, Weinstein does many things differently from other judges. It should be noted that his manner of conducting business reflects his view of the function of courts and the role of the judge. Thus, he refuses to wear judicial robes most of the time and he dispatches a considerable amount of business at eye-level with attorneys and defendants rather than sitting above them on the "bench."[74] He also finds that cases are handled more efficiently when motions are dealt with around a table in his courtroom or in his chambers when the judge and attorneys sit in chairs arranged in an intimate circle.[75] As for sentencings, he explains:

. . . in the case of criminal defendants, very often they are so overwhelmed that they don't really understand what's going on. It seems to me that every person appearing before the judge is a human being and entitled to be treated with dignity and that often requires that we speak face to face and try to appreciate that we have a human being before us.[76]

However, in his courtroom, there is no doubt he is in control. He puts it this way:

I have never used a gavel. I have never had to. When I come into a courtroom I don't think there is anybody that doesn't know that I am in charge. I don't need help. I never felt a need for it.[77]

But Weinstein's independence is not just in sartorial matters. In 1988, Weinstein argued in a law review article that the Courts of Appeals had very little power to remove judges from cases they were remanding.[78] Some years later, he simply refused to follow an order of the Administrative Office of U.S. Courts to stop

---

[73] Weinstein Oral History, at 20.

[74] He does wear robes when he gives the oath of allegiance to new citizens to give the proceedings dignity and when he sits with the Court of Appeals because the others do and it is not his court.

[75] WEINSTEIN, INDIVIDUAL JUSTICE IN MASS TORT LITIGATION, *supra* note 8, at 91 (1995).

[76] Kenneth P. Nolan, *Weinstein on the Courts*, LITIG. 24, 26 (Spring 1992).

[77] Glaberson Interview, *supra* note 45, at 24.

[78] Jack B. Weinstein, *Limited Power of the Federal Courts of Appeals to Order a Case Reassigned to Another District Judge*, 120 F. R. D. 267 (1988) (available on Westlaw).

impaneling juries at a time of financial stringency for the federal government. He got his juries.[79]

Weinstein has not been deterred from publicly criticizing the ideas of prominent "judicial superiors." In the late 1970s, he was a forceful opponent of proposals to establish court rules and of proposals to impose new standards on trial and appellate advocates by mandating that certain courses be taken in law school and/or that trials be observed. The effort was led by Chief Justice Warren E. Burger and Chief Judge Irving Kaufman of the Second Circuit.[80] Weinstein saw these proposals as an attempt to make it more difficult to obtain access to the federal courts.[81] Weinstein disagreed strongly with Burger and Kaufman over whether the weakness of trial advocates was a major problem in the district courts. "I have found," he said, "the quality of representation in my court to be generally high."[82] The problems that did exist, he thought, were due to character and competence rather than defects in training and insufficient experience. Weinstein believed that any real problems could be handled by normal appellate and grievance procedures.[83]

The point of judicial independence for Weinstein is that judges are there to take risks, such as granting bail to unpopular defendants who nevertheless are entitled to it under the law. It certainly means deciding cases the way a judge believes, without worrying about reversals or public opinion.[84] In a *cause celebre* discussed in Chapter 9, Weinstein presided over the trial of two corrupt New York City policemen, who had been on the payroll of the Mafia and had even committed murders for them. The men were convicted of racketeering and Weinstein sentenced them to life imprisonment. Then, however, he voided their convictions on statute of limitations grounds. He explained that, if had not acted on the statute of limitations problem and the appeal was just on the conviction, that,

> ... that they would just affirm. They wouldn't take the heat. But if I take the heat I think it's more likely they will affirm my dismissal because then they can blame me. But I think that is appropriate. I don't care. If you're going to claim the Rule of Law then we have the Rule of Law.[85]

---

[79] N.Y.L.J., Apr. 8, 1993. Later, he said he would have issued an order to the President, Congress, or to the Treasury, had it been needed. Weinstein Oral History, at 611ff.

[80] Kaufman would block his elevation to the Second Circuit. *See* Weinstein Oral History, at 373.

[81] Letter to Editor, NEW YORK TIMES, Mar. 22, 1975.

[82] Jack B. Weinstein, *Don't Make a Federal Case Out of It*, 318 A.B.A. Student Law 17 (1974–75).

[83] *Id.*; Jack B. Weinstein, *Proper and Improper Interactions between Bench and Law School: Law Student Practice, Law Student Clerkships, and Rules of Admission to the Federal Bar*, 50 ST. JOHN'S L. REV. 441, 452 (1976) [hereinafter Weinstein, *Proper and Improper Interactions*].

[84] Weinstein Oral History, at 253, 1408.

[85] *Id.* at 1747.

As it happened, the Court of Appeals reversed Weinstein's statute of limitations decision and the two men are now serving their life sentences.[86]

The eighth characteristic of Jack Weinstein's judging is his *extensive involvements in extrajudicial activities*. From the outset, Weinstein would not be limited to deciding cases. Throughout his career he has been teaching, writing, speaking, and engaging in a variety of other extrajudicial activities.

There has been a symbiotic relationship between his judging, teaching, writing, speaking, and other off-the-bench activities. Just look at his "evidence industry." During his first decade on the bench, Weinstein, together with his former law clerk, Margaret Berger (who became a professor at Brooklyn Law School), produced a seven-volume treatise on evidence. Together with Berger, he updated it thrice and produced annual supplements for it. By himself, he undertook a major updating of Edward R. Morgan's *Basic Problems of State and Federal Evidence*.[87] Weinstein's involvement with his casebook, *Cases and Materials on Evidence*,[88] "traces its lineage back to James Bradley Thayer's, *Select Cases on Evidence at the Common Law* (1892). Weinstein joined John M. Maguire and Edmund M. Morgan for the fourth edition (1957). Later editions were edited by Weinstein and other collaborators including Margaret Berger. The case book also had annual supplements. Weinstein was applying rules of evidence as a judge, teaching evidence, reworking treatises and casebooks on evidence, and serving on the Advisory Committee drafting the Federal Rules of Evidence. Similarly, there were new editions of *Elements of Civil Procedure* (first published with Maurice Rosenberg in 1962, then with Rosenberg and Hans Smit in 1970, and then with Rosenberg, Smit, and Harold Korn in 1976).

Weinstein had secured his position on the Advisory Committee on the Rules of Evidence, which produced the first set of federal evidence rules, with the assistance of Columbia Law School Dean William Warren.[89] Weinstein was one of two professors on the committee, which was made up of "relatively conservative litigators."[90] It was chaired by Albert E. Jenner, Jr., a distinguished Illinois attorney, and included such luminaries as Judge Simon E. Sobeloff of the U.S. Court of Appeals for the Fourth Circuit, and the famed litigator, Edward Bennett Williams. The committee met four to five times a year for three years from March 1965 to December 1968 to produce a working draft. A year was given over for comments from the outside followed by the drafting of revised rules.

Weinstein believes that the committee created "a moderate and workable classification of the rules of evidence which [would] somewhat improve the truth-finding

---

[86] *See* Chapter 9, *infra*.

[87] BASIC PROBLEMS OF STATE AND FEDERAL EVIDENCE BY EDMUND M. MORGAN (5th ed. 1976). By Jack B. Weinstein. The book was a practice-oriented treatise. [hereinafter WEINSTEIN, BASIC PROBLEMS].

[88] *See, e.g.*, 6th edition with Maguire, Chadbourn, & Mansfield (6th ed. 1973).

[89] As a professor, Weinstein had written the *Probative Force of Hearsay*, 46 IOWA L. REV. 331 (1961); *Some Difficulties in Devising Rules for Determining Truth in Judicial Trials*, 66 COLUM. L. REV. 223 (1966).

[90] WEINSTEIN, BASIC PROBLEMS, *supra* note 87, at x.

capacity of the courts." As he explained it, the major principles of the rules were simplicity in application; greater discretion for the trial judge; a bias in favor of admissibility; greater flexibility; and discretion to avoid harsh, unjust results which might flow from mechanical application.[91] He saw some benefit in uniformity and in increased ability to find the rules more quickly.[92] Generally, the bar strongly objected to the new Rules because they increased the discretion of trial judges considerably.[93] After the Rules were adopted by the Supreme Court, Congress delayed their effective date, concerned about policy judgments in politically sensitive areas. It then deleted the section on privilege (as Weinstein preferred[94]) and made some other changes.[95]

During his first decade on the bench, Weinstein wrote law review articles which were mini-treatises on various evidentiary problems.[96] When the preliminary draft of the Rules of Evidence was published and the Rules finally approved, Weinstein made a series of speeches preparing the way for acceptance of the rules. Speaking and writing later in the decade permitted him to influence the way the rules were being interpreted.[97] Trials gave him the opportunity to use the rules in action.[98] Indeed, throughout his career, Weinstein wrote important evidence opinions and books and articles and continued to give speeches on aspects of evidence. From time to time, he also taught evidence at Columbia Law School. A second area for Weinstein where judging was linked with his off-the-bench writing, speaking, and other activities was the availability of counsel for the poor, an issue that has concerned him throughout his entire career.

---

[91] Jack B. Weinstein, An Overview of the New Federal Rules of Evidence, New Rules of Evidence Course, New York County Lawyer's Ass'n (Sept. 23, 1975).

[92] Jack B. Weinstein, *Introduction to a Discussion of the Proposed Federal Rules of Evidence*, 48 F.R.D. 39, 41 (1969) (available at Westlaw).

[93] Jack B. Weinstein, *Rules for Courts: The Role of Lawyers, Judges, Professors and Government*, 13 ISRAEL L. REV. 459, 473 (1978).

[94] Weinstein had been "almost alone in the committee in proposing the Federal Rules not cover privileges . . ." Jack B. Weinstein, *The Role of the Chief Judge in a Modern System of Justice*, 28 REC. ASS'N. B. CITY N.Y. 291, 292 (1973).

[95] Geoffrey C. Hazard, Jr., *Reform of Court Rule-Making Procedures*, 87 YALE L. J. 1284, 1292FF (1978); Charles Alan Wright, Book Review of JACK B. WEINSTEIN, INDIVIDUAL JUSTICE IN MASS TORT LITIGATION, 9 ST. MARY'S L.J. 652, 654–56 (1977–1978).

[96] Jack B. Weinstein & Margaret A. Berger, *Basic Rules of Relevancy in the Proposed Federal Rules of Evidence*, 4 GEORGIA L. REV. 43–109 (1969); Jack B. Weinstein, *The Uniformity-Conformity Dilemma Facing Draftsmen of the Federal Rules of Evidence* [with Appendix by Paul Sherman], 69 COL. L. REV. 353–76 (1969); Jack B. Weinstein, *Alternatives to the present Hearsay Rules*, 44 F.R.D. 375 (1968) (available on Westlaw).

[97] *See* Jack B. Weinstein, Introduction to the Federal Rules of Evidence, Federal Litigation Lecture No. 6, Association of the Bar of the City of New York, Dec. 2, 1976. He spoke, for example, at the New York County Lawyer's Association on Sept. 23, 1975.

[98] *See United States v. King*, 73 F.R.D. 103 (1976) [Rule 502], 75-CR-973, 1976 Op. 5 (Rules 402 and 403). Also a member of the Special Committee on New York Evidence, Weinstein recommended that the state undertake a revision of its rules of evidence. Press Release, Sept. 27, 1972, at 1.

Jack Weinstein's entire judicial career has been marked by *innovation* and experimentation in methods of managing cases, in techniques used in the courtroom,[99] in the application of procedural rules, and in the development of the substantive law. Weinstein's innovativeness has encompassed the use of special masters and magistrates, the audacious use of the district judge's equity powers, and pioneering work in complex civil litigation.[100]

Few district judges see themselves as "innovators."[101] Those who do make a reputation as innovators generally do so as case managers.[102] Those who have innovative tendencies in areas other than case management tend either to restrain themselves or camouflage their handiwork as fidelity to settled law.[103]

Although Weinstein has said, "I don't think my chambers are particularly more innovative than anybody else's,"[104] his reputation is of a man who "never saw an innovation he didn't like."[105] In a light vein, Weinstein has said, "Sometimes innovations are successful, sometimes they are more successful."[106]

A long and early advocate of televising judicial proceedings—in order to open the courtroom "to all the people"—Weinstein permitted arguments to be televised in the

---

[99] Michael Hoenig, *Products Liability: Computer Generated 'Pedagogical Devices' Admissible or Not?*, Commenting on *Verizon Directories Corp. v. Yellow Book USA, Inc.*, 331 F. Supp. 2d 136 (2006), N.Y.L.J., Nov. 8, 2004, at 3.

[100] Weinstein has been relatively cool to another area of reform, alternative dispute resolution. Undoubtedly, because it can be used to keep the poor out of court. Weinstein does not make use of the new method of dealing with *habeas corpus* petitions in the Eastern District—farming cases out to magistrates, the court's *pro se* clerk, and one of the judge's law clerks followed by a memorandum and recommendation to the judge. Weinstein prefers the traditional adversarial mode. N.Y.L.J. Aug. 9, 2002, at 3.

[101] In Kitchen's interviews of district judges, eleven described their willingness to innovate as rare; seven as moderate, but only three as frequent.

[102] Some do both. Frank Johnson, though he made statements to the contrary, fashioned equitable relief in relatively new ways. Larry W. Yackle, Federal Courts 19 (2nd ed. 2003). Judge Robert R. Merhige, Jr. used his equity powers extensively and bypassed lawyers to involve the parties in settlement negotiations. RONALD J. BACIGAL, MAY IT PLEASE THE COURT: A BIOGRAPHY OF JUDGE ROBERT R. MERHIGE, JR. 144 (1992). see Reynaldo Garza of the Southern District of Texas developed jail delivery days where he would try hundreds of illegal immigrants en masse; LOUISE ANN FISCH, ALL RISE: REYNALDO G. GARZA, THE FIRST MEXICAN AMERICAN FEDERAL JUDGE 94–95 (1996). See also RICHARD CAHAN, A COURT THAT SHAPED AMERICA: CHICAGO'S FEDERAL DISTRICT COURT 16 (2002); VERNA C. CORGAN, CONTROVERSY, COURTS, AND COMMUNITY: THE RHETORIC OF JUDGE MILES WELTON LORD 4–5, 44 n.29 (1995); FRITZ, *supra* note 35, at 63.

[103] James Zagel & Adam Winkler, *The Independence of Judges*, 46 MERCER L. REV. 795, 818 (1995); POSNER, *supra* note 62, at 13. This seems unusual for judges who are innovators would seem to have the best opportunity to become well-known and widely respected. See LAWRENCE BAUM, JUDGES AND THEIR AUDIENCES 108–09(2006).

[104] P. Nolan, *supra* note 76, at 25.

[105] Judge Joseph McLaughlin quoted in James L. Oakes, *Jack Weinstein and His Love-Hate Relationship with the Court of Appeals*, 97 COLUM. L. REV. 1251 (1997).

[106] Nolan, *supra* note 76, at 24, 25.

class action suit dealing with the sale of guns. He also allowed closed-circuit testimony of a witness in the federal witness protection program.[107]

Weinstein has relied heavily on magistrate judges, working with them closely and strongly favoring their greater integration into the court.[108] His expansion of the use of special masters has included their use to communicate with those affected by the litigation, to raise the profile of the litigation, to mediate, to interact with administrative agencies, to make use of social welfare, religious, and philanthropic groups in order to ease tensions and fund programs, and to explain the court's role to the public and build consensus and support for solutions.[109]

Believing that the Federal Rules of Civil Procedure "represent less a merger of equals than the conquest of law by equity,"[110] Weinstein has made audacious use of his equity powers and flexible use of procedure; for example, issuing a series of near path-breaking opinions on the power of his court to stay litigation in state and federal courts.[111] He has also taken the position that federal courts have the power to develop federal common law–equity remedies where the particular facts of a case fall outside the literal coverage of a federal statute, but the use of common law can fill gaps in the congressional statutory patterns or otherwise make that pattern effective.[112]

Weinstein has made major efforts to involve the U.S. government in important cases because such involvement raises the profile of the case and makes somewhat more likely the government purse will be used for settlement. He has also brought in the United States in cases where the government lacked statutory authorization to bring suit. He has invited the United States to appear as *amicus* in education, housing, and shareholder litigation.[113]

Weinstein has made considerable use of advisory juries. An advisory jury does not have decision-making power but does, as its name suggests, advise the judge. Weinstein believes it is "especially useful to a judge when his or her personal knowledge and general background may not permit him to appreciate fully all aspects of a problem and weigh its elements appropriately."[114] Among the cases where he has employed the advisory jury mechanism was a Federal Tort Claims Act case to determine damages where the government had opened and read the mail of private citizens. He used

---

[107] *See* N.Y.L.J., July 17, 1997. He has called for televising of Supreme Court arguments for over thirty years. *See* Morton Mintz, *High Court Taping Urged*, WASH. POST, Nov. 18, 1977, at A2.

[108] Weinstein Oral History, at 99–100, 1425, 1611–12, 1724.

[109] *See* Jack B. Weinstein, *Litigation Seeking Changes in Public Behavior and Institutions—Some Views on Participation*, 13 U. CAL. DAVIS L. REV. 231, 239 (1990); Curtis J. Berger, *Away from the Court House and into the Field: The Odyssey of a Special Master*, 78 COLUM. L. REV. 707, 728 (1978); *80th Birthday Roundtable, supra* note 51, at 149, 168–69.

[110] WEINSTEIN, INDIVIDUAL JUSTICE IN MASS TORT LITIGATION, *supra* note 8, at 127.

[111] Weinstein Oral History, at 1021.

[112] *Cutler v. The 65 Security Plan*, 831 F. Supp. 1008 (Jan. 30, 1993).

[113] Weinstein, *Litigation Seeking Changes*, *supra* note 109, at 231, 238.

[114] Jury charge in unpublished, untitled case, 1977 Op. NB 63-8 (copy in possession of author).

another advisory jury to determine if New York City's "nail and mail" system of citing landlords for sanitations violations was discriminatory and unjust.[115]

Weinstein's innovations in complex civil litigation, discussed in chapters 10 and 11, have been daring and influential. They have included pioneering work in case consolidation and quasi–class actions;[116] the appointment of a panel to select experts to review the scientific issues involved in silicon breast implant litigation;[117] and working jointly with state judges in mass tort cases, including the holding of integrated pretrial joint hearings, appointment of special masters/referees, and joint opinions.[118] He has employed a generous approach to party structure[119] and, at times, handled the difficulties of expert testimony by swearing in experts, seating them at a table with counsel and judge, and engaging them in recorded colloquies under court direction.[120]

In the area of criminal law, Weinstein created or at least facilitated the creation of the "Fatico hearing," employed when there is reason to question the reliability of material facts, having in the judge's view, a direct bearing on the sentence to be imposed, especially where those facts are essentially hearsay.[121] In a complex criminal case discussed in Chapter 7, Weinstein ordered the government to provide Spanish language translations of many court documents for sixteen Hispanic defendants in a drug trafficking case, so that they would have a "better understanding of what is transpiring."[122] In the same case, Weinstein appointed an attorney, Eleanor Jackson Piel, not to represent any single defendant, but to coordinate discovery and other administrative aspects of the large, complex criminal case for the defense in order to avoid enormous duplication of legal effort.[123]

Although Weinstein's innovative substantive jurisprudence is discussed throughout this book, it should be mentioned here that he was among the first American jurists to use the interpretation of human rights principles by high courts of other nations

---

[115] NEW YORK TIMES, Apr. 24, 1982; Weinstein Oral History, at 441–43. *See also id.* at 442f, 449f. *See* Birnbaum v. United States, 76-1837, 1977 Op. NB 61, 64.

[116] *See* NEW YORK TIMES, June 3, 1992; NEWSDAY, June 3, 1992; WALL STREET JOURNAL, June 3, 1992, at B6.

[117] Jack B. Weinstein, 1 ALMANAC FED. JUDICIARY 101 at 102.

[118] Stephen Breyer, *Tribute to the Honorable Jack Weinstein*, 97 COLUM. L. REV. 1497, 1948–49 (1997). Weinstein Oral History, at 983ff. *See In re Joint E. & S. Asbestos Litig.*, 129 F.R.D. 434 (Jan. 30, 1990) and *In re New York City Asbestos Litig.*, 1990 N.Y. Misc. LEXIS 38 (Jan. 30, 1990).

[119] Minow, *supra* note 59, at 2016, 2017–18.

[120] Jack B. Weinstein, *Improving Expert Testimony*, 20 UNIV. RICH. L. REV. 473, 485 (1986).

[121] *United States v. Fatico*, 441 F. Supp. 1285 (Dec. 1, 1977), *rev'd* 579 F.2d 707 (2d Cir. 1978: *Oakes*-WJF-Mans), *on remand*, 458 F. Supp. 388 (July 27, 1978), *aff'd*, 603 F.2d 1053, 1057 n. 9 (2d Cir. 1979: *Oakes*-Mesk-Stewart), *cert. denied*, 444 U.S. 1073 (1980).

[122] Peter Bowles, *Tough Talk from the Bench*, N.Y. NEWSDAY, Brook. Sunday, 1 at 5 (Nov. 14, 1993); N.Y.L.J., Jan. 11, 1993; Weinstein Oral History, at 1203ff.

[123] *United States v. Mosquera*, 813 F. Supp. 962 (Feb. 10, 1993); N.Y.L.J. Feb. 12, 1993; Weinstein Oral History, at 1206.

as authority. Weinstein has employed such authority in cases involving sentencing, extradition, and terrorism.[124]

A final characteristic of the Weinstein judgeship has been his *ability to attract attention* far beyond his district for his ideas, decisions, and activities, developing a national constituency for some of them. At least in comparison with other district judges, he has been a lightning rod for publicity.

Weinstein may be termed an "entrepreneurial judge," "alert to the opportunity for innovation, willing to invest the resources and assume the risks" of developing and "selling" genuinely new legal concepts.[125] Entrepreneurial judges are rare. Occasionally, issues that come before an unusual judge that fall within an area of his special expertise and interest may stimulate new ideas or approaches which may "move the law." Such a judge may then become a salesman for that idea, a "judicial entrepreneur." Such a judge, according to the scholars who have pioneered the use of the term, must have a grand vision of the law and where it should be headed. He must be creative and willing to make law. Since entrepreneurship runs contrary to prescriptions of judicial modesty, demeanor, and adherence to precedent, a judicial entrepreneur often is a bit of a renegade. He must have the self-confidence to be engaged and the capacity to endure criticism, reversal, and failure.[126]

Weinstein is such a judge. But while most entrepreneurial judges, rare as they are, have only one or two major ideas to "peddle," Weinstein has never been so limited. Weinstein is alert to the opportunity for innovation, willing to invest the resources and assume the risks of developing and selling generally new legal concepts.[127] He has a grand vision of the law and where it should be headed. He is creative, willing to make law, and self-confident. He also has the capacity to endure criticism and reversal and is a bit of a renegade. Acting as an "educator-entrepreneur," he has reached a national audience.

Weinstein comes easily to this role, arguably because he sees himself as an educator. There is always much on Weinstein's mind—much to learn, much to impart. Debating in his mind whether to speak at an occasion where he was to receive an award, he said to me only partially in jest: "I've never ignored the opportunity of a public forum to make a little substantive statement."[128]

Although at one point Weinstein seemed to suggest that there might be a conflict between his role as professor and that of judge, surely he has been both. The roles have

---

[124] *Ahmad v. Wigen*, 726 F. Supp. 389, 412–15 (Sept. 26, 1989); *Nicholson v. Williams*, 203 F. Supp. 153, 233ff (Mar. 18, 2002); *Mojica v. Reno*, 970 F. Supp. 130, 146–52 (July 11, 1997). *See also* Donald J. Sharpstein, *European Courts, American Rights: Extradition and Prison Conditions*, 67 BKLYN. L. REV. 719 (2002).

[125] WAYNE V. MCINTOSH & CYNTHIA L. CATES, JUDICIAL ENTREPRENEURSHIP at 4, 5, 13, 113 (1997).

[126] *Id.* at 10, 119.

[127] He admits that at times, he has written long opinions to get attention. Weinstein Oral History, at 409.

[128] *Id.* at 1091–92.

not proved incompatible but symbiotic, as when a case provided the opportunity to address the problem of the probative force of hearsay of which he had written.[129]

As an educator, Weinstein attempts to influence several audiences. One such audience is law students. For more than three decades while he was on the bench, Weinstein remained a law school professor, teaching law students in the classroom and in the court room and chambers, where his seminars often met.[130] The depth of his concern about teaching was exemplified by the fact that he has created a new set of materials for every course he has taught.

Conversely, insights from teaching have impacted upon Weinstein's judging. Having taught procedure, for example, Weinstein believes that procedure "is useful only to achieve a goal substantively." He adds, "My view, having taught it, is that it is flexible."[131] Weinstein has given draft opinions to his seminar students for criticism.[132]

In addition, teaching and judging have given Weinstein two different outlets for his ideas and scholarship. He has explained it: "Some things I can get off my chest in law reviews and some things I have to wait for the right case."[133] There have been some opinions written with the casebook in mind.[134] As a judge, he has used "compelling legal scholarship on intricate legal issues as leverage to attain a just result."[135]

With his scholarship, Weinstein has sought to influence law professors, attorneys, law students, and fellow judges. He has written hundreds of law review articles and delivered more than that number of speeches.[136] He has continued to attend and speak at major conferences of law professors and attorneys throughout the world. While some of Weinstein's scholarship could be termed "academic," whether acting as judge or scholar, most of Weinstein's work is intended to improve things in the real world. As Margaret Berger has written of his work:

> For although his theoretical innovations have profoundly shaped the law of mass torts, his work has always had an empirical grounding. He has always understood that solutions were dictated by the context in which problems arise and that answers must be rooted in reality if they are to succeed.[137]

---

[129] Weinstein Oral History, at 467.

[130] Weinstein was among the first judges to hire interns. *See* Weinstein & Bonvillian, *supra* note 21, at 276; Weinstein, Proper and Improper Interactions, *supra* note 21, at 446

[131] Weinstein Oral History at 944.

[132] *Id.* at 1130.

[133] *Id.* at 1588. Of course, most cases result in "nothing that can be traced from the library." Weinstein Oral *Id.* at 507.

[134] *Id.* at 801–02.

[135] Daniel Wise, *"Doing Justice" Never Ends for Eastern District's Chief Judge*, N.Y.L.J., Aug. 5, 1986, 1 at 2.

[136] Occupying 36 pages of his resume in 2006. A copy is in The possession of this author.

[137] Margaret Berger, *Eliminating General Causation: Notes toward a New Theory of Justice and Toxic Torts*, 97 COLUM. L. REV. 2117 (1997).

Many of Weinstein's opinions are mini-treatises, useful for judges, attorneys, law professors, and law students. He has prepared check lists on sentencing and materials on *habeas corpus* for other district judges.

Finally, he has attempted to reach the general public through interviews and op-ed pieces. Those on Weinstein's mailing list—it is a long list—may receive large envelopes with opinions, articles, speeches, and copies of correspondence, sometimes weekly, sometimes twice a week, sometimes even daily.

WEINSTEIN'S ACTIVISM

Virtually every observer of Jack Weinstein's career terms him a "judicial activist." So does this observer, but since "judicial activist" is a label often used as an epithet to discredit, it requires definition. It is usually a term of opprobrium spat at Supreme Court justices, applied to a host of sins. The term is used to criticize justices when they vote to strike down acts of Congress and state legislatures, thereby not demonstrating sufficient deference to the elected branches of government or to the federal system. It has also been used when precedent is overruled, evaded, weakened, ignored, or poorly distinguished, thereby undermining stability in the law. "Activism" has been employed when federal comity with the states is not respected, when Supreme Court justices decide cases with unnecessarily broad or restricted reading of statutes, when threshold doctrines are given short shrift, when justices decide cases by basing their decision upon principles larger than necessary, and when justices use their authority to make significant changes in public policy. Critics fault activist justices for reaching for a result that achieves a social policy the judges find desirable (and the critics do not). In sum, it is fair to say that in the great majority of cases, the term "activist" is thrown around by those whose ox has been gored.[138]

The label "activist" is used less often to criticize the work of lower federal court judges whose decisions are usually less visible. It has, however, been applied to judges who have ordered expansive remedies demanding affirmative conduct from the bureaucracy where schools, prisons, and mental hospitals have been involved with the kind of detail which, arguably, ought to been left to the agency or at least prescribed by the legislature.[139] That Weinstein has not really done, although he almost did so in the *Mark Twain* school case described in Chapter 5.

---

[138] *See* Stefanie A. Lindquist & Frank B. Cross, Measuring Judicial Activism 7 (2009). Bradley Canon, who has published useful scholarship in this area, has stated that "A Court is activist when its decisions conflict with those of other policy-makers . . . including predecessor courts." Bradley C. Canon, *A Framework for the Analysis of Judicial Activism, in* SUPREME COURT ACTIVISM AND RESTRAINT 385ff (Stephen C. Halpern & Charles M. Lamb eds.). *See also* CHARLES S. LOPEMAN, THE ACTIVIST ADVOCATE: POLICY MAKING IN STATE SUPREME COURTS 3 (1999).

[139] *See* American Enterprise Institute, Symposium: *Whom do Courts Represent* 29 (June 1, 1981) [hereinafter AEI Symposium].

It is important to distinguish between a hyperactive and an "activist" judge. No one can doubt that Weinstein is an extremely *active* judge. He handles more than his share of the work of the Eastern District and publishes an unusually large number of opinions for a district judge. Refusing to be limited to the briefs of the parties before him, he reads widely, takes judicial notice of what he has read, and provides attorneys before him a list of the sources he has used. His many involvements in extrajudicial activities have not been criticized as "activist"—except perhaps for his race for New York's Chief Judge in 1971. Certainly, no one has ever suggested that his activities have detracted from his judicial duties. Nor can Weinstein's fierce judicial independence, his approach to opinion writing, and his occasional accessibility to reporters translate into activism. Although attorneys have griped from time to time about the energy and creativity Weinstein has demonstrated in seeking settlements, strong management of a docket is an important requirement of a federal district judge.[140]

There is no question that Weinstein's instincts drive him toward rapid action. His temperament and energy level propel him to do more than judges usually do. Taking definitive action just comes naturally to him. "I just do," he said. "When I see something wrong, I tend to want to do something about it."[141] When, for example, there is a potential legal barrier to students attending school or something chargeable to the government which discourages students from attending school, he brooks no delay. Early in Professor Burt Neuborne's career, Weinstein called him at home to chide him for not having filed a discrimination case earlier.[142] When a public school in a disciplinary matter took a student's coat and mislaid it on a Friday afternoon, Weinstein immediately set a hearing for the next Monday by which time the authorities had given the mother funds to buy a new coat.[143]

Weinstein was aware of this at the time he was sworn in as a judge. At the ceremony, he said: "Not the least of the problems will be the necessity of applying a check rein . . . upon an activist seeker of troublesome issues . . . "[144] But if his temperament places no barriers to action, neither does his judicial philosophy or his view of his role.[145]

---

[140] Weinstein Oral History, at 288. *See* Chapter 5, for discussion of the *Coney Island* case. Weinstein has said that, "My theory is that settlements [are] better than trials and long litigations. For one thing, trials exacerbate animosities in ways that's undesirable." Weinstein Oral History, at 211.

[141] *Id.* at 37. Judge Jose Cabranes of the Court of Appeals for the Second Circuit has stated that " . . . the assertion of judicial power may as readily be a function of an individual jurist's disposition to command and to take charge as it is a result of ideology." José A. Cabranes, Judging: Some Reflections on the Work of the Federal Courts, Remarks at Touro College, Jacob B. Fuchsberg Law Center 27 (Mar. 1, 1995).

[142] Weinstein Oral History, at 1661; William Glaberson, *A Judge Shows He's Boss*, N.Y. Times, July 20, 1997, at 24.

[143] Weinstein Oral History, at 1659ff.

[144] *See id.* at 34.

[145] Barry Meier, *Bring Lawsuits to Do What Congress Won't*, N.Y. Times, Mar. 26, 2000, at K3; Weinstein Oral History, at 37. Peter G. Angelos, a leading lawyer for asbestos plaintiffs, said that Weinstein "would have been a more interesting and effective United States Senator from New York." Arnold H. Lubasch, *Jack Weinstein: Creative U.S. Judge Who Disdains Robe and High Bench*, N.Y. Times, May 28, 1991.

Some of Weinstein's efforts to protect those who might be protective of those who otherwise would be without power to protect themselves fall on the "hyperactivity" rather than the "activist" side of the line. For example, his handling of *habeas corpus* petitions personally without using his law clerks.[146] Nor should he be sharply criticized for construing *pro se* pleadings liberally and facilitating the amendment of complaints, enumerating their failings in a conditional order rather than entering a final order of dismissal at once, so that the pleading can be corrected. This is in compliance with Supreme Court precedent.

Concerns about activism are triggered by Weinstein's impatience with gate-keeping doctrines, his alleged abandonment of neutrality in the court room, his audacious use of procedure, his evasion of precedent, and because he admits that he "makes law." Because he believes that accessibility to the courts on equal terms is essential to equality before the law,[147] Weinstein has often powered past threshold doctrines. He says, "I'm not too excited by jurisdiction."[148] His general view of abstention sums up his (not always invariable) view of gate-keeping rules: "I don't want to abstain. I don't like to duck any of these things."[149] Thus, for plaintiffs, Weinstein may limit the effect of such doctrines as standing, mootness, abstention, and justiciability in order to reach, hear, and decide substantive contentions.[150] He often denies summary judgment even though he knows that the case will ultimately be dismissed, so, at least, the individual litigating will have had an opportunity to be heard.[151]

Once Weinstein gets a case, he says, "I like to decide it."[152] "Power should be exercised," he commented to me, "Otherwise, there's no point in having it."[153]

In his courtroom Weinstein has from time to time abandoned neutrality to help out a sympathetic party who has no attorney or whose attorney is particularly weak. It is,

---

[146] Jack B. Weinstein, Speech to Practicing Law Institute Prisoners' Rights Seminar, New York City 23 (Oct. 6–7, 1972) (in possession of author).

[147] Stephen B. Burbank, *The Courtroom as Classroom: Independence, Imagination and Ideology in the Work of Jack Weinstein*, 97 COLUM. L. REV. 1971, 2000ff (1997). *See also* Weinstein Oral History, at 148–49; In re Sabella, 315 F. Supp. 333 (June 22, 1970).

[148] *Id.* at 347. The context for this remark was a case where there was no doubt about Article III, but a question as to whether the case belonged in the Eastern District of New York or some other district.

[149] Weinstein Oral History, at 1625.

[150] Very early in his tenure, Weinstein wrote what ought to be called an advisory opinion in a naturalization case. The aspiring citizen seems to have slept with a woman whom he did not know was married. Under the existing immigration law this seemed to have been "adultery" and the petitioner, therefore, appeared to lack the "good moral character" to qualify for naturalization. Weinstein related that, when he was about to rule for the petitioner, the Immigration and Naturalization Service, which desired to take a more modern view of sexual chastity, asked him to write an opinion in the case. That he did, seizing upon a case where the facts were very good to, in effect, rewrite policy. *See* Weinstein Oral History, at 101f; Jack B. Weinstein, *Rendering Advisory Opinions—Do We, Should We?*, 54 JUDICATURE (Nov. 1970) 140, 142. *See In re Petition for Naturalization of Egbert William Johnson*, 292 F. Supp. 381, 384, 385 (Sept. 26, 1969). *See also Petition for Naturalization of Evangelina Bayer*, Pet. No. 734865 (1972).

[151] Weinstein Oral History, at 149–50.

[152] *Id.* at 1778.

[153] *Id.* at 350–51.

though, difficult to cavil at Weinstein's efforts during his first decade on the bench, to assist aged applicants for naturalization whose English was not strong and who hesitated in answering his questions, Weinstein would put questions this way: "You do know the President of the United States is so and so, don't you? They would say yes . . . " Then, they were naturalized.[154]

But sometimes Weinstein reaches too far. As an illustration, there was a Social Security disability case in which the government was arguing that the individual had not appealed in time. Weinstein commented on the case:

> I utilized all my guile to find this poor fellow probably had not received his notice
> in time and had a timely notice of appeal . . . . I had to be his lawyer as well as his
> judge. But I think I did fairly well for him in dealing with presumptions and mail
> delay and everything else.[155]

Weinstein, whose judicial and scholarly careers have been concerned with the modernizing of the rules of evidence and procedure, sees the federal courts and the modernization of procedure as having a substantial function in protecting the poor and those who do not have the means of obtaining lawyers and advisors.[156] Such reforms as the creation of the Federal Rules of Civil Procedure have, in Weinstein's eyes, demonstrated the personality of our legal system: "its compassion for people who claimed to have been wronged, its reliance on the good sense of judges, its faith in the usefulness of lawyers and, ultimately, its optimistic confidence that the people will use their political institutions for what is right and decent."[157] Thus, Weinstein-the-judge has taken the position that procedure both can and should be used creatively to achieve substantive justice.[158]

Nevertheless, Weinstein admits to playing "fast and loose with a lot of procedure."[159] His use of the powers of equity can be breathtaking: "My view, having taught it, is that it [equity] is flexible. I just don't feel inhibited."[160] In the asbestos litigation (discussed in Chapter 9), Weinstein enjoined every court in the country from settling

---

[154] Weinstein Oral History, at 103 ff. *See United States v. Ekwunoh*, 813 F. Supp. 168 (Jan. 14, 1993), *vacated*, 12 F.3d 368 (2d Cir. 1993). Weinstein placed a lower estimate on the amount of drugs the defendant had placed in her mouth in a case where she was charged with aiding the sale of drugs, rather than the amount the government had charged her with. Weinstein Oral History, at 749ff.

[155] *Id.* at 695–97; *Sinatra v. Heckler*, 566 F. Supp. 1354 (July 1, 1983).

[156] Weinstein Oral History, at 1625–26.

[157] Jack B. Weinstein, *The Ghost of Process Past: The Fiftieth Anniversary of the Federal Rules of Civil Procedure and Erie*, 54 BROOK L. REV. 1, 29 (1988). *See also* Gold & Eikenberry, *supra* note 47, at 1, 4.

[158] SCHUCK, *supra* note 7, at 118 (1987).

[159] Weinstein Oral History, at 945. *See United States v. Jonas*, 842 F. Supp. 1533 (Jan. 27, 1994); *c.f.* SCHUCK, *supra* note 7, at 137–38.

[160] Weinstein Oral History, at 945.

asbestos cases.[161] (The Court of Appeals reversed.[162]) In dealing with class actions, he took advantage of the lack of interlocutory appeals to protect some extremely innovative procedures from being reversed.[163]

Much of what has made Weinstein so controversial is his unabashed willingness to admit that judges do make law and the ways he finds to do so. As will be clear in the rest of this book, Weinstein does not shy away from reversal. In one case, he risked reversal by treating a case as a Federal Tort Claims Act case "because the law was wrong." He commented, "I was more interested in moving the law into what I considered the more modern and useful areas of tort law." He was reversed with Henry Friendly writing the opinion.[164]

Weinstein is quite aware that he often runs a serious risk of reversal and he is in fact often reversed. One of the gentlest reversals occurred in *Anchor v. Irizarry*:

> Instead of dismissing the case, the able District Judge sought to see done that which he thought should have been done. We might well wish we could deal with the problem in the same manner, but we can not do so.[165]

Weinstein has been so willing to ignore Court of Appeals precedent that one of its more easily exacerbated judges, Ellis Van Graafailand, excoriated him not so unjustly:

> . . . the proper administration of our judicial system requires that a District Court accept an appellate court's rejection of a theory of law which the lower court has announced.[166]

Weinstein seems less likely to respect the *work* of the court directly above him than most judges. If former Judge and Attorney General Griffin Bell said, "We cannot have a system of law unless judges follow the court above,"[167] Weinstein's reply would be: "[T]here is no overpowering reason for me as a judge to do something I think is wrong."[168] It should be noted, though, that when Weinstein was at his most activist

---

[161] *In re Joint E. & S.D. Asbestos Litig.*, 1993 U.S. Dist. LEXIS 10,700 (July 1, 1993). *See also* Weinstein Oral History, at 514–17.

[162] *In re Joint E. & S.D. Asbestos Litig.*, 14 F.3d 726 (2d Cir. 1993: *Wint*-VanG-Pollack).

[163] *See infra*, Chapters 10 and 11.

[164] *See* Weinstein Oral History, at 52ff. The case was *Bushey & Sons v. United* States, 276 F. Supp. 518 (Oct. 12, 1967).

[165] *Irizarry v. Anker*, 558 F.2d 1122, 1125 (2d Cir. 1977: *Danaher*-WJF-Dooling). The Second Circuit opinion reversing Weinstein in *Anchor v. Irizarry* is quoted by Weinstein in Weinstein Oral History, at 367.

[166] *In re United States*, 834 F.2d 283, 286 (2d Cir. 1987: *VanG*-Meskill-Card). *See also* Weinstein Oral History, at 868.

[167] AEI Symposium, *supra* note 139, at 7.

[168] Weinstein Oral History, at 480. A few smaller concerns should be mentioned. In one case he employed the rules for privilege of the Advisory Committee that drafted the Federal Rules of Evidence in his decision, even though Congress had rejected them. He called the "standards" "reflective of reason and

during the era of Guideline sentencing, he was one (if one of the most visible) of a large number of federal judges of various philosophies.[169]

Against these examples of judicial activism, one must set the efforts Weinstein has made to explain why he has done what he has done. Far, far more often than most trial judges, Weinstein takes great pains to explain his thinking. This can be seen in the unusual number of opinions as well as in their unusual length. It is in this way that Weinstein acknowledges his accountability for his judicial actions.

In addition, there are the great many treatise-like opinions Weinstein has written, exploring and illuminating murky areas of the law for other judges and for practitioners. No federal judge of the last fifty years has illuminated so many difficult areas of law in his opinions. Some of the subjects he has given this treatment to are: how to calculate damages for pain and suffering;[170] the admissibility at a trial for violation of civil rights governmental reports finding police and prosecutorial misconduct;[171] whether state or federal law is to be used for discovery in civil rights actions;[172] the admissibility as evidence of radioimmunoassay of hair analysis;[173] industry-wide liability in mass torts;[174] whether a contract between a cruise ship line and a passenger should be treated under admiralty law or under the law governing consumer contracts for resorts.[175] To this one should add the checklists he has prepared for other judges to use in sentencing[176] and his report recommending procedures for his colleagues to employ in dealing with *habeas corpus* petitions.[177]

Senator Oren Hatch relates that a nominee for a judgeship was asked, "If you had to choose between the law and your own conscience, what would you choose?" He said unequivocally, 'My conscience.'" Hatch commented, "We must get beyond that. Lower court judges ought to abide by the principles of *stare decisis*."[178] Jeffrey Toobin

---

experience" and gave less weight to some rather than other rules of procedure. *See* Weinstein Oral History, at 358; JACK B. WEINSTEIN & MARGARET A. BERGER, WEINSTEIN'S EVIDENCE MANUAL: A GUIDE TO THE UNITED STATES RULES BASED ON WEINSTEIN'S EVIDENCE 18-5-7 (1987); Jack B. Weinstein, Some Reflections on the 1983 Amendments, Seminar, The New Amendments to the Federal Rules of Civil Procedure 6 (Nov. 2, 1983) (copy in possession of the author). In another case, *Verizon Directories Corp. v. Yellow Book U.S.A.*, 338 F. Supp. 422 (2004), Weinstein wrote a tentative opinion that he never intended to publish making it fairly clear to one party that he was prepared to rule against them. In that manner, a settlement was achieved, probably quite a desirable one, part of which was an agreement that the opinion would not be published. *See* Weinstein Oral History, at 1663–64.

[169] Weinstein Oral History, at 886–87.

[170] *Geressy v. Digital Equip. Corp.*, 980 F. Supp. 640 (Sept. 16, 1997).

[171] *Gentile v. County of Suffolk*, 129 F.R.D. 435 (Feb. 15, 1990).

[172] *King v. Conde*, 121 F.R.D. Supp. 180 (June 15, 1988).

[173] *United States v. Medina*, 749 F. Supp. 59 (Oct. 22, 1990).

[174] *Hall v. E.I. DuPont & Co.*, 345 F. Supp. 353 (May 18, 1992).

[175] *Vavoules v. Kloster Cruise Line*, 822 F. Supp. 979 (June 9, 1993).

[176] Weinstein Oral History, at 1300.

[177] *In re Habeas Corpus Cases*, 03-Misc.-0066 (Dec. 11, 2003).

[178] AEI Symposium, *supra* note 139, at 4–5.

commented in the *New Yorker*: "Jack B. Weinstein is Oren Hatch's worst nightmare—the apotheosis of the liberal activist judge."[179]

While Weinstein's record does not support a statement as strong as Toobin's, the reader must judge for himself whether Weinstein is a judicial activist in the pejorative sense of the term. What this observer has found is a hyperactive judge, who surely does "seek troublesome issues"; a strong-minded judge of remarkable intellectual abilities, uncowed by the Court of Appeals, who sometimes comes close to insubordination. Weinstein spots problems and possibilities in the law far more than most and is unafraid to innovate, create and drive the law. A law-maker while he was a professor, he did not break that habit on the bench. Furthermore, one can not doubt that Weinstein makes far greater use of the tools available in his kit than other judges. Added to this is an unusually deep concern for the humanity of those who come before him; an emotion driven from the mainstream of American law during the years he has been on the bench. Whether Jack B. Weinstein will be viewed as prophet or anachronism may take decades to decide.

---

[179] [Jeffrey] Toobin, *Benchmark*, NEW YORKER. May 3, 1993, at 34, 35.

5

"An Activist Seeker of Troublesome Issues"[1]:

Jack Weinstein's First Decade on the Bench, 1967–1976

JACK WEINSTEIN WAS formally inducted as a district judge in a ceremony in the U.S. Courthouse in Brooklyn on May 5, 1969. (He actually had begun sitting on May 1.) Present at the ceremony were his eight colleagues, judges of the U.S. Court of Appeals for the Second Circuit, the District Court of the Southern District of New York and the New York State Court of Appeals, as well as a number of other government officials and members of the bar. Weinstein's wife and three sons, his mother, and no fewer than nine aunts and uncles by blood and marriage were also present.[2]

No fewer than fifteen persons (including Weinstein) spoke at the ceremony. Stanley Fuld called Weinstein "as thoroughly equipped as any judge who has ever graced this bench or any other."[3] Eugene Nickerson, later to join Weinstein on the bench, stated that Weinstein's counsel to him had been "wise and disinterested, his company delightful and stimulating and his friendship highly prized."[4] Louis Lefkowitz, whom Weinstein might have run against for Attorney General of New York State, praised Weinstein and spoke of the "phenomenal increase in recent years in federal litigation concerning the interests and operation of state and local government."[5] Dean William

---

[1] Transcript of Ceremonies Attending the Induction of Honorable Jack B. Weinstein as United States District Judge for the Eastern District of New York, May 5, 1967 at 54, 56 (hereinafter, Induction Ceremony) (copy in possession of author).

[2] Persons Assigned to Specific Seats in *id.*, n.p.

[3] Induction Ceremony, at 17.

[4] *Id.* at 23.

[5] *Id* at 28, 29.

proved to be a poor prophet when he regretted the faculty's "loss of 'Professor Weinstein's incisive and fruitful mind.'"[6] Chief Judge Joseph C. Zavett administered the judicial oath while William Rosenfeld, Weinstein's his former law partner, presented Weinstein with his judicial robe. It has already been mentioned that when Weinstein spoke, he noted, prophetically

> Not the least of the problems ahead will be the necessity of applying some of the check rein of mandated passivity upon an activist seeker of troublesome issues, and who is habituated to saying what is on his mind.[7]

Weinstein recalls that he was "fully comfortable the moment he got on the bench."[8] Right away, he insists, he felt that he was "an Article III judge . . . fully the equivalent of the President of the United States in my courtroom."[9] No doubt his adjustment was eased by his mastery of procedure and evidence, although he did receive the training the Federal Judicial Center was giving to new judges. Weinstein felt that, as an academic he had the advantage of having thought through problems as a teacher and had done so in a remarkable number of courses.[10] The only area in which Weinstein admits he lacked confidence was in knowing how a judge should interact with the "outside world."[11] There would be no "freshman effect"—acting cautiously in the early years on the bench, nor does it seem that Weinstein needed "socialization" from other judges.[12] Weinstein did not fall under the sway of a mentor or strong-minded colleague. John F. Dooling, Jr., a superb judge, had an office near his, and Orrin Judd, appointed shortly after Weinstein, was another colleague whose advice he would seek over the years, but they would be models not mentors.[13]

Weinstein would find the Eastern District a good place to work. His arrival spurred the transition to a very high-quality court. Three relatively undistinguished judges had taken senior status in 1966 and 1967. Jacob Mishler, appointed in 1960, was a jurist of real ability and he had been joined by Dooling in 1961. The able Judd would soon

---

[6] *Id.* at 36.

[7] *Id.* at 50, 54.

[8] Jack B. Weinstein Oral History, at 18.

[9] *Id.* at 20.

[10] *Id.* at 157.

[11] *Id.* at 21.

[12] On the freshman effect and socialization, *see* J. Woodford Howard, Courts of Appeals in the Federal Judicial System 222ff; J. Woodford Howard, Courts of Appeals in TAE FEDERAL JUDICIAL SYSTEM 222 (1981); Walter F. Murphy, ELEMENTS OF JUDICIAL STARATEGY 49–51 (1964); Ronald A Carp & Ronald Stribhm, THE FEDERAL COURTS 121–24 (2nd ed. 1991); Robert A. Carp & Russell Wheeler, *Sink or Swim: The Socialization of a Freshman District Judge*, 21 J. Pub. L. 359 (1972). Political scientists have suggested that the socializing agents of federal judges are their colleagues within the district, especially the Chief Judge; court staff including bailiffs and secretaries; local lawyers; new judge seminars; FEDERAL JUDICIAL CENTER, BENCHBOOK FOR U.S. DISTRICT JUDGES (1996; 4ed. with March 2000 revisions) and other judges met at circuit judicial conferences. *See* Carp & Wheeler, 347ff.

[13] *Id.* at 5.

be aboard. The court was small (seven judges in regular, active service and three on senior status at the time of Weinstein's investiture). Mishler, respected and loved by his colleagues, became Chief Judge in 1970 and served for a decade before being succeeded by Weinstein.

Weinstein possessed the characteristics that distinguish fine district judges—independence; patience, and efficiency with routine cases which reinforce appreciation of process; ability to handle a fast pace and take quick decisions in the courtroom even if wrong; the ability to act carefully and well under emergency conditions as well as to preside with dignity.[14] Time is at a premium in the district court. The very extensive research Stanley Fuld was able to do with a relatively light-loaded appeals court with control of its docket was not available in the district court. Even Weinstein was limited in the number of issues he could develop fully in an opinion in any one year.

Weinstein's work was greatly facilitated by the adoption of the individual calendar system early in his judicial career. Under the master calendar, which the judges were using when Weinstein arrived, whenever a judge was free, he was assigned to another case which needed immediate attention, even if earlier stages had been handled by other judges. Weinstein was the fastest of the judges in the District under this system and tried a tremendous number of cases, but, as he said, "it was like emptying a . . . never-ending chute. I would get in early, try cases, and there would be all the other cases coming from everybody else."[15] Weinstein found it overwhelming and psychologically unsatisfactory. As he said, "I like to keep a clean desk and I like to be responsible for my own mistakes."[16]

Weinstein discussed adoption of the individual calendar system with Chief Judge Joseph C. Zavatt. One of Weinstein's clerks was then sent around the country to investigate how the individual calendar was working elsewhere. Weinstein and the law clerk wrote a report which led to adoption of one of the first fully integrated individual assignment systems in the country. The adoption of the system of individual assignment in 1969 was critical to Weinstein's view of how cases should be handled—one judge "should take control [of] the case at the outset."[17] This permitted Weinstein to "utilize [his] own view of how procedure and substance should be integrated."[18]

In these early years, there was a richer variety of cases than today. The criminal docket included truck hijackings and bank robberies, and the civil docket held minor

---

[14] *See* José A. Cabranes, Judging: Some Reflections on the Work of the Federal Courts, Remarks at Touro College, Jacob D. Fuchsberg Law Center, Huntington, N.Y. at 11–12 (May 1, 1995); CHRISTIAN G. FRITZ, FEDERAL JUSTICE IN CALIFORNIA: THE COURT OF OGDEN HOFFMAN, 1871–1891 at 254–56 (1991).

[15] Weinstein Oral History, at 98.

[16] Jack B. Weinstein, Calendar Control and the Pre-Trial Conference, [Remarks] at Seminar for Newly Appointed Judges, Federal Judicial Center 3 (Sept.1976).

[17] *Id.* at 99.

[18] Weinstein Oral History, at 99. There would be times, however, when Weinstein would express reservations about the system, particular about its unfairness to slower, more thoughtful judges like Dooling. Weinstein, Calendar Control and the Pre-Trial Conference, *supra* note 16, at 3–4.

commercial arbitration cases, Federal Tort Claims Act cases, and more diversity actions. Some categories of cases to which Weinstein was partial have now largely or completely disappeared, among them cases involving labor relations and naturalizations. Weinstein thoroughly enjoyed handling these because it gave him the opportunity "to see all these different kinds of people."[19]

In retrospect, Weinstein views his early years as "fairly pedestrian," with "interesting little cases, almost finger exercises."[20] At a minimum these early cases, provided the judge with opportunities to learn about such areas and industries as air-conditioning, nail polish, insurance, electronics, and bombsights.[21]

EARLY CASES

Weinstein's first case, *Engel v. Tinker Nat'l Bank*,[22] involved contracts for land, vendors and vendees, an assignment, and tax liens. The five-page typed opinion was released twenty days after Weinstein's induction. It was quite technical and not an "important case," but even though it was Weinstein's first opinion, it showed a capacity to deal with legal complexity to produce a "just" result, and so it should be at least briefly described. The case had been filed in state court and removed to federal court on the petition of the United States. The case revolved around an unrecorded unconditional sales contract for two small houses, executed on December 1, 1957, with the deed not to be delivered until the monthly installments had been entirely paid after eight years. In the meantime, the buyers were occupying the houses and making substantial improvements. When the vendor was beset by creditors, he assigned the contract for the sale of the house to the Tinker Bank as collateral security for his loans, then in default. The buyers then paid their monthly installments to the bank. However, when the buyers attempted to exercise their right under the contract to pay the balance due and have the property conveyed to them, the bank refused to issue the deed, stating that it held the deed solely as collateral security and it was unable to convey title.

The buyers of the houses then sued the bank in a New York State court seeking specific performance of the contract. The court denied summary judgment to the buyers on the ground that the judgment creditors and lien holders of the contract should be joined as party defendants and the priorities and interests litigated in a single action. Seventeen defendants were joined. Later, the case was removed to federal court.

Applying New York law (except for the federal statutes dealing with the U.S. tax liens) "to unravel this tangle", Weinstein held that the contract vendees – the buyers – were the equitable owners *pro tanto* of their properties. Among the authorities

---

[19] *See* Weinstein Oral History, at 105. On the caseload, *see id.* at 56, 91–92, 97, 131,137, 308–09.

[20] *Id.* at 1.

[21] *See* Jack B. Weinstein Oral History, at 43, 74.

[22] 269 F. Supp. 199 (May 25, 1967). *See also* Weinstein Oral History, at 42.

Weinstein cited were one study and two reports of the New York Law Revision Commission. He also used legislative history to interpret the federal law involved (the Lien Law of 1966). Weinstein held that the contract vendees' rights were superior to the tax liens of the United States. Thus, the vendees were entitled to specific performance of the contract and the buyers could purchase the houses.

Wheeler v. Flood[23] was decided within a week of *Engel v. Tinker Bank*. A *habeas corpus* action, the case involved a typical problem facing federal and state courts during the early years of Weinstein's judgeship, that of speedy trials for criminal defendants. Hovering over the case were implications for federalism. The petitioners, Susan and Robert Wheeler, who had been indicted for illegally importing narcotics, had been in custody twenty and fifteen days respectively and sought a writ to compel a U.S. Commissioner[24] to hold a preliminary examination hearing to determine whether there was probable cause that they had committed the offense. Their preliminary hearing had been delayed nineteen days to allow the Assistant U.S. Attorney time to gather his evidence in a presentable form, something that was customary even though Rule 5 (e) of the Federal Rules of Criminal Procedure provided that the hearing shall be held "within a reasonable time" after the defendant had been brought before a U.S. Commissioner. Most courts denied the relief the petitioners were seeking because the issue of delay was mooted by the indictment, which was the result of a grand jury finding of probable cause.

Weinstein, however, thought differently. He pointed out that, from the defendant's vantage point, the preliminary hearing could serve as a valuable discovery device. Defense counsel could be present and cross-examine the witnesses for the prosecution as well as present evidence. Thus, he held that, while some delays in holding the preliminary hearing could occur, the hearing could not be put off for weeks. He ordered the defendants released from custody unless the hearing was held on the day he heard the petition.

The first case to really "grab" Weinstein's attention was *Clairol Inc. v. Gillette Company*,[25] a case involving trademark infringement and unfair competition. Clairol sought a preliminary injunction restraining Gillette from using the term "Innocent" on any hair dye product as Clairol was using the names "Innocent Ivory" and "Innocent Beige" on its hair dye products. Gillette was using the term "Innocent Color" for a hair coloring product.

Weinstein denied Clairol's request for a preliminary injunction finding, based upon the evidence that had thus far been presented, that Clairol had not clearly established that it had acquired common law trademark rights in "Innocent Ivory" and "Innocent Beige." The public had not been shown to associate "Innocent Ivory" or "Innocent

---

[23] *Wheeler v. Flood*, 269 F. Supp. 194 (June 1, 1967).

[24] The predecessor to Magistrate Judges with lesser responsibilities.

[25] 270 F. Supp. 371 (June 23, 1967).

Beige" with Clairol. Clairol had not shown that Gillette's use of "Innocent Color" had caused confusion in the market place. Weinstein explained:

> In a market like this, so heavily dependent upon highly competitive and alert advertising specialists, many ideas and names are afloat at any one time. The court should not discourage the entrepreneur who moves first to commit his resources in favor of a particular idea or word.[26]

Weinstein published a photograph of the packages of both companies in *Clairol*, his fifth opinion.[27]

The first Weinstein case with constitutional implications involved an attack on the zoning ordinances of the Town of Islip.[28] The town argued, that because zoning is "so peculiarly a matter of local concern," a federal court should abstain from exercising its jurisdiction.[29] Writing during the heyday of the Warren Court, Weinstein noted that recent cases suggested that the theory of abstention is "losing its charm."[30] He believed that the factors which had been invoked to justify withholding federal relief were not present and refused to dismiss the case. Weinstein later explained that he "was aware of the fact that very often a plaintiff could not get a square deal and that's what the federal courts were for, after all, to make sure that local corruption or politics didn't prevent the person getting his constitutional rights fairly adjudicated and so I stepped into that case on theoretical grounds."[31]

VIETNAM WAR RESISTORS

A submariner during the Second World War, Weinstein proved sympathetic to those who did not wish to serve in the Vietnam War, especially those with religious objections and those who fled the country. He almost never ruled for the government in these cases.[32] This was due in some measure because of his doubts about the war itself, but also because his experience made him fear that unenthusiastic soldiers might well endanger other combatants.[33]

---

[26] *Id.* at 382.

[27] In a beautiful turn of the phrase, Weinstein wrote: "There also seems little doubt that the word Innocent is capable of trademark protection where, as here, it is used fancifully and suggesting as a euphemism for guile in making hair appear what it is not, the very antithesis of innocent." *Id.* at 376.

[28] *Lerner v. Town of Islip*, 272 F. Supp. 664 (Aug. 10, 1967).

[29] *Id.* at 665.

[30] *Id.* at 666.

[31] Weinstein Oral History, at 15.

[32] *C.f. United States v. Mandell*, 67-Cr-294 (1968) (copy of typed manuscript in possession of author).

[33] Weinstein Oral History, at 64.

The *first* Weinstein opinion in a case involving those who refused to serve in the armed services during the Vietnam War was released on December 12, 1967, *United States v. Lybrand*.[34] In that case, Weinstein granted a judgment of acquittal on the charge of knowingly failing to comply with his draft board's order to report for civilian work in lieu of induction into the armed forces. This was because the government ordered the defendant, a conscientious objector, to report for civilian work ahead of the time he would have been ordered to report for military training. Weinstein held that the courts were not foreclosed from deciding if local draft boards had complied with Selective Service regulations and that: "the failure of a local board to call conscientious objectors in the order specified in the regulations was of sufficient significance to constitute a jurisdictional defect which renders void an order to report."[35] Weinstein considered the proper order of call an element of the criminal offense and, as he often would in his career, set a high bar for the government to prove all elements of *mens rea*. Weinstein refused to accept the government's reliance on a "presumption of regularity" of the proceedings of a local draft board. Nevertheless, he also made clear that the judgment of acquittal would not immunize the defendant from his obligation to report for civilian work.[36]

In spite of the fact that there was a highly deferential standard of review of the actions of Selective Service boards—whether the deciding body had any basis in fact for its decision[37]—Weinstein, like a number of other federal judges, invariably found ways to overturn their decisions. In a case of a pantheist opposed to war by reason of religious belief, Weinstein found that a general mimeographed form letter from a local board had not informed the registrant why his case for conscientious objection had been denied. As a result, the defendant had not had a reasonable opportunity to gather evidence to support his position.[38] In another case, Weinstein held that the fact that a registrant had sought deferments on a basis other than conscientious objection was not by itself a permissible basis for a decision not to grant a conscientious objector claim or to refuse to reopen a classification.[39] He also held that where registrants were denied counsel during the classification process, draft boards could not hold registrants to a strict use of technical statutory language.[40]

One important case involved transfers of members of the 62nd Army band. Regulations involving the band were being more strictly enforced and band members transferred, not only because some members had circulated and signed petitions opposing the war, but also because the wives of some of the members (and the girlfriend of one) had demonstrated against the war. David Cortright, a baritone

---

[34] *United States v. Lybrand*, 279 F. Supp. 74 (Dec. 12, 1967).

[35] *Id.* at 80–81.

[36] *Id.* at 83.

[37] *See, e.g., In the Matter of Les Lovallo*, 71 C 48 (Feb. 4, 1971), JBW Op. NB 55.

[38] *United States v. St. Clair*, 293 F. Supp. 337 (Nov. 20, 1968).

[39] *Kulas v. Laird*, 315 F. Supp. 345 (May 14, 1970).

[40] *United States v. Friedman*, 69-Cr-54 (Nov. 26, 1974).

horn player, had been transferred by the Army from New York to Louisiana. He brought suit against the Secretary of the Army and his commanding office for declaratory relief, an injunction prohibiting them from interfering with his First Amendment rights and for a writ of mandamus canceling his transfer orders and forbidding transfers without good cause. He also sought a writ of mandamus to cancel the order transferring him from New York to Texas. A general had testified at trial that the reason for Cortright's "precipitous" transfer was the desire to rid the band of a "troublemaker."[41] A number of former members of that band were permitted to intervene in the action to have their transfers to various posts cancelled since they had been made in circumstances similar to Cortright's.

Weinstein treated the case as a class action for purposes of some issues.[42] He steamrolled over a number of gate-keeping problems including jurisdiction, sovereign immunity of the United States, and the policy that federal civilian courts may not review the actions of the military. Weinstein held that, although the amount for purposes of general federal question jurisdiction—then $10,000—was not technically met, there had been financial costs to Cortright's transfer and that the plaintiffs were alleging violations of "one of the most cherished constitutional rights—freedom of speech." Furthermore, there would be no other forum and procedure to test whether rights had been violated. Weinstein found jurisdiction under the statute granting district courts the power to mandamus employees of the United States.

Although courts were reluctant to employ judicial review of military matters, in *Cortright v. Resor* Weinstein saw a trend toward limited exercise of judicial power to control abuses by military as well as civilian officials.[43] Refusing to be "bound to a narrow review of administrative proceedings when the proceedings involve[d] an important constitutional right,"[44] he found a lack of due process because of "a totally inadequate hearing."[45] Weinstein also held that servicemen were not deprived of "such basic constitutional rights as freedom of speech,"[46] even if the right might need to be balanced against the interests of the military in preserving discipline and providing protection for national security.[47] Finding that the changes in duty assignments "were for the purpose of halting the public expressions of disagreement with the Vietnam War by band members," he held that the findings and conclusion of the Army's investigating office were not supported by substantial evidence.[48] The remote contingency

---

[41] *Cortright v. Resor*, 325 F. Supp. 797, 801–02 (Mar. 23, 1971) *rev'd*, 447 F.2d 245 (2d Cir. 1091).

[42] *Id.* at 808.

[43] *Id.* at 815–16.

[44] *Id.* at 819.

[45] *Id.* at 820.

[46] *Id.* at 822.

[47] *Id.* at 823.

[48] *Id.* at 824.

of the members of the band actually taking up arms and defending the country was not enough to legitimize the suppression of speech.[49]

Weinstein ordered Specialist Cortright's transfer rescinded, dismissed the complaints of the intervening plaintiffs, and ordered that representatives of the defendants post copies of the correct official guidelines regarding dissent on bulletin boards utilized by the band, as well as a one-page statement of the facts and conclusions in the lawsuit. *Cortright v. Resor* seems to have been the first case where any civilian court revised duty orders of one lawfully in the armed forces on a finding that the duty order had transgressed statute and regulations.[50]

Six months later the Court of Appeals reversed, with the very highly regarded Henry Friendly writing the opinion.[51] Friendly was joined by Weinstein's colleague on the Columbia Law School faculty, Paul Hays. The higher court found that plaintiff's case was not strong enough to justify judicial intrusion into the area. While the Court of Appeals did not hold that a civilian court could *never* interfere with a transfer order or prescribe other relief to prevent the abridgment of First Amendment rights, it held that on the whole that the area of military orders to military personnel was confined by the Constitution to the President.[52] The Court of Appeals also challenged Weinstein's observation that the trend was away from reluctance to interfere in military affairs. It held "that the Army had a large scope in striking a proper balance between servicemen's assertions of the right of protest and the maintenance of the effectiveness of military units to perform their assigned task."[53] Judge James L. Oakes, beginning a distinguished career on the Second Circuit, dissented. Judge Oakes argued that civilian courts may review military findings in substance and effect and that the appellate court should uphold the decision of the trial judge unless "clearly erroneous."[54] The Supreme Court denied *certiorari*.[55]

One of the grand or maybe grandiose undertakings of Weinstein's first decade was his search to resolve the large number of cases on his (and other judges' calendars) of pending indictments against self-exiled draft evaders. These cases, on the dockets of federal judges throughout the country, could not be resolved unless the defendants appeared in court. But, if the defendants appeared in court, they were likely to be arrested. Weinstein gave a good deal of thought to devising a theory for dealing with these cases, even considering the possibility of a nationwide class action.[56] Finally, he arrived at a theory where he could cloak himself as protector of the constitutional rights of criminal defendants to a speedy trial.

---

[49] *Id.* at 825–26.

[50] *Cortright v. Resor*, 447 F.2d 245, 246 (2d Cir. 1971: *Friendly-Hays/Oakes*).

[51] *Id.*

[52] *Id.* at 246.

[53] *Id.* at 254–55.

[54] *Id.* at 255, 259.

[55] *Cortright v. Froehlke*, 405 U.S. 965 (1972).

[56] Weinstein Oral History, at 405. *See id.* at 63, 269, 355, 406.

In 1974, when the executive and the Congress were considering some form of amnesty for such fugitives, which might have affected their rights, Weinstein, on his own, acting, he said, to "protect" his docket, without consulting the defendants, appointed his Columbia colleague, Louis Lusky, as attorney for the draft evaders to argue the question of the sufficiency of their indictments. Weinstein's theory was that the fugitive cases were artificially inflating his caseload and that of the prosecutor. To guarantee prompt disposition of the cases, he proposed to call them up, determine if the government was making reasonable efforts to apprehend the fugitives and whether the public or defendants were being prejudiced by the delay. He then could dismiss invalid indictments. Although the defendants could not be tried in *absentia*, he argued that challenges to indictments could be made by the defendants' attorney (even if Weinstein and not the defendants had appointed him):

> The court's right to hear from counsel on behalf of a defendant on legal issues, even during the period when a defendant had no right to counsel, was established long before adoption of our Constitution.[57]

The government sought mandamus from the Second Circuit to prohibit Weinstein from conducting any further proceedings where the defendant had not appeared personally by counsel authorized to appear for him. The government also sought to vacate Weinstein's order to turn over Selective Service files to Lusky for discovery and inspection and to bar Weinstein from entertaining motions for the dismissal of the indictments by court-appointed counsel. It is possible that Weinstein's haste in this matter may have been the result of his concern that draft evaders with strong defenses might be coerced into alternate service under President Gerald Ford's amnesty plan.[58]

The Court of Appeals did not buy Weinstein's handiwork. A distinguished panel of judges—Walter Mansfield, Irving Kaufman, and Wilfred Feinberg—granted the mandamus, holding that Weinstein clearly had exceeded his powers. The Court of Appeals held that neither Lusky nor *amicus* counsel Michael Tigar had been authorized by the defendants to inspect their files or indeed had been authorized by any defendant to act at all.[59] No usage or custom existed that permitted a judge "to appoint himself or a stranger as the representative of a defendant who has fled the jurisdiction in order to not face criminal charges, at least without the fugitive's authority or consent."[60] The matter was essentially mooted when President Jimmy Carter issued a pardon for all such fugitives on the first full day of his presidency.

---

[57] *United States v. Lockwood* [and twenty-four related cases], 382 F. Supp. 1111 (Sept. 30, 1974). *See also United States v. Lockwood*, 386 F. Supp. 734 (Nov. 26, 1974), where Weinstein denied a blanket motion to dismiss twenty-six indictments on the ground of speedy trial.

[58] *United States v. Salzmann*, 548 F.2d 395, 398 (2d Cir. 1976).

[59] *United States v. Weinstein*, 511 F.2d 622, 628 (2d Cir. 1975).

[60] *Id.* at 628.

Weinstein was narrowly affirmed by the Court of Appeals in another Vietnam War case, *United States v. Salzmann*,[61] where a fugitive who had settled in Israel was ordered by his draft board to report to Livorno, Italy, for pre-induction processing. After failing to report for induction, Salzmann took the position that he could not financially afford such a trip. Although travel assistance was provided by the United States by regulation, it had never been offered to Salzmann. Weinstein held that the government had not exercised "due diligence" in bringing Salzmann to trial and dismissed the case with prejudice. The Court of Appeals in an opinion by Chief Judge Irving R. Kaufman affirmed on the narrow ground that the government should have informed Salzmann that he would have been provided free transportation, if necessary, back to New York. On the whole, Weinstein believed that the Court of Appeals in its own words, left "[c]ompassionate yet fair treatment of Vietnam era exiles" to the "imagination and energy of the political branches of government."[62]

CLASS ACTIONS AND MASS TORTS

Weinstein considers *Dolgow v. Anderson*[63] as "probably the first important case" he wrote on.[64] It was his first class action.

Some of Weinstein's earliest cases when he practiced law had involved stockholders' derivative suits. From these, he "got a sense that class actions were important in keeping people honest."[65] Weinstein strongly supported "a very vital class action system because I was aware that a lot of these poor people that I had dealt with one way or another . . . were not going to get any place . . . unless they were able to assemble their forces through the class action or other devices."[66]

The *Dolgow* litigation was brought by owners of common stock of the Monsanto Corporation, one of the world's largest producers of chemical synthetic fibers with assets and sales of hundreds of millions of dollars, against the corporation, its officers and directors. The plaintiffs argued that the officers and other insiders had deliberately driven up the price of its shares by issuing optimistic predictions as to the corporation's future and then sold their stock ahead of a precipitous fall from $80 a share to $40 a share. By the time Weinstein first dealt with the case, it already had sixty-one docket entries and, due to the master calendar system, aspects of the case had been before six judges.

The first significant issue Weinstein confronted involved a gate-keeping issue. The defendants moved to dismiss the case on jurisdictional grounds. The main office of

---

[61] 417 F. Supp. 1139 (July 16, 1976).

[62] *United States v. Salzmann*, 548 F.2d 395, 403 (2d Cir. 1976: *Kaufman*-Fein-VanG).

[63] 43 F.R.D. 21 (Aug. 24, 1967).

[64] Weinstein Oral History, at 48, 67.

[65] *Id.* at 50–51.

[66] *Id.* at 51.

the corporation was in Missouri but, because of the cost of serving defendants in St. Louis, the plaintiffs had served the summons and complaint directed to each defendant on an employee who worked in the New York office. Weinstein held that under the New York Civil Practice Law and Rules service could be made "in such manner as the court . . . directs," if the court finds that the specified modes of service are "impracticable" Weinstein found that, in this case, service in St. Louis was "impracticable." The principal author of the Civil Practice Law and Rules (CPLR) wrote:

> Reducing unnecessary burdens of process is particularly important in class actions. One of the purposes of this procedural device is to make it possible for individuals with modest claims and resources to redress wrongs which would otherwise go unchallenged.[67]

Weinstein would say later: "I took a very strong position there [in *Dolgow*] that the class action was important. It served a useful purpose and the courts ought not put too many clogs on it by making service and other requirements too onerous."[68]

Weinstein's first important opinion in the *Dolgow v. Anderson* litigation was another gate-keeping issue and involved the central question—whether the litigation could be maintained as a class action. On the issue of certification of a class action, Weinstein had to determine in *Dolgow* whether such an action was superior to other available methods for the fair and efficient adjudication of the controversy (joinder, intervention, consolidation, the test case, and the administrative process).[69] Weinstein invited the Securities and Exchange Commission to file *an amicus curiae* brief on this issue.[70]

Weinstein held that, if private enforcement affords relief to those injured by violations of the securities law and serves as a deterrent (as he found here), then, "[i]t is the duty of the federal courts to render private enforcement practicable because 'the other procedures available for handling proliferated litigation' cannot serve this function in a situation like the one here."[71] Since the costs of litigation in *Dolgow* would far exceed any damage award any individual plaintiff might gain, if the case did not proceed as a class action, it seemed unlikely that it would proceed at all. Weinstein, thus, saw the mission of the class action as taking care of the "smaller guy" and found it appropriate because there were tens of thousands of small Monsanto shareholders.

Weinstein, thus, gave strong support for class actions in the field of securities regulation where, he said, it serves "the same prophylactic function . . . that the shareholders derivative suit has in the area of general corporate law."[72] The class action had

---

[67] *Dolgow v. Anderson*, 43 F.R.D. 21, 23 (Aug. 24, 1967).
[68] Weinstein Oral History, at 49.
[69] *Dolgow v. Anderson*, 43 F.R.D. 472, 482 (Jan. 3, 1968).
[70] *Id.* at 478.
[71] *Id.* at 484.
[72] *Id.* at 487.

"substantial therapeutic value" by providing a primary means of enforcing desired standards upon corporate officials.

Weinstein had no trouble finding that *Dolgow v. Anderson* satisfied Rule 23 (b) (3); that there were "questions of law or fact common to the members of the class"; and that such questions "predominate[d] over any questions affecting only individual members."[73] The plaintiffs would be required at a hearing to show that statements emanating from the defendants relating to Monsanto's future prospects were "consistently over-optimistic."[74] The remaining questions involving individual situations could be determined after the common questions had been resolved. However, Weinstein found that the plaintiffs had defined the class they purported to represent too broadly and redefined the class of injured investors in a manner permitting utilization of the class action procedure.[75]

Nevertheless, on April 7, 1969, Weinstein granted defendants' motion for summary judgment from the bench and ordered that the class action be disallowed. After almost two years of intensive fact exploration and development, Weinstein held that, when construing all evidence favorably to the plaintiffs, there was no evidence to support the plaintiffs' claims and that no reasonable jury or court could find that plaintiffs' rights had been violated.[76]

The Second Circuit reversed the decision with the distinguished district judge, Edward Weinfeld, sitting by designation on the panel.[77] The court held that Weinstein had erred when he granted defendants' summary judgment motion for there were specific facts set out in plaintiffs' affidavit which required a trial, and plaintiffs' discovery had been restricted. The higher court said that it was unable to review the issues without detailed findings and conclusions by the trial judge. Weinstein, they suggested, had come to his conclusions too rapidly and had not laid out the material facts upon which he based his finding that no genuine issue of fact existed.[78]

Then, on a motion for rehearing, the panel modified its opinion, remanding for the preparation of findings and conclusions in accordance with Weinstein's intention at the time he ruled on the motion for summary judgment to write an opinion analyzing the claims and iformation for whatever assistance it may give to the parties and should an appeal be taken to the Court of Appeals."[79] Judge Moore dissented strongly.[80]

On remand, Weinstein rejected further discovery.[81] He held [again] that the action could not proceed as a class action because there was not a substantial possibility that

---

[73] *Id.* at 487.

[74] *Id.* at 489–90.

[75] *Id.* at 492.

[76] *See Dolgow v. Anderson*, 438 F.2d 825, 830–31 (2d Cir. Apr. 23, 1970; *mod.* Sept. 2, 1970: *Smith-Weinfeld/Moore*).

[77] *Id.*

[78] *Id.* at 830.

[79] *Id.* at 833.

[80] *Id.* at 833, 830 [*sic*].

[81] *Dolgow v. Anderson*, 53 F.R.D. 661 (Oct. 8, 1971).

the plaintiffs would prevail on the merits.[82] "The possibility of recovery on the merits was so slight, Weinstein held, as not to justify the enormous expense and inconvenience of trying this case as a class action."[83] He wrote that:

> . . . a rule of law too restrictive and inflexible may over- inhibit and dampen their [the managers of large enterprises] drive without providing gain to the investor in the form of more reliable prediction.[84]

At that point, the district court permitted the case to proceed as a suit by individually named plaintiffs, but later, Weinstein ultimately granted summary judgment because the indisputable evidence demonstrated that defendants bought and sold stock of the company in the good faith expectation of the company's success and based on the same information available to outsiders.[85]

Hall v. I.E., du Pont de Nemours & Co., Inc., and *Chance v. I.E., du Pont de Nemours & Co., Inc.* were Weinstein's first mass tort cases. The litigation arose out of eighteen separate accidents in which children were injured by blasting caps. The problem was the impossibility of determining which corporation had manufactured the particular blasting cap that had injured a given individual because, when the cap exploded, the only reliable evidence of its manufacturer—markings on the casting—were often reshaped in the explosion.[86] The national pattern of production and distribution of the product causing the industry was known. The fundamental allegation was that during the time of the accidents, the explosives industry had failed to place any warning upon individual blasting caps and had failed to take other safety measures thus creating an unreasonable risk of harm, including death. There had been a long-standing industry practice of not placing a warning message on individual blasting caps. Professor Linda Mullenix of the University of Texas has pointed out the significance of this litigation:

> The blasting cap litigation involved problems related to the ability of federal courts to join multiple individual claimants residing in different states in aggregate litigation; problems relating to consolidations of multiple claimants with different individual injuries into one case; problems with identification of the multiple defendant manufacturers; problems with substantive tort standards

---

[82] *Dolgow v. Anderson*, 53 F.R.D. 664, 667.

[83] *Id.* at 668.

[84] *Id.* at 686.

[85] *Id.* at 686. However, *see Feit v. Leasco Data Processing Equipment Corp.*, 332 F. Supp. 594 (Aug. 26, 1971), a class action bought by a shareholder of an insurance company to recover damages resulting from material omissions from its registration statement and prospectus, where Weinstein, in an opinion covering forty-five pages of Federal Supplement, rendered judgment for the class, holding that there was material error.

[86] Weinstein Oral History, at 378.

related to causation and liability; and problems in determining the relevant applicable state law that applies to these claims.[87]

The first decision Weinstein made in the cases was to dismiss on statute of limitations grounds those claims that were based on an antitrust theory—that there had been a conspiracy to inhibit the manufacture of safe blasting caps and to refrain from the proper labeling of these products in restraint of trade.[88] Weinstein then chose to delay confronting the difficult question as to which choice-of-law principles were to be applied by assuming the existence of "a national body of state law."[89]

Instead, he next turned to the issue of whether a group of manufacturers and their trade association, comprising virtually the entire blasting cap industry of the United States, could be held jointly liable for injuries caused by their product. Weinstein answered that they could be under the circumstances presented by developing a theory of industry-wide liability in a mass tort action, one he would use in the *Agent Orange* case.[90]

Although the individual liability of each manufacturer could not be determined because the evidence of the manufacturer's identity was destroyed by the explosion,[91] what was known was the national pattern of production and distribution of the product causing the injuries. Because each defendant had done something to cause the damage and because it was impossible to demonstrate which manufacturer was individually liable, Weinstein held all the wrongdoers jointly liable for the plaintiffs' harm.

Weinstein found that injuries to children were a foreseeable risk of the use and circulation of blasting caps and that this risk was known or should have been known to the individual manufacturers.[92] The manufacturers were jointly liable because the actions of the group created an unreasonable risk of harm, and there was joint control of the risk because the manufacturers had taken joint action with regard to warnings and other safety features. There had been a joint enterprise taken for the mutual benefit of the parties. The allegations in the case suggested that "the entire blasting cap industry and its trade association provide the logical locus at which precautions should be taken and liability imposed" in an industry composed of a small number of units.[93] Weinstein dismissed the joint liability aspects in those cases where the specific manufacturer was known, severing them and transferring two of the three to other districts.[94]

In *Chance v. E.I. du Pont de Nemours & Co., Inc.*,[95] another part of the blasting cap litigation, Weinstein decided the relatively novel question as to whether a jury was

---

[87] Linda S. Mullenix, Book Review, Individual Justice in Mass Tort Litigation, 5 L. & POL. 173 (1995).
[88] *Hall v. E.I. du Pont de Nemours & Co.* 312 F. Supp. 358 (Apr. 7, 1970).
[89] *Id.* at 360.
[90] Weinstein Oral History, at 146ff, 195ff.
[91] *Hall v. E.I. du Pont de Nemours & Co.* 345 F. Supp. 353.
[92] *Id.* at 365–66.
[93] *Id.* at 378.
[94] *Id.* at 378, 385–86.
[95] 57 F.R.D. 165 (Oct. 16, 1972).

required to decide issues of fact upon which choice of law depends, when that choice may determine decisions on motions to sever and to transfer. A recent Second Circuit opinion, *Marra v. Bushee*,[96] seemed to suggest that a jury was needed. Weinstein ruled the other way, making the assumption that "[h]ad the Court of Appeals had the benefit of full briefs and argument, we doubt that it would have stated the jury favoring rule so broadly."[97] He then held that a jury was not necessary, that a federal court might resolve preliminary issues of fact.[98] In his oral history, Weinstein commented that the Court of Appeals "were so wrong [in *Marra*] I ignored them."[99]

Weinstein's final opinion in the litigation dealt with choice of law issues regarding severance and transfer.[100] This was his first brush with the problem of trying to apply a single substantive rule in a mass tort consolidation.[101] The case had been brought in New York because the industry trade association maintained an office in the state. However, the association's activities in the state had been relatively limited, although the state was the locus for the decision that each explosive cap would not be marked.

Applying New York choice of law analysis—an area of the law heavily shaped by Stanley Fuld—Weinstein held that New York would not apply its own law on the question of joint liability. Those states where the accidents had taken place had a considerable interest. Still, to the extent that the blasting industry operated in unison on safety matters, it did so on a national basis. Weinstein stated that the choice of law analysis of the time was inadequate to determine a single determinative state law. That would have to be done by the Congress or uniform state legislation.[102] In the meantime, the case should be handled in the states which had the interest. He severed the actions and transferred each of the cases to the federal district court where the accident had taken place.[103] The remaining claims remained in the Eastern District.

Thus, in *Hall* and *Chance* Weinstein had created the doctrine of industry-wide liability where the manufacturer was not known in individual cases, disregarded possible Second Circuit authority on choice-of-law matters, and wrestled with difficult choice of law analysis in determining the state law to apply where plaintiffs, defendants, and the place of injury were diverse.

---

[96] 447 F.2d 1282 (2d Cir.1971).

[97] *Chance v. E.I. du Pont de Nemours*, 57 F.R. D. 165, 168 (1972).

[98] *Id.* at 169.

[99] Weinstein Oral History, at 199.

[100] *Chance v. E.I. du Pont de Nemours & Co.*, 371 F. Supp. 439 (Jan. 23, 1974).

[101] Weinstein Oral History, at 279. He had been, he said later, "thinking about it (the jurisdictional issue) for a long time and *Chance* . . . was a catalyst for my coming to firm conclusions about it." Weinstein Oral History, at 253, 256.

[102] *Chance*, 371 F. Supp. at 448.

[103] *Id.* at 449–51.

CONSTITUTIONAL CASES

The three most important constitutional cases Weinstein dealt with in his 1967–1977 decade on the bench were *Fiallo v. Levy*,[104] *Goldfarb v. Secretary of Health, Welfare, & Education*,[105] and *Kramer v. Union Free School District #15*.[106] They were all cases in which Weinstein was part of a three-judge district court.[107] In two of the three, the position he took was sustained by the U.S. Supreme Court.

Fiallo involved differential statutory treatment of the alien parents of illegitimate children. Unwed biological mothers and their children were spared from restrictive, nonnumerical immigration quotas and labor certification requirements, while unwed biological fathers and their illegitimate children were excluded by the Act's definition of parent and child. The majority of the three-judge district court, in an opinion written by Leonard Moore, held that such a classification came within Congress's exceptionally broad powers to make rules for the admission of aliens and held that the legislative classification was not patently unreasonable.

Weinstein saw it differently: "The Constitutional road to equality of the sexes is open to men as well as women," he wrote.[108] This statute discriminated between male and female parents and between legitimate and illegitimate children. Such a congressional classification did not escape traditional constitutional scrutiny "merely because it is set in alienage legislation."[109] For Weinstein, each of the plaintiffs— fathers and their children—was being "deprived of a critical part of his life" without due process.[110]

"Courts now recognize," Weinstein wrote, that "unwed fathers, like mothers often have strong ties of affection to their illegitimate children and desire a continuing relationship with them."[111] However, the Supreme Court did not agree with him, affirming the majority opinion of the three-judge district court by a vote of 6–3, resting on the broad deference the judiciary gives Congress over the admission of aliens.[112]

---

[104] 406 F. Supp. 162 (Nov. 28, 1975: *Moore*-Bramwell/*JBW*) (Equal Protection/Legitimacy). *See also* Weinstein Oral History, at 275.

[105] 396 F. Supp. 308 (June 17, 1975: *PC*: JBW-Judd-Moore©) (Equal Protection/Gender). *See* Weinstein Oral History, at 278.

[106] 282 F. Supp. 70 (Jan. 30, 1968: *Moore*-Bartels/*JBW*) (Equal Protection/Voting). *See* Weinstein Oral History, at 76.

[107] At the time of these three cases, Congress required the convening of three-judge district courts in several categories of cases including cases in which the constitutionality of federal statutes were at issue. At the time of the three cases discussed here, the decisions of three-judge district courts were subject to direct appeal to the U.S. Supreme Court.

[108] *Id.* at 168, 169.

[109] *Fiallo v. Levy*, 406 F. Supp. 162 at 170.

[110] *Id.* at 169.

[111] *Id.* at 172.

[112] *Fiallo v. Bell*, 430 U.S. 787 (1976). The case would be superseded by statute. *Miller v. Albright*, 523 U.S. 420 (1998).

Goldfarb v. Secretary of Health, Welfare, & Education[113] dealt with gender discrimination in the distribution of Social Security survivor's benefits. Under the existing law, a wife received Social Security benefits automatically upon the death of her husband, while under the reverse scenario, the husband received benefits from his wife's death only if he had received one-half of his support from his spouse. The three-judge district court upon which Weinstein sat held that the resolution of the case—that there was gender discrimination—was dictated by a recent Supreme Court decision, *Weinberger v. Wiesenfeld*.[114] Weinstein joined Judd in a two-column decision. Ruth Bader Ginsburg, arguing in the Supreme Court for the plaintiff, prevailed 5–4.[115]

Kramer v. Union Free School District #15 involved a section of the New York education law which limited voters in a school district election to those who owned property in the district or had a district school child permanently residing in his/her home or who were lessees in the district (although the spouses of the latter could not vote). A childless resident who lived with his renting parents sued, claiming violation of equal protection. Before Weinstein took the bench, Chief Judge Justice Joseph C. Zavatt denied the motion to convene a three-judge district court and dismissed the claim.[116] A petition for writ of mandamus to the Supreme Court to direct the convoking of a three-judge court was denied.[117] However, a panel of the Court of Appeals, rendering three opinions, reversed and remanded.[118]

A three-judge district court made up of Leonard Moore, John R. Bartels, and Weinstein then sat to decide the merits of the constitutional issue. Moore and Bartels held that states may require that those seeking to vote on school policy must have a direct interest at stake in the issues to be decided:

> . . . schools are erected and operated primarily for the education of children, and parents and those closely allied to the community by leases or property ownership are obviously the most interested and affected.[119]

Weinstein dissented, finding the statute honeycombed with "arbitrary and constitutionally indefensible distinctions."[120] He stated that "the right to vote on important governmental issues may not be denied to a citizen with intellectual and moral capacity who meets prescribed reasonable age and residence requirements."[121] Placing the

---

[113] 396 F. Supp. 308 (June 17, 1975: *PC*: JBW-Judd-*Moore*©).

[114] 420 U.S. 636 (1975). *See also Frontiero v. Richardson*, 411 U.S. 677 (1973).

[115] *Califano v. Goldberg*, 430 U.S. 199, 206 (1977).

[116] 259 F. Supp. 164 (May 10, 1966), *rev'd*, 379 F.2d 491 (2d Cir. 1967).

[117] Davis v. Union Free School District No. 7, 385 U.S. 807 (1966).

[118] *Kramer v. Union Free Sch. Dist. No. 15*, 379 F.2d 491 (2d Cir. 1967: *Hays-Kauf*©/*Lumb*).

[119] *Kramer v. Union Free Sch. Dist. No. 15*, 282 F. Supp. 70, 75 (Jan. 30, 1968).

[120] *Id.* at 75, 82.

[121] *Id.* at 75, 78.

case in the social, political, and economic milieu in which the challenged statute operated:

> Disallowance of the franchise in school board elections is a denial of equal power to control the expenditures of a major portion of locally raised funds and a substantial amount of state and federal money; it is a refusal of a voice in the administration of adult education, recreation, library and cultural enrichment programs which play an important role in the daily lives of citizens of voting age; it is a preclusion of effective participation in the decisions which determine the character and quality of the local community. It is, in short, a deprivation of one of the basic incidents of citizenship.[122]

The Supreme Court reversed the three-judge court by a vote of 5–3, thus striking down the limitation on voting.[123] In one of his last opinions, Chief Justice Earl Warren applied "exacting scrutiny" and held that the challenged statute had not been sufficiently narrowly tailored.

FIRST AMENDMENT CASES

Throughout his career, Weinstein has been a staunch friend to the First Amendment. During his first decade on the bench, he encountered a number of interesting First Amendment issues.

Weinstein was reversed in a case where he invalidated a $5 fee imposed by New York City for granting a permit to use a sound amplification device for addressing the public. The administrative cost to the city for issuing each permit – at least six forms were required – was more than ten dollars. The fee was challenged by the U.S. Labor Party. Weinstein held the fee unconstitutional. Rather than relying on a line of Supreme Court cases validating such fees where the amount of the fee was reasonably related to the "expense incident to the administration of the act,"[124] Weinstein rested on a line of cases declaring such fees unconstitutional as a "tax" on the exercise of a constitutional right.[125] He emphasized that what might be a relatively small fee by major party standards might cut off access to electoral politics for a minor party. "Even seemingly minor limits on the extent of political debate," he wrote, "must be subject to the strictest scrutiny."[126] He concluded:

> If a bureaucratic system is needed to protect the rights of the majority without inhibiting those of the minority, the question is who should pay for that bureaucracy.

---

[122] *Id.* at 75, 76.
[123] *Kramer v. Union Free Sch. Dist. No. 15*, 395 U.S. 621 (1969).
[124] *See, e.g., Cox v. State of New Hampshire*, 312 U.S. 569 (1941).
[125] *See, e.g., Murdock v. Commonwealth of Pennsylvania*, 319 U.S. 105 (1943).
[126] *United States Labor Party v. Codd*, 391 F. Supp. 920, 923 (Mar. 11, 1975).

It is the majority that appears to wish the protection so that there is no unfairness in paying the cost.[127]

In a very brief opinion, the Court of Appeals reversed, holding that a fee representing less than the actual cost of the municipal service was constitutional in the absence of proof that the payment of even this modest fee was beyond the reach of the political party.[128]

In 1968, two years before the landmark Supreme Court case of *Goldberg v. Kelly*,[129] Weinstein held that a decision not to consider a high school humanities teacher for tenure, allegedly because of his activities with the teachers' union, violated his constitutional rights. In a striking anticipation of *Goldberg*, Weinstein cited, as the Supreme Court would, a seminal law review article by Yale Professor Charles Reich.[130] Weinstein wrote:

Whether we state the matter in traditional terms—that government largess is a property right within the meaning of the Fourteenth Amendment . . . or whether we say that to deprive a government employee of his job for exercising constitutionally protected rights, is to deprive him of the liberty guaranteed by that Amendment, or whether we merely reason that all government action with respect to its employees must meet the standards imposed by the Amendment, our Constitution is the same, the federal government requires every level of government to afford non-discriminatory and fair treatment, both substantively and procedurally, to all its employees.[131]

Although Weinstein's decision broke new legal ground for protection of probationary teachers and expanded the scope of academic freedom, the plaintiff in the case still lost because he was not able to establish as a matter of fact that he had been denied tenure because of his union activity.[132]

---

[127] *Id.* at 924.

[128] *United States Labor Party v. Codd*, 527 F.2d 118 (2d Cir. 1975: *Gurfein*-Fein-Mans).

[129] 397 U.S. 254 (1970).

[130] Charles Reich, *The New Property*, 73 YALE L.J. 733 (1964).

[131] *Albaum v. Carey*, 283 F. Supp. 3, 9 (Mar. 15, 1968).

[132] *Albaum v. Carey*, 310 F. Supp. 594 (Dec. 18, 1969). A three-judge district court (Moore, Bartels, and Weinstein) dismissed the case holding that, although Albaum "was a devoted, highly skilled and imaginative teacher, he had difficulties in developing new programs and in carrying out school policies because of substantial and continuing disagreements with administrators and supervisors." *Id.* at 596. Nothing Albaum said or did in connection with labor negotiations had contributed to the decision.

    See also Krawez v. Stans, 306 F. Supp. 1230 (Dec. 3, 1969), where two students had been thrown out of the U.S. Merchant Marine Academy for admitting that they had been using marijuana, even though they had been assured by Academy officials that, if they spoke freely to federal narcotics agents, nothing would be used against them. Nevertheless, they were expelled after a hearing in which they were not represented by counsel. Weinstein ordered their reinstatement on a contract theory, refusing to defer to the expertise of the Academy administrators because the administrative record was inadequate. One other interesting

Weinstein dissented when sitting with a three-judge district court in *Mildner v. Gulotta*, an attack on the procedures used in New York State to discipline attorneys. The majority dismissed the complaint under the abstention doctrine. In his twenty-eight-page dissenting opinion (preceded by a table of contents), Weinstein argued that the attorney disciplinary system was unconstitutional on due process and equal protection grounds and suggested alternatives to the state's procedures which could be applied prospectively.[133] The Supreme Court affirmed the panel majority without opinion.[134]

CRIMINAL CASES

Criminal cases generally are more visible than civil cases. This was true during Weinstein's first decade on the bench, even though drug offenses were not yet dominating district court calendars, prosecutions of organized crime were relatively infrequent, and sentencing was more individualized. Throughout his career, Weinstein has eloquently enforced the Fourth Amendment and resisted efforts by prosecutors to achieve preventive detention by denying bail. Influenced by Stanley Fuld, he has employed the principles of *mens rea* and the Rule of Lenity[135] to protect criminal defendants. Weinstein has taken petitions for *habeas corpus* from state prisoners and Section 2255 motions by federal prisoners to vacate their sentences or release them as a result of constitutional errors with great seriousness. His deep concern about sentencing is the subject of Chapter 8.

Weinstein had relatively few organized crime cases during this decade.[136] Such cases would greatly increase after passage of the Racketeer Influenced and Corrupt Organizations Act of 1970 (RICO) and with the growing effectiveness of federal strike forces—specialized crime prosecutorial offices.[137]

First Amendment decision from this period was *Koppel v. Levine*, 347 F. Supp. 456 (Aug. 10, 1972), dealing with the impounding by school authorities of a student literary magazine allegedly "obscene."

[133] *Mildner v. Gulotta*, 405 F. Supp. 182, at 201, 227, 228–29 (Oct. 9, 1975: Neahen-Moore(c)/Weinstein).

[134] *Levin v. Gulotta*, 425 U.S. 901 (1976). *Apicella v. McNeil Labs*. 66 F.R.D. 78 (Feb. 24, 1975) raised an issue that Weinstein would often deal with in his career—that of one or more parties of a law to try to prevent information used in the litigation from being made public. *See Chapter 6*.

[135] In construing an ambiguous criminal statute, the court should resolve the ambiguity in favor of the defendant.

[136] Weinstein's first "mob" case was *United States v. Schipani*, 293 F. Supp. 156 (Nov. 8, 1968). *See* Weinstein Oral History, at 108. The Court of Appeals affirmed his refusal to dismiss the indictment of Carmine Persico, who later became head of the Colombo family. *See United States v. Persico*, 425 F.2d 1375 (2d Cir. 1970: Hays-Moore-Fein). Persico had been tried five times in the Eastern District of New York. Weinstein also wrote for the Court of Appeals in 1975 in *In re Grand Jury Subpoena of Alphonse Persico*, 522 F.2d 41 (2d Cir. 1975: JBW-Smith-Timb.). Alphonse Persico, too, would head the Colombo family.

[137] A Weinstein opinion written when sitting with the Court of Appeals upheld the power of the strike forces to effectively prosecute crime. *See In re Grand Jury Subpoena of Alphonse Persico*, 522 F.2d 41 (2d Cir. 1975: JBW-Smith-Timbers).

Weinstein heard a number of cases involving police misconduct, cases that, as Judge Walter Mansfield put it in an opinion affirming Weinstein, presented "a sordid picture of police extortion and misconduct."[138] The most prominent of these cases involved Frank King, a New York City detective who was linked to the theft of four hundred pounds of the "French Connection" heroin seized in 1962. Weinstein sentenced King to five years for income tax evasion. He would have given him twelve years, if the sentence could have been accumulated. Weinstein commented that "[t]he whole thing was a corrupt operation from beginning to end."[139]

Weinstein had one major political trial, that of Joann Chesimard (Assata Shakur) and a co-defendant who were tried for a bank robbery in Queens on August 23, 1971, the purpose of which seems to have been to fund the radical Black Liberation Army. Weinstein recalls Shakur as "a troublesome defendant." He wrote:

> The case was an extremely difficult one. The defendant herself was hostile both to her attorney and to the court. Only after many days of patient consultation with the defendant was it possible to conduct hearings and a trial in an orderly way.[140]

He kept order by allowing the defendant relatively broad rein to make political statements (though not allowing the case to be tried as a "black liberation" case), by not permitting her to be referred to under her original name (Chesimard), and by making it quite evident that he would exclude her from the courtroom, if she continued to be obstreperous. He told Shakur that she would be in contempt, if she refused to submit to photographs taken posing at the same angles as the bank photograph, something the prosecution needed.[141] Weinstein reflected in 1993 that:

> I do think now that if somebody wants to use the criminal case as a platform and it's the only real opportunity that some of them will get for that publicity, some flexibility should be afforded the defendant.[142]

Although Weinstein was "convinced that she was guilty," the jury acquitted Shakur.[143]

---

[138] *United States v. McClean*, 528 F.2d 1250 (2d Cir. 1976: Mans -Medina-And), *aff'd*, 1975 JBW Op. NB 815 (1976).

[139] *See* excerpt from transcript in *United States v. King*, 75-Cr-973, JBW 1976 Op. NB 63, 100 (copy in possession of author). *See also* Gregory Wallance, Papa's Game 282 (1981); Weinstein Oral History, at 360–63.

[140] *United States v. Chesimard*, 75-Cr-797, 1977 OP. NB 46off. In her autobiography Shakur describes Weinstein as "a notorious racist pig." Her attorney called him "a dull asshole." Assata Shakur, Assata: An Autobiography 160, 161 (1983).

[141] *United States v. Jackson and Shakur*, 75-CR-5, Oct. 14, 1975.

[142] Weinstein Oral History, at 340.

[143] *Id.* at 335.

Jack Weinstein has always taken the Exclusionary Rule seriously. In 1969, Weinstein heard a case in which two customs officers had opened a package mailed from Switzerland and found twelve illegally imported gold coins. When a second package was opened, it yielded fifteen gold coins. Four weeks later, customs agents with probable cause came to the defendant's apartment, placed him under arrest, advised him of his constitutional rights, and threatened to search his entire apartment unless he revealed where his coins were kept. He did so, and more coins were seized.

Weinstein upheld the opening of the mail, holding that "[a] quick and expeditious method of examining people and goods entering the country is essential if customs regulations and laws against smuggling are to be enforced without undue embarrassment and delay to travelers and without clogging mail and other conduits of goods from abroad."[144] While Weinstein held the search of the mail was constitutional, he found that the defendant's arrest appeared to have been a pretext for the search of his apartment. Weinstein excluded evidence gained from the warrangless search because the government had ample time and basis for obtaining the search warrant.[145]

In *United States v. Tarlowski*, a taxpayer was criminally prosecuted for failure to file income tax returns. During his hearing at the Internal Revenue Service (IRS), the man's accountant was asked to leave the room. The IRS special agent then gave some *Miranda* warnings. A second, somewhat similar incident occurred several years later. The defendant, poorly educated and unaware that he might be prosecuted criminally, was, Weinstein held, the target of a deliberate effort to obtain information while leaving him in ignorance of the seriousness of his case. Weinstein held that no statutory authorization permitted the decision of the Special Agent to exclude a man in whom the defendant reposed trust and confidence. The Special Agent's conduct rose to a violation of due process because a representative of the federal government may not, at his own behest, limit the right of an individual to demand the presence of others during an interrogation.[146] Weinstein said later, "This seemed to me to go far beyond what the civilized person would think as suitable."[147] The motion to suppress was granted.

Weinstein's most important Fourth Amendment opinion involved the constitutionality of the antihijacking system the government then used in airports.[148] His opinion spanned twenty-five pages in the Federal Supplement. The antihijacking system employed included warning signs, the use of a hijacker profile, a magnetometer (metal detection device), interviews by airlines personnel, a U.S. marshal, and a frisk. Testimony on the secret hijacker "profile" was given *in camera* with the defendant's lawyer present, but not the defendant.

---

[144] *United States v. Sohnen*, 298 F. Supp. 51, 54 (Mar. 10, 1969).

[145] *Id.* at 56.

[146] *United States v. Tarlowski* , 305 F. Supp. 112 (Aug. 4, 1969).

[147] Weinstein Oral History, at 130.

[148] *United States v. Lopex*, 328 F. Supp. 1077 (May 14, 1971).

Weinstein was impressed that in 6 percent of the frisks a weapon was discovered as well as by the fact that only one-tenth of all passengers screened were actually frisked.[149] He concluded that "contraband seized as a result of a properly circumscribed investigatory frisk predicated on information generated by a well administered federal hi-jacking system is admissible in evidence." He found that "measured against the air traveling population as a whole, the method is highly effective in narrowing the group which need particular attention."[150] He made clear that he was not deciding at that time "whether in the absence of some prior indication of danger, the government may validly require any citizen to pass through an electronic device which probes beneath his clothing and effects to reveal what he carries with him."[151] Nevertheless, in the case before him Weinstein threw out the evidence because it was based in part on an improper ethnic criterion and on individual judgment. The system he had approved had survived constitutional scrutiny only "by its careful adherence to absolute objectivity and neutrality."[152] In the decision, Weinstein stated that "[e]ven the state secret privilege may not be utilized in a way that will deny a defendant constitutional rights."[153]

Sentencing

The most controversial sentence Weinstein imposed in 1976 was given to Eugene Hollander, one of the two most visible defendants in the New York nursing home scandals of the mid-1970s (the other was Bernard Bergman, who was sentenced in the Southern District of New York by Weinstein's Columbia colleague, Marvin Frankel). After journalists had unearthed appalling conditions in nursing homes, state and federal prosecutions followed.

Hollander, who had been defrauding the federal government, pled guilty to filing a false statement with a federal agency. Hollander was a puzzling and tragic case. He was an observant Orthodox Jew, a survivor of Auschwitz, married to another Auschwitz survivor. Although he became wealthy, Hollander was a workaholic, who worked sixteen to eighteen hours a day. Committing fraud and profiting from the wretched conditions of his nursing homes, he appears to have given away much of the money he made in non–tax deductible charitable contributions. Sixty-eight years old, he had irreversible heart disease and was suffering from depression.

---

[149] *Id.* at 1084.

[150] *Id.*

[151] *Id.* at 1100.

[152] *Id.* at 1101.

[153] *Id.* at 1089. In *United States v. Marti,* 1970 op. NB op. 5, Weinstein denied a motion to suppress jewelry seized by customs agents under the "border search" exception to the warrant requirement.
    The right to a speedy trial was another conspicuous civil liberties problem during this period. *See United States v. Colitto,* 319 F. Supp. 1077 (Nov. 9, 1970). Although this was a period during which the "War on Drugs" began, Weinstein heard few drug cases of interest.

At the sentencing hearing, after Hollander's rabbi testified about the horrors Hollander had lived through, Weinstein asked: "As a rabbi, is there any way you know of for me to punish the bad Hollander without hurting the good Hollander?" Weinstein pointed out that others he sentenced also came from social situations that are "just terrible, horrible."[154] Weinstein ordered Hollander to divest himself of all connections, direct or indirect, with any nursing home. He sentenced him to the Manhattan Correctional Center on week nights for six months or as long as was necessary to divest himself of those connections. He was also required to make restitution for all his illegally obtained assets.[155]

Weinstein and State Supreme Court Justice Milton Mollen, who had sentenced Hollander in state court, were sharply attacked in the *Congressional Record* by Representative and Mayor-to-be Ed Koch.[156] Professing his high regard, Koch sent a copy of the criticism to Weinstein, hoping that it would not affect their relationship. Weinstein responded by writing: "I am never upset by anything you say since your judgment is much admired by me." Weinstein added, however, that the other Eastern District judges had agreed with the sentence and that there was blame enough in the nursing home scandal to include the public officials who permitted those conditions and even for the "children of those in nursing homes" who failed to visit their parents and even for Koch and himself. He added that "it would be most helpful if Congress would give its attention to providing appropriate facilities in our metropolitan area."[157]

The Kahane Case

During this period, the federal courts were hearing far more cases brought by prisoners—applications for resentencing, *habeas corpus* petitions and civil rights (Section 1983) actions—than ever before. Weinstein also handled litigation involving conditions in the Brooklyn House of Detention and the Suffolk County jail.

The prisoner case that gained the widest attention involved a right-wing Jewish leader, Rabbi Meir Kahane, whom Weinstein had sentenced in 1971 for conspiracy to violate the Federal Firearms Act after Kahane had pleaded guilty to attempting to make a bomb. After a crowd of Orthodox Jews held an all night vigil in the park across from the courthouse, Weinstein sentenced Kahane to five years' probation. There had been no proof that Kahane's activities had led to any physical damage, although there was some reason to believe that his rhetoric had influenced others to engage in violence. At sentencing, Weinstein warned Kahane not to become involved with guns

---

[154] *United States v. Hollander*, 75-CR-525 (May 4, 1976), 1976 Op. NB #6, at 12.

[155] *Id.* at 19ff. *See also* NEW YORK TIMES, April 23, 1981, at A1, B1.

[156] Cong. Rec., H4624 (daily ed. May 19, 1976); E3021 (June 2, 1976).

[157] Letters from Edward I. Koch to Jack B. Weinstein, May 20, 1976; Jack B. Weinstein to Edward I. Koch, June 1, 1976; Edward I. Koch to Jack B. Weinstein, June 7, 1976; Jack B. Weinstein to Edward I. Koch, June 9, 1976 (copies in possession of author).

or explosives. He told him: "In this country, at this time, it is not permissible to substitute the bomb for the book as the symbol of Jewish manhood."[158]

Later, Kahane was informed in more detail that he was to have nothing to do directly or indirectly, with weapons anywhere in the world, most particularly in Israel. However, Kahane violated his probation and was held in prison in Israel, and returned to the United States where he was prosecuted for violating probation and sentenced to one year in prison.

In his sentence, Weinstein directed that Kahane "be placed in an institution and in a setting so that he can obtain . . . kosher foods [and comply with] other religious requirements that he may reasonably have."[159] When Kahane was about to be transferred to prison, he alleged and the government confirmed, that, under its long-standing practice, it planned to deny him kosher food. Kahane then sued.

Almost twenty years later, Weinstein recalled that he "had a lot of fun" with his opinion "going into the background of Kasruth."[160] Because of the erosion of the "hands-off doctrine," under which courts had deferred to prison officials, Weinstein's decision was not difficult to make, particularly because there was an analogy to cases involving Muslim prisoners. Weinstein "found" that Jewish dietary laws were central to Orthodox Judaism. Stating a principle Weinstein would often repeat, he declared "[a] person does not lose his basic humanity and constitutional rights because he has been convicted or is serving a term in prison." Where the government has to take control over people's lives, as in prison, a niche has been carved into the Establishment Clause to require the government to afford opportunities for worship. The court would correct the sentence, if the government did not cooperate and continued to infringe upon Kahane's constitutional rights.[161] Weinstein's *Kahane* opinion was "flavored from beginning to end with a concern that the government's asserted need for uniformity not be permitted to outweigh the privilege of free exercise of religion of those whose lives have come wholly under federal control."[162]

The Court of Appeals remanded Kahane's case for consideration in light of its holding in July 1975 that a judge of the Southern District of New York in a similar situation had lacked jurisdiction.[163] The hearing before Weinstein on remand was a procedural tour de force in which the judge guided the attorneys through a labyrinthine procedural path too complex to fully explain here. At the hearing, the status of the parties was restyled; the claim for review was amended; there was a generous reading of jurisdiction; a pending action was dismissed; venue was found; issues not raised by the pleadings were treated as if they had had been raised; Rule 21 dealing with misjoinder

---

[158] *United States v. Kahane*, 1975 Op. NB Op. 2 (Feb. 20, 1975); 396 F. Supp. 687, 689 (May 7, 1975).

[159] *Id.* at 689.

[160] Weinstein Oral History, at 342.

[161] *Kahane, supra* note 158, at 690, 695, 698.

[162] Elvin L. Benton, *Prison Warden in a Kosher Pickle*, 71 LIBERTY (March–April 1976) n.p.

[163] *United States v. Huss (Hoss) and Smilow*, 520 F.2d 598 (2d Cir. July 25, 1975: *Gibbons*-Gurfein-Meskill©).

and nonjoinder or parties was considered; relief was granted although it had not been requested in the pleadings; and a writ of *habeas corpus* filed and consolidated with the pending case. The upshot was that, although the government preferred to incarcerate Kahane in the Allenwood prison, since it would not provide him with kosher food there, Kahane was able to stay at the Community Treatment Center in Manhattan, from which he could leave from time to time for prayer and to procure Kosher meals.[164]

The Second Circuit affirmed though it modified Weinstein's order to give the government more discretion in the kosher diet case[165] and Weinstein finally transferred Kahane's case, on the government's motion, to the Middle District of Pennsylvania where the Allenwood Prison was.

SCHOOL CASES AND CIVIL RIGHTS

New York City had the nation's largest school system with one million students, 60,000 teachers, 1000 public schools, and a $3 billion budget.[166] It was also the sixth most segregated city in the nation for black schoolchildren.[167] By the time Weinstein reached the bench, the public schools had become a major subject of political controversy in New York City.[168] Tough and politically unpopular decisions were left for judges to resolve, but the courts lacked electoral legitimacy as well as the technical expertise and staff resources necessary to keep track of a large bureaucracy.[169] Federal judges "sitting in a large northern city," Weinstein would write, "approached the legal problems in public education with a sense of inadequacy that often verges on despair."[170] The Eastern District court had a great many New York City school cases including those

---

[164] Hearing in *Kahane v. United States*, 75-C-624, Aug. 14, 1975, JBW 1975 Op. NB 798–827. There was another hearing on November 14, when it appeared that Kahane flouted the terms of his probation. *In the Matter of Kahane*, Hearing, Nov 14, 1975, 1975 JBW OP. NB. op. 24.

[165] *Kahane v. Carlson*, 527 F.2d 492 (1975: *Smith*-Kaufman-Friendly).

[166] Michael A. Rebell & Arthur R. Block, Equality and Education: Federal Civil Rights Enforcement in the New York City School System 69 (1988); Michael A. Rebell, *Jose P. v. Ambach: Special Education Reform in New York City*, *in* Justice And School Systems: The Role of the Courts in Education Litigation 25 at 29 (Barbara Flicker ed., 1990).

[167] Brief *Amicus Curiae* by Association of the Bar of City of New York In support of respondents, *Parents Involved in Community School Board v. Seattle School District No. 1*, U.S. (1979) (No. 65-908), at 8.

[168] Gary Orfield, *Unexpected Costs and Uncertain Gains of Dismantling of Desegregation*, *in* DISMANTLING DESEGREGATION: THE QUIET REVERSAL 73, 98 (Gary Orfield, Susan E. Eaton, & The Harvard Project on School Desegregation eds., 1996) [hereinafter ORFIELD, EASTON]. *See also* CHRIS McNICKLE, TO BE MAYOR OF NEW YORK 223ff (1993).

[169] Howard I. Kalodner, *Overview of Judicial Activism in Education Litigation*, *in* JUSTICE AND SCHOOL SYSTEMS, *supra* note 166, at 3,11 (hereinafter Kalodner, *Overview*); ORFIELD, EATON, *supra* note 168, at 349.

[170] Weinstein, *Equality, Liberty and the Public Schools*, 48 U. CIN. L. REV. 203 (1979).

with racial overtones because the headquarters of the New York City public schools system was then within its jurisdiction—indeed, a short walk from the courthouse. In Brooklyn, Weinstein was not the only judge to have New York City school cases, but his would have greater visibility than most because "he ran with them and they became bigger than they [otherwise] might have been."[171]

The first case before Weinstein, in the spring of 1969, was a class action against the New York City Board of Education and some of its officials on behalf of hundreds of students dismissed from Franklin Lane High School on January 27, 1969.

Franklin Lane was located in Brooklyn. It was primarily an African-American school with many white teachers. Terribly overcrowded, the school expelled some 670 students, who had been absent thirty days or more and had unsatisfactory academic records. Four hundred twelve of those students were seventeen years old and received no public education after their expulsion. Many of the others were receiving instruction at an "annex," which operated only three hours a day and gave no home work, examination, or grades.

The Board of Education asserted that the mass expulsion was an attempt to relieve overcrowded conditions. Although other schools in New York were equally overcrowded, such expulsions had taken place only at Franklin Lane. Weinstein said that, frustrated by the lack of discipline, school officials "decided to get rid of all of the kids they felt were interfering with the other children."[172] No procedures had been established to challenge the criteria for dismissal or their application to individual students.

An application for a temporary restraining order did not reach Weinstein until Friday, April 17. Weinstein "jumped right in as soon as it came to [his] attention" and acted aggressively. He recalls that he was "very upset because some of these kids had been out for three months, and I thought that the case had to be pushed as quickly as possible."[173] On his own motion, Weinstein ordered a hearing on the following Monday.

Weinstein held that the powers granted under Rule 23 of the Federal Rules of Civil Procedure were broad enough to permit the court to take action to protect the class beyond just giving notice to class members, particularly where a preliminary injunction or temporary restraining order had been sought.[174]

In order to learn the scope of the problem and the number of members of the class who were genuinely interested in continuing their education, Weinstein took an unusual step. He ordered the Board of Education to send a letter and questionnaire to each member of the class using franked envelopes supplied by the court.

---

[171] Weinstein Oral History, at 454; Jack B. Weinstein, *Equality, Liberty and the Public* Schools, 48 U. CIN. L. REV. 203 (1979); Interview of Jack B. Weinstein by Juan Williams, NPR News Interview, Thurgood Marshall: 50th Anniversary Brown v. Board of Education 27 (Nov. 20, 2003).

[172] Weinstein Oral History, at 110.

[173] Weinstein Oral History, at 112-13.

[174] *Knight v. Board of Ed.*, 48 F.R.D. 108, 112-13 (Apr. 21, 1969).

Nine days later, after hearing testimony from students, parents, teachers, and the principal and reading a report of his court-appointed panel of educational experts, Weinstein issued a preliminary injunction and findings of fact.[175] He found that: (1) decisions expelling the students had been approved by the highest authorities of the City and Board of Education; (2) the decisions were made at a time when there were serious threats of bodily injury to students and faculty; (3) it had become impossible to maintain discipline and control at Franklin Lane because of overlapping schedules, extreme overcrowding, and widespread truancy; and (4) there were insufficient educational facilities made available for the operation of high schools in New York City.

Weinstein held that the members of the plaintiff class had been denied their right to due process but that there had been no denial of equal protection. He ordered that: (1) all members of the plaintiff class who wanted a full daytime education be admitted to Franklin K. Lane or another appropriate high school; (2) specific efforts be made—including a summer makeup high school program—so that the plaintiffs could make up the work they had missed; and (3) any member of the plaintiff class who felt aggrieved by the failure of the Board of Education could seek a hearing with the court-appointed panel of experts.[176]

School Desegregation: The Mark Twain Case

The first New York City desegregation case to reach a federal court was the litigation before Weinstein involving the desegregation of Mark Twain Junior High School on Coney Island.[177] It was a class action brought on behalf of the children attending the school, one of six junior high schools in the district of Community Board 21 in South Brooklyn. The district stretched from Coney Island to Bensonhurst. The Mark Twain School was composed of 85 percent minority students. Five other junior high schools in the district were 65 percent white. The neighborhood of the Mark Twain School was largely made up of slums in which nonwhites lived. The rest of the district was predominantly white. The five other junior high schools in the district were 65 percent white.

The plaintiffs in the *Mark Twain* case argued that the local school board and the New York City Board of Education both had purposefully made Mark Twain a non-white school by making decisions which put whites in other schools and by refusing to adopt a plan that would have decreased the racial imbalance. The defendants argued that the segregated school was the result of residential segregation and white flight. Joined as third-party defendants were the federal, state, and city housing agencies

---

[175] *Knight v. Board of Ed*, 48 F.R.D. 115 (Apr. 30, 1969).

[176] When asked about the impact of the case thirty-four years later, Weinstein said he did not know whether the court intervention had made the school better or worse. Weinstein Oral History, at 115.

[177] *Hart v. Community School Bd.*, 383 F. Supp. 699 (Jan. 28, 1974).

responsible for urban renewal, whom, it was charged, had "dumped" low-income families on Coney Island.

Weinstein had known Coney Island "fairly well." He had often taken excursions there as a child with his family, and it had been part of his father's territory. However, when assigned the *Mark Twain* case, he had not been there for two decades. He immediately went out there with his clerk, Joan Wexler, to get a physical feel of the situation.[178] His opinion reflected his appreciation of the area:

> Broad sandy public bathing beaches and a wide boardwalk overlooking the ocean have been used by hundreds of thousands of people each summer for generations . . . . Sea breezes are still cooling in the summer and moderating in the winter. Fishing is pleasant off the pier . . . Walking the boardwalk and swimming is free [and] other physical attractions would seem to make this corner of New York an attractive place for children and their parents both to visit and live in.[179]

But, he added, "Much of Coney Island became one of the City's worst slums."[180]

A trial began in January 1973. In May, the plaintiffs sought preliminary relief—an order integrating the schools immediately—because of the delay caused by the trial. Weinstein denied the motion. The Court of Appeals remanded the appeal of denial of preliminary relief for findings of fact and conclusions of law.[181]

After a trial with thirty-nine witnesses (2471 pages of transcript), Weinstein held that the evidence demonstrated that Mark Twain was segregated and that illegal segregation in public housing was "partially" liable for helping to maintain segregation. Weinstein found that "a host of coordinated and uncoordinated actions by different governmental agencies had presented the school board with a junior high school almost entirely used by minorities in a predominantly white school district."[182]

In 1962, whites had comprised about 81 percent of Mark Twain's students. Ten years later, only 18 percent of its total enrollment was white.[183] By the fall of 1973, only 30.4 percent of all the students attending school in District 21 were nonwhite.[184] Further, the utilization rate of Mark Twain had dropped from 88 percent of capacity (1962) to 41 percent (1972) because of the "attrition" of white students.[185] This had happened

---

[178] The Weinstein Oral History devotes considerable space to the *Mark Twain* case. *See especially* at 278–95. *See also* NEW YORK SUN, July 9, 2007, at 4.

[179] *Hart v. Community School Bd.*, 383 F. Supp. 699, 709 (Jan. 28, 1974). *See* Weinstein Oral History, at 278ff.

[180] *Id.*

[181] *Hart v. Community School Bd.*, 487 F.2d 223 (2d Cir. 1974).

[182] Weinstein, Equality, Liberty, and the Public Schools, *supra* note 170, at 233.

[183] *Hatt v. Community School Bd.*, 383 F. Supp. 699, 711.

[184] *Id.* at 712–13.

[185] James J. Fishman, *The Limits of Remedial Power: Hart v. Community School Board 21, in* LIMITS OF JUSTICE: THE COURTS ROLE IN SCHOOL DESEGREGATION 115, 119 (Howard I. Kalodner & James J. Fishman eds., 1978) (hereinafter Fishman).

primarily because the school district had changed feeder patterns to Mark Twain so that graduates of predominantly white elementary schools were rezoned away from it.[186] Further, within the Mark Twain School there was a considerable amount of segregation based upon the equivalent of tracking.[187] New York City Board of Education officials had not taken strong action to force integration because of the well-founded fear that such action would cause white families with school-age children to move out of the district's integrated schools or even out of the district.[188] As Weinstein wrote, "[f]aced with the serious, urgent problem that Mark Twain is a severely racially imbalanced and under-utilized school, the Community Board and the Chancellor failed to act."[189]

Weinstein held that the [h]ousing and school patterns fed on each other.[190] Thus, the segregation had been "brought about partly through the ghettoization of the core of Coney Island", but also because white-middle class children had been deliberately zoned out of the school district. This enhanced segregative tendencies and led to gross underutilization of Mark Twain's physical facilities.[191]

Other decisions made at all levels of government also contributed substantially to city patterns of residential segregation. Nevertheless, even if segregation had resulted from a variety of causes, including housing, transportation, police, and parks, Weinstein stated that the answer still was to desegregate.[192] If the "schools cannot carry much of the burden of eliminating social and economic equality," Weinstein believed that "public schools remain, as classrooms in democracy, one of the primary institutions through which our society can promote interracial tolerance and understanding and, therefore, multi-racial harmony."[193]

For Weinstein, *Brown v. Board of Education* and subsequent cases had "touched the core of our constitutional ethos and must be construed with the breadth required of such fundamental pronouncements."[194]

Weinstein held that a school board which did not act to avoid racial segregation in its schools was itself causing or bringing about racial segregation. When racial characteristics determine place-of-residence, then the school board's use of a neighborhood or residential criterion for student assignment and school construction decisions, constitutes "a racial classification once removed."[195] "When residential segregation resulted from state action, then the school board's use of residential criterion constitutes

---

[186] *Id.* at 123.

[187] *Hart*, 383 F. Supp. 699, 713.

[188] *Id.* at 720.

[189] *Id.* at 721.

[190] *Id.* at 706.

[191] *Id.*

[192] *See also* JACK B. WEINSTEIN, INDIVIDUAL JUSTICE IN MASS TORT LITIGATION 92 (1995).

[193] *Hart*, 383 F. Supp. at 729.

[194] *Id.* at 732.

[195] *Id.* at 735.

'double discrimination.'"[196] Under the Fourteenth Amendment, school boards may not respond "to the fact and dilemma of segregation" with "indifference and inaction."[197]

Reading "an element of reasonableness" into the equation, Weinstein held that "the state must act to eliminate *de facto* racial imbalance unless it is clearly impracticable to do so."[198]

After holding that desegregation had to occur, Weinstein decided first to try voluntary cooperation among the parties for, as a general rule, desegregation plans generated by the parties were likely to be more effective.[199] He gave the school authorities a month (until March 1, 1974) to submit a detailed plan to eliminate the segregation, making clear to them that closing Mark Twain was not an option.[200] The plan was to ensure that the school would not deviate more than ten percent from the districtwide average of minority pupils in junior high and intermediate schools.[201] Tracking had to be sharply reduced. Students, parents, and the community had to be prepared for the change. Detailed programs to eliminate possible racial tension in Mark Twain had to be developed.

Weinstein's view of the *Mark Twain* litigation was that the totality of problems had to be attacked—education, housing, police, parks, and transportation.[202] He used the power of his court to involve a great variety of actors and institutions in the community.[203] Federal, state, and city housing authorities had to provide a joint plan to undo racial balance in publicly supported housing in Coney Island.[204] The Corporation Counsel, Police Commissioner, Metropolitan Transit Authority, and Parks Department were to be involved.[205] Weinstein was also looking for a plan which would involve the further physical development of Coney Island in ways that might attract a more varied population.

After the submission by the parties of a series of proposals, Weinstein postponed the deadline for desegregation from September 1974 to September 1975. Realizing that the court was "faced with a polycentric problem that cannot easily be resolved through a traditional court-room bound adjudicative process," Weinstein, in a supplemental opinion announced on April 2, 1974, appointed a special master to assist the parties

---

[196] *Id.* at 736.

[197] *Id.* at 737.

[198] *Id.* at 740.

[199] Committee on Education and the Law, *The Role of the Courts in Educational Policy Litigations*, 42 REC. ASS'N BAR N.Y. CITY 356 (1987) [hereinafter City Bar Committee Report]; Curtis J. Berger, *Away from the Court House and into the Field: The Odyssey of a Special Master*, 78 COLUM. L. REV. 707, 709 (1978).

[200] *Hart*, 383 F. Supp. at 756.

[201] *Id.* at 756.

[202] WEINSTEIN, INDIVIDUAL JUSTICE IN MASS TORT LITIGATION, *supra* note 193, at 92; Weinstein Oral History, at 203.

[203] Martha Minow, *Judge for the Situation: Judge Jack Weinstein, Creator of Temporary Administrative Agencies*, 97 COLUM. L. REV. 2010, 2012.

[204] *Hart*, 383 F. Supp. at 757.

[205] *Id.* at 758.

and the court in developing an appropriate and comprehensive remedy.[206] The special master he appointed was Professor Curtis J. Berger, his colleague on the Columbia Law School faculty and an expert in housing and community planning. Berger was to coordinate and evaluate remedial proposals, serve an investigatory function among the parties, and advise the court in technical areas. He was to "bridge the gap between the court as impartial arbiter of plans placed before it and advocates protecting their clients' positions that are often narrower than that of society at large."[207] The master's report was to include a comprehensive plan dealing not only with the elimination of the segregation of Mark Twain, but also with housing, nonresidential development, community social welfare, recreation, transportation, and protective facilities near the Coney Island neighborhood. Berger was given three months to provide the report to educate the judge.[208]

Weinstein's use of the special master was innovative. His appointment of Berger was intended largely to focus more attention to the housing part of the case. A bridge and buffer for Weinstein, Berger met with a great many people in order to learn all he could about community attitudes and the possibility of collaboration between different groups and government officials.[209] To Berger's surprise, Weinstein kept his special master at arm's-length, only speaking with him in open court or when counsel was present.[210]

Weinstein also held a number of public hearings. In dealing with the case, either he or the special master were in touch with parents, parents' groups, school officials, and federal, state, and city authorities including the mayor of New York City, the teachers' union, and religious leaders. One of the important insights that Weinstein gained from those hearings was that he would not be able to obtain approval from the African-American segment of the population for attempting to make Coney Island a fully integrated upper-class, middle-class, and lower-class community.[211]

Other opposition to Weinstein's first decision in the *Mark Twain* case began to build. Senator James Buckley of New York held hearings in Brooklyn, supposedly about anti-busing proposals before Congress, which turned into a forum to attack Weinstein's decision.[212] Weinstein allowed other opponents to intervene in the suit, granting an application by residents of the district with children in the public schools, who might have lost their public housing. He allowed a group which did not have children in

---

[206] *Hart*, 383 F. Supp. at 758.

[207] *Id.* at 764.

[208] Fishman, *supra* note 186, at 145.

[209] Berger, *supra* note 200, at 711ff.

[210] Berger, *supra* note 200, at 724. Of the role of the special master, Weinstein wrote: "The master acts to solidify the interest of a group that the court can deal with. He, she or they can also explain the court's role to the public during the litigation and build consensus and support for some solution. In effect, there is an attempt to create a new constituency." Jack B. Weinstein, *Litigation Seeking Changes in Public Behavior and Institutions*, 13 U.C. DAVIS L. REV. 231, 239 (1980).

[211] Weinstein Oral History, at 293.

[212] Fishman, *supra* note 186, at 146.

school, but which might have been adversely affected by the decision to participate in the litigation as an *amicus*.[213]

In the plan he submitted, Berger adopted and expanded a proposal of the community school board for a magnet school which would encourage white parents to send their children to Mark Twain by eliminating advanced instruction programs at the other schools in the district. If that wouldn't work, he offered an alternative plan for widespread busing.[214] However, only seventy-three double-spaced pages of Berger's report dealt specifically with the school. One hundred nine pages dealt with the neighborhood.[215] Berger offered a sweeping plan for the revitalization of Coney Island, a plan which would be bitterly attacked by City housing officials and by minority intervenors.

Berger commented wryly that his report served the certainly unintended purpose of educating a federal court on the difficulty, indeed impossibility, of directing neighborhood redevelopment. A consent decree would have involved the court and its surrogate (a special master) in what would have at least "meant a five-year involvement by the surrogate in 'every aspect of a massive real estate redevelopment from land acquisition and tenant relocation to the marketing of completed units.'"[216]

In the end, Weinstein issued a final order which was much more modest than he had anticipated.[217] Having become convinced that a federal judge could not practically oversee such a complex undertaking without political and economic resources available to him, he abandoned neighborhood renewal as a goal. The judge completely adopted Berger's magnet school plans, but ignored his housing proposals.[218]

Perhaps, as James J. Fishman wrote, Weinstein believed that, once he found liability, he could give impetus to various governmental agencies. But he had underestimated the difficulty of the housing problem and of instigating bureaucratic change. The district court was unable to generate enough political force.[219] While Weinstein said in retrospect that "consciously to some extent but mainly subconsciously, I was using this big master plan as a kind of stalking horse in order to threaten everybody and achieve a more modest but effective resolution,"[220] this may be a rationalization.

The plaintiffs and the community school board appealed. The Second Circuit upheld the findings about the school. It agreed that segregative intent can be inferred from

---

[213] Fishman, *supra* note 186, at 147. *See also* ROBERT M. COVER, OWEN F. FISS, JUDITH RESNIK, PROCEDURE 276, 290ff (1988).

[214] Fishman, *supra* note 186, at 147–49.

[215] Berger, *supra* note 200 at 726.

[216] *Id.* at 735–36.

[217] *Hart*, 383 F. Supp. 769. His order came down four days after the Supreme Court decided *Milliken v. Bradley*, 418 U.S. 717 (1974), which effectively made very ambitious judge-made resolution of Northern racial imbalance/segregation problems unlikely.

[218] Berger, *supra* note 200, at 733, 735, 736; Weinstein Oral History, at 285, 287.

[219] Fishman, *supra* note 186, at 162–63.

[220] Weinstein Oral History, at 288.

the foreseeable consequences of actions taken coupled with inaction in the face of ten-dered choices. It also upheld the use of magnet plans. However, the Second Circuit sharply criticized Weinstein:

> [The community school board] succeeded initially in getting the District Judge to convert a narrow issue, involving a single junior high school with a capacity of about 1,000 students into what could only become an issue so broad as to defy judicial competence, a matter which would require action by three governments, federal state and city, for a solution.[221]

The ultimate consent decree was the work of the parties.[222] The "modest but effec-tive resolution" the parties agreed upon was making Mark Twain into a magnet school with a balance of about 65 percent white and 35 percent minority. Mark Twain became one of the first magnet schools in the nation to result from a desegregation suit.[223]

Magnet schools have the potential to further desegregation and innovation,[224] but they may do more harm if extensive tracking is relied upon. And, even when the magnet schools work, as Weinstein has said, having one cannot magically erase years of racial prejudice and socio-economic discrepancies.[225] The closest student of the case has said that the court's resolve to integrate Mark Twain and Berger's adoption of a backup widespread busing plan "was a powerful impetus to make the plan work."[226] The scarce resources of District 21 were all poured into Mark Twain.[227]

Mark Twain turned out to be a success. The school itself was integrated with a mini-mum of community upheaval.[228] By 1983, with a student population that was 35 per-cent minority, Mark Twain led the city's junior high schools in reading scores.[229] By 1988, it was offering ten talent programs including microbiology, art, dance, mathe-matics, vocal music, and athletics.[230] The school was turning away two of every three applicants while maintaining its racial balance. The happy result would likely never have occurred without active court involvement.[231] Weinstein says that of the school cases he handled, *Mark Twain* "was the one success I had." "Kids [who] went through

---

[221] *Hart v. Community School Bd.*, 512 F.2d 37, 41 (2d Cir. 1975: *Gurfein*-Friendly-Timbers). *See* Jack B. Weinstein, *Equality, Liberty and the Public Schools: The Role of State Courts*, 1 CARDOZO L. REV. 343, 358 (1979).

[222] REBELL & BLOCK, *supra* note 166, at 163.

[223] Curtis J. Berger, *Jack Weinstein: The Fertile Septuagenarian*, 97 COLUM. L. REV. 1961, 1963 (1997).

[224] Kimberly C. West, A Desegregation Tool that Backfired: Magnet Schools and Classroom Segregation, 103 YALE L.J. 2567, 2569 (1993–1994).

[225] Jack B. Weinstein, *Education of Exceptional Children*, 12 CREIGHTON L. REV. 987, 1017 (1979).

[226] Fishman, *supra* note 186, at 159.

[227] *Id.* at 161.

[228] Fishman, *supra* note 186, at 162–63.

[229] NEW YORK TIMES, Feb. 22, 1983.

[230] NEW YORK TIMES, Nov. 10, 1988, at B17, B18.

[231] City Bar Committee Report, *supra* note 200, at 361.

that school over the years got a substantially better education than they otherwise would have. And everybody's morale was improved—both teachers and students."[232]

In 2007, the Supreme Court withdrew its support for continuing desegregation orders once the constitutional wrong had been cured.[233] Weinstein closed the case eight months later.[234]

ENVIRONMENTAL LAW

Threats to Long Island's fragile ecology have led to high visibility litigation in the Eastern District over the past four decades.

During his first decade on the bench, Weinstein heard one major environmental lawsuit,[235] yielding a decision that resonated in 2010. In the mid-1970s, the Nixon administration announced that it would lease ten million acres of seabed to oil companies for $1.3 billion, thus permitting oil drilling in the Baltimore Canyon area (sixty miles south of Long Island) and the George's Bank area (fifty miles southeast of Montauk Point). The following year, the Bureau of Land Management announced the selection of 154 tracts from that area. In May 1976, a four-volume environmental impact statement (EIS) was published and, on June 30, the Secretary of the Interior announced his intention to go forward with the leasing.

Within a matter of days, Nassau and Suffolk Counties and five Long Island towns, including Islip and Huntington, arguing that the National Environmental Protection Act (NEPA) had been violated, sued.[236] Since actual steps toward leasing were not imminent, Weinstein did not grant a preliminary injunction. But he denied the government's motion to dismiss, pointing out the potential damages to beaches, wetlands, the fishing industry, and tourist revenues as well as the potential to cause serious unemployment and pose a danger to the health of the inhabitants of Long Island.[237]

After hearings, Weinstein granted a preliminary injunction against the sale of leases, finding that the EIS had not adequately explored the possibility that state and local governments might bar pipelines on their shores and, therefore, make necessary the use of tankers, which generally spill far more oil than pipelines. The Second Circuit

---

[232] Weinstein Oral History, at 115.

[233] *Cmty. Schs. v. Seattle Sch. Dist.*, 551 U.S. 701 (2007).

[234] *Hart v. Cmty. Sch. Bd.*, 536 F. Supp. 2d 274 (Feb. 28, 2008). For other civil rights cases decided by Weinstein during this period, *see Boyd v. United States*, 345 F. Supp. 790 (June 7, 1972), discussed in *Boyd v. The Lefrak Organization & Life. Realty*, 509 F.2d 1110 (1975) [reviewing decision of another judge]; See also *Otero v. New York City Hous. Auth.* 354 F. Supp. 941 (Feb. 8, 1973), *rev'd* 484 F2d 1122 (1973: *Mans-Hays-Mull*). *See also* Weinstein Oral History, at 200ff.

[235] During this decade, there was an opening skirmish in the battle over the Shoreham Nuclear Reactor, which is discussed in Chapter 7. *See Lloyd Neck Harbor Study Group v. Seaborg*, 70-C-1253 (Apr. 2, 1971). *See* Weinstein Oral History, at 174ff.

[236] NEWSDAY, Oct. 15, 1975, at 5, 42; Weinstein Oral History, at 175ff, 274–75.

[237] Hearing of October 14, 1975, JBW Op. NB 1975, at 60 at 62–63.

stayed enforcement of the preliminary injunction and the Secretary accepted bids on ninety-three tracts within the sale area.[238]

After a trial, Weinstein again concluded that the requirements of NEPA had not been met and that the EIS was inadequate for a number of reasons.[239] The Court of Appeals, in an opinion written by Mansfield, administered one of the sharpest reversals given to Weinstein during his first decade on the bench. The appellate court employed a less deferential standard of review to Weinstein's determination, explaining that Weinstein's determination, that the EIS failed to contain sufficient information, was not related to testimonial credibility. Weinstein's decision was called "unrealistic,"[240] and his holding concerning the inadequacy of the EIS was characterized as "[a] more speculative exercise" than "can hardly be imagined."[241] The Court of Appeals overturned Weinstein's finding that "the economic costs and benefits of the planned action were seriously and grossly misrepresented by the Bureau of land Management." His holding that the EIS failed to consider the alternative of separating exploration of the tracts from production was called "a clear error." He was chided for sitting as a super-agency empowered to substitute scientific expertise, presented to it de novo for that considered by the agency[242] and criticized for implying bad faith on the part of the Secretary.[243] The Second Circuit stated that the court [Weinstein] "appears to have allowed its views regarding the substance of the Secretary's proposal to becloud its understanding of its reviewing function . . . and its adoption *sua sponte* of grounds for inadequacy that was not suggested by the parties."[244]

Weinstein did not accept the rebuke passively. Although the Second Circuit had granted costs on appeal against some of the plaintiffs, Weinstein declined to be bound by the court's "unexplained decision in this matter" and refused to allow trial costs against Nassau and Suffolk Counties and environmental interest groups.[245]

"MAKING LAW"

Weinstein's *first* audacious attempt to make law occurred less than a year after he assumed the bench. In *Spindel v. Spindel*,[246] a wife sought a declaratory judgment

---

[238] County of Suffolk v. Secretary of the Interior, 562 F2d 1368, 1374 (Aug. 27, 1977: *Mansfield*-Smith-Palmieri).

[239] Weinstein Oral History, at 176.

[240] *County of Suffolk,* at 1387, 1388–89.

[241] *Id.* at 1378, 1379. As a result of disqualifications, the Court of Appeals panel was made up of only one Court of Appeals judge, Walter Mansfield, Edmund L. Palmieri from the Southern District of New York, and Russell Evans Smith of the District of Montana.

[242] *Id.* at 1383.

[243] *Id.* at 1387, 1388–89.

[244] *Id.* at 1390.

[245] *County of Suffolk v. Secretary of the Interior,* 76 F.R.D. 469 (Oct. 26, 1977).

[246] 283 F. Supp. 797 (Apr. 11, E.D.N.Y. April 11, 1968).

that her Mexican divorce was invalid. Although the parties were before the court in a federal diversity action, the husband argued that the federal courts lacked subject matter competence because the case fell within the "domestic relations" exception to diversity jurisdiction. At the time, there was a long-standing judicially wrought limitation that the federal courts would not entertain domestic relations cases. That exception, originating in dicta in an 1859 Supreme Court case, *Barber v. Barber*,[247] was rooted in an understanding of the jurisdiction of the English courts of chancery, which the *dissenting* justices of the Supreme Court stated did not extend to the subject of divorce and alimony.

Weinstein held that his court had subject matter jurisdiction over the *Spindel* case. In his opinion, Weinstein went back not only to Article III of the Constitution and the 1789 Judiciary Act, but also inquired into the accuracy of the interpretation of the actions of the English courts of chancery. By looking at a number of British and American cases, he undermined the view that there had not been jurisdiction over divorce. He also pointed to Supreme Court cases arising on appeal from territorial courts in which "the Court said federal courts lacked jurisdiction, but then *acted* as if they possessed judicial power over divorce cases."[248]

Weinstein rejected the view that the federal courts were barred from entertaining not only actions involving matrimonial status, but also from hearing any cases concerned with "domestic relations" in the broad sense of the term, calling that broad interpretation "unwarranted by the Constitution, any statute, holding of the Supreme Court or current jurisdictional theory."[249]

Weinstein not only stated that the historical reasons relied upon by the Supreme Court were "not convincing," but also discussed or cited decisions from the eighteenth and nineteen centuries from the English Court of Common Pleas, Court of Chancery, and House of Lords as well as nineteenth-century treatises to demonstrate that those courts had decided questions of marital status incidental to the exercise of then established jurisdiction; that the chancery gave the ecclesiastical court substantial assistance in matters involving matrimonial status, that Chancery would, in effect, function as a domestic relations tribunal if some independent basis for the exercise of its jurisdiction were present and that the temporal courts would restrain the church tribunals from exceeding their jurisdiction.[250]

Finally, Weinstein reread *Barber* and demonstrated that the majority of the Supreme Court had recognized the distinction between the power to grant a divorce and the power to decide whether a divorce was valid.[251] He was also able to show that in the

---

[247] 62 U.S. 582 (1859).

[248] *Spindel v. Spindel*, 283 F. Supp. 797 (Apr. 11, 1968).

[249] *Id.* at 806.

[250] *Id.* at 806–09.

[251] *Id.* at 809.

nineteenth century, the lower courts had recognized that the federal courts were competent to determine some aspects of marital status.

At the time of *Spindel*, there was a flurry of interest in Weinstein's scholarly opinion, but then the decision languished until 2006.[252] Then in the case of *Marshall v. Marshall*[253] (which dealt with the estate of Anna Nicole Smith's wealthy husband), Justice Ruth Bader Ginsburg, writing for a unanimous Court, greatly eroded the domestic relations (and probate) exceptions to federal jurisdiction, stating that neither exception was "compelled by the Constitution or federal statute," but were "judicially created doctrines stemming in large measure from misty understanding of English legal history." *Spindel* was cited in her decision for "collecting cases and commentary revealing the vulnerability of historical explanation as an "exercise in mythography.""[254]

THE RACE FOR CHIEF JUDGE

Just as Weinstein was beginning to make his mark as a federal judge, he almost left the federal bench. In 1973 Weinstein ran for the Democratic nomination of the New York Court of Appeals and was barely defeated.

Traditionally, when the Chief Judgeship was vacant, both parties nominated the senior associate judge to the center chair. When Stanley Fuld was scheduled to retire in 1973, the senior associate judge was Charles Breitel, an able jurist.

Weinstein says that what primarily led to his decision to run for the Chief Judgeship was his concern about the condition of the state courts and what he considered an immediate need for an activist Chief Judge concerned with court administration.

That was not a description of Breitel. Weinstein had developed his views on the administration of justice in the state from his experience with the Tweed Commission and while serving as an advisor to the New York State constitutional convention.[255] He retained the deep affection for the Court of Appeals from his clerkship and for the state court system as a whole from much of his work. Another reason for running, Weinstein said, was that he felt strongly that Breitel had made Fuld's life "miserable up there with a lot of picayune complaints and attitudes."[256] But, most of all, there was a need for a Chief Judge concerned with administration. Fuld had not been that and there was little to suggest Breitel would be. Weinstein's activist temperament was attracted by that challenge. All of these facts "conspired to use running for this

---

[252] Weinstein Oral History, at 1732–33.

[253] 547 U.S. 293 (2006).

[254] *Marshall v. Marshall*, 547 U.S. 293, 299 (2006).

[255] Weinstein Oral History, at 1282. *See, e.g.*, Jack B. Weinstein, *Improving the Administration of Justice in New York through Constitutional Reforms, in* MODERNIZING STATE GOVERNMENT: THE NEW YORK CONSTITUTIONAL CONVENTION OF 1967 (Sigmund Diamond ed.), 28 PROC. ACAD. POL. SCI. 85, 102 (Jan. 1967).

[256] Weinstein Oral History, at 1282.

office as a basis for laying out to the public at large what the problems of the judicial system were."[257]

Weinstein says he was set off on that "crazy expedition" by a visit to the Brooklyn House of Detention, the result of either a *habeas corpus* or a civil rights case which he heard on that spot.[258] Weinstein had been appalled by what he had seen:

Guys had been sitting there for two years waiting for a trial. They had their arms through the bars when they found out I was a federal judge, begging me to do something about their case and let them out. A lot of them were, of course, con guys. But some were genuinely trapped in a system that couldn't handle them.[259]

He expressed his feelings with passion:

Within a few blocks of my courthouse in Brooklyn, there is a city jail housing more than 1,000 men presumed to be innocent, with the right to bail and a prompt trial on the charges lodged against them. Many of them wait for more than a year for their cases to be heard. There is a family court where people sit and wait interminably to be heard by a court which has inadequate facilities for treating children who probably become criminals if they continue to be deprived of the services required to cope with their problems. There is a housing court where people are not adequately informed of their rights. There is a civil court where the rate of defunct judgments against consumers is so high that it is clear that legitimate rights to a defense are often unknowingly waived.[260]

Weinstein says he began the race with no intention of being elected, rather he was hoping to "dramatize the problem" and then "he could just get off." "But," he said, "it was a little like mounting a tiger. Once you got on you can't just say I'm quitting."[261] He then added: "Evie and I had a ball and I learned an awful lot about the state and what people think and how politics works."[262]

Weinstein had consulted with his colleagues on the Eastern District bench, as well as Second Circuit Judge Irving Kaufman and Judges Henry Friendly and Edward Weinfeld, prior to running, and all had approved of it.[263] As it happened, not every federal judge would approve, and Kaufman had to temporarily block passage of a statement by the Judicial Conference that nobody who held a federal judicial office could

---

[257] *Id.* at 1285.

[258] *Id.* at 11–12.

[259] *Id.* at 11–12.

[260] Jack B. Weinstein, *Finding the Will and the Skill to Help People*, 2 STUD. LAW. 19 (1973–1974).

[261] Weinstein Oral History, at 1285.

[262] *Id.* at 1285–86.

[263] *Id.* at 1286.

run for state office. Such a resolution prohibiting political activity by judges was passed in the autumn of 1973.[264]

Weinstein began putting his views forth on the administration of justice in the fall of 1972 in various parts of the state. He did not declare his candidacy for the June 1973 primary until February 28. Six men were in the race for the Democratic nomination for Chief Judge. Four were state judges: Bernard Meyer, Francis T. Murphy, Vito Titone, and Irwin Brownstein; one was an attorney, Jacob Fuchsberg; and, of course, Weinstein. Breitel was the uncontested Republican nominee. James J. Leff would run on the Conservative Party line.[265]

When Weinstein announced his candidacy, he said:

New York's courts are in trouble. There is widespread loss of faith in the ability of New York's criminal justice system to deter, to rehabilitate, or to check the spread of crime. There is a readiness to be brutal to, to deny civil rights on the theory— wholly mistaken—that such steps are necessary if society is to protect itself. I cannot as a judge remain silent.[266]

He ran an issue-oriented campaign. Included among his proposal were the following: adoption of a class action procedure to protect large groups of consumers;[267] merit selection of all judges except the Chief Judge of the Court of Appeals; state financing of all judicial races;[268] merit selection of judge's law clerks; use of the individual assignment calendar;[269] a statewide commission to investigate charges of judicial misconduct, a majority of whose members would be nonjudges;[270] complete state funding for the courts; a task force to coordinate sentencing, federal and state judicial resources, and to help develop integrated policies for criminal justice in the metropolitan areas;[271] neighborhood courts; a simplified summons with a provision for response by mail; a center to assist the public in each courthouse; a penalty for businesses failing to pay

---

[264] *Id.* at 1289; John P. Mackenzie, The Appearance of Justice 206 (1974).

[265] On the race for Chief Judge, *see* Cynthia Owen Philip, Paul Nejelski, & Aric Press, WHERE DO JUDGES COME FROM? (1996).

[266] Jack B. Weinstein, Press Release, Feb. 28, 1973, at 1.

[267] Jack B. Weinstein, Press Release on Speech to the New York State Bar Association, Insurance, Negligence and Compensation Section, Jan. 25, 1973, at 1.

[268] Committee to Elect United States Judge Jack Weinstein, Chief Judge of New York State, Judge Weinstein Urges Government to Finance Judicial Campaigns, Press Release, May 22, 1973.

[269] Jack B. Weinstein, Statement on Family Court, in Committee to Elect United States Judge Jack B. Weinstein, Chief Judge of New York State, Press Release 4 (May 15, 1973) (draft) (copy in possession of author).

[270] Jack B. Weinstein, Press Release on Speech to 1973 Luncheon Meeting of the Columbia Law School Alumni Association 2–3 (Jan. 26, 1973).

[271] Weinstein press release, Nov. 29, 1972

judgments obtained by consumers in Small Claims Court;[272] and spreading vacations over the year so the courts would be effectively open twelve months.

To Weinstein, the centerpiece of his remedy for the ailments of the state court system was the Chief Judge of the Court of Appeals. That official already had powers to lead the judiciary. It was the Chief Judge who appointed and supervised the state court administrator, chaired the Administrative Board of the Courts and the Judicial Council, and who had the power to convene the Court on the Judiciary in disciplinary matters.[273] It was the Chief Judge who stood at the crucial point between substance and procedure, between administration and case-by case decision-making.[274] The administrative machinery was already there. "What has been lacking," Weinstein declared, was the "full utilization of that mechanism and exercise of that authority."[275] As he said in a speech to the Harlem Fight Back Organization: "More money, more judges, more personnel are meaningless unless there is tough administration and tight control over the whole process.[276] The Chief Judge, he said, "must be the one to lead the courts and make them operate well. He has the power, the moral position and the obligation to do so."[277] It was the Chief Judge who had to explain the needs of the court system to the public, the legislature, and the executive. It was he who had to be a prime focus for improvement and constructive innovation.[278] It was also the Chief Judge who had to be responsible for the effectiveness of court administration "all the way down the line."[279] Thus, the race had the potential for a high-level debate on what needed to be done to improve justice in New York, how it was to be done, and who would be responsible for it.

The debate turned out to be not on as high a level as Weinstein had wished, but it was not dirty or demeaning and Weinstein stuck to talking about judicial administration. While concern about crime became a part of the debate, there was no demagoguery about it in Weinstein's campaign. He made clear that, "The Bill of Rights does not cause crime." Indeed, cutting back on civil rights would make crime prevention even more difficult, Weinstein said.[280] Furthermore, the public had to be educated to the realities of constitutional law and judges should not cower in the face of

---

[272] Weinstein for Chief Judge, Committee to Elect United States United States Judge Jack B. Weinstein, Chief Judge of New York State, Jack B. Weinstein Charges N.Y. Civil Courts Deny Justice to over 100,000 Consumers Annually, Press Release 1 (May 2, 1973).

[273] Jack B. Weinstein, *The Role of the Chief Judge in a Modern System of Justice*, 28 REC. ASS'N B. CITY N.Y. (1973).

[274] *Id.* at 297.

[275] *Id.* at 294.

[276] Jack B. Weinstein, Press Release, Dec. 12, 1972, at 2 (copy in possession of author).

[277] Weinstein, *The Role of the Chief Judge*, supra note 274 at 295.

[278] *Id.* at 291.

[279] Committee for Effective Justice, Press Release, Feb. 28, 1973 [Jack B. Weinstein, announcing candidacy for Democratic Nomination for Chief Judge, at 3].

[280] Jack B. Weinstein, Press Release on Speech to Saddle Rock School, at 2–3 (Jan. 19, 1973) [hereinafter Saddle Rock Speech].

unjustified attacks.[281] There also had to be "serious concern given to the relationship between the prisoner and society."[282] There had to be residential community correctional centers, education in prison as well as psychological help and job training.[283] "We must," Weinstein said, "bring home to the public the fact that the safety of the people on the streets is directly and intimately linked to the success of our efforts at rehabilitating the inmates of our correctional institutions."[284]

Regarding Governor Nelson Rockefeller's proposal for mandatory life sentences for pushers, Weinstein said that it "may sound good and tough, but . . . had no real chance of working."[285] "The real task" was "not 'to express moral outrage by enacting higher penalties with self-defeating procedural straitjackets,'" but rather "to see that the existing penalties are applied consistently and swiftly to the people the Legislature intended to penalize when it enacted the present life-sentencing procedures."[286]

Weinstein was ranked "highly qualified" by the Committee on Judicial Screening of the Association of the Bar of the City of New York.[287] He was given the highest ranking of the New York State Bar Association.[288] The *New York Times* strongly endorsed him:

> The one Democratic candidate who combines great knowledge of the law, specific expertise in the intricacies of the entire state court system and, above all, an outspoken desire and will to administer all the courts is Judge Weinstein.[289]

He was also endorsed by such papers as the *New York Post*, the *Amsterdam News*, *Buffalo Evening News*, and *Syracuse Post-Chronicle*[290] and received the support of such leading attorneys as former U.S. Attorneys General Nicholas Katzenbach and Ramsey Clark, Burke Marshall, Pierre Leval, and Alan K. Hellerstein. There were endorsements from a number of liberal local politicians including Charles Rangel and Bella Abzug, as well as from the deans of all of the Schools of Social Work in New York State, the editors-in-chief of three law reviews, and a number of law students.[291]

---

[281] Jack B. Weinstein, Judging the Judges: The Crisis in Judicial Removal and Discipline in New York State, Speech to Columbia Law School Alumni Association 12 (Jan. 26, 1973).

[282] Committee to Elect United States Judge Jack Weinstein, Chief Judge of New York State, Weinstein Calls for Community Based Penal Facilities, Press Release (n.d.).

[283] Saddle Rock Speech, *supra* note 281, at 10ff.

[284] Saddle Rock Speech, *supra* note 281, at 13.

[285] Jack B. Weinstein, Press Release on Speech to Jamaica Lawyers Club (Jan. 18, 1973), at 1.

[286] Jack B. Weinstein, Judge Weinstein Claims Drug Problems in New York City Can Be Reduced, Press Release 4 (Apr. 8, 1973).

[287] Committee to Elect United States Judge Jack Weinstein, Chief Judge of New York State, Weinstein Endorsed by Solarz, Abrams, Press Release (n.d.), at 1.

[288] Committee to Elect United States Judge Jack Weinstein, Chief Judge of New York State, New York Bar Gives Judge Weinstein Its Highest Rating, Press Release 1 (May 14, 1973).

[289] NEW YORK TIMES, May 29, 1973.

[290] Committee to Elect United States Judge Jack Weinstein, Chief Judge of New York State, Weinstein Receives All Major Endorsements [press release, n.d.].

[291] Committee to Elect United States Judge Jack Weinstein Chief Judge of New York, Weinstein Receives All Major Endorsements, Press Release (n.d.); Committee to Elect United States Judge Jack Weinstein

In the end, Weinstein lost the primary by 755 votes. He had 242,039 votes, and Fuchsberg, 242,794. Weinstein had refused to challenge Fuchsberg's petition to get on the ballot and had decided not to use television advertising.[292] That made the difference. In the general election, Weinstein did not support Breitel publicly but he did so privately, turning over to him all his memoranda and research on improving the state judicial system.[293] Breitel won. Weinstein believes that the contested election probably stimulated Breitel to take a leadership role in court administration and make a lot of reforms he might otherwise not have made.[294] All of Breitel's successors have also attempted to lead on the administrative side. Fuchsberg made it to the Court of Appeals in 1974. His emergence as a leading contender for Breitel's center chair in 1978 ironically led to adoption of a merit selection system for the entire New York Court of Appeals.[295]

Just before the tenth anniversary of Jack B. Weinstein's investiture, the *New York Times* published an article which mentioned his most recent controversial rulings— *Salzmann*, *Kahane*, and the *Mark Twain* and *Offshore Oil* cases. He was described then in such terms as "likes attention," "brilliant," "turns out more work than anyone else."[296]

All of that was true, but his judicial career had just begun.

Chief Judge of New York, Students Support Weinstein in Race for Chief Judge, Press Release 1 (n.d.); Committee to Elect United States Judge Jack Weinstein Chief Judge of New York State, Democrats Endorse Weinstein, Press Release, May 23, 1973. *See also* Recorded Radio Advertisement, Times Endorsement, Transcript, May 29, 1973 (copy in possession of author).

[292] Weinstein Oral History, at 1287–88,

[293] *Id.* at 1290.

[294] *Id.* at 1286.

[295] Dan Diamond, *The Battle of the Bar Associations*, Juris. Dr., May 1978, at 29, 30.

[296] Frank Lynn, On the Beach and in The Limelight, New York Times, Mar. 20, 1977.

6

"Making the Unequal Equal through the Alchemy of the Law":

Growing Renown, 1977–1986

DURING JACK WEINSTEIN'S second decade, he grasped the potential of a number of potentially significant cases, enhancing his reputation within and outside the American judiciary. The most important of these, the *Agent Orange* class action, settled by Weinstein with a dazzling display of judicial power, left an enduring mark on mass tort cases and class action litigation (see Chapter 10). Weinstein's decisions on First Amendment matters marked him as a votary of free speech. His criminal docket yielded prominent mob defendants and several prosecutions for political corruption. Once again, there were cases raising important issues affecting the New York City public schools. Passed over for both the Chief Judgeship of the New York Court of Appeals[1] and for elevation to the U.S. Court of Appeals for the Second Circuit, Weinstein continued to pursue his work—both judicial and scholarly—with zest.

FIRST AMENDMENT JURISPRUDENCE

During this period, Weinstein handled a considerable variety of cases involving the First Amendment: cases raising such problems as access by interest groups to local Memorial Day parades, attempts to discourage door-to-door solicitation by religious

---

[1] *See* Weinstein Oral History, at 609.

groups, and litigation over the Central Intelligence Organization's opening and reading the mail of American citizens.

North Shore Right to Life Committee v. Manhasset American Legion Post No. 304,[2] involved a petition for an injunction filed by members of a right-to-life group who had been denied the right to march in a Memorial Day parade run by the American Legion. Weinstein had participated in many such parades on the North Shore of Long Island after his family moved to Great Neck while he was teaching at Columbia.[3] He saw the annual event as an occasion "[i]nfused with [the] aura of American history and surrounded by the beauty of spring," during which the residents of the towns "put aside their individual problems, and recall together those who gave their lives that we might enjoy this land and its freedoms."[4]

Receiving the petition on the eve of the parade, Weinstein acted with dispatch so that, if he denied it, the group would still have time to appeal. After spending the morning in the Great Neck Public Library reading American Legion magazines, he then heard two hours of arguments in a Nassau County courtroom, retired for five minutes, and issued a thirty-minute oral opinion finding a First Amendment violation and granting an injunction to allow the group to participate.[5]

Although the American Legion had invited various local organizations to participate in the parade, the Right to Life Committee's formal request to join had been denied because the Legion's constitution required it to be "absolutely non-political." There was a threshold issue—whether those responsible for the parade were "state actors" bound by the Constitution. Weinstein took an expansive view of state action, holding that the parade was in no sense "a private procession of the American Legion. It belongs to all the people."[6] Although, the town itself had not discriminated against the anti-abortion group, there was state action because public property was involved and the American Legion had been acting as the agent of the municipalities. Since the restrictions on the group had been predicated on the substance of their ideas, they were content-based. Excluding the group from the march "would be to exercise a form of ostracism reflecting a communal disrespect for their right to express their views," Weinstein wrote.[7] Weinstein did suggest to the anti-abortion group that it not *flaunt* its views because "[s]ometimes respect for the sensibilities of our fellow Americans suggests restraint in the unremitting and maximum enforcement of our constitutional rights. In a nation such as ours, its very pluralism requires some forbearance."[8]

---

[2] 452 F. Supp. 834 (June 9, 1978).

[3] Weinstein Oral History, at 498.

[4] *North Shore Right to Life Comm. v. Manhasset American Legion Post No. 304,* 452 F. Supp. 834, 836 (June 9, 1978).

[5] NEW YORK TIMES, May 30, 1978.

[6] *North Shore Right to Life Comm.* 452 F. Supp. at 836.

[7] *Id.* at 840.

[8] *Id.* at 840–41. *See, however, Hurley v. Irish-American Gay*, Lesbian, and Bisexual Group of Boston, 515 U.S. 557 (1995), holding that the state may not require private citizens who organize a parade to include among the marchers a group imparting a message the organizers do not want to convey.

In the late 1970s, Weinstein heard a number of related cases involving ordinances passed by various Long Island towns and villages to limit door-to-door solicitation. The major target was the Unification Church (the so-called "Moonies"). In one case, Weinstein, after trial, declared unconstitutional the application of the Town of Babylon's ordinance to the Unification Church. In several other cases, Weinstein helped the church, four towns, and two villages to reach agreement on solicitation guidelines. However, the challenge to the constitutionality of an ordinance carefully drawn by the Town of Southampton was set down for a full trial.[9]

The Southampton ordinance barred door-to-door distribution of religious literature. There was an exception, however, for any person who had resided or maintained a place of business in the town for at least six months. Weinstein did not see the ordinance as "ideologically neutral"; rather, it differentiated on the basis of content by precluding those with "foreign ideas" from availing themselves of a historically protected means of communication. This, then, was unconstitutional content discrimination.[10] In addition, he stated that the Equal Protection Clause and the right to travel had also been violated because there had been discrimination on the basis of residence.[11] Writing of the efforts of the several towns and villages, Weinstein said that the "open marketplace of ideas cannot be restricted to little stalls, each separately regulated by local officials."[12] Both the Second Circuit and the Supreme Court affirmed without opinion, although Justice William Rehnquist dissented in the High Court.[13]

Throughout his career, Weinstein has heard cases in which parties sought to keep some aspect of the judicial proceeding secret. During this decade, it was the settlement (which had been sealed) of litigation over the Franklin National Bank.

The insolvency of one of the nation's largest banking institutions precipitated major litigation in the Eastern District in the early 1970s. By the time the case was ready for trial, more than one hundred thousand pages of depositions had been taken and more than $10 million in legal fees had been collected. It was anticipated that the trial would last at least six months and involve millions of documents.

Just as the trial was getting under way, the case settled. As part of the settlement, it was agreed that the settlement itself would be sealed and kept confidential. Years later, a public interest group brought suit to unseal the settlement.[14]

Weinstein first ruled that the Freedom of Information Act (FOIA) did not apply to lawsuits. Then, after weighing conflicting considerations, Weinstein held that confidentiality had been a critical factor in avoiding enormous expenditures by both the

---

[9] NEW YORK DAILY NEWS, July 13, 1979; NEW YORK TIMES, Dec. 29, 1979; NEWSDAY, Dec. 29, 1979.

[10] *Troyer v. Town of Southampton*, 483 F. Supp. 1135, 1139 (Jan 4, 1980).

[11] *Id.* at 1140.

[12] *Id.* at 1141.

[13] *Troyer v. Town of Southampton*, 628 F.2d 1346 (1980), *aff'd sub nom, Town of Southampton v. Troyer*, 449 U.S. 988 (1980).

[14] *In re Franklin Nat'l Bank Sec. Litig.; Federal Deposit Ins. Corp. v. Ernst & Ernst*, 92 F.R.D. 468 (Dec. 7, 1981).

litigants and the courts. The balance struck at the time the settlement was sealed had not changed and so he would not unseal it. However, he did suggest that public interest groups might move to intervene early in cases of great public importance prior to settlement. In a short opinion, the Court of Appeals affirmed.[15]

For two decades, 1953–1973, the Central Intelligence Agency (CIA) illegally intercepted, opened, and read first-class mail of "suspect persons" and institutions as it passed in and out of the United States. At least 215,000 pieces of mail were copied and the CIA put 1.5 million names gleaned from the mail into a data bank. The rationale was anticommunism, but Weinstein thought that such operations were "only part of a general pattern of post–World War Two lawlessness and abuse of power exemplifying 'contempt for the law and the Constitution' by government."[16]

Several victims sued in the Eastern District of New York under the Federal Tort Claims Act[17] and the cases came to Weinstein. Weinstein ruled that both common law rights in New York State and U.S. constitutional rights of the plaintiffs had been violated. He held that, though a class action was not appropriate, the court had jurisdiction and the United States was liable under the Federal Tort Claims Act. But what was the measure of damages? Weinstein impaneled an advisory jury to offer its expression as to the appropriate amount of damages, because the plaintiffs had not suffered any of the "tangible indicia of harm for which a dollar value may be assigned," but had suffered actual mental pain, outrage, and shock for which damages should be assessed, This meant putting a value on individual rights of privacy and psychic damages when U.S. agents fail to obey the law and violate individual rights. Those jurors recommended damages of from $2500 to $10,000 and confirmed the opinion of the court "that the emotional distress these plaintiffs suffered was the sort that would be experienced by reasonable people under the almost unprecedented circumstances of these cases."[18] Weinstein, however, decided that $1000 plus "a suitable letter of regret and assurance of non-recurrence" was appropriate.[19] He concluded:

> The existence of a court system capable of protecting the right to privacy by granting money damages and other relief against the government and its agents

---

[15] *Federal Deposit Ins. Corp. v. Ernst & Ernst*, 677 F.2d 230 (1982: PC: Kauf-VanG-Lowe). These days Weinstein appends to his protective orders a note that "this order is subject to modification of the court in the public interest." Jack B. Weinstein, Individual Justice in Mass Tort Litigation 67ff (1995). Weinstein's opinion was followed in *Pansy v. Borough of Stroudsburg*, 23 F.2d 772, 778, 784–85 (1994) (Alito, J. on panel). *See also In re Agent Orange Prod. Liab. Litig.*, 821 F.2d 139, 198 (1987), *cert. denied*, 484 U.S. 953 (1987).

[16] Birnbaum v. United States, 436 F. Supp. 967, 971 (Aug. 17, 1977).

[17] 28 U.S.C. 1346 (b).

[18] *Birnbaum, supra* note 16, at 988.

[19] *Id.* at 989.

makes our Constitution and laws consequential to our citizens rather than pretentious, empty promises.[20]

Some months later, Weinstein tried three more mail-opening cases. Among the plaintiffs was one notable figure, the octogenarian Corliss Lamont, who had been a relatively prominent advocate for causes on the left for generations. The CIA had opened over 100 pieces of Lamont's correspondence to and from various people in the Soviet Union. Included were his "love letters" to his wife. (In an aside in one opinion, Weinstein said: "The court has not read the letters—it had more than enough of the demeaning process of reading other men's letters to their loved ones as a young naval officer assigned from time-to-time to censorship duties on his ship."[21]) Weinstein awarded Lamont $2000.[22] On reading the government's letter of apology to Lamont, Weinstein said:

> It is, perhaps, not as gracious a letter of regret as the plaintiff might have wished. But, taking into account the proud and upright attitude of government and their secret services and their reluctance to admit wrong doing, the letter serves its purpose. It expresses with some humility the possibility that even the mighty in Washington can do wrong.[23]

The Court of Appeals affirmed, although it disavowed Weinstein's censure of the government and reversed the order for a letter of apology, because no such remedy had been provided in the Federal Tort Claims Act. Judge Leonard Moore reluctantly concurred in part and dissented as to the damages.[24]

Weinstein was upheld by the U.S. Supreme Court in *Securities and Exchange Commission v. Lowe*.[25] Lowe had been convicted in state courts several times for offenses connected with securities peculations, including appropriation of funds and covering up fraud from investment clients. Yet, as Weinstein put it, "Lowe's urge to share his knowledge of finance continue[d] unabated."[26] After release from prison, Lowe created a number of newsletters and publications with information about stocks, none of which seem to have violated any law. Lacking, perhaps, a sense of humor, the Securities and Exchange Commission (SEC) instituted administrative proceedings which successfully revoked

---

[20] *Id.* at 990. *See also* WASHINGTON POST, May 10, 1977, at 1; NEW YORK TIMES, May 10, 1977, May 13, 1977.

[21] *Wilson v. United States*, 1978 U.S. Dist. LEXIS 19505, at 4 (1978).

[22] Weinstein reports that Lamont was much moved by the decision. *See* Weinstein Oral History, at 444, 485, 505.

[23] 1978 Op. NB 301a.

[24] *Birnbaum v. United States*, 588 F.2d 319, 332 (1978: *Gurfein*-Oakes-Moore (c/d)). *See also* NEW YORK TIMES, Nov. 11, 1978.

[25] 556 F. Supp. 1359 (Feb. 1, 1983).

[26] *Id.* at 1361.

the registration of Lowe Corporation as an investment advisor and barred Lowe from association with any investment advice. The Commission also sought a court order enjoining further publication of investment advisory materials and ordering Lowe to disgorge subscription moneys.

The case raised statutory and constitutional issues. The statutory issue involved the reach of Section 17 (b) of the Securities Act of 1933—whether newsletter publishers were to be treated differently from broker dealers and others who directed investments of clients. Employing the leading Supreme Court decision on commercial speech,[27] Weinstein held that prepublication restraints were not justifiable when the less drastic alternative of disclosure existed, as it did in this case. He also held that investment advisory publications might even be entitled to more constitutional protection than protected commercial speech because they were "a combination of fact, economic and political analyses, conjecture and recommendation."[28] Weinstein held that, in order to avoid such constitutional difficulties and permit continued regulation of securities markets, the Act should be interpreted as not extended to publishing, so long as publishers stayed away from giving advice to particular persons. If a publisher fully complies with the record reporting, and disclosure requirements of the Act, then he must be allowed to register for the purpose of publishing and to publish.[29] However, Weinstein stated that "narrowly drawn reasonable rules for divulgence of criminal activities or of deregistration of principals of a publisher would not be invalid."[30] The publication, therefore, could go on, but not any activity creating dangers of personal advice.[31]

Weinstein was reversed by the Court of Appeals. The higher court validated the prohibition on selling advice and counsel, analysis, and reports to clients as to the value of specific securities or the advisability of investing in, purchasing, selling, or holding specific securities.[32] Dissenting, Judge Charles L. Brieant, Jr., endorsed the Weinstein decision, taking the position that the Supreme Court's commercial speech cases went beyond mere advertising and protected expression of fact and opinion implicating "substantial individual and societal interests."[33]

The Supreme Court unanimously reversed the Court of Appeals, although three of the justices concurred narrowly and one did not participate. The High Court held

---

[27] *Central Hudson Gas & Electric Corp. v. Public Service Comm'n*, 447 U.S. 557 (1980).

[28] *Security & Exchange Comm'n v. Lowe*, supra note 15, at 1367.

[29] *Id.* at 1369.

[30] *Id.* at 1370. *See also* WALL STREET JOURNAL, Feb. 2, 1983, at 8.

[31] Years later Weinstein indicated that his approach in the *Lowe* case was also based on an issue that was never suggested in an opinion connected with the case. His view had been that under sentencing theory, a person who has served his sentence is presumed to be rehabilitated and entitled to return to a place in society and make a living. "And Lowe's knowledge was entirely within this area of stock markets. So I didn't see where he should be prevented from earning a living if it was possible to do so without great risk to the public." Weinstein Oral History, at 683.

[32] *Security & Exchange Comm'n v. Lowe*, 725 F.2d 892, 902 (1984: *Oakes-VanG©/Brient*).

[33] *Id.* at 902, 906, 910.

that the publications described fell within the statutory exclusion for *bona fide* publications.[34]

The most important Weinstein opinion in First Amendment matters during this period was *Greenberg v. Bolger*[35] in which Weinstein held that Congress's decision in 1980 to provide preferential third-class mail rates only to the two major political parties was unconstitutional.

Under the Postal Reorganization Act of 1970, the U.S. Postal Service was created as "an independent establishment of the executive branch of the Government of the United States." At that time and, in 1980 when the litigation took place, the U.S. Postal Service was a monopoly. In 1978, the benefit of reduced postal rates was extended to the Republican and Democratic Parties, as well as to minor political parties. However, under the 1980 Postal Service Appropriation Act, a rate of 3.1 cents per letter was allowed only to "major" parties—defined as parties whose candidate had received 25 percent or more of the total votes in the preceding presidential election. "Minor parties," parties which had received five to less than 25 percent of the vote, were to pay 8.4 cents per letter. The Act did not give any preferential rates to parties that had been successful in state or local elections or independent presidential candidates.[36]

Five political parties[37] and the National Unity Campaign for John Anderson sought an injunction either to invalidate the statute in part or an order directing the Postal Service to afford them the special reduced rates. None of these parties had approached the nationwide 5 percent figure in the 1976 presidential election.

After a lengthy hearing, Weinstein announced his decision on June 6, 1980. The 5 percent limitation was unconstitutional; the minor parties and the Anderson campaign were to be treated the same way as the major parties. Weinstein directed the Postal Service to use already appropriated funds to implement the same rates for the plaintiffs as the rates charged to the majority parties.[38]

The full opinion in *Greenberg v. Bolger* was issued two weeks later on June 20, 1980.[39] The nub of the opinion was its second and third paragraphs:

> A critical duty of the courts in our system of constitutional government is to protect a minority against a majority's attempt to reduce human rights. In our democratic republic it is essential that each person be afforded the right of equal access to the marketplace of political ideas and the opportunity of influencing governmental policy through election and persuasion of government officials.

---

[34] *Lowe v. S.E.C.*, 472 U.S. 181, 210 (1985).

[35] 497 F. Supp. 756 (June 20, 1980).

[36] In his oral history, Weinstein said that it "just seemed to me a completely unnecessary attempt to disadvantage third parties." Weinstein Oral History, at 565.

[37] Socialist Party of America, Libertarian Party, Peace & Freedom Party, Conservative Party of New York, and the Citizens' Party (an intervener).

[38] *Greenberg v. Bolger*, 80-CV-0340, Transcript of Hearing of June 6, 1980, 1980 NB 303f. *See especially* at 371–72.

[39] 497 F. Supp. 756.

The vital role played by third parties and independent candidates in changing the political environment; the programs, goals and candidacies; the monopoly that is enjoyed by the Postal Service; and the very real burdens denial of the preferred postal rates places on small or new political parties, require that the plaintiffs enjoy access to the mails equal to that of the Republicans and Democrats.[40]

In his opinion, Weinstein examined the history of independent candidates and third parties,[41] the obstacles against third parties, and the factors which contribute to their emergence. He held that restricting the postal subsidy based on the nationwide popularity of a political party was content-based and that by "subsidizing the mailings of the Republicans and Democrats, the government had chosen to benefit those with popular views and burden those with unpopular views."[42] There was no appeal.

SCHOOL CASES AND CIVIL RIGHTS JURISPRUDENCE

As early as 1979, Weinstein had written that "[f]or all practical purposes. . ., the [Supreme] Court's recent decisions insulate white suburbs from the integration effort.[43] He also said: "the noble, broad and generous words of the Warren Court in *Brown* have been replaced by the language of *Rodriguez* and *Dayton*."[44] But if broad desegregation orders were passé, there still would be important litigation involving civil rights in public education coming before Weinstein.

Lora v. Board of Education of City of New York[45] was one of three major lawsuits Weinstein handled involving the New York City school system during this period. It is an example of litigation that that turned out to be bigger than it might have been because of the way Weinstein handled it.[46]

Lora was a class action involving exceptionally handicapped children in New York City who attended special day schools (600 schools). In the mid-1970s, New York City's

---

[40] *Id.* at 764.

[41] *Id.* at 770.

[42] *Id.* at 776.

[43] Jack B. Weinstein, Equality, *Liberty and the Public Schools: The Role of the State Courts,* 1 CARDOZO L. REV. 343, 378 (1979).

[44] *Id.* at 343.

During this period, Weinstein gave a number of speeches and produced a number of articles on this general topic. *See, e.g.,* Jack B. Weinstein: *Equality, Liberty and the Public Schools: The Public Role,* 48 U. CIN. L. REV.203 (1979) [hereinafter Weinstein, *Equality, Liberty*]. These were the Robert S. Marx Lectures at the University of Cincinnati College of Law, April 19 and 20, 1979; *Education of Exceptional Children,* 12 CREIGHTON L. REV. 987 (1979) [Toepel Lecture]; *Litigation Seeking Changes in Public Behavior and Institutions—Some Views on Participation,* 13 U. C. DAVIS L. REV. 231 (1980) [hereinafter, Weinstein, *Litigation Seeking Changes*]. Weinstein also gave the commencement address at Mark Twain Jr. H.S., Brooklyn, July 28, 1978.

[45] *Lora v. Bd. of Ed. of City of New York,* 456 F. Supp. 1211, (June 2, 1978).

[46] Weinstein Oral History, at 454.

day school population represented only two-tenths of 1 percent of a total public school population of over one million. In 1977, 68 percent of the students attending day schools were black and 27 percent were Hispanic, while the total New York City school population was 36 percent black and 23 percent Hispanic. By comparison, New York City's special private schools receiving government subsidies were 45 percent white, 34 percent black, and 20 percent Hispanic. Certainly, one reason for the striking disparity between whites and minorities was the difficulty in communicating with parents of minority children and also the greater knowledge some middle-class families had of the availability of public funds for the private facilities. In addition, the system of diagnosis and classification of the public schools suffered from inadequate staffing.

The plaintiffs complained of the procedures and facilities afforded for the education of children whose emotional problems resulted in severe acting-out and aggression in school. They contended that, although the special day schools had smaller classes, specially trained teachers, support staff, and facilities, that they were intentionally segregated dumping grounds.[47] The students saw themselves as "emotional outcasts, left abandoned by the regular school system and 'remanded' to educational 'holding pens,' there to be incapacitated rather than rehabilitated, until such time as they can be conveniently dumped, untrained and unfit, into a society which holds no proper place for them."[48]

The lawsuit was filed in June 1975, after Congress had amended the Education of the Handicapped Act of 1970, which was intended to achieve appropriate public education for such children. The plaintiffs argued that their constitutional and statutory rights had been violated; that standards for identification, evaluation, and educational placement were vague, ambiguous, and overbroad and were being applied in a capricious, arbitrary, and racially discriminatory manner. Lawyers for the Legal Aid Society and the NAACP representing the plaintiffs, accused the Board of Education of operating a "dual system" of education in the special schools in which black and Hispanic children were reassigned to racially segregated schools that did not provide a special education.[49] The judge assigned the case, Walter Bruchhausen, denied class certification.

After Bruchhausen's death, the case was reassigned to Weinstein, who did certify the class. Weinstein had a special sensitivity to the *Lora* litigation because of his own history of disciplinary problems in school. The plaintiffs in *Lora* made a motion for discovery, seeking fifty randomly selected student files with names redacted, in order to provide evidentiary support for their charges. In his opinion on the motion for discovery, Weinstein balanced his broad and sympathetic view of the constitutional right to privacy against social and legal needs. He held that, under the Federal Rules of

---

[47] *Lora*, 456 F. Supp. at 1214.

[48] *Lora v. Bd. of Ed. of City of New York,* 74 F.R.D. 565, 586 May 12, 1977.

[49] *See* Keba Williams, U.S. Judge Visits "600" Schools, Finds Things Are Bad and Good, NEW YORK TIMES, May 18, 1977, at B3.

Evidence, the evidentiary privilege for communications made confidentially by students or their parents to psychiatrists, psychologists, or social workers had to give way to the need for full development of the facts so that the paramount public interest in the fair administration of justice would be served. "Remedial education of the emotionally disturbed and handicapped," Weinstein argued, "if tainted by capricious or discriminatory administration may have devastating consequences not only for the victimized student, but for society generally."[50] As it appeared that the files sought were the sole available reliable source of important information in this litigation, Weinstein ordered that the data be supplied to qualified personnel under strict controls.[51]

After extensive discovery, there was a trial with forty-nine witnesses spread over eleven months. yielding 3900 pages of transcript. Weinstein heard from experts, parents, and children. He also visited schools in all five boroughs.[52] In his most important *Lora* opinion,[53] Weinstein held that because there had been referrals to racially segregated schools, there had been the denial of equal opportunity under Title VI of the 1964 Civil Rights Act.[54]

In that *Lora* opinion, Weinstein also held that the segregation of the plaintiffs in a special day school without affording appropriate educational and therapeutic treatment would violate their constitutional rights.[55] When students in the special day schools go without therapeutic treatment, the rationale for confining them in the special day school collapses, and the students are entitled to the protection of the Due Process Clause. Weinstein also held that "[t]he isolation of minority students in special educational settings with small hope of truly fruitful educational movement into a less restrictive environment constitutes a denial of equal protection.[56]

Weinstein saw the role of the court in *Lora* as to "aid educators in providing the equality in education that is our constitutional goal." He held that the parties should meet with each other and then with the court to attempt to work out the specific terms of a decree, which presumably would involve the requisites of notice, evaluation, training, an independent advocate for parents or children, and understandable explanations for parents and teachers. The representatives of the state and federal governments were asked to participate in conferences with counsel and the court.[57]

---

[50] *Lora v. Bd. of Ed. of City of New York,* 74 F.R.D. 565, 579 (1977).

[51] *Id.* at 584. *See also* NEW YORK TIMES, May 3 and May 6, 1977.

[52] Weinstein Oral History, at 486ff. *See* NEW YORK TIMES, May 11, 1977, at B3. *See also* Weinstein, *Equality, Liberty, supra* note 44, at 222–23.

[53] *Lora v. Bd. of Ed. of City of New York,* 456 F. Supp. 1211 (June 2, 1978).

[54] The litigants were not writing on a clean slate. In the 1960s, the City day schools had been criticized for the inadequacies of their programs, an inadequate referral process prone to misidentification, failure to mainstream and for being a device for disposing of problem children with whom the largely white middle class teachers could not cope. *Id.* at 1220.

[55] *Id.* at 1274ff.

[56] *Id.* at 1276.

[57] *Id.* at 1294–95. *See also* Weinstein, *Equality, Liberty, supra* note 44, at 222–23.

Thirteen months later, in July 1979, relying upon a panel of educators, public hearings, and trips to the schools, Weinstein handed down a "final order," which dealt with evaluations, placement in the least restrictive environment, Individualized Education Programs (IEP), in-service training, special day schools, private-school funding at public expense, reporting, and monitoring.[58] He also insisted on a sensitivity course for teachers, something some of them resented.[59]

On May 19, 1980, Weinstein supplemented his July 1979 order by establishing a panel of independent experts to provide the Board of Education with technical expertise and recommendations in implementing the final order. Members of the panel were to be selected by plaintiffs, the Board of Education, the United States, and the Public Education Association. It was financed with funds from the United States and the Carnegie Foundation.[60]

On June 2, 1980, the Second Circuit affirmed Weinstein's 1978 opinion in part and vacated and remanded in part based upon standards announced by the Supreme Court *after* Weinstein had issued his final order. The remand was for a more searching inquiry into the issue of discriminatory intent, supported by specific findings, and appropriate conclusions of law stated separately.[61]

On September 4, 1980, Weinstein met with the *Lora* Advisory Panel of Experts to assist in the development of nondiscriminatory standards for the identification and placement of children with emotional hardships in special education programs in New York City.[62] Concerned by what appeared to be unsatisfactory progress by the Board of Education in developing nondiscriminatory standards and/or criteria and procedures, the panel began in 1981 to independently develop guidelines. Those guidelines played an important role in shaping the development of nondiscriminatory standards and procedures.[63]

On August 2, 1984, Weinstein upheld the stipulation (final order) between the parties which concluded a nine-year history of trial, appeals, judgments, consent decrees, and implementation of a program of nondiscriminatory standards.[64] The standards embodied such important principles as the student's right to placement in the least restrictive setting where an appropriate education would be assured.

---

[58] *Lora v. Bd. of Ed. of City of New York*, 75 Civ. 917, 1979 JBWNB 202–42 (July 2, 1979).

[59] Weinstein Oral History, at 115ff, 486f.

[60] *Lora v. Bd. of Ed. of City of New York*, 75 Civ 917, 1980 NB 187 (May 22, 1980).

[61] *Lora v. Bd. of Ed. of City of New York*, 623 F.2d 248 (June 2, 1980: *Pollack*-Mulligan-*Oakes*©). The Supreme Court decision(s) were *Dayton Bd. of Ed. V. Brinkman*, 99 S.Ct. 2971 (1979); *Columbus Board of Education v. Penick*, 99 S.Ct. 2941 (1979).

[62] Jack B. Weinstein Press Release, Sept. 4, 1980.

[63] Frank H. Wood, *The Lora Case: Nonbiased Reform, Assessment and Placement Procedures*, 52 Exceptional Child. 323, 327 (1986). Even while the case was being litigated, the New York City School system had implemented changes intended to correct the practices which had led to disproportionate placement of minorities in the special day schools and to improve the education programs provided in those schools. *Id.* at 324.

[64] *Lora v. Bd. of Ed. of City of New York*, 587 F. Supp. 1572 (Aug. 2, 1984).

In the *Lora* litigation, Weinstein let embarrassment of the school board become the impetus for change rather than legal sanctions.[65] He found *Lora* "frustrating, as much of this educational litigation is, because you're dealing with sociological problems, broken homes."[66] Yet, he also saw the case as a "wholesome example of how disputes of this kind can be peaceably resolved [with] [a] minimum of adversarial litigation by lawyers and maximum utilization of the good will of experts and others interested primarily in the welfare of children."[67] From *Lora* he learned that the more due process protections that are put in place, the more the middle class benefits because of its ability and opportunities to take advantage of the protections.[68]

A decade after *Lora*, a *New York Times* page one story stated that there was compelling evidence that black and Hispanic students were harmed rather than helped by special education, that tens of thousands of children may be funneled into that system unnecessarily and that 84 percent of the city's 130,000 special education students were black and Hispanic.[69] Some months before the *Times* article was published, Weinstein was asked what the impact of *Lora* was; he replied that "as in many of these education cases, the court's impact is relatively slight. There are just too many factors that are much more important."[70] Speaking about another education case around the same time, he said "It's hard to know what the benefit of all this is, because you're in a moving stream and the whole sociology is changing, and was changing. . . You have to ask, what would have happened, if this hadn't been done. It's impossible to do that."[71]

In the mid-1970s, the Office of Civil Rights of the Department of Health, Education, and Welfare (HEW) decided to seriously get into the desegregation business by turning its attention to bilingual education issues, second-generation racial discrimination problems, and the rights of the handicapped.[72] *Caulfield v. Board of Education* was part of a series of cases in which the federal government threatened to cut off federal funding because of the way the Board of Education was employing English teachers and conducting bilingual education. HEW had found that there had been a pattern of assigning teachers in a way that tended to relate the race of the teacher to the predominant race of the teachers in the school. It insisted that an illegally segregated system of teacher assignment was being maintained and that to desegregate there had to be assignments made by race.

For its part, the Board of Education contended that it was caught in a whirlpool of circumstances from which it could not escape—state law, demographic changes in the

---

[65] Wood, *supra* note 63, at 329–30.
[66] Weinstein Oral History, at 488ff.
[67] *Lora v. Bd. of Ed. of City of New York*, 587 F. Supp. 1572, 1574 (Aug. 2, 1984).
[68] Weinstein, *Equality, Liberty, supra* note 44, at 232.
[69] N.Y. TIMES, Apr. 7, 1994, at 1A, B5.
[70] Weinstein Oral History, at 493.
[71] Weinstein Oral History, at 115f.
[72] Michael A. Rebell & Arthur R. Black, Equality and Education: Federal Civil Rights Enforcement in the New York City School System 64 (1985).

student population of the City schools, collective bargaining agreements, a low inci-dence of minorities in the relevant available teacher work force and the incidence and distribution of vacancies.[73]

The imminent threat of a massive cutoff of funds led to the Board of Education to accept an agreement with HEW in a related case to spread minority teachers evenly throughout the system to reflect student and population ratios. The agreement pro-vided that each individual school must reflect the racialethnic composition of the sys-tem's teacher corps as a whole within a range of 5 percent, with only educationally-based exceptions.[74] While this averted the cutoff of federal funds, the only interested group consulted during the negotiations was the United Federation of Teachers.[75] Weinstein held that the City's compliance was non-voluntary, a result for which Title VI of the Civil Rights Law did not contain procedures.[76]

Teachers, supervisors, and administrators challenged the memorandum of under-standing between HEW and the Board of Education. At issue were the rights of indi-vidual teachers to have their assignment made without respect to race.[77] Weinstein held that there had to be some form of public participation in the process that produced the HEW-School Board agreement because to comply with the memorandum of under-standing, which had kept federal funding flowing, would require sweeping changes in the City's school system. He held that Title VI mandated some form of hearing when there was such critical decision-making. At stake was whether the "voluntary" remedial agreement between the United States and New York City had impermissibly infringed on the rights of third parties. Weinstein's fundamental assumption was that "those persons who may be affected by a court decision should have the right to be heard before their fate is sealed."[78] The right of notice and hearing was indispensable in protecting the individual against abuse by government. He held that "the law does not permit procedural rights of beneficiaries to be eroded by local and federal officials who characterize a process as 'informal compromise' rather than strict enforcement."[79] Even though due process procedural protection might inhibit the use of the fund cutoff device to enforce federal policy requiring desegregation, "the people have a right to know what is going on and to express their views, however misguided they appear

---

[73] *Caulfield v. Board of Ed.* 449 F. Supp. 1203, 1217 (Mar. 15, 1978).

[74] The *Caulfield* litigation spawned another lawsuit handled by Weinstein. It dealt with the Department of Education's cut-off of funds to New York City under the Emergency School Aid Act. *See Board of Ed. v. Califano*, 77-C-1928 (Nov. 18, 1977). In that suit, Weinstein held that the Department had failed to adhere to constitutionally mandated procedures and statutory standards and remanded the case to it.

[75] *Id.* at 1212.

[76] *Id.* at 1221.

[77] *Caulfield*, 449 F. Supp. 1203, 1214 (Mar. 15, 1978).

[78] Weinstein, *Litigation Seeking Changes*, *supra* note 44, at 232.

[79] *Caulfield*, 449 F. Supp. at 1203.

to those who control [the] government's operation."[80] Weinstein left it to HEW to determine what procedural protections plaintiffs were entitled to under Title VI.[81]

On September 5, 1978, the Court of Appeals reversed Weinstein's order for further administrative proceedings.[82] Finding no HEW regulations for public participation or a hearing when the department acts informally,[83] Judge Oakes reasoned that:

> The complex scientific, technological, social and economic issues presented in so much of current administration are often ill-suited for resolution by adjudicatory procedures. . . . Judicialization of agency procedures and the expansion of participation rights may also aggravate the tendency for the agency to assume a passive role.[84]

A bench trial followed. As the Second Circuit had termed the agreement "voluntary," the issue for determination was whether the parties that entered a remedial plan had a reasonable basis for believing that the practices at issue might result in liability and whether the remedial measures adopted were reasonable in view of the perceived liability. In an opinion that spanned sixty-five pages in the Federal Supplement, Weinstein held that the agreement was valid and had not violated the teachers' rights. The parties had a reasonable belief that the Board's hiring and assignment practices violated Title VI, Title IX, and the Constitution. The remedial measures in the agreement were a reasonable means to cure inequities and those measures did not violate the rights of third parties.[85] This time, the Court of Appeals affirmed,[86] and the Supreme Court denied the petition for certiorari.[87]

CIVIL RIGHTS

Probably the most important noneducation civil rights action Weinstein tried was an employment discrimination case brought under both Title VII (employment

---

[80] Id.

[81] Id. at 1225–26.

[82] Caulfield v. Board of Ed., 583 F.2d 605 (1978: Oakes-VanG-Pierce). The Court of Appeals upheld Weinstein on a related matter—his denial of a motion by teachers, principals, and others for an injunction to prevent city, state, and federal officials from conducting a survey of the ethnic identification of teachers and supervisors.

[83] Id. at 613–14.

[84] Id. at 615.

[85] Caulfield v. Board of Ed., 486 F. Supp. 862, 924 (Aug. 27, 1969).

[86] Caulfield v. Board of Ed., 632 F.2d 999 (1980: Oakes-Lumb-Mesk). Judge Oakes would have affirmed on Weinstein's theory while the other two judges affirmed on the ground that the case in its present posture did not contain an allegation that any individual's liberty or privacy interest had been invaded by state action.

[87] Caulfield v. Board of Ed., 450 U.S. 1030 (1981).

discrimination) and Section 1983 (violation of constitutional rights) against the Suffolk County Department of Corrections. In *Snell v. Suffolk County*,[88] black and Hispanic police officers claimed first that the County discriminated against minorities in hiring and promotion. Of particular interest in *Snell* is the manner in which Weinstein transformed the case as well as his unusual opinion where he included a serious discussion of ethnic humor based on nonlegal sources and mentioned his own experiences as a young man. At least that part of the opinion is a good example of Weinstein writing an opinion because he was interested in the subject.

The Section 1983 action was tried to a jury while the Title VII action was given a bench trial. Midway through the plaintiffs' case, when it appeared that they lacked sufficient proof, Weinstein related for the record the substance of a conference with the attorneys in which he suggested that the hostile work involvement within the jail was an independent cause of action under both Title VII and Section 1983.[89] The plaintiffs had stated that they repeatedly had been subject to demeaning ethnic quips and offensive racial epithets, such as "nigger," "coon," and "spic," while they were on the job. In addition, they had been denied access to a locked bathroom for officers and also had received applications for the Ku Klux Klan.

Weinstein thought that the case presented a very basic issue of substantial infection of the workplace by pervasive race hatred, something that reminded him of what he had seen on the docks as a teenager. He "set the case up in a way that would make the superiors liable for not controlling that because they must have been aware."[90]

The jury found for the County on the claims of discrimination in assignment and promotion and awarded damages to three of sixteen plaintiffs based upon the sheriff's failure to correct the atmosphere of racial and ethnic hostility.

Deciding the Title VII claims, Weinstein found that the plaintiffs had been subject to vicious, frequent, and reprehensible instances of racial harassment.[91] He granted an injunction ordering the warden to appear before all corrections officers and declare that the County would not tolerate discrimination by any correction officer against any other corrections officer. The warden was instructed to forbid the use of racial epithets and the posting or distribution of derogatory bulletins, ethnic phrases, or jokes and to appear before all corrections officers to announce this policy against racial epithets.[92]

In his opinion in the Title VII case, Weinstein dealt at some length with the problem of banning racial epithets. The court, he said, "would have to repair to some soundproof

---

[88] 611 F. Supp. 521 (May 24, 1985), *aff'd*, 782 F.2d 1095 (1986: *Kauf*-Timb-New).

[89] *See* Weinstein Oral History, at 796ff.

[90] *Id.* at 796.

[91] *Snell v. Suffolk County*, 611 F. Supp. 521, 526 (May 24, 1985).

[92] *See* Jack B. Weinstein, Reflections on Book IV of the Torah, Speech at Temple Emanuel, Great Neck (May 24, 1985), 1985 Sp. NB 14 at 10.

ivory tower not to recognize that racial clues, ethnic jokes and hostility still manifest themselves in a large variety of ways."[93] He went on:

> A good deal of the persiflage in rough humor—ethnic or otherwise—observed during the presiding judge's youth working around the New York City docks is not without some utility. It may provide ventilation for suppressed hostility and fear.
>
> Sanitizing the workplace may detract from the cathartic value ethnic slurs sometimes have. . . . Given, however, the harsh and crude way in which racial animosities have regularly been expressed by corrections officers in the Suffolk County Jail, an absolute prohibition on racial "joking" there is mandated by law. Only a radical shock to the mores can succeed in bringing home to these officers the necessity of eschewing overt hostility so that equal working conditions for all employees can exist as Congress intended.[94]

The Court of Appeals affirmed Weinstein and "[n]oted with approval that his order relies on available resources and does not unduly burden Suffolk County."[95] It refused to reverse on the grounds of the "somewhat uncommon use of judicial notice" by Judge Weinstein.[96] It rejected the claim that Weinstein impermissibly manipulated the substantive ground for the lawsuit by injecting a new issue—the atmosphere of racial harassment that had not specifically been added in the complaint.[97]

CRIMINAL CASES

During this period, Weinstein presided over several visible organized crime trials and handled two important political corruption cases. He fought battles against bail being used as preventive detention and wrote several important opinions involving the Fourth Amendment.

Organized Crime

District judges who agree on many issues differ over bail for organized crime defendants who can afford to pay it. If released on bond, they may continue their criminal

---

[93] *Snell v. Suffolk County*, 611 F. Supp.521, 528 (May 24, 1985).

[94] *Id.* at 529.

[95] *Snell v. Suffolk County*, 782 F.2d 1095, 1105 (1986: *Kauf*-Timb-New). *See also* Weinstein's decision in *Hill v. Berkman*, 635 F. Supp. 1228 (May 15, 1986), where Weinstein held that, although the military could permissibly exclude women from combat and combat support positions, that under Title VII—the law prohibiting discrimination in employment—the federal courts had jurisdiction to review the classification of the position.

[96] *Id.*

[97] *Id.* at 1102. Two interesting civil rights suits dealing with housing were decided by Weinstein during this period. *See Wycoff Gardens Tenants Ass'n, Inc. v. New York City Hous. Auth.* 78 Civ 113, 1979 NB 444 (Apr. 2, 1979), *remanded to* 1979 NB 711 (Nov. 21, 1979: 2dC: Mull-Oakes-New); *Haakmat v. Pierce*, 82-Civ-1614, 1982 NB 296). On *Haakmat*, see *Staten Island Advance*, July 9, 13, 16, 1982. *See also* Weinstein Oral History, at 636ff.

involvements. On the whole, Weinstein generally trusted to Mafia discipline to ensure that defendants would not flee, and usually was more generous in the bail he set than many of his colleagues and the judges of the Court of Appeals for the Second Circuit. This led to many reversals.[98]

In 1985, Weinstein released Anthony Colombo, head of the Colombo organized crime family, on bond because his trial was not to begin and be completed within three months to two years of his bail application. He held that the government had failed to establish by clear and convincing evidence that detention was necessary. Reading the statutory bail provisions (amended in 1984),[99] together with the Constitution and the Speedy Trial Act, Weinstein held that "[s]uch a long period of preventive detention without a finding of guilt, based solely on possible damage to the public is anathema to American ideals of due process."[100] He was reversed. Commenting almost a decade later, he said: "I've been through this with the Court of Appeals a dozen times. And I lose each time. And I do it each time because I think I'm right."[101]

Another battle over bail involved Anthony Vitta and Salvatore Migliorisi, members of a Mafia family charged with extortion. Vitta was also alleged to have engaged in loan sharking and to have been a member of a criminal enterprise in violation of RICO. Both men were placed in custody because they were a magistrate found them to be a danger to a potential witness, referred to as "X." At first, Weinstein affirmed the magistrate's detention order and, in turn, was affirmed by the Court of Appeals.[102]

Later it became clear that the trial would not take place for nine months and would last many months. This case was one of the growing number of extraordinarily complex criminal cases brought during and after this period in the Eastern District; cases which had many defendants and attorneys, difficult legal issues, a large volume of materials disclosed through discovery, and extensive pretrial motions.[103] The trial of Vitta and Migliorisi involved two defendants who had been severed from a case which originally had sixteen defendants. There was a seventeen-count indictment (including a complex RICO count) and over 1000 hours of wiretap recordings.[104]

Without bail, the defendants, presumed innocent, would be incarcerated for over a year until a jury verdict. After the two men moved for reconsideration of the detention order, Weinstein learned that witness X, whose protection provided the basis for finding that the defendants' custody was required, was not a "blameless victim." X was a convicted criminal, accused of income tax evasion, who had had an intimate social relationship with the defendants and might even have been profiting financially from

---

[98] *See* Jack B. Weinstein letter to Wilfred J. Feinberg, May 5, 1981. Responding to a question for the oral history, Weinstein could only recall one Mafia defendant who, when released by him on bond, fled the jurisdiction. Weinstein Oral History, at 736.

[99] Bail Reform Act of 1984, 18 U.S.C. 3141 *et seq.*

[100] *United States v. Colombo*, 616 F. Supp. 780 (Aug. 22, 1985), *rev'd*, 777 F.2d 96 1985 (*Pierce*-Pratt-Metzner).

[101] Weinstein Oral History, at 738.

[102] *United States v. Vitta*, 653 F. Supp. 320 (Nov. 14, 1986).

[103] *See United States v. Vitta and Migliorisi*, 86 CR 452, 1986 Op. N.B. 644 (1986).

[104] *Id.*

the incarceration of the defendants. This derogatory information suggested to Weinstein that it would be in the defendants' best interest to have X appear at trial, rather than to kill him.[105] The other possible grounds for holding the defendants—risk of flight and danger to the community—did not, he thought, seem to be present. Thinking it doubtful that continued detention of the defendants would substantially decrease the potential of harm to X, the lengthy detention of the defendants seemed to Weinstein to "assume a punitive character" when significantly prolonged and thus would offend the Due Process Clause.[106]

In his opinion, Weinstein argued that all of the hardships of pretrial detention, "including deterioration of morale, demeanor, finances, resources, reputation, and quality and thoroughness of the legal defense," might combine to disadvantage the defendants at the judgment and sentencing stages of the proceedings. Congress, Weinstein wrote, did not consider the constitutionality of long pretrial detention under the Bail Reform Act of 1984 because it assumed that such concerns would be *de facto* allayed by the conjunction of that law with the Speedy Trial Act. However, extended imprisonment had become the rule rather than exception whenever pretrial litigation was used in complex multicount, multidefendant actions. Weighing all the factors, Weinstein determined that "[t]he balance is clearly in favor of release now." He fixed bail at $100,000 for each defendant and added conditions to limit the activities of each defendant while out on bail.[107]

The most dramatic organized crime case Weinstein tried during this period involved Richard Mastrangelo and Joseph Dazzo, who, with nine other defendants, were accused of conspiracy to import marijuana. Most of the defendants had been tried before Judge Henry Bramwell, but Mastrangelo and Dazzo had been severed Mastrangelo had been indicted for obstruction of justice for attempting to intimidate the key witness, James Bennett. With the case virtually complete against Dazzo, the government was ready to begin its case against Mastrangelo. Bennett flew to New York from Florida, where he was living, and stayed over one night at his daughter's home in Brooklyn. The next morning, on his way to the courthouse, Bennett was chased by two men and shot dead. The murder was announced to a stunned courtroom of participants and spectators.[108]

Weinstein immediately initiated a process of deliberation that spanned several hours, seeking the advice of the parties as to how best to proceed under the circumstances. He was aware that this was "a special emergency situation" when the judge has got to react immediately and can't be held "to the same kind of dispassionate analysis that the Court of Appeals will undertake years or months after the event."[109] The jury

---

[105] *United States v. Vitta and Migliorisi* , 653 F. Supp. 320, 336 (Nov. 14, 1986).

[106] *Id.* at 337, 338.

[107] *Id.* at 345.

[108] *See* trial transcript, 1981 NB 269, 269–70. The year before, when Alphonse (Allie Boy) Persico was to be sentenced by Weinstein for loan-sharking, his attorney, George Gold, was gunned down.

[109] Trial Transcript, *United States v. Dazzo*, 1982 NB 269, 293.

was sequestered.[110] The case against Mastrangelo was severed. The defendants' bail was revoked.[111] Weinstein could have exercised his option to introduce a tape recording of a conversation between Mastrangelo and Bennett, but stood by his pretrial ruling excluding the tape as prejudicial to Dazzo.

Dazzo's trial continued and he was convicted for drug offenses. His conviction was affirmed, although Judge John R. Bartels would have vacated the sentence and remanded for resentencing, believing Weinstein had sentenced Dazzo while outraged over the murder.[112] (Weinstein had given Dazzo fifteen years in prison and a $4000 fine.[113])

The Second Circuit upheld Weinstein's declaration of a mistrial for Mastrangelo on the basis of "manifest necessity," so that a new trial would not be prevented by the Double Jeopardy Clause of the Constitution. Judge James L. Oakes, writing for the court, concluded that there was the possibility that Mastrangelo had participated in making the witness unavailable and that the government was without fault. Therefore, the trial judge's determination in favor of a mistrial was, entitled to "special respect."[114]

Weinstein's take on the case years later was that it was a "strange situation where I supposed I pushed things by attributing the murder to this guy as a basis for the mistrial... I think I acted with some impropriety to save the case because I was so outraged by what they had done, but it did succeed. And I think probably rightly so."[115]

Political Corruption

One of the most important functions of a U.S. Attorney is to try to keep politics and politicians as clean as possible. Over the past forty years, one Vice President and a number of members of Congress, four federal judges, and a great many state and local officials have been convicted of federal crimes. During his second and third decades on the bench, Weinstein handled four significant trials of politicians and government officials accused of corruption. Two are considered in this chapter and two in Chapter 7.

One of the prosecutions involved a New York State Supreme Court Justice, William S. Brennan of Queens, who had solicited and accepted bribes of $3,000 to $10,000 in order to fix cases in his own court. The prosecution put on more than forty witnesses and offered 150 pieces of evidence in the fifteen-day trial. The key witness against Brennan was a close friend, Anthony J. Bruno, described by the *New York Daily News* as a "baggy-eyed saloon keeper."[116] Bruno said he testified because his wife had unwittingly become an accomplice. The sixty-seven-year-old Brennan, a former transit police

---

[110] *Id.* at 311–12.

[111] New York Daily News, Apr. 30, 1981; New York Times, Apr. 30, 1981.

[112] United States v. Dazzo, 1982 NB 97 (Feb, 22, 1982: *WJF*-Lumb/*Bartels*).

[113] New York Daily News, July 6, 1981.

[114] *United States v. Mastrangelo*, 1981 NB 320 (Sept. 17, 1981: *Oakes*-Blumenthal/*Meskill*).

[115] Weinstein Oral History, at 603.

[116] New York Daily News, Nov. 21, 1985.

officer, state assemblyman, and state senator, did not testify in his own defense, which largely consisted of character witnesses. In his closing statement, the prosecutor told the jury that Brennan was so corrupt that he once sent a man to jail because a bribe offer had been withdrawn.[117] The jury deliberated for eleven hours over one day and a half and found Brennan guilty of all charges in the twenty-six-count indictment. He was the first New York judge convicted of a crime for over a decade.[118]

At sentencing in a crowded courtroom, Weinstein described Brennan as "casually corrupt and amiably dishonest."[119] Discussing the seriousness of Brennan's crime, Weinstein referred to the Old Testament, the medieval Jewish commentator Rashi, Sir Francis Bacon, and Martin Manton. He wrote:

> No crime is more corrosive of our institutions. In the final analysis the judicial system depends upon the trust of the people and the impartiality of the judges. . . Were the public to lose faith in the honesty of the judges, much of the law's barrier to vigilantism and chaos would crumble.[120]

Along with the nature of the crime, Weinstein saw other aggravating circumstances: a lack of appreciation of the degree to which his behavior deviated from being acceptable, the need to assure the public of the fairness of the system, the adverse impact on the exercise of discretion by at least some judges, and violation of the great trust placed in judges. Yet, as we might expect, Weinstein found mitigating factors: a harmonious marriage; a closely knit family, living on a modest scale; industriousness; substantial contributions to the welfare of the community; poor health; Brennan's compassionate sentencings as judge.

In the end, the sentence Brennan was given was not heavy: five years of prison (he would be eligible for parole in twenty months), five years further probation, a $209,000 fine, and a mandatory assessment of $1300.[121] The government was disappointed, hoping for a stiffer penalty in order to pressure Brennan into cooperating with other investigations.[122] The *Daily News*, sharply critical, said that the sentence Brennan received "made one wonder if Weinstein is in the right line of work."[123] Many of the

---

[117] NEWSDAY, Dec. 10, 1985.

[118] On the Brennan trial and sentencing, *see* NEW YORK TIMES, Nov. 15, 1985, Nov. 21, 1985, Dec. 13, 1985, Feb. 3, 1986; NEWSDAY, Nov. 13, 1985, Dec. 4, 1985, Feb. 4, 1986; NEW YORK DAILY NEWS, May. 21, 1985, Feb. 4, 1986; NEW YORK POST, Dec. 13, 1985, Feb. 4, 1986; N.Y.L.J. Dec. 13, 1986.

[119] New York Daily News, Feb. 4, 1986.

[120] *United States v. Brennan*, 629 F. Supp. 283, 302 (Feb. 3, 1986). In his opinion, Weinstein placed a chart of judges convicted in federal courts over the preceding twenty-five years, their crimes and the sentences they received.

[121] *Id.* at 306–07.

[122] NEW YORK TIMES, Feb. 3, 1986, at A1, B3.

[123] NEW YORK DAILY NEWS, Feb. 4, 1986. *See also* Murray Kempton's criticism, NEW YORK POST, Feb. 4, 1986.

students from Grear Neck High School who attended the sentencing also felt that the penalty was not stiff enough.[124]

A four-term member of Congress, Frederick W. Richmond, was sentenced by Weinstein for income tax evasion, possession of marijuana, and supplementing the salary of a federal employee. A highly successful businessman, Richmond's wealth at the time of his sentencing was estimated at $18.9 million. He also had a long record of philanthropy, especially in the areas of education, mental health, and culture— Richmond was one of those who stepped in to save Carnegie Hall from the wreckers' ball. He also had served as president of the Urban League, played a role in the development of the Food Stamp program, and helped many persons individually. Yet Richmond had also indulged in drugs brought for him by his staff, been arrested for solicitation, and had been involved with a man who had been convicted for attempted murder and escaped from prison.

Weinstein had to determine whether or not to accept the plea agreement between the U.S. Attorney and Richmond. Under part of it, Richmond agreed to resign from Congress and promised that he would not serve were he reelected. Weinstein held that part of the agreement was unconstitutional because it (1) conflicted with the fundamental right of the people to elect their representatives, (2) interfered with the principle of separation of powers, and (3) contravened public policy by utilizing a technique latent with the possibility of executive domination of members of Congress through the threat of forced resignation.[125]

In his opinion, a penetrating analysis of the separation of powers, Weinstein reasoned that the right of the people to elect their representatives was embodied in the Constitution by prescribing only a limited number of qualifications for congressional office.[126] The separation of powers was fostered in the Constitution by keeping the power to strip a member of Congress of elective office away from both the judiciary and the executive. Weinstein thought that the possibility of the executive utilizing the threat of prosecution of a Congressman "involves particularly dangerous political consequences," representing "an opportunity for an assault on the composition and integrity of a coordinate branch of government."[127] Taken together with the investigative techniques such as those used in the ABSCAM case,[128] the enormous spectrum of criminal laws that can be violated, the powerful investigative and prosecutorial

---

[124] NEW YORK TIMES, Feb. 3, 1986, at A1, B3. An intervening Supreme Court decision led Weinstein to grant a postconviction motion to dismiss the fraud counts. However, the other counts stood. *United States v. Brennan*, 685 F. Supp. 884 (May 13, 1988).

[125] *United States v. Richmond*, 550 F. Supp. 605 (Nov. 10, 1982).

[126] *Id.* at 607.

[127] *Id.* at 608.

[128] Where an FBI sting operation captured on tapes political officials (including members of Congress) involved in taking bribes.

machine available to the executive forced resignations through plea bargains would provide "an intolerable threat to a free and independent Congress."[129]

Ultimately, Weinstein sentenced Richmond to a year and a day in prison (making him eligible for parole after four months) and a fine of $20,000. At sentencing, while he was seated at a table without wearing robes, Weinstein told Richmond:

> You have done commendable things for most people. For this you received personal gratification, affection, respect and high office. You have committed criminal acts. For this you must be punished.[130]

Protection of the Rights of Criminal Defendants

Weinstein wrote several concise Fourth Amendment opinions during this period that are models of the genre. *United States v. Robles*[131] involved a method being used by Drug Enforcement Administration (DEA) agents to deal with defendants who were avoiding the more stringent drugs searches at Kennedy Airport by bringing drugs to New York from other cities. Weinstein had to determine whether, at different points of the chronology, the special agent had sufficient suspicion to first, stop the defendants and, later, to detain them. The case, Weinstein said, raised very serious questions of due process, equal protection, and of the right of the people to travel freely within the United States.[132]

In *Robles*, a trained DEA special agent was monitoring domestic flights. The defendants, flying from Chicago to New York, attracted the agent's interest "because of the fast pace at which they proceeded and the fact that they kept their eyes and head facing down."[133] Weinstein found this observation "without significance." On leaving the plane, Robles "grabbed Arroyo by the hand, pulling her sharply towards him" and the couple began walking "at a fast pace." This, too, was unremarkable. Robles then stopped

---

[129] *Id.* Weinstein did try the case of the tenth and last ABSCAM defendant Joseph Silvestri—not a member of Congress, but a New Jersey real estate consultant and developer, who was accused of making arrangements for two members of Congress to meet with FBI agents positing as representatives of an Arab sheik. Weinstein told the defendant and attorneys that he did not believe Silvestri's entrapment defense—"the defendant had his tongue hanging out to commit crimes." A jury found Silvestri guilty. NEWSDAY, Dec. 22, 1982; NEW YORK TIMES, Jan. 29, 1983.

[130] NEW YORK TIMES, Nov. 10, 1981, at 1. *See also* Transcript of sentence, *United States v. Richmond*, 82-CR-416, 82-CR-418, 1982 Op. NB, at 281–91. At the time he had a presentencing conference with Judges I. Leo Glasser and Mark Costantino. Weinstein would have given Richmond one year (to serve six months) and a $20,000 fine. Glasser would have given him eighteen months or one year and one day, five years' probation, and a $10,000 fine. Judge Costantino would have given him two years in prison, three years' probation, and a $15,000 fine. This is based on Frederick W. Richmond Sentencing Material provided to me by Judge Weinstein. *See also* Weinstein Oral History, at 646.

[131] 78 CR 70, 1978 Op. NB 701 (May 15, 1978).

[132] Hearing transcript, *United States v. Robles*, 78 CR 70, 1978 NB (May 15, 1998).

[133] *Id.* at 704.

at a pay telephone and made a call, speaking in Spanish. "This is unexceptional," wrote Weinstein.[134] At this point, however, "Robles' composure seemed to change. Instead of looking straight down he began to turn around and survey the entire area" and "looked nervous." Weinstein, however, pointed out that "[m]ost people are nervous when they are milling around the carousel at La Guardia. A large proportion of the baggage never turns up and everybody is anxious about whether they will get their bag and whether they are in the right spot."[135]

Once the bags were retrieved the couple left the baggage claim area. "Any other activity would have been suspicious," said Weinstein. Weinstein continued to analyze the behavior of Robles as described by the DEA agent as cause to hold Robles and Arroyo up. The Robles stopped and surveyed the area, attempted to hail a cab, then waited on the proper taxi line. It was at this point that Agent Whitmore stopped the couple identified himself as an agent, and asked several ordinary questions. "None of this was suspicious," said Weinstein.

Weinstein stated that, after receiving the answers to his questions, the agents had no right under the case law to detain the couple and ask any additional questions.[136] At this point, "[e]ven if, in a purely technical sense the arrest was not made, these people, given their social status and the official status of the agent, were prevented from proceeding further. At this point, they were effectively under arrest" and "[s]ince the stop or investigation was illegal everything that followed flowing directly from the stop was illegal."[137]

Weinstein dismissed the indictment, but recommended that the case be appealed because the enforcement technique used in the case was part of a special program. Weinstein thought that "[t]he courts responsible for trying these cases are entitled to a decision by the Court of Appeals. . . in view of what appears to be a developing divergence among the District Judges of the Circuit."[138] He added:

> . . . except for the fact that these people were Hispanic, their actions are probably exactly the actions of many of the Judges arriving at La Guardia Airport from Chicago and other places within the United States.[139]

United States v. Seinfeld[140] was another important Fourth Amendment case. A police officer had been properly executing a search warrant at a residence which was also used for doing business, selling kits to manufacture gun silencers. During the course of the search, incoming business calls were answered by one of the police officers. One caller

---

[134] *Id.* at 705.
[135] *Id.* at 705–06.
[136] *Id.* at 707.
[137] *Id.* at 707.
[138] *Id.* at 708.
[139] *Id.*
[140] 632 F. Supp. 622 (Apr. 15, 1986).

said that the two .22 caliber silence kits he had previously purchased worked well. Based on that information, federal agents procured another search warrant for the caller's residence, executed it, and discovered a large quantity of illegal firearms.

Weinstein held that the second search was valid. The "relatively minor trickery" of a policeman posing as an employee of the business he was searching "does not," he said, "create a constitutional impediment to use of the defendant's voluntary statements as a basis for a search warrant."[141] There may be occasions when a caller to a business phone has an expectation of privacy, but this was not one of them.[142]

COMMERCIAL DISPUTES

It is too easily forgotten that one of the valuable roles the federal courts perform is the resolution of commercial disputes. During this period, Judge Weinstein handled a variety of interesting cases. In *Russo v. Texaco, Inc.*, Weinstein upheld the Federal Trade Commission's approval of the acquisition of Getty Oil by Texaco and Texaco's divestiture of Getty's previous franchise relationships with Getty service station dealers. Holding that that protection against corporate overreaching which harmed gasoline consumers and small businesses was assigned to the FTC, not judges, Weinstein observed that:

> In a rapidly changing economy, fixed preservation of business relationships may spell financial death to the detriment of franchisees as well as franchisors. Change may be required for survival.[143]

Denby v. Seaboard World Airlines, Inc.[144] involved insurance for silver that had been stored in a warehouse at John F. Kennedy Airport. To resolve the case, Weinstein had to define the meaning of a French word used in the Warsaw Convention. To do so, he looked to decisions of a court in the Netherlands and the House of Lords. Another commercial case involved a barge fully loaded with oil which ran hard aground when the depth of water was exceptionally low.[145] Among the labor cases of interest was one involving district court jurisdiction over suits brought under the Employee Retirement Income Security Act (ERISA) by union pension funds.[146] Another involved the National Labor Relations Board's refusal to exercise jurisdiction over labor disputes involving

---

[141] *Id.* at 625.

[142] *Id.* at 626. *See also United States v. Morales*, 568 F. Supp. 646 (Aug. 3, 1983), where Weinstein upheld a search warrant that was executed after the law enforcement officer received new material information suggesting that a material fact in the warrant was inaccurate.

[143] *Russo v. Texaco, Inc.*, 630 F. Supp. 682, 688 (Feb. 21, 1986).

[144] 575 F. Supp. 1134 (Dec. 8, 1983).

[145] *Pittston Marine Transport Co. v. G.A.T.FX. Terminals Corp.*, 1985 Op NB 280 (Oct. 2, 1985).

[146] *Local 807 Labor-Mgmt. Pension Fund v. Owens Trucking, Inc.*, 585 F. Supp. 616 (May 25, 1984).

the association which operated thoroughbred racing in New York State.[147] In a case that Weinstein had to decide in a matter of hours, the issue was whether the Long Island Railroad was part of the national railway network. If so, it was covered by the Norris-LaGuardia Act, so a strike against it could not be enjoined.[148]

An unfair competition case yielded a very important opinion on jurisdiction. It occurred in a suit between Bulova Watch Company, a New York corporation whose principal place of business was New York, and K. Hattori & Co., Ltd., a billion dollar multinational corporation using subsidiaries to penetrate the American market and to keep its home production going at a huge volume and profit. Bulova charged Hattori with unfair competition and disparagement as well as with engaging in a conspiracy to raid its marketing staff in order to appropriate Bolivia's trade secrets.[149]

Hattori was a Japanese corporation which owned all the stock of the Seiko Corporation of America. It contracted for the manufacture of its watches in Japan and sold them under Seiko, Pulsar, and other brand names in the United States. Watches and clocks accounted for 90 percent of Hattori's sales, and the United States was its largest foreign market. In 1978, six members of Bulova's staff—regional sales managers and more senior executives—left Bulova to join either a Seiko subsidiary or a Seiko distributor. Later, a number of Bulova's salesmen were hired by Pulsar. Bulova contended that these hirings had caused serious dislocations at Bulova's corporate headquarters and damaged its sales.

Weinstein's seventy-seven-page opinion on jurisdiction has been described as "a primer on the development of multinational marketing techniques."[150] Deciding the case, Weinstein took extensive judicial notice based partly upon his own research and issued a preliminary memorandum upon which the parties were entitled to be heard as to notice. Hattori took up the invitation.

Weinstein first examined the business relationship from the practical viewpoint of businessmen rather than "through the distorting lens of a legal conceptual frame work established in an earlier era."[151] Weinstein explained that:

[A]side from their magnitude, today's multinationals are unique in the way vast investment in myriad locations are made to serve the interests of a single organization. Large advantages lie in the possibility of making centralized management and

---

[147] *New York Racing Ass'n v. N.L.R.B,* 95 Lab. Cas.13785, 1982 WL 1964 (July 28, 1982), *rev'd,* 708 F.2d 46 (1983: *Fein*-Lumb-Kearse). Weinstein ordered the Labor Board to make a reasoned decision as to its jurisdiction over the association. He was reversed. *See also Local 807 Mgmt. Pension Fund v. Owens Trucking, Inc.,* 585 F. Supp. 616 (May 25, 1984).

[148] Weinstein issued a restraining order so that the point could be argued. *Metropolitan Transp. Auth. v. United Transp. Union,* 77-Civ-2358, 1978 Op. NB 68 (Mar. 31, 1978).

[149] *Bulova Watch Co. v. K. Hattori & Co.,* 508 F. Supp. 1322 (Feb. 12, 1981).

[150] *Jewelers' Circular–Keystone* (Feb. 1981) at 360, 361.

[151] *Bulova Watch,* 508 F. Supp. 1322.

investment decisions on the basis of the situations and opportunities prevailing in various host countries.[152]

He looked to the cumulative significance of all activities of a foreign corporation within the state (New York) in order to determine whether the corporation was doing business within the state for jurisdictional purposes.

An important question in assessing presence for jurisdictional purposes is whether a multinational has reached a stage in its evolution when it can be said that its sales and marketing subsidiaries truly have a "life of their own." In his analysis, Weinstein commented:

> It would be helpful were the law to provide some grand jurisdictional ledger sheets upon which formal points such as these could be assigned weights and totted up. That is not possible in our real world where so much depends on nuances, on a sense of interrelationships and on a realistic appraisal of subtle economic and power connections. Real rather than formal relationships must be considered.[153]

It was the integrated international operation of Hattori affecting activities in New York that was the primary focus of concern. Weinstein found Hattori "a highly effective export manufacturer, not a fully developed multinational." It is "very much the hub of a wheel with many spokes."[154] It is appropriate, therefore, "to look to the center of the wheel in Japan when the spokes violate substantive rights in other countries."[155] Weinstein found that "'Hattori and its American subsidiaries do maintain some independence—about as much as the eggs and vegetables in a Western omelet.'"[156] In the end, therefore, Weinstein held that the district court had jurisdiction over Hattori both on the theory that it was "doing business" in New York and under New York State's long-arm statute. However, the district court would not exercise that jurisdiction over the individual defendants who were sued.[157]

---

[152] *Id.* at 1336.

[153] *Id.* at 1340.

[154] *Id.* at 1341.

[155] *Id.*

[156] Jewelers' Circular–Keystone (April 1981) 246.

[157] During this decade, Weinstein called for a national standard for service in federal cases instead of the system where federal judges determined state long-arm jurisdiction on a state by state basis. Jack B. Weinstein, *Coordination of Judicial Resources*, 12 JUDGES J., Oct. 1973, at 22–24, 33–34 (1982). Weinstein also had an important standing case where he was reversed by the Second Circuit. *RBK Instruments, Inc. v. United States*, 715 F.2d 713 (1983: HJF-Card-Oakes). Weinstein only entered an order dismissing the action. In a suit over race horses brought against the Aga Khan, Weinstein held that the courts of France were a more appropriate forum than the Eastern District. *Murty & Murty Bros. Sales v. S.A. Prince Aga Khan*, 92 F.R.D. 478 (1981). In *Harris v. VAO Intourist, Moscow*, 481 F. Supp. 1056 Weinstein held that a suit against Intourist over the alleged wrongful death of an American tourist in a fire in a Moscow Hotel was barred by the Foreign Sovereign Immunities Act. In *Perkins Elmer (Computer Sys. Div.) v. Texas Mediterranean Airways*, 107 F.R.D. 55 (July 30, 1985), where the defendant moved to dismiss the

Probably the most important of the economic disputes which came to Weinstein was *Hydrolevel Corp. v. American Society of Mechanical Engineers,*[158] an antitrust case that questioned the practices of voluntary standard-setting organizations and wound up costing the American Society of Mechanical Engineers (ASME) $4.5 million.

The ASME was a tax-exempt technical and scientific society which set safety standards for mechanical devices such as boilers through a highly developed system of four hundred codes and standards. Much of the research for the society was done by volunteers who came from its members. The question in the *Hydrolevel* case was whether such an organization could be held liable as an unwitting member of a conspiracy in restraint of trade.

In the case before Weinstein, ASME was sued for restraint of trade when two of its highly placed volunteers combined to issue a misinterpretation of one of its codes. At issue was a water-level control device for boilers Hydolevel had developed to shut off the supply of boiler fuel when it dropped too low. A major competitor and a leading underwriter of commercial boilers joined with others to write the ASME Boiler and Pressure Vessel Committee asking if a time-delay feature would meet the code. The two men who were then the chair and vice chair of the subcommittee which evaluated the device replied that the cutoff could prove to be dangerous. The written reply was then used by a major competitor of Hydrolevel in its advertising. Hydrolevel's business declined.

After a seven-day trial, Weinstein charged the jury that, when a society was doing quasi-public work, that in order to be held liable the society in effect had to have approved, in some way or made itself a part of the manipulation by one of the members of its committees for the advantage of a private party. The jury found that ASME had conspired to restrain trade in the shut-off market and awarded Hydrolevel $3.3 million damages. Weinstein reduced the damages by promoting the settlement of related suits, and then trebled the remaining damages as it was an antitrust suit. The final judgment was for $7.5 million.[159] Weinstein did not write an opinion in the case.

The Court of Appeals affirmed the judgment on liability, although on a theory different from that embodied in Weinstein's instructions to the jury. The appellate court took the position that the normal rules of agency applied and that, if the actor was an agent of the society, as those in the committees were, then the Society was liable.

---

complaint because the plaintiff had responded to the summons by letter rather than by a form acknowledging that there had been service of the summons. Weinstein wrote: "It does not serve any end of justice to penalize a plaintiff for failure to secure the 'proper' talismanic piece of paper from defendant if a substantially equivalent writing has been obtained. . ." *Id.* at 59–60.

[158] On the *Hydrolevel* case, *see* Charles W. Beardsley, The Hydrolevel Case—A Retrospective, Mechanical Engineering 66 (June 1984).

[159] *Hydrolevel Corp. v. Am. Soc'y Mech. Eng'rs,* 75-C-1360 (Feb. 13, 1979), 1979 NB 48. Ironically, after being told of his victory, the president of Hydrolevel suffered a fatal heart attack. NEWSDAY, Feb. 5, 1979.

Hydrolevel had only to demonstrate that ASME's agents had acted within their apparent authority when participating in the conspiracy.[160]

Fifteen professional societies filed amicus briefs in the Supreme Court on behalf of ASME, arguing that voluntary nonprofit organizations should not be subjected to liability for treble damages on the basis of a principle as tenuous as apparent authority. The Supreme Court upheld the Court of Appeals by a 6–3 vote, although Chief Justice Warren Burger, concurring, took Weinstein's view of the case.[161] The High Court stated that the facts of the case dramatically illustrated the power of ASME to restrain competition.[162]

The fact that ASME was a nonprofit organization did not alter its liability under the antitrust laws. Since the antitrust violation in the case could not have occurred without ASME's codes and ASME's method of administering the codes, it was not inappropriate that the society be liable for the damages. The Court also held that the apparent authority theory was consistent with the congressional intent to encourage competition. It criticized Weinstein's jury instructions that required proof that ASME ratified the acts in question and that these acts were meant to benefit the society. A ratification rule in antitrust cases would encourage other organizations to close their eyes to potential member abuses.

Weinstein then retried the damages issue. The jury awarded Hydrolevel $1.1 million which was to be trebled. When the money from settlements was deducted, the award came to $2.5 million, not counting attorneys' fees. At this point, the case was settled for $4.75 million.

JUSTICE WITH A HUMAN FACE: SOCIAL SECURITY DISABILITY CASES

Weinstein's belief that the law must show a human face—to understand, respect, and protect "little people"—is best demonstrated during this decade in two areas: the battle over the bureaucratic treatment of the physically and mentally disabled[163] and his effort, primarily in extrajudicial activities, to see that the law gives the poor a fairer shake, to "level the playing field."

Under considerable political pressure during the Carter and Reagan administrations (especially during the latter), the Social Security Administration (SSA) threw large numbers of individuals receiving Social Security disability payments off the rolls. The federal judiciary reacted negatively to these policies. Weinstein was by no means alone, but his voice was one of the loudest. Not only did he make several of the most important

---

[160] *Hydrolevel Corp. v. American Society of Mech. Eng'rs*, 635 F.2d 118 (1980: *Lumb-HJF-Mesk*).*See also* Weinstein Oral History, at 540.

[161] 456 U.S. 556, 578 (1982). Powell, White, and Rehnquist dissented.

[162] *Id.* at 571.

[163] A similar battle occurred in 1997, but is not treated here. *See* Robert Post, *U.S. Challenges Courts on Disabilities*, NEW YORK TIMES, Apr. 21, 1977.

decisions but, with a law review article pointing the way, he provided assistance to other judges.[164]

In 1980, at the behest of the Carter administration, Congress amended the Social Security Act to require periodic review of disability rules and authorized a stepped up review of the benefits of Social Security disability recipients to determine whether they remained eligible. The SSA interpreted that law as a directive to reduce the number of disability payment beneficiaries

When the Reagan administration came to office, it initiated a vigorous search for recipients who, it thought, were not entitled to the payments. Weinstein described it this way:

A zealous administration . . . believed it had congressional sanction to cut costs at the expense of what some believed was an impotent constituency.[165]

The Agency's administrative law judges (ALJs) were under pressure to reduce the number of those receiving Social Security disability payments.[166] Between March 1981 and November 1983, the SSA conducted one million reviews of disability awards and terminated awards in 45 percent of the cases. Weinstein put it this way:

Within the ranks of the ALJs, there is diversity. Some function as sieves, approving the majority of claims they hear, others function as dikes turning back with regularity the rush of claims that come before them.[167]

Of the cases that were appealed to the courts, the Agency's decisions was overruled 50 percent of the time.[168]

The Secretary of Health and Human Services (for practical purposes, this meant the Agency) was required to make a realistic, individual assessment of each individual's ability to engage in substantial gainful activity. A worker was considered disabled if he were unable, considering his age, education, and work experience, to engage in substantial gainful work that existed in the national economy. Such SSA decisions were made "far more quickly than the precious values at stake seem[ed] to warrant."[169]

Many of those who were mentally ill did not receive a meaningful individual assessment. Rather, from 1978 at least until the early months of 1983, there was overwhelming

---

[164] Jack B. Weinstein, *Equality and the Law: Social Security Disability Cases in the Federal Courts*, 35 SYRACUSE L. REV. 897 (1984).

[165] *Id.* at 913. *See also* JEFFREY B. MORRIS, ESTABLISHING JUSTICE IN MIDDLE AMERICA 271–72 (2007).

[166] *Id.* at 902. *See also* CHRISTOPHER E. SMITH, UNITED STATES MAGISTRATES IN THE FEDERAL COURTS 82 (1980).

[167] Jack B. Weinstein, *Equality and the Law*, *supra* note 164, at 915.

[168] JEFFREY B. MORRIS, TO ADMINISTER JUSTICE ON BEHALF OF ALL THE PEOPLE: THE UNITED STATES DISTRICT COURT FOR THE EASTERN DISTRICT OF NEW YORK 57 (1992).

[169] PETER SCHUCK, SUING GOVERNMENT 65 (1983).

"evidence 'of a fixed clandestine policy against those with mental illness'"[170] Further, Weinstein found that the SSA relied on bureaucratic instructions rather than on individual assessments and overruled the medical opinions of its own consulting physicians.[171] Not only the harsh decisions, but the process itself was "devastating since the mentally ill are particularly vulnerable to bureaucratic error. The communications from the SSA were difficult for them to understand and frightening to many."[172]

A multitude of individual lawsuits asked the federal courts to reverse the disability determinations.[173] Weinstein considered this "the most troublesome of his duties,"[174] encompassing heartbreaking decisions as to whether particular individuals were sufficiently disabled. Many of those affected were very poor and appearing *pro se* without either attorneys or expert medical assistance. Weinstein wrote: "Unless and until we furnish the poor with adequate medical and legal advice and representation, there will be unacceptable inequality in the system."[175]

Although by statute the decision of the administrative law judge had to be upheld if supported by substantial evidence, many decisions were challenged. Because of political pressure, the SSA refused to accept federal court rulings as precedents. Until late 1983, the SSA appeared to have a policy of resisting every Social Security claim no matter how justified.[176] In the 1982–1983 fiscal year, for example, the 905 cases constituted 17 percent of the civil caseload of the Eastern District of New York. In September 1983 the Eastern District disposed of sixty-six Social Security cases; only twenty-two were won by the government.[177]

In 1982, Weinstein stated the manner in which the Social Security Act should be interpreted: "The purpose of the Social Security Act is to benefit those who are in need by providing a remedy for certain problems seriously affecting a person's life. To fulfill its purpose, the act should be broadly construed and liberally applied."[178]

By the end of August 1984, the *New York Times* reported that forty-five states were under court orders that blocked them from carrying out terminations without using a medical improvement standard—placing the burden on the Agency to show an improvement in the beneficiary's medical condition before benefits could be terminated.[179] By the beginning of 1985, federal courts had ordered the SSA to restore benefits to more

---

[170] Weinstein, *Equality and the Law*, *supra* note 164, at 921–22.

[171] *Id.* at 922, 908.

[172] *Id.* at 922.

[173] Ultimately, there were some class actions.

[174] Weinstein, *Equality and the Law*, *supra* note 164, at 897.

[175] *Id.* at 938.

[176] *Zimmerman v. Schweiker*, 575 F. Supp. 1436, 1441 (Dec. 5, 1983).

[177] Weinstein, *Equality and the Law*, *supra* note 164, at 900, 911.

[178] *Suarez v. Schweiker*, CY-82-0935, 1982 NB 399, 404 (Nov. 2, 1982).

[179] Susan Gluck Mezey: no Longer Disabled: The Federal Courts and the Politics of Social Security Disability 152–53 (1988).

than 200,000 persons.[180] Strikingly, there was very little difference in the results between the Reagan judicial appointees and those of Nixon or Carter.[181]

As the district courts were virtually unanimous in holding against the SSA and, in time, were joined by the Courts of Appeals, an unseemly situation developed as the Agency refused to acquiesce in court decisions because of the lack of a *national* standard. The Social Security Administration obeyed rulings only in so far as they affected the individual plaintiff.[182]

In *Suarez v. Schweiker*, Weinstein remanded the case to the Agency because the administrative law judge (ALJ) had refused to listen to the claimant's own testimony as to her mental state.[183] In *Edwards v. Secretary of Dept. of H & HS*,[184] the ALJ had found that a woman who had had gall bladder surgery, a hysterectomy, and an ileostomy was capable of working. The woman had one working kidney and frequently had to empty her ileostomy bag. To "suggest that a person with such hygiene and medical problems would be acceptable in any work-place setting constitutes an unsupported flight of fancy,"[185] Weinstein said while reversing the Agency.

In *Sinatra v. Heckler*,[186] the Social Security Administration had thrown out the claimant's request as "untimely." Under SSA regulations, a claimant has to request a hearing no later than sixty days from the day he received notice of the decision. The agency employed a presumption that its notice arrived at the claimant's address five days after the agency dated it. The claimant had received the notice on December 21, 1979, and requested the hearing seventy-three days later (March 3, 1980).

In previous cases, the Second Circuit had held that there could be judicial review of an adverse determination *only on the merits*. The problem in *Sinatra v. Heckler* was that there was no final decision to be reviewed. The problem here was that the petitioner's request for review within the agency was not timely filed. With that door closed, Weinstein based his decision on a petition for the writ of mandamus. He overcame the tardiness in requesting the hearing by holding that the five-day presumption placed the ultimate burden of proof on the issue delay on the agency. He stated: "To force a claimant to negotiate the bureaucratic maze of the Social Security and postal system to uncover an administrative mishap would place upon him an inordinate burden."[187]

Weinstein found that the agency presumption could be overcome by "a glance at the calendar." He found it "not unreasonable that a letter dated December 21, 1979, would be belatedly dispatched and then delayed in the mail [because of the holidays] so that

---

[180] *Id.* at 122.

[181] C. K. Rowland & Robert A. Carp, Politics and Judgment in Federal District Courts 129–30 (1996).

[182] Mezey, *supra* note 179, at 126–27.

[183] 82-CV-0935, 1982 NB 399, 403 (1982).

[184] 572 F. Supp. 1235 (Oct. 19, 1982).

[185] *Id.* at 1243.

[186] 566 F. Supp. 1354 (July 1, 1983).

[187] *Id.* at 1359.

it would not have been received before January 3, 1980."[188] Having made the thirteen days disappear, Weinstein then remanded the case to the agency for a hearing!

One of Weinstein's most remarkable accomplishments was, with the aid of able attorneys, to transform a case that began in Small Claims Court in Queens into a national class action.[189] In deciding it, Weinstein's prose captured considerable press attention.

In *David v. Heckler*,[190] Joseph David sued over the government's underpayment of Medicare reimbursement claims for his cancer-ridden wife. Begun in the lowest state court, the United States removed it to district court. There, it was expanded into a class action on behalf of hundreds of thousands of older Americans in the Borough of Queens whose Medicare Part B claims had been subject to diminution and who alleged that the notice and appeal procedures available to them violated due process.[191] Because there was a general bar to judicial review of Medicare Part B claims, the case was heard on constitutional grounds.

Under Medicare, a beneficiary can be denied partial or full reimbursement for payments made for medical treatment, if the treatment is deemed not necessary or not covered or if the doctor's charge is not "reasonable." Evidence at trial demonstrated that the notices to patients explaining denials of reimbursement did not meet the standard of due process. "The review letters defy understanding by the general public," Weinstein wrote. They were "written in a specialized Medicare vocabulary" They were "unintelligible to the average beneficiary." They "could not be understood by the great majority of the beneficiaries who received them."[192] Not only were the review letters incomprehensible, but the information they attempted to convey was "insufficient and misleading."[193] The "information needed to decide whether the reasonable charge figure was correct [was] unavailable or inaccessible."[194] Descriptions of the procedure allegedly used to determine "approved charges" were often concealed. Instead, there was "incomplete data, human and computer error, subjective decisions and sometimes pure guesswork."[195]

---

[188] *Id.* at 1360.

[189] One of the attorneys was the very able former U.S. Attorney in the Southern District, Whitney North Seymour, Jr. Another case transformed, though ultimately not successfully, involved a fingerprint lifted from the wheel of a hijacked truck. Weinstein suggested that the prosecution call in the FBI and obtain a duplicate. He then invited the defense counsel to object, putting the word "hearsay" into his mouth, and laid out the issue and overruled the objection, with the hope that the Court of Appeals would limit the relevant precedent. However, the appellate court did not seem to see the hearsay issue. Jack B. Weinstein, "Is there Scholarship After Death Or Are Evidence Teachers Needed After the Federal Rules?," Address, AALS Workshop on the Teaching of Evidence, 15–16 (Oct. 17, 1981) [hereinafter Weinstein, "Are Evidence Teachers Needed?"].

[190] 591 F. Supp. 1033 (1984).

[191] *See also* Weinstein Oral History, at 762ff.

[192] *David v. Heckler*, 591 Supp. 1033, 1042 (July 11, 1984).

[193] *Id.* at 1037.

[194] *Id.* at 1036.

[195] *Id.* at 1038.

Perhaps the best example of Weinstein's gift for the catchy phrases reporters love comes from this case. Responding to the government's argument that the review notices were sufficient, Weinstein wrote that:

> The language used is bureaucratic gobbledygook, jargon, double talk, a form of officialese, federalize and insurancese and doublespeak. It does not qualify as English.[196]

That quotation, or more generally, his opinion, got wide play. It was picked by newspapers such as the *New York Times, Los Angeles Times, Toronto Globe & Mail, Houston Post, Torrance (California) Daily Breeze*, and the *International Herald Tribune*.[197] Weinstein held that the notices Medicare recipients received were constitutionally inadequate. The information provided was not sufficient to enable a beneficiary to determine either the actual basis of a denial of reimbursement or whether reimbursement had been calculated correctly.[198]

Though he did not rule entirely for the plaintiffs, Weinstein ordered prompt action to ensure that notice be improved. He directed the defendants to cooperate with Legal Services for the Elderly in furnishing necessary information to ensure that the statute is properly administered for the benefit of the class.[199]

However, Weinstein's most important opinion in the Social Security disability area occurred in another class action brought by New York City, state officials, and eight named individuals. The unpublished internal policy of the Secretary of Health and Human Services as applied to the mentally ill was challenged in the litigation as unlawful. The policy mandated a presumption that a failure to meet or equal its "listings of impairments" was tantamount to a finding of ability to do at least unskilled work. That presumption led to routine denial of benefits to claimants eligible under the Social Security Disability Insurance Program (SSDI) and the Supplemental Security Insurance Program (SSI). The covert policy was challenged as arbitrary, capricious, violative of the Constitution, the Social Security Act, and applicable regulations.[200]

By regulation, the Secretary had adopted a five-step process to determine whether an individual's impairments were of such severity that, considering his age, education, and work experience, he would be unable to engage in any other kind of substantial gainful work existing in the national economy. Yet, Weinstein found that from 1978

---

[196] *David v. Heckler*, 591 F. Supp.1033, 1043 (July 11, 1984).

[197] NEW YORK TIMES, July 11, 1984, at B3; LOS ANGELES TIMES, July 12, 1984; TORONTO GLOBE & MAIL, July 30, 1984; HOUSTON POST, July 12, 1984, at 5B; TORRANCE DAILY BREEZE, July 12, 1984, at A5; INTERNATIONAL HERALD TRIBUNE, July 16, 1984. The *Pensacola Times Tribune* suggested Weinstein as a vice presidential candidate: "Who? Well, Weinstein isn't a household name and probably never will be. But in our view, he should be." PENSACOLA TIMES TRIBUNE, July 15, 1984, at C2.

[198] *David*, 591 F. Supp. at 1043.

[199] *Id.* at 1048.

[200] *City of New York v. Heckler*, 578 F. Supp. 1109 (Jan. 11, 1984).

to at least the early months of 1983, the SSA clandestinely and consistently had employed the presumption that mentally disabled claimants who did fulfill the listings of impairments necessarily retained sufficient residual functional capacity (RFC) to do "unskilled work." The covert policy eliminated steps from the sequential evaluation process, thereby ignoring the requirement of an individualized RFC assessment. The policy was changed only after the filing of this lawsuit before Weinstein and another in the Eighth Circuit.[201]

After a seven-day trial, Weinstein held that the Secretary had not made "a realistic, individual assessment of each claimant's ability to engage in substantial gainful activity," but had relied on bureaucratic instructions and overruled the medical opinions of its own doctors. The resulting supremacy of bureaucracy over professional medical judgments and the flaunting of published, objective standards were contrary to the spirit and letter of the Social Security Act.[202] Weinstein ordered that all decisions denying benefits or terminating them be reopened and that, while the cases were determined using proper standards, benefits be reinstated (but not at that time made retroactive).[203]

The Secretary raised no challenge on appeal to the substance of Weinstein's decision. The Court of Appeals then affirmed Weinstein's decision as to all of the claims of procedural infirmities.[204] The Supreme Court unanimously upheld the Second Circuit, focusing on a statute of limitations and exhaustion of remedies issues. It stated: "like the Court of Appeals, [w]e have no reason to disturb Chief Judge Weinstein's conclusion that the harm caused by wrongful denials was irreparable."[205]

One of the aspects of the Social Security disability cases which greatly troubled Weinstein was the inequality in the battle between the agency and the claimant. A huge, cumbersome bureaucracy was violating the law while U.S. Attorneys, pressured by political leaders, had to contest every suit brought by an ill individual who often had neither legal and nor medical expertise at hand.

JUSTICE WITH A HUMAN FACE: THE POOR IN THE COURTS

Besides the Social Security disability cases, many of which were argued *pro se*, Weinstein was troubled by the "enormous" problems presented by prisoner *pro se* litigation where the courts "find themselves unable to rely on traditional adversary processes to develop

---

[201] *Mental Health Ass'n of Minnesota v. Schweiker*, 554 F. Supp. 157 (D. Minn. 1982), *aff'd*, 720 F.2d 965 (8th C. 1983).

[202] *City of New York v. Heckler*, 578 F. Supp.1109, 1124 (Jan. 11, 1984).

[203] *Id.* at 1125. Weinstein claims that this decision was the first time a judge had revealed the hidden nature of the SSA's policy. Weinstein Oral History, at 727.

[204] *City of New York v. Heckler*, 742 F.2d 729 (1984: New-Lumb-Pratt). *See also* N.Y.L.J. Aug. 29, 1984, at 1; NEW YORK TIMES, Aug. 29, 1984, at 1.

[205] *Bowen v. City of New York*, 476 U.S. 467, 484 (1986), citing *City of New York v. Heckler*, 742 F.2d at 736.

and clarify the legal and factual issues."[206] He found civil rights cases brought by prisoners more difficult to deal with than the average *habeas* petition, "since in the latter there is usually some kind of record that tends to focus the factual issues. Prisoners' civil rights actions run the gamut."[207]

The period 1977 to 1986 was a particularly dismal time for the poor to be in U.S. courts. The Burger Court was trimming back access to the federal courts. Conservative and many moderate jurists were arguing that the federal courts were being clogged by Section 1983 (civil rights) suits, prisoner petitions, and Social Security disability cases. There were also strong pressures to reform class actions, stop discovery "abuse" and abolish diversity jurisdiction.[208]

During these years, Weinstein was devoting a great deal of time and attention to the problem of meaningful access to the courts by the poor (an important personal concern at least going back to his days as County Attorney), giving many speeches, publishing articles, and trying to do something practical about it as Chief Judge.[209] Weinstein argued that the pressure to reform class actions, stop discovery abuse, abolish diversity jurisdiction, and eliminate judicial review of disability awards because of their burden on the federal courts were not based on factual evidence, but rather part of efforts occurring in all three branches to keep the poor out of court.[210]

Weinstein did not find it "unfortunate" that actions to enforce statutory and constitutional rights on behalf of the poor, the weak, and the disadvantaged had taken the place of traditional straight forward commercial cases on the federal civil calendar.[211] Judges themselves, said Weinstein, "must struggle against their status to wall off

---

[206] As discussed in a 1972 speech. *See* Jack B. Weinstein, Speech to Prisoners' Rights Seminar, Practicing Law Institute, New York City, Oct. 6–7, 1972 at 13, 11 [hereinafter, Weinstein, *PLI Speech*].

[207] *Id.* at 8.

[208] Weinstein, *Right to Equal Access Speech*, The Poor's Right to Equal Access to the Courts, Speech at University of Connecticut Law School, Apr. 22, 1981 [hereinafter *Right to Equal Access Speech*], reprinted in 13 CONN. L. REV. 651 (1981 [hereinafter, Weinstein, *Right to Equal Access article*]; *The Court's Stake in Lawyer's Pro Bono Work*, at 10–11.

[209] *See* Reforming the Poor out of Court, Speech at Columbia Law School, Mar. 28, 1981, reprinted in N.Y.L.J., Mar. 30, 1981; Speech at the Association of the Bar of the City of New York, Oct. 6, 1981 [hereinafter Weinstein, *The Court's Stake*], reprinted N.Y.L.J. Oct. 23, 1981; *The Law School Community's Obligation to Equal Justice for the Poor*, Speech to Columbia Public Interest Foundation, Mar. 31, 1982 (1982 NB Speech 13) [hereinafter Weinstein, *Law School Community's Obligation*]; Ensuring Equality Before the Law, COLUMBIA (June 1982), at 48; Introductory Remarks at Civil Rights Seminar, Association of the Bar of the City of New York, Sept. 14, 1982 (1982 NB Speech 29); Justice and Mercy—Law and Equity, Speech at New York Law School Law Review Annual Banquet, Apr. 13, 1983, reprinted 28 N.Y.L.S. L. REV. 817 (1984). The last mentioned was also used as a commencement address at the University of Connecticut Law School, May 21, 1983. Excerpts from that were published in NEWSDAY, June 2, 1982. See also his Remarks at Volunteer Celebration, City Bar, Oct. 18, 1985.

[210] Weinstein, *Right to Access article*, *supra* note 208, at 657.

[211] Weinstein, *Reforming the Poor out of Court*t, *supra* note 209, at 7.

public access to the courts"—both jurisprudentially and in opening their work to the media.[212]

The federal courts were, he said, the "one group powerful and independent enough to speak out—and to act—when our country deviates from its ideals."[213] They were "the final institutional barrier to prevent the violation of the rights of the weak and oppressed." Unlike some of the leading spokesmen for the federal courts, men like Chief Justice Burger and Chief Judge Kaufman, Weinstein felt that the courts were "really not busy enough." He thought that judges should be figuring out ways to bring even more cases—and more deserving parties—into court.[214] Based upon his experience, he doubted that "liberality in reviewing correspondence, taking judicial notice, granting friend-of-the-court status, use of masters or their equivalent, considering the needs of the press, or freely granting intervention, would produce costs in terms of complexity that would outweigh the advantage of access to the courts of those who might be protected by judicial decisions."[215] "Judges," he said, "should be encouraged to construe *pro se* prisoners' pleadings more liberally . . . facilitate amendments of complaints by enumerating their failings in a conditional order rather than entering a final order of dismissal at once" and require answering papers from the state.[216]

From the many cases he had tried where parties represented themselves—*habeas corpus* petitions, prison suits, Section 1983 actions, and the Social Security disability cases—Weinstein had become even more aware of the vulnerability of *pro se* litigants as well as the burdens placed on the court when individuals without legal training represent themselves:

> The inability of the unskilled litigant to prepare pleadings, conduct adequate investigation, work with the rules of evidence, research decisional law, or persuasively argue the case in court render fair and expeditious disposition of most civil litigation virtually impossible.[217]

A judge, Weinstein said at the 1981 Brooklyn Law School commencement, presiding over a case involving a *pro se* litigant, is deprived of the help of counsel in understanding and disposing of the case expeditiously.[218]

---

[212] Jack B. Weinstein, Open Courts—An Antidote for the Dangers of False Elitism, Speech on 20th Annual Dean's Day, New York Law School (Mar. 8, 1980) 2–3 [hereinafter, Weinstein, *Open Courts*].

[213] Jack B. Weinstein, Equality, Liberty and the Public Schools: The Role of State Courts, 1 Cardozo L. Rev. 343, 378 (1979).

[214] Weinstein, *Reforming the Poor*, supra note 209, at 3.

[215] Weinstein, *Litigation Seeking Changes*, supra note 44, at 246.

[216] Weinstein, *PLI Speech*, supra note 206, at 23.

[217] Weinstein, All People Are Entitled to the Assistance of Lawyers in Civil as Well as Criminal Matters, Speech at Association of the Bar of the City of New York 3 (Mar. 30, 1976).

[218] Weinstein, Commencement Address, Brooklyn Law School, June 11, 1981, at 8.

Only a small portion of the actual and potential legal problems of the poor were being handled by professionals.[219] In 1980, fully 26.9 percent of all civil filings in the federal district courts were prisoner petitions, civil rights actions, and claims under the Social Security laws, but in a majority of these cases the poor lacked counsel.[220] In six hundred of 3550 civil cases—*habeas corpus*, Section 1983, Title VII age and sex discrimination cases, and appeals from administrative determinations—brought in the Eastern District, the poor were unrepresented.[221]

Thus, without access to the courts, without these foundational protections, "most of the rest of our promises of liberty and justice for all remain a mockery for the poor and the oppressed."[222] "Equal Rights for some," he said, "is no equal rights at all."[223] "Accessibility to the courts on equal terms" was essential to equality before the law, he argued.[224] The poor federal court litigant did not have accessibility on equal terms when he or she lacked counsel.

As Chief Judge of the Eastern District, Weinstein was in a position to do something about it. He appointed a committee which recommended forming a panel of lawyers who would volunteer to be randomly assigned to *pro se* litigants in the District. To recruit volunteers, Weinstein mailed 20,000 letters to members of bar associations. He set up the Eastern District Pro Bono Panel and created the Eastern District Civil Litigation Fund to provide some money for medical examinations and other needs of poor litigants.[225] He endowed both, providing funds for expenses of counsel and medical reports for litigants. He then came to the bar "like a modern mendicant—seeking services rather than alms."[226] Training seminars were sponsored for volunteer lawyers.[227] Weinstein himself participated in programs training lawyers to handle Social Security disability cases.[228]

SOME FURTHER THOUGHTS ON WEINSTEIN'S WORK, 1977–1986

Weinstein was extraordinarily innovative in the use of tools when trying cases. He was one of the first judges, if not the first, to permit a witness to give testimony

---

[219] Weinstein, *Law School Community's Obligations, supra* note 209, at 3.

[220] Weinstein, *Right to Equal Access article, supra* note 208, at 657.

[221] Weinstein, *The Court's Stake, supra* note 209, at. 3.

[222] Weinstein, *Right to Equal Access Speech, supra* note 208, at 8.

[223] Weinstein, *Law School Community's Obligations, supra* note 209, at 10.

[224] Weinstein, *Right to Equal Access article, supra* note 208, at 655.

[225] COLUMBIA LAW SCH. NEWS (December 1981); NEW YORK DAILY NEWS, Apr. 9, 1981, at 22; NEW YORK POST, July 9, 1981 (editorial praising the plan).

[226] Jack B. Weinstein, *The Court's Stake, supra* note 209, at 9. Though far from alone, Weinstein offered an eloquent and prestigious voice to the ultimately partially successful campaign to save the Legal Services Corporation from the mischief of its enemies. Weinstein, *Right to Access article, supra* note 209, at 657.

[227] Jack B. Weinstein, *Equality and the Law, supra* note 164, at 928, 935.

[228] He participated in the New York State Bar Association program of December 1, 1983. Letter from John S. Hogg to Judge Weinstein, Aug. 4, 1983, Weinstein 1983 Speech #37.

by picture phone. The witness was the eminent heart specialist, Dr. Denton Cooley.[229] In bench trials he occasionally swore in all the experts, seated them at a table with him and counsel and engaged them in a colloquy under his direction.[230] Having used a special master in the *Mark Twain* case, where a political solution was required, he used several of them in *Lora*, but this time to employ their technical knowledge.[231] He invited the government to appear as *amicus curiae* in stockholder litigation (SEC), education suits (HEW), and in a housing case (HUD), which raised the visibility of those cases.[232]

On the other hand, Weinstein was slapped down when he attempted through a decision to create a new privilege for scholars. At issue was a motion to quash a grand jury subpoena[233] to a Ph.D. candidate at the State University of New York at Stony Brook, who was working on a dissertation entitled, "The Sociology of the American Restaurant." The jury was investigating a suspicious fire and explosion at a restaurant where the student was working. Weinstein quashed the subpoena on the basis of a limited federal common law privilege he created, derived from the qualified reporter's privilege. "Compelled production of researcher's notes," Weinstein said, "inhibit prospective and actual sources of information, thereby obstructing the flow of information to the researcher, and through him or her, the public."[234]

The Second Circuit reversed and remanded.[235] Judge Ralph Winter, himself a distinguished professor of law, regarded the record in the case as "far too sparse to serve as a vehicle for consideration of whether a scholar's principle exists, much less to provide grounds for applying it to Brajuha [the young scholar]."[236] Lacking was "a detailed description of the nature and seriousness of the scholarly study in question, of the methodology employed, of the need for assurances of confidentiality to various sources to conduct the study, and of the fact that the disclosure requested by the subpoena would seriously impinge upon that confidentiality."[237] The record also lacked documentary or testimonial evidence from scholars of the nature of the work or of its role in the scholarly literature of sociology.[238] There also was not "evidence of a considered research

---

[229] *Dresdner v. Cutter Lab*, 76-CV-1837, 1977 NB 1, 2.

[230] Weinstein, Weinstein, *Improving Expert Testimony*, 20 RICH. L. REV. 473–97 (1986).

[231] Transcript (unofficial), Second Circuit Conference [included in letter to Kenneth Feinberg, Dec. 1, 1985], 1986 Sp.67, pp. 74ff.

[232] Weinstein, *Open Courts, supra* note 212, at 5–6. Once again Weinstein used an advisory jury. This time he used a six-person jury, which found discriminatory and unconstitutional New York City's "nail and mail" system of citing landlords. However, after an intervening Supreme Curt decision, he found the system constitutional on its face. *Greene v. Lindsay*, 102 S.Ct. 874 (1974).

[233] *In re Grand Jury Subpoena Dated January 4, 1984*, 583 F. Supp. 991 (Apr. 5, 1984).

[234] *Id.* at 993.

[235] *In re Grand Jury Subpoena*, 750 F.2d 223 (1984: *Winter-Oakes-Clarie*).

[236] *Id.* at 224.

[237] *Id.* at 225.

[238] *Id.* at 225.

plan, conceived in light of scholarly requirements or standards, contemplating assurance of confidentiality for certain parts of the inquiry."[239]

Weinstein's independence and his receptiveness to innovation produced decisions he must often have known would be reversed. Although his overall reversal rate was relatively low—he was affirmed on most everything in the *Agent Orange* case,[240] and some Court of Appeals reversals in his cases were overturned by the U.S. Supreme Court—as we have seen, his relationship with the Court of Appeals became rockier. While he could speak of reversals in jest,[241] some reversals seem to have hurt, including that in *Lora*.[242]

One reversal in an evidence case that must have hurt occurred in *United States v. Jamil*.[243] There, Weinstein had issued a pretrial order suppressing and excluding a tape recording of a conversation among the defendant, the defendant's attorney, and an informer. He suppressed the evidence because of its slight probative force, its cumulative nature, the time required to deal with it in court, its probable interjection of prejudice, and for other reasons. When it reversed, the Court of Appeals cited to the Weinstein-Berger treatise: "'Since the trial judge is granted such a powerful tool by Rule 403, he must take care to use it sparingly.'"[244]

That Weinstein was using his scholarship on intricate legal issues as ways to attain a just result should not be a surprise.[245] But, concurrently, he was also revising his treatises and casebooks[246] and writing law review articles in a wide variety of legal fields and subjects including class actions, education, expert witnesses, statistics, and access of the poor to legal services. Many of the articles were derived from speeches he gave. He was also preparing special materials for courses and lectures he was giving.

---

[239] *Id.* at 225.

[240] *See* Chapter 10, *infra*.

[241] In one speech he said, "Another thing wrong with the Federal Rules of Evidence is that we can understand them, so, too, can the appellate judges. We now get opinions reversing the district courts. Previously neither the district nor the court of appeals judges would have comprehended the point and the ruling below would have been sustained." Jack B. Weinstein, Reform, Speech to Columbia Law School Alumni Association, New York City Jan. 17, 1986, at 5.

[242] "As you will see, I was sort of depressed last week since we have a series of reversals of our court's work including the reversal of Judge Dooling's *Jackson* case. Last week, they reversed my *Lora* decision." Jack B. Weinstein to Michael Perry, June 10, 1980. See the reversal in *Korek and Korek v. United States*, 734 F.2d 923 (1984: *Fein*-Mans-Card), a particularly sharp one. Weinstein could hardly be faulted in *B.K. Instruments, Inc. v. United States*, 83-6124 (1983: HJF-Card-Oakes), where he followed Second Circuit law, but the Court of Appeals, anticipating a Supreme Court decision, changed its rule.

[243] *United States v. Jamil*, 546 F. Supp. 646 (1982), *rev'd*, 707 F.2d 638 (1983: *Pierce*-Timbers-Kearse).

[244] *Id.*; citing *Weinstein's Evidence* Sect. 403[01] at 403–07 (1982). Rule 403 of the Federal Rules of Evidence authorizes judges to exclude evidence if its probative value is substantially outweighted by the danger of unfair prejudice etc.

[245] Daniel Wise, "Doing Justice" Never Ends for District's Chief Judge, N.Y.L.J., Aug. 5, 1986,

[246] Jack B. Weinstein, J. J. Mansfield, N. Abrams, & M. A. Berger, *Rules and Statute Supplement* [for California Practitioners] for 1984 ed. EVIDENCE; Jack B. Weinstein, J. H. Mansfield, N. Abrams, M. Berger, 1986 *Professors Update for Use with Cases and Materials on Evidence* (7th ed.), *Rules & Statute Supp.*, 1984 ed.

Weinstein continued to devote considerable attention to the field of evidence. He taught evidence at Columbia Law School and for bar groups. He updated treatises, wrote major law review articles on problems resulting from expert testimony and on the use of statistics in court,[247] as well as continued to give lectures to try to influence the manner in which the Federal Rules of Evidence were interpreted. He extended his efforts to jurisdictions such as Ohio, which had adopted rules similar to the Federal Rules, bringing his desire that the federal and state courts "should provide an integrated system of justice a little closer."[248] He addressed law school professors of evidence on the topic: "Is there Scholarship after Death or Are Evidence Teachers needed after the Federal Rules?"[249]

Weinstein paid tribute to the eminent scholar, James H. Chadbourn, in the *Harvard Law Review*,[250] reviewed a book on eyewitness testimony,[251] and, stimulated by a note in the *Harvard Law Review*, wrote an interesting letter on hearsay to its student author.[252] Further, he also continued to write opinions with his casebook in mind.[253] At least once, however, he was unable to convince his former law clerk and co-editor, Margaret Berger, to put an opinion of his in the book.[254] He continued to use his cases to teach his students.[255]

One of Weinstein's particular concerns, undoubtedly spurred by the *Agent Orange* case, was dealing with expert testimony.[256] He was concerned that an expert "can be found to testify to the truth of almost any factual theory no matter how frivolous,"

---

[247] Discussed in Chapter 9.

[248] Jack B. Weinstein, *The Ohio and Federal Rules of Evidence*, 6 Cap. U. L. Rev. 517, 518. As of January 1977, eight states had adopted the Federal Rules of Evidence in various forms. *Id.* at 517.

[249] Jack B. Weinstein, Is There Scholarship After Death or Are Evidence Teachers Needed After the Federal Rules? Speech at Association of American Law Schools, Workshop on the Teaching of Evidence, Washington, D.C., Oct. 17, 1981 (copy in the possession of the author).

[250] Jack B. Weinstein, *Writings of James H. Chadbourn*, 92 Harv. L. Rev. 364 (1982). Chadbourn's revision of Wigmore's ten-volume treatise, Weinstein wrote, "was equivalent to completely rebuilding the Brooklyn Bridge while traffic flowed over it. . . ." *Id.* at 368.

[251] Jack B. Weinstein, Review of Elizabeth F. Loftus, Eyewitness Testimony (1979), 81 Colum. L. Rev. 441 (1981).

[252] Jack B. Weinstein to Stuart Singer [Note to be forwarded to main author of The Theoretical Foundation of Hearsay Rules], April 3, 1981. A chapter Weinstein had written for a book was republished in *The Practical Lawyer* and again in the *Civil Advocates Manual*. The chapter, "The Examination of Witnesses," was published in Morgan's Basic Problems of State and Federal Evidence 51ff (5th ed. by Jack Weinstein, 1976), then in Ali-Aba Committee on Continuing Education, The Practical Lawyers' Manual of Trial and Appellate Practice, No. 2, at 91ff (1979) and in Civil Advocates Manual 195ff (Guy O. Kornblum, Joseph W. Rogers, Jr., & Charles Van Orden eds.).

[253] *United States v. Obayabona*, 627 F. Supp. 397 (Dec. 27, 1985) on admissibility of a FBI Special Agent's prior consistent statement.

[254] Weinstein Oral History, at 617.

[255] *Id.* at 457f, 468.

[256] Weinstein gave the Emanuel Emroch Lecture at the University of Richmond Law School, April 3, 1986, which appeared as *Improving Expert Testimony*, 20 Rich. L. Rev. 473–97 (1986) He also lectured on the subject at the annual meeting of the Association of American Law Schools. "Experts in the Courts," Jan. 4–7, 1981. *See also* Jack B. Weinstein, Litigation and Statistics, Ninth Symposium on Statistics and the

thus validating the case sufficiently to avoid summary judgment and force the matter to trial.[257] Weinstein thought that solutions to the problem had not crystallized, but he laid out a number of ideas, suggesting, in part, that judges had to become more familiar with the scientific background of issues, appoint special masters, question expert witness, and express their views more forcefully to guide the jury. He even suggested that the court might even have inherent power "to deny an expert a fee for spouting nonsense."[258]

During this period, Weinstein wrote a book on the rule-making process in which he traced the evolution of the rule-making power of courts from the early English experience to present day practices with which he was dissatisfied. His prescription was to get the Supreme Court out of the rule-making process (except for its own Rules) and have the Judicial Conference take over in a more open, publicized way with more representative advisory committees. Weinstein was also critical of rule-making by individual federal courts, when the bar, law schools, and the citizen were given no opportunity to comment on proposed drafts.[259]

Weinstein continued his most traditional pedagogy at Columbia Law School, though in unconventional ways. He not only was teaching four credit courses in subjects like Evidence, but also team teaching seminars on such subjects as "Some Dilemmas of Equality and Freedom." In Columbia's summer program in The Netherlands he gave a course focusing on complex litigation, which included discussion of the *Mark Twain* case, *Hall v. DuPont*, and Judge George Pratt's rulings in the early stages of *Agent Orange*. In 1984, he taught a course in judicial administration with the Eastern District executive. Students came from six metropolitan area law schools.[260]

Weinstein's ties to law schools went far beyond his teaching at Columbia. Geographic proximity to Brooklyn Law School and the growing influence in that law school of his former clerks, Margaret Berger and Joan Wexler, gave him a second law school for pedagogy. He was also a member of the board of Cardozo Law School. One year (1981), he gave the commencement addresses at Brooklyn, Salmon P. Chase, and Cardozo Law Schools. He also spoke or acted as toastmaster at annual law review banquets and alumni association events at Columbia, N.Y.U., Cardozo, and St. Johns' Law School.

Weinstein remained devoted to the work of the legal academy throughout the country. He also spoke at the annual meeting and workshops of the Association of

Environment, Speech to National Academy of Sciences, Washington D.C. (Oct. 27, 1986); Jack B. Weinstein, *The Role of the Court in Toxic Tort Litigation*, 73 GEO. L. J. 1389 (1985).

[257] Weinstein, *Improving Expert Testimony*, *supra* note 230, at 482, 486.

[258] *Id.* at 473, 484–86.

[259] JACK B. WEINSTEIN, REFORM OF COURT RULE-MAKING PROCEDURES (1977). The book was derived from previous law review articles: Jack B. Weinstein, *Reform of Federal Court Rulemaking Procedures*, 76 COLUM. L. REV. 905 (1976); Jack B. Weinstein, *Reform of the Rule-Making Process*, 63 ABAJ 47 (1997). *See also* Julius Isaacson, Book review of JACK B. WEINSTEIN, REFORM OF COURT RULE-MAKING PROCEDURES, 8 U.BALT. L. REV. 164 (1978–1979); Charles Alan Wright, Book Review, ST. MARY'S L.J. 652, 658 (1978).

[260] Jack B. Weinstein, Legal Education: A Partnership among Law Schools, Law Firms and the Courts, Speech at New York Law School Alumni Association Annual Dinner 1 (Nov. 20, 1984).

American Law Schools. He saw the need for a partnership between law schools, law firms, and courts and praised the "more healthy balance between the theoretical and practical in law schools."[261] He was a strong supporter of the trend of students learning at courts in addition to law school.[262] In Barbados for a meeting of the Federal Bar Council, he found time to write a two-and-one-half-page letter to Dean Jesse Choper reviewing with praise an article by a candidate for tenure at Boldt Hall.[263] He also found the time to read law review articles and to praise or, in some cases, question their authors.[264] Sometimes, he wrote to congratulate students on their work.

Weinstein also participated in educational programs sponsored by bar associations and other groups.[265] He organized and taught training sessions for lawyers in his court, especially attorneys serving the Eastern District in a *pro bono* capacity.[266] In 1982–1983, there were one-day courses offered free of charge for those handling Social Security disability, Section 1983, employment discrimination, and prison cases.[267] At the August 1986 American Bar Association meetings, he spoke at five different forums.[268]

CHIEF JUDGE OF THE EASTERN DISTRICT

Toward the end of Jimmy Carter's presidency, Weinstein was considered for appointment to the U.S. Court of Appeals for the Second Circuit. He wrote his colleague at Columbia, Herbert Wechsler, that he would not have applied had not a member of the bar sent him an application. He was not chosen, at least in part because of the opposition of the chronically ambitious Second Circuit Chief Judge Irving R. Kaufman.[269]

However, Weinstein did make a mark during the next eight years (1980–1988) as Chief Judge of the U.S District Court for the Eastern District of New York. The position of Chief Judge of a district court is a position gained by seniority. It provides little power or much statutory authority, but does offer the holder the capacity for leadership

---

[261] *Id.*

[262] Weinstein, Legal Education: A Partnership among Law Schools, Law Firms and Courts, Speech at Benjamin N. Cardozo Law Review Reception for Alumni 12, 18 (Mar. 31, 1985).

[263] Jack B. Weinstein letter to Jesse Choper, Feb. 23, 1986 (in possession of author).

[264] *See* Jack B. Weinstein to Prof. Ronald J. Allen, June 7, 1981; to Prof. John C. Cooper, July 29, 1986; to Paul Spiegelman, Aug. 15, 1985.

[265] *See, e.g.,* Association of the Bar of the City of New York Panel on Modern Federal Discovery Practice Oct. 1, 1984; Demystifying Federal Civil Practice, Speech before Brooklyn Council of Women Lawyers, Nov. 23, 1982; Annual Seminar of the New York State Attorney General's Staff, Albany, NY, published as *Some Reflections Between Government Attorneys and Clients*, 1 TOURO L. REV. 1 (1985).

[266] *E.g.,* Seminar on Comprehensive Crime Control Act of 1984, Courthouse, 1984 Sp. 21.

[267] *See, e.g.,* Press Release, Oct. 26, 1983, 1983 Sp. 29.

[268] The subjects were: lawyers' professionalism; jury charges in complex litigation; the use of experts in toxic tort cases; the settlement of complex cases; and the impact of Gramm-Rudman budget reductions.

[269] On the history, see Jack B. Weinstein to Herbert Wechsler, Jan. 9, 1979; Jack B. Weinstein to Michael Perry, June 10, 1980 (copies in possession of the author). The characterization of Chief Judge Kaufman is not Weinstein's, but my own. At the time Kaufman was still angling for a Supreme Court appointment.

in matters of judicial administration. The predominant view among judges is that the Chief Judge is ultimately responsible for seeing that the court is administered effectively and in compliance with statutes, policies of the U.S. Judicial Conference, and the Circuit Judicial Council, as well as the regulations of the Administrative Office of the U.S. Courts (AO).[270] The Chief Judge of a district court oversees the work of the district executive, clerk, and the heads of probation and pretrial services.

Court budgets have grown throughout the past forty years, the number of court employees has greatly increased so the and reliance on information technology has become much greater. As a result, the concerns of the Chief Judge of a large district court, such as the Eastern District of New York, have greatly increased. In Weinstein's time as Chief Judge, matters came before him including security, space acquisition and allocation, daily building operations, the budget, and the appointment and reappointment of magistrates.

The Chief Judge of the district court also has a variety of duties connected with case management, oversight of case assignments, the local rules and rule-making, and jury and grand jury utilization. He has to ensure that the court is functioning appropriately under the Speedy Trial Act of 1974 as amended. A Chief Judge may also have to deal with sensitive issues of judicial performance.[271]

As Chief Judge of the district court, Weinstein was the external voice of the court. Thus, he was responsible for the court's relations with the Judicial Conference, Circuit Council, Administrative Office of the U.S. Courts, U.S. Attorney, and the General Services Administration. He testified before before congressional committees.[272] As Chief Judge, Weinstein was liaison with outside groups including state and local courts, law schools, and the press. He represented the court at various public events and official ceremonies, spoke before bar and civic groups and was responsible for ceremonies in which new judges were sworn in and elderly judges memorialized. As Chief Judges do, he spoke out about delays in filling vacant judgeships as well as on the adverse effects of budget cuts.[273]

As one would expect, Jack B. Weinstein was an activist Chief Judge. Weinstein's major aims as Chief Judge were to maintain collegiality,[274] defend judges against interference or threats to their independence, spare his colleagues the "junky bureaucratic stuff," and "make it as comfortable for them as [he] possibly could."[275] There were also

---

[270] Federal Judicial Center, Deskbook for Chief Judges of U.S. District Courts 5–6 (3rd ed. 2003).

[271] *Id.* at 6ff, 112ff.

[272] *See* Testimony on the funding of Pre-Trial Service Agencies before Subcommittee on Crime of House Committee on Judiciary Concerning Authorization of the Pretrial Services Agencies, April 16, 1981.

[273] During his eight-year tenure, Weinstein presided over many inductions, retirements, memorial ceremonies, dedications of court facilities, and the presentation of awards. He also gave the oath of office to the court's marshal and head of the Probation Office and to Elizabeth Holtzman when she became District Attorney of Kings County in 1981.

[274] To foster collegiality among the judges, Weinstein set up morning coffee, Tuesday lunches, and a lecture series, entertained at home, and held retreats with judges and advisory committees.

[275] Weinstein Oral History, at 1297.

other goals: to assist the poor in using the courts, maintain close relationships with the bar and improve its quality, fight off the division of the district, and create and/or modify the court's rules for handling civil and criminal cases.[276]

Among the major achievements of Weinstein's chief judgeship were the creation and modification of the court's rules for handling civil and criminal cases. Weinstein appointed a committee, chaired by an old friend, Edwin J. Wesley of Winthrop, Stimson, Putnam & Roberts, to develop orders governing discovery. The adoption of the Standing Orders on Effective Discovery was intended to maximize cooperation between lawyers during discovery, provide for easy access to the court with respect to discovery disputes, and to set forth the standards presumptively to be applied in discovery disputes.[277] After the rules went into effect, a committee was established to monitor their operation and make further proposals.[278] A similar process was used for criminal cases.[279] Ultimately, the Southern and Eastern Districts issued joint rules for the conduct of civil and criminal cases.[280]

One matter that was important to Weinstein was to resist pressures from eastern Long Island for division of the District. For Weinstein, the beauty of the Eastern District of the court was and is its diversity, "containing the farms of the East" and "the industry of Brooklyn," a district with "city lawyers and country lawyers." Splitting the circuit, Weinstein believed, would not only duplicate court bureaucracy, but reduce the heterogeneity of cases, judges, lawyers, and jurors. Instead, he supported a seat of the Eastern District in Uniondale. At the dedication of a temporary courthouse in Uniondale in 1982, he reaffirmed his support for a permanent federal courthouse with more extensive facilities on the East End, something which finally came about in Central Islip.[281]

Weinstein's fierce independence showed up in his Chief Judgeship. Weinstein opposed what he considered to be encroachments in the administrative sphere by the

---

[276] While he was Chief Judge, the Eastern District's Clerk of Court, Richard A. Weare, was named the District's first District Executive and Robert C. Heinemann succeeded Dodge as Clerk of Court. *See* U.S. District Court Eastern District of New York Press Release, July 28, 1983.

[277] Revised Report of the Special Committee on Effective Discovery in Civil Cases for the Eastern District of New York to the Honorable Jack B. Weinstein, 102 F.R.D. 339, 352 (available on Westlaw).

[278] Jack B. Weinstein, A Few Nice Things about Lawyers, Speech before Alumni Association, St John's University School of Law, New York City, 1984 Sp 5 at 3–8 (Apr. 27, 1984); Press Release on Report of the Discovery Oversight Committee on Eastern District of New York, June 25, 1986.

[279] *See* Report of the Eastern District of New York Criminal Procedure Committee on the Assignment of Cases to Judges Including Related Case Designations and an Arraignment Function. Peter Zimroth, Press Release, Jack B. Weinstein Released Today Two Draft Reports of the Eastern District Criminal Procedure Committee, June 17, 1986. Report of the Eastern District of New York Criminal Procedure Committee on Case Management and a Uniform Pre-Trial Order (Tentative Draft, June 17, 1986).

[280] N.Y.L.J., Mar. 4, 1986. As Chief Judge, Weinstein also formed a Committee on Potential Uses of Technology chaired by Douglas Dodge. U.S. District Court Eastern District of New York Press Release, Nov. 29, 1985.

[281] 15 SUFFOLK ACAD. LAW NEWS (November–December 1980), at 2.

Second Circuit Judicial Council. He strongly opposed giving the judicial councils the power to modify or abrogate local district court rules.[282] He warned the Council:

> We would like to continue our Eastern district experiments in collegial self-regulation and support with the help of the bar and our law schools. Do not press us into a mold that will impair rather than improve our effectiveness.[283]

He also strongly opposed having the courts draw up five-year plans, believing that adoption of the Second Circuit Advisory Committee's proposals for planning would "lead our court in the direction of over-administration, excessive paper work and loss of time better spent in trying and disposing of cases."[284] He stated that ". . . the judges of our district who preside over clam and potato diggers see almost no utility in spending our energies in this way."[285]

Weinstein's independence was demonstrated by refusing to go along with leaders of the federal judiciary in important matters of judicial administration. He was at odds with Chief Justice Burger and/or Chief Judge Kaufman (although these battles were not personal) over such matters as special certification for trial advocates, television in the courts, and, most importantly, over the condition of the dockets of the federal courts and what should be done about it.

When the Judicial Conference, acting under the Judicial Councils Reform and Judicial Conduct and Disability Act, certified to the Speaker of the House of Representatives that Judge Harry E. Claiborne of the District of Nevada had engaged in conduct which might constitute grounds for impeachment, Weinstein would not go along with his colleagues on the U.S. Judicial Conference. He refused to vote for several reasons, but the most important of them was judicial independence. "The protection of judges by Article III of the Constitution required," he thought, "the courts to proceed in this area only when it is absolutely essential to do so."[286] In this case, the House Judiciary Committee had already recommended that the House vote Articles of Impeachment.

---

[282] Jack B. Weinstein to Steve Flanders, Feb. 10, 1986, 1986 Sp. NB. #7.

[283] Jack B. Weinstein, Annual Judicial Conference, Second Judicial Circuit of the United States, May 9, 1981, 93 F.R.D. 673, 779 (available on Westlaw).

[284] *Id.* at 673, 778.

[285] *Id.* Weinstein was also a gadfly within the Circuit Judicial Conference. He opposed increasing the length of the annual meeting—presumably a time for relaxation and fellowship because of the loss of trial-judge days. Jack B. Weinstein, Remarks, Remarks at Proceedings of the 1981 Annual Judicial Conference of the Second Circuit, Buck Hill Falls, PA, 93 F.R.D. 673, 777–78 (available on Westlaw). See also Weinstein's draft remarks for panel presentation on the Topic: Perspectives on Improving the Work of our Courts, Judicial Conference of the Second Circuit, at 1(Scheduled for May 9, 1985) (copy in possession of author). Responding to a questionnaire on the value of the conference, he wrote, "Minor. May have been useful in permitting some R and R and some preening by bench and bar invited." Survey on Second Circuit Judicial Conference 1 (1980) (copy in possession of author).

[286] *In re Harry E. Claiborne*, 1986 NB 495a and following pages. It appears that this draft opinion expressing his objections was never published. A copy of the document is in the possession of the author.

Weinstein was also appalled by the recommendation of the Executive Committee of the Judicial Conference to suspend civil jury trials when the federal government ran out of money. Weinstein wrote to the head of the Administrative Office of the U.S. Courts that he would support any Eastern District judge who decided in an individual case that hardships and the proper administration of justice required an immediate civil jury trial.[287]

Finally, Weinstein saw his court as a "bridge" to the law schools, the poor, and the community. His beliefs that "courts are for all the people" went beyond his deep concern about counsel for the poor. He was proud that in the Eastern District, the poor could walk right in off the streets and not be blocked by porticos and columns as the Southern District of New York was. He sought to open the courts to the community with art exhibitions and high school moot courts.

CONCLUSION

During Jack Weinstein's second decade on the bench, he became an increasingly prominent with bench and bar. Although we have not yet explored the most important litigation before him (Agent Orange), Weinstein's work in the areas of the First Amendment, the criminal law, New York City litigation and his handling of matters coming from the Social Security Administration deserved attention. Regarded as one of the nation's foremost authorities on evidence, he also made a significant mark with his book on rule-making and his penchant for innovation. There is no sign that he grieved over being bypassed for "promotion" to the U.S. Court of Appeals or appointment to the Chief Judgeship of the New York Court of Appeals and he proved an effective chief judge of the Eastern District of New York.

---

[287] Jack B. Weinstein to L. Ralph Meacham, June 18, 1986 (copy in possession of author).

7

"Imaginative Reformer" and "Vindicator of the Ideal of the Judge":

Jack Weinstein's Work, 1987–1996

JACK WEINSTEIN BEGAN to reap those honors which come with a career of great distinction during the decade which commenced when he was in his sixty-sixth year. In 1993, Weinstein received notice that he had won the judiciary's highest award, the Devitt Award, was named "National Law Journal's Lawyer of the Year,"[1] and received an honorary doctorate from Yale. Among those honored with him at Yale were Mario Vargas Llosa and Kurt Masur. Weinstein's citation read in part:

> ... At a time when the law's promise and performance are being called into question, you are truly its Renaissance figure. A brilliant teacher of generations of law students, you are also a trenchant scholar in an outstanding variety of legal fields, a tireless gadfly of the legal profession, and an imaginative reformer of legal institutions. Above all, you vindicate the ideal of the judge, uniting lofty principle, practical wisdom, and passion for justice. . .[2]

Possibly even more gratifying, Weinstein spoke at the twenty-fifth anniversary dinner of the Nassau-Suffolk Law Services Committee. The organization, which he had an important hand in founding, now had a budget of $4.5 million.[3] Weinstein also reached another milestone in 1993. On February 8, 1993, he notified the clerk of the

---

[1] 16 Nat'l L.J. No. 17-18 (Dec. 27, 1993–Jan. 3, 1994).
[2] Yale (Summer 1994), 64 at 66; New York Times, May 23, 1993.
[3] Nassau Lawyer, Feb. 1992, at 6.

Eastern District that he would take senior status effect March. He made clear, though, that he intended "to carry a full judicial load."[4] Certainly, there was no indication that he had slowed down during this decade.

THE MANY SIDES OF WEINSTEIN

Reviewing Weinstein's work during this decade, one sees many sides. There was the staunchly independent judge again challenging the authority of the Administrative Office of the U.S. Courts to order cancellation of civil jury trials because of a funding crisis.[5] There was Weinstein, the educator, going full speed ahead: on the one hand, accepting students from several area law schools into his course in mass torts while, on the other, permitting a group of kindergarten children to sit in the jury box during the trial of a Columbo family capo.[6]

Weinstein's powerful prose was often on display. It occurred, for example, in his dismissal of two claims in a suit between Rupert Murdoch's news corporation and Time-Warner after the latter corporation chose to carry MSNBC rather than Fox News:

> These were not Adam-and-Eve-like innocents slipping naked into the cable television and broadcast jungle to negotiate with each other and the serpent.[7]

His flashing wit and sense of irony often appeared as when a *New York Times* reporter asked Weinstein his opinion of two of the leading candidates for a seat on the U.S. Supreme Court, Jon O. Newman and Stephen G. Breyer. Weinstein replied, "I'd be proud to be reversed by either one of them."[8] His wit lit up a sentencing opinion, where he argued that the crime the defendants were convicted of was so ineptly planned and executed that the "real offense" was far less heinous than the Sentencing Guidelines suggested. Weinstein stated that "[t]he ineptitude of the criminals is undisputed." The conspirators were unable to obtain a handgun ("Although almost any child in most grade schools in New York City could have told them how to procure one"). One conspirator had to be forcibly awakened to join the team and another had to be awakened so that the FBI could read him his Miranda rights. "The conspirators were recorded discussing whether the pedestrians would notice someone carrying a rifle on 42nd Street [and] whether it would be effective to shoot the gun into the air to distract police officers from noticing the robbery in progress."[9]

---

[4] N.Y.L.J., Feb. 8, 1993.

[5] N.Y.L.J., Apr. 18, 1993.

[6] N.Y.L.J. Oct. 8, 1992, at 2; NEW YORK DAILY NEWS, Jan. 26, 1993.

[7] NEW YORK TIMES, May 17, 1997, at 33, 45.

[8] NEW YORK TIMES, May 30, 1993, at 24.

[9] The quotations are from *United States v. Vasquez*, 791 F. Supp. 348, 349, 350 (Apr. 23, 1992). *See also Lunz v. Senkowski*, 1995 NB 903 (1995).

There was Weinstein-the-advisor-to-attorneys. While dismissing a *habeas corpus* petition as moot, he recommended a damage action, pointing to a particular case as a model.[10] He still had so much stored-up knowledge that he could decide some cases based on knowledge from his earlier career. In one case, the question was whether the New York State practice regarding the docketing of judgments discriminated against the judgments of federal courts. The ruling depended upon the reading of New York's Civil Practice Rule 5018 (b). Weinstein called the New York rule "considerably more sensible than Missouri's was" (a statute voided by the U.S. Supreme Court) and stated that "[t]he drafters of the CPLR were well aware of the practical and theoretical issues posed by Section 1962,"[11] citing the third Preliminary Report of the Advisory Committee on Practice and Procedure and 5 H. Korn & A. Miller, *New York Civil Practice*, a later edition of Weinstein, Korn, and Miller.[12]

The areas of the law Weinstein had the greatest impact upon during this period were class actions (see Chapter 10), criminal justice, and the environment. Among the important class actions before him in addition to *Agent Orange*, were mass tort cases involving asbestos, repeated stress injuries (RSI), breast implants, and the effects of the drug DES. Important criminal cases involved the mob, political corruption, and terrorists. He also dealt with a number of civil forfeitures, where the government was seeking the return of all ill-gotten gains. His battle against the Sentencing Guidelines is left for Chapter 8. There were two highly political cases, one a battle over the budget for the state judiciary between Governor Mario Cuomo and the Chief Judge of the Court of Appeals, Sol Wachtler. The other, far more important litigation, involved closing the Shoreham nuclear plant on Long Island. There was a wide range of other civil cases, although, unlike during his first two decades, there few cases of particular interest involving either the New York City school system or racial civil rights.[13]

CRIMINAL CASES

The Comprehensive Crime Control Act of 1984[14] made major changes in federal criminal law. Making bail was made more difficult. Penalties applicable to narcotics offenses were strengthened and clarified, including the use of criminal and civil forfeitures. Federal laws designed to prevent international money laundering were improved.

---

[10] *Diaz v. Henderson*, 1989 WL 106896 (Sept. 12, 1989).

[11] 28 U.S.C. 1962 (1988). *See also In re Sterling Die Casting Co.*, 132 B.R. 99 (Oct. 3, 1991). Prior to the enactment of the Bankruptcy Abuse Prevention and Consumer Protection Act of 2005 (BAPCPA), a litigant in a bankruptcy case was permitted to appeal, under certain circumstances, "to the district court for the judicial district in which the bankruptcy judge sits." Laura B. Bartell, *The Appeal of Direct Appeal - Use of the New 28 U.S.C. S 158(d)(2)*, 84 Am. Bankr. L.J. 145, 145 (2010) (explaining a "litigant could appeal a final judgment, order or decree (and certain interlocutory orders and decrees) to the district court for the judicial district in which the bankruptcy judge sits.").

[12] *Id.* at 102, 104.

[13] *Cuno, Inc. v. Pall Corp.*, 729 F. Supp. 234 (Dec, 19, 1989).

[14] P.L. 98–473, 98 Stat. 1976. *See also* Criminal Fine Enforcement Act, P.L. 98–596, 98 Stat. 3134.

The process of sentencing was radically changed. The number of criminal cases filed in the federal district courts throughout the country rose as a result of drug, immigration, and firearms prosecutions. Weinstein's made important contributions in cases involving bail, searches and seizures, forfeitures, and sentencings.[15]

Bail

Weinstein continued to be reversed by the Court of Appeals on bail matters. One such case involved Jack Ferranti, accused of arson for setting fire to a Queens building in which he had a clothing boutique. A firefighter died in the blaze. When bail was at issue, the government contended that Ferranti was attempting to intimidate the tenants in the building he owned and allegedly had ordered the murder of a tenants' rights activist. Weinstein, reversing the magistrate judge, held that the proffer and proof as to Ferranti's danger to the community was "equivocal." The bail package Weinstein shaped contained (with one exception) no special conditions to assure the community's safety. The Court of Appeals reversed, holding that the government had established by clear and convincing evidence that Ferranti was a danger to the community and stated that "No conceivable conditions could ensure the safety of the community."[16]

Searches and Seizures

Weinstein's concern about erosion of Fourth Amendment protections surfaced in a number of cases. In 1989, he warned:

> If we do not soon solve the drug problem that affects our land, we can expect further deterioration of all our constitutional rights as part of the price we pay for our failure.[17]

Weinstein was not reflexively against the government in Fourth Amendment cases. He understood the employment of new technology and knew that "[a]s law enforcement officials' knowledge of the narcotics industry expands and the tools and techniques of the trade shift, the indicia of suspicion and degree of import attached to each will also change."[18] "A virtuoso," he wrote, "may draw reasonable inferences and suspicions of criminal involvement that would elude the amateur."[19] In *United States v. Ceballos*, he upheld a stop, pat-down, and frisk finding reasonable suspicion as the result of calls

---

[15] Weinstein granted petitions for *habeas corpus* from state prisoners during this period, but there was no major case. *See Rivera v. King*, 1995Op. 1134 (June 30, 1995); *Perez v. Irwin*, 766 F. Supp. 90 (June 27, 1991), *aff 'd*, 963 F.2d 499 (Card-WJF-New). *See Mitchell v. Hoke*, 745 F. Supp. 874 (Sept. 5, 1990), which is discussed in the evidence section of this chapter.

[16] *United States v. Ferranti*, 1990 NB 1628, 1632 (1995: *Alti-Mesk-Calab*).

[17] *United States v. Ceballos*, 719 F. Supp. 119 (June 30, 1989).

[18] *Id.* at 123.

[19] *Id.* at 124.

to a beeper made from a pay phone in a known narcotics location, evasive driving and, deliberately furtive actions, a suspicious transaction, and flight.[20]

Weinstein has observed that "Courts should not lightly second guess the on-the-spot observations of police officers, nevertheless scrutiny of the factors supporting the reasonableness of the officer's suspicions is required." In *United States v. Restrepo*, he held that a protective sweep on the sidewalk in connection with a *Terry* stop[21] did not extend to the interior of the suspect's home.[22]

In *United States v. Giraldo*,[23] Weinstein excluded twelve-and-one-half kilos of cocaine seized as the result of a search, which had resulted from the agents' trickery. The agents had secured admission to an apartment by claiming to be gas company workers searching for a gas leak. When they entered the apartment, the agents asked for permission to search it, ostensibly looking for the leak. The defendant, believing that there was a life-threatening emergency, gave written consent. Weinstein held that the defendant had not voluntarily admitted the agents. Rather, the original entry was illegal and the permission to search had not been freed of the taint of deceptive entry. "Defendant's ability to effect and exercise the right to refuse consent was overwhelmed by the continuing shock of the gas company threat and the police presence," Weinstein wrote.[24] There were also sound public policy reasons for not sanctioning this type of deception: "in order to insure cooperation in truly life-threatening situations, it is vital to maintain the public trust in emergency services."[25]

While sitting with the Court of Appeals, Weinstein delivered a powerful dissent in *United States v. Riley*,[26] which seems to have drawn the ire of Chief Judge Jon Newman. In *Riley*, agents had received a very broad warrant to search a home. In the home, they found thirty-six pounds of marijuana, firearms, and an agreement for the rental of a storage locker. The agents then asked for and received a warrant to search the locker, where they found three kilograms of cocaine. The trial judge, Chief Judge Franklin S. Billings of the District of Vermont, had held the residence warrant was partially unsupported by probable cause and insufficiently particularized. Two of the three members of the Court of Appeals panel disagreed, upholding broadly worded categories of items that could be seized. Once a category of seizable papers had adequately been described, Newman stated, the Fourth Amendment was not violated because those executing the warrant "must exercise some minimal judgment."[27]

---

[20] *Id.* at 123–26.

[21] A Terry stop is a stop of a person by law enforcement officers based on reasonable suspicion.

[22] *United States v. Restrepo*, 890 F. Supp. 180 (May 30, 1995). The opinion covered forty-five pages in Federal Supplement.

[23] 743 F. Supp. 152 (Aug. 24, 1990).

[24] *Id.* at 155.

[25] *Id.* at 154. *See also* NEWSDAY, Aug. 25, 1990; NEW YORK TIMES, Aug. 26, 1990, at 45.

[26] 906 F.2d 841 (*New-Mesk/JBW*: June 22, 1990).

[27] *Id.* at 845.

Dissenting, Weinstein called the majority opinion "one small step forward in the current war on drugs and one giant leap backward in the centuries-old struggle against general search warrants."[28] Construing the "vague boilerplate language" of the portion of the warrant listing "other items that constitute evidence of the offenses of conspiracy to distribute controlled substances," Weinstein said that it

> gives the police carte blanche to search every nook and cranny of a home from basement to attic, to allow every item including clothing, linens and the like, to open and rifle every closet, cabinet, drawer, brief case and piece of luggage; to remove bedding, carpets, floors and walls; to seize garbage and the residue in plumbing drains; and to read every book and piece of paper[29]

Weinstein also discussed the implications of a warrant such as this for contemporary and future searches. In light of the increasing sensitivity and sophistication of forensic science, this use of a "general warrant" would mean "that almost any object in a person's house could provide evidence of drug activity."[30]

Judge Newman replied angrily in the majority opinion that "[t]he breadth of Judge Weinstein's alarms is exceeded only by their distance from the holding in this case."[31] With no sense of regret, Weinstein reflected in 1994, "I really got under his [Newman's] skin when I started by saying 'the majority opinion constitutes once small step forward on the war on drugs and one giant leap backwards. . .'; he was really infuriated." Weinstein added that, as with other cases he had heard with the Court of Appeals, there was no discussion in conference—just conversation taking two minutes.[32] He added, "I find the practice very disappointing and intellectually barren."[33]

Organized Crime

Weinstein had high-profile cases involving the Gambino and Colombo crime families and the Colombian drug cartel during this period. He handled much of a complex criminal trial involving the Gambino crime family. The twenty-two count indictment, greatly oversimplified here, named sixteen defendants accused of a Racketeer Influenced and Corrupt Organizations (RICO) conspiracy as well as conspiracy to engage in murder,

---

[28] *Id.* at 846.

[29] *Id.* at 847.

[30] *Id.* at 853.

[31] *Id.* at 845.

[32] Weinstein Oral History, at 999.

[33] *Id.* at 1000. Weinstein, sitting with the same two judges, dissented in another drug case involving two young African-Americans, who claimed they had "accidentally" crossed the border at Niagara Falls on a bus and then, realizing their mistake, had gotten off the bus and walked back to the United States. The majority found probable cause from the fact that the two entered the U.S. Immigration officer together and told the same "unusual" story. Weinstein found this "an example of drug war zealousness infringing on constitutional rights." *See United States v. Patrick*, 899 F.2d 169, 172, 173, 175. (1990: Mesk-New/JBW).

extortion, loan sharking, labor racketeering, bribery, and other offenses. The seventy-two predicate acts in the RICO conspiracy consisted of forty-six separate specified offenses.[34] By August 28, 1987, the indictment had been the subject of five written and many oral opinions. Six pages of charts explaining the cases were published in Federal Supplement.[35] While the "boss" of the family, Paul Castellano, was an unindicted co-conspirator and the under-boss was no longer alive, the indictment included the consigliore (Joey Gallo), capos (including John Gotti), and associates of the family.

Weinstein put a good deal of thought into how to handle such a megacriminal case. As he put it, "These huge, complicated RICO cases require specially tailored proceedings if the court is to properly control the litigation in a way protective of both the public's and the defendants' interests."[36] Among the hardships of this kind of "monster" case was its effect on the life of the jurors and its radical disruption of their work and home life. The trial judge, too, faced great problems of trial management and its possible consequences for his or her health. Moreover:

> . . . the judge's and attorneys' fatigue, as long trials grind on, results in more mistakes, shortened tempers and reduced ability to smooth over the inevitable conflicts of counsel and court under our adversary system.[37]

Weinstein wrote a number of "Weinstein-like" opinions in *Gallo*. The first major opinion in the *Gallo* litigation involved the bailability of defendants because of their possible danger to a potential witness, "X." Weinstein did not believe that the risks to X would be increased by the release on bail of certain *Gallo* defendants even though "neither was a gentle soul."[38]

His second opinion, a major one, dealt with the pretrial discovery of statements made by co-conspirators. Weinstein explained that because "a RICO case may hinge on a relatively vague or abstract sense of involvement or constructive knowledge, evidence concerning alleged co-conspirators can have an enormous impact on the determination of culpability."[39] Weinstein then examined the Federal Rules of Criminal Procedure, the Federal Rules of Evidence, the Jencks Act,[40] the production of material under *Brady v. Maryland*,[41] the ABA Standards for Criminal Justice, and the Second Circuit opinion in *United States v. Percevault*.[42] He held that the government would have to produce all statements made by defendants as co-conspirators, except for statements made

---

[34] *United States v. Gallo*, 668 F. Supp. 736, 738 (Aug. 28, 1987).

[35] *Id.* at 740–43; 745–46.

[36] *United States v. Gallo*, 654 F. Supp. 463, 465 (Feb. 19, 1987).

[37] *United States v. Gallo*, 668 F. Supp. 736, 755 (1987). *See generally id.* at 754–56.

[38] *United States v. Gallo*, 653 F. Supp. 320, 326 (Nov. 14, 1986).

[39] *United States v. Gallo*, 654 F. Supp. 463, 466 (Feb. 19, 1987).

[40] 18 U.S.C. §3500.

[41] 373 U.S. 83 (1963).

[42] 490 F.2d 126 (1974).

by co-conspirators who were prospective witnesses and statements made by co-conspirators which had not been made during the course and in furtherance of the conspiracy. The decision followed from Weinstein's view that "broadened discovery in criminal cases should be encouraged whenever possible, particularly where fairness and efficiency were so severely handicapped by the scope, length, and complexity of labyrinthine RICO cases." If expanded discovery was of debatable value in everyday cases, it was essential in unwieldy RICO cases. Discovery, thus, was necessary not only for the defendants, but for the judge in dealing with severance and other preliminary motions.[43]

The Court of Appeals issued a mandamus blocking Weinstein's discovery order, later followed by a full opinion. (The opinion chiding Weinstein for inattentiveness to precedent is also discussed in Chapter 4.)[44] A panel consisting of Van Graafeiland (writing), Meskill, and Cardamone sharply rebuked Weinstein, stating that he had "misinterpreted the Rules, prior decisions of this court and the nature and extent of its inherent authority."[45]

Weinstein denied defendants' misjoinder motion because the gravaman of this conspiracy was agreement on the overall objective—to participate in the affairs of the enterprise. However, in spite of the strong presumption against splitting an indictment, he severed some defendants for reasons of efficiency. The case was initially divided up into seven trials, a number ultimately reduced to four. Weinstein was troubled by the potential incompatibility of defense theories and trial strategies and the fact that evidentiary decisions might result in prejudice to some defendants. He wrote:

> There are conspiracies within conspiracies, and conspiracies to conceal other conspiracies, conspiracies which are discrete and finite, and those which are amorphous and indefinite, involving conspirators joining and leaving the conspiracy at various times.[46]

But it was the jury which really worried him. This case, he said, was a contest in which the risk that the jury could [not] follow instructions was so great and the consequences of failure so vital to the defendants that the practical and human limitations of the jury system cannot be ignored.[47] The jury would be required to make almost a gross (144) of separate decisions of guilt and innocence after a long and arduous trial. It would be difficult for the jury to consider the evidence as to each defendant separately, independent of the evidence against his or her co-conspirators.[48]

[43] *United States v. Gallo*, 654 F. Supp. 463, 480 (Feb. 19, 1987).
[44] *In re United States*, 834 F.2d 283 (Dec. 1, 1987).
[45] *Id.* at 284.
[46] *United States v. Gallo*, 668 F. Supp. 736, 751 (Aug. 20, 1988).
[47] *Id.* at 753.
[48] *United States v. Gallo*, 668 F. Supp. 736, 749, 750 (Aug. 28, 1988).

Weinstein handled the most important of the trials growing out of the "monster case," that of Joey Gallo, Joseph Armone, Anthony Vitta, and Salvatore Migliorisi for extortion and obstruction of justice. In that case, the government called over thirty witnesses and introduced over thirty-three exhibits. The defense had eight witnesses and over fifty exhibits. Each man was convicted. Saying, "It's not easy sentencing an old man," Weinstein sentenced the seventy-six-year-old Gallo to ten years and Armone (who was seventy) to fifteen years and an $820,000 fine.[49]

In one of the severed trials, which dealt with parts of the labor union aspects of the conspiracy, Julius Miron and two other defendants were found guilty of racketeering activity and obstruction of justice, as well as several non-RICO counts. After the trial, Weinstein dealt a second time with Miron's motion for acquittal on the grounds that the government had improperly used some of his immunized grand jury testimony. Weinstein concluded that:

> No one like Miron, who is granted limited use immunity in a good faith attempt to develop leads into past criminal acts of third parties, should receive an "immunity bath" as well as an "invisible shield" against prosecution for future crimes, particularly where the defendant's compelled testimony is of absolutely no significance in that prosecution.[50]

The Second Circuit upheld Weinstein's determination on Miron's use immunity, although each member of the panel wrote a separate opinion.[51] Judge Winter thought Weinstein had erred, but that the error was harmless. Though he joined Winter, Judge Van Graafeiland also affirmed on the alternative ground[s] advanced by the district court.[52] Judge Altimari dissented, believing that such use of tainted evidence in a criminal prosecution violated the federal immunity statute.[53]

The second important mob trial Weinstein handled during this period involved the Colombo family. But, in Weinstein's words, Michael Sessa and Victor ("Little Vic") Orena, were "'low-level hoodlums' rather than 'superstar[s]' like John Gotti."[54] Sessa and Orena had been involved in the internecine war within the Colombo family, which took place after Carmine Persico went to prison and resulted in at least one dozen murders. Orena and Sessa were charged with racketeering, conspiracy, and murder.

---

[49] NEW YORK DAILY NEWS, Feb. 10, 1988; Newsday, Feb. 23, 1988. Prior to sentencing him, Weinstein offered to release Joseph Armone, the under boss of the Gambino family on a $1 million bond pending the sentencing, if he publicly renounced any connection with the family and resigned any position he might hold. NEW YORK TIMES, Dec. 24, 1987. Armone turned down the offer, saying that he was a man of pride and honor.

[50] *United States v. Gallo*, 671 F. Supp. 124, 138 (Aug. 7, 1987).

[51] *United States v. Gallo*, 859 F.2d 1078 (Sept. 22, 1989: *Winter-VanGc/Alti*).

[52] *Id.* at 1084.

[53] *Id.* at 1092.

[54] NEW YORK DAILY NEWS, Sept. 15, 1992.

Weinstein rejected a government attempt to prosecute the warring family members together, threw out several incriminating statements made by Orena to an FBI agent after his arrest, and would not let the jury be told that Orena was a convicted felon.[55] Nevertheless, with the prosecution's case built on informers, surveillance photographs, and taped conversations, Orena was found guilty of murdering a one-time friend and underling, loan sharking, racketeering, and weapons possession.[56]

When the jury came in with a verdict of guilty of racketeering, conspiracy, and murder, Sessa berated it: "'I can't believe youse (sic) believed those rats.'" His wife and mother burst into tears and his mother cried out, "'Oh my boy! Oh my God! What am I going to do?'"[57]

Weinstein sentenced the defendants to life, gave them fines of well over $1.5 million, and ordered them to pay for the cost of their imprisonment.[58] "Harsh terms of imprisonment," he wrote, "are required to incapacitate defendants and extricate them from the net of criminal activity in which they have been ensnared for their adult lives and to which they no doubt would return at the first opportunity."[59] In addition, he thought that severe sentences might by general deterrence save youngsters who might be seduced into the criminal lifestyle of these mobsters.[60]

Weinstein also handled cases involving Colombian organized crime figures. When American authorities apprehended Dandeny Munoz-Mosquera, with a reputation as an assassin in Colombia and for carrying out the orders of drug kingpin, Pablo Escobar, the best they could do at first was to charge him with the crime of making false and fraudulent statements to federal authorities and unlawful possession of a false identification document.[61] After Munoz-Mosquera was convicted, however, Weinstein departed from the Sentencing Guidelines and imposed a severe sentence on the basis of his criminal history in Colombia including a conviction for armed robbery and charges of murder. The cumulative sentence of six years was harsh given the nature of the crime for which he had been convicted.[62]

---

[55] DAILY NEWS, Sept. 15, 1992; NEW YORK TIMES, Sept. 15, 1992. N.Y.L.J. Dec. 14, 1992. One of the witnesses at the Orena trial was the notorious Salvatore (Sammy Bull) Gravano. NEW YORK TIMES, Dec.11, 1992.

[56] In the Sessa-Orena cases, Weinstein wrote opinions dealing with a psychologist's opinion on a witness's credibility (not admissible in the case), *United States v. Sessa*, 806 F. Supp. 1063 (Nov. 20, 1992); the ability of a defendant to stipulate that he had been previously convicted of a felony (a firearms charge) so that proof of that would not go to the jury. (He could.) *United States v. Orena*, 821 F. Supp. 870 (May 24, 1993).

[57] NEWSDAY, Nov. 13, 1992.

[58] Weinstein was affirmed. *United States v. Orena*, 32 F.3d 704 (1994: Mahoney-Miner-Meskill). As part of their sentence, Orena's sons agreed to leave the Mafia. Weinstein Oral History, at 1222. In a 101-page decision in 1997, Weinstein held that Orena did not deserve a new trial. N.Y.L.J., Mar. 11, 1997, at 1. In 2004, Weinstein rejected a claim that Gregory Scarpa had framed Orena for a 1989 murder. NEW YORK POST, Jan. 8, 2004, at 19.

[59] *United States v. Orena*, 821 F. Supp. 870, 874 (May 24, 1993).

[60] *Id.*

[61] NEW YORK TIMES, Nov. 25, 1991.

[62] NEW YORK TIMES, Mar. 1, 1992, at B3; Weinstein would not let the jury be told about the Colombian charges. NEW YORK TIMES, Nov. 25, 1991.

The Munoz-Mosquera sentencing led to a rare recusal by Weinstein in another Munoz-Mosquera case. When Munoz-Mosquera was accused of being involved in drug-related murders including the bombing of an Avianca flight in which 110 persons had been killed (capital crimes), he moved to substitute a judge other than Weinstein. Weinstein although a strong opponent of recusal, disqualified himself, stating "[f]or the state to kill a defendant using procedures which might have been tainted, or seem to have been tainted by prejudice is not acceptable in a constitutional democracy such as ours."[63] Weinstein held that, while there appeared to be no precedent, "given the heavy weight of special protection in capital cases, the defendant should have the right to strike the first judge assigned to the case without giving any reason."[64] He also held, seemingly in the alternative, that the case had been erroneously assigned to him as a "related case" and, thus, even if he had denied defendant's motion to strike, he would have returned the case to the clerk to be placed back in the wheel for reassignment. He directed the clerk to notify the press "so that the impartiality of the process of assigning judges can be publicly observed in a capital case."[65] Weinstein, no friend to capital punishment, said in his oral history that he was "just delighted to get out from under the case."[66]

However, in 1993, Weinstein did preside over a major criminal trial which involved Mosquera. A "mega-case," *United States v. Mosquera*, had eighteen Spanish-speaking defendants. Ten thousand documents were introduced into evidence and five hundred fifty tape recordings. The case stimulated two important Weinstein innovations. To help deal with its complexities, Weinstein appointed Eleanor Jackson Piel "coordinating counsel" to "coordinate efforts among defense counsel, to maximize efficiency and economy and to comport with the requirements of due process." Although there was no explicit authorization for the appointment of coordinating counsel in federal law, Weinstein held that the Federal Rules of Criminal Procedure "were to be flexibly interpreted to avoid unjust results" and also cited to a provision of the Criminal Justice Act.[67] "Urgent measures," he said, "are needed to move cases along more swiftly. Modern techniques, special equipment and innovative use of limited personnel are essential to achieving that goal."[68]

Weinstein broke new ground in a second area. The eighteen defendants spoke no English. As a result, they confronted profound obstacles in fully understanding

---

[63] *United States v. Escobar and Munoz-Mosquera*, 803 F. Supp. 611 (Oct. 13, 1992). *Id.* at 616.

[64] *Id.* at 618.

[65] *Id.* at 620.

[66] Weinstein Oral History, at 1173. Many years previous, he had handled a capital case involving a policeman who had hijacked a plane claiming he had bombs on him. The jury hung on the capital charge. On February 18, 1994, there was a story in the *New York Daily News* that Mosquera was intending to kill Weinstein, Judge Sterling Johnson, and former U.S. Attorney Andrew Maloney. Fortunately, nothing came of it.

[67] N.Y.L.J., Feb. 1, 1993, at1.

[68] *United States v. Mosquera [sic]*, 813 F. Supp. 962, 968, 966, 965 (Feb. 10, 1993); N.Y.L.J., Feb. 12, 1993, at 1. Professor Gerald Lynch of Columbia Law School was asked to evaluate the project. *See also* Weinstein Oral History, at 1203, 1206.

the proceedings. They lacked even a copy of the original indictment "in a language they could understand and discuss with their friends, relatives and counsel."[69]

Weinstein ordered the government to supply each defendant with a copy of the indictment translated into Spanish. When the government moved for reconsideration of the order, Weinstein invited several civil rights groups to file *amicus* briefs. The New York Civil Liberties Union, Puerto Rican Legal Defense Fund, and Asian-American Bar Association did so.[70] Weinstein then responded with a twenty-seven-page opinion discussing the Sixth Amendment, the Court Interpreters Act, the Federal Rules of Criminal Procedure, and, naturally, the inherent power of the court. Every non-English speaking criminal defendant was to be provided with a translation of the indictment, relevant portions of the statutes, the plea agreement, and the presentence report. Other documents would be translated as ordered by the court.[71] If this would cost the government money, Weinstein response was that the "price for the publicity in 'tough on crime' slogans must now be paid." Presumably, Congress and the President would now review the laws and appropriations to "increase congruence between pretension and reality."[72] The costs would be paid via the Criminal Justice Act.[73] Weinstein also urged civil rights organizations and the bar to produce a pamphlet for defendants explaining the federal judicial system.[74]

Forfeitures

During this period the government began making increased use of forfeiture in both civil and criminal procedures, particularly where drugs were involved. As early as 1970, Congress strengthened civil forfeiture as a means of confiscating illegal substances.[75] In 1978, it amended the earlier act to authorize the seizure and forfeiture of the proceedings of illegal drug transactions.[76] In 1986 Congress passed the Money Laundering Control Act to try to stop the flow of illicit money back to drug suppliers.[77] By the 1990s, Weinstein would be hearing cases in which the United States initiated forfeiture proceedings without first obtaining a criminal conviction.

---

[69] *United States v. Mosquera*, 816 F. Supp. 168, 170 (Mar. 16, 1993). *See* N.Y.L.J., Jan. 11, 1993, at 1.

[70] N.Y.L.J., Jan. 11, 1993, at 1 and Jan. 22, 1993; NEW YORK DAILY NEWS, Mar. 3, 1993.

[71] *Id.* at 178. In *Mosquera*, the coordinating counsel would decide which documents required translation.

[72] *United States v. Mosquera*, 816 F. Supp. 168, 176–77 (Mar. 16, 1993).

[73] *Id. See also* Weinstein Oral History, at 1203–06.

[74] *United States v. Mosquera*, at 178.

[75] Comprehensive Drug Abuse Prevention and Control Act, P.L. 91–513, 84 Stat. 1236.

[76] P.L. 95–633, 92 Stat. 3777.

[77] P.L. 99–750, 100 Stat. 570.

The use of forfeiture, as Weinstein has said, "skirts the edge of due process."[78] Once probable cause is shown to the court by instituting a suit—that there are "reasonable grounds" to believe that the property is subject to suit—hearsay is admissible to support the finding of probable cause. The burden of proof then rests upon the claimant who must prove by a preponderance of the evidence either that the funds did not have their source in illegal drug transactions and money laundering, or that they did not know or constructively know the source and nature of the funds as drug-related. Weinstein was troubled that under the civil forfeiture statute, police might "create nonexistent violations, or. . . trump up minor violations, to support searches that may lead to forfeitures of assets for their departments."[79]

In 1992, Weinstein handled several forfeiture cases aimed at the Cali cartel, which allegedly was importing 3000 kilograms a month of cocaine into the United States. One involved more than $10 million in wire transfers. The money laundering involved such actions as driving cars filled with cocaine from Florida to New York, shell corporations in Panama and Colombia, flying money to Panama, the exchange of drug dollars in the black market, electronic funds transfers from companies nominally in the clothing manufacturing business, loans made and paid the same day, electronic transfers in and out of bank accounts in many countries including the United States, and the literal *washing* of money. The jury rendered a verdict of forfeiture of eighteen of twenty-two seized amounts.[80]

In a related case, *Manufacturas International, LTDA v. Manufacturers Hanover Trust Co.*[81] claimants sued intermediary banks for loss of the use of their funds as well as violation of various federal and state statutes. Weinstein granted summary judgment for the banks, holding that they could not be held liable for following government orders respecting government funds. For this case Weinstein wrote a major opinion on forfeiture. Beginning with discussion of the ancient theory that forfeiture occurs simultaneously with the tainting of the object by the crime, he went beyond the time the opinion was written (the age of electronic fund transfers) to discuss problems which might be caused by future technological advances. In his opinion, Weinstein considered issues raised by the Federal Reserve Act, the Foreign Intelligence Surveillance Act, the Uniform Commercial Code, and New York law, while also dealing with a cause of action for conversion, a third-party beneficiary issue, negligence claims, and the reduction of privacy protections occurring because of the war on drugs.[82]

---

[78] *United States v. All Funds on Deposit in Any Account Maintained at Merrill, Lynch Pierce Fenner & Smith*, 801 F. Supp. 984, 989 (Aug. 5, 1992).

[79] *Id.* at 989ff.

[80] *United States v. All Funds on Deposit in Any Accounts Maintained at Merrill, Lynch, Pierce, Fenner & Smith*, 801 F. Supp. 984 (Aug. 5, 1992).

[81] 792 F. Supp. 180 (Feb. 27, 1992).

[82] *See also* Weinstein's casebook-like opinion in *United States v. United States Currency in the Amount of One Hundred forty-five thousand One Hundred-thirty-nine Dollars*, 803 F. Supp. 592 (Aug. 12, 1992), *aff 'd*, 18 F.3d 73 (1994: VanG-Card/Kearse), *cert. denied sub nom., Efiong v. United States*, 513 U.S. 815 (1994).

Dealing almost exclusively with constitutional and statutory matters and not with Weinstein's handling of the trial, the Second Circuit affirmed, stressing the need for courts to ensure what little due process is provided in the statutory scheme.[83]

Weinstein wrote the first published opinion applying a 1992 amendment to the forfeiture laws giving subject matter jurisdiction and venue to district courts over forfeiture cases, so long as *any* acts or omissions giving rise to the forfeiture had occurred in the district (even though the property was located in a foreign country).[84] Weinstein held that his court had jurisdiction over funds on deposit in London where the High Court of Great Britain had restrained the property pending the outcome of the civil forfeiture in the Eastern District.[85] The Court of Appeals affirmed.[86]

Political Corruption

Weinstein had political corruption prosecutions involving two well-known New York City politicians,—cases, he said, "bred in greed, arrogance and vanity."[87] Mario Biaggi, a congressman from the Bronx, who had once been a serious candidate for mayor of New York City, was found guilty by a jury of three crimes: receiving private supplementation of his salary, the use of interstate travel and telephone in aid of that crime, and obstruction of justice. Biaggi had sought to induce a possible witness to his crimes to lie if he was called before a grand jury. The leader of the Brooklyn Democratic organization, Meade Esposito (Amedeo Henry Esposito), was also convicted before Weinstein of providing a member of Congress with substantial benefits because of official acts performed and to be performed, as well as for the use of interstate travel and telephones in aid of that crime. The Biaggi and Esposito cases led to four Weinstein opinions. Two were sentencing opinions. The third held that the exclusion of Italian-Americans from the jury had not been the result of purposeful discrimination.[88] In the fourth, Weinstein considered the meaning of the statutory term "bribery" while rejecting a motion to set aside the convictions under the Travel Act.[89]

The first opinion dealt with double jeopardy, collateral estoppel, and the Eighth Amendment, and analyzed the shifting views of the Second Circuit. He ultimately upheld this forfeiture.

[83] *United States v. Daccaret*, 6 F.3d 37 (Sept. 10, 1993: Pratt-Oakes-Pierce). On remand, *see Organizacion JDLTDA v. U.S. Department of Justice*, 1996 Op. NB 255 (Apr. 2, 1996).

[84] *United States v. All Funds on Deposit in Any Accounts Maintained in the Names of Heriberto Castro Meza*, 856 F. Supp. 759 (July 8, 1994). *See* 28 U.S.C. §1335(b).

[85] *See* N.Y.L.J., July 13, 1994, at 1.

[86] *United States v. All Funds on Deposit in any Accounts Maintained in the names of Heriberto Casta Meza*, 94–6179, (2nd C.: Alti-Oakes-Card); N.Y.L.J., Aug. 17, 1995, at 1. *United States v. Jurado-Rodriguez*, 1995 NB 1751 (1995), decided by Weinstein, involved men linked to Jose Santacruz-Londono, the head of the Cali cartel, who sought to dismiss a criminal indictment on the grounds that the indictment violated the terms of Luxembourg's extradition decree and constituted double jeopardy.

[87] *United States v. Esposito*, 1987 NB 743, 745 (Oct. 23, 1987).

[88] *United States v. Biaggi*, 673 F. Supp.96 (Nov. 6, 1987).

[89] *United States v. Biaggi and Esposito*, 674 F. Supp. 86 (Nov. 25, 1987).

When sentencing the two men, Weinstein spoke of Biaggi's lack of remorse, evidenced by his taking satisfaction that the jury had not found him guilty of "corruption." Weinstein stated that "[w]hile accepting supplementation of income may not reveal as much corruption as outright bribery, it is corrupt. This action tends to cause a deterioration of the political system."[90] He expressed his concern that legislators, writing on Biaggi's behalf, had professed shock over the interpretation of the statutes he was convicted under. Employing the Sentencing Guidelines, Weinstein sentenced Biaggi to two years and six months in prison and a $500 fine.[91] Of Biaggi, Weinstein remarked in his oral history:

> I knew Biaggi, and I liked Biaggi, but, unlike Esposito, [he] had a very bad reputation as a crook, right from the time that he was a police officer.[92]

Weinstein gave Esposito a suspended sentence of two years, as well as two years' probation, a $500,000 fine, and five hundred hours of community service on behalf of the aged. The punishment was reduced because of Esposito's age (eighty-three) and his poor health and that of his wife. The "compelled public service" was made part of the probation "so that the public will be presented with a more positive model of the defendant and political figures" and as "a form of restitution for the harm to the public confidence in our government from the crimes of the defendant."[93] Esposito was also barred during his period of probation from giving anything of value to any public official. Weinstein said:

> It was a very difficult sentence for me to impose because he was a charming man and I was very fond of him. And I just couldn't see a man of that age and so sick in prison.[94]

Weinstein dismissed further corruption charges against Esposito seven months later because he found Esposito—by now legally blind, suffering memory losses after three minor strokes, and fighting colon cancer—too old to stand trial. Weinstein believed that Esposito would never have been able to assist properly in his defense.[95]

---

[90] *United States v. Biaggi*, 1987 NB 754, 757 (Nov. 5, 1987).

[91] *United States v. Biaggi*, 1987 NB 754, 759–60 (Nov. 7, 1987).

[92] Weinstein Oral History, at 865.

[93] *United States v. Esposito*, 1987 NB 743, 746 (Oct. 23, 1987).

[94] Weinstein Oral History, at 864.

[95] NEW YORK POST, July 1, 1988, at 4; NEW YORK TIMES, July 1, 1989. During this period Weinstein also presided over the conviction of the special counsel to the Speaker of the New York State Assembly, who had used Assembly funds to compensate his secretaries for private law practice work. A divided Court of Appeals affirmed the mail fraud and tax conviction. *United States v. Rubin*, 844 F.2d 979 (Apr. 15, 1988: Kearse-IRK/Mesk (d in part)).

Terrorist Cases

Weinstein had two major cases involving terrorists from the Middle East. The first involved Israel's request for the extradition of Mahmoud Abed Atta, a/k/a Mahmoud El-Abed Ahmad ("Ahmad"), a naturalized U.S. citizen and Palestinian terrorist implicated in a 1986 attack on an Israeli passenger bus. Ahmad sought *habeas corpus* to prevent his extradition. Magistrate John L. Caden had denied extradition on the grounds that it was for a political offense.[96] A second request was made to Judge Edward Korman, who granted extradition.[97] A petition for *habeas corpus* on due process grounds followed. Weinstein received the case by random selection.

In an international extradition case, judges typically defer to the judgment of the State Department as to whether the person extradited would receive fair treatment in the country requesting the extradition.[98] Weinstein transformed what probably would have been a simple *pro forma* case of judicial deference into a potentially significant human rights precedent. The court itself would be required to determine that the person extradited was granted due process and treated humanely.[99]

On May 16, 1989, Weinstein ruled from the bench that he would consider the due process claim and permit both parties to submit further evidence on that and any other issue. The government unsuccessfully sought mandamus to prevent the hearing and prevent the court from receiving evidence on the probable nature of the judicial procedures of the requesting nation in an extradition matter.

Weinstein held fourteen days of hearings in July and August, with extensive arguments based upon full briefs, in order to make sure that, if extradited, Ahmad would not be subjected to procedures or treatment "so offensive to our nation's sense of decency as to obligate the court to block his extradition." He heard from six witnesses on the Israeli judicial process and conditions of detention; four for the petitioner and Professors Alan Dershowitz and Monroe Freedman for the United States. Ahmad was represented by former U.S. Attorney General Ramsey Clark.

In a thirty-four-page opinion in the Federal Supplement,[100] Weinstein ruled first that terrorism and acts of war against civilians cannot be defined as political acts. In his second, unprecedented ruling, Weinstein held that U.S. courts must review the judicial process in the foreign country independently of the State Department to determine whether the individual would be treated fairly on return. He then held that Ahmad would be treated fairly in Israel.[101]

---

[96] *In re Extradition of Atta*, 1988 WL 66866 (June 17, 1988).

[97] *In re Extradition of Atta*, 706 F. Supp. 1032 (Feb. 14, 1989).

[98] Sometimes there is also a question as to whether the crime the person to be extradited is alleged to have committed is an extraditable offense.

[99] *Ahmad v. Wigen*, 726 F. Supp. 389, 394 (Sept. 26, 1989).

[100] *Id.*

[101] *See* WALL STREET JOURNAL, Oct. 18, 1989; JEWISH WEEK, Oct. 27, 1989.

Weinstein saw some merit in an expansive view of the political offense exception under which someone who commits a "political offense" cannot be extradited. He would not say that the State Department's view, that the political offense exception was not applicable to violent attacks on civilians, was "wrong as a matter of law or policy," but only that "as a corollary to limiting the protection of the political offense doctrine, there is the need for increased vigilance of the courts and expansion of their power of inquiry."[102] "In a sense," he said, "to characterize an act as terrorism is to recognize its political nature while at the same time excluding it from the category of *protected* political crimes."[103] He held that "[s]poradic acts of violence cannot justify deliberately waylaying a civilian bus operating on a regularly scheduled run and deliberately attempting to kill the civilian driver and civilian passengers." If the alleged attack took place as charged, it "must be characterized as a random act of murderous terrorism, rather than a protected political offense."[104]

Regarding deference to the State Department's presumption that a foreign nation will exercise its powers in good faith, Weinstein thought that the presumption might require greater scrutiny.[105] Holding that the courts have an obligation "not to extradite people who face procedures or treatment that 'shock the conscience' of jurists acting under the United States Constitution and within our current legal ethos," Weinstein said that "[t]he courts are not and cannot be, a rubber stamp for the other branches of government in the exercise of extradition jurisdiction."[106] In coming to this position, Weinstein drew upon court decisions, treaties and international precedent, including the *Soering* case,[107] in which the European Court of Human Rights in 1989 prevented the United Kingdom from extraditing an accused murderer to the Commonwealth of Virginia because of the risk that he would languish for years on death row. He called *Soering* "a persuasive though non-binding international standard" on the refusal to extradite.[108]

Weinstein found that it was improbable that Ahmad would be, if extradited, abused after his extradition in order to obtain information, that he would serve his term of imprisonment under humane conditions, and that trials by civilian courts within Israel were conducted by professional and independent jurists sensitive to the rights of defendants. Thus, the evidence established "that he will receive full and satisfactory due process protections afforded under the laws of Israel."[109] The petition for *habeas corpus* was denied.

---

[102] *Ahmad v. Wigen*, 726 F. Supp. 389, 405 (Sept. 26, 1989).

[103] *Id.* at 407.

[104] *Id.* at 409.

[105] *Id.* at 415.

[106] *Id.* at 412.

[107] *Soering v. United Kingdom*, 11 Eur. Ct. H. R. 439 (1989).

[108] Ahmad, 726 F. Supp. at 414.

[109] *Id.* at 420.

The Court of Appeals affirmed, but questioned Weinstein's decision to explore the merit of Ahmad's contention that he would be treated badly by the Israeli justice system. That, the court thought, was improper. "The interests of international comity are ill-served," Judge Van Graafeiland wrote, "by requiring a foreign nation such as Israel to satisfy a United States district judge concerning the fairness of its laws and the manner in which they are enforced."[110]

Five years later the Israeli Supreme Court, sitting as a Criminal Court of Appeal, reversed a Jerusalem court and held that there was insufficient evidence to convict Ata [sic].[111]

Weinstein also handled the trial of alleged terrorist, Khaled Mohammed El-Jassem, a PLO official linked to Black September and Fatah, who was accused of attempting to explode three powerful car bombs on March 4, 1973, when Prime Minister Golda Meier was visiting New York City. The targets were two Israeli banks on Fifth Avenue and an El Al terminal. El-Jassem, indicted in 1973, was arrested in Italy during the 1991 Persian Gulf War.[112] El-Jassem was represented by radical attorneys William Kunstler and Ronald Kuby.

Although there had been a bombing at the World Trade Center, just before the trial was to begin,[113] Weinstein refused to delay the trial, although when a defendant with a Middle Eastern connection was arrested, he sequestered the jury and continued the trial on Saturday and Sunday, though not on Friday in consideration of the defendant's religion.[114] Weinstein ordered that the PLO not be mentioned in front of the jury and that El-Jassem be described as a member of a "Palestinian rights group." A three-and-one-half-day trial and three hours of jury deliberation produced a verdict that El-Jassem was found guilty.[115] After the verdict, Weinstein allowed El-Jassem to make a lengthy political statement.[116] When Weinstein sentenced El-Jassem to thirty years, Kunstler denounced him as a Zionist with a lack of compassion for anyone associated with the PLO.[117] The Court of Appeals affirmed.[118]

---

[110] *Ahmad v. Wigen*, 910 F.2d 1063, 1067 (Aug. 10, 1990: *VanG*-New-Kearse).

[111] *Case of Ata*, Israel Supreme Court, 1995 NB 5.

[112] DAILY NEWS, Mar. 3, 1993, at 28; NEWSDAY, Apr. 17, 1993.

[113] The trial began twenty years to the day the bombs were to go off. NEW YORK TIMES, Mar. 5, 1993.

[114] DAILY NEWS, May 5, 1993, at 24.

[115] NEW YORK TIMES, Mar. 9, 1993.

[116] Weinstein Oral History, at 1212.

[117] NEWSDAY, Apr. 17, 1993,

[118] *United States v. El-Jassem*, 819 F. Supp. 166 (Apr. 20, 1993), *aff'd*, 48 F.3d 1213 (1994). For an interesting case involving extradition, money laundering, double jeopardy, the interpretation of the law of Luxembourg, and the use of expert witnesses in interpreting that law, *see United States v. Jurado-Rodriguez*, CR-94-547 (Nov. 15, 1995).

First Amendment/Privacy

Weinstein heard few First Amendment cases in this period. The most interesting involved a conflict raising First, Fourth, and Fifth Amendment concerns. In March 1992, a U.S. magistrate judge issued a warrant authorizing U.S. Secret Service agents to enter the apartment of defendant Babatunde Ayeni to search for evidence related to credit card fraud. The agents came accompanied by a CBS television news crew that filmed twenty minutes of the search during which the defendant's wife and child were present. Nothing of significance was found in the search.

CBS, which did not broadcast the tape, refused to give it to Ayeni and moved to quash a subpoena on the basis of its newsgathering privilege. Ayeni contended that he needed the tape because it might contain information relevant to his motions to dismiss his indictment and suppress evidence and to aid his defense at trial. Weinstein suggested an *in camera* review of the tape and CBS consented.

Holding that Ayeni was entitled to the tape, Judge Weinstein stated that the Fourth Amendment was "designed to prevent the wrong that Ayeni and his family had suffered. 'The Fourth Amendment and the problems that gave rise to its adoption,' Weinstein wrote, 'teach that the execution of a search warrant is a serious matter. Only for limited and necessary purposes does the ordinary inviolability of the home temporarily give way". "Participation by the media in the invasion of privacy must be scrutinized carefully," he wrote.[119]

While assertion of the newsgathering privilege by CBS as a ground for quashing the subpoena was appropriate, the *in camera* review of the tape revealed that it contained potentially exculpatory evidence. It proved a graphic indication of the government's zeal to arrest Ayeni and its failure to produce any evidence after tearing apart his home. Weinstein thought that "[t]his tape with the gripping pictures of a cowering wife and child and lack of any evidence supporting the government's case, is likely to be strongly relied on by the jury in weighing the government's charges."[120] The judge was "reluctant in a criminal case to substitute [his] judgment for a defendant's on the question whether such evidence is 'necessary or critical' to a defense. It is sufficient that a compelling argument of cogency can be made."[121]

Weinstein also believed that the news-gathering privilege operated weakly, if at all, in the case before him. Ayeni's home had been entered without his consent or that of his family. That CBS had trespassed and engaged in conduct directly contrary to Fourth Amendment principles bore upon the court's evaluation of the privilege. "Even a reporter must accept limits on how far upon another person's privacy he or she may intrude."[122] Further, in the case, the government had failed the public trust.[123] The U.S.

---

[119] *United States v. Sanusi*, 813 F. Supp. 149, 158 (Dec. 7, 1992).

[120] *Id.* at 160.

[121] *Id.*

[122] *Id.*

[123] *Id.* at 160–61 (finding that "[i]nviting private citizens . . . to the execution of the warrant to join the search party is a failure of public trust - one that indicates a disregard of the important values at stake when the government enters a private person's home.").

Attorney was ordered to bring the matter to the attention of the highest authority in the Secret Service.

In March 1994, CBS reached a settlement with the Ayenis, paying them $100,000.[124] Although CBS had settled, Weinstein refused to dismiss the individual government defendants from the Ayenis' civil suit. In what may have been a case of first impression, Weinstein held that the agent who allegedly arranged for CBS's involvement was not entitled to qualified immunity for it would be "grossly unreasonable for a government agent not to have known that the presence of private persons he invited, they could titillate and entertain others, was beyond the scope of what was lawfully authorized by the government."[125] The Second Circuit affirmed.[126] Certiorari was denied.[127]

In another case, Weinstein recognized the right of U.S. taxpayers to file tax returns "under protest." When Laurence P. McCormick had filed such a return, the Internal Revenue Service (IRS) treated it as a nullity, then charged him penalties both for a frivolous filing and for a late return. Weinstein held that the First Amendment protects the right of protest to any branch of the government. "A protest," he wrote, "is an expression of grievance, seeking redress that the Internal Revenue may not throttle or mute by threats of penalties."[128]

Cuomo v. Wachtler

In *Cuomo v. Wachtler,* very high-profile parties were employing the courts as part of a political struggle. Chief Judge Sol Wachtler of the New York Court of Appeals and Matthew Croson, New York's chief administrative judge, brought suit in state supreme court in Albany. The judges sued Governor Mario Cuomo, claiming that he was violating the state constitution by not providing necessary funding for the operation of New York's courts. Cuomo counter-sued in the Eastern District and removed the state case there, alleging that Wachtler was violating federal civil rights laws and the U.S. Constitution.

Weinstein, who knew both men personally, offered to recuse himself. He expressed "dismay and sadness" at "the possibility of these titans of New York, upon whose wisdom rests the welfare of almost twenty million New Yorkers contending with each other personally in the courts."[129] Weinstein urged both sides to withdraw from what would become "a public spectacle" and asserted that the issues at stake—budgetary

---

[124] Weinstein Oral History, at 1357; NEW YORK TIMES, Mar. 20, 1994; U.S.A. TODAY, Mar. 21, 1994.

[125] *Ayeni v. CBS Inc.,* 848 F. Supp. 362, 368 (Mar. 17, 1994).

[126] *Ayeni v. Mottola,* 35 F.3d 680 (Sept. 12, 1994: New-Pierce-Leval). *See also* NEW YORK TIMES, Sept. 13, 1994, at B2.

[127] 514 U.S. 1062 (1995).

[128] *McCormick v. Peterson,* 94-1 U.S. Tax. Cas. (CCH), at 50, 026, 73 A.F.T.R. 2d (RIA). 597 (Dec. 1, 1993).

[129] *Cuomo v. Wachtler,* 1991 NB 562, 564 566.

issues—were not well suited for courts to decide.[130] Weinstein asked former Secretary of State and City Bar president Cyrus Vance to mediate,[131] but the mediation was not successful, and Vance left for Europe to mediate a larger conflict, the civil war in Yugoslavia.[132] With the principals unwilling to settle, Weinstein said the case "became an embarrassment." The federal courts lacked jurisdiction and the Eastern District was the wrong venue. The suit then was removed to the Northern District of New York, where the federal suit was dismissed and the state litigation removed to the state courts.[133] Three months later the case settled.[134]

Miscellaneous Civil Cases

The civil cases that came to Weinstein during this period exemplified the remarkable range of subjects that come before the federal district courts. They a patient case for microporous nylon membrane filters, which involved the collateral estoppel effect of factual findings by a British court dealing with a patent of the European Patent Office (a case in which Weinstein called for a universal patent system[135]); a contest between a satellite television and a cable TV company over access to the North Shore Tower apartment complex in Little Neck;[136] a suit raising the issue whether it was unfair competition for a business to acquire a telephone number identified by the spelling of a generic term that a competitor was using (with a spelling modification) to identify its telephone number (it was unfair competition; the number was 1-800-MATTRESS);[137] whether a contract between a cruise ship line and a passenger should be treated under admiralty law or under the law governing consumer contracts for resorts, which would have provided a longer statute of limitations. (Weinstein answered "admiralty law," although he suggested that courts might well consider whether outmoded admiralty concepts should be replaced, since a cruise ship is arguably "a consumer floating luxury hotel.").[138] Spiro Agnew and Jean-Bertrand Aristide, the former president of Haiti, were parties in cases

---

[130] *Id.* at 564.

[131] N.Y.L.J., Oct. 8, 1991, at 1; NEW YORK TIMES, Oct. 8, 1991, at B1, B2; NEW YORK TIMES (editorial) Oct. 9, 1991.

[132] N.Y.L.J., Oct. 17, 1991.

[133] *Wachtler v. Cuomo*, 1991 U.S. Dist. LEXIS 17069 (N.D.N.Y. *McAvoy*: Nov. 21, 1991). *See also* N.Y.L.J., Nov. 1, 1991; 1991 NB 1018 (Nov. 4, 1991); NEW YORK TIMES, Nov. 22, 1991; NEWSDAY, Nov. 23, 1991.

[134] The state judiciary was protected from cuts for the next fiscal year and received a $19 million increase in funding, while the legislature created an additional $15 million in savings for the courts. NEW YORK TIMES, Jan. 17, 1992, at B4. On the lawsuit, *see* Weinstein Oral History, at 1049–55, 1057. *See also Oral History: Judge Richard D. Simons, New York Court of Appeals (January 1983–December 1997)*, 1 N.Y. LEGAL HIST. 53, 131–33 (2005).

[135] *Cuno, Inc. v. Pall Corp.*, 729 F. Supp. 234, 239–40 (Dec. 19, 1989).

[136] Weinstein Oral History, at 1055–57.

[137] *Dial-A-Mattress Franchise Corp. v. Anthony Page DBA Easy Assocs.*, 880 F.2d 675 (July 27, 1989: *New*-Miner-Ward).

[138] *Vavoules v. Kloster Cruises Ltd.*, 822 F. Supp. 979, 983 (June 9, 1993).

before Weinstein,[139] until he ruled that Aristide in his case was entitled to state immunity.[140]

Weinstein had two ugly cases involving children that had international implications. In *United States v. Georgescu*,[141] a Romanian national had molested a nine-year-old Norwegian girl on a flight to the United States while the plane was over the Atlantic Ocean. Congress had established "special aircraft jurisdiction" over specified crimes, including sexual abuse crimes, taking place on a foreign aircraft scheduled to stop in the United States. The United States had ratified an international convention encouraging punishment of crimes aboard a foreign aircraft in international airspace. This seems to have been the first case unrelated to hijacking brought under the U.S. which did not involve an American or an American airline. Weinstein denied a motion to dismiss the case, although he expressed reservations about the wisdom of further prosecution in the United States, believing that prosecution in the child's home county might be a lesser burden for her. Weinstein encouraged the parties and the Romanian government to agree to let the defendant take a plea in the United States, serve no time, then return to Romania where he would lose his job. The Romanian government agreed to make him available for any further proceedings. While theoretically the judge is not supposed to be directly involved in plea bargaining and Weinstein technically wasn't, he "made clear to the parties what I expected them to do."[142]

Weinstein also became embroiled in an international *cause celebre* involving a Zimbabwean diplomat, who allegedly had abused his nine year old son. Representatives for the child fought against his return to Zimbabwe. President Ronald Reagan became personally concerned with the case. Weinstein held that the courts had no jurisdiction, which cleared the way for the transfer of the matter to the State Department. Ultimately, the Supreme Court lifted a stay, and the boy was flown home accompanied by a State Department psychiatrist and a Zimbabwean social worker.[143]

During this period Weinstein did not as a *district judge*, have before him important civil rights cases nor did he have New York City Board of Education cases. He did sit as an appeals court judge to hear the controversial Yonkers desegregation case involving housing and public schools, *United States v. Yonkers Branch NAACP*,[144] Weinstein joined Judges McLaughlin and Jacobs in a *per curium* opinion affirming Judge Leonard Sand, who had rejected the City's plan and issued a modified remedial order of his own.

Siegel v. Board of Education of City of New York, a Title VII lawsuit, did come to Weinstein. Weinstein rejected the contention that the differential in the salaries of

---

[139] *Agnew v. Alicanto, S.A.*, 125 F.R.D. 355 (Apr. 25, 1989).

[140] N.Y.L.J., Dec. 14, 1993.

[141] 723 F. Supp. 912 (Oct. 25, 1989). *See also* NEW YORK TIMES, Nov. 17, 1989.

[142] Weinstein Oral History, at 965–67.

[143] NEW YORK TIMES, Jan. 2, 1988, at A27; Jan. 13, 1988; Mar. 2, 1988, at B2; DAILY NEWS, Jan. 5, 1988; Jan. 10, 1988; Jan. 13, 1988; Jan. 16, 1988; MANHATTAN LAWYER, Jan. 12–18, 1988; NATL. L.J., Jan. 18, 1988, at 6.

[144] 29 F.3d 40 (July 5, 1994).

elementary school and high school principals was the result of gender discrimination, holding that the difference was related to the complexity of their jobs.[145] In *Michael M v. Board of Education of New York City School District,*[146] Weinstein held that Congress could, under the Education of All Handicapped Children Act, constitutionally provide that cities and states could be sued for attorneys' fees for successful suits brought against them.

Among the particularly thorough evidence opinions, there was one involving the business records exception to the hearsay rule,[147] another answering the question whether radioimmunoassay (RIA) hair analysis could be used in a hearing on probation violation to determine whether a probationer had been using drugs,[148] and a third, a petition for habeas corpus involving whether the petitioner's confrontation rights were violated by the introduction of identification hearsay.[149]

Perhaps the most influential evidence opinion arose in a civil rights action against Suffolk County and individual County police officers. *King v. Conde,*[150] a much cited Weinstein opinion, occurred at a time when the Suffolk Police Department had a particularly notorious reputation for claims of police misconduct—for using excessive force and covering up bad police behavior. At the time, the Suffolk District Attorney and police were being investigated by the State Investigation Commission headed David Trager (later, judge of the Eastern District).[151]

King resulted from a late night scuffle between rowdy police and rowdy civilians. Discovery in these civil rights actions were marked by a distinct lack of cooperation from the police. Weinstein's opinion in *King v. Conde* dealt with the discoverability of police personnel records and other information sought by plaintiffs.

In a tightly reasoned opinion clearly intended to guide his colleagues in cases involving the Long Island police, Weinstein discussed the applicability of state privacy rules and offered detailed procedures for applying a balancing test.[152] He emphasized that the "great weight of the policy in favor of discovery in civil rights actions supplements the normal presumption in favor of broad discovery. . ."[153] If the materials were to be available, Weinstein suggested that both sides consider the effect of a protective

---

[145] 713 F. Supp. 54 (May 9, 1989); Weinstein Oral History, at 953; N.Y.L.J., May 16, 1989.

[146] 686 F. Supp. 995 (May 27, 1988).

[147] *United States v. Chan,* 680 F. Supp. 520 (Feb. 9, 1988).

[148] *United States v. Medina,* 749 F. Supp. 59 (Oct. 22, 1990); N.Y.L.J., Oct. 24, 1990, at 1. One unexpected effect of the *Medina* case was that Weinstein received invitations to deliver speeches on hair analysis. Weinstein Oral History, at 1029.

[149] *Mitchell v. Hoke,* 745 F. Supp. 874, 878 (Sept. 5, 1990).

[150] *King v. Conde,* 121 F.R.D. 180 (June 15, 1988). *See also* Weinstein Oral History, at 897–906.

[151] Kenneth D. Levine, Civil Rights Litigation-Plaintiffs' Perspective (paper done under academic supervision of Jeffrey Morris Dec. 2, 1994 in possession of Jeffrey B. Morris), at 2.

[152] *King,* 121 F.R.D. at 190. *See also* Levine, *supra* note 151, at 25.

[153] *King,* 121 F.R.D. at 195.

order limiting use of the materials to the instant litigation.[154] Weinstein also emphasized that the

> ... Lawfullness of police operations is a matter of great concern to citizens in a democracy and protective orders must be considered with that public interest in mind.[155]

King v. Conde demonstrate that Weinstein's patience (and, presumably, that of his colleagues) had worn thin. He raised *sua sponte* the notion of sanctions against the Suffolk County Department of Law:

> If civil rights cases involving the police in Suffolk County cannot be amicably handled in the future, the court will consider appropriate educational programs to assist the attorneys involved in acquiring the appropriate cooperative attitude.[156]

Rather than obey Weinstein's order, the defendants continued to refuse disclosure, ultimately settling with King out of court.[157] In a little over twenty years, *King v. Conde* was cited in 196 opinions.[158]

THE LITIGATION OVER THE SHOREHAM NUCLEAR REACTOR

One of the most important cases Jack Weinstein has handled involved the closing of the Shoreham Nuclear Reactor, *County of Suffolk v. Long Island Lighting Co.* (the "*Shoreham* case"). The *Shoreham* case was important, not for black letter law nor for anything extraordinary that happened in the courtroom. Rather, it was a case growing out of an explosive political controversy. In such cases, there is the possibility that the district judge may have the leverage to represent the public and forge a workable, statesman-like solution. *Shoreham* was, therefore, both complex litigation and an intense political battle. Jack Weinstein played a very important role in the Shoreham litigation, ultimately achieving a legal and political settlement.

---

[154] Levine, *supra* note 151, at 28.

[155] *King*, 121 F.R.D. at 190.

[156] *Id.* at 197.

[157] Levine, *supra* note 151, at 30.

[158] In *Gentile v. County of Suffolk*, 129 F.R.D. 435 (Feb. 21, 1990), Weinstein permitted the introduction of part of the State Investigation Committee's report into evidence with strong limiting instructions. In *Browning-Ferris Indus. v. Muszynski*, 899 F.2d 151 (Mar. 26, 1990: JBW-Mes-New), Weinstein, writing for the Court of Appeals, dealt with the situation where the court is faced with the problem that determining jurisdiction was far more difficult then deciding the case on the merits. Weinstein wrote that while it is customary to resolve subject matter jurisdictional issues before reaching the merits, there were exceptions to the rule and this court had found one. The rationales for such rare decisions were judicial efficiency and restraint.

The battle over Shoreham attracted the attention of the nuclear power industry, the national media, and Congress.[159] A good half-dozen government agencies—county, state, and federal—were heavily involved and so was the governor of New York (and potential presidential nominee), Mario Cuomo, environmental groups, businessmen, and many "ordinary" Long Islanders.[160] The federal government had an important interest in safe nuclear power. The state had an important interest in stable and predictable electric rates. Both state and local interests were concerned about the viability of the company that furnished electric power on Long Island, the Long Island Lighting Company (LILCO).[161]

In his major opinion in the lawsuit over closing Shoreham, Weinstein summed up the rich background of the case.

> This case... brings to the surface private agendas for publicly owned power and deep antipathy towards large corporations, particularly utilities. It has elements of xenophobia and hysteria. It reflects a deep populist strain of our citizens and an urge to stand up for what they believe in, to speak out on public issues and be heard by public officials. Stronger than the other rational and emotional aspects of the case is a pervasive fear of atomic energy generally and the Shoreham Nuclear Power Station (Shoreham) in particular. . . . To understand this case is to appreciate that money alone and [the] economic theory of litigation do not fully explain the dynamics of mass tort litigation.[162]

In 1965 LILCO announced that it would construct a large nuclear power plant on the north shore of Long Island. It was a time of high public confidence in nuclear power. Although many technological problems had yet to be solved, the number and size of nuclear reactors were growing rapidly.[163] LILCO, Long Island's biggest taxpayer, was a seasoned utility experienced in fossil-fuel plant construction and operation.[164] It had a firm lock on the supply of energy on Long Island as it was the sole supplier of natural gas within its electric franchise area.[165]

In 1965, LILCO expected that the plant would be operational in four and one-half years and would cost $65–75 million. By 1969, that estimate had increased to $261 million. The real cost would top $5 billion,[166] due to astronomical increases in cost, the product of enhanced safety requirements, LILCO's lack of experience in constructing atomic plants, and, as Weinstein said, "some bad luck."[167]

---

[159] Susan Beck, *Ken Feinberg: Kaye Scholer's King Solomon,* AMERICAN LAWYER 119–21 (May 1989).

[160] Weinstein Oral History, at 925, 928.

[161] *County of Suffolk v. Long Island Lighting Co.,* 710 F. Supp. 1407, 1419 (Feb. 13, 1989).

[162] *County of Suffolk v. Long Island Lighting Co.,* 710 F. Supp. 1428, 1431 (Mar. 22, 1989).

[163] DAVID P. MCCAFFREY, THE POLITICS OF NUCLEAR POWER: A HISTORY OF THE SHOREHAM POWER PLANT 254 (1991).

[164] *Id.* at 44; DIANE KETCHMAN, LONG ISLAND: SHORES OF PLENTY; AN ECONOMIC CELEBRATION 60 (1988).

[165] *Id.* at 33.

[166] MCCAFFREY, *supra* note 163, at 49; Richard Michael Strean, Nuclear Power Politics (Ph.D. dissertation in Political Science, Cornell University, Aug. 1993), at 78.

[167] Weinstein Oral History, at 923–24.

Construction of Shoreham was delayed for many reasons. One major factor was environmental hearings, hearings which may have been an important factor in the creation of the antinuclear movement nationally.[168] However, there were other causes of delay: a turbulent regulatory environment, engineering problems, poor labor productivity, and general mismanagement. Shoreham also lacked unanimous support from the business community.[169] As costs skyrocketed (854 percent from 1966 to 1981[170]), LILCO had to borrow money and increase its rates, producing a serious public relations problem for a company with the second-highest electric rates in the nation.[171]

Opponents of Shoreham used public hearings and the need for an environmental impact statement to keep delaying the opening of the reactor.[172] Public opinion throughout the nation began to cool to nuclear power because of scientific disagreements over safety, the growth of environmentalism, and an economic downturn. Safety concerns mounted after the nuclear accident at Three Mile Island on March 4, 1979, when a reactor boiled dry, failed to cool, and began to disintegrate.[173] The belief grew in the early 1980s that, because of the immense difficulties of evacuating Long Island, if there were an accident, Shoreham would create unacceptably dangerous risks.

By 1983 the plant was almost complete, but on Long Island, opposition to Shoreham was wearing down its proponents, financially and politically.[174] Governor Cuomo, the Suffolk County Executive, and the county legislature all came to the view that the plant was unacceptably dangerous.[175] In February 1983, Suffolk County refused to participate in the design and testing of an evacuation plan for Shoreham. In the absence of county approval, the state declined to approve the plan. LILCO ratcheted up tensions in January 1984 by withholding a $26 million property tax payment due the County.[176]

By 1985, the plant was complete, but unable to get a commercial license because the state and county were still unwilling to engage in emergency planning.[177] By 1986, political careers on Long Island generally depended upon opposition to Shoreham.[178] While the county government and LILCO's ratepayers did not want Shoreham ever to open, they also opposed allowing LILCO to recoup its immense losses through large rate hikes. In April 1986, the explosion and fire at the Chernobyl Nuclear Plant in the Soviet Union focused world attention on the dangers of nuclear power.

---

[168] McCaffrey, *supra* note 163, at 51.

[169] McCaffrey, *supra* note 163, at 180–81.

[170] Rick Eckstein, Constraint and Discretion: The Political Economy of the Shoreham Nuclear Plant (unpublished Ph.D. dissertation in Sociology, State University of New York at Stony Brook, 1990), at 147.

[171] *Id.* at 155; McCaffrey, *supra* note 163, at 217.

[172] Strean, *supra* note 166, at 57.

[173] New York Times, Feb. 12, 1989, at 1, 42.

[174] McCaffrey, *supra* note 163, at 207; Strean, *supra* note 166, at 145.

[175] Weinstein Oral History, at 925; Eckstein, *supra* note 170, at 69.

[176] McCaffrey, *supra* note 163, at 123–24.

[177] New York Times, Jan. 22, 1989.

[178] McCaffrey, *supra* note 163, at 135.

In May 1986, Suffolk County ("the County") and a class of ratepayers joined in filing a $5.4 billion civil RICO suit against LILCO, arguing that LILCO had obtained rate increases by fraud and misrepresentation.[179] The case came to Weinstein.[180]

Governor Cuomo, portraying the issue in starkly moralistic terms and reinforcing public fears about nuclear power, had committed the full force of the state executive and, by employing his appointment power, the Public Service Commission, against the opening of Shoreham. Cuomo, though, was willing to compensate LILCO for most of those costs that had been prudently incurred and otherwise assist the company in its post-Shoreham life.[181]

On May 18, 1988, Weinstein refused to dismiss the civil RICO suit against LILCO, with potential damages possibly reaching $8.7 billion. Weinstein was unimpressed with defendants' arguments that plaintiffs lacked standing and that the charged pattern of racketeering activity did not relate to a continuous criminal enterprise, although he indicated that establishing the factual basis for that argument might be difficult, if not impossible.[182] Years later he explained why he let the case go forward:

> . . . there was enough basis for the claim, so that the people of Long Island had a right to see the case unfold. If I had dismissed it earlier, in a matter of importance to three and a half million people where the press was involved and constant charges of lying were involved, the setting up of an atomic plant was involved, an atomic plant with all its dangers, it would have been a mistake. There are some cases that should not be dismissed as a matter of summary judgment. In this case, it wasn't clear what the evidence would be. I would not have been comfortable dismissing it at this stage.[183]

More succinctly, he put it this way: "Political matters of this kind cannot be treated the same way as intersection accidents."[184]

In September 1988, Weinstein let the lawsuit based upon RICO brought by Suffolk go ahead, but also held that because the County had interests which might differ

---

[179] There had been some previous litigation over the plant. *See, e.g., In re LILCO* Sec. Litig., 111 F.R.D. 663 (Aug. 25, 1986), where Judge Leonard Wexler certified a class of shareholders suing over common law fraud and negligent misrepresentation. In *LILCO v. County of Suffolk*, 625 F. Supp. 1500 (Feb. 10, 1986), Judge Wexler barred the county from trying to block the exercise of LILCO's emergency plan for impermissible intrusion on federal regulatory authority. There was also some litigation in state courts.

[180] In a related case, *Long Island Lighting Co. v. Barbash*, 625 F.2d 221 (Nov. 8, 1985), Weinstein refused during a proxy fight to enjoin an advertisement sponsored by Citizens to Replace LILCO. He would not treat the ad as a proxy solicitation because he saw it as an advertisement purchased in connection with a serious public debate with political implications. He said: "To muffle the voice of the less affluent public by allowing suits such as these to go forward dangerously hobbles the public debate that is our democracy's first line of defense." *Id.* at 226.

[181] McCaffrey, *supra* note 163, at 24–25.

[182] *County of Suffolk v. Long Island Lighting Co.*, 685 F. Supp. 38 (May 18, 1988); Newsday, May 19, 1988, at 7, 35.

[183] Weinstein Oral History, at 895.

[184] Id.

considerably from the ratepayers, that the County could not serve as a proper class representative. Further, the individual ratepayers could not represent the class since their substantial legal costs had been paid by the County. Weinstein did not preclude a new class action by appropriate parties.[185]

The individual ratepayers then petitioned for the substitution of Judith Vladek as attorney for the class. That motion was granted but all plaintiffs except Suffolk were then severed from the action for the purposes of participating in the impending trial over the RICO claims of Suffolk County.[186]

The trial of the civil RICO suit brought by the County which was now the sole plaintiff began on October 3, 1988, and lasted thirty-six days.[187] On November 2, Weinstein in jacket, tie, and LILCO hardhat toured Shoreham with six jurors and four alternates. A court reporter tagged along as judge and jurors wound their way up and down narrow staircases and through cramped crawl spaces.[188] In his oral history, Weinstein described what he saw:

> All in all it was an extremely complex political, social, economic [and] science case and I just loved it. I went out to Suffolk to Shoreham and I crawled into all of the boilers. It was just an incredibly complex plant. It was probably the most complex single engine produced in this world, up to that point. Millions of miles of wires and electronically controlled units. [Sic] It was just mind boggling when you got in there. . . . I crawled through some parts like in the old submarines. You had to crawl through safety hatches. It was kind of scary for me because at one point we went into the diesel room and they turned on the huge diesels to show how they were working. I had my clerks there. I had the lawyers there. We were all in this little room and the diesels were turned on. I said, "Turn those G_ Damned things off." Because I had been on a submarine. A diesel, if it doesn't have access to air, will in a matter of a fraction of a second, pull all of the air out of the room, a relatively small room, and kill people immediately. . . . I just didn't trust engineers [chuckle] having had all of this testimony about ineptitude.[189]

What did Weinstein actually think of the safety of the plant? In his oral history, he reflected: ". . . it was clearly the safest atomic plant in the world. It was a beautiful engine. . ."

---

[185] *County of Suffolk v. Long Island Lighting Co.*, 710 F. Supp. 1405–06 (Sept. 6, 1988); NEWSDAY, Sept. 7, 1988, at 1. Weinstein Oral History, at 929. *See also County of Suffolk v. Long Island Lighting Co.*, 710 F. Supp. 1407, 1411 (Feb. 13, 1989).

[186] *County of Suffolk v. Long Island Lighting Co.*, 710 F. Supp. 1407 (Feb. 13, 1989).

[187] NEWSDAY, Oct. 4, 1988; NEW YORK TIMES, Oct. 4, 1988.

[188] NEWSDAY, Nov. 3, 1988.

[189] Weinstein Oral History, at 932–33.

. . . I thought it was as safe as those things can be made. But, I never have complete confidence in any kind of man made object. I think, as I recall when I visited the plant, there was this beautiful large very impressive control room with all of the boards, levers, switches, valves and everything. I looked over and there was one of the engineers, I don't know who he was—off duty or what, he had his feet on the desk and he was reading a magazine.[190]

It was a safe plant but at that time I was fairly convinced that it wasn't really needed. . . . it was better from a safety point of view as well as from a sense of security point of view as well as from a[n] economic point of view, to shut it down.[191]

Speaking outside the hearing of the jury, Weinstein called the County's case "thin."[192] Yet, the jury on December 5 found LILCO guilty of racketeering, fraud, and misrepresentation.[193] Several days later, the jury set damages as $7.6 million. Trebled under RICO, the utility's liability was $23 million.

The jury verdict opened up LILCO to billions of dollars of further liability in the ratepayer class action. It also gave Suffolk County what seemed to have been a potentially decisive role in settlement talks. On December 9, Weinstein set an expedited schedule for motions in the ratepayer case[194] Motions were to be heard on February 2, 1989. Besides that pending trial, Weinstein had to decide whether to certify the class of ratepayers. He also had to deal with the motion to set aside the verdict in the County's case that had just been decided and consider the possible bankruptcy of LILCO.

Settlement talks began in the middle of December.[195] He has explained what was "on his table" at the time:

There were all kinds of problems in circumventing the Suffolk legislature and getting the County Executive to come along, sub rosa in getting the governor to coordinate his press releases and his statements with what I was doing in Suffolk, Nassau and Brooklyn; and in working something out that had the appearance [of] being fair to all sides. LILCO was at that point in very serious financial straits so that the settlement had to be worked out permitting them to make minimum payments for the first year or two and then increasing the payments towards the end when they would become more financially stable.

I couldn't take away from the Public Service Commission the control of fees and rates. . .

---

[190] Weinstein Oral History, at 935.

[191] Weinstein Oral History, at 935–36.

[192] NEWSDAY, Dec. 6, 1988.

[193] NEWSDAY, Dec. 6, 1988, at 1; NEW YORK DAILY NEWS, Dec. 6, 1988, front page (headline was: LILCO LIED JURY FINDS); NEW YORK TIMES, Dec. 6, 1988.

[194] *County of Suffolk v. Long Island Lighting Co.,* 710 F. Supp. 1406 (Dec. 9, 1988).

[195] NEWSDAY, Dec. 21, 1988, at 6.

The problem of those people who moved out of the area so that they wouldn't get rate reductions provided a big hurdle. . .

I had to take care of the United States. . .

I had to deal with a *qui tam* action. . .

Then there were all kinds of applications for fees by everybody who was involved.[196]

It was clear to Weinstein that the settlement had to accomplish, if possible, the amelioration of the tax consequences, the elimination of the liability for the suit as well as the state issues with respect to rates, and the closing of Shoreham.

Weinstein offered the parties the assistance of Kenneth Feinberg, who was close to the governor, close to Weinstein, and a superb mediator. The judge expressed his hope that the parties would work through the holidays to resolve the matter.[197] He would later say that he could have negotiated a settlement quickly had it not been for difficulties in dealing with the Suffolk legislators.[198]

Weinstein felt the governor's political clout was essential for the number of difficult issues to be resolved. As a result, negotiations had to be coordinated closely with the governor. For his part, Cuomo wanted the state legislature to share political responsibility, but that body lacked enthusiasm for such a commitment. Weinstein knew that the [federal] Nuclear Regulatory Commission was determined to go ahead and license the plant. He was also aware that the State Public Service Commission would refuse rate increases unless they were linked to key elements of the settlement and the proposed sale of Shoreham to the Long Island Power Authority (LIPA), which had been created in 1986 to see to the decommissioning of the reactor.[199]

As the date for the hearing of motions, February 2, neared, Weinstein intensified pressure. He ordered several experts in utility finance to prepare reports on how much LILCO could afford to pay to settle the suit.[200] One Sunday there was an all-day session in his chambers.[201] On January 22, there were ten hours of negotiations with Feinberg spending most of the day shuttling between rooms. At the end of the day, Feinberg gave each party a nine-page document that could have been used either as the basis for

---

[196] Weinstein Oral History, at 930ff.

[197] NEWSDAY, Dec. 18, 1988, at 5, 10 and NEWSDAY, Dec. 25, 1988. NEW YORK TIMES, Dec. 17, 1988, at 6; Dec. 22, 1988, at B2; and Dec. 25, 1988.

[198] Weinstein Oral History, at 928.

[199] NEWSDAY, Dec. 29, 1988, at 3, 37; WALL STREET JOURNAL, Jan. 12, 1989, at A10; NEW YORK TIMES, Jan. 24, 1989; Weinstein Oral History, at 934; NEWSDAY, Jan. 26, 1989.

[200] NEW YORK TIMES, Jan. 19, 1989.

[201] NEWSDAY, Jan. 19, 1989.

a global resolution or at least as talking points.[202] On the eve of the hearing, there were six hours of discussion, but no deal.[203]

The seven-hour hearing on February 2 was held in a crowded courtroom. Weinstein appeared to be enjoying himself lecturing and debating points with the thirty lawyers present. At the hearing, he admitted to being troubled about aspects of the case— "among the most troubling cases I've ever had," he said. He said that he would not have decided the case the way the jury did, but it was very difficult to overturn the jury's findings. He also said that the case did not have the value some of the attorneys thought it had. What Weinstein was doing was making both sides nervous, creating more pressures for settlement. He reserved decision at the hearing and didn't say how he would rule on the motion to dismiss the racketeering case.[204]

On February 11, he dismissed the racketeering case against LILCO by holding that RICO did not apply to a rate regulation case. RICO, Weinstein said, cannot "and should not be applied in a case like this to permit a federal jury in a civil case to question the ratemaking authority of the state."[205] Congress intended state ratemaking to be free from federal court intrusion. A construction of RICO which permitted a jury to retroactively reduce electric rates, thus, might violate the Tenth Amendment.[206] While he agreed with the jury that there was sufficient evidence to support the conclusion that LILCO'S misrepresentations caused injury, he nevertheless found that there had not been fraud, just inexperience and incompetence. He denied LILCO's jury verdict based on a claim of insufficiency of the evidence, but granted its motion to set aside the jury verdict as a matter of statutory construction of the RICO Act. Thus, were he reversed over his reading of RICO, the jury verdict would stand.[207]

Two days later, Weinstein approved class action status for the ratepayers suit and stated that it was "vitally important" that the suit be resolved because at it had "broad implications" for the economic stability of Long Island.[208] In so holding, Weinstein refused to follow the New York rule which prevented attorneys from paying litigation costs, even though the plaintiffs in this case would not be liable if they lost. He held that "[u]nder the Supremacy Clause, state laws [that] are 'an obstacle to the accomplishment and execution of the full purpose and objectives of Congress' are invalid."[209]

---

[202] NEW YORK TIMES, Jan. 23, 1989, at B3; NEWSDAY, Jan. 23, 1989.

[203] NEWSDAY, Feb. 2, 1989.

[204] NEWSDAY, Feb. 3, 1989, at 3, 27; NEW YORK TIMES, Feb. 3, 1989, at B1, B 4.

[205] *County of Suffolk v. LILCO*, 710 F. Supp. 1387, 1393 (Feb. 11, 1989). *See also* NEW YORK TIMES, Feb.12, 1989, at 1, 42.

[206] *Id.* at 1399.

[207] *See* NEWSDAY, Feb. 12, 1989, at 17.

[208] *County of Suffolk v. LILCO*, 710 F. Supp. 1407 (Feb. 13, 1989); NEWSDAY, Feb. 14, 1989, at 1, 3, 17; NEW YORK TIMES, Feb. 14, 1989, at A1, B4.

[209] *Id.* at 1414.

The next day, February 14, 1989, a settlement was reached between the ratepayers and LILCO, which included $390 million in givebacks. Weinstein has said that ". . . the essential theory of the settlement was mine," but a lot of the details were "Ken's and Judith's and LILCO's." The class action representatives did not like the deal, which Weinstein approved.[210]

Pressures now increased greatly for a global settlement. After announcement of the settlement with the ratepayers, the Suffolk County legislature voted to close the nuclear plant immediately.[211] The following day, the Public Service Commission granted LILCO a 5.4 percent rate increase conditioned on not operating Shoreham while negotiations were going on about its future.[212] LILCO now was under great economic pressure. The total cost of Shoreham had reached $5.5 billion and was increasing at the rate of $1 million a day.[213] The utility was $3.5 billion in debt. Each passing month cost LILCO more in finance charges, taxes, operating expenses, and legal fees. (Shoreham had paid $35.2 million in attorneys' fees since 1982.) LILCO's costs would continue to increase as a result of the settlement with the ratepayers.[214] After the County legislature on February 27 voted unanimously to appeal and to oppose the settlement, LILCO knew there would be further litigation costs.

However, on February 28, 1989, a deal was reached between the governor and LILCO. The major parts of the settlement follow: LILCO was sold to LIPA for $1, and Shoreham was to be decommissioned. LILCO'S ratepayers were to pay for the decommissioning. LILCO would continue to seek a license to operate Shoreham, but would not operate it. Most of the prudently incurred costs of Shoreham would go into the utility's rate base. Electric rates were expected to increase 5 percent per year for ten years. The state would support LILCO's application for $500 million in industrial bonds. LILCO would take a $2.5 billion federal tax write-off for Shoreham, and LILCO could pay back dividends. Its debt was to be restored to investment grade rating. The New York Power Authority would assume authority to meet new demands for Long Island power.[215]

Fairness hearings[216] on the ratepayers settlement took place in Brooklyn, Hauppauge, and Uniondale early in March. The Hauppauge hearing was crowded. Weinstein has spoken of the abuse he took, "which was, perhaps warranted."[217]

---

[210] *County of Suffolk v. LILCO*, 710 F. Supp. 1422 (Feb. 15, 1989).

[211] NEW YORK POST, Feb. 14, 1989, at 37.

[212] NEW YORK TIMES, Feb. 16, 1989.

[213] NEW YORK TIMES, Feb. 17, 1989 (editorial); Feb. 18, 1989; NEWSDAY, Feb. 21, 1989, at 7, 25.

[214] NEWSDAY, Feb. 28, 1989.

[215] MCCAFFREY, *supra* note 163, at 154.

[216] At the conclusion of every class action, a judge must hold a fairness hearing and assess the reasonableness of the outcome. The fairness hearing is a device to moniter class counsel. *See* William B. Rubenstein, *The Fairness Hearing: Adversarial and Regulatory Approaches*. The Fairness Hearing: Adversarial and Regulatory Approaches, 53 UCLA L. REV. 1435 (2006).

[217] Jack B. Weinstein, Explanation of *Shoreham* litigation to class in civil procedure, Columbia Law School, New York City, March 1989, as related by Jack B. Weinstein to Jeffrey B. Morris, Dec. 3, 2010. *See also* NEWSDAY, Mar, 3, 1989, at p. 6, 39; Mar. 4, 1989, at 3m 10.

On March 22, 1989, Weinstein approved the $400 million settlement in an opinion which paraphrased Shakespeare and quoted Shelley. He also wrote:

> Shoreham is dead. Those who refuse to acknowledge the obvious only make it more difficult to bury the controversy and get on with life. This nuclear plant, in all its technical glory, will be torn down because the people will it."[218]

The final judgment was issued on April 14.[219]

In the *Shoreham* case Weinstein "worked closely with Cuomo and Ken Feinberg in extricating LILCO and the state and everyone else from the disaster."[220] He made settlement more likely by maneuvering in such a way as to raise the potential damage of each payer, if they fought on.[221] He was willing to serve as a lighting rod for politicians who were afraid of accepting responsibility for closing the plant.[222]

"JUSTICE WITH A HUMAN FACE": WEINSTEIN'S HUMANITY

In *Allegra v. Bowen*, 670 F. Supp. 465 (Sept. 29, 1987) an administrative law judge had denied child disability benefits for muscular dystrophy to a thirty-three-year-old woman who had immigrated to the United States from Italy at the age of twenty-five. The woman had been unable to satisfactorily prove to the Social Security Administration that she had been disabled at age twenty-two (the age at which a child must be disabled to receive the benefits). She had reports from her Italian physician and her American doctor, but she lacked the original documentation of her diagnosis. She also had overwhelming documentation of present, advanced muscular dystrophy.

---

[218] *County of Suffolk v. LILCO*, 710 F. Supp. 1428, 1444 (Mar. 22, 1989). *See also* NEWSDAY, Mar. 23, 1989, at 5.

[219] *County of Suffolk v. LILCO*, 710 F. Supp. 1487, (1989) aff'd with different reasons, modified and rev'd in part (as to Suffolk County's application for attorneys' fees), 907 F.2d 1295 (June 29, 1990: Pierce-Card-VanG). Weinstein's attorneys' fees opinion was issued on March 23, 1989, *County of Suffolk v. LILCO*, 710 F. Supp. 1477. His dismissal of a *qui tam* action came on April 14. *U.S. ex rel. Dick v. LILCO*, 710 F. Supp. 1485, *aff'd*, 912 F.2d 13 (Aug. 14, 1990: Pierce-VanG-Card.). Weinstein himself thought he should have been reversed on this phase of the case. Weinstein Oral History, at 1022. In 1995, when LIPA was considering the takeover of LILCO, Weinstein extended the life of the Citizens Advisory Panel, a group organized to help improve electric and gas service on Long Island. *County of Suffolk v. LILCO*, 1995 U.S.Dist.LEXIS 18946 (Dec. 19, 1995), *aff'd*, 106 F.3d 1112 (Feb. 11, 1997: Mesk-Kearse).

[220] Weinstein Oral History, at 175.

[221] Eckstein, *supra* note 221, at 282.

[222] NEW YORK TIMES, Feb. 18, 1989. In 1998, Weinstein refused on constitutional grounds to modify his decree in order to accelerate payments and greatly alter who would receive the most compensation. *County of Suffolk v. LILCO*, 14 F. Supp. 2d 260 (July 28, 2998). Two years later, handling litigation involving LILCO rates and deductions, he interpreted his own settlement order, ruling for ratepayers. However, he was reversed by the Second Circuit! *See County of Suffolk v. LILCO*, 87 F. Supp. 2d 187 (Mar. 9, 200), 2000 U.S. Dist. LEXIS 215419 (Mar. 27, 2000), *rev'd, County of Suffolk v. Alcorn*, 266 F.3d 131 (Sept. 28, 2001: Wint-Kearse-Oakes). *See also* Weinstein Oral History, at 1505, 1560.

Weinstein said that it was "quite unreasonable to require a claimant to obtain original records from abroad when good sense suggests that they were probably destroyed
many years ago."[223] The treatise-writing professor-judge saw the legal issue as a "best
evidence" question—whether the production of the treating physician's documents
was required or whether a sworn letter from a doctor located abroad would be sufficient. As muscular dystrophy was a "malady of progressive degeneration," an expert
treating such a condition "would be capable of extrapolating backward in time to reli-
ably conclude the patient's previous condition." Weinstein added that "[r]equiring
severely handicapped people to produce clinical records, which are clearly unnecessary
and unobtainable, constitutes a perversion of the administrative process."[224] He
ordered the matter remanded for computation of benefits.[225]

Then, there was the case of the great-grandmother, opposed to drugs, but overwhelmed by the problems of a four-generation all-female household that included two
of her children (one on drugs) and two great-grandchildren. Everyone in the apartment was on public assistance. The U.S. government was seeking to evict them all from
public housing. Weinstein wrote a fifty-two-page opinion, blocking the eviction. He
issued an injunction to keep the drug sellers out, but let the grandmother hold on to
the apartment. The eviction, Weinstein said, "would have been disastrous because the
only hope of saving the largest part of the group was in saving the apartment and the
grandmother's control of the children."[226]

A more controversial demonstration of humanity involved the Mafioso captain,
Gregory Scarpa, Sr., who was facing charges which included three murders. Scarpa was
dying of AIDS. He had been released to house arrest by a magistrate judge, whereupon
he made an unauthorized exit, during which he was shot. In the shooting, he lost an
eye and the surrounding area of his face and skull. The magistrate judge then revoked
bail.By the time, Scarpa reapplied for bail, he was having difficulty walking and standing and was suffering from an infection on the left side of his face that threatened to
spread to his brain. He required immediate hospitalization and nursing care. If impris-
oned, Scarpa was likely to die in pain and without adequate medical care. Weinstein
released him on a $1.2 million bond for confinement in Beekman Hospital to be watched
constantly by U.S. marshals (whose services were to be paid for by Scarpa's family).
"Despite the defendant's dreadful murderous conduct and that of his gang," Weinstein
said, "he is a person, a human being." He also said, "We do not punish those who have
not been proven guilty. When we do punish, we do not act cruelly." The fact that the
defendant may have been a cruel and vicious murderer does not permit the law to

---

[223] *Allegra v. Bowen*, 670 F. Supp. 465, 468 (Sept. 29, 1987).

[224] *Id.*

[225] *Id.* For a similar decision in another SSA case, see *Brown v. Bowen*, 668 F. Supp. 146 (Aug. 25, 1987).

[226] *United States v. Leasehold Interest in 211 Nostrand Ave.*, 760 F. Supp. 1015, (Mar. 26, 1991). *See also* Weinstein
    Oral History, at 1080–82; N.Y.L.J., Mar. 27, 1991; NEW YORK TIMES, Mar. 27, 1991, at B1.

descend to his level of depravity, said Weinstein. Several weeks later, Weinstein modified the order to permit Scarpa to be released to Cabrini Hospice.[227]

Weinstein later commented that he looked "like he had been dug up from the grave—just a horrible picture. He was a human being. I couldn't let him out on house arrest, but I could allow him to go into a hospital where he would be supervised and controlled and get, at least, some treatment that would be helpful."[228]

Scarpa would live a lot longer than it appeared at the time. Some months later, Weinstein sentenced him to ten years in jail.[229]

---

[227] *See United States v. Scarpa*, 815 F. Supp. 88, 89, 93 (Feb. 19, 1993 amend. Feb. 23, 1993); *Bay Ridge Paper*, Dec. 24–Jan. 6, 1994, at 1. *See also* NEW YORK TIMES, Feb. 23, 1993, at B2; NEW YORK POST, Feb. 23, 1993.

[228] Weinstein Oral History, at 1208.

[229] *Bay Ridge Paper*, Dec. 24, 1993–Jan. 6, 1994, at 1.

8

"Under the Blindfold, Does Justice Weep?"[1]:

Jack Weinstein and Sentencing

ON THE DAY he sentenced Colombo capo Michael Sessa to life imprisonment, Michael Sessa's mother screamed out to the judge, "You can't do that to my son. Oh my God, you killed me." Her husband walked out of the courtroom and collapsed.[2] The night before Jewish Defense League founder Meir Kahane was sentenced by Jack Weinstein, a large group of Orthodox Jews camped out in front of the Eastern District courthouse in Brooklyn, praying and fasting. After he was sentenced, Kahane told Weinstein, "The Judge of all will judge you, Judge Weinstein."[3] Such dramatic experiences connected with sentencings are not unusual in the lives of federal district judges. Sentencing traditionally has been the function of the district courts with almost no appellate review. But for two decades district judges were deprived of most their sentencing discretion and were often forced to impose very harsh prison terms.

During this period, most federal judges were highly critical of the Federal Sentencing Guidelines imposed by a Sentencing Commission created by Congress in 1984. So was Jack Weinstein, but what was unique about his role was the extent of the battle he waged. Among the most visible, energetic, and vehement opponents of guideline sentencing, Weinstein not only devised ingenious ways to circumvent the Guidelines, but used his opinions to apprise other federal judges of his techniques. Weinstein marshaled his craft, reputation, energy, and stubbornness to attempt to thwart policies he

---

[1] *United States v. Molina*, 94 CR 576, at 7, 1997 Op. 10 (Apr. 30, 1997).
[2] NEW YORK DAILY NEWS, May 25, 1993.
[3] Weinstein Oral History, at 243.

viewed as lacking in humanity. In that battle, he employed opinions, speeches, law review articles, op-ed pieces, attendance at meetings of judges, and even a well-publicized refusal to handle the sentencing of drug defendants to rally opposition to the Guidelines. Weinstein attempted to educate judges appointed after Guideline sentencing as to how sentencing should be done, attempted to teach defense lawyers how to maximize their role at sentencing hearings, put words into the mouths of defendants at those hearings so as to give himself the ammunition to impose a lighter sentence, and began videotaping sentencing hearings in order to influence the Court of Appeals.

Weinstein was far from alone in the struggle to overcome the work of the Sentencing Commission, Congressional will, and the oversight of the Court of Appeals. Many federal judges were against the Guidelines and guideline sentencing. But if his efforts were not unique, they were significant. Weinstein would remind his audience, whomever it was, that those being sentenced were not numbers, but real people: pregnant Ghanaian women, struggling immigrant mothers from the Dominican Republic, Pakistani restaurateurs.

This chapter is devoted to the evolution of Weinstein's views of the Guidelines, the efforts he made to minimize the impact of the Guidelines in sentencing, and the reactions to his work by the Court of Appeals.

The District Court for the Eastern District of New York had long had a heavy criminal caseload. Like other courts it was greatly affected by the enormous and unsuccessful "War against Drugs," the wielding of the Racketeer Influenced and Corrupt Organizations Act (RICO) and growing federal involvement in areas of criminal law that previously had been the sole province of the states. In addition to the growth of drug crimes and RICO prosecutions, the Eastern District was affected by the presence of an Organized Crime Strike Force which led to important prosecutions as well as by considerable improvement in the caliber of the U.S. Attorney's Office.[4] Weinstein has said, "When I first began practice, the Eastern District prosecutor had a poor reputation. It shifted about the time I became a judge. We then had first-rate U.S. Attorneys. They were able to induce some of the best lawyers to come down here as Assistants."[5]

Weinstein often fondly recalls what sentencing was like in his early years on the court before the war against drugs, the great increase in the number of judges, and the Guidelines. In his early years on the bench, no sentence was imposed without several judges conferring. In complex situations all the judges participated. "Individual justice," Weinstein said, "meant something to each of us."[6] This, of course, was true in

---

[4] *See, e.g.,* STEVEN HARMON WILSON, THE RISE OF JUDICIAL MANAGEMENT IN THE U.S. DISTRICT COURT 95 (2001).

[5] Videotaped interview of Jack B. Weinstein by Gordon Mehler, Oct. 10, 20066, at 5 (Oral History for Federal Bar Council). Among those "first-rate" U.S. Attorneys were Weinstein's colleagues Edward R. Korman, Raymond J. Dearie, Reena Raggi (now judge of the U.S. Court of Appeals for the Second Circuit), and David G. Trager.

[6] Jack B. Weinstein, "Judge Jacob Mishler—Coffee, Cake and Sympathy," Memorial, Eastern District New York Courthouse, May 21, 2004, at 2

other districts as well.[7] Other things were also different. A trial judge could give a hefty sentence for the purpose of general deterrence, and then reduce it within ninety days (when the case would be less visible), thus blending sentencing for deterrence with less harsh long-run outcomes.[8] Furthermore, the sentencing judge had a variety of weapons in his arsenal beyond prison, among them probation and treatment under the Youth Correction statute. Most important, though, was that the district judge was the principal figure in sentencing, but shared his or her discretion with his or her colleagues.[9]

THE FATICO HEARING

Weinstein's most important contribution to sentencing practices prior to the Guidelines involved the conduct of the sentencing hearing. Prior to *United States v. Fatico*,[10] it was possible to introduce hearsay testimony into the sentencing hearing, material which would not have been admissible in a criminal or civil trial.

The *Fatico* case involved two brothers, Carmine and Daniel Fatico, who were charged with "fencing" two truckloads of furs and zinc. The two men had pled guilty to receiving stolen goods. In order to have their sentences enhanced, the government intended to demonstrate at the sentencing hearing that the Faticos were "made" members of the Gambino family. By demonstrating the Faticos' connections to organized crime, they would be labeled "special offenders," which would work a serious alteration in the conditions of their confinement. To achieve this, the government intended to put an FBI agent on the witness stand to testify concerning information furnished to him by a confidential informant. However, the government objected to cross-examination of the agent about matters that might lead to the disclosure of his identity and risk his life.

The case provided Weinstein with an opportunity to address the probative force of hearsay, a subject to which he had given a good deal of thought. At the time, he had been revising his evidence treatise and casebook and had already written many hearsay opinions. He was also teaching evidence and believed that *Fatico* could also serve as a springboard for discussions with his students when they came to court.[11]

---

[7] WILSON, *supra* note 4, at 2.

[8] Weinstein Oral History, at 1376. *See also id.* at 610; RONALD J. BACIGAL, JR., MAY IT PLEASE THE COURT: A BIOGRAPHY OF JUDGE ROBERT R. MERHIGE, JR. 121 (1992).

[9] Sentences, however, in the Eastern District were more severe on the whole than the median sentences for the entire circuit according to a study published in 1974. C.K. ROWLAND & ROBERTA A. CARP, POLITICS & JUDGEMENT IN FEDERAL DISTRICT COURTS 78 referring to ANTHONY PARTRIDGE &WILLIAM B. ELRIDGE, THE SECOND CIRCUIT SENTENCING STUDY: A REPORT TO THE JUDGES OF THE SECOND CIRCUIT (1974).

[10] 441 F. Supp. 1285 (Dec. 1, 1977), *rev'd*, 579 F.2d 707 (June 12, 1978).

[11] Weinstein Oral History, at 467–68.

Traditionally, a federal sentencing judge had been able to use information from a very wide variety of sources. However, in *Fatico*, Weinstein would not allow the testimony of the FBI agent, stating that it was "a violation of the Due Process and Confrontation Clauses of the Constitution to base a critical decision affecting liberty on information from a person whom the government would not permit to be cross-examined." Allowing the second hand account by the government without cross-examination deprived the defense not only of knowing who the informers were, but also of the information upon which they relied.[12] Although the Federal Rules of Evidence did not apply to sentencing proceedings, Weinstein held that the Constitution did apply.[13] Weinstein avoided following a Supreme Court precedent which appeared to be on point[14] by finding that there had been "a clear drift away" from the absolute no-due-process-at-sentencing position. He bolstered his position with recent Supreme Court decisions on confrontation and cross-examination in parole revocation and probation revocation hearings. There was, he held, no informer's privilege at sentencing, if the testimony was necessary to a material issue on the merits.[15]

The government sought interlocutory review. Weinstein was reversed by a distinguished panel of the Court of Appeals (Oakes writing, Feinberg, and Mansfield), who found no violation of either the Confrontation or Due Process Clauses. The law seemed to be that out-of-court declarations by an unidentified informant were usable when there was good cause for nondisclosure of his identity and sufficient corroboration by other means.[16]

On remand involving only Daniel Fatico,[17] the government sought to prove Fatico's strong links to organized crime at a sentencing hearing by producing the testimony of *seven* federal and state law enforcement agents, who cumulatively testified that seventeen different informers had told them that the defendants were "made" members of the Gambino family.

Weinstein remained troubled by the multi-layered hearsay because the defense was unable to subject the informers to cross-examination. Further, as a result of narrow statutory construction by the Second Circuit, the court was able to order revelations of only a trial witness' statement.[18] As it was, therefore, impossible for the defense to obtain the prior statements of law enforcement officers, they could not be impeached by prior inconsistent statements.

Weinstein also dealt with another issue at Fatico's sentencing—the standard of proof on controverted issues. Traditionally, the standard had been "preponderance of the evidence." In *Fatico*, Weinstein held that "when the fact of membership in organized

---

[12] Weinstein Oral History, at 467.

[13] *United States v. Fatico*, 441 F. Supp. 1285, 1289 (Dec. 1. 1977).

[14] *Williams v. New York*, 337 U.S 241 (1949).

[15] *United States v. Fatico*, 441 F. Supp. 1285, 1290.

[16] *United States v. Fatico*, 579 F.2d 707, 713 (June 12, 1978).

[17] *United States v. Fatico*, 458 F. Supp. 388 (July 27, 1978).

[18] *Id.* at 399–400.

crime will result in a much longer and harsher sentence, the standard should be 'clear, unequivocal and convincing evidence.'"[19]

With these substantial preliminaries out of the way, Weinstein held that the government had met its burden of proof. Without that finding, the sentence would have been no more than three years running concurrently with a gambling sentence. His finding that Daniel Fatico was a made member of an organized crime family led to a sentence of four years to be served consecutively with the separate three-year sentence for gambling. Weinstein said, "All in all, the result of the finding of organized crime membership 'will probably be five extra years of hard service in a high security prison far from his family."[20] Carmine Fatico received five years' probation and a $100,000 fine.

The Second Circuit affirmed the sentence, although it said that it was "by no means . . . endorsing all the rules of the District Court."[21] While the Court of Appeals did not believe that a sentencing hearing (already known as a "Fatico hearing") would be necessary every time a defendant disputes facts in the presentence report, it "certainly would not hold it an abuse of discretion on the part of a district judge to hold such a hearing where there is reason to question the reliability of material facts having in the judge's view direct bearing on the sentence to be imposed, especially where those facts are essentially hearsay."[22] The Supreme Court denied certiorari.[23]

Over a thirty-year period, the *Fatico* hearing has been a part of the sentencing process in the Second Circuit. It is a mini-trial that can take place before sentencing where the prosecution has the opportunity to prove that the defendant had in fact committed more serious crimes than those to which he pled. The defendant has the right to contest such allegations, which the government must prove by a preponderance of the evidence. Credit for the hearing seems to have gone to the Court of Appeals, but it was Weinstein who made it happen. Weinstein's second opinion has been followed or cited forty-three times by the Courts of Appeals of the First, Second Third, Fourth, and Seventh Circuits and district courts in the Second Circuit and the District of New Jersey.[24] The Court of Appeals for the Fourth Circuit has disapproved its use.[25]

---

[19] *United States v. Fatico*, 458 F. Supp. 388, 408 (July 27, 1978). The issue of the standard of proof and how that standard might be quantified is something Weinstein has often reflected upon during his career. In *Fatico*, Weinstein gave his colleagues a questionnaire in which they were asked to put in numerical form what their standard for "preponderance of the evidence was." *Id.* at 410. The consideration Weinstein gave to the "preponderance of the evidence" standard in *Fatico* and his survey of his colleagues as to what the burdens meant to the judges themselves eventually led to an interesting publication. Jack B. Weinstein, *Symposium on Federal Sentencing: Comment: A Trial Judge's Second Impression of the Federal Sentencing Guidelines*, 66 SO. CAL. L. REV. 357, 360–63 (1992). *See also* Weinstein Oral History, at 467.

[20] *United States v. Fatico*, 458 F. Supp. at 413.

[21] *United States v. Fatico*, 603 F.2d 1053, 1056 (Aug. 13, 1979: *Oakes-Meskill-Stewart* 1979), *cert. denied sub nom., Fatico v. United States*, 445 U.S. 1073 (1980).

[22] *Id.* at 1057 n. 9.

[23] 444 U.S. 1073 (1980).

[24] *United States v. Rosa*, 841 F.2d 1074 (3d Cir. 1989).

[25] *United States v. Urrego-Linares*, 879 F.2d 1234 (4th Cir. 1989).

A SHORT HISTORY OF THE SENTENCING GUIDELINES

Three concerns led to the Federal Sentencing Guidelines: political hay being made out of crime and the belief that it resulted from soft-sentencing judges, growing skepticism of rehabilitation as a major goal of sentencing, and concern about wide disparities in sentencing practices.

During the mid-1960s and early 1970s there was considerable political mileage to be gained from tough crime policies and by appointing tough-on-crime judges such as Chief Justice Warren Burger. In New York State, Governor Nelson Rockefeller promoted extremely harsh drug laws. The "War on Drugs" began in the Nixon administration, but it was greatly accelerated by the Reagan administration, which sought to prosecute drug offenders in the federal courts and greatly increased funds for their capture and prosecution. Federal drug cases increased more than 270 percent during the 1980s.[26] Massive expenditures on prisons were made by the federal and state governments. Ironically, the street price for drugs climbed so high that professional criminals were attracted to the business.[27] Drugs became the primary engine of crime and of the growth of the prison population.[28]

By the 1980s, there was a growing belief that rehabilitation as a goal of imprisonment was not working. Politicians pointed the finger at light sentences and recidivism, and many also expressed concern about wide variations in sentencing.

The concern about sentencing disparities was spurred by wide attention to an unusually readable book by a well-regarded judge, Marvin Frankel of the Southern District of New York (a law school classmate and, later, faculty colleague of Weinstein). In *Criminal Sentences: Law without Order* published in 1973, Frankel, in a crisp, careful, and hard-headed manner, discussed the disparities resulting from sentencing as it was then practiced and what should be done about it.[29]

Frankel's primary concern was with lawlessness—permitted by legislators, participated in by administrators, but "especially that perpetuated by judges operating with unchecked and sweeping powers under vague statutes offering no criteria to properly consider the length of or the reason for sentencing."[30] Frankel's major suggestion was for legislatures to set specific guidelines for employment of the sentencing power and for appellate courts to review the exercise of that power by trial judges. Frankel sought a prescription of the purposes and justification for criminal sentences from the legislature and a detailed chart or calculus to be used by those involved in sentencing.

---

[26] G. ALAN TARR, JUDICIAL PROCESS AND JUDICIAL POLICY MAKING 38 (4th ed. 2006).

[27] WILSON, *supra* note 4, at 119. *See id.* at 114–15; 138–39; 233–34; 396ff.

[28] Jack B. Weinstein & Christopher Winner, Sentencing in the United States (draft chapter in my possession) [hereafter referred to as WIMMER & WEINSTEIN], at 38.

[29] Reviewing the book, this author believed that it "might be the most influential and important book . . . by a sitting judge since [Cardozo's] *The Nature of the Judicial Process.*" *See* Jeffrey B. Morris, Book Review of FRANKEL, CRIMINAL SENTENCES: LAW WITHOUT ORDER, 19 N.Y. LAW FORUM, 704 (1974).

[30] *Id.* at 704.

He also called for "*some* system of open, thorough, straight-forward review on appeal of sentencing decisions."[31] Finally, he recommended a permanent commission responsible for the study, formulation, and enactment of rules.[32] In these years, Weinstein was not against sentencing guidelines or against appellate review of sentencing. In January 1973, when he was campaigning for state Chief Judge, he pointed out that "[d]evelopment of detailed sentencing guidelines should prevent appellate review of sentences from being overly burdensome on our appellate courts."[33]

Frankel's ideas were grossly distorted in Congress when it turned its attention to sentencing in the 1980s. A thoughtful consideration of a very difficult problem was overcome by a simplistic view that an important reason for crime was sentencing by "soft" judges, and the way to cure it was to limit judicial discretion. What began in Congress as a liberal reform measure sponsored by men like Senator Edward Kennedy became in a few years the tough, antijudge, law and order measure, the Sentencing Reform Act of 1984.[34]

That law (Title II of the Comprehensive Crime Control Act of October 12, 1984[35]) provided for the creation of a sentencing commission housed in the judicial branch, named by the President and staffed both by judges and nonjudges. The Commission was to be responsible for creating sentencing guidelines which would function as an adjunct to substantive criminal statutes created by Congress.[36] The Sentencing Reform Act divested the district courts of a power that not only had been essentially unchecked, but also had been an exclusively judicial function for hundreds of years.[37]

Congress did not give the newly created Commission much guidance. It did not even adopt a particular purpose for criminal sentencing, though it was clear that rehabilitation in prison was abandoned as a major goal. Into the vacuum would step the Commission.

The Guidelines that the Commission produced were harsh and sharply limited judicial discretion. The scheme was basically a grid based upon two axes. The vertical axis of the sentencing table was composed of forty-three levels representing the severity of the offense. The horizontal axis represented the criminal history of the offender,

---

[31] Marvin Frankel, Criminal Sentences: Law Without Order 82 (1973).

[32] *Id.* at 704.

[33] Jack B. Weinstein, Can We Have Safe Streets and Protect Civil Liberties Too?, Speech at Saddle Rock School, Great Neck, N.Y. 10 (Jan. 19, 1973).

[34] Kate Stith & Jose A. Cabranes, Fear of Judging: Sentencing Guidelines in the Federal Courts 38–48.

[35] 18 U.S.C. §3551 *et seq.*

[36] The separation of powers problem led to constitutional challenges before many district judges. Weinstein and the Supreme Court upheld the constitutionality of the composition of the Sentencing Commission, Weinstein ruling orally from the bench that the Commission was constitutional. Jack B. Weinstein, *A Trial Judge's First Impression of the Sentencing Guidelines*, 52 Albany L. Rev. 1, 3, 10 (1987) [hereinafter Weinstein, First Impression]. *See Mistretta v. United States*, 488 U.S. 361 (1999); *see also* Weinstein, First Impression, *supra*, at 3, 10. In the Eastern District, Weinstein agreed with Judges Charles P. Sifton, Eugene Nickerson, and Edward Korman, while his colleagues Judges Leo Glasser and Raymond Dearie held that it was unconstitutional. See Weinstein, First Impression, at 3 n. 14, 15.

[37] Michael Goldsmith & James Gibson, *The U.S. Sentencing Guidelines: A Surprising Success*, 12 Occasional Papers, Center for Research on Crime & Justice, N.Y.U. L.S. 6 (1988).

adjusting the severity of the sentence to six categories of the offender's past behavior. Both the offense and the criminal history could be adjusted upward or downward. For example, the prosecution could recommend a downward departure on the basis of substantial assistance provided it by the offender, while there could also be departures for factors or circumstances that had not been adequately considered. Ultimately, though, the judge had to choose the sentence range in the box in which the particular criminal history category and the offense met. There were a total of 258 boxes in the grid, each with a narrow sentencing range.

The Commission was never required to provide an explanation of its rules or respond to criticism of its proposed Guidelines. Nor did the Commission provide an analysis in terms of any of the traditional theories of punishment. The Guidelines had the force of law.

While the Commission attempted to eliminate disparities in sentencing, the overall effect of its work was harsh. Congress eliminated the possibility of parole. The Commission, in addition, would greatly limit decreasing sentences to probation and reduction for good time. The grid dominated. The sentencing judge was primarily expected to provide mathematical calculations. In 2004, Weinstein stated that, "The modern judge and his or her law clerks spend far more time with the Sentencing Guidelines Manual than the Federal Rules of Evidence or Criminal Procedure."[38]

Between the 1982 fiscal year and the 2002 fiscal year, the percentage of defendants sentenced to imprisonment jumped from 49 percent to 80 percent.[39] The average sentence increased from thirteen months to forty-three months.[40] The number receiving probation dropped from 39 percent to 17 percent.[41]

This harsh regime generally was made harsher as Congress periodically passed laws requiring mandatory minimum sentences, which forced the Commission to jack up penalties for all related offenses, while plugging those loopholes that still existed for downward departures. One rare exception was the "safety valve" provision of the Violent Crime Control and Law Enforcement Act of 1994, which limited application of the statutory minimums to the most serious drug offenders. Courts could sentence nonviolent drug offenders who cooperated with the government to Guidelines sentences rather than the mandatory minimums.[42]

The combination of the War on Drugs with the Sentencing Guidelines proved particularly harsh. Drug sentences were very high. Generally, it was the small fry that were arrested, tried, and sentenced: the "swallowers" and the small-time addicts who possessed drugs and sold them to finance their habit.[43] Sentences of from five to thirty

---

[38] *In re Sentencing*, 219 F.R.D., 262, 263 (Jan. 30, 2004).

[39] 35 *The Third Branch*, No. 10 (October 2003).

[40] WIMMNER & WEINSTEIN, *supra* note 28, at 13.

[41] 35 *The Third Branch* (October 2003).

[42] 18 U.S.C. §3553 (f).

[43] The "swallower" swallows dozens or even hundreds of small sealed bags of drugs to escape detection when entering the country. The "mules" attempt to bring drugs into the country on their person or in suitcases, valises etc.

years often had to be imposed on the couriers because of the amount of drugs they carried when they were caught. The "kingpins," who, if caught could turn over their couriers, were able to receive lengthy reductions of their sentences for cooperating with the government.

The incarceration of the mules did nothing to stop the flow of drugs to the streets. There was an endless flow of impoverished couriers who brought drugs into the United States undeterred by the harsh penalties, often because they never had heard about them. Most of the couriers had little previous background in drug crimes or other criminal activity.[44]

Among the other effects of the Guidelines was that, as judicial discretion declined, prosecutorial discretion grew. In drug cases where the offense level was based on the quantity of drugs, prosecutors determined just how much to charge. U.S. Attorneys also controlled the major reason for downward departure—substantial assistance to the prosecution. Evidence of prior crimes, which only needed to be proved at sentencing by a preponderance of the evidence, could greatly enhance the sentence, thereby giving the government more power to coerce testimony.[45]

During the Guidelines regime, Congress reduced funding both for educational programs within prisons and for treatment of drug abusers outside. Responding to passage of the PROTECT Act[46] in 2003, Attorney General John Ashcraft directed that federal prosecutors seek maximum charges and sentences whenever possible. He had previously directed prosecutors to appeal those criminal cases in which judges departed downward from the presumptive range described by the Guidelines.[47]

As a result of all this, the population of the prison system swelled during the Guidelines era. Most of that expansion involved drug and nonviolent property offenders and technical parole and probation violators.[48] In 1984, there were 34,263 inmates in the federal prison system, 29.5 percent of whom were drug offenders. By the end of 2002, the federal prison system had 163,528 inmates, 55 percent of whom were drug offenders.[49]

WEINSTEIN AND SENTENCING IN AN ERA WHERE
JUSTICE LACKED A "HUMAN FACE"

The Sentencing Guidelines and Judge Weinstein probably could never have been reconciled. First, the Guidelines limited judicial discretion, an inherently unattractive result for Weinstein. More important was Weinstein's belief that justice should have a

---

[44] Weinstein Oral History, at 981.

[45] Weinstein Oral History, at 412, 583–84, 1292.

[46] Prosecutorial Remedies and Other Tools to End the Exploitation of Children Today Act of 2003, 108 P.L. 21; 117 Stat. 650.

[47] 72 U.S.L.W. 2085 (Aug. 19, 2003); 72 U.S.L.W. 2168 (Sept. 30, 2003).

[48] WIMMER & WEINSTEIN, *supra* note 28, at 17.

[49] 35 *Third Branch*, No. 10 (October 2003).

human face. Weinstein believes that when the judge faces the task of passing judgment upon someone, he "must think about the defendant as a human being, about his or her situation in life, about his or her family and background."[50] For Weinstein, the Sentencing Guidelines were "a failure because—unlike some state equivalents—they largely banish humanity from the sentencing process."[51]

Weinstein believes that it is not possible for judges to "rigidly apply a general two-dimensional set of sentencing standards to each individual case in a just and beneficial manner," particularly when those standards mandate incarceration across the board.[52] The imposition of appropriately effective punishment "requires personal attachment to the individual."[53]

Wearing a business suit and sitting across a table from the defendant and his attorney when sentencing, Weinstein, from time to time, may put the defendant's hand in his or he may put his arm around members of the defendant's family. He sees that the defendant's young children have dolls and coloring books.[54] He has said that, "I try always to keep in mind that I'm dealing with people. I'm just like them. I'm not some instrument of the Lord."[55] Weinstein assumes that *all* people, and that includes "bad people," have good traits and that many of the defendants he sees "are so borderline . . . . They are just poor, very poor people that get sucked into these things because they lose their business or they had a death in the family and they are just over the line."[56] The roots of his empathy run very deep. He said to me, "You get a sense sometime for the desperation of some of these people. They are real people."[57]

Writing of the Guidelines, he asked: How else do courts contend with the mechanistic computations of the Guidelines?

He responded:

They attempt to humanize each sentencing. Judges talk to the defendant. They find out how he or she is doing in prison. They make sure that they are being treated properly. They talk with the defendant's family members if they are present. They let a weeping child or wife sit next to a defendant being sentenced. They try to give anyone who is in court on the defendant's behalf an opportunity to address the court. Not only does this let the defendant know that in the judge's eyes he or she is more than a statistic, but it often brings to light some mitigating

---

[50] Jack B. Weinstein, *Avoiding Cruelty at Sentencing while Protecting the Public*, 7 N.Y.S.B.A. Crim. Just. J. 8 (Winter 1999) [hereinafter, Weinstein, *Avoiding Cruelty*].

[51] Wimmer & Weinstein, *supra* note 28, at 42.

[52] Jack B. Weinstein, *A Judge's Dilemma*, Fortune News (February 1992).

[53] Wimmer & Weinstein, *supra* note 28, at 29.

[54] Weinstein Oral History, at 1680.

[55] Benchmark, New Yorker, May 3, 1993, 34 at 36.

[56] Weinstein Oral History, at 1611

[57] Weinstein Oral History, at 307.

circumstances that probation or defense counsel may have overlooked—a ground for departure.[58]

He has written:

> The sentencing proceeding is the prototypical situation in which face-to-face contact and empathy are essential. At sentencing, the judge's body language and visage must convey: "I respect you as a human being and I regret having to impose this heavy sentence. None of us likes to send anyone to prison, but that is my duty in this case."[59]

Weinstein's stress on the humanity of defendants is not mere rhetoric. It affects Weinstein's sentencings and his treatment of defendants. When Mafia leader Gregory Scarpa was dying of AIDS but under indictment on murder and racketeering charges, Weinstein believed that he should spend his final days in a hospital despite his "proven dangerous propensities." This way it would be easier for his family to visit him because "Despite the defendant's dreadful murderous conduct and that of his gang, he is a person, a human being."[60] Weinstein referred to another case, where he sentenced the defendant in a hospital so he could continue to receive treatment. He recalled, "I put my arms around the wife and daughter who were just completely broken up. I tried to pat them on the shoulder."[61] Where he can, Weinstein gives community treatment sentences "so that these people can be with their families. Otherwise you completely destroy them."[62]

One defendant was a twenty-year-old African-American with a two-year-old daughter. Weinstein had to sentence him to 123 months. What he wished he could do was give him six months of intensive work in a prison run under military discipline and "get him off drugs; get him started in education . . . . The sentence in state court would have been six months."[63] Weinstein couldn't do that because of the Guidelines. At the sentencing, he sent his clerk out to get some cookies for the child. When they were leaving, he said to his clerk, "give her the whole tin of cookies," a great big tin. I said, "She doesn't have a father, maybe at least she ought to have a tin of cookies." And, he added, "I did it primarily to assuage my own sense of the cruelty I had just become party to."[64]

Weinstein has written that a sentence runs the risk of being excessively cruel if it does not take into account those factors that make the person sentenced a

[58] Weinstein, *Avoiding Cruelty, supra* note 50, at 9.
[59] WIMMER & WEINSTEIN, *supra* note 28, at 45–46.
[60] NEW YORK TIMES, Feb. 23, 1993, at B2.
[61] Weinstein Oral History, at 1208.
[62] Weinstein Oral History, at 738. *See also id.* at 593.
[63] Weinstein Oral History, at 316–17.
[64] Weinstein Oral History, at 316–17.

unique individual.[65] The sentencing Weinstein did under the Guidelines tortured him: "This sense of the cruelty" that he was involved in was overwhelming.[66] He said to me that during this period of many years, he was "happy if I can get through the day without creating too much injustice or cruelty."[67] In *United States v. Adaze*, he sentenced the defendant to a substantial prison term. As he tells it, "... and then it worried me and finally in the middle of the night I said, 'God, I can't let this happen. I don't have any power under Rule 35 to correct it,[68] but I'm going to do it anyway.' To get around that, he used the excuse of failure of proper counsel."[69]

EARLY IMPRESSIONS OF THE GUIDELINES

After passage of the Sentencing Reform Act and the release of the Draft Guidelines by the Sentencing Commission, Weinstein expressed his reactions in a letter to Commission Chairman William W. Wilkins, Jr. While he was critical, his letter hardly foreshadowed his later feelings. He did point out that:

> The prison penalties to be imposed would require many times more prison time than at present. The result would be unnecessary cruelty, unacceptable costs in prison and welfare and for his rehabilitation than we now accomplish.[70]

In particular, he pointed out that while at present sentences for mules (couriers) were around three years (which meant prison for less than two years), under the new regime, they would be 168 to 210 months (fourteen to seventeen and one-half years). This, he thought, was very harsh, for "[m]any of these mules are ignorant women from undeveloped countries who cannot resist the lure of a few thousand dollars. In view of the extreme poverty of their families, I doubt that heavy penalties will deter them."[71]

In the statement Weinstein made at a Commission hearing fifteen days later, Weinstein spoke more strongly: "Because of a relatively few disparate sentences at either end of the spectrum, you propose a rigid, inflexible, procrustean bed . . ."[72]

---

[65] Weinstein, *Avoiding Cruelty, supra* note 50, at 8.

[66] Weinstein Oral History, at 325.

[67] Weinstein Oral History, at 886.

[68] Rule 35 permits a judge to correct clerical and technical errors in sentences for seven days after sentencing. After that a sentence may be reduced only on the government's motion and only for substantial assistance to the government.

[69] Weinstein Oral History, at 1157–58; *United States v. Adaze*, CR 92-0037 (1992). Weinstein Opinions Notebook 457–58. Rule 35 of the Federal Rules of Criminal Procedure governs the correcting or reducing of a sentence.

[70] Letter from Jack B. Weinstein to William W. Wilkins, Jr., Oct. 6, 1986 (copy in possession of the author.)

[71] *Id.*

[72] Jack B. Weinstein, Statement to United Sates Sentencing Commission, Hearing on Preliminary Draft Sentencing Guidelines, New York City, Oct. 21, 1986 [delivery copy], at 3.

"Imprisonment is not," he said in his formal statement, "and cannot be, the primary solution to our serious crime problem."[73] He attacked the deemphasis upon alternate methods of control—strict probation, fines, and institutional treatment in the community. The proposals would not only add to taxpayer costs, but would "destroy families, adding to the risk of yet another generation of criminals from amongst those children growing up unsupervised by incarcerated parents."[74]

In a 1987 lecture at Albany Law School, Weinstein was relatively positive, although he expressed some concerns.[75] He defended the Sentencing Reform Act on both policy and constitutional grounds. If the Commission's first proposals had been, he thought, "impossibly rigid and doctrinaire," after their modification, they were sufficiently "flexible to be workable."[76] He was not worried about due process problems[77] and thought that "one of the great unexpected benefits of the Guideline sentencing process [was] that it has forced the judges and courts to rethink what has been done in sentencing."[78] He also welcomed the right to appeal sentences.[79]

Weinstein seemed content then with the trade-off of "[r]eplacing human empathy and judgment with computer-generated calculation" which "cuts the sentence loose from the three-dimensional defendant and promises to reduce the number of sleepless nights and painful choices for judges than the old system fostered."[80]

This is not to say that he didn't have any concerns. One concern was the failure to eliminate enormous prosecutorial discretion.[81] He also worried that the Commission had chosen but three factors relevant to sentencing—criminal history, dependence on crime for a livelihood, and acceptance of responsibility for wrongdoing—rather than the eleven specific offender characteristics Congress had listed in the statute.[82] He also warned against applying the rules of the new system blindly for "the mathematical matrix operates in a human context. The web of humanity is spun with compassion."[83]

Another concern was the requirement of incarceration for all but the most minor offenses. Weinstein warned of the costs of excessive use of long-term incarceration in prison construction and on the welfare rolls as well as the breakup of families due to long-term incarceration.[84] Weinstein also presented alternatives "to achieve positive results which prolonged incarceration cannot—particularly because of its increased

---

[73] *Id.* at 4.

[74] *Id.*

[75] Weinstein, *First Impressions, supra* note 36.

[76] *Id.* at 2.

[77] *Id.* at 9.

[78] *Id.* at 30.

[79] *Id.* at 9.

[80] *Id.* at 10–11.

[81] *Id.* at 5.

[82] *Id.* at 12.

[83] *Id.* at 11.

[84] *Id.* at 14, 17–19, 22.

tension, idleness and terrible brutality casting a pall over our prisons today."[85] Among the alternatives were a network of community-based treatment centers (which doesn't seem to have existed at the time), the development of prison furlough programs, halfway houses, home detention, intensive supervision by probation, community service, other probation and supervised activities such as intensive drug treatment and job placement workshops, and work with programs created by religious institutions and day prisons.[86]

Most of all, he argued that "'[t]hough lulled by the case and seeming certainty of guideline dictation, we must still listen for the voice of the individual defendant, struggling to be heard amidst the cacophony clamoring for a crackdown on crime and increased incarceration.'"[87] "We must insist," he concluded, "that in the interest of justice and humanity, the Commission not board up the windows of compassion and understanding left open by the departure exceptions."[88]

Nevertheless, even in 1987, Weinstein was already charting the potential for departures, among them "the good a defendant had done in his lifetime," very elderly defendants, the extreme illness of a child, the loss of a job, and potential longterm unemployment, as well as the effect of imprisonment on substantial postcrime rehabilitation.[89]

"LIVING" WITH THE GUIDELINES

By the time the Sentencing Institute for the Second and Eighth Circuits met on March 2, 1992, Weinstein was finding the Guidelines harsh, inflexible, ineffective, and expensive. He thought that the Guidelines had overburdened the entire system for processing criminal defendants while imposing dreadful costs on individual defendants. In published comments, Weinstein stated that the emphasis on prison in guideline sentencing was too great and there was too little concern for many ameliorating circumstances, rehabilitative possibilities, and community and family needs. He found "deeply troubling," the Commission's tendency "to try to stamp out whatever remains of the trial court's power to take into account the exigencies of the particular case and the relevant differences among the people before it."[90]

---

[85] *Id.* at 30

[86] *Id.* at 20–28.

[87] *Id.* at 30.

[88] *Id.*

[89] *Id.* at 16–17.
  Between Feb. 28 and July 25, 1988, 38.6 percent of all departures in the United States (25 of 70) occurred in the Eastern District of New York. *Id.* at 16.

[90] Jack B. Weinstein, *A Judge's Reflections on Departures from the Federal Sentencing Guidelines*, 5 Fed. Sent'g. Rep. (July-Aug. 1992), at 6 [hereinafter *Weinstein, Reflections on Departures*]. At the time, the percentage of departures nationally was 17 percent of which 80 percent were downward. In the Second Circuit,

Judicial opposition to the Guidelines increased because most of the criminal defendants judges saw—certainly in the Eastern District—were drug mules. Thousands were
being sentenced while the illegal drug business thrived. Weinstein was not alone in
seeing that the harshness in drug cases was not working. In the Eastern District, prison
time for "mules" had increased threefold, but there also had been a threefold increase
in gastric drug importation. The harsher prison terms for swallowers and mules were
doing no good because the drug "lords" didn't care about what would happen to their
carriers and there was a huge surplus of potential carriers in the Third World willing to
take the risk.[91] In an op-ed piece in the *New York Times* in July 1993, Weinstein recommended a nonpartisan federal commission on drugs "to report candidly on the costs,
benefits, risks and advantages of present and potential drug policies."[92]

Yet, Weinstein also said that *he* was not having that much trouble working with the
Guidelines. He said that heretofore he had not been forced to impose a sentence that
he found offensive. He credited the Court of Appeals for the Second Circuit for not
ordering him to commit what he perceived as injustices.[93] Citing to his own decisions,
he stated that "[t]here are almost invariably adequate guideline permitted reasons to
depart when the guidelines seem unfair."[94] "Where a trial judge believes a sentence
outside the Guidelines is desirable and necessary for the judge and the system to retain
their integrity, the departure rarely proves to be unjustified."[95] He listed ways open for
district judges to work around the Guidelines, including judicial jaw-boning with the
U.S. Attorney because the "claws [of the judge] still remain."[96] He also suggested that
opinions could be used to "help clarify" the thinking of the U.S. Attorney in deciding
whether to appeal as well as give pause to the Court of Appeals.

Still, he said back in 1993, that there was "some cause for pessimism about the future
of departures," among them mechanistic probation reports, passive defense attorneys,
and post-1987 appointed judges coming to the bench without having had the experience of individualized sentencing. They were instead being trained in the mechanics of
guideline sentencing at the Federal Judicial Center.[97]

At a symposium later that year, Weinstein was more negative. He observed:

Our judges now spend less time discussing with each other the substantive issues
of punishment that concern us all. We have fewer occasions in which to share our

---

23 percent of the sentencings were departures, of which 90 percent were downward. In the Eastern
District of New York, thirty percent of the sentences were departures, 80 percent downward.

[91] *Id.*

[92] Jack B. Weinstein, *The War on Drugs Is Self-Defeating*, NEW YORK TIMES (op-ed), July 8, 1993. *See also*
FORTUNE NEWS, February 1992, at 11.

[93] Weinstein, *Reflections on Departures, supra* note 90, at 7.

[94] *Id.* at p. 8.

[95] *Id.*

[96] *Id.* at 7.

[97] *Id.* at 8.

thoughts and concerns about the appropriateness of our sentences and their effects on the people whom we are sentencing and the general public. Discussion and argument between attorneys and the court about individual sentences have also atrophied.[98]

He also said "use of the guidelines does tend to deaden the sense that a judge must treat each defendant as a unique human being." "We judges," he said, "are becoming rubber-stamp bureaucrats."[99]

Still, Weinstein in the early 1990s seemed to be able to find his way around the Guidelines with few problems. In two cases in 1992, he was able to capitalize on the fact that two couriers were pregnant at the time of their arrests. In *United States v. Pokuaa*,[100] the Guidelines would have produced a prison sentence of from 27 to 33 months for Lucy Pokuaa, a twenty-three-year old Ghanaian woman (though a resident alien) who had swallowed balloons containing about ninety-two grams of heroin prior to boarding a plane to Kennedy Airport. If Pokuaa, who was bedridden because of a difficult pregnancy, had been given that sentence, under New York law she would have lost her child after she had given birth. Weinstein departed from the Guidelines for "an aggravating or mitigating circumstance of a kind or to a degree not adequately taken into consideration by the Sentencing Commission," the boiler plate for not following the Guidelines.[101] For Pokuaa, the circumstances were the potential loss of parental rights and the risk of injury or death to mother or fetus posed a by complicated pregnancy brought to term in prison. Weinstein sentenced Pokuaa to time served and ordered her immediate transportation to Ghana in a manner "that is safe for mother and fetus—even if this requires a berth or a first class airplane seat."[102]

That Weinstein's sentencing opinions were so often gripping was the result not only of the situation of the convicted defendants, but also of his ability to write stirring narratives, rather than bloodless findings of fact. These narratives usually accompanied downward departures, but even when he did not depart, Weinstein illuminated the human factors which illustrated the severity of the Guidelines. One of the most

---

[98] Symposium: Federal Sentencing: Jack B. Weinstein, Comment: *A Trial Judge's Second Impression of the Federal Sentencing Guidelines*, 66 SO. CAL. L. REV. 357, 361 (1992).

[99] *Id.* at 364.

[100] 782 F. Supp. 747 (Jan. 31, 1997).

[101] 18 U.S.C. §3553(b) (1988).

[102] *United States v. Pokuaa*, 782 F. Supp. 747 (Jan. 31, 1992). The second sentencing involving a pregnant mother was *United States v. Arize*, 792 F. Supp. 920 (June 24, 1992). There, Weinstein departed on his own motion to sentence a defendant who had swallowed balloons of heroin not knowing she was pregnant. He sentenced Peace Arize to twenty-three months; with a sentence one month longer she would have automatically lost custody of her child under New York law. In *United States v. Perez*, 756 F. Supp. 698 (Feb. 19, 1991), Weinstein sentenced a defendant whose child died while she was confined in prison awaiting trial for dealing crack, to time served, stating: "Even the most inhumane would consider this cruel punishment dealt by the fates sufficient retribution for her transgression. There are occasions where the law's implacability must bend and give homage through compassion to humanity's frailties and nature's cruelties. This is such a case." *Id.*

moving occurred in *United States v. Gaviria*,[103] in which the defendant was sentenced in October 1992. In that opinion, Weinstein took the reader to the poverty-stricken neighborhoods of Medellin where the defendant had grown up. She was abandoned by her father when she was four. The man who then moved into her home beat her with cables and pieces of wood. A babysitter also beat her, as did her aunt who did so while young Maria's hands and feet were being held by her aunt's friends.

Gaviria had learned how to survive in the streets where she begged for clothes. At sixteen, Gaviria married a twenty-four-year-old man who used drugs, stole, beat and stabbed her, and was involved with other women. The beatings continued after they moved to New York. Moneyless, unable to speak English, and not knowing how to travel, Gaviria feared death from the man who by now had become her husband, who was insisting that she assist him in his drug operation. She gave in and ultimately was arrested, while possessing 67.7 grams of cocaine base. The Guidelines dictated a sentence of between seventy and ninety-seven months. Pointing out that "nowhere in the Guidelines . . . is there room to consider how the facts of the life of a woman abused in this fashion should bear upon her sentence"[104] Weinstein looked to the effect of Gaviria's circumstances on the decisions she made:

> Until her arrest, defendant's life had been an extraordinary trial of physical and emotional abuse and coercion. Her actions were legally voluntary, but they were not the result of free rational decisionmaking . . . . She had long suffered from anxiety and depression, lacked any self-esteem, blamed herself for her suffering and greatly feared her husband and his associates.[105]

After examining and finding wanting the defenses of duress and coercion, Weinstein thought that Gaviria's "subservience" was relevant to blameworthiness. A "woman living in a relationship of complete subservience to a man deserves less punishment than the usual defendant when that man orders her to commit a crime and she obeys," he wrote. Yet, the Guidelines had no place for "subservience" and Weinstein could not do anything to help Gaviria because of the five-year minimum sentence for the crime. While some minimum sentences might be unconstitutional when applied, he thought that, in this case, the minimum sentence is not "so shocking and disproportionate as to warrant addressing the constitutional issue."[106]

By 1992, Weinstein clearly was actively searching for ways to depart from the Guidelines, or, as he put it, "constantly trying to get a technical base for departing."[107]

---

[103] 804 F. Supp. 476 (Oct. 22, 1992).

[104] *Id.* at 479.

[105] *Id.* at 481.

[106] *Id.* at 479, 481. On Weinstein's references in sentencing opinions to the effect of a history of beating on a woman, *see also, e.g., United States v. DeRoover*, 36 F. Supp. 2d 531 (Feb. 16, 1999).

[107] ". . . my constant effort is to increase the scope of the departure power." Weinstein Oral History, at 1107.

In addition to pregnancy, in *United States v. Cotto*, Weinstein found that a downward departure was warranted by a combination of the defendant's near retardation, vulnerability, efforts at rehabilitation, and the incompetence reflected in the execution of the crime.[108]

Sometimes Weinstein could achieve what he viewed as the appropriate result without coming up with departures. The very first line of attack was with the U.S. Attorney: to reduce the degree of the crime by charging a lesser amount of drugs carried. Next, the defendant might demonstrate exceptional contrition and make an attempt to cooperate with the U.S. Attorney.

Yet, sometimes Weinstein was manipulative. In one case, Weinstein twisted the facts to hold that the government had not proven that the young man involved, Scott Jonas, was a participant in the charged conspiracy *beyond* the period the Guidelines took effect.[109] Such a finding of fact was unreviewable. But Weinstein said:

> ... if I had not found this as a basis for avoiding the guidelines, I would have had no difficulty in finding two or three other ways of circumventing the guidelines. I've become fairly adept at finding ways of doing it.[110]

In another case, where he departed downward on account of defendant's exemplary life raising two children while working, he attempted to reinforce his position by demonstrating the defendant's assistance to her daughter-in-law. To do so, he laid the groundwork by asking, or more accurately, "leading" the defendant at the sentencing hearing:

> Do you help your daughter-in-law at all with the children? ... Do your daughters-in-law work? ... I think the family needs her help ... Do the children relate closely to you? What do they call you?[111]

In other cases, Weinstein advanced rehabilitation (not a Guidelines goal) as the appropriate goal for sentencing. He did this with a defendant, Saul Ramirez, who was eighteen when arrested for importing narcotics.[112] The young man had come from a broken home where his father had beaten his mother. The boy had taken on "the role of provider for the family," preparing meals and caring for three siblings, one of whom had Down's syndrome. He completed high school and worked steadily at regular jobs and had received a police commendation for trying to save the life of a young gunshot victim.

---

[108] *United States v. Cotto*, 793 F. Supp. 64 (June 5, 1992).

[109] *See United States v. Jonas*, 842 F. Supp. 1533 (Jan. 27, 1994).

[110] Weinstein Oral History, at 1262. *See also id.* at 263, 39.

[111] *United States v. Rodriguez*, 1995 NB 1911 (Dec. 27, 1995), at 17.

[112] *United States v. Ramirez*, 792 F. Supp. 922 (June 24, 1992).

Weinstein used information not taken into account by the Guidelines, such as the boy's excellent employment history, devotion to his family, and endeavors to raise himself from a difficult personal situation through education. He gave the boy five years' probation and 250 hours of community service, but attached the condition that he was to live with his uncle in New Jersey rather than in "his drug-and crime-ridden neighborhood." Weinstein commented sometime later, "This was a kid who would have been chewed up in prison. Rehabilitation was what was required."[113]

One of Weinstein's most important efforts to limit the effect of the guidelines, although it would prove futile, was his attempt to import traditional principles of *mens rea* (guilty mind; criminal intent) into sentencing. *United States v. Cordoba-Hincapie*[114] involved two separate Colombian nationals who thought the drug they were smuggling into the United States was cocaine, but in both cases it turned out to be heroin. The sentencing range for the amount of drugs they imported was much greater for heroin than for cocaine. The offense they had been charged with and had been convicted of was knowingly and intentionally importing heroin into the United States. However, at the sentencing hearing, Weinstein found beyond a reasonable doubt that the men thought they were importing cocaine.

Weinstein applied the principles of *mens rea* to the case and held that the defendants' punishments had to be limited by extent of their culpability. His opinion, close to fifty pages, was one of his finest, one of the most important opinions on *mens rea* written by an American judge. In it he discusses the history of *mens rea*, the present state of the doctrine; the degree to which the Constitution limits departures and the unsettled state of the law resulting from the Supreme Court's rare confrontation with the difficult issues connected with *mens rea*.

Weinstein held that: (1) *mens rea* constitutes a fundamental protection against the abuse of criminal statutes by the state; (2) *mens rea* continues to reflect the deep commitments within our culture regarding the individual's relationship to the community; (3) there is a continuing constitutional importance of the *mens rea* principle; and (4) to assume that Congress would adopt a heightened penalty without requiring a showing of a defendant's knowledge would be to assume that Congress acted irrationally. After posing a threefold test to take account of *mens rea* at sentencing, he held that the two Colombians could only be sentenced for the amount of *cocaine* they brought in.

Weinstein also relied on *mens rea* in the prosecution of Carolina Ekwunoh, a twenty-eight-year-old Nigerian immigrant, separated from her husband and living modestly with her three children on her own earnings from a clothing and jewelry boutique in Brooklyn.[115] Using Weinstein's word, Ekwunoh had just been a "greeter" who met a

---

[113] Weinstein Oral History, at 1158.

[114] 825 F. Supp. 485 (July 7, 1993).

[115] Transcript of Proceedings, *United States v. Ekwunoh*, CR-91-684 (Feb. 23, 1994) (in the possession of the author], at 3. The government stated that Ekwunoh had been in the Nigerian Witness Security Force for many years.

drug courier at the airport and took an attaché case from him. Ekwunoh claimed that she had believed the amount she was to receive at the airport was 400 grams. The brief case actually contained 1.013 kilograms of cocaine. The punishment for the latter weight was much greater.

Ekwunoh pled guilty to knowingly and intentionally possessing heroin with the intent to distribute an amount of heroin in excess of one kilogram. That offense carried a mandatory sentence of ten to forty years. In spite of her plea, Weinstein said that "the sentencing judge must find the quantity of drugs involved in order to determine the applicability of the mandatory minimum term of imprisonment."[116]

Weinstein applied the rules of *mens rea* and the principles of conspiracy to the attribution of quantities of drugs. He held by a preponderance of the evidence that a reasonable person in the position of the defendant with the knowledge and experience she had as an obedient underling would not necessarily have foreseen that the individual at the airport would be carrying over a kilogram of cocaine when she expected only 400 grams. Weinstein imposed a sixty-month sentence followed by five years supervised release and a fine of $50,000. In addition, it was likely that Ekwunoh would forfeit her house and permanently lose custody of her child.[117]

The Court of Appeals held that Weinstein's finding of fact as to the drug quantity was clearly erroneous and ordered that he sentence her to the minimum sentence for possession of cocaine (ten years).[118]

On remand, Weinstein said that the Court of Appeals decision was "mistaken on the facts and constitutes a gross departure from traditional principles of criminal law."[119] Privately he said that, if he had put the figure of 400 grams into Ekwunoh's mouth, he really believed her when she said she thought the quantity of drugs was relatively small.[120] He also said on remand that much of the difficulty with guideline sentencing and minimum sentences "lies not so much in the fault of the legislature or even the sentencing commission, but in the decisions of our courts and their self-imposed barriers to justice."[121]

Quite remarkably, both the defense counsel *and* the Assistant U.S. Attorney were "appalled" by "this draconian and unnecessary result" and called for modification of the Court of Appeals order. Weinstein held that he could not defy the Court of Appeals mandate, but gave both counsel one month to apply to the higher court for amendment of that mandate.[122] Although the Court of Appeals denied the petition, a *deus ex machina* arrived. Congress passed the Violent Crime Control Criminal Law Enforcement

---

[116] *United States v. Ekwunoh*, 813 F. Supp. 168, 172 (Jan. 14, 1993).
[117] *Id.*
[118] *United States v. Ekwunoh*, 12 F.3d 368 (Dec. 17, 1993).
[119] *United States v. Ekwunoh*, 888 F. Supp. 364 (Feb. 23, 1994).
[120] Weinstein Oral History, at 1198ff.
[121] *Ekwunoh*, 888 F. Supp. at 365.
[122] Transcript of Proceedings, *United States v. Ekwunoh*, CR 91-684 (Feb. 23, 1994), at 8.

Act,[123] which had the "safety valve" provision limiting the application of statutory minimums to the most serious offenses.[124] The fact that the Court of Appeals had vacated her sentence and remanded permitted Weinstein to sentence anew. When he did, he made additional findings requiring downward departure—the emotional difficulties of Ekwunoh's eleven-year-old child and the effect of the legal system on Ekwunoh's state of mind. A "prepossessing, articulate woman" was now "emaciated, inarticulate, with a visible tic and an expression that can only be described as a permanent cringe." Weinstein made a thirteen point departure downward which required a sentence with a range of between thirty and thirty-seven months. As Ekwunoh had already been incarcerated for thirty months, Weinstein sentenced her to time served plus supervised release.[125]

CONCEPCION AND ABBADESSA-DERIGGI

In two large multidefendant cases involving municipal scandals Weinstein put forward a legal theory which, had it been adopted, would have greatly undermined the efficacy of the Guidelines. Both scandals involved municipal services in New York City—welfare payments and inspections of taxicabs for safety. Neither scandal produced defendants well-suited to sentencing under of the Guidelines.

United States v. Concepcion, the case of the welfare-cheating Dominican mothers, a case of massive fraud, was the largest criminal case in the history of the Eastern District. Over one thousand persons were involved, though many fewer were prosecuted. Weinstein sentenced fifty-five defendants. While sentencing, Weinstein saw the defendants repeatedly.[126] He viewed the case as involving more than prosecutions and sentencings. To him, the case represented a profound failure of the government of New York City as well as a failure within the Dominican community. Paradoxically, as indicated earlier, he believed that the women were "very good mothers who were stealing "to give the children something better."[127]

The defendants, primarily women who had emigrated from the Dominican Republic, bought, sold, and used false identity documents and bribed government employees. The typical defendant applied for multiple welfare benefit packages (Aid for Dependent Children (AFDC), food stamps, and Medicaid) using false birth certificates for mothers and children, Social Security numbers not yet issued by the Social Security Administration, false immigration records, and other forged documents. While some city employees were bribed, the success of the scheme was often due to the administrative ineptitude

[123] 18 U.S.C. §3553(f).
[124] *See infra*, p. 250.
[125] *See* N.Y.L.J. Dec. 8, 1994, at 1.
[126] Weinstein Oral History, at 1151.
[127] *Id.* at 1150.

of city employees: " . . . in effect, the government made it easy for these people to cheat . . . by not using better methods.[128] Some of those connected with the scheme netted hundreds of thousands of dollars each. The total amount lost by city, state, and federal government was around $45 million.[129]

Generally, the defendants' in *Concepcion I* and *II* (twenty defendants were sentenced six months later)[130] had been raised in poverty in the Dominican Republic. Their parents generally had not married or had married and then separated. The defendants came to New York in their youth. Almost all had children, in most cases by fathers to whom they were not married and who were not supporting the children. Many lived in poverty in some of New York City's poorest neighborhoods. Some, but probably not the majority, had been drug users. Most of the women had taken responsibility for raising their children.

The Guidelines were not well adapted to these prosecutions because of their stress on incarceration and Weinstein did not use them. Most of the defendants were single mothers with young children. As Weinstein said, "[r]emoving the mothers in such a matriarchical setting destroys the children's main source of stability and guidance and enhances the possibility of their engaging in destructive behavior."[131] He emphasized: "[y]ou can't want to destroy those mothers because you destroy the family."[132] No correctional facilities in the New York metropolitan area allowed children to live with their parents. Since the cases were all related, each defendant could have been charged the full cost of the scandal leading to extremely harsh sentences. On the other hand, the most culpable could receive lighter sentences because of cooperation with the government.

Weinstein's approach to sentencing in these cases involved interpreting three statutory sections in a way that would minimize their influence. The end result of the three-step test Weinstein drew from the statute was a lack of a clear preference for sentencing under the Guidelines scheme.[133]

Turning to the individual sentences in the welfare fraud case, Weinstein indicated the difficulties with sentencing these defendants. The defendants with children

---

[128] Weinstein Oral History, at 1231. Trying a criminal case involving the president of the Flushing Federal Bank, Weinstein believed that the failures of government almost induced people to get involved in the criminal conduct. Weinstein Oral History, at 1065ff. *See especially* at 1068.

[129] *United States v. Concepcion*, 795 F. Supp. 1262, 1270 (June 30, 1992).

[130] *United States v. Concepcion*, 808 F. Supp. 166 (Dec. 11, 1992).

[131] *Concepcion*, 795 F. Supp. at 1282.

[132] Weinstein Oral History, at 1150.

[133] The three sections were (1) 18 U.S.C. §3551 which mandated that the court impose sentences to achieve the general purposes listed in Section 3553(1); (2) Section 3553(a) which lists purposes for punishment; and (3) 18 U.S.C. §3553(b) which states that the court shall impose a sentence of the kind, and within the range referred to [by the Guidelines] "unless the court finds that there exists an aggravating or mitigating circumstances of a kind . . . not adequately taken into consideration by the Sentencing Commission."

"have each displayed a strong maternal feeling for them."[134] This is his description of one of the mothers at sentencing:

> One mother, typical of the group, shook with fear at the possibility that prison would wrest her from her children . . . the family had come for the allocution directly from the younger child's junior high school graduation which took place on a beautiful June day. When the family arrived, the older sister and the graduate—still clad in a white robe and sporting a medal for her accomplishments in English class—displayed the high spirits of two young, successful women looking forward to future accomplishments. Their mother, by contrast, quailed at the prospect of having to leave these children without her guidance in a crime and drug-ridden section of the Bronx.[135]

Weinstein pointed out that the women would serve their sentence in a place where family visitation would be almost impossible. Furthermore, they "would be thrown in with drug 'mules' and habitual criminals of sharply different economic and cultural backgrounds from their own . . . Most are middle-aged, conservative women, primarily housewives, who have never been involved in crime and who have worked at menial jobs out of economic necessity and with little concern for their own careers or egos."[136]

Weinstein's explanation of each sentence takes about a page and is compelling reading. One mother had, back in Santo Domingo, "supported the family by washing clothes and cleaning houses while her father lolled in the streets."[137] Another woman had a father who "became a drug addict who stole from the family's house to support his habit." Her "mother is in a coma after surgery from cancer."[138] Still another defendant had divorced her first husband because of physical abuse to both herself and their daughter and was divorced from the second because of his drug use. She had another two children by former boy friends.[139] One had only one child, but no one in the extended family to care for it.[140]

Weinstein gave terms of imprisonment to five of the first twenty he sentenced; probation to the other fifteen. Nine were also given community service or home detention; five were given supervised release. He ordered fines and/or restitution ranging from $23,000 to $200,000 from them all.[141] The sentences presented considerable

---

[134] *Concepcion*, 795 F. Supp. at 1284.

[135] *Id.* at 1285.

[136] *Id.*

[137] *Id.* at 1289.

[138] *Id.* at 1290.

[139] *Id.* at 1294.

[140] *Id.*

[141] *Id.* at 1306–07.

complications and burdens for probation—bed space, child care placement, job placement.[142]

After he completed his sentencings of the *Concepcion* women, Weinstein issued an "amended sentencing memorandum," which consisted largely of ruminations.[143] In it, he praised the way the U.S. Attorney had handled the case—for understanding from the beginning that unduly harsh sentences for the lowest-level criminals would have accomplished little.[144]

He then sharply criticized the public officials responsible for welfare in New York City. The failures of government had made it too easy for the defendants to commit their crimes. The government employees had not even checked whether given Social Security numbers in fact corresponded to given names.[145]

Finally, he turned to the issue of deterrence. Although he said that he had sentenced with the aim of general deterrence, he thought the deterrence value of the sentences was "minimal." The ease with which the crimes had been committed and the clear sense of impunity with which the defendants had acted suggested that the prospect of penal sanctions was remote or nonexistent in the minds of such low-level offenders.[146] The defendants lived in an isolated and insulated community, spoke English poorly if at all, had little understanding of the workings of American government, and were "intro-duced to welfare fraud by peers who had themselves learned from others that it is an easy source of income." Further, "[n]early all stole to provide somewhat better lives for their children."[147]

Weinstein then turned to a theme he would develop in several other criminal cases with different ethnic communities. There had been, he said, a failure of general deter-rence in the Dominican-American community, which "must assume responsibility for dealing with unacceptable criminal behavior."[148] The answer, he thought, lay not in the criminal law, but in "[s]ocial sanctions administered by peers and those institutions of which members of the community are themselves members and to which they look for guidance."[149] This theme aroused considerable media interest,[150] as had a comment in another case connecting the Mafia and the Italo-American community in the sentenc-ing of mob figures.[151] The sentences imposed in *Concepcion* held up as there were no appeals.

---

[142] *Id.* at 1306-07.

[143] *United States v. Concepcion*, 825 F. Supp. 19 (June 23, 1993).

[144] *Id.* at 24.

[145] *Id.* at 25.

[146] *Id.* at 24.

[147] *Id.*

[148] *Id.* at 25.

[149] *Id.* at 24.

[150] NEW YORK TIMES, June 24, 1993, at B2; NEWSDAY, June 24, 1993.

[151] After imposing life sentences on three Mafia figures who had been convicted of murder and racketeer-ing, Weinstein said that there was "a large part of the young Italo-American community who should be

Shortly after *Concepcion*, when Weinstein attempted to employ the same statutory theory to avoid penalizing the little guys more than the "big fish," in a multidefendant scandal involving the bribing of taxicab inspectors, the Court of Appeals for the Second Circuit roundly rejected it.

The tax inspectors' scandal involved thirty employees of the New York City Taxi and Limousine Commission who accepted bribes in exchange for overlooking defects and for certifying taxicabs that had not been inspected. The defendants included line inspectors, senior inspectors, and their supervisors. Weinstein was especially troubled that some of the young line inspectors had been drawn unwillingly into the corruption by more senior colleagues. Once again, such endemic corruption appears in large measure to have been the result of the incompetence of high city officials.

Weinstein sought to sentence the defendants in proportion to their culpability. His primary goal was to deter future corruption, not only of the Taxi Commission, but in other governmental agencies responsible for enforcing safety standards.[152] In the taxi inspectors' scandal, using the Guidelines the small fry would have ended up with the greatest prison time, twenty-four to thirty months, because each could be held responsible for the total amount of money received by all the inspectors. Meanwhile, the bigger fish could cooperate with the government and sell everyone out, thereby receiving 5K1.1 letters from the U.S. Attorney and lower sentences.[153] Indeed, the government wanted to give the chief culprit the best deal. Weinstein believed in the taxicab inspectors' scandal that the twenty-four to thirty month Guidelines range for these offenses was greater than necessary to achieve general deterrence[154]

The United States appealed four sentences and two defendants appealed. The Court of Appeals with Judge Frank Altimari writing vacated and remanded the sentences of the four defendants.[155] The Appeals Court held that a court must sentence within the applicable Guidelines range unless a departure is appropriate. The cases were remanded to allow the district court to determine whether there were supplemental permissible bases for downward departures. The sentences of other defendants who appealed were vacated by other panels.[156]

---

discouraged from going into this line of work." NEW YORK TIMES, May 25, 1993; NEW YORK POST, May 26, 1993. Governor Mario Cuomo, asked to comment, said, "I can't imagine . . . Judge Weinstein saying anything that wasn't intelligent or fair." NEW NEWSDAY, May 26, 1993, at 3. Weinstein softened his comments in a revised sentencing memorandum.

[152] *United States v. Abbadessa*, 848 F. Supp. 369, 380 (Mar. 24, 1994).

[153] In a 5K 1.1 letter the prosecution informs the sentencing judge that the defendant rended substantial assistance in the investigation or prosecution for which the judge may depart downward from the Guidelines in sentencing.

[154] Weinstein Oral History, at 1373. *See also id.*, at 1259.

[155] *United States v. DeRiggi*, 45 F.3d 713 (Jan. 26, 1995).

[156] *Id.* at 719. The sentences of other defendants who appealed were vacated by other panels. *United States v. DeRiggi*, 54 F.3d 765 (Apr. 5, 1995); *United States v. Deriggi*, 50 F.3d 3 (Feb. 22, 1995).

Weinstein was not fazed. On remand, he interpreted the Guidelines in light of the traditions and purposes of sentencing, while also considering the facts *as he found them at the time of resentencing*.[157] This time he "found" another important factor, which he said had not adequately been considered by the Sentencing Commission—the hardship created when a defendant (released or soon to be released) is sentenced to a long term *after appeal*. Since postoffense conduct can constitute grounds for departure and criminal history scores can be adjusted to account for postoffense conduct, an order vacating a sentence required the district judge to resentence as if sentencing de novo.[158]

Weinstein then sentenced four of the six defendants to time served, another to continue his sentence in a halfway house. However, he gave Nicholas DeRiggi, the supervisory inspector of the Woodside inspection station and the chief organizer of the taxi inspection scheme, what he had given him before – thirty-six months in prison, two years' supervised release, $10,000 restitution, a $7500 fine, and a special assessment of $50.

Of the six, only DeRiggi appealed, and this time the Court of Appeals affirmed, stating that "there is no basis for finding that the Guidelines analysis employed here was perfunctory or pretextual, or that our mandate was disregarded."[159] One wonders. Weinstein himself related that, after the first Court of Appeals decision in *Abbadessa/DeRiggi*, he had run into Judge Frank Altimari, who had written that opinion. Altimari told Weinstein that he had had "a lot of trouble with *Concepcion* and *Abbadessa*." As Weinstein tells it: "So I said to him [chuckle], 'Don't worry about it, Frank . . .' You won't let me jump through the hoop frontwards, I'll go through the hoop backwards. And you can be sure the sentence is going to be exactly the same when they come back because there are other bases for doing it. If I apply the Guidelines, there's sufficient basis for departures."[160]

ABJURING DRUG CASES

But in 1993, the cruelty of sentencing drug defendants had become too great for Weinstein. He would write some years later, that "the drug system" was "in crisis," adding that these policies constitute "a form of cannibalism" whereby "we are eating the lives of our young people particularly in minority communities."[161] In the spring of 1993, Weinstein sent a memorandum to his colleagues, district judges, and magistrate

---

[157] *United States v. DeRiggi*, 893 F. Supp. 171, 174 (Jul. 12, 1995).

[158] *Id.* at 176ff.

[159] *United States v. DeRiggi*, 72 F.3d 7, 9 (Dec. 8, 1995: PC: Altimari-Jacobs-Cabranes).

[160] Weinstein Oral History, at 1323-24.

[161] Jack B. Weinstein, Standing Down from the War on Drugs, Remarks on Receiving the Award for Service to the Bar and Community of New York State Bar Association, Criminal Justice Section (Jan. 23, 2003), at 2.

judges on the bench of the Eastern District. In it, he said that he would not *now* handle any more drug cases because he could no longer tolerate meting out harsh sentences to low-level drug smugglers.[162] The penalties for drug offenses had increased enormously without having any impact. The endeavor appeared futile.

Weinstein sought to maximize attention on the drug problem by adding to his memorandum to his colleagues, a speech at Cardozo Law School, and a widely publicized statement, issued with Judge Whitman Knapp of the Southern District of New York, on why they would no longer hear drug cases.[163] In his law school speech, Weinstein called himself "a tired old judge who has temporarily filled his quota of remorselessness."[164] In response, eight Republican members of the House of Representatives called for Weinstein and Knapp to resign or be impeached.[165] But Weinstein and Knapp were not alone—senior judges of the U.S. District Court for the District of Columbia had asked not to be assigned any new *criminal* cases. The Weinstein-Knapp statement focused public attention—at least for a short time—on the problem.

Weinstein did eventually go back to drug cases.[166] He reflected about the decision to return: "So I decided to take them. I'm glad I did. Because, since I went back, I probably have had at least a hundred sentences. On many of them I've provided for rehabilitation and kept people out of prison and kept families together. I think I made the right decision by going back."[167]

BATTLES WITH THE COURT OF APPEALS

Around the time Weinstein announced that he would no longer hear drug cases, he complimented the Court of Appeals for the Second Circuit for its role in sentencing cases, saying that it "has been particularly imaginative in allowing new grounds for

---

[162] NEW YORK L.J., 1 (Apr. 15, 1993).

[163] Apr. 17, 1993. A sampling of the places where either Weinstein's Cardozo speech or the Weinstein-Knapp statement either appeared as a news story or in an editorial: NEW YORK LAW JOURNAL, Apr. 15, 1993, at 1; NEW YORK LAW JOURNAL, Apr. 17, 1993; WASHINGTON POST, May 1, 1993 (editorial); SAN FRANCISCO CHRONICLE, July 18, 1993; SUNDAY PUNCH; GAINESVILLE (FLORIDA) SUN, Aug. 15, 1993; NATIONAL LAW JOURNAL, May 17, 1993; HARPER'S (July 1993). *See also* Linda Himmelstein & Eva M. Rodriguez, *Panel Approves More Leeway in Drug Sentencing*, 15 LEGAL TIMES No. 49, at 2, 7 (week of Apr. 26, 1993).

[164] Jack B. Weinstein, *Why I Won't Try Any More Drug Cases*, 15 LEGAL TIMES 14 at 15 (week of Apr. 26, 1993) (repr. Weinstein Speech at Aleph Institute, Cardozo School of Law, Apr. 14, 1993).

[165] NEW YORK L. J. Apr. 29, 1993.

[166] Weinstein Oral History, at 1494–95. It should be noted that Weinstein does not believe in complete decriminalization of drugs because he is fearful as to what might happen in ghetto communities. Alex F. Maurice, *Judges Say: No Mandatory Jail for Minor Drug Offenders*, BROOK. HEIGHTS COURIER, Nov. 22, 1993, at 6.

[167] Weinstein Oral History, at 1495.

downward departures" in cases appealed by the government.[168] At the same time, he criticized that court for "failing to understand that it is their duty to interpret the law in the light of lenity, *mens rea*, and all the standard techniques that have been used by the courts over the years to mitigate punishment."[169] In his oral history, Weinstein admitted that there were times when they [the Court of Appeals] were probably right on the law, but that they should have struggled more.[170] Tensions grew in the mid-1990s between Weinstein and the Court of Appeals over sentencing, some of which was related to cases where the Court of Appeals thought Weinstein's sentences *were too long* or had not been properly justified.

One such case, a remarkable one, was *United States v. Shonubi*. Shonubi involved a drug swallower who was arrested carrying 103 balloons of heroin (estimated from a sample of balloons at 427.4 grams). Shonubi proved to be his own worst enemy. Had he pled guilty, he probably would have received *thirty* months imprisonment. Instead, but he decided to go to trial, where he lied and was found guilty.

Under the Guidelines, Shonubi's sentence could have been enhanced for the amount of heroin he had brought into the country on seven trips made before he was caught The prosecution calculated that the total amount of heroin Shonubi had brought into the country by multiplying the number of grams found on Shonubi when he was caught on his eighth trip by eight, the number of trips. This came to 3419 grams of heroin.

Weinstein accepted the manner in which the government had aggregated the trips involving drugs, but was troubled about enhancing the sentence for Shonubi's perjury at trial. Shonubi had lied about the amount of times he had traveled to Nigeria and stated that those trips did not involve drugs. Weinstein thought that "where the defendant arguably testifies to what he could not at the moment bring himself to disbelieve, an obstruction of justice enhancement for perjury is not warranted."[171] Weinstein then sentenced Shonubi to 151 months. The Guidelines permitted a range of 151 to 188 months.

The Court of Appeals reversed and remanded.[172] It overturned Weinstein's decision not to enhance Shonubi's statement for his perjury at trial, but took strong issue with Weinstein's aggregation of drugs. There simply was no proof, the Court of Appeals said, that Shonubi had imported 427.4 grams of heroin (the amount of the last trip) on each of his seven previous trips. It was necessary for the government to have "specific evidence"—drug records, admissions, or live testimony—in order to calculate drug quantities for sentencing purposes. Weinstein's fact-finding, the panel said, had been predicated on "surmise and conjecture" and was "clearly erroneous."[173]

---

[168] Jack B. Weinstein, *Why I Won't Try Any More Drug Cases*, *supra* note 164.
[169] Weinstein Oral History, at 979.
[170] Weinstein Oral History, at 606.
[171] *United States v. Shonubi*, 802 F. Supp. 859, 862 (Oct. 9, 1992).
[172] *United States v. Shonubi*, 998 F.2d 84 (June 30, 1993: *Card*-Oakes-Newman).
[173] *Id.* at 89, 90.

Weinstein responded with an opinion of 177 typed pages, which primarily was an essay on how a trier of fact reaches a decision. For the writing of it, he had posed questions to his Eastern District colleagues, and he used data from their responses in his opinion. Weinstein also appointed a panel of expert witnesses for the court under Rule 706 of the Federal Rules of Evidence. He submitted a draft of the opinion, not only to the parties for comment, but also to a number of scholars. Based on responses to his draft memorandum, he requested the parties to provide additional information on the *economics* of heroin smuggling.

It is not possible, even in a book about Weinstein, to offer more than a thimbleful of description of Weinstein's opinion in *Shonubi-III*.[174] The narrow issue at the heart of the opinion was: "How likely is it based on all available information, that the seven smuggling trips about which little was known were similar to the eighth, about which a great deal is known?"[175] The opinion included an unsparing, critical analysis of the manner in which the Second Circuit Court of Appeals had treated estimates based on extrapolation in various of its opinions.[176]

In *Shonubi-III*, Weinstein labeled the Court of Appeals request for "specific evidence" of drug transactions as akin to the "discredited notion" that the body must be produced in a murder prosecution. He lauded the value of demeanor evidence, something "generally unavailable to the court of appeals," and discussed what had been learned from Shonubi's demeanor and character at trial and sentencing. He also discussed how decision-makers learn and decide and the way hypotheses are patched together to make a problem intellectually tractable.[177]

Weinstein then turned to an area which he might have been the best qualified person in the United States to discuss—the rules favoring the admissibility of evidence.[178] On this issue, he looked at the testimony of the various expert witnesses and presented the results of his survey of his colleagues whom he had asked to rate five hypotheses about heroin swallowers.[179]

Among the other subjects discussed in the *Shonubi* opinion was (1) the floor below which heroin smuggling does not make economic sense; (2) the use of statistical evidence in mass torts and employment discrimination cases; (3) the need for protection of defendants when statistics are used in criminal cases.[180]

Weinstein concluded in his *Shonubi III* opinion that the defendant had carried a total of between 1000 and 3000 grams of heroin on his trips (considerably less than the previous estimate of 3419 grams). Applying under duress from the Court of Appeals

---

[174] *United States v. Shonubi*, 895 F. Supp. 460 (Aug. 4, 1995).

[175] *Id.* at 470.

[176] *Id.* at 476.

[177] *Id.* at 478–79.

[178] *Id.* at 492ff.

[179] *Id.* at 509ff.

[180] *Id.* at 512, 517–18.

the enhancement for perjury, Weinstein sentenced Shonubi to 151 months, the same amount he had sentenced him to the first time![181]

The Court of Appeals was unimpressed with Weinstein's *tour-de-force*. Judge Jon Newman, writing for Judges Cardamone, Calabresi, and himself in *Shonubi-IV*, stated:

> Judge Weinstein considered this case to be an 'opportunity to observe, explain, and discuss forensic decision-making' . . . an opportunity he seized with his customary thoroughness and erudition. Though his comprehensive opinion is a valuable addition to the legal literature on the subject of evidence in particular and judicial decision-making in general, we concluded that he relied on evidence beyond the category of "specific evidence" that our prior opinion ruled was required for determination of a "relevant conduct" drug quantity for purposes of imposing a criminal sentence.[182]

The appellate court still wanted "specific evidence"—drug records, admissions, or live testimony—if the sentence was to be increased. The Court of Appeals remanded with directions to impose a sentence based on 427.4 grams of heroin per trip.

In *Shonubi-V*,[183] Weinstein complied with the Court of Appeals mandate and sentenced Shonubi to ninety-seven months for carrying 427.4 grams which included an upward adjustment of two levels required by the Court of Appeals for perjury. This was the lowest point in the Guidelines range of 97 to 121 months, lower than it would have been under pre-Guidelines practice, but "entirely appropriate" to the crime.[184] Weinstein, however, could not help pointing out, that "[t]he Guidelines have had the unfortunate ancillary result of creating unusual tensions among and between normally collegial trial and appellate judges as they struggle to conform to a system so many consider unjust, unfair and counterproductive."[185]

Weinstein did not think much of the requirement of "specific evidence" the Court of Appeals had used, calling it "a retrogressive step towards the practice relied upon from the Middle Ages to the late Nineteenth Century,"[186] still, he admitted, the result required by *Shonubi* was "compassionate." In *Shonubi II* and *IV*, the "Court of Appeals was acting in the highest tradition in seeking a just result."[187] While generally Weinstein's sentences are compassionate, he is quite capable of giving stiff sentences. There are times, he has said "when they [the Guidelines] are too soft and they don't

---

[181] *Id.* at 530.
[182] *United States v. Shonubi*, 103 F.3d 1085, 1092 (Jan. 6, 1997).
[183] 962 F. Supp. 370 (May 20, 1997).
[184] *Id.* at 371.
[185] *Id.* at 372.
[186] *Id.* at 375.
[187] *Id.* at 376.

take into account of the experiences of the judge to the extent they should."[188] Accordingly, Weinstein has given greater penalties to leaders of criminal enterprises, government officials, and those who lure youth into crime.[189] He has employed restitution, forfeiture, and fines to strip this class of people of their financial gain.[190] He has put it this way:

> I myself favor a rather cruel enforcement of forfeiture—particularly as to the higher-ups. The only way to get at them is by taking away their money. Since it is essentially a crime of greed, it seems to me it has to be handled as one.[191]

Sometimes Weinstein has been reversed by the Court of Appeals because he was too harsh. This was true in Shonubi. *United States v. Tropiano* was another case where the Court of Appeals thought Weinstein erred on the harsh side. Tropiano had been charged with altering the vehicle identification number (VIN) of an automobile and with being a felon in possession of a firearm. He was acquitted of the latter offense. However, the government demonstrated that Tropiano had also been heavily involved with drug trafficking and automobile theft. The presentence report recommended a range of twenty-seven to thirty-three months. The government moved for an upward departure on the basis of uncharged conduct—drug trafficking. Weinstein believed that Tropiano was "a one man crime wave"[192] and felt that he had to be incarcerated to prevent him from committing crimes:

> The defendant is a confirmed recidivist. He is twenty-five years old, he's at the peak of his criminal career, and he has to be sentenced primarily for incarceration because the court is convinced that he will continue with serious conduct when he's out of prison.[193]

Weinstein sentenced Tropiano to sixty months in prison, three years' supervised release, and a $50,000 fine.

---

[188] Weinstein Oral History, at 1372. Weinstein was interviewed for the position of Chief Judge of the New York Court of Appeals in 1980, the day after he had given a sentence of ten years to a jockey heavily involved in a betting scandal. The sentence was high to encourage him to cooperate with the government. Judith Kaye was a member of the interviewing panel and said to him, "'Ten years for fixing a horse race. You really are tough, aren't you Jack?" Weinstein Oral History, at 1375–76. Weinstein later reduced the sentence to five years. The jockey never cooperated. On the *Errico* case, see NEW YORK POST, Sept. 1, 1981; NEW YORK DAILY NEWS, Sept. 11, 1981; NEWSDAY, Dec. 18, 1981; NEW YORK TIMES, Sept. 29, 1982.

[189] Weinstein Oral History, at 1221, 1229.

[190] *See* Weinstein Oral History, at 189, 1194, 1221. On Weinstein's support for the use of restitution, see *United States v. Malpeso*, 943 F. Supp. 254 (Oct. 23, 1996).

[191] Weinstein Oral History, at 1277.

[192] Weinstein Oral History, at 1400.

[193] Quoted in *United States v. Tropiano*, 50 F.3d 157, 161 (Mar. 17, 1995: McLaughlin -Kearse-Parker).

The Court of Appeals held that Weinstein's departure was procedurally defective.[194] Weinstein later called the Court of Appeals decision "one of the stupidest decisions ever handed down under the Guidelines."[195] He pointed out that the process of crafting a reasonable departure to protect the public as well as the defendant and his family is a process that is:

> . . . three-dimensional and alive. Converting it through oversimplification and mechanization into a two-dimensional, cartoon-like exercise does a disservice to justice—the holy grail of the law.[196]

On remand, after a scrupulous discussion of Tropiano's conduct and criminal history, Weinstein sentenced him to fifty-one months imprisonment, three years of supervised release, and a $10,000 fine. The Court of Appeals then affirmed, noting that in Weinstein's "discursive opinion the court criticized our decisions in *Tropiano* and several other cases, but was 'nonetheless' faithful to our mandate."[197]

In *United States v. Naugle*, during sentencing Weinstein had made several sympathetic statements about the defendant's family situation, but had declined to depart. The Court of Appeals suggested that it was not clear that Weinstein had known he had the power to depart and had then chosen not to do so. On remand, Weinstein's lectured the Court of Appeals as to what actually happens at a sentencing, suggesting that the members of the Court of Appeals do not actually see the defendant. He explained that his statements about defendant's family situation were simply intended to convey the thought, "I am aware of your importance to your family and vice versa—I see your family members here today—but, given the seriousness of your offense, I am unable to reduce your sentence."[198]

In 1997, there was an unseemly battle between the Court of Appeals and Weinstein over the sentencing of a drug courier, Diego Lopez-Aguilar. Aguilar, in his late twenties, was a Colombian immigrant. While he could have been sentenced to a minimum term of ten years, he was entitled under the "safety valve" provision of the 1994 crime act to a lower sentence. Weinstein seriously considered the fact that the twenty-nine-year-old defendant and his thirty-three-year-old wife had made a serious and concerted effort to conceive a child. The defendant's wife, implicated in some way in the offense, had been pregnant through *in vitro* fertilization, but had miscarried. The government consented to her deportation instead of prosecution. Believing that following the Guidelines

---

[194] *Id.* at 162–63.

[195] Weinstein Oral History, at 1399ff.

[196] *Id.* at 102.

[197] *United States v. Tropiano*, 1996 U.S. App. LEXIS 2470 (Jan. 16, 1996: McLaughlin-Leval-Cabranes).

[198] *See United States v. Naugle*, 879 F. Supp, 262, 267 (Mar. 17, 1995), *aff'd without opinion*, 54 F.3d 765 (Apr. 13, 1995). The original Court of Appeals opinion was *United States v. Naugle*, 47 F.3d 1158 (Jan. 18, 1995). Another important case where Weinstein departed upward was *United States v. Bonventre*, 824 F. Supp. 328 (June 21, 1993), a case involving an insurance board rating inspector who had taken bribes from contractors to fraudulently induce insurance carriers to lower Workers' Compensation premiums.

would reduce the chance of the couple having a chance to have a child, Weinstein evoked the "extraordinary family circumstances departure" and sentenced Lopez-Aguilar to thirty-seven months.[199] Of the case, Weinstein said, "I have the sense that the ability to have children . . . is [a] vital a part of humanity and the human condition . . .."[200]

The government appealed. Unknown to Weinstein (and to the U.S. Attorney), Lopez-Aguilar had completed his prison term and been deported before his appeal had been decided or even argued. The Court of Appeals, in a scathing opinion by Judge Dennis Jacobs, which Weinstein called "particularly nasty and unfeeling,"[201] held that Weinstein's departure was clear error; the "extraordinary family circumstance departure" applied only where there were continuing onerous family obligations.[202] The Court of Appeals set aside the sentence.

Tensions with the appellate court erupted when the case came back to Weinstein for resentencing. Only then did it become known that Lopez-Aguilar had been deported before the appeal had been argued. The letters the U.S. Attorney had written to the three judges of the panel informing them of this never seemed to have arrived. Weinstein took the position that he could not resentence Lopez-Aguilar *in absentia*.[203] He then telephoned Chief Judge Newman of the Court of Appeals urging that the court withdraw its mandate and reinstate Weinstein's original sentence with an order that, if the defendant is ever in court, he should be resentenced.

The matter became public. The panel conducted a full investigation to find out whether the letters had been sent. The judges on the panel suggested that Weinstein had initiated the events to prevent an appeal from being taken. The panel reinstated the sentence, but ordered the matter assigned to a different judge. Weinstein contended that the remand constituted an unwarranted and illegal interference with the judicial power of fellow district judges. He sent his order to the entire Court of Appeals and to the district judges of the Southern and Eastern District. Ultimately, the matter was reassigned to Judge Frederic Block.

WEINSTEIN'S SECOND DECADE OF GUIDELINES SENTENCING

The thrust of Weinstein's sentencing efforts from 1995 until the Supreme Court ended the reign of the Guidelines a decade later was to find loopholes to ameliorate

---

[199] *United States v. Lopez-Aguilar*, 886 F. Supp. 305 (May 16, 1995). Weinstein said that a second reason for the sentence was that he didn't see the point of burdening the taxpayer to fund a ten-year sentence.

[200] Weinstein Oral History, at 1305–06. On the brouhaha, *see id.* at 1299–1321, 1413–14. *See also* James L. Oakes, *Jack Weinstein and His Love-Hate Relationship with the Court of Appeals*, 97 COLUM. L. REV. 1951, 1957.

[201] Weinstein Oral History, at 1305.

[202] *United States v. Londono*, 76 F.3d 33 (Jan. 5, 1996). The opinion was amended by the Second Circuit. *See United States v. Londono*, 100 F.3d 236 (Nov. 14, 1996). The panel was Jacobs (writing), Altimari, and Connor of the Southern District.

[203] Weinstein Oral History, at 1309.

harsh results. In *United States v. Liu*,[204] he held that a pathological gambling addiction can constitute significantly reduced mental capacity which would entitle the defendant to a downward departure. In *United States v. Hammond*, he held that HIV positive status could be considered as a basis for leniency and reduced a sentence from a range of thirty-seven to forty-six months to thirteen months.[205]

One approach Weinstein often used was to delay sentencing for six months or a year to allow the defendant to make a record of rehabilitation. In *United States v. Flowers*,[206] he held that the Guidelines did not prohibit a delay in sentencing to determine if the defendant had been rehabilitated.

It might be said that Weinstein attempted to "rehabilitate" rehabilitation as a goal of sentencing in *United States v. K*.[207] In that case, Weinstein deferred the sentencing of a twenty-one-year-old Asian-American for more than a year during which he had been enrolled in the Special Options Rehabilitation Services (SORS) program run by Eastern District Pretrial Services officers. In his opinion, Weinstein declared that the Sentencing Reform Act "retained a great deal of the district court's historic discretion" and that power to depart could be based upon significant presentence rehabilitation. Under appropriate circumstances, a judge should take adequate steps to allow for an opportunity for a defendant to rehabilitate himself by granting a request for deferred sentencing.[208] He then found that K's activities may well have placed him "squarely within the parameters of 'extraordinary rehabilitation.'" K had participated and progressed in the SORS program, where he had worked toward a General Equivalency Diploma, been a volunteer for the Fortune Society and Legal Aid, and been provided mental health counseling and drug testing. Weinstein granted a motion to postpone sentencing for yet another year for the court "to assure itself that K has been rehabilitated and to explore and consider acceptable sentencing options."[209]

There were several cases where Weinstein openly tried to reconcile the needs of the defendant, who would be debilitated rather than rehabilitated in prison, with those of the victim. In *United States v. Blake*,[210] the left hand of the victim, a bank teller, had been permanently damaged during a bank robbery. The defendant had a three-year-old daughter, had been abused by her lover, and suffered from major depression. Weinstein held a hearing and sent the minutes to the victim. While the victim had not fully forgiven the defendant, she had developed some understanding of the defendant and the defendant's tragic situation. The government recommended that the sentence be left to the direction of the court. Weinstein intentionally delayed sentencing for six months in order to provide a practical test of rehabilitation. Ultimately, he sentenced

---

[204] 267 F. Supp. 2d 371 (June 6, 2003).

[205] 37 F. Supp. 2d 204 (Feb. 18, 1999).

[206] 983 F. Supp. 2d 159 (Oct. 28, 1997).

[207] *United States v. K.*, 160 F. Supp. 2d 423 (June 1, 2001).

[208] *Id.* at 440.

[209] *Id.* at 445–47.

[210] 89 F. Supp. 2d 328 (Mar. 15, 1998).

Blake to time served, five years of strictly supervised release, and restitution of $5000 paid at $80/month and required her to remain in therapy throughout the period.

THE END OF THE GUIDELINES ERA

Early in the twenty-first century, Congress increased its efforts to restrain federal judges from straying from the Guidelines while the U.S. Supreme Court was bringing the era of mandatory guideline sentencing to an end. The Feeney Amendment of the PROTECT Act of April 30, 2003, rushed through Congress with little public awareness, prohibited departures based solely on the existence of a plea agreement and limited their availability based on family ties and responsibilities as well as on a number of other existing grounds. This was the first time Congress had bypassed the Commission by amending the Guidelines. The new law required exacting reporting requirements on any judge who departed from the Guidelines for any reason other than cooperation with the government. The statute authorized the Courts of Appeals to resentence defendants *de novo* where a downward departure by a district judge had been found unjustified.[211]

Weinstein was critical of the PROTECT Act.[212] He also announced in an opinion that he would videotape his sentencings to, he said, "assist the Court of Appeals in their new onerous task of more closely supervising trial judges in minimizing departures from the Guidelines."[213] He may have been the first judge in the country to do this.[214] If, in the past during sentencings, a young child of a certain age was present, Weinstein would give then "a doll or doggie or stuffed animal to occupy them happily." After the PROTECT Act, Weinstein, at least partially, had a more Machiavellian concern. He put it this way:

> The defendant's words, his facial expressions and body language, the severity of an infirmity, the depth of his family's reliance, or the feebleness of his build cannot be accurately conveyed by a cold record. Many defendants are ill-educated and inarticulate. They do not have the intellectual capacity to articulate, as might a great novelist, what is in their heart. They are, after all, mere people.[215]

---

[211] P.L. 108-21, 117 Stat. 650 (2003), 18 U.S.C. §3742. *See also* 35 *Third Branch*, No. 11 (November 2003); 35 *Third Branch*, No. 10 (October 2003).

[212] *United States v. Khan*, 325 F. Supp. 2d 218, 233 (July 12, 2004). *See also* Peter R. Schlam & Harvey M. Stone, *Sentencing Guidelines, Enhancements, Employment Discrimination*, N.Y.L.J. 3 (Aug. 13, 2004). In this he was far from alone. Among judges in the Eastern District criticizing the Act were Thomas C. Platt and Sterling Johnson, Jr. A number of Southern District judges were critical including Chief Judge Michael B. Mukasey, John S. Martin, Jr., and Shira Scheindlin, Guido Calabresi and Roger J. Miner of the Second Circuit Court of Appeals were also critical.

[213] *In re Sentencing*, 219 F.R.D. 262 (Jan. 30, 2004).

[214] A.P. STATE AND LOCAL WIRE, Jan. 29, 2004.

[215] *In re Sentencing*, 219 F.R.D. 262, 264 (Jan. 30, 2004). *See also* NAT'L L.J. 4 (Feb. 9, 2004).

Meanwhile, the Supreme Court was moving to end the reign of the Guidelines. Four cases between 2000 and 2005 led to their demise.[216] That occurred on December 10, 2007, when the Supreme Court restored the broad sentencing discretion district judges once had by overturning a decision of the Court of Appeals for the Eighth Circuit and accepting the sentence of an able Iowa judge, Robert Pratt.[217] As a result of the decisions, judges were still expected to consult the Guidelines, but the Guidelines were just one factor among others. Trial judges were expected to consider the extent of the departure from the Guidelines and explain the appropriateness of an unusually lenient or harsh sentence.[218] The Courts of Appeals were to presume that sentences within Guideline ranges were reasonable, although such a presumption was not binding. The Courts of Appeals could only overturn "unreasonable sentences."

Weinstein and his fellow district judges had won their two decade long battle. Weinstein had understood a "great threat to humane civil rights is posed by such systems [the Guidelines] when they are crafted without concern for practical consequences or the fates of defendants or their communities."[219] Inflexibly harsh penalties did not work as a deterrent, at least where drugs, guns, sex, and violent crimes were involved.[220] One of the lessons learned from the Guidelines was "the need for modesty about our ability to manipulate and change institutions to better protect the public and improve the lives of criminals."[221] As we have seen, Weinstein believed that the Guidelines were a failure because "they largely banish[ed] humanity from the sentencing process."[222]

Weinstein worried that the Guidelines era was not dead and that traditional deference of courts to other branches might lead to continued guideline sentences. Weinstein urged the use of a jury on sentencing issues of fact and possibly on severity in order to provide a more humane and effective system of justice and as "a reflection of our government's dependence on the ultimate and residual sovereignty of the people."[223]

---

[216] *Apprendi v. New Jersey*, 530 U.S. 466 (2000); *Blakely v. Washington*, 542 U.S. 296 (2004); *United States v. Booker & United States v. Fanfan*, 543 U.S. 220 (2005). After *Booker*, Weinstein was quoted in the *New York Times*: "I'm really elated and I think most judges will be too." New York Times, Jan. 13, 2005, at A29.

[217] *Gall v. United States*, 552 U.S. 38 (2007). *See also* New York Times, Dec. 11, 2007, at A1. In a second decision the same day, the Supreme Court held that the sentencing judge could consider the disparity between the treatment of crack and powder sentences. (Congress had already modestly amended that statute.) *Kimbrough v. United States*, 552 U.S. 85 (2007).

[218] On November 1, 2007, the Sentencing Commission reduced the enormous disparity between sentences for crack and those for powder. New York Times, Dec. 11, 2007.

[219] Wimmer & Weinstein, *supra* note 28, at 16.

[220] Wimmer & Weinstein, *supra* note 28, at 20.

[221] *Id.* at 29.

[222] *Id.* at 42.

[223] *United States v. Khan*, 325 F. Supp. 2d 218, 224, 232 (July 20, 2004).

Even after the Supreme Court decisions of December 2007, Weinstein has continued to fight against arbitrary sentencing.[224] With the Guidelines largely gone, Weinstein turned his attention to the cruelty of mandatory minimum sentences especially in cases involving possession of child pornography. In *Polizzi v. United States*,[225] Weinstein held that, by not informing the jury of the five-year mandatory minimum sentence required on conviction of receipt of child pornography, *he* had committed constitutional error. Weinstein rested on original intent as to the role of the jury. The Court of Appeals vacated Weinstein's reversal of himself and remanded,[226] but the battle to defang at least the child pornography mandatory minimums had just been joined. On May 21, 2010, the *New York Times* made it a front page story.[227]

CONCLUSION

Jack Weinstein was far from alone in battling the Guideline regime, a battle the judges won. In that battle, he was one of the fiercest and most moving voices, pleading the cause on a variety of fronts. He used all his ingenuity for those he was sentencing in order to avoid results he found cruel and harsh. He succeeded often in mitigating the harshness of individual sentences, but also suffered a number of reversals. Through opinions, articles, and speeches, Weinstein attempted to educate his junior colleagues, defense lawyers, Assistant U.S. Attorneys, and members of Congress. In this, as with other aspects of Weinstein's judging, an observer can not but remark on legal creativity, eloquence, immense energy, and willingness to employ his prestige to attempt to achieve a result where the law could show a human face. In this area, unlike some others, judges do have special expertise and authority. Weinstein most assuredly was not afraid to use it.

---

[224] In *United States v. Handy*, 570 F. Supp. 2d 437 (Aug. 4, 2008) during, a seventy-one-page typed opinion, Weinstein held that the Commentary to the Sentencing Guidelines providing for enhanced punishment of a felon in possession of a stolen handgun even if the criminal does not know it is stolen, was "devoid of any mens rea connection," was "irrational, inconsistent with the Constitution and criminal laws of the United States and [was] void."

[225] 549 F. Supp. 2d 308 (Apr. 1, 2008), a 231-page typed opinion (not counting appendices).

[226] *United States v. Polouizzi*, [sic], 564 F.2d 142 (Apr. 24, 2009: *Katz*-Levl-Raggi).

[227] NEW YORK TIMES, May 21, 2010, at A1.

9

Feeling "Like the Man of La Mancha Pursuing Enamored Justice":

Weinstein's Judicial Work, 1997–2007 and Beyond[1]

AT THE AGE of seventy-five, Jack Weinstein began his fourth decade on the bench. His mind remained sharp, his energy level greater than that of those half his age. He did make a few concessions, the major one to give up teaching. That aside, he continued to speak and write as often as before and on a wide range of subjects.[2] He continued day after day to be fascinated with his job. During this period, there were two major sets of class actions and one important group of aggregated cases before him involving light cigarettes, gun injuries, and the drug Zyprexa. During this period, at the age of eighty-two, Weinstein volunteered to decide the entire backlog of *habeas corpus* cases in the Eastern District. Assigned a large chunk of that backlog—five hundred cases—Weinstein terminated them in less than nine months.

During this period, Weinstein handled two trials which attracted a great deal of media interest. Both were related to organized crime. In 1997, Vincent "Chin" Gigante, head of the Genovese family, who had ducked trials for years by feigning to be insane, was tried on homicide, racketeering, and conspiracy charges and convicted of conspiracy to kill two men. Almost a decade later, Weinstein presided over the trial of Louis Eppolito and Steven Caracappa, accused of committing murders for the Mafia while they were New York City police detectives.

Aside from the mass torts cases, Weinstein's most important case was probably that brought over the policy of New York City's Administration for Children's Services

---

[1] Jack B. Weinstein to Chief Judge Edward R. Korman, June 2, 2003, *re* Habeas Corpus Cases.

[2] Weinstein Oral History, at 1529.

(ACS) of removing children from battered mothers simply because they had been battered. In both the ACS case, and cases involving resident aliens who were being deported for committing crimes, Weinstein included norms of international human rights as relevant to his determinations.

Weinstein's scholarly activities continued, apparently without let up. Many of Weinstein's off-the-bench writings and speeches involved mass torts and the handling of scientific evidence in court. There were also telling discussions of what judges should do when confronted by an unjust law, clearly reflecting his continued agony about employing the Federal Sentencing Guidelines.

The characteristics of Weinstein's work in earlier decades were much in evidence, —among them, fecundity of output, scintillating prose, innovativeness, and deep commitment to the concern that the law show a human face. That there were once again reversals by the Court of Appeals in some major cases is no surprise.

The fiftieth anniversary of *Brown v. Board of Education* occurred in 2004, and Weinstein, among the few surviving attorneys who had worked on the cases, spoke on that subject at Yale, Harvard, and Cardozo Law Schools and to the Judicial Conferences of the Second and Ninth Circuits.[3] He continued to be invited to speak at graduations and to give named lectures. Not the least of the professional honors bestowed upon him was a Brooklyn Law School symposium devoted to his contributions to the law, which served as well to commemorate his eightieth birthday.[4] Weinstein not only attended the symposium which included many of his most distinguished admirers and critics, but also participated.

With *both* the Judge and Evelyn Weinstein in good health and celebrating their sixtieth wedding anniversary and beyond, the two continued to travel, including trips to Israel, Sicily, China, and Antarctica. They celebrated their sixtieth anniversary in 2006.

CRIMINAL CASES

The "Oddfather": United States v. Gigante

There were those who wondered whether Weinstein's domination of his courtroom would be shaken during the 1997 trial of Vincent [Vincenzo] "Chin" Gigante, the head of the Genovese Crime Family. Gigante had for three decades eluded prison by faking mental illness. As recently as March 1991, when Gigante was charged with sixty-nine

---

[3] *See, e.g.*, Jack B. Weinstein, *Brown v. Board of Education after Fifty Years*, 26 CARDOZO L. REV. 289 (2004).

[4] *Judge Jack B. Weinstein, Tort Litigation and the Public Good: A Roundtable to Honor one of America's Great Trial Judges on the Occasion of his 80th Birthday*, 12 J.L. & POL. 149 (2003).Weinstein was also selected to receive the New York State Bar Association's Gold Medal Award in 1998, its highest honor, whose recipients had included Justices Brennan, Marshall, Ginsburg, and Powell and Secretary of State John Foster Dulles. BROOK DAILY EAGLE, Jan. 26, 1998.

counts of mail fraud, extortion, and other crimes, psychiatrists had found Gigante mentally incompetent and that criminal case proceeded without him.[5]

Gigante was indicted again in 1993, this time for racketeering, seven mob murders, and conspiring to kill John Gotti and one other mobster. With his reputation for walking around Greenwich Village in pajamas and a bathrobe, defense lawyers presented Gigante to the court as a feeble old man, who watched cartoons on television during the day, claimed to be hearing voices, and insisted that God was his attorney. However, almost three years after the indictment, Mafia turncoat Salvatore "Sammy the Bull" Gravano and acting Lucchese boss, Alphonse D'Arco, testified that Gigante was faking. He was lucid when he was with the mob; the rest of the time he acted "nuts."

In August 1996, Judge Eugene Nickerson found Gigante competent to stand trial.[6] Several months later, however, Weinstein's colleague and old friend recused himself from the case because his wife had Alzheimer's.[7] The case was assigned to Weinstein, but was further delayed when Gigante underwent open heart surgery.[8]

Gigante was the only alleged major New York boss of his generation to have escaped trial and conviction.[9] A boxer as a youth, Gigante became Vito Genovese's chauffeur and "gofer" and worked his way up the mob ladder. By the time he was twenty-five, he had been arrested seven times. At twenty-nine, he tried unsuccessfully to shoot mob leader Frank Costello. As a leader, Gigante seems to have been effective. Under him, the crime family dominated the building trades industry—controlling windows, concrete, and trucking—as well as garbage collection and the convention trades.[10]

Weinstein immediately exerted control over the Gigante proceedings. Gigante came to his arraignment disheveled, unshaven, and mumbling. He shuffled into court where his legs trembled, his hands shook, and his eyes darted wildly. Weinstein ordered him to be clean shaven and presentably dressed and barbered.[11]

Initially, Weinstein cancelled the $1 million bail without a motion from prosecutors and committed Gigante to a hospital for examination, limiting visitors to "only his family members. I mean natural family."[12] After hearing five doctors on the issue of competency and rejecting evidence based on a brain scan, Weinstein said he had not heard anything that would persuade him to overturn Nickerson's ruling that Gigante was competent to stand trial. Weinstein found that when Gigante was "behind closed doors," he was savvy, "[that he] ... demonstrated normal and detailed concerns for those he loved [and] exercised meticulous and detailed control of the day-to-day

---

[5] NEW YORK DAILY NEWS, June 22, 1997, at 26.
[6] *United States v. Gigante*, 1996 WL 497050 (Aug. 28, 1996).
[7] NEW YORK TIME, May 15, 1997, at B2.
[8] NEW YORK POST, December 19, 1997, at 30.
[9] NEWSDAY, June 25, 1997.
[10] *United States v. Gigante*, 982 F. Supp. 140, 145 (Oct. 29, 1997) [hereinafter referred to as Main *Gigante* Opinion].
[11] NEW YORK DAILY NEWS, June 11, 1997, at 26.
[12] NEWSDAY, May 16, 1997, at A30; NEW YORK TIMES, May 16, 1997, at B3.

operations of a huge criminal enterprise."[13] The *New York Post* headlined: "JUDGE SAYS IT'S CRAZY TO BELIEVE CHIN'S MAD."[14] Nevertheless, Gigante was allowed to make bail and he moved into the Upper East Side home of his longtime girl friend.[15]

Weinstein rejected other defense motions for delay[16] and set the trial for June 26, 1997. He ordered that during the trial Gigante could sit in a wheelchair and have his vital signs checked, if necessary, during breaks every fifty minutes. However, so as not to bias the jury, medical personnel were to wear civilian clothes and neither stethoscopes nor life-saving equipment were to be visible. He issued an order forbidding lawyers from talking to the press, but granted a media request to set aside four rows in court for reporters.[17]

On the first day of the trial, Gigante showed up without a tie, unshaven, and wearing a blue windbreaker, baggy pants, and a sports shirt. Weinstein made clear then that he was "not satisfied with the dress of the defendant." The next day Gigante showed up cleanly shaven and neatly dressed.[18] He sat through the trial "mute, interacting with no one, staring off into space,"[19] but Weinstein believed the report from the Federal Corrections Center in North Carolina, where Gigante had been examined, that he was malingering.

As with other Mafia cases, the trial before an anonymous and partially sequestered jury was colorful. The courtroom echoed with names such as "Benny Eggs," "Big Louie," "Fat Tony Salerno," Vincent "Fish" Cafaro, Benny Squint, and "Matty the Horse." Gigante himself had another nickname, "The Robe." Less reverent observers dubbed him the "Oddfather."[20]

Almost three weeks into the trial, Weinstein blasted both sides: the prosecution for presenting witnesses who failed to tie Gigante to any crimes, the defense for cross-examining a witness who had provided no evidence against their client.[21] Weinstein would state that, although evidence relating to Gigante's participation in murders occurring before the mid-1980s was not strong, evidence regarding his later conduct demonstrated beyond a reasonable doubt that he had been the boss of the Genovese Crime Family since 1985 and was guilty of the crimes and predicate acts charged from that year forward. Weinstein stated that the evidence clearly revealed the "great lengths

---

[13] Main *Gigante* Opinion, *supra* note 10, at 152.

[14] New York Post, June 4, 1997, at 6.

[15] New York Times, June 20, 1997.

[16] *See* Main *Gigante* Opinion, *supra* note 10, at 148.

[17] Daily News, June 22, 1997, at 26.

[18] Newsday, June 27, 1997, at 7A; New York Times, June 28, 1997.

[19] Main *Gigante* Opinion, *supra* note 10, at 176–77.

[20] *See* Newsday, June 27, 1997, at 7A; New York Times, July 1, 1997; New York Daily News, July 9, 1997, at 29; New York Daily News, July 13, 1997; New York Post, July 15, 1997.

[21] New York Post, July 15, 1997; Newsday, July 15, 1997. *See also* Main *Gigante* Opinion, *supra* note 10, at 151.

to which defendant went to appear incompetent in order to avoid detection and prosecution."[22]

At the Gigante trial, Weinstein made a ruling that appears to be one of first impression by a federal court in a criminal case. He permitted the use of closed-circuit technology to permit the lawyers in the Brooklyn courtroom to examine a witness at an undisclosed location. The witness, who had been given a new identity through the Witness Protection Program and was terminally ill with cancer,[23] was the only one in three weeks of testimony to offer first-hand information implicating Gigante in any of the murders.[24]

During the Gigante trial, the government presented eighteen witnesses and entered well over two hundred fifty exhibits. The defense rested without putting on a single witness. After three days of jury deliberation, Gigante was acquitted of three of the murders. The jury divided over the other four. Gigante was convicted only of conspiracy to kill John Gotti and one other man. Weinstein ordered Gigante to surrender within twenty-four hours.[25] Two months later, he upheld the convictions, dismissing all the postverdict statute of limitations motions and all competency issues.[26]

On the day of Gigante's sentencing, Weinstein took the bench quickly and said, "Good morning, Mr. Gigante." Taken completely off guard, Gigante blurted, "Good morning, your honor."[27] As Weinstein stated in his main Gigante opinion, the issue of whether Gigante was competent to be sentenced had to be conducted "with scrupulous care."[28] There were seven days of testimony in the sentencing hearing. Rejecting a report from prison doctors, Weinstein ruled that Gigante was competent to be sentenced.[29] He stated that the "defendant has been found to be a malingerer whose claimed mental problems were exaggerated," and who was still feigning insanity in a shrewd attempt to avoid punishment for his crimes.[30]

In his sentencing opinion, Weinstein stated that "this [d]efendant must be sentenced both for what he was and what he is."[31] "Sentencing courts are permitted to take account of age and frailty," Weinstein said.[32] Gigante "is a shadow of his former self . . . an old man finally brought to bay in his declining years after decades of vicious criminal tyranny."[33] Believing that Gigante "has a substantial chance of surviving more than

---

[22] Main *Gigante* Opinion, *supra* note 10, at 152.

[23] N.Y.L.J., July 17, 1997, at 1–2.

[24] NEWSDAY, July 17, 1997, at A26; NEW YORK TIMES, July 18, 1977, at B1. *United States v. Gigante*, 971 F. Supp. 755 (July 21, 1997), *aff'd*, 166 F.3d 75 (Jan. 22, 1999). Main Gigante Opinion, *supra* note 10, *aff'd*, 85 F.3d 83 (May 30, 1996). *See also* 2 U.S.C. ADVANTAGE No. 6 at 1 (September 1997).

[25] NEW YORK TIMES, July 26, 1997, at 1, 25; NEW YORK DAILY NEWS, Sept. 25, 1997.

[26] Main *Gigante* Opinion, *supra* note 10, at 158ff, 168ff. *See also* NEW YORK TIMES, Sept. 25, 1997.

[27] JIMMY BRESLIN, THE GOOD RAT 30 (2008).

[28] Main *Gigante* Opinion, *supra* note 10, at 175.

[29] NEW YORK POST, Feb. 7, 1997, at 6; *see also United States v. Gigante*, 996 F. Supp. 194 (Jan. 5, 1998).

[30] *United States v. Gigante*, 989 F. Supp. 436, 440–41 (Jan. 5, 1998).

[31] *Id.* at 443.

[32] *Id.*

[33] *Id.* at 440.

ten years in prison,"[34] yet aware that to impose the maximum sentence—thirty years—on the sixty-nine-year-old Gigante, would be equivalent to a life sentence, Weinstein sentenced him to twelve years in prison, five years of supervised release, and a fine of $1.25 million.[35] The Assistant U.S. Attorney was satisfied with the decision.[36] The Court of Appeals affirmed.[37]

Five years later, when pleading guilty in April 2003 before Judge I. Leo Glasser to obstruction of justice, Gigante finally admitted his insanity had been a ruse. He died in prison in December 2005 at the age of seventy-seven. He had served a little more than seven years of Weinstein's sentence.[38]

Eppolito and Caracappa

In 2006, Weinstein presided over another mobster trial that attracted worldwide attention—a Racketeer Influenced and Corrupt Organizations Act (RICO) case brought against two ex–New York City detectives, Louis Eppolito and Stephen Caracappa. Eppolito was fifty-seven and Caracappa, sixty-four. The two men were accused of having been on the Mafia payroll while they were policemen. Not only had they turned over evidence to the gangsters, but they also committed at least eight murders at the mob's behest.

The trial attracted great interest. A parade of colorful mobster-witnesses testified: car thieves, drug abusers, pimps, lone sharks, and grave diggers.[39] The dénouement of the trial surprised most, possibly excepting close observers of Weinstein's career.

Eppolito and Caracappa, two decorated police detectives, were accused of having been on the payroll of Lucchese family gangster Anthony "Gaspipe" Casso, between 1986 and 1990. During those years the two policemen murdered at least eight men, seven closely related to the Mafia. One poor young man was "rubbed out" by mistake because he shared the same name as a mobster who had tried to kill Casso.[40] The trial's star witness, the go-between the detectives and Casso, was a wholesale clothier turned drug dealer, Burton Kaplan.[41]

The indictment charged the two men with racketeering, conspiracy, and narcotics trafficking and stated that they had participated in such racketeering acts as murder, attempted murder, kidnapping, tampering with a witness, bribery, and money laundering.

---

[34] *United States v. Gigante*, 989 F. Supp. at 442.

[35] *Id.* at 442–44.

[36] NEW YORK POST, Dec. 19, 1997.

[37] *United States v. Gigante*, 166 F.3d 75 (Jan. 22, 1999: *Walker*-Oakes-Knapp).

[38] Mob Boss Vincent "Chin" Gigante Dies in Prison, http://www.wnbc.com/investigations/5577860/detail.html. Among Weinstein's other published opinions in the *Gigante* case is that giving directions to expert witnesses. *United States v. Gigante*, 925 F. Supp. 967 (May 15, 1996).

[39] NEW YORK TIMES, Apr. 2, 2006.

[40] NEW YORK SUN, Apr. 22–24, 2006, at 3.

[41] For his testimony Kaplan was reward by being released from jail 216 months earlier. JIMMY BRESLIN, THE GOOD RAT 267–70 (2008).

There was a significant statute of limitations issue in the case. Virtually every criminal act had occurred before Eppolito moved to Las Vegas in the early 1990s, a few years after he retired from the police department. Caracappa moved to Las Vegas for personal reasons in 1996. There was but a single post-1990 transaction included in the racketeering indictment: Eppolito and Caracappa were accused of agreeing to help a man purchase an ounce of methamphetamines while they were living in Las Vegas. The entire case would eventually rest on whether that drug deal which occurred in 2004–2005 was part of the original conspiracy or just an "unrelated criminal act committed years later in an entirely different geographic area and milieu and under different circumstances."[42] If that act was "unrelated," the statute of limitations on the federal charges had run.[43]

At a hearing on bail before the trial, Weinstein indicated concern about the statute of limitations problem:

> This connection between the end of the action in New York and what's happening now in Nevada is questionable. The evidence is not strong on the statute of limitations. The charges seem to be relatively stale, and the statute of limitations problem is going to be a serious one.[44]

At another time, Weinstein spoke of the statute of limitations problem as a "ticking time bomb that can be exploded at any time."[45] In October 2005, Weinstein, however, denied a defense motion to quash, deciding to let the case go to trial and see if the government could prove that there had been an ongoing criminal enterprise stretching from the streets of Brooklyn to the casinos of Las Vegas.[46]

Weinstein set high, but manageable bail, $5 million for each man. He thought that while the offenses the defendants were accused of were very serious, the weight of evidence against them was not strong, given the statute of limitations problem. Neither, he thought, was likely to abscond before trial and, due to their ages, they were not likely to be serious threats to anyone.[47] The men were placed under house arrest and required to wear ankle bracelets so their whereabouts would be known.

Weinstein rejected the government's pretrial motion for an anonymous and escorted jury because he felt this might undermine the presumption of innocence and interfere with the defendant's ability to conduct an effective defense.[48] To use such devices in

---

[42] *See United States v. Eppolito and Caracappa*, 436 F. Supp. 2d 532, 569ff (June 30, 2006).

[43] The case had originally been a joint federal and state investigation. The murders could have been successfully prosecuted by the state because there was no state statute of limitations on homicides. However, the state required access to Burton Kaplan, who was a federal prisoner. Ultimately the feds completely took over the case. BROOKLYN DAILY EAGLE, July 5, 2006, at 1.

[44] Breslin, *supra* note 27, at 40.

[45] Michael Daley, *The Law Is Bigger than One Shocking Ruling in Brooklyn*, NEW YORK DAILY NEWS, July 2, 2006.

[46] NEW YORK TIMES, July 1, 2006, at 1.

[47] *United States v. Eppolito*, 2005 WL 1607192 (July 11, 2005).

[48] *United States v. Eppolito*, 2005 WL 220061 (Jan. 30, 2006).

order to prevent extensive publicity would not be successful, Weinstein felt, since there already had been more than one hundred articles published in New York City news-papers commenting on the case.[49] Furthermore, he felt that the use of an anonymous jury would be "demeaning" because juries in the Eastern District are "made up of solid citizens who do not frighten easily."[50]

Weinstein, who then was eighty-four years old, presided over the trial with full control. The lead defense lawyers, Bruce Cutler (for Eppolito) and Edward Hayes (for Caracappa) were perhaps the most publicized trial lawyers in New York.[51] The New York Times reporter covering the trial described Cutler as an "operatic presence, gruff and voluble and built like a tug boat" and Hayes as "lean and adrenal with the quick wit of a bookie and a closetful of alligator shoes."[52] Much less colorful, prosecutors Robert Henoch, Mitra Hormozi, and Daniel E. Wenner were extremely well-prepared and organized. Weinstein ran the trial tightly, reining in the lawyers of both sides.[53]

The trial was packed with members of the media. At least five books were being written about the case. Prospective authors included Eppolito's estranged son, a former Las Vegas call girl, and an investigator with the U.S. Attorney's Office.[54] Literary agents and Hollywood producers also attended.[55]

The trial began on March 13, 2006. At the trial, the milieu of the case, South Brooklyn, was painted in grim colors: a world of gangster bars and auto body shops. where people were forever swapping cars and passing envelopes and owed money to loan sharks and their mothers.[56]

Cutler opened with an attack on the turncoat witnesses for the government. He spoke of a moral cancer that had replaced men of honor in the mob with "reprobates" and "louts." Cutler tended to use polysyllabic words, rhythmic repetition, and strik-ing phrases, calling one witness, for example, "a gnome" Cutler called Kaplan, the pros-ecution's star witness, "a Fagin character," who had led one witness on a "spiral to perdition to hell."[57] Alan Feuer, covering the case for the New York Times, wrote that Cutler "proved himself a master not only of the metaphor," "but also of the pejorative," hurling insults such as "cretin," "bum," "thieving scurvy lowlife," and "sophisticated, unctuous, polished lowlife thief."[58]

[49] Id. at * 2.

[50] Id. at * 3.

[51] NEW YORK TIMES, Apr. 22, 2005, at B1, B6. See GUY LAWSON & WILLIAM OLDHAM, THE BROTHERHOOD (2006) and JIMMY BRESLIN, THE GOOD RAT (2008).

[52] Alan Feuer, Take 1 Trial. Add the Mob. Yield: 4–5 Books and a Film, NEW YORK TIMES, Mar. 7, 2006, at B3.

[53] NEW YORK TIMES, Apr. 2, 2006, at A28.

[54] NEW YORK TIMES, Mar. 11, 2006, at B6.

[55] The author of this book also attended parts of the trial.

[56] NEW YORK TIMES, Aug. 30, 2006.

[57] NEW YORK TIMES, Mar. 14, 2006, n.p.; NEW YORK TIMES, Mar. 28, 2006, at B3; NEW YORK TIMES, Apr. 5, 2006, at B2.

[58] Alan Feuer, Defense Closes with Style in Trial of 2 Ex-Detectives, NEW YORK TIMES, Apr. 5, 2006, at B2; NEW YORK TIMES, June 27, 2004, at B1, B5.

Over twelve days, the government presented thirty-four witnesses. The more important ones were criminals desperate for release under the federal witness protection program. The government also presented forensic reports, crime-scene reports, and secretly recorded audio and visual tapes. On the other hand, the defense rested after thirteen minutes, calling but two witnesses and introducing only eighteen pieces of evidence.[59]

On April 6, after about a day and one-half of deliberation, the jury came back with the verdict "Proved" on all seventy counts involving the two men. Weinstein released the jury, revoked bail, and ordered federal marshals to take the defendants away.

The proceedings, though, were far from over. Eppolito (and later, Caracappa, though only by motion) claimed that his counsel had been "ineffective" and hired other lawyers to make that case. At a hearing on June 24, Eppolito took the stand to press his ineffectiveness claim and by his testimony made clear the wisdom of Cutler's decision *not* to let him take the stand. One of the arguments Eppolito made was that he had been so afraid of Weinstein that he did not raise the issue in court: "I didn't want to tick off the judge," he said. Ironically, as a result of the posture of the litigation at that time, the lead prosecutor, Robert Henoch strongly defended Cutler's performance.[60] Weinstein indicated on June 26 that he would deny the ineffectiveness claim, that Cutler had put on a professional defense and Eppolito's immorality and lack of credibility had led Weinstein to give little (or no) weight to his testimony at the hearing.[61]

At the sentencing hearing Weinstein said that "[t]his is probably the most heinous series of crimes ever tried in this courthouse." On June 5, he gave both men life sentences.[62]While it seemed the two men had reached the end of the line and would receive their comeuppance. a month after the trial, on May 3, Weinstein reminded the attorneys of the statute of limitations problem: "It was not a strong case and the government was warned of that from day one."[63]

On June 30, Weinstein produced a stunning dénouement. In a seventy-seven-page opinion, he threw out almost all of the convictions because the statute of limitations had run. He ruled that the conspiracy had ended when the defendants retired to Las Vegas; rejecting the claim that the 2004–2005 drug deal had been part of the earlier conspiracy.[64] Weinstein granted a new trial to both men on the drug charges and to Eppolito on the charge of money laundering. However, since he had already sentenced the men, if the Court of Appeals reversed Weinstein, their sentences would be reinstated.

---

[59] New York Times, Apr. 1, 2006. B2.

[60] New York Times, June 24, 2006, at B1; Newsday, June 24, 2006, at A3.

[61] New York Times, June 27, 2006, at B1, B5.

[62] *United States v. Eppolito*, 436 F. Supp. 2d 532, 557 (June 30, 2006); Brooklyn Daily Eagle, June 6, 2006, at A1.

[63] N.Y.L.J., May 4, 2006, at 1.

[64] New York Times, July 1, 2006.

The press was stunned by the ruling, but, on the whole, not critical. Many were struck by Weinstein's quotation at the end of his opinion of words spoken by Sir Thomas More in Robert Bolt's play, *A Man for All Seasons:* "I'd give the Devil the benefit of Law for my own safety's sake."[65]

A little over a month later, Weinstein received a "fan letter" from Victoria Gotti, mother of John A. Gotti, stating that "it takes a tremendous amount of courage to do whatever you did" and that Eppolito and Caracappa "need thank their lucky stars for your wisdom and fairness."[66]

More than two years later the Court of Appeals reversed Weinstein and remanded the case to him for reinstatement of the jury's verdicts and imposition of the sentences.[67]

"THE MAN OF LA MANCHA PURSUING ENAMORED JUSTICE":
THE HABEAS 500[68]

One of the most remarkable feats of Weinstein's career accomplished when he was eighty-two, was clearing much of the backlog of *habeas corpus* petitions of all the judges of the Eastern District. Volunteering for the work, Weinstein was assigned five hundred of the nearly eight hundred backlogged cases. With the assistance of a former law clerk, Marc Falkoff, as special master, the cases were resolved in about nine months.

---

[65] *United States v. Eppolito*, 436 F. Supp. 2d 532, 602 (June 30, 2006). *A Man for All Seasons* was published in 1967.

[66] Alan Feuer, *A Gotti Approaches the Bench*, NEW YORK TIMES, Aug. 16, 2008.

[67] *United States v. Eppolito*, 543 F.2d 25 (Sept. 17, 2008: Kearse -Sack-Hall), *cert. denied*, 129 S. Ct. 1027 (2009). Weinstein gave Eppolito a life sentence plus one hundred years and a $4.5 million fine. Caracappa was given a life sentence plus eighty years and a fine of $4.25 million. *United States v. Eppolito*, 05-CR-192 (Mar. 6, 2009).

Between 2004 and 2008 Weinstein, no friend to capital punishment, handled the capital case of Humberto Pepin Taveras, an illegal immigrant from the Dominical Republic. Taveras, who had once been a butcher, but was in drug dealing in the United States, murdered two comrades in dealing, chopped up their bodies and put them in garbage bags. Taveras' past had included nine months in prison for a drug offense, abuse of women, and rape of his girlfriend's daughter, vaginally and orally.

Within four years, Weinstein had authored ten opinions in the *Taveras* case. *See particularly*, *United States v. Taveras*, 2006 U.S. Dist. LEXIS 7408 (Feb. 28, 206). *See also United States v. Taveras*, 436 F. Supp. 2d 493 (June 29/July 5, 2006). *And see United States v. Pepin*, 514 F.3d 193 (Feb. 6, 2008: Sack-Walk-Calab). Taveras is the name on his district court papers. In the Court of Appeals opinion, his name is Humberto Pepin.

In a sermon published in the *New York Law Journal*, Weinstein stated: "I oppose capital punishment for reasons personal and theoretical." Jack B. Weinstein, *Death Penalty: The Toran and Today*, N.Y.L.J., Aug. 23, 2000.A newspaper reported that Weinstein had informed the U.S. Attorney that the chance of getting a jury to deliver a verdict of death in the *Taveras* case was "virtually nil." Joseph Goldstein, *Judges Revolt over the Death Penalty*, N.Y. SUN, Mar. 4, 2008, at1. Taveras was convicted in a week-long trial. As the jury was not unanimous for death during the penalty phase, Weinstein gave Taveras a life sentence.

The reader will remember that early in his career, Weinstein unsuccessfully defended a half-mad capital defendant who wanted to be electrocuted so he could see his paramour in heaven and continue the discussion that he had started with her that had led to him killing her. The defendant got his wish. *See* Chapter 2.

[68] (Copy in possession of the author) Jack B. Weinstein memorandum to Chief Judge Edward R. Korman, June 2, 2003, *re* Cases.

Weinstein and Falkoff also prepared an instruction manual, which could be used in other chambers by law clerks and interns, with boilerplate for forty-eight frequently raised issues in deciding state *habeas* cases as well as forms for the orders. The five hundred cases occupy five feet of shelf space.

Despite Congressional efforts to limit prisoner use of *habeas corpus*, still, by the dawn of the twenty-first century, some 50,000 *habeas* petitions were being filed annually in the federal district courts. Some district judges were giving the petitions given short shrift or putting them on back burners.

We have seen that Weinstein has always taken *habeas* petitions particularly seriously. He reads the record himself and decides the cases without employing either law clerks or magistrate judges.[69] While most district judges have chafed at the number of *habeas* petitions and their frivolousness, Weinstein has not "discourage[d] these habeases because I think it's helpful to these people doing this kind of legal work, figuring out why they were unjustly convicted instead of why they should kill somebody when they get out."[70]

Yet, in 2002 Weinstein had been considering abandoning *habeas* cases completely. There were several reasons. His senior judge colleagues in the Eastern District were refusing to take *habeas*, *pro se*, and Social Security cases. Weinstein also felt that the judges of New York State had absorbed "the revolution in criminal due process" and "the quality of New York's judges is quite high." Indeed, Weinstein believed that "state procedural protections may be greater now than in federal courts," and Congressional and Supreme Court policy had "made this part of our jurisdiction increasingly irrelevant." Weinstein was also concerned that he was being increasingly reversed for deciding *habeas* cases on procedural grounds when a decision on the merits was required. Finally, the rest of the Eastern District judges were handling *habeas* cases through initial reference to a specialized magistrate judge, a very different procedure than that Weinstein had always used. Weinstein wrote to his law clerks asking them, if he should abandon the cases. The law clerks generally said "no."[71]

When Weinstein saw the statistics on the backlog in the district, he decided to undertake the *habeas* project. Some judges had as many as forty cases and were not doing anything with them. Weinstein proposed to Chief Judge Edward Korman that he would be willing to voluntarily take any of the *habeas* cases from his eighteen colleagues because he thought it "unfair to make prisoners wait for years":

> People are entitled to whatever psychic benefit they get from having somebody hear their case and from having a sense that it's not some bureaucratic hole the complaint goes down.[72]

---

[69] Weinstein Oral History, at 1404.

[70] Weinstein Oral History, at 1329.

[71] Jack B. Weinstein to "Dear Clerks," June 18, 2002. *See* Weinstein Oral History, at 1660.

[72] William Glaberson, *Lost Causes Get a Last Hearing*, NEW YORK TIMES, July 30, 2003, at B1, B6. *See also* John Marzulli, *Appeals Put on Fast Track*, NEW YORK DAILY NEWS, May 5, 2003, at A25. *See* Weinstein Oral History, at 1643–44.

Elsewhere he explained:

So much self-hatred and hatred of others seethes in our streets and prisons. At the very least, those unjustly convicted need to be promptly released.[73]

In his memorandum and order providing directions to the special master, Weinstein told Falkoff:

In expediting dispositions, the court should consider the psychic costs that result from delays in disposition for a class of generally poor, uneducated and unrepresented prisoners. Usually they are incarcerated far from their families. Many await the court decision without any explanation for any delays. Except in unusual cases, petitions are entitled to be heard by the court, at least by telephone.[74]

While he was working on the project, Weinstein wrote Korman:

In the wee hours of the night I feel like the Man of La Mancha pursuing enamored Justice—a role endemic to the federal district judge.[75]

Reporting to the court when the project was completed, Weinstein wrote of the tragic stories of many victims of crimes and of many defendants—impoverished in mind, spirit, and ethical values—who robbed, burglarized, assaulted and murdered, committed forced sodomy and preyed on adults and infants alike. "So many lives—both those of the victims and those of the convicts . . . —are unnecessarily destroyed."[76]

Disposing of the cases in about nine months, Weinstein granted the petition in 9, dismissed it in 441, closed 44 administratively, reassigned 3, and consolidated 3 with their earlier petitions.[77] Sixty-eight cases were certified for appeals to the Court of Appeals.[78] He would say later that he had found only one case where he thought

---

[73] Jack B, Weinstein, How Should We React to Hate?, Sermon, Temple Emanuel, Great Neck, Sept. 5, 2003, at 6–7.

[74] In re Habeas Corpus Cases, Memorandum & Order with Directions to Special Master, 03-Misc-66 (May 1, 2003). See also In re Habeas Corpus Cases, 216 F.R.D. 45 (May 1, 2003), (available on Westlaw) See also 216 F.R.D. 52 (May 12, 2003), (available on Westlaw) regarding promptness. See generally, In re Habeas Corpus Cases 298 F. Supp. 303 (Report on 500 Habeas Cases), 03-Misc.-0066 (Dec. 11, 2003) [hereinafter Report on 500 Habeas Cases]. Marc Falkoff had his B.A. degree from the University of Pennsylvania, a M.A. from the University of Michigan, a Ph.D. from Brandeis, and a J.D. from Columbia.

[75] Jack B. Weinstein to Chief Judge Edward R. Korman, June 2, 2003, re Habeas Corpus Cases.

[76] Report on 500 Habeas Cases, supra note 70, at 307.

[77] See Edward Korman, Report for Fiscal Year 2003, U.S. District Court for the Eastern District of New York, n.p.

[78] In a speech to the Great Neck Lawyers Association, Weinstein said that in a dozen of the 500 habeas cases constitutional rights had been violated. Jack B. Weinstein, Convicting the Innocent and Acquitting the Guilty, Speech to Great Neck Lawyers Association, 2007 Speech 18 (Nov. 14, 2006).

there was a clear miscarriage of justice and about a dozen where there were serious constitutional errors warranting a retrial.[79]

It is appropriate to describe at least one case where Weinstein granted the writ. In *Thomas v. Kuhlman*,[80] the petitioner had been convicted fifteen years before of the second-degree murder of a woman with whom he had a romantic relationship. The primary evidence against him was the testimony of a drug addict who said that she had observed Thomas on a fire escape in front of the victim's window. Had the defense counsel visited the crime scene, he would have discovered that was a factual impossibility. On the ground of ineffective assistance of counsel, Weinstein granted the writ for petitioner's release unless steps were taken to retry him within four months. Subsequently, Thomas accepted a plea bargain in satisfaction of his indictment.

Weinstein also granted the writ in cases involving sodomy and attempted rape where the victim was a chronic schizophrenic who experienced hallucinations and was a convicted pedophile, and the prosecution had not turned over "Brady" materials to the defense;[81] where the attorney not only had a serious conflict of interest in representing a defendant, but was also bilking defendant's family of exorbitant sums of money;[82] where there had been a violation of the Confrontation Clause; and where the defense attorney did not call a critical witness[83] or introduce critical impeachment evidence.[84]

After the experience handling the five hundred *habeas* petitions, Weinstein's judgment on New York State's criminal justice system continued to be favorable. The paucity of petitions granted was, he said, "reflective of the high level of criminal justice administered in New York State courts."[85] He said that in dealing with the five hundred cases, he had been:

Impressed by the fact that in many respects New York provides more extensive procedural and substantive protections for criminal suspects and defendants than do the federal trial and appellate courts. The five district attorneys in the Eastern District of New York are, in general, scrupulous in enforcing state and federal limitations on prosecutions. The police in these counties, in general, do not violate constitutional rights in their investigations and properly preserve evidence. The New York trial and appellate judges are energetic, fair and learned,

---

[79] Jack B. Weinstein, *The Role of Judges in a Government Of, By and For the People: Notes for the Fifty-eighth Cardozo Lecture*, 30 CARDOZO L. REV. 1, 88 (2008).

[80] 2003 U.S. Dist. LEXIS 5498 (Apr. 7, 2003).

[81] *Benn v. Greiner*, 402 F.3d 100 (Mar. 9, 2005: *Soto*-WJF-Winner). *Brady v. Maryland*, 373 U.S. 83 (1963), stands for the proposition that suppression by the prosecution of evidence favorable to a defendant who requests it violates due process.

[82] *Eisemann v. Herbert*, 274 F. Supp. 2d 283 (July 31, 2003), *rev'd and remanded*, 401 F.3d 102 (Mar. 11, 2005).

[83] *Batten v. Greiner*, 2003 WL 22284187 (Aug. 26, 2003).

[84] *Harris v. Artuz*, 288 F. Supp. 2d 247 (Aug. 26, 2003).

[85] Report on 500 Habeas Cases, *supra* note 70, at 306.

following the law with the help of excellent charge books and well-drawn statutes. Defense counsel, whether appointed or retained, are usually effective and highly professional in protecting the rights of their clients in the state courts.[86]

Indeed, Weinstein commented to me that "in general, I would say that given the chance of being tried in state or federal court, I'd prefer the state court for crime."[87]

In a final report, Weinstein discussed the adverse effects of unnecessary delays in handling *habeases*. He wrote of problems assembling and duplicating long scattered records and unanswered correspondence from prisoners.[88] Naturally, he made a series of recommendations. The goal for handling *habeas* petitions, Weinstein thought, should be one hundred days from filing to decision. He recommended administrative reforms in chambers, the clerk's office, and New York's counties, which would allow for more expeditious processing.[89] His most important recommendation was that magistrate judges should be permitted to exercise their powers as if they were Article III judges.[90] Half of each Article III judge's allocation of incoming *habeas corpus* cases should—without screening—be diverted to a specific magistrate judge's docket as soon as they arrive. The magistrate judge would then write reports and recommendations on the petitions in the form of proposed judgments. The proposed judgment would then be adopted by the district judge "in almost every case."[91]

Miscellaneous Criminal Cases

Weinstein was greatly concerned over the intense pressure on defendants generally to plead guilty because of lengthy pretrial incarceration. While the number of criminal cases per judge had increased considerably in the 1990s, the average number of criminal jury trials per judge nationally had dropped from nine to five.[92] This in large measure was the result of increased prosecutorial power under the Sentencing Guidelines. Weinstein argued that one of the "seismic modifications" of the criminal law in recent decades was that the defendant might need the freedom bail provides to effectively prepare a defense—not for trial—but rather to strengthen this position for plea

---

[86] *Id.* at 306–07.

[87] Weinstein Oral History, at 1643. *See, e.g., Rodriguez v. Mitchell*, 208 F. Supp. 2d 381 (June 14, 2002). where Weinstein recused himself because the petitioner rejected the help of an assigned counsel. For Weinstein counsel's assistance was essential in complex matters. Of the court's newly adopted method which placed considerable responsibility with a qualified specialist in *habeas* as magistrate, he said that it "seems to work well," results in less strain on the district judge and "may well be more thorough," but it was not his preference. *See also* N.Y.L.J., Aug. 9, 2002, at 3.

[88] Report on 500 Habeas Cases, *supra* note 70, at 312.

[89] *Id.* at 313f.

[90] *Id.* at 316.

[91] *Id.* at 317. On the Habeas Report, *see also* N.Y.L.J., Dec. 11, 2003, at 1, 7.

[92] *United States v. Joyeros*, 204 F. Supp. 2d 412, 427–34 (May 9, 2002).

bargaining. If a court denies a defendant bail, he or she is placed in a weaker bargaining position over the plea.[93] Weinstein thought that the acceptance of guilty pleas required particularly close supervision by the court to make sure they were voluntary.[94]

During this decade, money laundering cases and other cases involving forfeitures came in increasing numbers. *United States v. Speed Joyeros, S.A.*[95] involved money laundering by the defendant, Yardena Hebroni, making use of her jewelry business in Panama. One of Weinstien's serious concerns was the ability of the defendant to prepare her case. The judge assigned to the case before Weinstein had denied bail because of the fear that she would leave the country. After Weinstein was given the case, it bogged down over a large number of unavailable business records. Weinstein ordered the defendant released on bail, but his order was vacated by the Court of Appeals. Given the difficulty Hebroni was having examining documents in prison as well as her apparent physical and emotional deterioration, Weinstein granted bail once again, but was once again reversed.[96]

In Hebroni's case, Weinstein was concerned about both her capacity and her desire to plea. He was also concerned about the possible conflict of interest of her defense counsel. As a result, he ordered a psychiatric evaluation of her and appointed additional defense counsel. Ultimately, though, he accepted the plea. In sentencing her, Weinstein considered three reasons which took the case outside of the "heartland" of cases—the length and rigor of her pretrial detention, the destruction of her livelihood, and the repeated denial of bail, which had prevented her from effectively preparing her defense and from seeing her child. He departed downward two levels and credited Hebroni with good behavior in prison, reducing the time she still had to serve to approximately twenty-seven months, while also fining her $250,000.[97] Further, she had to forfeit $6 million of assets in her company and $600,000 in a U.S. bank.[98]

CIVIL CASES

Battered Wives and Their Children

Nicholson v. Williams was a non–mass tort class action, which it appears will have a substantial national impact. One observer of the case has remarked, "*Nicholson v. Williams* has had wide-ranging positive effects on both the policies and practice of ACS [New York City's Administration for Children's Services] and on New York's

---

[93] *United States v. Speed Joyeros, S.A.*, 204 F. Supp. 2d 412, 426ff (May 9, 2002).

[94] *Id.* at 417–18.

[95] *United States v. Speed Joyeros, S.A.*, 204 F. Supp. 2d 412 (May 9, 2002).

[96] *United States v. Hebroni*, 25 Fed. Appx. 85 (Feb. 8, 2002: Leval-Calab-Stein); 187 F. Supp. 2d 75 (Feb. 12, 2002), *rev'd*, 37 Fed. Appx. 549 (Mar. 13, 2002: Leval-Calab-Katz).

[97] *United States v. Speed Joyeros, S.A.*, 204 F. Supp. 2d 412, 446 (May 9, 2002).

[98] *United States v. Speed Joyeros, S.A.*, 204 F. Supp. 2d at 445–46. On the Hebroni case, see Weinstein Oral History, at 1583–88, 1593–95.

lower courts.[99] Because of its visibility, the result to some degree of the way Weinstein handled it, *Nicholson* is also likely to lead to modification of similar policies in other states.[100]

New York City's Administration for Children's Services (ACS) had a policy that when domestic violence against a mother was found, her children would be taken away and placed in foster care. Shawline Nicholson, a thirty-two-year-old mother of two, who was attending college classes, was badly beaten by her boyfriend one night while her year-old daughter lay in a crib. That night, her children were removed from her apartment. The City put the children into foster care the next day. Five days later, a neglect petition was filed against both Nicholson and the batterer. At the court hearing, Nicholson did not have counsel.[101]

Shawline Nicholson then filed a complaint on behalf of her two children against officers and employees of ACS. In January 2001, the Nicholsons and others moved for class certification. Weinstein broadened the litigation by asking the Juvenile Rights Division of the Legal Aid Society to act as a friend of the court in the case. He broadened it further by requesting that the parties consider *amici* representation for the children as well as for alleged perpetrators who might have an interest in not being separated from the children or their mothers.[102]

By the beginning of 2002, *Nicholson v. Williams* had attracted *amici* from across the country. Among the *amici* participating were the National Network to End Domestic Violence, the Missouri Coalition Against Domestic Violence Against Women, the National Coalition for Child Protection Reform, the Ohio Domestic Violence Network and the Citizens Committee for Children.

With certification of the class pending, Weinstein ordered the parties to be prepared for immediate trial whether or not he had certified the class.[103] His haste was the result of his belief that children and parent-child relationships are particularly vulnerable to delays in repairing rifts. Bonding and experience in learning how to relate during critical growth years may be adversely affected by even relatively short separations.[104]

On July 9, 2001, a trial began to determine whether class certification was appropriate and whether and in what form a preliminary injunction should issue. After two

---

[99] *See also* Kathleen A. Copps, The Good, The Bad and the Future of Nicholson v. Scoppetta: An Analysis of the Effects and Suggestions for Future Improvements" 72 ALB. L. REV. 497. 510 (2009 [hereinafter Copps, The Future of Nicholson v. Scoppetta]).

[100] *Id. See also* Weinstein Oral History, at 1554; NEW YORK TIMES, Dec. 18, 2004, at B1, B6; Interview with Prof. Myra Berman, May 2009. *See also* NEW YORK TIMES, Feb. 5, 2002, at B3.

[101] *Nicholson v. Williams*, 203 F. Supp. 2d 153, 168–69 (Mar. 18, 2002); N.Y.L.J., Mar. 5, 2002, at 1, 4.

[102] He noted in an opinion that an advertisement had been placed in the *New York Law Journal* stating that the court was prepared to recognize a subclass of alleged batterers who might have an interest in not being separated from the children or their mothers. However, no representative of alleged batterers came forward. *Nicholson v. Williams*, 202 F.R.D. 377 (Aug. 16, 2001). *See also Nicholson v. Williams*, 2001 NB (Mar. 20, 2001). *See* N.Y.L.J., Mar. 22, 2001.

[103] *Nicholson v. Williams*, 2001 NB (June 14, 2001).

[104] *In re Shawline Nicholson et al.*, cv 00-2220, 2001 NB (Oct. 25, 2001), at 5.

months of evidentiary hearings, Weinstein certified a class of mothers who claimed that they had been physically abused by the men in their lives, that their children have been removed from their custody and kept separated from them by ACS on the ground that they had been subject to domestic violence by those men and the federal constitutional rights of both the mothers and the children had been violated in the process.[105] The evidence indicated that the practice resulted from benign indifference, bureaucratic inefficiency, and outmoded institutional biases.[106]

On August 13, in the middle of the trial with ACS Commissioner Nicholas Scoppetta on the witness stand, Weinstein stated that, while he believed that improper removals had occurred, he would delay issuing an order for six months. Weinstein may have intended to remedy an injustice without placing the "heavy hand of federal oversight" over ACS.[107] Scoppetta called the ruling, "an absolutely wonderful result."[108] The next day, Scoppetta circulated within his agency a memorandum directing a change in the standard language used in Family Court applications to remove children. That language had, in effect, accused the battered victims of committing domestic violence.[109]

In March 2003, Weinstein issued a 188-page typed opinion explaining why he had granted a preliminary injunction to prevent ACS from using its policy.[110] In that opinion, Weinstein wrote that the "evidence reveals widespread and unnecessary cruelty by agencies of the City of New York toward mothers abused by their consorts."[111] One section of the opinion presented modern perspectives on domestic violence and child welfare, as well as on the effects of domestic violence and removal on the children.[112]

Weinstein stated that the "limiting factor on what a battered mother does to protect herself or her children from the batterer is usually a lack of viable options, not a lack of desire."[113] Accusing battered mothers of "neglect" aggravates the problem.[114] The "'one-size-fits-all'" approach is especially inappropriate in cases of domestic violence. Separating battered mothers from their children ought to be the alternative of last resort. Indeed, removing the child from the mother might be more damaging to the child than doing nothing at all and could aggravate the occurrence of domestic violence by discouraging women from reporting it at early stages.[115]

Most of ACS's policies were, Weinstein wrote, driven by fear of an untoward incident of child abuse that would result in the criticism of the agency and some of

---

[105] *Nicholson v. Williams*, 205 F.R.D. 92 (Aug. 16, 2001).

[106] NEW YORK TIMES, Mar. 15, 2002, at B3.

[107] N.Y.L.J., Aug. 20, 2001. *See also* N.Y.L.J., June 20, 2001, at 1.

[108] NEW YORK TIMES, Aug. 18, 2001, at B3.

[109] N.Y.L.J., Aug. 20, 2001, at 1, 2.

[110] *Nicholson v. Williams*, 203 F. Supp. 2d 153, 168–92 (Mar. 18, 2002).

[111] *Id.* at 163.

[112] *Id.* at 193–205.

[113] *Id.* at 200.

[114] *Id.* at 201.

[115] *Id.* at 202–04.

its employees.[116] There was an agency-wide practice of removing children from their mother without evidence of a mother's neglect and without seeking prior judicial approval.[117] There was no indication that ACS effectively and systematically pursued removal of the abuser before seeking removal of the battered victim's child.[118] The practice and policies of ACS often led to the abuser being left unaccountable because it was administratively easier to punish the mother by separating her from her children.[119] Weinstein said that "many more separations of abused mothers and their children are made by ACS than are necessary for protection of the children."[120] Indeed, "neither the existing ACS written policies nor proposed changes proffered to the court included a clear set of standards and guidelines" to aid a caseworker in determining when the danger from domestic violence in a household reaches the point of creating immediate danger.[121] Further, there were "long and unnecessary delays in returning children to the mother, which often was disastrous to the physical and emotional well-being of the children."[122]

Weinstein held that the constitutional right of families against state interference in their affairs was buttressed by a number of U.S. Supreme Court decisions.[123] Even a temporary separation triggers constitutional protections.[124] The rights of family and parental authority are fundamental liberty interests, a core value of American society and constitutional law, protected by both procedural and substantive due process and possibly also by the Fourth, Ninth, and Thirteenth Amendments. Weinstein also looked to international human rights authority and suggested that the rights were also protected by international law, the Universal Declaration of Human Rights, the International Covenant on Civil and Political Rights, and the Convention on the Rights of the Child.[125]

Nicholson was appealed. A divided U.S. Court of Appeals certified three questions of law to the New York Court of Appeals,[126] which the latter court only partially answered. The Court of Appeals held that simply showing that a child was exposed to domestic violence is insufficient to show neglect; "plainly more is required." The state court, thus, rejected a presumption of child neglect and removal from the home whenever a

---

[116] *Id.* at 205.

[117] *Id.* at 215.

[118] *Id.* at 211.

[119] *Id.* at 210.

[120] *Id.* at 212–13.

[121] *Id.* at 220. The New York statute defined a "neglected child" was a child less than eighteen years old "whose physical, mental or emotional condition has been impaired or is in imminent danger of being impaired as a result of the failure of his parent . . . to exercise a minimum degree of care." N.Y. Family Court Act § 1012 (f).

[122] *Nicholson v. Williams*, 203 F. Supp. 2d 153, 216 (Mar. 18, 2002).

[123] *Id.* at 233ff.

[124] *Id.* at 235.

[125] *Id.* at 233–35.

[126] *Nicholson v. Scoppetta*, 344 F.3d 154 (Dec. 16, 2003: *Katz-Oakes-Walk*).

parent allows her child to witness domestic abuse of that parent.[127] Two days after that decision, the suit was settled.[128] New York City essentially conceded that children could not be placed in foster care just because their mothers had been abused.[129]

Nicholson would become an influential case because Weinstein made use of experts from all over the country, because he insisted that persons involved the administration of the policy come to court, and because of his extensive opinion laying out the problems.[130] As a result of the litigation, the City completely reorganized the handling of this class of cases.[131]

Education

Once again there were New York City school cases before Weinstein. Some of the schools he dealt with decades before reappeared in litigation.

More than thirty years after Weinstein enjoined the mass dismissal of African-American students with unsatisfactory academic records from Franklin K. Lane High School because of widespread disciplinary problems at the overcrowded school,[132] it happened again. This time the so-called "push-outs" involved Franklin K. Lane and two other high schools. In 2003, a class action was brought against Franklin Lane[133] and

---

[127] *Nicholson v. Scoppetta*, 3 N.Y. 3d 357 (2004). *See* Roy L. Reardon & Mary Elizabeth McGarry, *New York Court of Appeals Round Up: Child Witnessing Domestic Violence Not by Child Neglect*, N.Y.L.J., Dec. 15, 2004, at 3. Weinstein also held that unwed fathers were entitled to due process rights as well. *Nicholson v. Williams*, 203 F. Supp. 2d 153, 240–41 (Mar. 18, 2002).

[128] Stipulations and order of settlement, *Nicholas v. Williams*, No. 00-cv-5155 (Dec. 17, 2004).

[129] NEW YORK TIMES, Dec. 18, 2004, at B1, B6.

[130] Weinstein Oral History, at 1554–55.

[131] There was a second important issue in the *Nicholson* case—the pay of New York States 18B attorneys who were supposed to represent the mothers in such proceedings—$40/hour for work in court; $25/hour for out-of-court work with a cap on compensation for any single case of $800. The pay was so low, that mothers usually could not secure an attorney. Weinstein signaled that he might order a rise in such pay and granted *amicus* status to the New York County Lawyers Association. In January 2002, Weinstein ordered that in proceedings in which children could be taken from their mothers, that appointed counsel should be paid $90/hour for work in and out of court. *Nicholson v. Williams*, 203 F. Supp. 2d 153, 260 (Mar. 18, 2002). In another case, Weinstein held that the subclass A mothers in the class action were entitled by virtue of the Due Process Clause of the U.S. Constitution to effective counsel as well as a statutory right to counsel. *Nicholson v. Williams*, 203 F. Supp. 153, 260 (Mar. 18, 2003). *See also* N.Y.L.J., Nov. 26, 2001. In *Nicholson v. Scoppetta*, 116 Fed. Appx. 313 (Nov. 29, 2004: Katz-Walk-Oakes), the Court of Appeals vacated the hourly rate for 18B attorneys because the New York Legislature had increased the rate to $75/hour for representation in felony cases, family court, and some others. There was a cap of $4,400. However, the legislature did not make the money available until 2005. Jack B. Weinstein, *The Role of Judges in a Government Of, By and For the People: Notes for the Fifty-Eighth Cardozo Lecture* 1, 54.

[132] *Knight v. Board of Ed.*, 48 F.R.D. 108 (Apr. 21, 1969); 48 F.R.D. 115 (Apr. 30, 1969). *See* Chapter 4.

[133] *Ruiz v. Pedota*, 2004 U.S. Dist. LEXIS 50 (Jan. 6, 2004).

lawsuits were brought against Martin Luther King, Jr.[134] and Bushwick High Schools.[135] The students were predominantly African-American and Hispanic.

Weinstein took these cases with utmost seriousness as he had thirty-five years before. This time he appointed a former law clerk, Josh Hill, an African-American graduate of Yale Law School, as special master and advised him "to work very gingerly; not to say too much, to listen, to bear in mind that the school system was short of funds . . ." and to be aware that "any rigid decree sweeping back all the kids would break this school down and might break down other schools."[136] The cases settled. The litigation was resolved without unnecessary conflict and costs, without an admission of fault or liability, and with the rights of the students protected. Weinstein thought Hill did "a wonderful job."[137]

The most important of the education cases Weinstein handled in his early years on the bench returned for a brief coda. The days of the decree in *Hart v. Community School Board*,[138] the Mark Twain school case, were numbered after the 2007 Supreme Court decision in a Seattle School case.[139] The Supreme Court had held that judicial supervision of local schools as a result of past discrimination was not intended to operate in perpetuity. District courts were to look for good faith compliance with the decree by the school board and also see whether the vestiges of past discrimination had been eliminated to the extent practicable. Employing the narrowest ground taken by the Supreme Court majority, Weinstein held that the school board had complied in good faith with *Hart* over a long period of time. He held that the City was entitled to a certificate of closure, writing: "The defendants have complied with the 1974 order. Mark Twain has been desegregated. The court has no jurisdiction. The case is closed."[140] That, however, did not prevent Weinstein from visiting the school and suggesting in the opinion dissolving the decree that the rusted metal gates at the entrance of the school should be painted and the magnet school's sign should be restored and freshened up.[141]

First Amendment Law

Probably the most interesting First Amendment case Weinstein decided during this period was one that appeared to be of first impression and raised an interesting

---

[134] *SG v. New York City Bd. of Ed.*, 03-CV-5152. *See Rv. v. New York City Bd. of Ed.*, 321 Supp. 2d (2004).

[135] *Rv. v. New York City Dep't of Ed.*, 321 F. Supp. 2d 538 (June 17, 2004). NEW YORK TIMES, Dec. 24, 2003.

[136] Weinstein Oral History, at 1598.

[137] *Id.* at 1737.

[138] 383 F. Supp. 699 (Jan. 28, 1974).

[139] *Parents Involved in Cmty Sch. v. Seattle Sch. Dis. No. 1*, 551 U.S. 701 (2007).

[140] *Hart v. Community Sch. Bd.*, 536 F. Supp. 2d 274 (Feb. 28, 2008).

[141] *Id.* at 284.

separation of powers problem in a state context. In *Gordon v. Griffith*,[142] a New York State assemblyman had fired a legislative aide after she spoke out publicly (and, according to the assemblyman, inappropriately) on a controversial matter. The aide then sued for violation of her civil rights. Weinstein's opinion, clearly drawing upon his experiences with the New York State legislature more than forty years before, combined an essay on republican governance with an analysis of two strands of First Amendment law.[143]

Weinstein began the opinion by staking out a judicially modest position. He thought that, because of the requirements of republican government and the principle of separation of powers, judges with lifetime tenure should exercise restraint in overseeing the staffing decisions of legislators who periodically stand for office.

The defendant, Edward Griffith, had hired the plaintiff, Diane Gordon, as his community relations director. Technically a salaried employee of the State, Gordon properly engaged in partisan activity on Griffith's behalf. In her own right, she was a delegate from the same assembly district to the State Democratic Party.

The controversy that led to Gordon's firing occurred in the spring of 1999 when the New York City's Police Department was under intense scrutiny because of several incidents in which the police viciously beat Abner Louima, a Haitian, while he was in custody, and killed Amadou Diallo an unarmed West-African immigrant in a hale of bullets.[144] When the incidents were at the forefront of public attention, Gordon took part in a protest and press conference against "police brutality." The next day Griffith summoned her to his office, criticized her for going against his "friends" at the 75th precinct and fired her.

Weinstein upheld the firing, granting the motion to dismiss the complaint. He believed that public employees were entitled to a substantial measure of "asylum" from dismissal for speech, but that had to be weighed against the relationship between officials elected to core democratic institutions of the government and their constituents. To extend free speech tenure to legislative aides would "run headlong into the State's authority to prescribe the operation of its legislative body" and "jeopardize the vital and dynamic relationship that must exist between elected legislators and their constituents."[145] Extending full First Amendment protection to the speech of legislative aides might well impede "legislators' authority to base staffing decisions on appropriate political considerations."[146] Furthermore, since the close affiliation of aides and the legislators they serve generates a strong public perception of association between

---

[142] 88 F. Supp. 2d 38 (Mar. 16, 2000).

[143] The two strands were (1) that involving a public employer's ability to take an adverse employment action against a public employee for speaking out on matters of public concern and (2) that of a public employer's ability to terminate a public employee based on political affiliation—patronage dismissals.

[144] Abner Louima was viciously beaten and sodomized by police officers while in custody. Amadou Dialo had suffered multiple bullet wounds in a police shooting.

[145] *Gordon v. Griffith*, 88 F. Supp. 2d 38, 44 (Mar. 16, 2000).

[146] *Id.* at 51.

the two and elected officials often rely on their aides as surrogates speaking on their behalf, the public assumes that their views are identical. If legislators are mistakenly held accountable for the speech of their political staffers, the channels of communication between legislators and constituents can be distorted. "On balance," Weinstein thought that "the negligible chilling effect on free speech which may result by permitting legislators to dismiss political aides for their public comments is substantially outweighed by potential benefits in the effective operation of the state legislators and in the representative process generally."[147]

By terminating Gordon, Griffith was acting to protect his relationship with local police officers and with his electorate generally. In firing her, he publicly disassociated himself from her comments in an attempt to undo the political damage he believed—whether correctly or not—she had caused.[148]

The Treatment of Immigrants

Weinstein began to use international human rights norms as authority[149] in a series of cases resulting from two laws enacted in 1996: the Anti-Terrorism and Effective Death Penalty Act of April 24, 1996 (AEDPA)[150] and the Illegal Immigration Reform and Immigrant Responsibility Act of September 30, 1996 (IIRIRA).[151] Weinstein was among the first federal judges to employ these norms in interpreting and deciding upon the constitutionality of statutes.

Prior to AEDPA, permanent legal residents of the United States, if convicted of certain crimes, were entitled to what was known as a fairness hearing (so long as they had seven years of permanent residence in the United States by the time of the hearing) where they could argue that they should not be deported because of humanitarian factors such as family ties, evidence of hardship, or of service to the community.

AEDPA provided that legal permanent residents convicted of certain enumerated crimes (including aggravated felonies, controlled substance violations, a firearms offense, and two or more crimes of moral turpitude) were barred from seeking such a discretionary waiver of deportation based on humanitarian conditions and equity. That had been provided for in Section 212(c) of the Immigration and Naturalization Act of 1952,[152]

The Attorney General was interpreting section 440(d) of AEDPA[153] to apply retroactively, thus denying legal permanent residents convicted of certain crimes *before* review of a final order of deportation.[154]

---

[147] *Id.* at 52.

[148] *Id.* at 58.

[149] *See also* the discussion of *Nicholson v. Williams in this chapter*, p. 298.

[150] P.L. 104-132, 110 Stat. 1214 (1996).

[151] P.L. 104-208, 110 Stat. 3009 (1996).

[152] 8 U.S.C. §1182 (c).

[153] 110 Stat. 1277, 8 U.S.C. 1182.

[154] Provided for in 28 U.S.C. §2241.

In a trilogy of cases involving the retroactive application of AEDPA, Weinstein construed the statutes to, as he put it, "give as much due process as I could."[155] The first decision, *Mojica v. Reno* dealt with the retroactive effect of AEDPA on an alien who had committed crimes and been convicted prior to enactment of AEDPA, but who had a waiver hearing pending at the time of the enactment. Guillermo Mojica, a legal permanent resident of the United States since 1992, had pled guilty to conspiracy to distribute cocaine and served a year in prison. The Immigration and Naturalization Service (INS) determined that he could not be excluded from the United States when he returned from travel abroad, but that he could be deported.[156] After Mojica brought suit, Weinstein held that the Department of Justice could not retroactively employ AEDPA to summarily deport aliens with criminal records awaiting hearings.

In the 103-page *Mojica* opinion, Weinstein discussed the history of immigration in the United States, the nation's human rights obligations the role of *habeas corpus* and the scope of *habeas* review. The opinion also covered the presumption against retroactivity, judicial review of administrative action, venue and the protections of legal permanent residents against arbitrary deportation.

First, Weinstein had to demonstrate that, in spite of the fact that AEDPA placed jurisdiction of judicial review of final orders of deportation in the Court of Appeals, the district court retained *habeas corpus* jurisdiction under its general *habeas corpus* powers.[157] AEDPA and IIRIRA, he held, had neither repealed nor narrowed the scope of the *habeas* powers of a district judge. There was no indication that Congress intended to take the dramatic—and arguably unconstitutional—step of repealing the *habeas* statute with roots traceable to our nation's beginnings. Congress, Weinstein held, had just intended to speed up the process of deportation by restricting judicial review of orders of deportation. Further, repeal of *habeas* jurisdiction was barred by the rule against repeals by implication.[158]

At a time when most federal courts were holding that the two immigration statutes were repealing or amending the power of district courts and the rights of lawful permanent residents, *Mojica v. Reno* stood alone in holding that the *habeas* power of 28 U.S.C. §2241 remained unaffected by enactment of the 1996 immigration laws.[159]

Weinstein then held that Section 440(d) of AEDPA did not retroactively eliminate the right of the petitioner to a fairness hearing, pointing to the common law presumption against retroactivity, "the default rule underlying all judicial interpretation of

---

[155] Interview of Jack B. Weinstein by Jeffrey B. Morris, n.d.

[156] 970 F. Supp. 130 (July 11, 1997), *aff'd in part and dismissed in part, question certified sub nom, Henderson v. INS*, 157 F.3d 106 (Sept. 18, 1998), *cert. denied sub nom, Navas v. Reno*, 119 S. Ct. 1141 (1999). *See* NEW YORK DAILY NEWS, June 25, 1997.

[157] *Mojica v. Reno*, 970 F. Supp. at 157.

[158] *Id*. at 157, 159–60.

[159] Colleen Caden, Mojica v. Reno: *Upholding District courts' Statutory Habeas Power under the Immigration Laws of 1996*, J. L. & POL. 16, 9 173–75, 207 (1999).

statutes" as well as the constitutional aversion to retroactivity.[160] In the absence of explicit language, because of the default rule, the statute could be read only to deprive one of rights prospectively because the rule of statutory construction required an interpretation that favored the alien.[161]

In 2001, the Supreme Court essentially took Weinstein's position by holding that an alien whose conviction predated the 1996 laws was entitled to a Section 212(c) hearing, if the law would have permitted it at the time of conviction.[162]

In *Mojica*, besides employing statutory construction, constitutional interpretation and looking to the common law, Weinstein also drew strength from various international human rights conventions, among them the Universal Declaration of Human Rights and the 1969 American Convention on Human Rights and Fundamental Freedom.[163] These, he asserted, protected the rights of the alien to be treated fairly and the right of the alien's family legally within the country not to suffer unduly because of expulsion.[164] Weinstein stated that to ensure that U.S. law does not conflict with international law, an act of Congress should never be construed to violate the law of nations, if any other possible construction remains.[165]

The footprints of Weinstein's values are all over *Mojica*, including his discussion of the disturbing problem of retroactivity where the result is banishment:

Retroactive application would create a situation in which people who have lived in the community, have established themselves as valuable members of society and who are needed to support their families, are summarily deported without regard to the present and future interests of their families or the community at large.[166]

One is reminded of the history of Weinstein's family where a large number of his relatives were killed in the Holocaust while others survived by being smuggled into the United States. He wrote:

Ours is a nation of immigrants and their descendants . . . this country has grown and prospered in a climate of constant refreshment by the introduction into our midst of adventurous spirits willing to leave the security and predictability of what they knew in their lands and rulers they adjured for the hope of full equality of rights and opportunities within our borders . . . Our treatment of aliens is rooted deeply in the fertile soil of constitutional and statutory design.[167]

---

[160] *Mojica*, 970 F. Supp. at 154–644, 168, 169, 179.
[161] *Id.* at 154, 180.
[162] *United States v. St. Cyr*, 533 U.S. 289 (2001).
[163] *Mojica*, 970 F. Supp. at 146–52.
[164] *Id.* at 148.
[165] *Id.* at 152.
[166] *Id.* at 170.
[167] *Id.* at 143.

Mojica had held that Congress had not designed Section 440(d) for persons whose deportation proceedings were pending at the time AEDPA was signed into law. In *Pottinger v. Reno*,[168] a case of first impression, Weinstein held that AEDPA did not apply to *pre-enactment criminal conduct and conviction*, where deportation proceedings were brought *after* the 1996 laws became effective. In his opinion, Weinstein employed standard statutory interpretation as "further informed by constitutional and international human rights principals."[169] The Court of Appeals affirmed in a summary order.[170]

Maria v. McCelroy[171] involved a person who had pled to attempted armed robbery and had been sentenced to two to four years in prison *before enactment* of the two 1999 laws. After his guilty plea, IIRIRA was enacted, which lowered the sentence necessary for that crime to be considered an "aggravated felony" from five years to one year. Maria, thus, was now an "aggravated felon," which was not the case when he committed the crime or when he had been sentenced.

Weinstein argued that Section 440(d) and the new permanent aggravated felony law which replaced it should be interpreted to avoid offending due process principles. The reasons he mustered to hold that the statute did not apply to Maria included: (1) avoidance of constitutional conflicts with other branches;[172] (2) the ambiguity of the statute;[173] (3) the rule of lenity;[174] and because (4) "an act of Congress should be construed in accordance with international law where it is possible to do so without distorting the statute."[175] On appeal, the parties stipulated that Mojica was entitled to a hearing. This result is found in *Pottinger v. Reno*, a Court of Appeals affirmance of another Weinstein case.[176]

Beharry v. Reno,[177] was decided several years after the trio of cases just discussed, but only a few months after 9/11. In *Beharry*, Weinstein read constitutional and international law to require a hearing in a deportation case. Don Beharry was a twenty-six-year-old man born in Trinidad, who had lived most of his life in Westchester County, just north of New York City. Beharry, a legal permanent resident who had not applied for citizenship, was convicted of robbery in the second degree—an aggravated felony—and was apparently not entitled to a hearing. As most of Beharry's family lived in the United States, Weinstein saw in the case a violation of the fundamental right of familial integrity. The nub of his ruling was that an immigrant cannot be deported

---

[168] 51 F. Supp. 2d 349 (Aug. 2, 1999).

[169] *Id.* at 352, 360–62. *See also* N.Y.L.J., Aug. 3, 1999, at 1, 6.

[170] *Pottinger v. Reno*, 2000 U.S. App. LEXIS 33521 (Dec. 18, 2000: Card-Wint-Pool).

[171] 68 F. Supp. 2d 206 (Aug. 27/Oct. 7, 1999).

[172] *Id.* at 230. *See also id.* at 224, 231.

[173] *Id.* at 228ff.

[174] *Id.* at 230.

[175] *Id.* at 231–34.

[176] Pottinger v. Reno, 2000 U.S. App. LEXIS 33521, at * 6 (Dec. 18, 2000) Weinstein's *Pottinger* opinion can be found in *Pottinger v. Reno*, 51 F. Supp. 2d 349 (July 30, 1999).

[177] 183 F. Supp. 2d 584 (Jan. 22, 2002).

because he is a felon unless officials first consider the impact of a child left behind. Weinstein directed INS to hold a hearing to consider the effect deportation might have on Beharry's daughter.[178]

In *Beharry*, Weinstein pulled together four different lines of reasoning for the hearing in *Beharry*: the international guarantee against arbitrary interference with one's family, the due process right to family integrity, "the best interests of the child," and the right under international law for an alien to be allowed to submit reasons against expulsion. Thus, in *Beharry*, Weinstein wove immigration statutes "into the seamless web of our national and international law."[179] Immigration law, like admiralty, is founded on international law and, therefore, Congress's powers might be limited by changing international law norms, even though Congress does have the power to override the provisions of customary international law. However, courts should "interpret legislation in harmony with international law and norms whenever possible," Weinstein wrote.[180] In this particular case, Weinstein held that Congress had not paid heed to the Convention on the Rights of the Child which, in spite of Congress's failure to ratify, was customary international law.[181] The American statute was incompatible with international law because of its "Draconian punishment of aliens."[182] Summary deportation of Beharry without allowing him to present the reasons why he should not be deported violated the International Covenant of the Rights of the Child's guarantee against unreasonable separation of families and the provision that aliens should be allowed to submit the reasons against their expulsion. The statute, Weinstein stated, "should be interpreted in a way not inconsistent with international law to permit a compassionate hearing." That would also remedy possible incompatibility with the Universal Declaration of Human Rights. Weinstein felt that the United States "as a moral leader of the world" should construe its statutory programs to make them compatible with international protective norms.[183] The Court of Appeals overturned Weinstein's ruling in *Beharry*, stating that he had not exhausted his administrative remedies.[184] On the whole, though, Weinstein emerged well from appellate review of the deportation decisions.

---

[178] New York Times, Feb. 11, 2002, at B1, B2; New York Times, Feb. 12, 2002.

[179] *Beharry v. Reno*, 183 F. Supp. 2d 584, 591 (Jan. 22, 2002), *rev'd sub nom, Beharry v. Ashcroft*, 329 F.3d 51 (July 24, 2003).

[180] *Id.* at 598.

[181] *Id.* at 600.

[182] *See, e.g., id.* at 602.

[183] *Id.* at 601. *See also* Jack B. Weinstein, Cardozo Graduation Address, Cardozo Law School, New York City, June 7, 2002, at 5–7 (copy in possession of the author).

[184] *Beharry v. Ashcroft*, 329 F.3d 51 (July 23, 2003: Soto-Caleb-Jacobs).

By the REAL ID Act of May 11, 2005, P.L. 109-13, 111 Stat. 231, 311, Congress mandated that district courts transfer pending *habeas corpus* petitions challenging orders of removal to the Court of Appeals. Once again, Weinstein attempted to carve out plenty of room for *habeas* challenges in other areas of immigration. *See Maiwand v. Ashcroft*, 2005 WL 2340466 (Sept. 26, 2006). *See also* Weinstein Oral History, at 1453.

A Miscellany of Civil Cases

Several cases, though not earthshaking, deserve mention in order to illuminate the breadth of the dockets of district courts and, with the last three, to offer a window on aspects of Weinstein's judging in less-charged cases.

Although liberal in most ways, Weinstein is no enthusiast about employment discrimination claims, because of their ambiguity and subjectivity and the difficulty of distinguishing between racial or ethnic prejudice and office politics, difficult bosses, and "the kinds of frustrations that often arise when strangers are forced closely on a daily basis. This can be true whether the claims are sexual harassment, hostile work environment, disparate treatment or retaliation." On the other hand, he has also cautioned against the "robust" use of summary judgment in these cases.[185]

However, Weinstein rendered the first reported decision in which it was held that an employee, who though herself never discriminated against on the basis of sex, had standing to bring a claim that her rights had been violated by the sexual harassment of other women in her shop, which she alleged had caused her emotional distress.[186] The Court of Appeals reversed.[187]

A dispute between Verizon and Yellow Book (the *Yellow Book* case) led to a suit over false and misleading advertising with antitrust overtones. Yellow Book had been insinuating in its advertising that more people were using Yellow Book than the "yellow pages." The suit required extensive discovery and testimonial evidence. Appointing Ken Feinberg to help settle the suit, Weinstein also wrote a tentative opinion which facilitated the settlement, making it clear that he was prepared to find against Yellow Book and give the case to a jury to determine damages (which he suggested could have been substantial). He had no intention of issuing that opinion.[188]

The settlement agreement provided for a new method to stabilize the industry: an independent auditor to determine comparative and actual usage figures for potential advertisers so each company could provide to advertisers an accurate percentage of people using their books. Weinstein settled the case, withdrew his opinion, and, in effect, encouraged everybody to go into the new mode. In his findings of fact and law, memorandum, order, and final judgment, Weinstein stated:

> They have thus turned this private dispute into a socially useful accord that will permit prospective advertisers in, and users of, yellow page directories to determine the value of these important merchandising tools.[189]

---

[185] *Gallagher v. Delaney*, 139 F.3d 338, 342 (Mar. 19, 1998: *JBW*-Kearse-Walker), *c.f.* Shira A. Scheindlin & John Elofson, *Judges, Juries and Sexual Harassment*, 17 YALE L. & POL. REV. 813 (1999).

[186] *Leibovitz v. New York City Transit Auth.*, 4 F. Supp. 2d 144 (May 5, 1998). *See* Christopher M. O'Connor, *Stop Harassing Her or We'll Both Sue: Bystander Injury Sexual Harassment*, 50 CASE-WESTERN RESERVE L.R. 501, 517 (1999).

[187] *Leibovitz v. New York City Transit Auth.*, 252 F.3d 179 (June 6, 2001: *Jacobs*-McLaughlin-Sack).

[188] Weinstein Oral History, at 1663–64.

[189] *Verizon Directories Corp. v. Yellow Book U.S.A., Inc.*, 338 F. Supp. 2d 422, 423 (Oct. 7, 2004). On the litigation, *see* N.Y.L.J., July 27, 2004, at 1, 3. *See also* Weinstein Oral History, at 1662–65.

Less monumental was the copyright action over a rag doll which Weinstein decided with a thirty-eight-page opinion. The case boiled down to whether the plaintiff's twenty-inch doll and the defendant's forty-eight-inch doll were "significantly different."[190] In applying the test for substantial similarity from the perspective of the "ordinary observer," Weinstein pointed out that "an ordinary eighty year old judge is bound to see a 48 inch rag doll somewhat differently than an ordinary 8 year old child."[191] The forty-eight-inch doll he described as "attractive, perky looking and the 20 inch doll as 'sweet and cuddlesome.'"[192] He held that "the 20 inch Sweetie-Mine doll has a considerably younger, winsome look than the defendant's 48 inch doll."[193] Weinstein found that they were different and that the forty-eight-inch doll did not infringe upon the twenty-inch doll.

Finally, there was the "fluke case," in which commercial and recreational fishermen sued federal and state administrative officers and agencies challenging a regulation that controlled the amount of fluke that could be taken from the waters of the East Coast of the United States during the 2006 fishing season. Weinstein rendered summary judgment for the government. He pointed out that the administration of the summer flounder (fluke fisheries) "is exceptionally complex necessitating a sensitive balancing and cooperation among many interests."[194] "The fish," he said, "move freely across boundaries . . . The effects on the tourism industry, fishing fleets, rod, tackle and bait shops as well as fishing devotees and gastronomes requires the exercise of substantial political wisdom."[195] There would be that summer, he said, "sufficient fluke available commercially to almost satisfy the public's appetite for this delectable fish" and "[f]or recreational fishermen, the size and abundance of fish this spring, summer and fall, and predicted sunny skies, warm breezes and calm seas off our beautiful beaches promise ample delight for sports-fishing. There is no reason to delay the opening of the season because of this litigation."[196] His opinion had a glossary of principal agencies and laws implicated in setting quotas for fluke fishing.[197] The opinion closed with a quotation from Izaak Walton.[198]

Evidentiary Matters

Although Weinstein continued to write and speak on many topics during this period, one of those that most concerned him was the use of scientific evidence in the courtroom. During this period Weinstein was considering mountains of epidemiological

---

[190] *Well-Made Toy Mf'g Corp. v. Goff Int'l Corp.*, 210 F. Supp. 2d 147, 168 (June 26, 2002).

[191] *Id.* at 154.

[192] *Id.*

[193] *Id.* at 168.

[194] *United Boatmen v. Gutierrez*, 429 F. Supp. 2d 543, 546, 550–52 (May 17, 2006).

[195] *Id.* at 546.

[196] *Id.* at 549.

[197] *Id.* at 550–52.

[198] *Id.* at 550. The opinion was republished in the *New York Law Journal* (May 10, 2006).

evidence in class actions before him. Further, in 1993 the Supreme Court overturned the seventy-year-old precedent for testing the admissibility of expert testimony. In *Daubert v. Merrill Dow Pharmaceuticals*,[199] the High Court created a broad, general test for the admissibility of expert testimony. The evidence or testimony had to be scientific knowledge arrived at by the scientific method, and had to assist the trier of fact in understanding the evidence in the case. The judge is required to make a threshold determination that the scientific knowledge would indeed assist the trier of fact— that it was scientifically valid and the methodology could be applied to the facts in issue. *Daubert* emphasized reliance and reliability, leaving trial judges considerable discretion. The Supreme Court often cited the Weinstein-Berger evidence treatise as authority for propositions in the *Daubert* opinion.[200]

Weinstein's scholarly career, work on the Federal Rules of Evidence, experience as trial judge and lifetime interest in science fitted him particularly well to ponder the new challenges facing judges after *Daubert*.[201]

The broad issues for the judge dealing with scientific evidence were, as Weinstein saw them: how to get good evidence in, how to present it in a way that was comprehensible to the jury, how to deal with slanted testimony, and how to protect scientists from abuse in the courtroom. The primary challenge for the law was not to keep out bad evidence, but how to get good evidence and present it in a manner the jury will understand.[202] A complementary concern was how a lay judge or jury evaluates the credibility of scientific presentations by experts who present opposing conclusions?[203]

Weinstein's view was that judges should be more like "gate-openers" than "gate-closers."[204] He does not believe that scientific evidence is beyond a juror's comprehension. His approach to *Daubert* in both civil and criminal cases has been to allow experts to come in and testify as freely as possible. The issue of false proof can be dealt with later by way of a delayed motion for summary judgment, if there is not enough evidence to support the case.[205]

---

[199] 509 U.S. 579 (1993). *Daubert* replaced *Frye v. United States*, 293 F. 1013 (D.C. Cir. 1923).Weinstein suggests that the rejection of *Frye* in the third edition of his treatise on evidence led to a Third Circuit decision which, in effect, became the rule in the United States. *See* Weinstein Oral History, at 181.

[200] *Daubert v. Merrill Dow Pharmaceuticals*, 509 U.S. 579, 587 n. 5; 588; 591 n. 12; 594; 594, n. 11, 12 quoting from either Weinstein himself or from WEINSTEIN & BERGER, WEINSTEIN'S EVIDENCE.

[201] Jack B. Weinstein, *Scientific Evidence in the United States Federal Courts: Opening the Gates of Law to Science, in the First Worldwide Common Law Judiciary Conference Report Held at Williamsburg, VA. & Washington, D.C. 138 (May 23–28)*, published in the First Worldwide Common Law Judiciary Conference, held at Williamsburg, Va. and Washington, D.C., May 23–28, Chapter 3, at 137, 145 [hereinafter Weinstein, *Opening the Gates*].

[202] Weinstein, *Opening the Gates, supra* note 196, at 145.

[203] Jack B. Weinstein, *Enhancing the Relationship of Science and the Courts*, Inaugural Address, American Academy of Forensic Science, New York City, Feb. 20, 1997, at 1 [hereinafter Weinstein, *Enhancing the Relationship*].

[204] Weinstein, *Opening the Gates, supra* note 196, at 137, 141–42.

[205] Jack B. Weinstein, Some of My Case Histories Regarding Science, Speech to Oregon Defense Lawyers Association, Eugene Oregon, Dec. 7, 1997, at 22.

Weinstein warned judges against seeking certainty where and when there is none.[206] It was important to police expert witnesses to prevent charlatans. Stating what judges must expect from expert witness, he used one word, "Honesty."[207] Weinstein advised against scientists giving more definite answers than the science allows, saying "I don't know" more often—to make doubt and uncertainty respectable again.[208] He urged the scientific community to regulate itself, to develop ethical standards for expert testimony, and to have expert testimony reviewed by other scientists.

CHARACTERISTICS OF WEINSTEIN'S JUDGING

Many, if not all, of the characteristics of Weinstein's judging already discussed, continued to be apparent during his fourth decade of judging. There can be no better example of his ethic of hard work than his handling of the five hundred *habeas* cases while carrying an otherwise full load. His zest for his job was obvious. His opinions, if anything, had become more thorough and longer, but the superb prose style was still there. His ability to write powerful narratives was particularly in evidence in the battered mothers' case[209] and in his report on the five hundred *habeas* cases.[210] One example of vivid prose will have to suffice. It comes from an opinion in a commercial dispute between two large corporations. Granting a motion for summary judgment in a suit between Fox News Network and Time Warner, Inc. on claims for fraud and promissory estoppel, Weinstein wrote:

> The parties did participate in intensive and complex negotiations, but they never reached—or even approached—agreement on the essentials to a contractual relationship in this esoteric field. The cajolery, as well as the blandishments, honeyed phrases and assurances that are to be expected in many negotiations between parties of this sort in this media-entertainment field did not constitute fraud or promissory estoppel under the circumstances.[211]

The *Nicholson* case is also a fine example of Weinstein's shaping of a case, moving it from a simple lawsuit about one city's administrative policy onto a national stage.

Weinstein's ability to effectively use the craft of judging to achieve a compassionate result was on particular display in his attempts to tame the congressional statutes in

---

[206] Weinstein, *Opening The Gates, supra* note 199, at 145.

[207] Weinstein, *Enhancing The Relationship supra* note 158, at 11.

[208] *Id.* at 25.

[209] *Nicholson v. Williams,* 203 F. Supp. 2d 153 (Mar. 18, 2002).

[210] *In re Habeas Corpus Cases,* 03-Misc-0666 (2003).

[211] *Fox News Network v. Time Warner, Inc.,* 1997 WL 271720 (May 16, 1997).

the immigration trilogy decisions which gave heart to beleaguered younger, liberal judges elsewhere in the country.[212]

Weinstein's abiding concern that justice show a human face was evident again in speeches and articles as well as in opinions. In a speech given at a synagogue on the medieval Jewish philosopher Maimonides, Weinstein spoke of the "invisible aspect to justice that cannot be ignored." That is "the aspect of humanity, of the human spirit, and of the empathy we feel for our fellow men and women," that "is the gate to justice that gives life and reason to our work as lawyers and judges."[213] "We must," he said, "try to open the gate between the head of the law and the hearts of those who seek justice from us."[214]

In many off-the-bench speeches and articles during this period, Weinstein posed the question of how a judge should respond when asked to do evil.[215] Why did he return so often to this question? This observer, although without clear support, sees this as a form of expiation, not only for the cruelties Weinstein believes he was forced to perform in sentencing, but also for the unsettling conflicts that led him so often to evade the authority of the Sentencing Commission, the Court of Appeals, and Congress.

In discussing the range of options for a judge faced with the prospect of enforcing unjust laws, Weinstein ruled out only one: "silence-acquiescence."[216] The other alternatives Weinstein considered were: resignation; disobedience; interpreting the law in such a way as to conform with precedent while satisfying one's conscience; applying the law, but pointing how unjust it is; distinguishing cases; under-ruling; criticism; dissents, if on the appellate court; out-of-court speeches.

Judges have, Weinstein wrote, "a duty . . . to expose injustice where they can."[217] Trial judges must, even where it is clear that the appellate courts seem to be going in a different direction, "be true to an inner core of responsibility. They must sometimes risk, even court, reversal when necessary to make certain that the appellate courts, the bar, academia and the public are fully aware that there is a strong opposing view."[218]

One should say, though, that with the important exception of the class actions, Weinstein has fared relatively well with the Court of Appeals during this period. In the two really big trials he handled, the troublesome *Gigante* and that of the Mafia cops,

---

[212] *See, e.g.,* Paul Comment in *Judge Jack B. Weinstein and the Public Good: A Roundtable Discussion to Honor One of America's Great Trial Judges on the Occasion of His 80th Birthday,* 12 J. LAW & POL'Y 149, 161, 162 (2003); John Banzhaf's comment in Judge Handling Law Suits Against Big Tobacco and His Reputation of Favoring Plaintiffs overlarge Companies Accused of Causing Harm, National Public Radio, Morning Edition 2 (June 5, 2000) (copy in possession of author).

[213] Jack B. Weinstein, Maimonides' Tempering of a Justice too Rigid and Cruel for Humanity, Speech at Temple Emanuel, Great Neck, NY, Aug. 6, 1999, at 6.

[214] *Id.* at 7.

[215] *See especially,* Jack B. Weinstein, *Every Day Is a Good Day for a Judge to Lay Down His Professional Life for Justice,* 32 FORD. URB. L.J. 131 (2004) [hereinafter, Weinstein, *Every Day*].

[216] *Id.* at 133.

[217] *Id.* at 169.

[218] Weinstein, *Every Day, supra* note 210, at 154.

his courtroom work emerged unscathed. If he was reversed on the statute of limitations issue in the *Eppolito/Caracappa* case, he had to sentence them once again to life sentences, and that surely could not have troubled him much. His work in the *Habeas 500* also survived. His work in *Nicholson* was generally validated and led to more humane policies toward battered women with children in New York and elsewhere. His decisions in the trio of deportation cases were also upheld, although he was slapped down in the later *Beharry* case.

In his eighties, Weinstein continued to be an innovator in and out of the courtroom. In the *Yellow Book* case,[219] for example, both sides presented almost all their exhibits in computer-generated formats as well as in hard copy. Both sides stipulated to their use and their admission to evidence pending, of course, the judge's agreement. Weinstein, the witness, the court reporter, and lawyers had computer monitors and there was a large screen in the courtroom. Michael Hoenig, writing in the *New York Law Journal*,[220] called the relevant *Verizon Directories* opinion, a "forcefully advocative, articulate and visionary statement as to why theory and practice should support admission of pedagogicals into evidence." Weinstein did not seem to have any doubt that the approach could also be used with juries.[221] Weinstein made innovative use of his former law clerk, Josh Hill, as a special master in the push-out cases and collaborated with his former law clerk, Marc Falkoff, in the *Habeas 500*.

Weinstein advocated and employed criminal restitution as a bridge to avoid extensive civil litigation in the *Cheung* case. Borrowing from Swedish and French practice, he succeeded in compensating victims of fraud through an integrated civil settlement and criminal restitution order. The remedy was in effect a civil quasi-class action coordinated with a criminal proceeding to assure maximum recovery by the victims with minimum transaction costs. Weinstein's opinions in *United States v. Cheung* and *Chau et. el. v. Cheung*[222] constitute a road map for other judges.

CONCLUSION

During his fourth decade on the bench, the period between his seventy-fifth and eighty-fifth birthdays, Weinstein retained the mindset of a young man. His legal mind was still operating brilliantly. One commentator wrote that his briefing orders read

---

[219] *Verizon Directories Corp. v. Yellow Book U.S.A., Inc.*, 331 F. Supp. 134 (Mar. 22, 2004).

[220] *Computer-Generated "Pedagogical" Devices: Admissible or Not*, N.Y.L.J., Nov. 8, 2004, at 3.

[221] *Id.*

[222] *United States v. Cheung, and v. Cheung*, 952 F. Supp. 148 (Jan. 13, 1997). *See also* the discussion in Jack B. Weinstein, *Compensation for Mass Private Delicts: Evolving Role of Administrative Criminal and Tort Law*, 2001 U. ILL. L. REV. 961–62.

like law review articles.[223] If often called upon to speak at funerals and memorial occasions, he did so eloquently, but often with a light touch. Honoring his ever-young colleague, John R. Bartels, who was ninety-nine years old when he died, Weinstein spoke of: "Sex, or as we now refer to it in federal court, gender is one of the great inventions of a whimsical God."[224] He remembered Eugene Nickerson, a particularly dear colleague, as one who "helped keep us from weeping over life's injustices by laughing at its incongruities" and remembered Curtis Berger as a "master of human relationships and law."[225]

Weinstein's unique style continued to mark his work and his life: utter independence; remarkable self-assurance mixed with dollops of self-criticism, humility, and ease in giving praise to others,[226] both the meek and the great; awesome in action, yet never far from humor; powerful in conviction, though rarely personal in disagreement; inexhaustible in work habits, yet patient with others; and, even in his eighties when his country was going through an era during which his liberal values were being heartily rejected, unquenchably optimistic.

His optimism, wit, and stress on human relationships was evident at the fortieth anniversary of his investiture, celebrated at a party at Brooklyn Law School, the dean of which was his former clerk, Joan Wexler. The large attendance included Weinstein family and close friends, colleagues from the Eastern and Southern Districts and Second Circuit Court of Appeals, former law clerks, his own staff, and members of the Brooklyn Law School faculty.

Weinstein spoke lightly and briefly at the occasion, telling a fictional story about an encounter with current Chief Judge Raymond Dearie, who was trying to teach him how to wear a robe. Using the acting skills learned in his childhood, Weinstein acted out Dearie's a "quick back kick, a low front clutch and back grab." Then Weinstein inquired of Dearie how to avoid getting his robe caught under his bench chair and tearing it: "Jack, it's simple. Keep the front clutch in your left hand sitting down.

---

[223] EDNY Judge Sets Stage for Notable Decision on Restitution and Forfeiture, http://www.nyfederalcriminalpractice/2008/02/edny-judge-sets-stage-for-nota.html.

[224] Proceedings of Memorial Ceremony for Senior Judge John R. Bartels, 1897–1997, 977 F. Supp. LXIII, LIX at LXXII (May 20, 1997).

[225] On Nickerson: Celebrating the Life of Eugene Nickerson, Memorial Speech, Eastern District ceremonial Courtroom, April 19, 2002, at 2002 (Apr. 2, 2004) (draft of law review article) (copy in possession of author).On Berger: Jack B. Weinstein, *In Memoriam: Scholar and Teacher, People Person and Institutional Conciliator,* 99 COLUM. L. REV. 273, 275 (1999); Jack B. Weinstein, *Scholar and Teacher, People Person and Institutional Conciliator,* (draft of article for COLUMBIA LAW REVIEW, July 28, 1998).

[226] For example, in 2002, he said to the winners of Legal Service Awards for *pro bono* practice: "I hold each of you in awe. You and your work reflect the core of the ethical obligation and commitment to humanity of our legal profession." Jack B. Weinstein, Presentation of Association of the Bar Legal Service Awards, Remarks at Association of the Bar of the City of New York, May 7, 2002, p. 1.

And transfer the back grab forward with your right. And keep both hands in your lap while you're sitting." "Yes, chief, but sometimes I listen and take notes. I forget to hold the robe." "Jack, shape up. We're trained to appear to be listening when we don't hear a word. We have clerks and a reporter to listen." "Yes, chief, I'll practice. I'll try." "All right, Jack. Remember even an old judge can learn."[227]

---

[227] Jack B. Weinstein, "Stream of Consciousness," Remarks delivered at Brooklyn Law School 40th Anniversary Party 5–6 (Apr. 16, 2007) (copy in possession of author).

10

Bringing Justice to Large Groups of People:

Mass Torts and Class Actions (I)

JACK WEINSTEIN HAS had an enormous impact on the way the U.S. legal system has dealt with mass torts. Weinstein has been a central figure in the development of class actions for mass tort litigation and a pioneer in the use of other methods of aggregating mass tort cases. In his opinions, he has illuminated the many corners of class actions, including, but not limited to, jurisdiction, choice of law, lawyer ethics, industry-wide liability, and the uses of experts and statistics. His broader views on mass torts and class actions and the management of complex cases have also been given wide currency through his book, *Individual Justice in Mass Tort Litigation*,[1] many articles and speeches, as well as from other involvements such as his work as an advisor on the American Law Institute Complex Litigation Project. In this area, he has been a federal district judge with marked national influence, extending even to state courts. This chapter will present a background on class actions and other mass tort actions and then focus on Weinstein's most celebrated case, *Agent Orange*. Weinstein's involvements since *Agent Orange*, where he often has been frustrated by the Court of Appeals, is the subject of Chapter 11.

---

[1] JACK B. WEINSTEIN, INDIVIDUAL JUSTICE IN MASS TORT LITIGATION: THE EFFECT OF CLASS ACTIONS, CONSOLIDATIONS, AND OTHER MULTIPARTY DEVICES (1995) [hereinafter, WEINSTEIN, INDIVIDUAL JUSTICE].

A SHORT HISTORY OF CLASS ACTIONS AND
AGGREGATED CASES IN MASS TORTS

Mass tort cases often arise from widespread use of or exposure to products or substances.[2] If there is a high volume of repetitive litigation involving the same or similar products involving uncertain groups of potential claimants and defendants,[3] there often is pressure to aggregate or combine cases to save money, avoid delays, and deal with congested dockets. Plaintiffs' lawyers, in particular, may have considerable financial incentive to aggregate cases.

Mass tort cases often have multiple issues, some requiring individual presentation and some appropriate for group litigation. Mass tort cases test the mettle of a judge, both his or her intellect and his or her managerial abilities, because the volume, diversity, and complexity of claims often require the adaptation of traditional procedures to new contexts.[4]

While class actions have a long history in the federal courts, their use was greatly enhanced by the 1966 amendment of Rule 23 of the Federal Rules of Civil Procedure. Before that, class actions had usually involved antitrust, securities, price-fixing, and cases involving the Fair Labor Standards Act. The major purpose of the 1966 reform was to increase the capacity of the federal courts for civil rights actions.

The use of class actions for mass torts was neither intended nor expected by the framers of amended Rule 23, who assumed that common issues of fact and law would be outweighed by differences in the circumstances of the injuries, the injuries themselves, and in state laws.[5]

To certify a class for a class action, there must be a great number of suits and common questions of fact or law or both. In addition, the named plaintiff must adequately represent the class, and the named plaintiff's claims must be typical of the class as a whole.[6]

The advantages of class actions are the reduction of duplicative litigation, allowing a single judge to familiarize himself with legal and factual issues; allowing plaintiffs' attorneys to generate enough capital to conduct the litigation on a level playing field with what usually are large corporate defendants; an enhanced possibility of global settlement allowing small recoveries; consistency of result; and judicial control of legal fees. Disadvantages include attenuation of the usual individual client-attorney relationship; removal of local issues from their normal venue and superceding the role of the local jury; an increase in complexity; forcing defendants to settle because of the

---

[2] MANUAL FOR COMPLEX LITIGATION, FOURTH 344 (2004).

[3] *Id.* at 344.

[4] *Id.* at 344–47.

[5] DEBORAH HENSLER, CLASS ACTION DILEMMAS: PURSUING PUBLIC GOALS FOR PRIVATE GAIN 24 (2000).

[6] ALBA CONTE & HERBERT B. NEWBERG, NEWBERG ON CLASS ACTIONS 319–35 (4th ed. 2002).

threat of huge awards; and problems protecting the rights of individual class members.[7] However, in class actions, the judge has a particular responsibility for the welfare of the litigants.

Weinstein takes issue with the view that the substantive law is not changed by aggregation of classes.[8] He has said that "class actions favor plaintiffs. There is no doubt about it."[9] For tort plaintiffs, class actions make it far easier to find attorneys who can advance the cost of the litigation. At the same time, the pressure on defendants to settle is much greater because the ultimate stakes are far greater.[10] Class actions also give plaintiffs more leverage in dealing with the government because it is more difficult for the government to dismiss a group grievance than an individual one. Yet, where there is scientific uncertainty as to whether a product has caused the harm alleged, the defendant has the advantage because the burden of proof lies with the plaintiff.[11]

The use of class actions in mass torts became more feasible in the 1970s because of changes in products liability law and in ethical rules governing attorneys.[12] The first judge to certify a class action in mass tort was Carl B. Rubin of the Southern District of Ohio, who did so in a case involving a nightclub fire.[13] After that, mass tort litigation began to be used for airplane crashes, hotel fires, and building collapses.[14]

The case which exploited the potential for the use of class actions in mass torts and set precedents for handling most of its aspects was Weinstein's *Agent Orange* litigation, which began in 1980.[15] Kenneth Feinberg, who headed the fund created by Congress for the victims of 9/11 and who was appointed by President Barack Obama to oversee the $20 billion BP compensation fund, called the *Agent Orange* case "the fundamental pillar, the precedent for all of the subsequent compensation schemes."[16] *Agent Orange* was the first time that a trial judge certified and an appellate court upheld the certification of a huge class, whose members alleged injuries varying in severity and types, incurred

---

[7] Jack B. Weinstein, Compensating Large Numbers of People for Inflicted Harm, Speech at Duke University & University of Geneva Conference on Group Litigation in Comparative perspective (July 21, 2000 at 16ff).

[8] Weinstein Oral History, at 1751.

[9] Jack B. Weinstein, *Some Reflections on the "Abusiveness" of Class Actions*, 58 F.R.D. 299 (n.d.) (available on Westlaw) [hereinafter Weinstein, *Abusiveness*].

[10] MANUAL FOR COMPLEX LITIGATION, FOURTH 25off (2004).

[11] David B. Luban, *Heroic Judging in an Antiheroic Age*, 97 COLUM. L. REV. 2064, 2087 (1997).

[12] PETER SCHUCK, AGENT ORANGE ON TRIAL 26ff (1987).

[13] *See In re Beverly Hills Fire Litig.*, 639 F. Supp. 915 (E.D. Ky. 1986). *See also* ROBERTA SUE ALEXANDER, A PLACE OF RECOURSE: A HISTORY OF THE U.S. DISTRICT COURT FOR THE SOUTHERN DISTRICT OF OHIO, 1803–2003, 189–90 (2005). *See also Coburn v. 4-R Corp*, 44. F.R.D. 43 (E.D. Ky. 1977).

[14] SCHUCK, *supra* note 12, at 33.

[15] *See* Kenneth R. Feinberg, *Lawyering in Mass Torts*, 97 COLUM. L. REV. 2177, 2178 (1997). Originally, Judge George Pratt handled the case, but he was forced to give it up after promotion to the Court of Appeals.

[16] Elizabeth Stull, *Judge Weinstein's 40th Anniversary on the Bench*, BROOK. DAILY EAGLE (Apr. 24, 2007), http://www.brooklyneagle.com/categories/category.php?category_id=4&id=12473.

under similar but not identical circumstances. The size of the settlement of *Agent Orange*, $184 million, also attracted widespread attention from bench and bar.[17]

In the 1980s, mass tort class actions emerged as a permanent part of the landscape for claims flowing from negligent, defective, or toxic products which affected groups of similarly situated defendants.[18] *Agent Orange* was followed by a number of high-profile mass tort actions in the 1980s.[19] District judges began begun to warm to class certification in this area, recognizing the value of centralized decision-making and of aggregation of claims for pretrial discovery, settlement, and disbursement of funds.[20] Furthermore, Weinstein had demonstrated in *Agent Orange* that there was a sufficient consensus of state law on common liability issues to support class treatment. In addition, the creation of subclasses eased the problem of certain differences within the class.[21]

In Chapter 11, we will see that the use of class actions for mass torts slowed in the 1990s, as appellate courts were troubled by the lack of control individuals had of their own cases, the use of class actions to extort high judgments from defendants, and by enormous fees earned by plaintiffs' attorneys with claimants left only piddling amounts.[22] By the first decade of the twenty-first century, the trend in the federal courts, with a few notable exceptions, was to reject certification of nationwide mass tort personal injury class actions. This included several decisions of the Second Circuit reversing Weinstein.[23] Contemporaneously, Congress sent mixed messages about litigating class actions in the federal courts, limiting the power of federal district judges by providing for interlocutory appeals in class actions, but also making it easier to remove class actions from state to the federal courts.[24]

Class actions require close judicial oversight and active management.[25] The stakes can be enormous: hundreds of millions of dollars, the survival of large corporations, and the expectations plaintiffs have that someone will listen to their concerns and treat them fairly. Many of the same problems exist with aggregations shy of class actions—"quasi-class actions" and consolidations—where the judge may consolidate

---

[17] HENSLER, *supra* note 5, at 24–25.

[18] CONTE & NEWBERG, *supra* note 6, at 309.

[19] *See, e.g., Benedictin* class action, *In re Richardson-Merrell, Inc., Benedictin Prods. Liab. Lit.*, 624 F. Supp. 1212 (S.D. Ohio 1985), *aff'd*, 857 F.2d 290 (6th Cir. 1988).

[20] Francis E. McGovern, *Judicial Centralization and Devolution in Mass Torts*, reviewing MICHAEL D. GREEN, BENEDECTIN BIRTH DEFECTS: THE CHALLENGE OF MASS TOXIC SUBSTANCES LITIGATION and WEINSTEIN, INDIVIDUAL JUSTICE IN MASS TORTS LITIGATION, 97 MICH. L. REV. 2077,

[21] CONTE & NEWBERG, *supra* note 6, at 309. *See In re "Agent Orange" Prod. Liab. Lit.*, 100 F.R.D. 718 (Dec. 16, 1983).

[22] Jack B. Weinstein, *Compensation for Mass Private Delicts: Evolving Roles of Administrative, Criminal & Tort Law*, 2001 U. ILL. L. REV. 947 [hereinafter Weinstein, *Delicts*].

[23] MANUAL FOR COMPLEX LITIGATION, FOURTH 347 (2004).

[24] The Class Action Fairness Act focused on the rights of individual class members, ensuring an objective assessment of the fairness of proposed settlements. Greenberg Taurig, LLP, *GT Alert: New Federal Legislation: The Class Action Fairness Act of 2005* (March 2005), available at http://www.gtlaw.com/pub/alerts/2005/0302.asp.

[25] MANUAL FOR COMPLEX LITIGATION, *supra* note 2, at 243, 343.

cases for the purpose of discovery, try test cases, and transfer many of the remaining cases to other judges.[26]

Whether or not there is class certification, mass tort litigation is complex litigation in which the judge must define problems and actively shape the litigation.[27] There may be hundreds of thousands of plaintiffs, multiple defendants and numerous lawyers to ride herd on during discovery (or at least to back up the magistrate judge). Third, fourth, and fifth parties such as insurance companies and governments may be involved.

The judge and/or magistrate judge must decide hundreds of procedural and evidentiary motions. The judge must decide whether to certify a class; determine subclasses and decide how future mass tort claimants are dealt with. He must grapple with complex issues of jurisdiction, choice of law, preemption, statutes of limitations, burdens of proof, and attorneys' fees.[28] He must attempt to understand and try to help the jurors understand scientific evidence and separate "good science" from "junk science";[29] coordinate with state judges; appoint settlement masters; decide whether a settlement is fair; determine proper attorneys' fees; and hold "fairness hearings."

WEINSTEIN, MASS TORTS, AND CLASS ACTIONS

Jack Weinstein's fingerprints are all over the field of mass torts. His *Agent Orange* case proved to be the watershed event in the use of Rule 23 for mass personal injury litigation. Weinstein has been a great, but not uncritical, booster of class actions; an influential educator and role model in handling them, as well as the object of considerable criticism from professors specializing in that field, defense attorneys, and interest groups. He has also been reversed a number of times.[30]

Weinstein sees class actions and consolidations along with contingency fees and lawyer advertising as "essential in a society as complex as ours."[31] From his short time in practice dealing with shareholders derivative cases, Weinstein got his "sense that

---

[26] CONTE & NEWBERG, *supra* note 6, at 300ff.

[27] Indeed, in 2002, the Judicial Conference changed class action rules to give the judge greater ability to shape class actions, including more influence over the selection of lawyers to represent the class and greater control over lawyers fees. NEW YORK TIMES, Sept. 25, 2002, at A18.

[28] KENNETH R. FEINBERG, WHAT IS LIFE WORTH? 12 (2005); WEINSTEIN, INDIVIDUAL JUSTICE, *supra* note 1, at 148.

[29] Joseph M. Price & Ellen S. Rosenberg, *The Silicon Gel Breast Implant Controversy: The Rise of Expert Panels and the Fall of Junk* Science, 93 J. ROYAL SOC'Y. MED. 31 (2000).

[30] *See* David Lauter, *Making a Case with Statistics*, NAT'L L. J. 1, 10 (Dec. 10, 1984).
 In previous chapters of this book, there has been discussion of Weinstein's handling of non-mass tort class actions including those dealing with New York City schools, battered wives who lost custody of their children, and the Shoreham Nuclear Reactor. He also had class actions involving labor matters and prisons. WEINSTEIN, INDIVIDUAL JUSTICE, *supra* note 1, at xi.

[31] Weinstein, *Compensation for Mass Private Delicts: Evolving Roles of Administrative, Criminal, and Tort Law*, Paul V. Van Arsdel, Jr. Lecture, University of Illinois 50 (Oct. 17, 2000).

class actions [were] important in keeping people honest" offering the less well-to-do a forum where they could assemble their claims.[32]

Weinstein believes that the class action (and/or the aggregation of mass claims) makes feasible bringing justice to the individual flexibly, efficiently and apolitically.[33] Class actions offer help with expert witnesses, allow for presentation of cases in a single forum, foster a quick and conclusive decision, and help in achieving settlement.[34] They can lead not only to some financial recovery, but also recognize that the plaintiff has a legitimate grievance.

Weinstein believes that the judge in mass tort cases is "the community's guardian,"[35] the central actor who has "the capacity, in a sense, to bind the whole system."[36] He believes that resolution of a mass tort dispute must take into account broader public policy considerations tied to the social, economic, and political needs of the community at large, even if the particular needs and interests of individual lawyers and litigants in these cases may have to be sacrificed for the good of the larger community.[37] Limited resources should be distributed as equitably as possible causing the least possible economic disruption.[38] This "communitarian-communicatarian" approach requires both judge and attorneys to actively consult with the putative victims, governmental authorities, defendant corporations, and insurers.[39]

Weinstein's views and actions have been sharply criticized by some legal academics and lawyers and have been looked at askance by the Court of Appeals for the Second Circuit.[40] Critical academics say that Weinstein's emphasis on his notion of individual justice does not compensate for what the individual loses.[41] Defendants' attorneys see him as having a "big strike zone for plaintiffs."[42]

---

[32] Weinstein Oral History, at 50–51. However, Jack B. Weinstein, *Revision of Procedure: Some Problems in Class Actions*, 9 BUFF. L. REV. 433 (1960). *See* WEINSTEIN, INDIVIDUAL JUSTICE, *supra* note 1, at 135.

[33] Jack B. Weinstein, *Some Reflections on the "Abusiveness" supra* note 9.

[34] Jack B. Weinstein, *What the Courts Should Offer in Mass Complex Torts*, Remarks to American College of Trial Lawyers, Del Coronado CA (Apr. 9, 1986) (handwritten copy in possession of author).

[35] Scott Fruehwald, *Individual Justice in Mass Tort Litigation: Judge Jack B. Weinstein on Choice of Law in Mass Tort Cases*, 31 HOFSTRA L. REV. 323, 327 (2002).

[36] Weinstein Oral History, at 396.

[37] Feinberg, *supra* note 15, at 2177; Helen E. Freeman & Kenneth R. Feinberg, Book Review, 80 JUDICATURE 44 (1996–1997) (reviewing JACK B. WEINSTEIN, INDIVIDUAL JUSTICE IN MASS TORT LITIGATION (1995)).

[38] Freedman & Feinberg, *supra* note 37, at 44.

[39] Weinstein, *Ethical Dilemmas in Mass Tort Litigation*, 88 NW. U. L. REV. 470, 488 (1994).

[40] Fruehwald, *supra* note 35, at 345. Judges Ralph Winter, Jon O. Newman and Joseph M. McLaughlin have been particularly unsympathetic to Weinstein's views. *See* Weinstein Oral History, at 657–58.

[41] Professor Linda Mullenix of the University of Texas Law School, a powerful critic, considers that "Judge Weinstein's description of communitarianism can be maddeningly vague." Linda S. Mullenix, *Mass Tort as Public Law Litigation: Paradigm Misplaced*, 88 NW. U. L. REV. 579, 584 (1992). The author of this book, a more sympathetic observer, agrees with Mullenix on this.

[42] Joseph Goldstein, *Federal Judge Lands at Center of a New York Legal Mystery*, N.Y. SUN, Dec. 3, 2007.

It cannot be doubted that Weinstein's work in class actions is that of a man with a penchant for engineering big solutions to big problems.[43] Certainly, the view that the class action requires some central authority to take control and help guide the litigation fits snugly with Weinstein's judicial philosophy, temperament, and intellectual abilities.[44] Weinstein's work in class actions and aggregations are another example of his active and activist judging, where he has been more than willing to make use of the equitable powers of the judge.[45] Weinstein has also been criticized for avoiding accountability to higher courts by making preliminary decisions which may greatly affect the outcome of the litigation and be of import beyond the litigation (for example, on jurisdiction or choice of law) which end up not being reviewed because the case settles.[46]

Weinstein's contributions to the development of class actions have included major opinions and writings on the problem of jurisdiction, severance, and choice of law (where he has sought a single national law).[47] His innovations as a judge, to be described herein, have stretched from, on the one hand, the use of computer technology in his courtroom for the retrieval of evidence to consideration of the proper role of experts (including concern for the availability of experts for the indigent and lower middle class), and the use of statistics. He has made innovative use of special masters, who he has used to handle discovery, to achieve settlement, and to ensure that his decisions are properly carried out.[48] Weinstein has also offered striking examples of close coordination with state judges and, demonstrated how to administer huge settlements, and conduct fairness hearings. He also invented the concept of quasi-class actions to avoid appellate strictures on class actions, while permitting district judges to control fees and settlement.[49] In his writings, he has administered criticism and praise to defendant corporations and executives, plaintiffs' and defense attorneys, judges, the scientific community, regulatory agencies, Congress, and the public.[50] He has written about such matters as alternative dispute resolution in class actions, the integration of bankruptcies into class actions, the integration of restitution orders in criminal cases, and recoveries in civil suits and expert testimony. He also has given considerable thought to the ethical problems of class actions and taken action in the

---

[43] Bob Van Voris, *A Carload of New Tobacco Trials: Going Against the Grain Brooklyn Judge Sets One a Month*, NAT'L. J., Apr. 24, 2000.

[44] WEINSTEIN, INDIVIDUAL JUSTICE, *supra* note 1, at 102.

[45] *See, e.g.,* Fruehwald, *supra* note 35, at 323, 344; Weinstein Oral History, at 481; WEINSTEIN, INDIVIDUAL JUSTICE, *supra* note 1, at 128; *Judge Jack B. Weinstein, Tort Litigation, and the Public Good*, J. LAW & POL'Y 164 (2003) [hereinafter *80th Birthday Roundtable*].

[46] Fruehwald, *supra* note 35, at 344.

[47] Fruehwald, *supra* note 35, at 329; 200 F.R.D. 21 (Feb. 8, 2001). *See generally, 80th Birthday Roundtable, supra* note 45.

[48] Discussion on Class and Multiple-Party Actions [between Atsuo Nugano and Jack B. Weinstein, New York City, Feb. 25, 2010], at 35–36 (original version) (copy in possession of the author) [hereinafter Nugano-Weinstein Discussion].

[49] *See, e.g., In re Zyprexa Prods. Liab. Lit.,* 424 F. Supp. 2d 488 (Mar. 28, 2006).

[50] *See, e.g.,* Weinstein, *Ethical Dilemmas, supra* note 39, at 472.

cases before him to keep fees down.[51] His efforts have been to control the abuses in class actions, but not "to really kill this little beastie" or "so entangle it so that it cannot be used effectively."[52]

One other aspect of Weinstein's treatment of class actions has been his deep belief that part of a judge's role in class actions is that the judge must meet with the victims, the plaintiffs, and listen to them. This is, of course, Weinstein's insistence on the "human face of the law." "The judge must," he suggested, "expose himself or herself to the emotional and other needs of the litigants."[53] And that "sympathetic connection" is one that should be replicated in the relationship between the lawyers and those injured.[54]

For his endeavors and views, there has been considerable criticism for moving away from the traditional lawyer-client model, for making decisions where he is free of accountability from the Court of Appeals, for being pro-plaintiff, and because lawyer use of the "related case" rule in the Eastern District has given him "an outsize influence" in some class actions.[55] In spite of the criticism and the fact that at the time of this writing Weinstein's approach to class actions and consolidations is beleaguered in the Second Circuit and elsewhere, there can be no doubt that Weinstein has played a vital role in the development of class actions. James L. Oakes, former Chief Judge of the Court of Appeals for the Second Circuit has said:

It is . . . . in the area of mass tort litigation that Judge Weinstein has been the most thoughtful, may I say the most profound and certainly the most innovative of trial judges.[56]

Kenneth Feinberg has spoken even more strongly:

Beginning with the Agent Orange litigation . . . Judge Weinstein has almost single handedly written the modern law of mass torts.[57]

Burt Neuborne, who handled major Holocaust cases, has said:

Every time I did any research, every time I confronted a problem, every time we thought about how to structure, what to do, what the problems were, the

---

[51] WEINSTEIN, INDIVIDUAL JUSTICE, *supra* note 1, at 81.

[52] Weinstein, *Abusiveness*, *supra* note 9, at 304.

[53] WEINSTEIN, INDIVIDUAL JUSTICE, *supra* note 1, at 50.

[54] Weinstein, *Ethical Dilemmas*, *supra* note 39 at 470, 527.

[55] Goldstein, *supra* note 42.

[56] James L. Oakes, *Jack Weinstein and His Love-Hate Relationship with the Court of Appeals*, 97 COLUM. L. REV. 1951 (1997).

[57] Kenneth R. Feinberg, *Lawyering in Mass Torts*, *supra* note 15 at 2178.

parameters of both the law and the problems were set in Judge Weinstein's remarkable corpus of work.[58]

Thus, in the areas of class action and mass torts, Weinstein's influence has been national. His decisions and writings have been followed by judges and large numbers of practitioners. His influence has been reinforced by his articles and by his speeches at circuit conferences, law schools, and elsewhere. Criticism of his work in Congress and by the defense bar have spread his ideas still further while legal academics have seen him as a central figure in this area.

Agent Orange

At the time Weinstein was assigned the *Agent Orange* case, he already was familiar with class actions as a judge. During his first year on the bench, he had written a short treatise on class actions in *Dolgow v. Anderson*.[59] In *Feit v. Anderson*, decided in 1971, he found class actions useful in vindicating the rights of a great many dispersed small-claim holders.[60] He had developed the concept of industry-wide liability in the blasting cap litigation, *Hall v. E. I. du Pont de Nemours & Co.*, when it was impossible to trace which company had manufactured the blasting caps that were maiming children.[61] The blasting cap litigation had anticipated such difficulties that arose in the *Agent Orange* litigation such as the ability of the federal courts to join multiple claimants residing in different states in an aggregate litigation, issues relating to consolidation of multiple claimants with different individual injuries in one case, problems with substantive tort law standards relating to causation, and problems in determining the relevant applicable state law that applied to the classes.[62]

Agent Orange is probably the most important litigation Weinstein handled. Presiding over an action with tens of thousands of plaintiffs, his procedural dexterity, mastery of substantive law, and administrative abilities revealed to judges and practitioners the enormous potential of the class action for massive tort litigation. The practical results were that the lives of thousands of Vietnam veterans were improved and a nagging political problem diffused.

During the Second World War, chemical companies developed the herbicide, Agent Orange. After the war, at the request of the U.S. government, the herbicide was marketed commercially. One of the ingredients of Agent Orange was dioxin, which was a highly

---

[58] *80th Birthday Roundtable, supra* note 45, at 149, 184 (2001).

[59] 43 F.R.D. 472 (Jan. 3, 1968).

[60] *Feit v. Anderson*, 332 F. Supp. 544 (Aug. 26, 1971); Weinstein Oral History, at 184.

[61] 345 F. Supp. 353, 378 (May 18, 1972). See chapter 5, Infrol. *See also* Weinstein Oral History, pp. 146ff; 153, 253–56, 274, 795ff.

[62] Linda S. Mullenix, review of Jack B. Weinstein, Individual Justice in Mass Tort Litigation: The Effect of Class Actions, Consolidations and Other Multiparty Devices, 5 Law & Pol. Book Rev. 173 (1995) [hereinafter Mullenix Review].

toxic substance. During the Vietnam War it was used by the U.S. armed forces to defoli-
ate jungles and mangroves. Agent Orange was used on an estimated 10 percent of
Vietnam's forests and 36 percent of its mangroves.[63] Between 600,000 and 2.4 million
veterans are believed to have had some exposure to the herbicide.[64] During the 1970s,
veterans and their families began to attribute a variety of illnesses and reproductive
problems to exposure to the herbicide.

On January 8, 1979, a lawsuit was brought for damages from exposure to Agent
Orange. As a result of multidistrict procedures, the *Agent Orange* litigation became
the largest mass tort case up to that time. No earlier case had been quite like it in terms
of scale, novelty, and difficulty of the questions presented and the widespread public
interest. Six hundred lawsuits were filed by 15,000 individuals. The defendants—
ultimately, seven corporations—spent $100 million preparing for trial. Fifteen hundred
attorneys were involved. By the late 1980s, the docket sheet for the cases was four
hundred twenty-five single-spaced pages.[65]

Agent Orange was not a typical mass accident case, where a number of people are
simultaneously harmed in the same way by the same cause. Unlike litigation over airplane
crashes or oil spills, *Agent Orange* involved multiple occurrences of various related harms
over a considerable amount of time and space. The plaintiffs' class was indeterminate;
in the future, other individuals might suffer injuries that could be attributed to Agent
Orange. The defendants, too, were indeterminate. Because the armed forces mixed
defoliants produced by different companies together before they used them, it was
impossible to attribute a particular injury to a specific company's product.[66] The *Agent
Orange* case was more than a lawsuit. It was "a searing morality play projected onto a
national stage."[67] Many plaintiffs believed deeply that they had been "mistreated by the
country they loved."[68]

The *Agent Orange* litigation, as Professor Peter H. Schuck of Yale Law School, its
leading student, described it, involved "dedicated, but deeply divided veterans; flamboy-
ant trial lawyers; class-action financial entrepreneurs; skillful, Machiavellian special
masters; a Naderesque litigation organizer" and "a brilliant, crafty judge."[69] Some of
the attorneys saw the litigation as a vehicle for fame and fortune. Others viewed the

---

[63] Grant B. Herring, *Judge Weinstein and the Agent Orange Case*, DEL. LAW. (Fall 1985) 56.

[64] Shira A. Scheindlin, *Discovering the Discoverable: A Bird's Eye View of Discovery in a Complex Multi-District Class Action, Litigation*, 52 BROOK L. REV. 397, 448 (1986).

[65] SCHUCK, *supra* note 12, at 4–5, 12–13, 45, 262. *See also* David W. Leedom, *To Jack, Son of Columbia*, 97 COLUM. L. REV. 1965, 1966 (1997); Vincent Robert Johnson, *Ethical Limitations on Creative Financing of Mass Tort Class Actions*, 54 BROOK. L. REV. 539 (1988). *In re "Agent Orange" Prod. Liab. Lit.*, 597 F. Supp. 740, 750ff (Sept. 25, 1984).

[66] Aaron D. Twerski, *Essay: With Liberty and Justice for All: An Essay on Agent Orange and Choice of Law*, 52 BROOK. L. REV. 341, 353 (1986); Paul Sherman, *Agent Orange and the Product of the Indeterminate Plaintiff*, 52 BROOK. L. REV. 369, 391 (1986).

[67] SCHUCK, *supra* note 12, at 11.

[68] *In re "Agent Orange" Prod. Liab. Lit. (Fairness Opinion)*, 597 F. Supp. 740, 747 (Sept. 25, 1984).

[69] SCHUCK, *supra* note 12, at 15.

litigation as part of a larger struggle to control the threat of toxic chemicals. The manufacturers of Agent Orange saw the case as a fundamental test of strength against a vicious, implacable plaintiffs' bar and a crucial indicator of their future economic viability.[70] The "crafty judge" would, in the face of all this, use his power to bring the parties to a reasonable settlement. In so doing, he transformed modern class action tort litigation.

Initially, the *Agent Orange* litigation did not come to Weinstein. The cases were consolidated by the Panel on Multidistrict Litigation[71] and referred them to Weinstein's colleague, George Pratt who, in a number of respects, anticipated much of Weinstein's work while he had the case. Pratt is a quiet, decent, bright, modest, and straight arrow of a man.[72] Pratt was a very able judge, who had to give up the case because of his elevation to the Court of Appeals.[73] With an important exception, Pratt's rulings in the case held up, although Weinstein's immense energy and legal imagination would transform the case after it was reassigned to him.

Pratt had dismissed the claims against the United States and had indicated that he would certify a Rule 23(b)(3) class action.[74] He had stated that the defendant chemical companies could use the government contract defense (e.g., that the circumstances surrounding the manufacture and use of the herbicide were so clearly controlled by the government that the manufacturer should be protected from liability). He held that discovery would proceed and that he would hold trials first on issues common to all litigants—the government contract defense and matters of causation.[75] In February 1982, Pratt appointed a special master and set a date for trial, June 13, 1983. In May 1983, Pratt rendered summary judgment for the defendants on some, but not all, issues connected with the government contract defense and dismissed several companies from the litigation. At the same time, however, he abandoned his plan for litigation organized by a well-defined set of issues beginning with a trial in one month. The litigation appeared to be turning "into a completely open-ended free-for all involving a defuse highly interrelated tangle of issues that would be subject to discovery, trial and decision at some unspecified time in the . . . future . . . ."[76]

Nevertheless, Pratt received one major setback from the Court of Appeals. In 1979, he had ruled that the law he would apply in the case would be federal common law because there were substantial federal issues and applying various state laws could cause great uncertainty and possible injustice. The Court of Appeals reversed Pratt,

---

[70] *Id.* at 255ff.

[71] The U.S. Judicial Panel on Multidistrict Litigation, is made up of seven federal judges, determines whether civil actions pending in different federal districts involve one or more common questions of fact so that the actions should be transferred to one federal district for coordinated or consolidated pretrial proceedings.

[72] George Pratt was a colleague of mine on the Touro Law School faculty for about a decade. I found him a marvelous colleague.

[73] *See* SCHUCK, *supra* note 12, at 110.

[74] *In re "Agent Orange" Prod. Liab. Lit.*, 506 F. Supp. 762, 787ff (Dec. 29, 1980).

[75] SCHUCK, *supra* note 12, 67–68.

[76] SCHUCK, *supra* note 12, at 101. *See also id.* at 98ff, 56.

raising both analytical problems and potentially immense difficulties in administering the litigation.[77]

The class action began to drag. Pratt was heavily involved in handling political corruption cases arising out of the ABSCAM scandal. When, in mid-1982, he was elevated to the Court of Appeals, he originally held on to *Agent Orange*, but he surrendered it on October 14, 1983, probably at the request of Chief Judge Wilfred Feinberg of the Court of Appeals, who was concerned with his court's docket.[78]

The case was reassigned to Weinstein, and the Weinstein touch was immediately seen. Professor Schuck states that, at his first meeting with the attorneys, Weinstein infused the case with renewed vitality. It was clear that he had already mastered the essentials of the litigation.[79] It was evident that he viewed the litigation not as a product liability case multiplied many times over (which some have argued Pratt did[80]), but as a major social problem needing settlement. He knew well, as he said more than five years later, that mass tort cases, although different in detail, have "the same kind of political and emotional aspects" as civil rights suits, and have mass media appeal. "They're not like intersection-collision cases."[81]

Yet, at his first meeting with attorneys on October 21, 1983, Weinstein had also said of *Agent Orange*, "it's just one old case to be disposed of. That's the way it will be treated."[82] By that, he meant he would not be fazed by the size of the litigation.

Weinstein saw the case through a "wide lens,"[83] the law of the communitarian ethic. He would say that poisons were put into the atmosphere through carelessness by producers:

... There was an injury in some sense to the community .... Payment should have been made under these circumstances, money utilized in some community care[sic] way that would permit those who might have been injured to benefit.[84]

Resolving the case on a technical issue would not, he thought, end the dispute, but rather cause it to fester.[85] Although he never confided it to the attorneys, Weinstein's

---

[77] *In re "Agent Orange" Prods. Liab. Lit.*, 506 F. Supp. 737 (Nov. 20, 1979), *rev'd*, 635 F.2d 987 (Nov. 24, 1980: Kearse-VanG/WJF), *cert. denied*, 454 U.S. 1128 (1981). *See also* SCHUCK, *supra* note 12, at 67, for strong criticism of the decision of the Court of Appeals.

[78] SCHUCK, *supra* note 12, at 110.

[79] *Id.* at 117.

[80] SCHUCK, *supra* note 12, at 54.

[81] Andrew Blum, *It's Best to Hang Together*, 12 NATL. L.J. 1, 55 (Sept. 11, 1989).

[82] SCHUCK, *supra* note 12, at 115.

[83] Martha Minow, *Judge for the Situation: Judge Jack Weinstein, Creator of Temporary Administrative Agencies*, 97 COLUM. L. REV. 2010, 2013,

[84] *80th Birthday Roundtable*, *supra* note 45, at 177.

[85] SCHUCK, *supra* note 12, at 117.

underlying objectives were to see that the veterans not be left without a sense of recourse and the defendants be charged only for harms they might have caused.[86]

To push the parties toward settlement, Weinstein imposed an early, immovable trial date, May 7, 1984, with little more than six months away before jury selection. He announced that the trial would run four months, that the plaintiffs were to select a small number of their best cases to try, that while government liability would also be tried before a jury, the jury's verdict would only be advisory.[87] And he warned the attorneys, "I like very dull trials, everything laid out before hand, everybody revealing everything."[88]

At that first meeting, Weinstein told the attorneys that he'd keep all parties in the case, including the United States. He indicated he was dubious of the chemical companies' government contractor defense. The issue, he said, was not just what the manufacturers knew, but what they should have known. However, the foremost issue was causality, which the plaintiffs' had to prove by statistical analysis.[89]

Besides the looming trial date, the parties had their own reasons to give serious attention to the possibility of settlement. The plaintiffs had severe problems in financing their case and the difficult job of persuading a jury to believe that the herbicide had caused their health problems. The defendants feared a jury trial because Weinstein had announced that he was moving the litigation from Uniondale, where Pratt had handled it, to Brooklyn, where a jury was more likely to award large damages.

From the first meeting, Weinstein took a comprehensive role in managing and structuring the *Agent Orange* litigation. At court hearings, Weinstein first "hammered" away at plaintiffs to produce medical evidence of causation, then hammered at the defendants, threatening to apply theories of enterprise liability, which would shift the burden of proof back to the defendants.[90] Weinstein would say years after the litigation that his own view, based largely on his reading of every available scientific study, was that no jury verdict for the plaintiffs could stand up. Therefore, if a jury went ahead and did find for the plaintiffs and the verdict then was overturned, the result "would have made everybody much more bitter . . . ." However, there were also serious risks for the defendants. Thus, "all in all, I thought the settlement was in everybody's favor."[91]

Weinstein sought to move the case rapidly. In January 1984, he appointed Magistrate Shira Scheindlin, an able former prosecutor and commercial lawyer (and, later, a federal judge who made a national reputation for her work on discovery matters), as special master and directed her to take the lawyers on a "forced march" to trial.[92] Three years

---

[86] Weinstein, *Ethical Dilemmas, supra* note 39, at 505.

[87] SCHUCK, *supra* note 12, at 113, 149.

[88] SCHUCK, *supra* note 12, at 115.

[89] *Id.* at 113–14.

[90] Herring, *supra* note 63, at 57.

[91] Weinstein Oral History, at 1281.

[92] SCHUCK, *supra* note 12, at 122.

of normal discovery would have to be telescoped into three months.[93] Scheindlin devoted practically full time to the case, holding daily, nightly, and Sunday meetings with the attorneys.[94] Among the varied issues Scheindlin dealt with were privileges (executive, state secrets, medical record), expert witnesses, and case management.[95]

Meanwhile, on December 16, 1983, Weinstein, because the affirmative defenses and questions of general causation were common, certified a Rule 23(b)(3) and 23(b)(1)(B) class for all issues.[96] Class certification, he indicated, was even more desirable than in most mass tort litigation because of the huge size of the plaintiff class. Notice could be given by mail and by advertisements on radio, television, and the newspapers as well as by telephone.[97] As generally was the case in the *Agent Orange* litigation, the Court of Appeals declined to overturn his order.[98]

The major significance of the class action certification was that, by joining the claims together in a class action, a classwide determination of the total harm to the entire body of plaintiffs could be made. Proof of that harm could be based on epidemiological and statistical evidence. Then, each individual defendant corporation could be held liable to each plaintiff exposed to injury for a pro rata share of plaintiffs' injuries[99] based upon the enterprise liability theory that Weinstein had set forward more than a decade before in *Hall v. E. I. du Pont de Nemours & Co.*[100] The certification order created the special relationship between the judge and plaintiffs that occurs with class actions.[101]

Weinstein saw the major vulnerability of the plaintiffs as the lack of material evidence on causation.[102] While the science on Agent Orange was far more advanced then the science in some later cases (such as the breast implant class action, discussed in Chapter 11), there remained much doubt. Dioxin harmed rodents, but did it harm people? Weinstein was dubious. (Subsequent research suggests that dioxin does more harm than found in the research Weinstein relied upon.[103]) But beyond the need to convince Weinstein intellectually, the plaintiffs' vulnerability on causation gave Weinstein a weapon to push the plaintiffs toward settlement. He could give them the impression that their proof as to causation was so weak that he might not allow the issue to go to the jury. Indeed, years later, when Weinstein handled the case of those plaintiffs who had opted out of the settlement, he did decline to submit the causation

---

[93] SCHUCK, *supra* note 12, at 140.

[94] Unofficial transcript of Second Circuit Judicial Conference enclosed in letter from Jack B. Weinstein to Kenneth Feinberg, Dec. 1, 1985 (in possession of this author).

[95] *See generally*, Scheindlin, *supra* note 64.

[96] *In re "Agent Orange" Prod. Liab. Lit.*, 100 F.R.D. 718 (Dec. 16, 1983).

[97] *In re "Agent Orange" Prod. Liab. Lit.*, 100 F.R.D. at 720–21.

[98] *In re Diamond Shamrock Chemical Co.*, 725 F.2d 858 (Jan. 9, 1984: Winter-New-MacMahon), *cert. denied*, 465 U.S. 1067 (1984). The chemical companies had asked the Court of Appeals to mandamus Weinstein.

[99] SHERMAN, *supra* note 66, at 369, 377ff.

[100] 312 F. Supp. 358 (Apr. 7, 1972).

[101] SCHUCK, *supra* note 12, at 125–28, esp. 127–28.

[102] HERRING, *supra* note 63, at 56–58.

[103] *See* LUBAN, *supra* note 11, at 2064 n.127.

to the jury. The low award Weinstein ultimately gave the plaintiffs' lawyers in the main *Agent Orange* action may have also reflected a conviction that the plaintiffs had a weak case and that such cases should be discouraged in the future.[104]

Besides class certification and causation, another of the problems of the *Agent Orange* litigation was whether to give the U.S. government immunity. This was not analytically difficult. Under the *Feres-Stencel* doctrine,[105] it seemed clear that the government was immune from suit. Weinstein said that only "a path-breaking appellate court," could change that.[106] Whether or not the U.S. government was legally immune from suit, Weinstein believed that morally it owed recourse to the veterans. Thus, he kept the government in the case; even assigning government counsel a front table in the well of the court presumably to dramatize the centrality of the government's role. He was hoping that the government would be forced to devise a more comprehensive political solution than would be achieved through litigation and, if not that, then at least the government might help behind the scenes.[107] These hopes were futile. Weinstein was very critical of the government's position, writing in an opinion that, although the government was within its legal rights to refuse to contribute to the settlement, its "benign detachment" might be cruel to veterans who served their country and now would feel that the government had turned its back on them.[108]

There remained the problem of which jurisdiction's manufacturers' liability law to apply in a case where the plaintiffs hailed from all over the country. The Court of Appeals' reversal of Judge Pratt's decision to apply one single law to the case—federal common law—was the law of the case and binding on Weinstein.[109] Confronting the problem of having to apply many different state laws and thereby of treating veterans differently based solely on their different domiciles, Weinstein found an ingenious solution. He chose to apply what he called a "national consensus" standard as the

---

[104] *See* SCHUCK, *supra* note 12, at 201, 206, 234, 238.

[105] *Feres v. United States*, 340 U.S. 135 (1950); *Stencel Aero Eng'g Corp. v. United States*, 431 U.S. 666 (1977). The doctrine prevents people who are injured as a result of military service from successfully suing the federal government under the Federal Tort Claims Act.

[106] *In re "Agent Orange" Prod. Liab. Lit.*, 580 F. Supp. 1242, 1247 (Feb. 16, 1984). Yet, Weinstein did brush aside the holdings of six Courts of Appeal and Judge Pratt, when he held in a "tentative memorandum" that family members of the veterans could sue for their independent genetic injuries. Later, he dismissed claims against the U.S. brought by veterans' wives on the basis of epidemiological evidence. *See In re "Agent Orange" Prod. Liab. Lit.*, 580 F. Supp. 1242, 1244 (Feb. 16, 1984); *mandamus denied*, 733 F.2d 10 (Apr. 13, 1984), *cert. denied*, 465 U.S. 1067 (1984). *See also* SCHUCK, *supra* note 12, at 137. He also dismissed the cases brought by minor children without prejudice so they could sue again, if evidence developed showing a valid claim against the government. *In re "Agent Orange" Prod. Liab. Lit.*, 603 F. Supp. 239, 247–48 (Feb. 11, 1985); SCHUCK, *supra* note 12, at 247–48.

[107] Weinstein Oral History, at 523.

[108] *In re "Agent Orange" Prod. Liab. Lit.*, 611 F. Supp. 1221, 1222 (May 9, 1985). *See also* SCHUCK, *supra* note 12, at 118, 131–32; Weinstein Oral History, at 523.

[109] SCHUCK, *supra* note 12, at 128. The "law of the case" principle is that if an appellate court has determined a legal question and returned the case to the court below for further proceedings, that the question will not be determined differently on a subsequent appeal in the same case where the facts remain the same.

appropriate governing law. Weinstein theorized there was a consensus among the states as to the rules of conflict of laws and the applicable substantive law of manufacturer's liability and punitive damages.[110] Weinstein distinguished between federal law applying of its own force under the Supremacy Clause of the Constitution and that of *Agent Orange* where he was applying national consensus law because *that was what a state court would do in choosing a rule of decision*.[111]

Weinstein's application of national consensus law in *Agent Orange* was without precedent. Professor Schuck called Weinstein's his handling of the choice of law wise and fair, but also involving "prestidigitation and insubordination." It left Weinstein with breathtaking flexibility in the application of legal principles to the case.[112]

Pursuing the goal of settlement, Weinstein "did everything he could to make sure that the train he was conducting was not derailed by the Court of Appeals."[113] He denied certification of the interlocutory appeal from his order certifying a class action, because it would not "materially advance the ultimate termination of the litigation," and because, if reversed, he would "still proceed with a trial in essentially the same manner."[114] He avoided writing formal opinions, instead giving many [unappealable] signals from the bench "revealing his 'preliminary' thinking to the lawyers without really committing himself to a position or inviting time-consuming appeals."[115] Thus, he was able "to innovate in the interlocutory space created by the final judgment rule, allow[ing] the parties to use his courtroom as a venue for a negotiated resolution."[116]

Weinstein appointed three special masters to hammer out the details of settlement. The appointment of special masters for settlement at the time was most unusual, perhaps unprecedented.[117] He did so because he thought the case was too overwhelming for a single judge to handle. Two of the special masters Weinstein selected were chosen in some measure for their potential clout in Washington.[118] Unlike the Coney Island school case, when he had kept his distance from the special master, in *Agent Orange*, Weinstein was constantly on the telephone with his masters.[119] Kenneth Feinberg would develop the plan for the settlement and its distribution. Leonard

---

[110] *In re "Agent Orange" Prod. Liab. Lit.*, 580 F. Supp. 690 (Feb. 21, 1984).

[111] *Id.* at 698.

[112] SCHUCK, *supra* note 12, at 128, 130–31.

[113] Stephen B. Burbank, *The Courtroom as Classroom: Independence, Imagination and Ideology in the Work of Jack Weinstein*, 97 COLUM. L. REV. 1971, 1989 (1997).

[114] *In re "Agent Orange" Prod. Liab. Lit.*, 100 F.R.D. 735–36 (Dec. 19, 1983).

[115] SCHUCK, *supra* note 12, 124–25.

[116] Burt Neuborne, *Innovation in the Interstices of the Final Judgment Rule: A Demurrer to Professor Burbank*, 97 COLUM. L. REV. 2091, 2098 (1997).

[117] SCHUCK, *supra*, note 12 at 144.

[118] Kenneth Feinberg was close to Congressional Democrats; Leonard Garment to Republicans both in Congress and the executive branch. The third special master, David Shapiro, an attorney knowledgeable about class actions, was chosen to negotiate the settlement.

[119] Transcript of Second Circuit Judicial Conference, *supra* note 94, at 81ff.

Garment explored what the government might contribute. David Shapiro and Feinberg actually negotiated the settlement.[120]

The weekend before trial, around the clock negotiations took place. An entire floor had been reserved in the courthouse for this purpose. The special masters shuttled between the two sides. Weinstein met separately with the parties and exploited the leverage he had—his ambiguous role as both mediator and decision-maker. He played upon the fears of the parties and wore down their resistance. None of the attorneys felt fully prepared for the trial.[121] The defense lawyers were warned of the risks of a Brooklyn jury verdict. The plaintiffs were advised that, even if they obtained a jury verdict, the Court of Appeals might prove to be less open to legally creative solutions than Weinstein.[122]

The principal terms of the settlement seem to have been quite literally dictated by Weinstein.[123] The plaintiffs argued for a settlement of $200 million. The defense offered $150 million. Although the defense lawyers were willing to give in to $200 million, Weinstein himself insisted on $180 million, probably because he did not want the settlement to send a message that the case was stronger than it really was.[124]

Thus, after six weeks of mediation, the case settled a few hours before the trial was to begin.[125] The complaints were dismissed with prejudice and the defendants were not to be subjected to liability in the future to any member of the 23(b)(3) class.

The settlement provided for a compensation fund of $150 million for U.S. veterans and $5 million for Australian and New Zealander veterans. A foundation was set up with $45 million to aid the *families* of Vietnam veterans. The interest on the money accumulated, increasing the fund to $240 million of which $170 million went for compensation and $55 million for class assistance.[126]

Prior to execution of the award, six days and nights of fairness hearings took place—three in Brooklyn, one each in Houston, Atlanta, and San Francisco. During these hearings, Weinstein listened to young widows who had seen their husbands die of cancer; mothers with testifying with tears in their eyes and their children in wheel chairs beside them; and men who had completely lost their memory in their thirties.[127] In all, Weinstein listened to five hundred people and received hundreds of telephone and written communications.[128] Weinstein was in a difficult position during these

---

[120] SCHUCK, *supra* note 12, at 144ff; Luban, *supra* note 11, at 2086.

[121] Herring *supra* note 63, at 56, 57.

[122] SCHUCK, *supra* note 12, at 160ff; NEW YORK TIMES, May 11, 1985, at I, 1; Herring, *supra* note 63, at 56, 58.

[123] SCHUCK, *supra* note 12, at 178.

[124] SCHUCK, *supra* note 12, at 159.

[125] The settlement was approved by Weinstein, *In re "Agent Orange" Prod. Liab. Lit.*, 597 F. Supp. 740 (Sept. 25, 1984), subject to the fairness hearings. The final judgment was approved on July 9, 1985. *In re "Agent Orange" Prod. Liab. Lit.*, 618 F. Supp. 623 (July 9, 1985).

[126] WEINSTEIN, INDIVIDUAL JUSTICE, *supra* note 1, at 157.

[127] *See* SHUCK, *supra* note 12, at 173ff.

[128] *See* SHUCK, *supra* note 12, at 177; Weinstein Oral History, at 216.

hearings—caught between a desire to hear the veterans and their families out and frustration at being able to do little for them. He was guarded by U.S. marshals because there were threats against his life.

At the end of the process, on September 25, 1984, he issued his "fairness" opinion, upholding the settlement. In that "fairness" opinion, which occupies more than a hundred pages of Federal Supplement (without counting the appendices), Weinstein tentatively upheld the settlement in "one of the most complex litigations ever brought."[129] He wrote of deep feelings inherent in the litigation:

> Vietnam veterans and their families desperately want this suit to demonstrate how they have been mistreated by the country they love. They want it to give them the respect they have earned. They want it to protect the public against future harm . . . They want a jury "once-and-for-all" to demonstrate the connection between Agent Orange and the physical, mental and emotional problems from which many of them clearly do suffer.[130]

Weinstein said that he'd "been deeply moved by his contact with members of the plaintiffs' class from all over the nation. Had the court the power to rectify past wrongs—actual or perceived—it would do so. But no single litigation can lift all of the plaintiffs' burdens."[131] He then "tentatively" held that the settlement gave the class more than it would likely achieve by attempting to litigate "to the death."[132]

Weinstein wrote of the "moving sights and sounds of the hearings" and discussed concerns that had repeatedly been voiced, among them, the need for information on possible genetic damage to veterans and their children, and the need for improvement of the Veteran's Administration and its hospitals. He noted the disappointment of the chemical companies and government to admit fault. Weinstein also acknowledged the sharp split of opinion among class members as to whether the court should accept the settlement.[133]

Weinstein then discussed the factual problems of the plaintiffs' case.[134] This was the nub of it:

> The critical problem for the plaintiffs is to establish that the relatively small quantities of dioxin to which service persons were exposed to in Vietnam caused their present disabilities. Here, adequate proof is lacking.[135]

---

[129] In re "Agent Orange" Prod. Liab. Lit., 597 F. Supp. 740, 749 (Sept. 25, 1984).

[130] Id. at 747.

[131] Id. at 747.

[132] Id. at 747.

[133] Id. at 775.

[134] Id. at 775ff.

[135] Id. at 782.

He stated that the "government contract defense in this case is powerful." Thus, there were "enormous legal problems that plaintiffs would have to overcome before they could succeed in obtaining relief from the courts."[136] The procedural frustrations, expense and delays required to resolve the issues and the problems connected with the statutes of limitations provided, Weinstein wrote, "another good reason for settlement."[137] Weinstein concluded:

> Based on all the information presently available, the procedural posture of the litigation, the difficulty any plaintiff would have in establishing a case against any one or more of the defendants, the uncertainties associated with a trial, and the unacceptable burden on plaintiffs' and defendants' legal staffs and the courts, the proposed settlement appears to be reasonable. It appears to be in the public's as well as the parties' interest.[138]

There was this coda:

> Whether or not that pain was caused by Agent Orange, it is shared by a disproportionately large number of Vietnam veterans. They and their families should receive recognition, medical treatment and financial support. Many lives have been broken by the Vietnam experience. The suffering ones deserve succor.[139]

Two and one-half years after the fairness opinion was issued and a little more than a year after oral argument, a panel of the Court of Appeals (Winter, Van Graafeiland, and Miner) affirmed Weinstein's *Agent Orange* rulings in nine separate, unanimous opinions totaling two hundred pages. Winter began the lead opinion this way:

> We are a court of law and we must address and decide the issues raised as legal issues. We do take note, however, of the nationwide interest in this litigation and the strong emotions these proceedings have generated among Vietnam veterans and their families.[140]

Weinstein was affirmed on the most significant issues: class certification, settlement amount, summary judgment against those opting out of the class action, and, generally,

---

[136] *Id.* at 799.

[137] *Id.* at 816.

[138] *Id.* at 857.

[139] *Id.* at 857.

[140] *In re "Agent Orange" Prod. Liab. Lit.*, 818 F.2d 145, 148 (Apr. 21, 1987). The Second Circuit's opinions were handed down a little more than one year after oral argument before it. It appears that the ultimate release was hastened as Chief Judge Wilfred Feinberg, aware that Kenneth Feinberg was about to let the *New York Times* know about the delay, put pressure on the panel to issue an immediate opinion before his court was criticized. *See* Weinstein Oral History, at 847.

as to attorneys' fees. He was reversed only as to the fee-sharing arrangement between the plaintiffs' lawyers and over control of the foundation created from part of the settlement monies. As to the latter, the appellate court insisted that the foundation be more tightly controlled by Weinstein.[141]

Writing for the Second Circuit in the leading opinion, Judge Ralph Winter indicated his reservations about using class actions for massive tort litigation, by stating that the litigation "justifies the prevalent skepticism over the usefulness of class actions in so-called mass tort cases and, in particular, claims for injuries resulting from toxic exposure."[142] In this litigation, though, the class action was justified by the centrality of the military contractor defense to the claims of the plaintiffs.[143] To subject defense contractors to full tort liability "would inject the judicial branch into political and military decisions that are beyond its constitutional authority and institutional competence."[144]

Winter called the settlement "almost as inevitable as the sunrise" and the size of the settlement "a payment of nuisance value."[145] He wrote of Weinstein's analysis of choice of law issues as "bold and imaginative," while suggesting that "the intellectual power of his analysis alone would not have been enough to prevent widespread disagreement among the jurisdictions in dealing with the cases of individual plaintiffs."[146] The Supreme Court denied review of three *Agent Orange* cases on January 12, 1988.[147]

Weinstein's opinion on the award of attorneys' fees in *Agent Orange*, which was reversed in part, is of particular interest. His fee award was extremely low and bitterly attacked by plaintiffs' lawyers. Out of a settlement of $180 million, of which the lawyers could have expected at least 20 percent ($36 million), they received only $10.7 million. The low fee award presumably reflected Weinstein's conviction that plaintiffs had a very weak case. Weinstein later came to believe that he had not compensated the attorneys who represented individual plaintiffs fairly.[148] On the other hand, Weinstein held that those attorneys who had advanced funds to finance the litigation were entitled to what had been agreed among the plaintiffs' steering committee, a 300 percent return on the amount they had advanced.[149] Weinstein viewed the plaintiffs' steering committee as an ad hoc law firm formed for the purpose of prosecuting the *Agent Orange* multidistrict litigation. Their award was, however, to be taken from the total amount of

---

[141] *In re "Agent Orange" Prod. Liab. Lit.*, 818 F.2d 179 (Apr. 21, 1987).

[142] *In re "Agent Orange" Prod. Liab. Lit.*, 818 F.2d at 164.

[143] *Id.* at 151.

[144] *Id.* at 191.

[145] *Id.* at 166, 151.

[146] *Id.* at 165.

[147] *In re "Agent Orange" Prod. Liab. Lit.; Pinkney v. Dow Chem.*, 484 U.S. 1004 (1988) (dealing with class certification); *Adams v. United States*, 484 U.S. 1004 (1988) (governmental immunity); *Fraticelli v. Dow Chem.*, 484 U.S. 1004 (1988) (opt-outs).

[148] WEINSTEIN, INDIVIDUAL JUSTICE, *supra* note 1, at 82.

[149] Weinstein had been unaware of that agreement until he received the applications for fees.

attorneys' fees awarded, not from the compensation for the victims. Overall, Weinstein argued for flexibility in dealing with attorneys' fees in mass tort litigation.[150]

Dealing with this issue of first impression, the Court of Appeals reversed Weinstein over his indulgence of the lawyers' creative financing. The agreement within the plaintiffs' steering committee had, the Court of Appeals believed, placed class counsel in a potential conflict in relation to the class.[151] The court thought the steering committee was merely a group of individual lawyers and law firms associated for the prosecution of a lawsuit and was disturbed about the appearance such an award would give.[152]

The plan for distributing the money judgment in *Agent Orange* was largely the work of Kenneth Feinberg, who also oversaw its implementation.[153] The $180 million judgment grew because of interest. Over nine years, $330 million was distributed. Fifty-two thousand veterans and their families received compensation payments of which $181 million went to U.S. veterans, $5 million were distributed to Australian and New Zealander veterans, $13.8 million to the plaintiffs' attorneys. Seventy million dollars in grant awards were given in ways that were to assist members of the veterans' families. Administrative costs were in the neighborhood of 10 percent.[154]

Weinstein played a major role, not only in overseeing the processing of individual claims, but also the grant applications made to the foundation. This cannot fairly be connected to judicial activism. Weinstein originally envisioned that the foundation would be free-standing, but it was the *Court of Appeals* that insisted that he had to supervise it himself or through a special master.[155] Weinstein said, "I would have preferred to decide it all and get out";[156] instead he found himself running a foundation with assets of hundreds of millions of dollars. His comment to me was revealing: "So, I'm controlling it and I had more fun than I've ever had in my professional life."[157] The Agent Orange Class Assistance Program set up a national network of social and medical agencies to assist the families of the veterans in community settings. It published manuals and treatises on government benefits, and, after five years, held a national conference recording the experience, insights, knowledge, and skills of thousands who

[150] *In re "Agent Orange" Prod. Liab. Lit.*, 611 F. Supp. 1452 (June 27, 1985). *See also* NEW YORK TIMES, Mar. 8, 1985; SCHUCK, *supra* note 12, at 192, 196; Weinstein Oral History, at 1038, 1045.

[151] *In re "Agent Orange" Prod. Liab. Lit.*, 818 F.2d 216, 233–34 (Apr. 21, 1987: *Minor*-Winter-VanG), *cert. denied*, 484 U.S. 926 (1987). *See also* Victor Robert Johnson, *Ethical Limitations on Creative Financing of Mass Tort Class Actions*, 54 BROOK. L. REV. 539, 550, 552, 584 (1988). *See also* Mullenix, *supra* note 41, at 588 n. 31.

[152] *In re "Agent Orange" Prod. Liab. Lit.*, 818 F.2d at 226.

[153] The distribution plan was approved on May 28, 1985. *In re "Agent Orange" Prod. Liab. Lit.*, 611 F. Supp. 1396, 1400 (May 28, 1985).

[154] N.Y.L.J., Sept. 30, 1997, at 1; PALMYRA (PA.) PALM ADVERTISER, Nov. 30, 1994; STARS AND STRIPES, week of May 23–29, 1994, at 1, 15. Originally, there was a $10 million indemnity fund to protect the companies. It turned out not to be needed, so the money went back into the pool.

[155] *In re "Agent Orange" Liab. Lit.*, 818 F.2d at 185.

[156] Weinstein Oral History, at 577.

[157] Weinstein Oral History, at 836.

had helped veterans and their families.[158] Weinstein felt, all in all, that his settlement "was utilized . . . fairly effectively to help a very large portion of the veterans' community."[159]

The federal government did finally act, although not until 1991, when legislation was passed providing payments for diseases "presumptively" caused by Agent Orange.[160] Weinstein offered this perspective: "we got out a little money in order to permit the government ultimately to step in and do what the government had to do that was right."[161] For his work, Weinstein himself became known, in the words of Professor Martha Minow of Harvard Law School, not uncritically, as a "creator of temporary administrative agencies—a judicially supervised structure for processing individual claims."[162]

Agent Orange Postsettlement Litigation

Since 1985, there have been a number of attempts to reopen the *Agent Orange* judgment for "new" claimants. After settlement most of the 2500 veterans who had opted out of the class action chose to come back to the class; 282 did not.[163] When he tried the cases of those who ultimately had opted out, Weinstein offered sympathy, but not generosity. In a thorough opinion dealing with epidemiological studies and expert testimony, he held that plaintiffs had not offered sufficient proof of causation, and could not overcome the government contract defense. Accordingly, summary judgment against them was required.[164]

"Phase-II Cases" were brought by plaintiffs who argued that their claims were based on medical problems that had occurred *after* the settlement agreement, but during the period the Agent Orange fund was distributing money ended the same way. Those

---

[158] On the foundation, *see* Weinstein Oral History, at 577, 780, 1247–39; Jack B. Weinstein, The Struggle to Define, and to Be, a Good Judge in a Secular Society, unpublished "Musings," Oct.6, 1998 (in possession of the author), at 18; WEINSTEIN, INDIVIDUAL JUSTICE, *supra* note 1, at 158; STARS AND STRIPES, week May 23–29, 1994, at 1. One grant, for example, went to the National Legal Services Project, which brought suit in the Northern District of California to challenge the Agent Orange regulations of the Veterans' Administration. That court held that the VA had discriminated against Vietnam veterans under the 1984 Dioxin Act.

A large volume containing forty-one papers discussed at the conference was published. *See* Jack B. Weinstein, Preface: *Lessons from the Agent Orange Class Program for Families and Children of Vietnam Veterans*, in THE LEGACY OF VIETNAM VETERANS AND THEIR FAMILIES xi, xii (Dennis K. Rhoades, et al. eds., 1995).

[159] Weinstein Oral History, at 128.

[160] *See* Agent Orange Act of 1991, P.L. No. 102-4, 105 Stat. 111, 39 US.C.A. §1116 (2002).

[161] *80th Birthday Roundtable*, *supra* note 45, at 225; N.Y.L.J., Apr. 9, 2004, at 3; Minow, *supra* note 83, at 2023.

[162] Minow, *supra* note 83, at 2019.

[163] *In re "Agent Orange" Product Liab. Legislation (Isaacson v. Dow)*, 304 F. Supp. 2d 404, 419 (Feb. 9, 2004).

[164] *In re "Agent Orange" Prod. Liab. Lit.*, 611 F. Supp. 1223, 1229 (May 8, 1985). *Id.* at 1263. *See also In re "Agent Orange" Prod. Liab. Lit.*, 611 F. Supp. 1263, 1267 (July 3, 1985). *But see* Second Circuit order, 818 F.2d 179 (Apr. 21, 1987); *on remand*, 689 F. Supp. 1250 (July 5, 1988).

suits, originally brought in Texas state courts, raised the question of whether a class of plaintiffs whose action was brought and still pending in federal court could circumvent the effect of a federal judgment by bringing new actions in a state court relying exclusively on state law. The answer was "No." The Phase II lawsuit was removed to federal court, and Weinstein refused to reopen the settlement, even though all fifty State Attorneys General supported the plaintiffs. The Second Circuit affirmed Weinstein, and the Supreme Court denied review.[165]

Several years later, the "Phase III" cases were brought by veterans who claimed that their injuries had manifested themselves *after the settlement fund had closed* (1994). Weinstein rejected those suits as well. However, the Court of Appeals reversed, holding that these *Agent Orange* claimants had not been adequately represented in the prior litigation and therefore could not be bound by the settlement of the 1984 class action. It was, therefore, possible for them to relitigate the adequacy of their class representation through a collateral attack on the global settlement. The Supreme Court affirmed by an equally divided court.[166] The suit returned to Weinstein who dismissed it on the basis of the government contract defense.[167]

On March 10, 2005, Weinstein dismissed suits Agent Orange claims brought on behalf of millions of Vietnamese under the Alien Tort Claims Act, the War Crimes Act, the Geneva and Hague Conventions, and customary international law. In his 233-page opinion, Weinstein agreed with many of the plaintiffs' contentions, referring often to historical, military, scientific, and legal writings. In this opinion, Weinstein held that corporations can be sued under the Alien Tort Claims Act, eviscerated the Political Question Doctrine, and stated that Congress and the executive are not entitled to unswerving deference when it comes to national defense and military affairs.[168] Weinstein also held that presidential powers are limited in wartime,[169] and that the President has no power to violate international law or authorize others to do so.[170] He further held that authorization by a head of a government does not provide *carte*

---

[165] *Ryan v. Dow Chemical Co.*, 781 F. Supp. 902 (Oct. 4, 1991), *aff'd*, 996 F.2d 1425 (June 24, 1993: VanG - Kearse-Card), *cert. denied sub nom, Ivy v. Diamond Shamrock Chems. Co.*, 510 U.S. 1140 (1993). *See* Weinstein Oral History, at 29, 941, 1231–33. *See also* Minow, *supra* note 83, at 2031.

[166] *Stephenson v. Dow Chem.*, 273 F.3d 249 (Nov. 30, 2001: Park-Card-Spatt), *aff'd in part and vacated in part sub nom, Dow Chem. v. Stephenson*, 539 U.S. 111 (2003). *See also* Ellen B. Unger, *Back to the Futures: The Supreme Court's (Non) Ruling in* Dow Chemical v. Stephenson, CLASS ACTION & DERIVATIVE SUITS NEWSLETTER, Oct. 13, 2003, at 3ff.

[167] *Isaacson v. Dow Chem. Co.*, 304 F. Supp. 2d 404 (Feb. 9, 2004), *aff'd*, 517 F.3d 129 (Feb. 22, 2008), *cert. denied*, 129 S.Ct. 1523 (2009). *See also In re "Agent Orange" Prod. Liab. Legislation: Twinam v. Dow Chem. Co.*, 344 F. Supp. 2d 873 (Nov. 16, 2004), *aff'd*, 517 F.3d 129 (Feb. 22, 2008), *cert. denied*, 129 S.Ct. 1523 (2009).

[168] *In re "Agent Orange" Prod. Liab. Lit., Vietnam Ass'n for Victims of Agent Orange/Dioxin v. Dow Chem. Co.*, 373 F. Supp. 2d 7, 71–75 (Mar. 10, 2005).

[169] *Id.* at 64.

[170] *Id.* at 72.

blanche for a private defendant to harm individuals in violation of international law,[171] and that necessity was no defense under the circumstances of the case.[172]

After all this, however, Weinstein still ruled against the Vietnamese. He held that the use of a defoliant is not a war crime; that there was no treaty to which the United States was a party, nor statute, nor binding declaration of the United States nor a rule of international or human rights law that applied to limit the spraying of herbicides by the United States in Vietnam during the period up to April 1995.[173]

On February 22, 2008, the Court of Appeals affirmed Weinstein in the Vietnamese Agent Orange case, *Vietnam Ass'n for Victims of Agent Orange v. Dow Chemical Co.*[174] Judge Miner's opinion was narrow. Its thrust was that the sources of international law relied on by the plaintiffs did not support a universally accepted norm prohibiting the wartime use of Agent Orange defined with the specificity demanded by a leading Supreme Court opinion.[175]

The success of *Agent Orange* was largely responsible for convincing plaintiffs' attorneys that it was better to handle mass torts via class actions or consolidated cases than by individual litigation.[176] The defense bar, too, may have begun to realize with *Agent Orange* that class actions could be useful to them. Those who might be liable for mass torts could quantify and satisfy their liability in one fell swoop through aggressive use of class action procedures.[177]

The size and complexity of claims in *Agent Orange* "have made it a paradigm of emerging problems in product liability."[178] Weinstein's work in *Agent Orange* became a model for managing class actions for the way special masters and magistrates were used, for handling class certification, and for determining the appropriate law to apply, the handling of fairness hearings, and how to deal with attorneys. His opinions of over one hundred pages on such matters as the effect of sovereign immunity on the government contract defense, or the use of summary judgment where the first issue was whether epidemiological evidence sustained causation, became important resources for judges dealing with later "big" class actions.

Weinstein's work in *Agent Orange* has not been free of criticism. Professor David Luban expressed concern about just how far Weinstein had departed "from the passive, neutral umpire of song and story." He had bluffed plaintiffs and defendants alike, retained Democratic and Republican consultants to help pressure the legislative and executive branches, unilaterally revised the dollar amount of the settlement, kept

---

[171] *Id.* at 64.

[172] *Id,* at 121.

[173] *Id.* at 105ff.

[174] 517 F.3d 104 (Feb. 22, 2008: Miner-Sack-Hall).

[175] The Supreme Court opinion is *Sosa v. Alvarez-Machain,* 542 U.S. 692 (2004).

[176] Blum, *supra* note 81, at 1, 54.

[177] Brent Rosenthal, *When Opt-out Class Actions Are Charades,* LEGAL TIMES, week of July 12, 1993, at 24.

[178] Sherman, *supra* note 66, at 369.

parties in the case by brute force, and rode circuit to conduct public hearings.[179] Kenneth Cohen, a practitioner and lecturer at Boston University Law School at the time, criticized Weinstein for using a class action to focus the attention of Congress, sweeping away tort law rules with his national consensus law, employing a different view of the law for individual opt-out cases, certifying a class only to hold claims together long enough to hammer out a settlement, and using provisional hearings without announcing how funds would be allocated.[180] Linda Mullenix, a prolific scholar at the University of Texas Law School, accused Weinstein of "judicial overreaching and procedural unfairness."[181] Aaron Twerski, Brooklyn Law School professor and an attorney in the case, called the *Agent Orange* case "an example of where the judge as philosopher-king fashioned something out of nothing."[182] Others expressed concern about potential unfairness to future claimants and were troubled that economic loss had been redistributed without regard to causation.

Overall, though, Jack Weinstein emerged from *Agent Orange* with his reputation burnished. The attorneys in the case, surely a potentially critical audience, agreed that he had handled the litigation well. Special Master Kenneth Feinberg has written that *Agent Orange* "initiated the modern era of mass torts." It was the "fundamental pillar, the precedent for all subsequent schemes" in mass tort litigation.[183] *Agent Orange*, according to Feinberg, was the "most complicated and thorny" of all mass tort cases and what Weinstein did "was fashion a remedy that only a handful of judges would have been able to or [had] the courage to do."[184] In future class actions, Weinstein continued to use a number of techniques and theories pioneered in *Agent Orange*, even as he created new ones. However, his subsequent innovations and techniques would not fare as well with the Court of Appeals.

---

[179] Luban, *supra* note 11, at 2087.

[180] Kenneth A. Cohen, Book Review of PETER SCHUCK, AGENT ORANGE ON TRIAL: MASS TORT DISASTERS IN THE COURTS, 67 B.U. L. REV. 581 (1987).

[181] Mullenix, *supra* note 41, at 579, 589 (1999).

[182] Aaron Twerski, *With Liberty and Justice for All: An Essay on Agent Orange and Choice of Law*, 52 BROOK. L. REV. 341.

[183] Elizabeth Stull, *Judge Weinstein's 40th Anniversary on the Bench*, BROOK. DAILY EAGLE (Apr. 24, 2007), http://www.brooklyneagle.com/categories/category.php?category_id=4&id=12473.

[184] *See* Blum, *supra* note 81, at 54.

11

Bringing Justice to Large Groups of People:

Mass Torts and Class Actions (II)

IN THE YEARS since the *Agent Orange* settlement, Jack Weinstein has continued to make important contributions to the field of class actions and aggregate litigation. However, the Court of Appeals has frustrated his attempts to achieve grand resolution of particular mass tort litigations.

During the 1990s, the atmosphere for class actions became less favorable because of the visibility of abuses by the plaintiffs' bar as well as continued reservations about departing from the traditional lawyer-client model. Appellate courts, including the Court of Appeals for the Second Circuit, became increasingly skeptical about class actions. The Supreme Court avoided facing class action issues until 1997 and 1999 and, when it did so, its decisions appeared to disfavor class aggregation.[1] A change in Rule 23 of the Federal Rules of Civil Procedure made judicial oversight of mass actions easier, while Congress provided for interlocutory appeals in class actions.

Jack Weinstein's ventures with asbestos litigation and later mass tort cases proved much less successful than *Agent Orange*. However, he continued to innovate and made significant contributions, including reconstruction of the Manville Personal Injury Settlement Trust, which came to be a paradigm for compensating asbestos victims; stimulating the first use of a panel of experts in the breast implant litigation; writing an opinion in the DES litigation which was a small treatise on determining damages; sitting jointly and sharing decision-making with state judges; writing major opinions attempting to modify traditional limits on personal jurisdiction where mass torts were

---

[1] *Amchem Prods v. Windsor*, 521 U.S. 591 (1997); *Ortiz v. Fibreboard Corp.*, 527 U.S. 815 (1999).

involved and engaging in a fascinating (and, finally, losing) battle with Congress over the use of federal agency data in litigation involving the importing of guns into New York City. He also wrote an influential book on the subject, *Individual Justice in Mass Tort Litigation*.[2] However, his attempts to fully resolve class actions involving asbestos, DES, light cigarettes, and victims of gun sales were unsuccessful.

ASBESTOS LITIGATION

Weinstein's attempts to reach a grand resolution of asbestos claims failed, as did his efforts to achieve an innovative class action settlement with claimants to a restructured Johns Manville trust and to avoid bankruptcy for two smaller companies which had produced asbestos.

Certainly, no mass tort problem has so bedeviled the courts as the claims against asbestos manufacturers.[3] In the first half of the twentieth century, asbestos was employed in a variety of ways including for shipbuilding, boiler linings, and building materials. Recent estimates indicate that more than 100 million people in the United States were occupationally exposed to asbestos during the twentieth century.[4] Asbestos proved toxic and caused early deaths from mesothelioma and lung cancer. Tens of thousands suffered from other asbestos-related diseases.[5] If asbestos caused illness and death, suits brought over it threatened the viability of industries, unions, and insurance companies.

Litigation over asbestos involved long delays, inconsistent verdicts, inadequate payments to the most seriously afflicted, and huge transaction costs.[6] By the late 1970s, when it became clear that asbestos plaintiffs could be successful in court, cases surged.[7] Early in the 1980s, approximately ten thousand asbestos suits were being filed annually in the federal courts.[8] The Johns Manville Corporation, the largest manufacturer of asbestos, overwhelmed by asbestos claims, filed for bankruptcy in 1982. Bankruptcy was a technique by which a company could stay in business while its creditors could be

---

[2] Published in 1995 by Northwestern University Press.

[3] *See* DEBORAH H. HENSLER ET AL., ASBESTOS IN THE COURTS: THE CHALLENGE OF MASS TOXIC TORTS (1985).

[4] AMERICAN ACADEMY OF ACTUARIES, MASS TORTS SUBCOMMITTEE, OVERVIEW OF ASBESTOS CLAIMS: ISSUES AND TRENDS 1 (August 2007).

[5] Jack B. Weinstein & Katherine Aschenbrenner, *Notes for Remarks on Asbestos: New Problems and Proposed Solutions*, 30 PROD. SAFETY & LIAB. RPTR. 1053 (Nov. 25, 2002).

[6] *See* Georgene M. Vairo, *Symposium: Reinventing Civil Procedure: Will the New Procedural Regime Help Resolve Mass Torts?*, 59 BROOK. L. REV. 1065, 1078 (1993); Peter H. Schuck, *Judicial Avoidance of Juries in Mass Tort Litigation*, 48 DE PAUL L. REV. 479, 481 (1998).

[7] HENSLER, *supra* note 3, at 112; WASHINGTON POST, Nov. 29, 1990, at B1, B4.

[8] By the latter part of the decade, the number of annual filings nearly quadrupled. *See* Weinstein & Aschenbrenner, *supra* note 5, at 1053, 1054 (Nov. 25, 2002); Vairo, *supra* note 6, at 1065, 1072; Hensler, *supra* note 3, at 41 n. 72.

partially satisfied.[9] Almost a decade after Manville's bankruptcy, when Weinstein was dealing with asbestos cases connected with the Brooklyn Navy Yard, he became involved with the problems of the trust for asbestos victims created from the Manville bankruptcy. The trust was stalling settlements.[10]

The Manville trust had emerged as the result of an agreement forged by Southern District Bankruptcy Judge Burton Lifland and attorney Leon Silverman. Manville had surrendered a majority of its stock as well as future payments to it to satisfy the claims of asbestos victims. The trust had been funded with $817 million in cash, notes, and Manville stock.[11] By the time the corporation emerged from bankruptcy in 1988, the trust owned 80 percent of the company.

The behavior of the first trustees of the Manville Trust was profligate. Perhaps as much as two-thirds of the trust funds expended went for transaction costs—paid out in fees to plaintiffs' lawyers and for the expenses of running the trust. When Weinstein first looked into the trust in the spring of 1990, he found it was out of money even though 152,000 claims were pending.[12] By 1990, $900 million had been spent to settle some 22,000 claims at an average at $43,509 per claimant. A short time later the value of the trust was estimated at from $2.1–2.7 billion, but current and future claims were estimated at $6.5 billion.[13] Some two dozen attorneys may have received as much as $200 million of the $900 million the trust had spent.

In the asbestos cases, Weinstein was at his most innovative and activist. Having considered the powers of the chancellors of Medieval England and how their techniques were carried over into modern times and the American context,[14] Weinstein wielded extraordinary equitable powers. When, for example, he realized the state of the trust, he immediately enjoined all pending cases against the trust in *every state and federal court*.[15]

In the asbestos cases related to the Brooklyn Navy Yard, Judge Helen E. Freedman of the New York State Supreme Court and Weinstein acted together, probably the first time a state court and a federal court had jointly exercised federal and state power.[16] Weinstein and Freedman held hearings together, issued orders together, and were

---

[9] ROBERT M. COVER, OWEN M. FISS, & JUDITH RESNICK, PROCEDURE 1707–08 (1988); Jack B. Weinstein, Preliminary Reflections on Managing Disasters, Speech to American College of Trial Lawyers, Lake Buena Vista, FL, Mar. 19, 1985, at 37–38; Brent Rosenthal, *When Opt-Out-Class Actions are Charades*, LEGAL TIMES 23 at 24 (week of July 12, 1993); Andrew Blum, *It's Best to Hang Together*, 12 NAT'L L.J. 1, 55 (Sept. 11, 1989); Weinstein Oral History, at 384–85.

[10] NEWSDAY, May 17, 1991, np.

[11] BUSINESS WEEK, June 25, 1990, pp. 28ff.

[12] NEW YORK TIMES, May 16, 1990, at D1, 2 and July 8, 1990, Sect. 3, at 1, 6. Weinstein Oral History, at 673.

[13] In re Joint Eastern & Southern Asbestos Litigation, 982 F2d 721, 727 (1992).

[14] WEINSTEIN, INDIVIDUAL JUSTICE IN MASS TORT LITIGATION xii (1995).

[15] Weinstein Oral History, at 1009.

[16] N.Y.L.J., Jan. 31, 1990, at 1, 6.

intending to try cases together, though ultimately that did not prove necessary.[17] Weinstein explained his view of federalism:

> I revised New York State Civil Practice and taught federal and state procedure at Columbia University, so that I think of our system of state and federal courts in unitary, cooperative terms as delivering justice to all our people.[18]

In June 1990, Freedman and Weinstein ordered Bankruptcy Judge Burton Lifland to dramatically alter the procedures for compensating asbestos victims by giving priority to plaintiffs on the basis of the date of their diagnosis, rather than the date they filed the lawsuit.[19]

On July 9, 1990, the judges ordered the complete overhaul of the Manville Trust. The trust was prevented from spending any more moneys in settlement or legal costs for the immediate future except for victims in "extreme financial hardship as a result of asbestos-related diseases."[20] Weinstein staked out broad authority over all problems arising out of the Manville reorganization plan.

The new class action settlement with the Manville Trust was the first instance of a major corporation's bankruptcy plan being rewritten years after it had been approved. The settlement provided for more funding, but smaller payouts. An injunction barred anyone from introducing evidence in any court case involving other asbestos defendants which would hold the Manville Trust jointly liable or in any way responsible.[21]

On June 27, 1991, in one of his longest opinions (503 pages), Weinstein approved the bitterly disputed revision of the Trust.[22] Critical of both Congress and the courts for not devising an affirmative solution to the asbestos cases, Weinstein attempted to treat all current and potential claimants of the trust as members of a single class. Because the revised plan had not been agreed to by the claimants and the manufacturers,

---

[17] The cases would have proceeded simultaneously, separating only when rules of evidence or other procedural differences required the juries to be separated. In the asbestos cases, Weinstein also worked closely with his Eastern District colleague, Charles Sifton, with Southern District Bankruptcy Judge Burton Lifland and Judge Robert W. Sweet, of the Southern District of New York.

[18] Discussion on Class and Multiple-Party Actions [between] Atsuo Nugano and Jack B. Weinstein, New York City, Feb. 25, 2010 [original version] (copy in possession of the author) [hereinafter Nugano-Weinstein Discussion].

[19] NEW YORK TIMES, June 2, 1990, at 1, 29. See also WASHINGTON POST, July 18, 1990, at H1, H6.

[20] In re Joint E. & S. Dist. Asbestos Litig., 982 F.2d 721 (Dec. 4, 1992: New-Wint/WJF(c/d)). A petition for mandamus seeking to overturn the injunction on the payment of claims was denied by the Court of Appeals.

[21] Other manufacturers could then file a claim with the Manville Trust. The settlement was to be reviewed by the general counsel of the AFL-CIO for fairness. See N.Y.L.J., Nov. 21, 1990; WASHINGTON POST, Nov. 20, 1990 and Nov. 29, 1990, at B1, B4. See also WALL STREET JOURNAL, Aug. 2, 1990, at B2; NEW YORK TIMES, Aug. 15, 1990, at D5; Weinstein Oral History, at 1019.

[22] In re Joint E. & S. Dist. Asbestos Litig., 129 B.R. 710 (June 26, 1991). See Weinstein Oral History, at 1086–87.

it was effectuated by filing and settling a class action that provided for a mandated non-opt-out class under Rule 23(b)(1)(B).[23]

However, in December 1992, the Second Circuit "unwound the restructuring of the Manville Trust in its entirety."[24] The *Manville* reversal was one of a number of setbacks at the time for trial courts handling class actions around the nation.[25] In essence, the Court of Appeals vacated the judgment because claimants with adverse interests had been improperly grouped together. It objected particularly to placing co-defendant manufacturers and the health claimants in the same class, because their interests were profoundly adverse to each other.[26] Judge Jon Newman's lengthy opinion for the Court of Appeals (he was joined by Judge Ralph Winter; Judge Wilfred J. Feinberg dissented in part) is believed to have been the first detailed examination of the mandatory class action settlement. The appellate court spoke of the "extraordinary efforts in crafting [an] ingenious set of arrangements" and said that it set aside the settlement "with considerable regret."[27] In 1994 a settlement was reached through which claimants of the Manville Trust would be paid only 10 percent of the value of their injuries, but would receive that compensation ten times faster than in the past.[28]

Although more than 10,000 new asbestos cases were filed in the federal courts every year,[29] the Judicial Panel on Multidistrict Litigation had refused four times to consolidate federal asbestos cases before a single judge for pretrial purposes. There were particular difficulties to dealing with asbestos through a class action or consolidation. Victims had been exposed to asbestos at different times under different circumstances. Their illnesses varied. There were also many (some four hundred) corporate defendants.

Weinstein was looking for a global resolution to the whole asbestos problem—a national class action lumping together all complainants with a pool of money from the corporate defendants.[30] He was not alone in the search. In the summer of 1990, some of the strongest personalities on the federal bench, judges such as Robert M. Parker of the Eastern District of Texas, Thomas D. Lambros of the Northern District of Ohio, and Weinstein, all seemed to be vying for the power to achieve a global settlement.

---

[23] *In re Joint E. & S. Asbestos Litig.*, 129 B.R. 710 (June 26, 1991). Liz Spayo, *Judge Approves Plan on Asbestos Claims*, WASHINGTON POST, May 17, 1991, at F1, F4; Barnaby J. Feder, Manville's *Fund to Get More Cash*, NEW YORK TIMES, May 17, 1991, at D1, D3. *See also* NEW YORK TIMES, Nov. 12, 1990, at D2.

[24] Barnaby J. Feder, *Appeals Court Blocks Plan for Asbestos Compensation*, NEW YORK TIMES, Dec. 5, 1992.

[25] Barbara Franklin, *Class Action Confusion*, N.Y.L.J., Dec. 10, 1992.

[26] 982 F.2d 721, 725 (Dec. 4, 1992). N.Y.L.J., Dec. 10, 1992. *See* H. FINK, L. MULLENIX ET AL., FEDERAL COURTS IN THE 21ST CENTURY: CASES AND MATERIALS 623.

[27] The court did uphold Weinstein's supervision of the trial preparation of the asbestos cases and noted that he was surely entitled to be concerned with the viability of the trust and to take remedial steps. *In re Joint Eastern & Southern District Asbestos Liability Litigation*, 982 F2d 721, 733, 743, 749 (1992).

[28] N.Y.L.J., July 28, 1994, at 1, 2.

[29] NEW YORK TIMES, Aug. 6, 1990, at D2.

[30] The *New York Times* reported on November 12, 1990, at D2, that the judge's goal had been the creation of one huge fund from contributions by asbestos makers and their insurers that would give something to all victims. *See also* NEW YORK TIMES, July 21, 1990, at 3.

In the summer of 1990, Weinstein flew to Texas and Cleveland to meet with Parker and Lambros.[31] Weinstein and Parker agreed that Weinstein would stop the bleeding of the Manville Trust so it could pay judgments. For his part, Weinstein would try to protect Parker's judgments or at least 75 percent of each of Parker's judgments.

Ten district judges with many asbestos claims on their dockets then met at the Federal Judicial Center in Washington. Though no judge emerged from the meeting charged to attempt global settlement, an attempt was made to consolidate most of the asbestos claims into three groups. Weinstein was to handle Manville and cases involving six other financially insecure defendants who did not have the money to pay off potential claimants. Lambros was to oversee a national settlement of two class actions. Parker was to be responsible for oversight of those cases where the defendants had been unwilling to settle and, if need be, to try them.[32]

Weinstein's memory of the meeting in Washington is that he had not pressed the matter of global settlement for, if he had, there would have been no agreement. The *New York Times* reported that Weinstein had told colleagues and friends that he agreed to the judges' plan because he was not convinced that broader class actions would survive appellate review. Another time, he gave a different reason: "Our country is too diverse, too large and too exciting for a single solution for asbestos claims."[33] Nevertheless, it is likely that he it considered a mistake not to consolidate everything into a single federal class action.[34]

In any event, the Court of Appeals for the Sixth Circuit, considering an application to mandamus Lambros, made clear that the group of judges had no jurisdiction, and Judge Lambros backed down from putting his part of the plan into effect.[35]

The Multidistrict Panel, prodded by a letter from eight judges[36] finally acted at the end of July 1991. The Panel consolidated more than 26,000 cases and transferred them to Judge Charles Weiner of the Eastern District of Pennsylvania, a very well regarded judge with a track record of innovation and accomplishment with asbestos cases.[37] Between 1991 and July 2003, Weiner presided over 105,000 asbestos-related lawsuits, closing out 78,000.[38] No global solution ever occurred. Asbestos-related cases are still with us in large numbers.

Nevertheless, Weinstein still was responsible for the asbestos cases brought by those who had worked at the Brooklyn Navy Yard. For Weinstein, the Brooklyn Navy

---

[31] Weinstein Oral History, at 667ff; 675ff.

[32] NEW YORK TIMES, Aug. 1, 1990, at 1, 35; Aug. 11, 1990, at A1.

[33] Weinstein Oral History, at 656–57; NEW YORK TIMES, Aug. 14, 1990, at D1, D2; *A Conversation with Judge Jack B. Weinstein*, BUS. INS., Oct. 30, 1992, at 88.

[34] *See* WEINSTEIN, INDIVIDUAL JUSTICE, *supra* note 14, at 87.

[35] *In re Allied-Signal, Inc.*, 1990 U.S. App. LEXIS 16573 (6th Cir. 1990).

[36] Weinstein did not technically "sign" the letter, but contacted the Panel's staff and requested that he be a signatory. *In re Asbestos Prods. Liab. Litig.*, 771 F. Supp. 415, 417 n. 3 (J.P.M.L. 1991).

[37] *In re Asbestos Prods. Liab. Litig.*, 771 F. Supp. 415 (J.P.M.L. July 29, 1991); NEW YORK TIMES, July 30, 1991, at 1A.

[38] 35 *Third Branch*, No. 7 (July 2003).

Yard cases triggered deep feelings. For Weinstein, the Brooklyn Navy Yard was a place for which he had a "strong sense of affection and attachment." His maternal grandparents had made their home in its neighborhood, and Weinstein remembered walking to buy food at a market which became a part of the Naval Yard.[39] He had worked at the Naval Yard while attending Brooklyn College at night. This strong but emotional man remembered that the plaintiffs had worked as young men during the Second World War building battleships and aircraft carriers urgently needed to defeat the Japanese. They had "labored in clouds of asbestos."[40] Reflecting on the Texas cases Judge Parker had settled, Weinstein said of the Navy Yard plaintiffs: "I felt that these were my people. Why should all the money go to East Texas? Let's take care of some of our own people. They were the kind of people that I knew when I grew up—ironmongers and painters and others."[41]

Weinstein's jurisdictional authority for handling the Navy Yard cases was dazzling. He sat not only as a judge of the Eastern District of New York, but also by designation as judge of the Southern District of New York. When he wanted to consolidate the Southern District asbestos cases with those in the Eastern District, he literally walked across the Brooklyn Bridge, sat as a designated Southern District judge, and granted a motion to transfer the cases to himself.[42] He was also working in tandem with Helen Freedman who had the state cases.

Attorneys claimed that having the state and federal cases proceed together with trials beginning on September 10, 1990, was "a cleverly designed move to maximize pressure for settlement."[43] A few cases were tried while settlement talks went on. Plaintiffs won thirty-four *state* asbestos cases tried to a jury with damage awards averaging $2 million. Weinstein tried sixty-four Navy Yard cases, including fifty cases in one sitting.[44] The defendants won twelve. The average award in the fifty-two other cases was $478,000.[45] Weinstein said that trying the cases "had a great effect on me, just seeing these people and how their lives had been destroyed."[46]

By March 17, 1992, the courts in New York City had disposed of almost all their asbestos related cases. With the assistance of Charles P. Sifton (Eastern District) and Robert W. Sweet (Southern District), Weinstein and Freedman had resolved a total of nearly 2,400 federal and state cases.[47]

---

[39] Weinstein Oral History, at 1348.

[40] Weinstein & Aschenbrenner, *supra* note 5, at 1053.

[41] Weinstein Oral History, at 673–74.

[42] Alison Frankel, *Waiting for Weinstein*, AMERICAN LAWYER 22–23 (February 2003).

[43] N.Y.L.J., Sept. 13, 1990, at 1, 4. Kenneth Feinberg was appointed jointly by Freedman and Weinstein to settle the approximately 550 Navy Yard cases. WALL STREET JOURNAL, Sept. 13, 1990.

[44] Kenneth P. Nolan, *Weinstein on the Courts*, 18 LITIG. 24, 25 (Spring 1992). *See also* Weinstein Oral History, at 673.

[45] N.Y.L.J., Mar. 22, 1991, at 1, 2.

[46] Weinstein Oral History, at 755.

[47] All but 8 of the 1096 Navy Yard power plant cases. Four hundred fifty-seven cases were transferred to the Eastern District of Pennsylvania. WALL STREET JOURNAL, Mar. 17, 1992; N.Y.L.J., Mar. 17, 1992; NEW YORK DAILY NEWS, Mar. 17, 1992.

Weinstein was also responsible for the cases brought against the Eagle-Picher Company, a small player in the asbestos world. He attempted, but did not succeed, in having Eagle-Picher become the first company to have all asbestos litigation against it consolidated into a single case without declaring bankruptcy.[48] To achieve this, Weinstein issued a series of near-path-breaking opinions on the power of the court to stay litigation in state and federal courts.[49]

In December 1990, Weinstein approved a class action settlement covering 175,000 claimants (65,000 current and an estimated 100,000 future claimants). He also ordered a suspension of cases involving an estimated 70,000 claimants in other state and federal courts.[50] The settlement under which the company would have had to pay an estimated $500 million, regardless how many claims turned up in the future, limited attorneys' fees. It was "bitterly and almost unanimously" opposed by plaintiffs' lawyers and failed.[51] In January 1991, after a last minute collapse of a deal to sell one of its divisions, Eagle-Picher filed for Chapter 11 bankruptcy protection.[52]

Weinstein's work with asbestos cases was not nearly as dazzling as his work in *Agent Orange*. He did reconstruct the Manville Trust, which came to be regarded as a paradigm for compensating asbestos victims. Ironically, the procedures of the trust became so efficient that people who might not have filed claims came to do so. Weinstein exercised extraordinary equity powers, including an order to stay all state and federal actions through the device of a mandatory class action. He also continued to innovate in the use of special masters and wrote the first opinion addressing the ethics of a mediator in a class action.[53] He also exercised powers jointly and effectively with a state judge and continued to innovate in the use of court-appointed experts.[54] However, his class

---

[48] NEW YORK TIMES, Dec. 11, 1990.

[49] Weinstein had appointed Marvin Frankel as a special master to determine if the company had enough funds to pay all claims and ordered the company to begin settlement talks with Feinberg as special master. WALL STREET JOURNAL, Nov. 6, 1990; NEW YORK TIMES, Oct. 2, 1990, n.p. See also NEW YORK TIMES, Aug. 14, 1990, n.p.

[50] WALL STREET JOURNAL, Dec. 11, 1990, at B4.

[51] NEW YORK TIMES, Dec. 13, 1990; Weinstein Oral History, at 1021–22.

[52] WALL STREET JOURNAL, Jan. 8, 1991; PROD, SAFETY & LIAB. RPTR., Jan. 31, 1991, at 36. Weinstein was also unsuccessful in attempting to use a Rule 23(B)(1)(b) class action to save the Keene Corporation from bankruptcy because the Court of Appeals, which generally preferred disposition of claims through bankruptcy rather than class actions, vacated, and dismissed his decision. *See In re Joint District Asbestos Litig. (Keene Corp. v. Fiorelli)*, 1993 WL 604077 (July 1, 1993), *vacated and dismissed*, 14 F.3d 726 (Dec. 1, 1993: Winter-VanG-Pollock); WEINSTEIN, INDIVIDUAL JUSTICE, *supra* note 14, at 6. 2081; Weinstein Oral History, at 514ff; WALL STREET JOURNAL, Dec. 6, 1993, at 38. WALL STREET JOURNAL, Dec. 2, 1993 and Dec. 6, 1993, at 38; Weinstein Oral History, at 1230.

[53] *See* Alison Frankel, *Waiting for Weinstein*, AM. LAW. 22–23 (Feb. 2003); Weinstein Oral History, at 983–89, 1370; In re Joint Eastern & Southern Asbestos Litig., 134 F.R.D. 32 (Dec. 12, 1990). *See also* 151 F.R.D. 540 (Nov. 5, 1993); 830 F. Supp. 686, 693 (Aug. 12, 1993); 151 F.R.D. 540, 542, 545–46 (Nov. 5, 1993).

[54] Mention should be made of *Rummo v. Celotex Corp.*, 726 F. Supp. 426 (Dec. 7, 1989), which proved to be an important case in determining what asbestos claims were worth. Weinstein held that the measure of an asbestos victim's damages for loss of future income should under New York law be based on the many years he might have lived but for exposure to asbestos rather than based on the one year he might be

action settlement for Manville claimants, as did his efforts to avoid bankruptcy for Eagle-Picher (and the Keene Corporation), failed. Weinstein's greatest failure was his ambitious effort to resolve all of America's asbestos claims in one class action. At the time this book is written, at least one company in nearly every U.S. industry was involved in asbestos litigation.[55]

THE DES CASES

Weinstein was responsible for the suits in the Eastern District related to the harm caused by the drug DES. Two opinions are of particular interest.

DES, a synthetic estrogen, was developed in the late 1930s and marketed by about three hundred pharmaceutical companies. In 1947–1948 the FDA gave manufacturers permission to market DES to prevent miscarriage and fetal death. Millions of pregnant women ingested DES in the 1950s and 1960s without knowing its dangers or the identity of the manufacturers of the particular drug they took. By 1971, DES was found responsible for the appearance of a rare form of vaginal cancer.The Food and Drug Administration (FDA) disapproved its marketing in the United States for use during pregnancy. As time went on, evidence accumulated that DES caused other serious problems including uterine deformities, ectopic pregnancies, and defects in the female children of those who had taken it. Litigation over alleged DES-related injuries began in the 1970s.

Generally, state courts do not have jurisdiction over a defendant unless he can be served in the estate or receive service of process in the state or is "doing business" in the state. In the *DES* cases, one of the defendants, Boehringer Ingelheim Pharmaceuticals, Inc., had not produced or sold DES *at all*. Rather, it had merged with a company that had obtained its supply of DES from chemical companies located in states (*other than New York*); had manufactured DES tablets in a few states (*but not New York*); and had sold the tablets in several states (*but not New York*). The company was never licensed to do business in New York, it never maintained an office in New York and it never shipped DES to New York. Under the traditional tests, the plaintiffs would not have had personal jurisdiction over Boehringer. Yet, its DES tablets were part of the national market for DES.

In Weinstein's opinion on jurisdiction in the DES cases, *Ashley v. Abbott Laboratories*[56] he held that New York could exercise personal jurisdiction over a nonresident manufacturer of DES without a showing that a manufacturer had minimum contacts or any

---

able to live. The plaintiff, a Brooklyn Navy Yard worker, received $775,000. *See also* N.Y.L.J., Dec. 14, 1989; Weinstein Oral History, at 968.

[55] *Judge Jack B. Weinstein, Tort Litigation and the Public Good: A Roundtable Discussion to Honor One of America's Great Trial Judges on the Occasion of his 80th Birthday*, 12 J. L.& POL.149, 177.[hereinafter *80th Birthday Roundtable*]; AMERICAN ACADEMY OF ACTUARIES, *supra* note 4, at 25.

[56] *In re DES Cases (Ashley v. Abbott Labs.)*, 789 F. Supp. 552 (Apr. 13, 1992), *appeal dismissed*, 7 F.3d 20 (Oct. 4, 1993) (2d C. 1993).

territorial connection with New York. Although his opinion was limited to *DES* cases, the decision set forth an analytical framework, which Weinstein asserted should be used to modify traditional limits on personal jurisdiction where mass torts were involved.[57] The opinion is a fine example of creative judicial activism rendered by a brilliant craftsman. Weinstein perceived the case before him an ideal vehicle for rethinking and altering an area of law he believed was "all fouled up."[58] That area is so technical and prickly that few judges would wish to tread in it. Yet for Weinstein, it was one he understood since his work revising the New York Civil Practice Act and Rules and one to which he had continued to give much thought. Although the field was arcane, its application was quite practical.

Weinstein approached the case not only with the desire to modernize the law, but with a politico-economic philosophy – that the United States should be treated as a common economic pond – and with awareness that his reform would benefit some litigants (plaintiffs) and disadvantage others (some defendants). (It is not clear that a redistribution of strategic advantages was a motivating factor.) Weinstein thought that, if the case had been reviewed, there "would have been an almost sure reversal in the Court of Appeals,"[59] because it was at odds with Supreme Court precedents on personal jurisdiction.[60] But it seemed likely that the case would settle. As a result, Weinstein employed his skill as a treatise writer to create a brilliantly wrought, scholarly and, in many ways, highly persuasive opinion. As it happened, there would be an appeal in the case, but the appeal would be dismissed.[61]

Weinstein had been a strong critic of the rules of jurisdiction in the United States since his revision of the Civil Practice Law and Rules (CPLR). He said in his oral history: ". . . the present position on jurisdiction in the United States is all wet . . . . It's wrong in principle. It's wrong in history. It's wrong in practice. It ought to be modified."[62] Rather than viewing the market on a state-by-state basis and determining jurisdiction over companies doing business in a particular state, Weinstein's view, evident in the blasting cap cases,[63] was that "the United States constitutes a common economic pond that knows no state boundaries. A substantial interjection of products at any point of the national market has ripple effects in all parts of the market."[64] Thus, a corporation that

---

[57] Sheila L. Birnbaum & Gary E. Crawford, *Jurisdiction Ruling Charts New Course*, NAT'L L.J. 18 (June 22, 1992).

[58] Weinstein Oral History, at 1128–29.

[59] 7 F.3d 20 (Oct. 4, 1993). Weinstein Oral, at p. 1133. See Stephen B. Burbank, *The Courtroom as Classroom: Independence, Imagination and Ideology in the Work of Jack Weinstein*, 97 COLUM. L. REV. 1971, 1990 (1997),

[60] *See World-Wide Volkswagen Corp. v. Woodson*, 444 U.S. 286 (1980); *Asahi Metal Indus. Co. v. Superior Court*, 480 U.S. 102 (1987) (plurality opinion). Birnbaum & Crawford, *supra* note, at 20. Weinstein attacked many of the underpinnings of the Supreme Court's personal jurisdiction jurisprudence including *Pennoyer v. Neff*, 95 U.S. 714 (1877) and *International Shoe v. Washington*, 326 U.S. 810 (1945).

[61] 7 F.3d 20 (Oct. 4, 1993).

[62] Weinstein Oral History, at 1128–29.

[63] Weinstein Oral History, at 255–56. *See infra*, p. Ch. 5.

[64] *In re DES Cases (Ashley v. Abbott Labs.)*, 789 F. Supp. 552, 576 (Apr. 13, 1992).

sells only in states west of the Mississippi River would be subject to personal jurisdiction in New York because of its participation in the DES national market. The ripple effects provide the foundation for jurisdiction.

In *Ashley v. Abbott Laboratories*, Weinstein perceived that he had an excellent vehicle to attack the problem. He had to apply New York State substantive law in the case. The New York Court of Appeals, in deciding a *DES* case, had employed an expansive market-share theory.[65] Under New York law, it did not matter whose pills a plaintiff had taken. The only way for a defendant to escape liability was to prove that it never marketed DES for use by pregnant women. To limit personal jurisdiction, thus, would be inconsistent with New York's interest in providing recovery based on a market-share rationale. Thus, Weinstein had a perfect vehicle to express himself on jurisdiction. As he said, ". . . this was the ideal case, I thought, to take a whack at it. I took the opportunity to do so."[66]

The first part of Weinstein's *Ashley* opinion dealt with New York's long arm jurisdiction. He fudged his handling of that issue to get to his new standard for jurisdiction. He explained: "I think what I did here was not supportable in theory or practice and I knew it wasn't, but I wanted to get to the second point. I knew it wasn't [correct] because when I had originally drafted the New York Long-Arm statute . . ."[67]

In *Ashley*, Weinstein wrote a 103-page treatise in which he explained why the traditional "territorial nexus" approach should be abandoned and then put forward an approach he thought more appropriate for modern life. What Weinstein was attempting to do was to fashion "a revolutionary new standard for judicial jurisdiction in DES and 'perhaps' other mass tort cases that focuses on the forum state's interest in vindication of its law, rather than its territorial contacts with the defendant alone."[68] Weinstein's new rule meant that a defendant could be served for a mass tort in any state which has "an appreciable interest in the litigation," so long as the defendant is able to mount a defense in the forum state without suffering relatively substantial hardship.[69] The effect of Weinstein's approach would be helpful to plaintiffs because it would nullify a "particularly pernicious advantage used by foreign competitors who could fashion their corporate structure to avoid significant contacts for jurisdictional purposes."[70]

The *Ashley* opinion was a tour de force which received considerable praise. One who applauded the decision was Weinstein's colleague, friend and seminar-collaborator,

---

[65] *Hymowitz v. Eli Lilly & Co.*, 73 N.Y.2d 487, *cert. denied*, 494 U.S. 944 (1989). *See also* Weinstein Oral History, at 1130.

[66] Weinstein Oral History, at 1130.

[67] Weinstein Oral History, at 1128.

[68] Harold Korn, *Rethinking Personal Jurisdiction and Choice of Law in Mass Torts*, 97 COLUM. L. REV. 2183 (1997).

[69] A state has an appreciable interest in a case if it raises issues whose resolution would be affected by, or has a probable impact on the vindication of, policies expressed in the substantive, procedural or remedial law of the forum. LAWYERS ALERT, June 8, 1992.

[70] NATIONAL L.J., Apr. 22, 1992.

Harold Korn of Columbia Law School, who called it "one of Judge Weinstein's most brilliant and prophetic ... decisions," added that Weinstein had "arrived at the right answer in the *DES cases* because he asked the right question in the right order, not withstanding existing doctrines pointing the other way."[71] Professor Burt Neuborne of New York University Law School thought that:

> In the DES cases, Judge Weinstein tried to push the outer envelope of *in personam* jurisdiction in an effort to create a single forum in which all the significant players could be united ...[72]

However, the opinion has not yet been influential.[73] Weinstein would return to his expanded view of personal jurisdiction in the light cigarette class action in 2000.[74]

Weinstein's second important opinion in the *DES cases* was his ninety page opinion on the defendants' motion for summary judgment on the ground that the statute of limitations had run. The opinion is an excellent example of how technically complex legal questions may have a dramatic effect on outcomes.[75] The New York Statute of Limitations began to run from the time the plaintiff discovered "her injury." But when would that be for the daughters of DES mothers who were now experiencing reproductive problems? Did the discovery of the "injury" run from the time they first found out that their mothers had taken the drug twenty years before? At that time, the daughters could well not have known that their *potential* infertility problems, miscarriages, and reproductive track abnormalities might be the result of DES. Weinstein held that awareness of the medical problem alone did not by itself trigger the statute of limitations. The statute of limitations was triggered when the daughters had a good reason to conclude that a human-made product had led to the difficulty.[76] This was a favorable, but not unrealistic, reading of the statute for the plaintiffs, as the whole picture of the class of injuries emerged "gradually."[77]

Weinstein held four meetings in his chambers with DES plaintiffs. They left a profound mark on him.[78] The meetings were held so that the judge could hear the stories

---

[71] Korn, *supra* note 68, at 2184, 2200.

[72] Burt Neuborne, *Innovation in the Interstices of the Final Judgment Rule: A Demurrer to Professor Burbank*, 97 COLUM. L. REV. 2091, 2097–98. *See also* LAWYERS ALERT, June 8, 1992, n.p.

[73] Weinstein Oral History, at 1132. On the *DES* jurisdiction opinion, see Comment: *Throwing Personal Jurisdiction into the Pond: Mass Tort Defendants' Rights Ripple Away in* Ashley v. Abbott Laboratories, 59 BROOK. L. REV. 1617 (1994).

[74] *Simon v. Phillip Morris, Inc.*, 86 F. Supp. 2d 95 (Mar. 3, 2000).

[75] *Braune v. Abbott Labs.*, 895 F. Supp. 530 (Aug. 9, 1995).

[76] *Id.* at 545.

[77] *Id.* at 547.

[78] He held an additional meeting after he had closed out his cases; letting DES daughters tell their stories and then offering a perspective on the legal background. *In re DES Litigation*, July 14, 2009.

of DES daughters and one DES son and those of a number of family members. The meetings were on the record with counsel for both sides were present. Weinstein heard stories such as that of a thirty-eight-year-old woman who had countless surgeries and eight years of infertility treatments and of a woman who developed lymphedema which caused her body to swell to such gross proportions that she was unable to sit or stand. Weinstein listened intently to story after story and expressed his compassion after each.

After defendants moved that Weinstein recuse himself for bias, he wrote an opinion with great care refusing to recuse himself. Weinstein also made sure to publish his opinion quickly, before the case settled.[79] He stressed that the conferences were conducted "in the court's role as settlement judge . . .."[80] The persons he saw were "representative plaintiffs, engaged in settlement negotiations, who desired to share their DES experiences with the court, to express their views about the litigation and to hear from the court how the cases might be resolved without trial."[81] He wrote that "the fact that a judge empathizes with other human beings does not render him or her partial. Were that the case, the only judges who would be able to preside over cases involving serious injury and suffering would be those who lack compassion."[82] Then Weinstein gave his view of one of the most important functions of courts:

> During the settlement process there is often a need for the court to communicate with the parties. Plaintiffs, particularly in mass cases, may feel alienated and disenfranchised . . . They have a need to vent, to express their frustrations, to feel that the system really cares about what happened to them."[83]

Weinstein said that there was "no basis in fact for a claim of partiality," that he had "maintained neutrality at all times,"[84] but he went on, "It would be unreasonable for defendants to expect this judge, or any other human being, not to be moved by such tragic tales of years of suffering."[85] Indeed, he pointed out, defense counsel "themselves have evinced much sympathy during settlement conferences as well as trial."[86] At another time, however, he admitted that he had "a very strong feeling for these people," as he had for the Brooklyn Navy Yard asbestos victims and those at the Suffolk County

---

[79] *Bilello v. Abbott Labs.*, 825 F. Supp. 475 (July 2, 1993). *See* 1992 Scrapbook, May 28, 1992, n.p.; Weinstein Oral History, at 1233–34; WEINSTEIN, INDIVIDUAL JUSTICE, *supra* note 14 at 276 n. 45.

[80] *Bilello*, 825 F. Supp. at 476.

[81] *Id.* at 476.

[82] *Id.* at 481.

[83] *Id.* at 480. On the meetings, see Pamela Newkirk, *Victims of DES Testify*, NEWSDAY, May 28, 1992, at 6.

[84] *Id.* at 477.

[85] *Id.* at 476.

[86] *Id.* at 481.

Developmental Center.[87] Weinstein's encounters with the victims of Agent Orange and DES and their families continue to affect, perhaps even to haunt, him.[88]

BREAST IMPLANT LITIGATION

Weinstein made one important contribution to the breast implant litigation—the creation and naming of a panel of neutral experts to guide judges in dealing with the medical issues. That appears to have stimulated Judge Sam Pointer, assigned by the Multidistrict Litigation panel to handle the case nationally, to do the same.

From the early 1980s, there were reports that women who had silicone breast implants were suffering connective tissue disease. The first multimillion dollar breast implant suit was filed as early as 1982.[89] In June 1992, the Multidistrict Litigation panel certified a multidistrict class action lawsuit against major implant manufacturers.[90] Attempts to settle the litigation were unsuccessful. Dow Corning, the largest manufacturer of the product, filed for bankruptcy protection.[91]

The problem with this class action was that it was "immature." There was little reliable science connecting the product to potential health problems. Not until 1994 were there a series of well-controlled, well-conducted epidemiological studies. The studies, however, failed to reveal any association between silicone gel breast implants and various connective tissue diseases.[92] Not until 1996 could it be said with "reasonable confidence" (on the basis of about ten epidemiological studies), that the links between breast implants and a variety of systemic diseases and symptoms was *very small, if it existed at all.*[93]

Judge Pointer of the Northern District of Alabama conditionally certified a nationwide class of women claiming compensation for injuries associated with silicone gel breast implants. In 1994, 400,000 claimants stepped forward.[94]

---

[87] Weinstein Oral History, at 675.

[88] To settle the *DES* cases, Weinstein worked with Justices James B. Cane and Ira Gamerman of the state courts. Kenneth Feinberg was appointed special master to report to the courts on the use of a panel of expert witnesses on market shares and individual causality. *In re DES Cases*, 789 F. Supp. 552 (Apr. 13, 1992).

[89] David E. Bernstein, Review Essay: *The Breast Implant Fiasco:* SCIENCE ON TRIAL: THE CLASH OF MEDICAL EVIDENCE AND THE LAW IN THE BREAST IMPLANT CASES BY MARCIA ANGELL (1996), 87 CAL. L. REV. 457, 485 (1999) [hereinafter Bernstein, Review Essay]; Joseph M. Price & Ellen S. Rosenberg, *The Silicone Gel Breast Implant Controversy: The Rise of Expert Panels and the Fall of Junk Science*, 93(1) J. ROYAL SOC'Y MED. 31 (Jan. 2000), James E. Rooks, Jr., *Science on Trial: The Clash of Medical Evidence and Law in the Breast Implant Case*, TRIAL (Nov. 1, 1996).

[90] Bernstein, Review Essay, *supra* note 89, at 477.

[91] MARCIA ANGELL, SCIENCE ON TRIAL: MEDICAL EVIDENCE AND THE LAW IN THE BREAST IMPLANT CASE IN MANHATTAN INSTITUTE FOR POLICY RESEARCH, Civil Justice Memo. No. 28, at 1 (1996) [hereinafter ANGELL, SCIENCE ON TRIAL].

[92] Price & Rosenberg, *supra* note 89, at 31.

[93] *Id. See also* ANGELL, SCIENCE ON TRIAL, *supra* note 91, at 4.

[94] DEBRA HENSLER, CLASS ACTION DILEMMAS 27 (2000).

The Multidistrict Panel assigned for trial pending cases in the Southern District of New York to Judge Harold Baer and those in the Eastern District to Weinstein. New York State Judge Joan B. Lobis was assigned to handle the New York State cases. The three judges coordinated the management of their cases with each other.

On April 3, 1996, Weinstein and Baer named a team of three special masters to help *identify* what *science* the judges *needed to* know to deal with the connection between breast implants and serious health problems—the state of the scientific evidence on the connection between silicone gel and exacerbated connective tissue diseases or immune dysfunction—as well as to help select the panel of experts to advise the court.[95] Contemporaneously, Judge Robert E. Jones of the U.S. District Court of the District of Oregon also appointed a panel of experts on causation of connective tissue disease by breast implants.[96]

After Weinstein and Baer had acted, Judge Pointer, acknowledging the use of Weinstein's procedures, employed Rule 706 of the Federal Rules of Evidence,[97] and appointed his own panel. Pointer appointed the three members of Weinstein's panel and added three experts of his own. Pointer's panel then identified four persons to deal with the scientific literature relevant to the breast implant litigation—specialists for toxicology, immunology, epidemiology, and rheumatology.[98] A report and videotaped testimony was to be produced, intended to become part of the record in all federal breast implant cases.[99]

In assessing the experiments by Pointer and Jones, scholars at the Federal Judicial Center were cautious about the use of such panels, yet strongly supported their use here:

> In the two cases presented here, the complexity of the evidence and the importance of establishing an accurate foundation for future litigation argued strongly for such extraordinary procedures.[100]

---

[95] *See In re Breast Implant Cases,* 942 F. Supp. 958 (Oct. 23, 1996: E.D.N.Y. & S.D.N.Y.: Weinstein & Baer). Judge Lobis encouraged all parties to participate with the panel. NEW YORK TIMES, April 4, 1996. The three special masters Weinstein selected each had a prior connection to Weinstein or to litigation Weinstein had handled: Margaret Berger (former law clerk, professor of law, and co-author of the evidence treatise), Joel E. Cohen (mathematician and scientist at Rockefeller University, who had participated in the Johns Manville bankruptcy litigation), and Alan Wolfe (professor of physics at Cooper Union and an adjunct professor at Cardozo Law School, who had once interned for Weinstein and served as an expert for a party in Manville). Joint Order No. 1, Appt. Special Master, *In re Silicone,* 96-BI-1 (1996); Laura L. Hooper et al., *Assessing Causation in Breast implant Litigation, The Role of Science Panels,* 64 LAW & CONTEMP. PROBS. 139, 146, 150, 155n, 155, 158. *See also* Weinstein Oral History, at 1415–34.

[96] *Hall v. Baxter Healthcare Corp.,* 947 F. Supp. 1387 (D. Or. 1996). *See also* Howard M. Erichson, *Mass Tort Litigation and Inquisitorial Justice,* 87 GEO. L. J. 1983 (1999).

[97] Rule 706 deals with court-appointed expert witnesses.

[98] Price & Rosenberg, *supra* note 89, at 33; Hooper et al., *supra* note 95, at 142. *See also In re Breast Implant Cases,* 942 F. Supp. 958 (Oct. 23, 1966).

[99] Price & Rosenberg, *supra* note 89, at 157–58.

[100] *Id.* at 182. Such panels were endorsed by Justice Stephen Breyer in his concurring opinion in *General Electric Co. v. Joiner,* 522 U.S. 136, 149–50 (1997).

The mere anticipation of the Pointer panel report led to a $3.2 billion settlement with Dow Corning.[101]

In October 1996, Baer and Weinstein denied motions for summary judgment and chose to sever the trials of systemic injuries (autoimmune and connective tissue disorders) and local injuries (pain and suffering arising from capsular-contracture, rupture, leakage, permanent disfigurement) and to try the local injuries first.[102]

Weinstein presided over the settlement of the Eastern District's breast implant cases, which were settled without an adequate scientific basis.[103] His conclusion was:

> The hundreds of symptoms associated with this undifferentiated disease, the lack of any acceptable agreed upon definition, the inadequacy of any satisfactory supporting epidemiological or animal studies, the lack of a scientifically acceptable showing of medical plausibility, and the questionable nature of the clinical conclusions of the treating doctors, all point to a failure of proof in making a *prima facie* case that silicone implants cause any of the syndromes claimed.[104]

REPETITIVE STRESS INJURY CASES

The repetitive stress injury cases (RSI) proved to be a lost opportunity for Weinstein. The cases involved injuries arguably caused by the routine use of computers, supermarket checkout scanners, and other devices. The central legal problem was whether there could be consolidation of cases covering a number of different ailments for which there might have been numerous different causes.[105] Scientific evidence about the problem was limited.

Weinstein had the earliest filed RSI case in the district. When the initial assignment was made to Weinstein, forty-four cases were pending. Ultimately, there were more than a thousand and Weinstein chose to consolidate them, the first time many RSI cases had been consolidated.[106] As the judge of the earliest-filed case, Weinstein heard its pretrial motions.

---

[101] Howard M. Erichson, *Mass Tort Litigation and Inquisitorial Justice*, 87 GEO. L.J. 1983 (1999).

[102] Burbank, *supra* note 59, at 2001. *See also* N.Y.L.J., Oct. 21, 1996, at 1, 5.

[103] Weinstein Oral History, at 658. *See* NEW YORK TIMES, Nov. 9, 1998, at A1.

[104] Quoted in Price & Rosenberg, *supra* note 89, at 31.

[105] *See Debruyne v. National Semiconductor Corp.: In re Repetitive Stress Injury Litig.*, 11 F.3d 368 (Dec. 9, 1993: Winter-Mesk-Pratt) [hereinafter *Dubruyne II*]. The Judicial Panel on Multidistrict Litigation declined to consolidate the RSI cases for unified pretrial proceedings. *In re Repeated Stress Injury Prod. Liab. Litig.*, 1992 WL 463023 (Nov. 27, 1992).

[106] *In re Repetitive Stress Injury Cases*, 142 F.R.D. 584 (June 2, 1992). *See also* Donatella A. Lorch, *Hand Injuries in Workplace Ignites Battle*, NEW YORK TIMES, June 3, 1992. *See also* NEW YORK TIMES, July 7, 1992.

By this time, the Court of Appeals, especially Judges Winter, Newman, and Van Graafeiland, were extremely skeptical of Weinstein's approach to mass torts, which was "to try to get as many cases under one roof as possible." A panel of Judges Winter (writing), Meskill, and Pratt, while dismissing appeals of Weinstein's consolidation order, granted mandamus *sua sponte*, overturning it.[107] Judge Ralph Winter wrote that "[t]he district court substituted a discussion of so-called mass torts for precise findings as to what are the 'common questions of law or fact justifying consolidation;' a sufficiently clear abuse of discretion to warrant mandamus relief."[108]

Weinstein believed that the Court of Appeals' dislike of consolidations resulted from the view that consolidations were too costly for defendants who are forced to settle. He thought that the appellate court did not understand his views as consolidation "would have really saved the defendants and the country a good deal if we could get this thing settled fast and get the proper science in and avoid a great deal of problems in the future."[109] He saw the litigation as "an ideal case for indicating the limits and the capacity to handle some of the cases in the federal court system."[110]

After the Second Circuit's order, Weinstein only played a small role in the RSI cases.[111] He did try the first RSI case where a plaintiff won a significant award from the makers of computer keyboards.[112] To determine the appropriateness of the amount of the verdict under New York law, Weinstein published an opinion that essentially was a small treatise on the manner in which a court should go about determining whether a damages award is reasonable, that is how to find if such an award deviates materially from what is appropriate. This opinion has proven very influential in both federal and state courts.[113]

---

[107] The panel was Winter (writing), Meskill, and Pratt. Weinstein said that, "It never occurred to me that they would mandamus in this kind of situation or I would have covered it by saying that this is not a consolidation, but that they are being banded together for purposes of discovery only." Weinstein Oral History, at 1144–45.

[108] *Dubruyne-II*, *supra* note 105, at 373.

[109] Weinstein Oral History, at 1142. As the judge assigned to try the cases, Weinstein was entitled to be heard at the Court of Appeals on the mandamus. The Second Circuit overlooked this initially, but offered the opportunity when it was dealing with the petition No one exercised that option. *See Debruyne v. National Semiconductor Corp.*, 35 F.3d 637 (July 24, 1994). *See also* 35 F.3d 640 (Aug. 29, 1994).

[110] Weinstein Oral History, at 1144. *See also id.* at 1141.

[111] In *Dorsey v. Apple Computers, Inc.*, 936 F. Supp. 89 (Oct. 22, 1996), Weinstein read the New York State statute of limitations favorably to a claimant who tied her injuries to work at her computer.

[112] NEW YORK TIMES, Dec. 10, 1996, at D1. Patricia Geressy was awarded $5.3 million, but Weinstein ordered a new trial when it was discovered that she had not disclosed before or during trial that she had a nerve injury prior to her experience at the computer. *See also Geressy v. Digital Equip. Corp.* 980 F. Supp. 640 (Sept. 16, 1997). *See also* NEWSDAY, June 16, 1998. *And see Gonzalez v. Digital Equip. Co.*, 8 F. Supp. 2d 194 (June 8, 1998), *rev'd sub nom. Rotolo v. Digital Equip. Corp.*, 150 F.3d 223 (July 24, 1988: *VanG-Mesk-Cab*). *And see* N.Y.L.J., Sept. 30, 1996.

[113] *Geressy v. Digital Equip. Corp.*, 980 F. Supp. 640, 653ff (Sept. 16, 1997).

GUN CASES

Beginning in 1995, Weinstein handled a series of cases aimed at limiting the flow of illegal guns into New York City. For his efforts, which bucked the national pro-gun trend, Weinstein was sharply attacked by the gun lobby, and there were calls for his impeachment.[114] Yet, none of these cases produced a victory for plaintiffs.

Weinstein has heard two types of gun cases. The first were private suits for damages brought by plaintiffs whose husbands or children were killed with guns which, it was alleged, reached New York as the result of the negligence in distributing the weapons by manufacturers and later sellers. The other suits were brought by the National Association for the Advancement of Colored People (NAACP) and the City of New York and were based on a theory of nuisance.

Hamilton v. ACCU-TEK, the lead negligent marketing suit, was a private action predicated upon the theory that the gun manufacturers were knowingly oversupplying the market in states with weak gun laws, which thereby permitted distributors to make illegal sales to out-of-state purchasers.[115] Forty-nine gun manufacturers and thirty-four gun distributors were sued,—the first cases dealing with the marketing practices of gun manufacturers and the first cases attempting to hold the industry collectively liable.[116] Weinstein ruled that, as in the blasting cap cases, manufacturers may be collectively responsible for damages resulting from gun-related violence.

When he denied the defendants' motion to dismiss in Hamilton *v. ACCU-TEK*,[117] Weinstein accepted plaintiff's theory that defendants' negligence in marketing handguns and flooding the market had fostered the development of an extensive underground market where it was easy for youths to illegally obtain handguns. The guns would be used, ultimately killing such individuals as the decedents. In October 1996, Weinstein refused to certify an interlocutory appeal of that decision without a more extensive factual underpinning.[118]

While the *Hamilton* case was pending, Weinstein dealt with a very visible local gun case, *Halberstam v. S.W. Daniel*.[119] In that case, Weinstein became the first judge to allow

---

[114] *See* Weinstein Oral History, at 1415–43.

[115] NEW YORK TIMES, Feb. 12, 1999; Mar. 14, 1998, at B3; Timothy D. Lytton, Halberstam v. Daniel *and the Uncertain Future of Negligent Marketing Claims against Firearms Manufacturers*, 64 BROOK. L. REV. 681ff (1998).

[116] NEW YORK TIMES, May 3, 1996.

[117] 935 F. Supp. 1307 (May 2, 1996).

[118] Transcript of Hearing on Motions, Oct. 25, 1966, *Hamilton v. Accu-Tek*, 95 CV 0049.

[119] *Hallberstam v. S.W. Daniels*, No. 96-5254. The case involved a Jewish boy, riding in a van across the Brooklyn Bridge, who was shot by a livery-cab driver retaliating for a massacre of Muslim worshippers in Hebron. The gun used had been available to criminals because the manufacturer evaded federal and state regulations by developing a gun kit advertised in a way that made it feasible for that to happen. *See* NEW YORK TIMES, Mar. 25, 1998, at B5; NEW YORK DAILY NEWS, Mar. 14, 1998, at 12. *See also* N.Y.L.J., Mar. 13, 1998, at 1, 11.

a negligent marketing claim in a gun case to go to a jury.[120] After trial, the jury decided against the plaintiff. While they had reservations about the practices of the gun industry, jurors indicated that "'they [the defendants] didn't pull the trigger.'"[121]

In *Hamilton v. ACCU-TEK*, Weinstein also ruled that the plaintiffs could attempt to prove the theory of industry-wide negligence without the need to identify the manufacturer.[122] In an opinion similar to that in the *DES* cases, Weinstein held that there was jurisdiction over the gun manufacturers and distributors, even if they had not done business in New York or maintained an office there. The plaintiffs identified the liability of gun makers by matching them to their share of the market.[123]

After trial, the jury rendered a special verdict. It found that the manufacturers had oversupplied states with weak gun laws, leading to illegal sales in states with stricter gun laws. Nine of the fifteen companies were found to have proximately caused the deaths of the decedents of two of the plaintiffs, but no damages were awarded against them. Damages of a little over $500,000 were awarded against three defendants for injuries caused one plaintiff. The damages were apportioned according to the defendant's share of the national gun market.[124] Later, Weinstein said that he might have gone the same way as the jury for the plaintiffs had not made a strong enough case.[125]

On appeal, the U.S. Court of Appeals certified two questions to the New York Court of Appeals.[126] But in contrast to its holding in the state *DES* case, New York's highest court did not hold the gun industry liable. It held that the manufacturers did not owe the plantiffs a duty of reasonable care in marketing and distributing the guns and that liability could not be apportioned on a market share basis.[127] Based on the opinion of the New York Court of Appeals, the Second Circuit vacated the judgment of the district court with instructions to enter judgment dismissing the complaint.[128]

The first gun case the NAACP brought was based on a theory of nuisance,[129] and prayed for injunctive relief. That suit occupied much of Weinstein's time in 2003, when he wrote dozens of memoranda and orders in the case.[130] The NAACP's theory was that the widespread access to guns and gun violence had a disproportionate effect on the

---

[120] NEW YORK TIMES, Mar. 13, 1998.

[121] NEW YORK POST, Mar. 28, 1998, at 12.

[122] NAT'L L.J., Feb. 15, 1999, at A1, A9.

[123] *Hamilton v. Accu-Tek*, 32 F. Supp. 2d 47 (Dec. 10, 1998). Weinstein disagreed with Magistrate Judge Pollack on the underpinnings of jurisdiction. *See also* Robert Kolker, *High Caliber Justice*, NEW YORK, Apr. 5, 1999, 33 at 35.

[124] NEW YORK TIMES, Feb.12, 1999; AMERICAN RIFLEMAN, July 2003, at 80.

[125] Weinstein Oral History, at 1459.

[126] *Hamilton v. Accu-Tek*, 222 F.3d 36, 46 (Aug. 16, 2000: *Card*-Trager/Cab).

[127] *Hamilton v. Beretta*, 96 N.Y. 2d 222 (2001).

[128] *Hamilton v. Beretta, USA Corp.*, 264 F.3d 21 (Aug. 30, 2001: *Card*-Cab-Trager).

[129] The use of property or course of conduct that interferes with the legal rights of others by causing damage.

[130] Weinstein Oral History, at 1621.

African-American community, both because African-Americans were more likely to be victims of crime and because African-Americans were more likely to be under some kind of criminal justice supervision. The NAACP also argued that membership in the organization was discouraged by the high levels of gun violence.

The NAACP case was tried over six weeks in the spring of 2003. For the trial, Weinstein chose to use an advisory jury to determine whether there was a "nuisance" and for advice on the shape of the injunction.[131] The case had serious jurisdictional problems.[132] Because some of the distributor defendants neither did business in New York nor had an office in the state, they might have been under a severe burden to defend the suit. As in other cases discussed in this book, Weinstein took flexible and modern view of personal jurisdiction. Strict territorial jurisdiction, he said:

> . . . is no longer a strong principle in a world where boundaries are increasingly fluid and borders are determined more through the conduct and agreement of individuals, organizations and governments than by the lines drawn on maps . . .
> A jurisdictional analysis may result, appropriately, in the inclusion of defendants for which appearing at trial could present some burdens."[133]

On the merits, the advisory jury found that forty-five of the defendants had no liability. The jury was unable to agree about twenty-three others.[134]

Weinstein found that there was a public nuisance, but one which the defendants could abate through easily implemented changes in marketing and more discriminating control of sales practices.[135] However, under New York law, a private plaintiff must demonstrate that it suffered harm [due to nuisance] *different in kind* from that suffered by the public at large. Since the NAACP had not demonstrated such a harm, Weinstein dismissed the action.[136] However, Weinstein made clear that suits brought by a governmental entity—the state Attorney General, the City Corporation Counsel or the U.S. Attorney—would not have to overcome the burden that had sunk the NAACP's case. He laid out clearly in his opinion the facts that a public litigant could use in a suit to enjoin this particular nuisance.

Even before Weinstein's *NAACP* opinion came down, the City of New York had, in June 2000, brought a nuisance action against defendant manufacturers and importers of guns and firearms. The suits were delayed for several years as a result of 9/11 and because decisions on several appeals in related litigation were anticipated. Over time,

---

[131] *NAACP v. Accusport,* 99 CV 7037 (Oct. 1, 2002).
[132] *NAACP v. A.A. Arms, Inc.,* 2003 WL 2124293 (Apr. 1, 2003).
[133] *NAACP v. A.A. Arms, Inc.,* 2003 WL 2124293, at *2 (Apr. 1, 2003).
[134] N.Y.L.J., May 15, 2003.
[135] *NAACP v. Accusport, Inc.,* 271 F. Supp. 2d 435 (July 21, 2003).
[136] *Id.* at 451.

the City's case evolved into solely an equitable claim seeking an injunction to abate a nuisance.[137]

In the New York City litigation, Weinstein rendered a number of important opinions dealing with jurisdiction over small, out-of-state gun shops. In his denial of a motion to certify the class action, he refused to dismiss dozens of out-of-state gun dealers for lack of personal jurisdiction.[138] Weinstein set out in extensive detail statistics supporting the City's claim that the defendants were serving the New York market through regular sale to straw purchasers and by multiple gun sales in states with weak gun laws. The City's evidence, he wrote, demonstrated that guns regularly arrived in New York via commercial channels. The defendants had done more than place handguns in the stream of commerce, which would be sufficient to provide the minimum contacts necessary for personal jurisdiction.[139] By June 2008, twenty of twenty-seven defendants had settled with the City, agreeing to allow their sales practices to be monitored and to attend training sessions on how to avoid practices that could lead to the sale of guns in New York.[140]

Perhaps the most important part of the gun case involved the strength of the gun lobby. Between 2004 and 2008, Congress sought to deny the plaintiffs access to records of the Bureau of Alcohol, Tobacco, Firearms, and Explosives (ATF). The data the plaintiffs sought traced sales histories of weapons that became the subject of law enforcement investigations, thefts of weapons, and multiple sales. While gun litigation was also going on elsewhere, it appears that Congress was particularly concerned with Weinstein's cases.

Four times Congress either barred disclosure of ATF data necessary for New York City's case or barred actual continuance of the litigation. Several times Weinstein, attempting to avoid challenging the constitutionality of Congress's actions, was able to find narrow, technical, or clever reasons to keep the lawsuit alive. Once he held that all Congress had done was simply to cut off the funds needed to disclose the data, so he held that the court would reimburse the ATF.[141] A second time he implied that Congress might be encroaching on state power to regulate the sale and use of guns, but to avoid the constitutional issue he held that Congress's bar didn't apply because his discovery order had preceded it.[142] Still another time he held the law inapplicable because the data was in the City's possession.[143] The fourth time, Weinstein held that the New York

---

[137] *City of New York v. Jennings*, 219 F.R.D. 255 (Jan. 13, 2004).

[138] *City of New York v. A-1 Jewelry and Pawn, Inc.*, 501 F. Supp. 2d 369 (Oct. 29, 2007). *See also* N.Y.L.J., Aug. 16, 2007.

[139] *City of New York v. A-1 Jewelry and Pawn Inc.*, 501 F. Supp. 369, 425ff (Oct. 29, 2007).

[140] New York Times, June 13, 2008. *See also* N.Y.L.J., Aug. 16, 2007.

[141] *See* Act of Jan. 23, 2004, P.L. 108-99, 108 Stat. 3 (2004); *City of New York v. Beretta U.S.A. Corp.*, 222 F.R.D. 51 (May 19, 2004); *Johnson v. Bryco Arms*, 222 F.R.D. 48, 51 (June 14, 2004). The Court of Appeals denied the ATF petition for mandamus to overturn the district court decision.

[142] *City of New York v. Beretta U.S.A. Corp.*, 228 F. R.D. 147 (Apr. 27, 2005). The statute involved was P.L. 108–199, 118 Stat. 3 (2004).

[143] *City of New York v. Beretta USA Corp.*, 429 F. Supp. 2d 517 (Apr. 27, 2006). In his reading of the rider, Weinstein rendered a decision contrary to a recent Seventh Circuit decision. *See City of Chicago v. Dep't of the Treasury*, 423 F.2d 999 (7th Cir. F.3d 775).

City litigation fell under an exception to the Act.[144] Finally, on April 30, 2008, the Second Circuit, reversing Weinstein, called an end to the duel by holding that a legislative bar to litigation was applicable to the New York City case. A panel of Judges Roger Miner, Jose Cabranes, and Robert A. Katzmann (dissenting) held the statute constitutional and applicable to the New York City gun case.[145] The Supreme Court then denied review.[146]

THE LIGHT CIGARETTE LITIGATIONS

Weinstein unsuccessfully sought a global solution in the litigation against the cigarette companies for the marketing of light cigarettes. There were around a dozen big, complex tobacco cases for which Weinstein attempted to engineer a nationwide judicial resolution. The central theory of plaintiffs was that, when the companies marketed light cigarettes, they misrepresented that they were less of a health hazard than regular cigarettes. While some settlements did occur—in 1998, for example, five tobacco companies reached a $20 billion settlement with the Attorneys General of forty-six states—a master solution could not be achieved through the courts in spite of Weinstein's efforts.[147]

The jurisprudential background was never favorable. The cases raised difficult jurisdictional problems and choice of law issues. The Second Circuit, now clearly no friend to such class actions, was particularly unsympathetic to the use of statistics in them.[148] Many third-party lawsuits, brought by health maintenance organizations and asbestos trusts for their expenditures on behalf of those they covered, had been thrown out by other courts.

Nor have juries been enthusiastic about finding the cigarette companies liable for smoker deaths or other liability. Weinstein himself had reservations about some of the cases. The first time Big Tobacco had been successfully sued by a third party was before Weinstein in *Blue Cross & Blue Shield of New Jersey v. Philip Morris, Inc.* The forty-four day trial had thirty-four witnesses, 1632 demonstratives, and 100 depositions. On June 15, 2001, the jury held against the cigarette manufacturers. The trial established, apparently for the first time, that the tobacco industry had engaged in statutorily banned deceptive practices, although the jurors rejected civil fraud and racketeering charges and, after five days of deliberation, came in with a minuscule verdict—damages of $17.78 million for Blue Cross and $11.8 million for Blue Cross Blue Shield's subsidiaries.

---

[144] Act of Oct. 26, 2005, P.L. No. 109-108, 119 Stat. 290. *City of New York v. Beretta U.S.A. Corp.*, 401 F. Supp. 244, 298 (Dec. 2, 2005), *aff'd in part and rev'd in part*, 524 F.3d 384 (Apr. 30, 2008).

[145] *City of New York v. Beretta USA Corp.*, 524 F.3d 384 (Apr. 30, 2008).

[146] 129 S. Ct. 1579 (2009). *See also* NEW YORK TIMES, Mar. 10, 2009, at A23.

[147] Through October 2001, Weinstein had already written over forty opinions. See list in *Blue Cross & Blue Shield of N.J., Inc. v. Philip Morris, Inc.*, 178 F. Supp. 2d 198, 206–07 (Oct. 19, 2001).

[148] Weinstein Oral History, at 1492.

But even that small victory was pyrrhic as the Second Circuit and the New York Court of Appeals made it impossible for the plaintiffs to collect.[149]

The *Simon II* class action grew out of a traditional class action (*Simon-I*) brought by lung cancer victims seeking compensation from tobacco companies. After Weinstein suggested in court that the case could be restructured to deal with tobacco issues in a much broader way, plaintiffs filed a new suit asking for a once-and-for-all determination of punitive damages.[150]

On September 19, 2002, Weinstein granted class certification to provide a procedural solution to the problem of repetitive and unrelated judgments for punitive damages. Weinstein ordered that millions of injured smokers be lumped into a nationwide class that would share a single pot of punitive damages from cigarette manufacturers.[151] Professor Stephen Gillers of New York University Law School called Weinstein, "probably the most procedurally creative judge sitting in the United States today," but added, "he's asking the court system to do what I think is beyond its competence."[152]

The Court of Appeals agreed. On May 6, 2005, it overturned Weinstein, considering the class action "unworkable."[153] The case was remanded, the Court of Appeals holding that punitive damages could not be tried without trying underlying damages.[154] That was the end of *Simon-II*. The plaintiffs' attorneys thought it too hard to prove medical causation liability and then, after that, the punitives.[155]

The remaining light cigarette action before Weinstein, *Schwab v. Philip Morris*, a suit for $2.4 trillion, survived a little longer. There, Weinstein certified a nationwide class action under the Racketeer Influenced and Corrupt Organizations Act (RICO) with tens of millions of plaintiffs who had purchased light cigarettes from the date of their introduction into the market place. The theory was that the cigarette manufacturers fraudulently obtained money from smokers by marketing their light cigarettes as safer than regular cigarettes.

In a 540-page typed opinion accompanied by a 986-page appendix, Weinstein dealt with certification, fraud, RICO conspiracy, causation, the computation of damages, the statute of limitations, expert evidence, allocation of damages, collateral estoppel, and other issues. In the appendix he wrote a long treatise on the history of the cigarette

---

[149] NEW YORK POST, June 5, 2001, at 22; NEW YORK DAILY NEWS, June 5, 2001, at 4. *See also* Weinstein Oral History, at 1462.

[150] William Glaberson, *U.S. Court Considers a Once-and-for-All Tobacco Law Suit*, NEW YORK TIMES, Sept. 14, 2006, at B1, B6.

[151] *In re Simon II Litig.*, 211 F.R.D. 86 (Oct. 15, 2002) (155-page printed opinion).

[152] LOS ANGELES TIMES, Sept. 21, 2002, at C1, C8.

[153] *Simon II Litig. v. Philip Morris USA Inc. (In re Simon II Litig.)*, 407 F.3d 125 (2005: *Oakes*-Pool-Wes). *See also* N.Y.L.J., May 19, 2005.

[154] Weinstein Oral History, at 1575.

[155] Weinstein Oral History, at 1575, 1751.

companies, so that the appellate courts, the parties, and the public had before them "all" the relevant facts.[156]

On April 3, 2008, the Court of Appeals reversed the grant of class certification because the "putative class action suffers from an insurmountable deficit of collective legal or factual questions."[157] The class of "light cigarette" smokers, alleging fraud under RICO, was decertified because individual issues outweighed issues susceptible to common proof. The appellate court also held that the use of fluid recovery in the action would violate due process rights.[158] The Court of Appeals added that Rule 23 "is not a one-way ratchet, empowering 'a judge to conform the law to the proof.'"[159]

So, Weinstein had little to show for over a decade of work with the light cigarette cases. Although he insisted that he was not emotionally invested in either side of the cigarette litigation, he did say to me:

> … it's outrageous that a group of companies whose products led to the early death of millions of people through alleged fraud which is fairly clearly based, but it's really my last gasp attempt to bring justice, I think, to millions of people.[160]

ZYPREXA

The most recent major class action before Weinstein has involved Zyprexa, a drug with a record of proven success in treating schizophrenia and depression. For its manufacturer, Eli Lilly & Co., Zyprexa has been an enormous money-maker. Although the drug has been approved by the FDA for schizophrenia, the company offered it for other conditions without alerting physicians and patients to the possibility it might lead to increases in weight that risked the onset of diabetes.[161] Weinstein's most important achievements in *Zyprexa* have been to create a "quasi-class action" and to preside over a global settlement of Medicare and Medicaid liens.

---

[156] *Schwab v. Philip Morris USA, Inc.*, 449 F. Supp. 2d 992 (Sept. 25, 2006). LEXIS had to split the opinion into sixteen parts to accommodate its large size.

[157] *McLaughlin v. American Tobacco Co.*, 522 F.3d 215, 219 (Apr. 3, 2008: Walker-Pooler-Winter).

[158] Jim Copland, *Smoke Test for Supremes*, N.Y. Sun, Apr. 4, 2008, at 9. Fluid recovery is a means of distributing class funds to their "next best use" where individual recoveries for all class members is impractical, such as where a large number of consumers have suffered small monetary losses. It can also be used as a means of distributing unclaimed funds remaining in a settlement or damage fund.

[159] *McLaughlin*, 522 F.3d at 219.

[160] Weinstein Oral History, at 1773–74.

[161] Weinstein Oral History, at 1671.

The thousands of suits in federal courts against Lilly were aggregated by the Panel on Multidistrict Litigation in 2004 because they involved common questions of fact. They were referred to Weinstein.[162] In its transfer order, the Panel said:

> In concluding that the Eastern District of New York is an appropriate forum for this docket, we note that centralization in this district permits the panel to effect the Section 1407 assignment to an experienced transferee judge who can steer this litigation on a steady and experienced course.[163]

Under the rules for multidistrict cases, Weinstein controlled the pretrial proceedings for all federal cases, but could only try those in the Eastern District of New York. While most of the cases before Weinstein involved victims or alleged victims who claimed they had gained weight while taking Zyprexa, there were also suits by State Attorneys General, U.S. Medicaid and Medicare liens, cases brought by third parties who had subsidized patients for the medication, and by owners of Lilly stock.

With the increasing skepticism of class actions by federal appellate judges, Weinstein sought another way to achieve settlements on a consolidated and cooperative basis without the formalities of a class action.[164] He noted the large number of plaintiffs and the need for coordinating the activities of attorneys (including the creation of a plaintiff's steering committee). Even though the settlements in a case like *Zyprexa* are in the nature of private agreements between individual plaintiffs and defendants, Weinstein stated that the litigation had many of the characteristics of a class action.[165] Just as supervision is required to prevent exploitation of absent class members in a Rule 23 action, so too was supervision necessary in the *Zyprexa* cases.

Weinstein called the aggregation of cases before him a "quasi-class action."[166] The cases had a large number of plaintiffs subject to the same settlement matrix. Specialized masters were used to control discovery. There was an escrow bank and a designated, independent law firm to negotiate and administer lien allocations to the federal government and the fifty states.[167] The role of the court was fiduciary in nature.

---

[162] *In re Zyprexa Prods. Liab. Litig.*, 314 F. Supp. 2d 1380 (J.M.P.L. Apr. 14, 2004).

[163] *Id.* at 1382. The substantial number of state cases could not, of course, be transferred to Weinstein.

[164] *In re Zyprexa Prod. Liab. Litig.*, 424 F. Supp. 2d 488, 490 (Mar. 28, 2006); 433 F. Supp. 2d 268 (June 8, 2006).

[165] *In re Zyprexa Prods. Liab. Litig.*, 233 F.R.D. 122 (Jan. 9, 2006).

[166] Suits brought by State Attorneys General were called "structural class actions." *In re Zyprexa Liab. Litig.*, 671 F. Supp. 2d 397 (Dec. 1, 2009). Weinstein wrote to Professor Stephen P. Burbank on January 24, 2006, about his problem trying to use less than perfect "'quasi-class action'" concepts to control fees and provide national consensus on liens for Medicare and Medicaid where there was a constantly expanding universe of cases without class action limits. Jack B. Weinstein to Stephen P. Burbank, Jan. 24, 2006 (copy in possession of author).

[167] Jack B. Weinstein, *The Role of Judges in a Government Of, By, and For the People: Notes for the Fifty-Eighth Cardozo Lecture*, 30 CARDOZO L. REV. 1, 115.

The parties were subject to the general equitable power of the court.[168] The judge would have enough control to protect litigants and vital industries and also to make sure that the general public would not view the action as abusive. Furthermore, duplicative discovery could be limited by granting copies in electronic form to all lawyers in federal and in state courts.[169]

Thus, for Weinstein, *Zyprexa* in many respects resembled a class action. He appointed his former law clerk, Peter Woodin, to handle discovery. He pressed the lawyers before him to coordinate discovery with the attorneys in state courts to minimize the number of times witnesses would have to appear for a deposition. A depository in Colorado housed *six million* documents with web-based access to discovery materials for the attorneys, which eliminated an enormous amount of copying.

Lilly decided to settle on an individual settlement basis, and Weinstein appointed four settlement masters (including Kenneth Feinberg) to work out the distributions. He pressed for a settlement that was simple, quick and fair for the victims. Weinstein exerted the pressures he had: ". . . I know my powers are limited, but since I have my hand in the spigot of seven hundred million dollars that gives me a certain amount of power."[170] As he said to me at the time: "They will be able to get the money out within months. This is always what I want. I want to get the money out."[171] He pressed for lower attorneys' fees and made it difficult for litigants to leave the settlement.[172] In 2005, the average settlement was about $90,000 covering 8,000 plaintiffs. In 2007, after the FDA changed the label on Zyprexa, the 18,000 settlements averaged $25,000.[173]

One part of the litigation of considerable interest involved Medicare and Medicaid liens for their share of individuals' recovery based on the amount "advanced" for Medicare health benefits or for other sums laid out by the state or federal government for the purchase of Zyprexa. On September 11, 2006, there was a global settlement, largely the work of State Attorneys General, which Weinstein thought "may provide a model for the handling of Medicare and Medicaid liens in future mass actions on a uniform national basis."[174] The settlement permitted "limited variations arising from the application of state laws," but not so much variation because, as Weinstein said, "A federal district court cannot allow variations in state law to interfere with the fair and efficient administration of a federally controlled national litigation."[175]

---

[168] *In re Zyprexa Prod. Liab. Litig.*, 424 F. Supp. 2d 488 (Mar. 28, 2006).

[169] *Id. See* Weinstein Oral History, at 1533.

[170] Weinstein Oral History, at 1742.

[171] Weinstein Oral History, at 1533.

[172] Weinstein Oral History, at 1140. On Weinstein's efforts to expedite the distribution of the settlement, see *In re Zyprexa Prod. Liab. Litig.* 2005 WL 3117302 (Nov. 22, 2005); 2006 WL 898105 (Apr. 6, 2006); *In re Zyprexa*, 433 F. Supp. 268 (June 8, 2006).

[173] Alex Berenson, *Lilly Settles with 18,000 over Zyprexa*, NEW YORK TIMES, Jan. 5, 2007.

[174] *In re Zyprexa Prod. Liab. Litig.*, 451 F. Supp. 458, 461 (Sept. 11, 2006).

[175] *Id.* at 477.

Plaintiffs and states must be treated equitably with respect to payment of the costs of a litigation from which they all benefit. Attorneys' fees were capped at 20 percent in certain small lump-sum claims and 35 percent in all others. The states and federal government modified their demands to provide a national equitable system.

The first phase of the *Zyprexa* litigation was largely over by December 2006. Eight thousand claims were settled and the money distributed. Attorneys' fees structure had been approved as had the national system for resolving Medicare and Medicaid liens.

Phase I was followed by a second and larger wave of lawsuits. A new plaintiff's steering committee was established on August 16, 2006. Thousands of cases were transferred to the Eastern District by the Multidistrict Panel. Many suits were brought by third parties—health insurance companies, unions, and others seeking compensation for reimbursements they had made—and also state and federal governments for moneys they had spent via the Medicare and Medicaid payments. The court, magistrate judges, and special masters continued to administer the litigation as a quasi-class action. Discovery went forward.

On June 11, 2007, Weinstein decided Lilly's motions for summary judgment in four Phase II cases. Weinstein granted one of the four. He allowed the other three cases to proceed, though he considered the question very close.[176] He was aware that allowing such suits to proceed could increase the cost of pharmaceuticals and efficacy of medical treatment, but could also furnish protection against underregulated potentially dangerous activity by markets where *caveat emptor* rules.

In 2008, Weinstein granted limited class certification to a group of third party-payers including labor unions, insurance companies, and pension funds. However, on January 15, 2009, the Court of Appeals agreed to hear an appeal of that certification, which augured badly for its future in view of the Court of Appeals decision in the light cigarette case and a recent Supreme Court decision.[177] On September 10, 2010, the Second Circuit decertified the class of third party-payers and vacated Weinstein's order denying Eli Lilly's motion for summary judgment regarding overpricing claims.[178]

---

[176] *In re Zyprexa Prod. Liab. Litig.,* 489 F. Supp. 2d 230 (June 11, 2007),

[177] *Zyprexa Prods. Liab. Litig.,* 253 F.R.D. 69 (Sept. 5, 2008), *rev'd sub nom. UFCW Local 1776 v. Eli Lilly and Co.,* 620 F.3d 121 (Sept. 10, 2010), *Zyprexa Prod. Liab. Litig.,* 04-5685-mv (Jan. 15, 2009). *McLaughlin v. American Tobacco Co.,* 522 F.3d 215 (Apr. 3, 2008); *Bridge v. Phoenix Bond & Indem. Co.,* 553 U.S. 639 (2008). In the *Zyprexa* litigation, Weinstein's protective order on documents produced in civil discovery was evaded by a *New York Times* reporter in collusion with one of the plaintiff's experts. A series of lead articles in the *Times* followed. Weinstein upheld the validity of his order and enjoined eight persons from disseminating the materials. Lilly, however, did not seek an injunction against the *Times* or the particular reporter involved. *See* opinion of Feb. 13, 2007, at 6, 73–75. *See also In re Zyprexa Prod. Liab. Litig.,* 242 F.R.D. 29 (Mar. 30, 2007).

[178] *UFCW Local 1776 v. Eli Lilly Co.,* 620 F.3d 121 (Sept. 10, 2010: Katz-Living-*Lynch*).

THE "RELATED CASE" CONTROVERSY

In recent years, there has been curiosity about the high concentration of important class actions that have come to Weinstein. Lawyers for the cigarette companies and gun industries have fulminated, while even some judges have raised their eyebrows. Sitting on several appeals in class actions before Weinstein, Jose Cabranes of the Court of Appeals has asked, "Is there a rule or practice in the Eastern District of New York that Judge Weinstein is assigned all mega-cases?" At a memorial for Judge Jacob Mishler, former Second Circuit judge George Pratt praised Mishler, pointedly noting that with Mishler there were "no manipulations of the related-case rule."[179]

Under the operation of the "related case" rule in the Eastern District, when a plaintiff's attorney files a case, he or she can indicate that the case is "related" to another case already in court. The tobacco suits went to Weinstein because the Manville Trust was suing the tobacco industry and Weinstein had the Manville Trust asbestos cases. The industry-wide gun case was marked related because of two cases Weinstein had had—one where the trigger pull on the shotgun had been too light; another, because of the plaintiff's theory of market share liability was similar to that in the *DES* cases.[180]

Because of this kind of successful forum shopping by plaintiffs' lawyers, Weinstein became the central arbiter of litigation against the tobacco and firearms industries even though the alleged harms are nationwide and no major manufacturer in either industry is located in the Eastern District.[181]

CONCLUSION

On the whole, Weinstein's work in mass torts has shown how tort doctrine can be made more flexible, how a judge can innovate in what has been the huge interlocutory space presented by the final judgment rule and by demonstrating how courts can be more sensitive to people's needs than government agencies. He has seen the problem of redress for mass torts whole—looking not only at civil court actions, but also at possible relief through criminal justice (restitution) and administrative agencies.[182]

Since the settlement of *Agent Orange*, in an environment very cool to class actions, Weinstein has settled many thousands of mass tort cases, presided over many trials, and written hundreds of opinions. From his work, we might single out in particular his reinvigoration of the Manville Trust; his opinions on jurisdiction; his stimulus for the use of a panel of experts appointed by the courts; his opinion on damages in the

---

[179] N.Y. Sun, Dec. 3, 2007.

[180] The *Zyprexa* cases had been assigned to Weinstein by the Multidistrict Panel.

[181] When asked how so many major cases ended upon his docket, Weinstein said, "I'm lucky." Joseph Goldstein, *Judge Lands at Center of a New York Legal Mystery*, N.Y. Sun, Dec. 3, 2007.

[182] Weinstein, *80th Birthday Roundtable*, *supra* note 55, at 213–14.

Repetitive Stress Injury cases; his ability in the gun cases to overcome the gun lobby and Congress to get at least some cases tried and to achieve settlements with gunshop owners helpful to New York City. One might wish to add to this the pioneering of joint decision-making with state judges; the use he has made of equity powers; his hearings for plaintiffs in the *DES* cases; and the probably short-lived creation of the quasi-class action. Nevertheless, at least at the time of this writing, one must say that, while Weinstein continues to be greatly respected as a commentator on mass torts and class actions, his grand style has not been winning acceptance within or outside the Second Circuit.

Conclusions

DISTRICT COURTS AND DISTRICT JUDGES

The federal district courts are both legal and political institutions. All federal judges, not just Jack Weinstein, "make" law as part of their work (although some may make more law than others). The broad range of cases discussed in this book are representative of the varied work of district judges: from desegregation of a school district in Coney Island to the prison diet; from a dispute over publishing the yellow pages of telephone directories to the closing of a nuclear reactor; from the restrictions placed on fluke fishing to the sentencing of Mafia dons.

Looking at district judging through the career of an individual judge has provided an alternative to bloodless statistical analysis, permitting examination of how the background and values of one district judge affected his decision-making. The choice of a particularly candid and accessible judge has produced an extraordinary amount of information about the effect of life experience and values on particular decisions. While, it has not been contended that Weinstein is a "typical" district judge, the effects of life experiences and values simply cannot be overlooked.

This book has shown not only judges resolving disputes, but also the making of law in cases large and small. It has demonstrated the number of opportunities a district judge has to settle conflicts and/or make policy in the course of litigation. The most significant opportunities would seem to occur on the motion for summary judgment and on the decision on the merits after a bench trial. Yet, we have also seen how a judge can affect the result by narrowing or expanding the scope of the dispute, by transforming the case through hints to the lawyers, by controlling the breadth and depth of discovery, by pressing hard for settlement, and by rulings on the admissibility of evidence. It is also clear that the judge's role is crucial in devising remedies in equitable actions and, at least traditionally, in determining sentences. Some opportunities lurk in areas where the trial judge is seldom reviewed by the Court of Appeals: in making findings of fact, issuing opinions in cases the judge expect will settle, and in controlling the pace of the litigation.

Earlier chapters showed many examples of Weinstein's mastery of the job of trial judge—finding jurisdiction, pushing a case along, controlling discovery, shaping cases and transforming little cases into big ones. They also demonstrated how he could settle highly political cases; how he could handle facts in an opinion, and protect the record to avoid reversal. We also saw how he used magistrates and special masters, and made sure information got on the record so that new law could be made by an appellate court.[1]

THE JUDGING OF JACK WEINSTEIN

Jack Weinstein brought to the bench a brilliant mind, super-human energy, and encyclopedic knowledge of procedure and evidence. He brought from the classroom a deep grounding in many areas of substantive law. He brought to his judgeship enormous intellectual curiosity, extraordinary energy, decisiveness and tenacity, considerable self-confidence, an excellent prose style, a habit of thoroughness, and the experience gleaned from an apprenticeship with one of the nation's finest judges. When he came to the bench, he was already an accomplished scholar, most of whose scholarship had been devoted to modernization of the law. He was experienced as a government lawyer and possessed practical knowledge of the legislative process.

Weinstein was fortunate to be a federal rather than a state judge for he did not have to worry about reelection, party bosses, or retirement at age seventy. Instead, he had independence, prestige, and strong staff support. He also had the facilities he needed— the newest technology, his own secretary, very high-caliber law clerks, and the availability of magistrate judges and special masters. He was even spared the one problem that greatly affected the morale of many colleagues throughout the nation—the parsimonious salary—not because he was a federal judge, but because he was independently wealthy from his writings.

There is no doubt then, that Weinstein's defeat in the election for Chief Judge of the New York Court of Appeals in 1971 was a great blessing. It is probably also fortunate that Weinstein was passed over for appointment to the Court of Appeals for the Second Circuit. He was and is far better suited for the work of a trial court than that of an appellate court. His brilliant grasp of evidence and procedure and the rapidity with

[1] *See, e.g.,* STEPHEN T. EARLY, CONSTITUTIONAL COURTS OF THE U.S. 68 (1977); WALTER F. MURPHY, ELEMENTS OF JUDICIAL STRATEGY 25–26 (1964).

which his mind works make him an ideal trial judge. Nor did he ever, save for the relatively few times he sat with the Court of Appeals by designation,[2] have to rely upon others for opinion assignments or negotiate about the substance of an opinion. That there was a Court of Appeals "above" him seems not to have been a major constraint on his judging, although over the long run it limited his efficacy in the class action field.

Yet a judge can only be as effective as his or her jurisdiction permits and his or her times allow.[3] He must also understand both the people whom he serves and the age in which he lives. As John Phillip Reid wrote, "If he and the people are estranged, he will pass without honor in his own land. If he is out of touch with the times, he will go unnoticed in his own community."[4] Jack Weinstein was well matched to the cosmopolitan district to which he was appointed and was, although far from the mainstream, in touch with his times.

Weinstein is a man to whom roots mean much. He was a third-generation Weinstein with roots in the Eastern District of New York. He remembers growing up amidst the farms of Bensonhurst, the excursions he took to Coney Island as a boy, and working at the Brooklyn Naval Yard as a teenager and when he was in college. Much of his professional career before he was appointed to the bench had been spent close by in Manhattan. The dominant traits of his personality—brilliance, self-confidence, outspokenness, liberalism, and a very high energy level—were unlikely to raise eyebrows in New York City, the heart of the Eastern District. The relative anonymity that New Yorkers are generally accorded has lessened the possibility that what he might do as a judge would make him a continuing target for political or press criticism Nor was it likely that he would confront the terrible community pressures with which judges who sat in Montgomery, New Orleans, or Little Rock had to contend.

To the extent that the docket and characteristics of the Eastern District of New York differed from those of other districts, Weinstein was fortunate. His grasp of evidence and procedure, his habit of command and self-confidence would allow him to manage effectively highly complex and visible cases, civil and criminal. New York City's central role in immigration produced naturalization and deportation cases which greatly engaged his sympathies. Because the headquarters for many years of the New York City Board of Education was located in Brooklyn, the Eastern District was the locus of important cases involving the city's schools.

Weinstein has always stressed the importance of good lawyering to good judging. The dynamic quality of the practice of law and the relatively high quality of the bar in the New York metropolitan area was another factor helping to maximize Weinstein's talents. All of the judges of the Eastern District profited from the noticeable increase in the quality of the U.S. Attorney's Office in the early years of Weinstein's tenure,

---

[2] Early in his career, he also sat on several three-judge district courts. *See* Chapter 5.

[3] *See* JOHN PHILLIP REID, AN AMERICAN JUDGE: MARMADUKE DENT OF WEST VIRGINIA 17 (1968).

[4] *Id.*

while the creation of an Organized Crime Strike Force in the district in the 1970s yielded increased numbers of challenging criminal cases.

Weinstein's timing was also fortunate. He arrived on the federal bench just about the time that the lower federal courts were replacing state courts as the for important public law litigation and commercial cases. He arrived as one of a large number of politically liberal appointments to the bench made by Presidents John Kennedy and Lyndon B. Johnson at the time that Warren Court jurisprudence was at its high point. Those appointments, as well as laws passed by Congress in the 1960s and early 1970s, made it possible to sustain moderate liberal activism in the lower federal courts into the 1980s. In addition, Weinstein, in particular, would be a beneficiary of the 1966 change in Federal Rules of Civil Procedure, which led to greatly expanded use of class actions. Although the nation and its leaders became increasingly conservative, the growth of political and judicial conservatism would not seriously intrude on Weinstein's judging until the mid-1980s, when the War on Drugs was enlarged and the Sentencing Guidelines created. While Weinstein's relation with the Court of Appeals became increasingly fraught during the 1990s, as profound differences developed over class actions and sentencing, it is likely that conflicts would have been even greater with a number of other, more conservative courts.

All in all, Weinstein meshed well with his district and his times.

SOME RUMINATION ABOUT JUDICIAL ACTIVISM

We have attempted to separate Weinstein's activeness as a judge from his "judicial activism." Weinstein is active in many ways. He is managerially active, having little hesitation about trying new methods to manage cases. He has been active in settling cases. He is a geographic activist who visits sites of his cases and holds hearings in various parts of his district. He is intellectually active, often going far beyond lawyers' briefs to inform himself on the problems before him. He also has been extraordinarily active as an educator.

On the whole, the activities of Judge Weinstein just described have not been controversial. What has been controversial has been his application of his philosophy of law and judging to the cases before him. We have seen that Weinstein does not even give lip service to the myth that judges do not make law. He knows that judges make law and that law is shaped by changing circumstances. Regarding law as a dynamic process, Weinstein has admitted that he is greatly interested in "moving" and modernizing the law. Beyond that, he identifies himself with what he says has been the postwar role of the federal courts: "protect[ing] the injured that c[o]me before them against those who have caused or are causing unjustifiable harm"[5] "I try," he has said, "wherever I see

---

[5] Jack B. Weinstein, Individual Justice in Mass Tort Litigation 127 (1995).

a chance to improve the administration of justice or to correct an injustice to utilize whatever powers I have. . ."[6]

It must be emphasized that Weinstein is not simply a reflexively liberal judge, as, for example, Miles Lord of the District of Minnesota was.[7] He is a subtle thinker who sees all sides of legal problems. He does not "shoot from the hip" in handling cases, but prepares carefully. With his mastery of procedure, ability to shape and transform litigation, capacity for innovation, audacious use of the powers of equity, and historical learning, Weinstein has formidable weapons to wield. Liberal judges may not be rare, but a liberal (or a conservative) judge with such mastery of the craft and willingness to risk reversal is. Time and time again Weinstein has devised new solutions to substantive legal problems and employed procedure flexibly at the risk of reversal. Thoroughly conversant with the techniques district judges typically use to protect their judgments, he has also developed others, such as "tentative opinions" and the denial of certificates of appealability. In the words of one observer, "this is not a guy you can just name a case to and expect him to acquiesce and walk away."[8] He is tenacious. "'Winning an appeal with one of these cases with Weinstein,'" an Assistant U.S. Attorney told one of Weinstein's clerks, "'is just the beginning not the ending.'"[9]

This, however, is where the criticism kicks in. Weinstein, not entirely unfairly, is said to be too innovative, too loose with precedent and procedure, and not sufficiently accountable to the courts above him. Many times, that "check-rein of mandated passivity" has been missing from the "activist seeker of troublesome issues."[10]

Weinstein to some degree sees himself as holding a "roving commission" as a problem solver,[11] for he is by nature, a man who loves solving problems.[12] Referring to Weinstein, Dean Martha Minow of Harvard Law School has written of the risks of what she calls "judging for the situation," that is, creating procedures tailored for particular circumstances. Weinstein, Minow says, looks beyond the parties and the purely legal issues they present to the underlying problem, views the problem from the standpoint of the various communities that it affects, and attempts to solve the problem by settling the case out of court.[13] Another critic, Professor Stephen Burbank of the University of

---

[6] Interview of Jack B. Weinstein by William Glaberson 2 (July 7, 1997) (copy in possession of author).

[7] *See* SHELDON ENGELMAYER & ROBERT WAGMAN, LORD'S JUSTICE (1985); FRANK D. SCHAUMBURG, JUDGMENT RESERVED: A LANDMARK ENVIRONMENTAL CASE (1976).

[8] Joseph Goldstein, *New View of Brown v. Board Unlikely to Sway One Judge*, N.Y. SUN, July 9, 2007.

[9] As recounted in Weinstein, Oral History, at 1402.

[10] Transcript of Ceremonies Attending the Induction of Honorable Jack B. Weinstein as United States District Judge for the Eastern District of New York, May 5, 1967, 50 at 54. *See also* Weinstein Oral History, at 34.

[11] Alexander, M. Bickel, quoted in DONALD L. HOROWITZ, THE COURTS AND SOCIAL POLICY 9 (1977).

[12] *Judge Jack B. Weinstein, Tort Litigation, and the Public Good: A Roundtable Discussion to Honor One of America's Great Trial Judges on the Occasion of his 80th Birthday*, 12 J. L. & POL. 149, 172 (2003) [hereinafter 80th Birthday Roundtable]. He has little hesitation about using power; has a tendency to act rapidly; has no embarrassment about making law or innovating. He is not a judge to "just sit back passively."

[13] Martha Minow, *Judge for the Situation: Judge Jack Weinstein, Creator of Temporary Administrative Agencies*, 97 COLUM. L. REV. 2010 (1997).

Pennsylvania Law School, chides Weinstein for being as unaccountable as a tenured professor.[14]

Weinstein may be a little too quick to use power. He may have tried too often to achieve "global resolution" of large problems. Perhaps, in spite of his great loyalty to the Eastern District, he has found it too small a canvas on which to paint. While Weinstein's performance in *Agent Orange* was truly remarkable, perhaps he subsequently went to the well too often. Already in the early 1970s, he was looking toward a national solution of the problem of draft evaders in exile. In the *Coney Island* school case he was originally looking for a solution involving not just reform of school districts, but one that would involve changes affecting transportation, housing, parks, and other areas of government services. More recently, his attempts to seek global resolutions of the asbestos and light cigarette cases have failed.

Weinstein's most powerful (although not always effective critics) have been the judges of the U.S. Court of Appeals for the Second Circuit.[15] Reversal rates are often not a measure of quality on the bench and that is true of Weinstein's. During his first two decades, there were a few important reversals—the *Army Band* case, the Baltimore Canyon oil digging case, and *Lora* among others. But Weinstein was to a very large degree upheld in *Agent Orange*. However, by the mid-1990s, he had gotten under the skin of such able circuit judges as Jon O. Newman and Ralph K. Winter, Jr.,[16] suffered important reversals, and was mandamused from time to time. In one case involving sentencing, the higher court not only mandamused him, but assigned the case on remand to another judge.[17] Since the mid-1990s Weinstein has been consistently reversed in class actions and sentencings (mostly, though not completely, for downward departures) and on bail. While he shakes off reversals and verbal spankings, some of his most important efforts have not been successful.

AN "ENTREPRENEURIAL JUDGE"

It was suggested in Chapter 4 of this book that one model useful in understanding the importance of Weinstein's judicial career is that of the "entrepreneurial judge"—a judge who is "alert to the opportunity for innovation, willing to invest the resources

---

[14] Stephen B. Burbank, *The Courtroom as Classroom: Independence, Imagination and Ideology in the Work of Jack B. Weinstein*, 97 COLUM. L. REV. 1971 (1997).

[15] Weinstein Oral History, at 945. Writing about another federal judge, the *New York Times* stated that Weinstein "on occasion repeated with evident pride a colleague's statement to still another judge: 'You must be doing something right. You're getting reversed about as much as Jack Weinstein.'" NEW YORK TIMES, Oct. 26, 1977, at 31–32.

[16] Although not under the skin of two other very able judges, Wilfred Feinberg and James L. Oakes.

[17] *See* Chapter 8.

and assume the risks to develop a genuinely new legal concept."[18] The judge does not have to be the author of the idea or concept, but he must become its chief salesman. Wayne V. McIntosh and Cynthia L. Cates defined the judicial entrepreneur as an innovator, policy-maker, maverick, and renegade. It is such judges whose opinions "make and move the law."[19] McIntosh and Cates, describe four entrepreneurial judges: Louis D. Brandeis, Jerome Frank, Hans Linde, and Sandra Day O'Connor. They see Louis Brandeis, for example, as an entrepreneur who was successful in developing and "selling" his concept of the right to privacy, first in the area of tort, then in the First Amendment, and, finally, in the Fourth Amendment.

According to McIntosh and Cates, we have few entrepreneurial judges because the task requires an important commitment of time, willingness to endure criticism and reversal, and possibly even professional marginalization. In addition, lower court judges generally view their role to be to apply the law, not to be creative.[20] McIntosh and Cates stated, "Few are the judges who have a grand vision of where the law, writ large, ought to be headed and the self-confidence to craft opinions that they think will help nudge it in that direction."[21] According to McIntosh and Cates, entrepreneurship runs contrary to all prescriptions of judicial modesty, demeanor, and adherence to precedent.[22]

Weinstein-the-educator is the quintessential entrepreneurial judge, although he has not (and probably could not) limit himself to the "selling" of a single idea. He has a strong sense of where the law should be headed, creativity, the willingness to invest the time, and the self-confidence to expose himself to strong criticism and reversal. Throughout his career, he has been an educator to fellow judges, to law professors, to the class-action, public-interest, and defense bars as well as to law students. He has used scholarly opinions, treatises, law review articles, speeches at law schools, newspaper interviews as well as participation in the annual meetings of the Association of American Law Schools, Society of American Law Teachers, and the American Law Institute to "push" new ways of dealing with old doctrines as well as new ideas and innovations. Criticism, reversals, and the risk of not being elevated to the Court of Appeals, have not held him back.

Weinstein has been an entrepreneurial judge who, because of his work in class actions and extrajudicial writings has captured a nationwide constituency. One might say that his district in many ways has been the nation.

---

[18] W. V. McIntosh & C. L. Cates, Judicial Entrepreneurship: The Role of the Judge in the Marketplace of Ideas 5 (1997).

[19] *Id.* at 4, 5, 13.

[20] *See* William Kitchin, Federal District Judges: An Analysis of Judicial Perceptions 77ff (1978).

[21] McIntosh & Cates, *supra* note 18, at 13.

[22] McIntosh and Cates, *supra* note 18, at 10.

WEINSTEIN'S LEGACY

Trial judges have been history's footnotes, generally remembered, if at all, for presiding over some extremely celebrated trials. There are at least two comparatively recent district judges who, one feels confident, will continue to have an important place in history, John J. Sirica and Frank M. Johnson. Sirica handled what may have been America's greatest "state trials"—those connected with the illegalities of Watergate. Frank Johnson will be remembered for his long and successful duel with Alabama's government over resistance to civil rights and state institutions which were not living up to constitutional norms. Weinstein never presided over a trial of truly great importance, and his battles over conditions in institutions of government in New York City and State have never risen to the significance of Johnson's.

What then will be the legacy of Jack B. Weinstein? Certainly, his treatises will keep his name alive for a long time to come. *Weinstein's Evidence* is the leading authority in that field, the successor to *Wigmore on Evidence*. His treatise on New York Civil Practice and Rules is also one of the leading sources of authority in applying the CPLR. Then, there is his *uncontroversial* work as lawmaker. He was the central figure in drafting the practice rules of one of America's most influential jurisdictions. He played a significant role in the devising of the Federal Rules of Evidence. There is as well his work as judge and scholar in the fields of mass torts and class actions. Weinstein, part treatise writer, part creator of practice rules, and part judge is a throwback to nineteenth-century figures such as John Forrest Dillon.

What about his opinions as a district judge? It is not likely, apart from his opinions in class actions, that very many will survive the effects of time. Case law seems to turn over every generation with only a few seminal cases surviving and seminal cases are the work of appellate courts. As with all judges (save perhaps John Marshall, Benjamin Cardozo, and a couple others), in spite of thoroughness and elegance, opinions are evanescent, regardless how much value they have had during the judge's lifetime. Although Weinstein's may linger somewhat longer than those of his contemporaries becasue of his treatise-like exploration of difficult problems.[23] There may even be a few which may survive as a Supreme Court dissent might, because of their relevance in the future. Those survivors may include his opinions on jurisdiction and those where he treated international law, treatises, human rights conventions, and human rights precedents from courts outside the United States as authority, which may lead to a greater penetration of those norms into American law.

The author is more confident that Weinstein's work in the field of class actions and mass torts will have a continuing influence on the field. With the progress of science, there is little doubt that the number of mass torts is likely to increase with time. Unless Congress chooses to establish one or more administrative agencies to deal with these

---

[23] Practitioners and academics have certainly stated to me that Weinstein's opinions on privilege and discovery may have "a long shelf life."

problems or there are dramatic changes in tort law, there will be great aggregations of cases impossible to tackle on an individual basis. In spite of the present hostility of appellate courts to class actions and other aggregative litigation, it seems likely that these society-wide issues will have to be dealt with by the courts with mechanisms not so different from class actions. If and when that happens, judges will have as a resource the dozens upon dozens of opinions and articles Weinstein has written discussing virtually the entire range of problems in the field.[24]

What Weinstein should be most remembered for are the ways in which he has placed a human face on the law. In a different, better-spirited era than ours, his belief that "to aid the weak and suffering delineates the primary duty and soul of American law,"[25] might become more widely accepted. Perhaps then it can be said openly that compassion has to be part of the law.[26] If that kind of America comes about, Weinstein's deepest concerns as a judge and the effort he made to live up to them will serve as a model for judges and lawyers.

To that one might add that it is not just the words that survive but the speaker's life and judicial career which will serve as the model. For many judges, Weinstein has become, as Paul D. Rheingold, author of *Mass Tort Litigation*,[27] has written, a model who "emboldens younger, less experienced mass tort judges who get assigned a case that there has to be some way. . . to get to the point where the parties want to resolve the case. And, after all, if there is a resolution, that's what the judge is about."[28]

To many, Weinstein is a "heroic judge."[29] To others, he is a lawless judge. Kenneth Feinberg (the nation's most prominent non-judge dispute resolver) has said, "I think Judge Weinstein had more of an impact on American law than any judge alive."[30] Others may assume that Weinstein's jurisprudence will not survive his passing. Perhaps this book should end with the citation that went along with the federal judiciary's highest award, the Edward J. Devitt Award in 2003:

> Recipients are selected whose decisions are characterized by wisdom, humanity, and commitment to the rule of law; whose writings demonstrate scholarship and dedication to the improvement of the judicial process; and whose activities have helped to improve the administration of justice, to advance the rule of law, to reinforce collegial ties within the judicial branch, or to strengthen civic ties within

---

[24] Helen E. Freedman & Kenneth R. Feinberg, Review of JACK B. WEINSTEIN, INDIVIDUAL JUSTICE IN MASS TORT LITIGATION, 80 JUDICATURE 44 (1996–1997).

[25] Jack B. Weinstein, Can the Law's Soul Survive the Law's Success?, Commencement Ceremonies, Salmon P. Chase College of Law, 4 (May 11, 1985).

[26] *See* Jack B. Weinstein, *The Myth of the Law as Universal Absolute, University of Connecticut Commencement Address*, excerpts pub. NEWSWEEK, June 1, 1983, n.p.

[27] PAUL D. RHEINGOLD, MASS TORT LITIGATION (1996).

[28] *80th Birthday Roundtable, supra* note 12, at 149, 162.

[29] *See* David Luban, *Heroic Judging in an Antiheroic Age*, 97 COLUM. L. REV. 2064, 2089 (1997).

[30] Quoted in Elizabeth Stoll, *Judge Weinstein's 40th Anniversary on the Bench*, BROOK. DAILY EAGLE, Apr. 26, 2007.

local, national, and international communities. According to the award criteria, bench, bar and community alike would willingly entrust that judge with the most complex cases of the most far-reaching import."[31]

The chair of the three-person committee which chose the 2003 recipient was Antonin Scalia.

---

[31] 35 *Third Branch*, No. 3 (March 2003).

INDEX

⌒

CPSIA information can be obtained
at www.ICGtesting.com
Printed in the USA
BVHW041937250719

554168BV00020B/340/P

9 780199 772414